Pidgin and Creole Linguistics
expanded and revised edition

Peter Mühlhäusler

Westminster Creolistics Series - 3

UNIVERSITY OF WESTMINSTER PRESS

1997

i

Other titles in this series:
volume 1: *From contact to Creole and beyond* (P Baker, ed.)
volume 2: *Changing meanings, changing functions* (P Baker & A Syea, eds)

Forthcoming titles:
Spreading the word (M Huber & M Parkvall, eds)
From French to Creole (C Corne)
St Kitts and the Atlantic Creoles (P Baker & A Bruyn, eds)

Series editor: Philip Baker

Published by the University of Westminster Press
for the Creole Linguistics Research Group,
School of Languages,
Faculty of Law, Languages and Communication,
University of Westminster,
9-18 Euston Centre, London NW1 3ET.

ISBN 1 85919 083 9

First edition published by Basil Blackwell 1986.
This completely revised and expanded edition (including three additional
chapters) first published in 1997.

Cover illustration: Scenes of life at the Dutch factory at Deshima (*detail*).
Silk handscroll painting, 18th century. Height 33 cm.
By courtesy of the Department of Japanese Antiquities, the British Museum.

Cover design: Rajesh Kumar

Printed in the UK by Hobbs the Printers Ltd, Totton, Hampshire, SO40 3YS.

Contents

Dedication   vi

Preface to the first edition   vi

Preface to the second edition   vii

Acknowledgements   viii

1 Names and definitions
   The term 'Pidgin'   1
   Terminological issues: 'Pidgin'   3
   The term 'Creole'   6
   The terminological debate in Creole linguistics   6
   The identification of Pidgins and Creoles   13
   An illustration: counting Pidgins and Creoles in the Pacific   16
   Conclusions   21

2 The study of Pidgins and Creoles
   Introduction   22
   Grammar as a gentleman's pastime   24
   Studies in defence of Pidgins and Creoles   27
   Early missionary and pedagogical grammars   28
   Pidgins and Creoles in philology   31
   Anthropological linguistics and sociolinguistics   35
   Structuralist studies   36
   Transformational generative grammar   38
   Post-generative models   42
   Pidgin and Creole studies as a separate field of inquiry   45
   Outlook   47

3 The sociohistorical context of Pidgin and Creole development
   Introduction   51
   Non-verbal communication and Pidgin development   51
   Verbal means of communication: general remarks   53
   Social forces as constitutive factors in Pidgin formation   55
   Nature and nurture   60
   Variability of contextual factors   63
   The social typology of Pidgins and Creoles   72
   Summary   92

4 Theories of origin

Introduction	93
Nautical jargon theories	94
Baby talk and foreigner talk theories	96
Relexification theory	103
Universalist theories	108
Common-core theories	113
Substratum theories	114
Conclusions	125

5 Linguistic development of Pidgins and Creoles

Introduction	127
The jargon stage	128
Stabilization	138
The phonological component	138
Loss of inflectional morphology	142
Syntax	144
The lexicon	153
Stabilization - a summary	162
The expansion stage	163
The phonological component	163
Inflectional morphology	166
The syntactic component	167
The lexical component	175
The development of stylistic flexibility	182
The expansion stage: a summary	186
Creolization	186
The phonological component	187
Inflectional and derivational morphology	192
Syntax	198
Lexicon and lexical semantics	205
Conclusions	210
Post-Pidgin and post-Creole continua	211
Phonology	212
Inflectional and derivational morphology	214
Syntax	216
The lexicon	219
Conclusions	221
Linguistic development of Pidgins and Creoles: summary	221

6 The relevance of Pidgin and Creole studies to linguistic theory

Introduction	222
The comparative method and the family-tree model of historical relationships	223
Continuity and discontinuity in language development	225
Systematicity and rule-governedness	227
Nature and nurture in linguistic structures	228
Qualitative differences between linguistic systems	229
Language learning, Pidgins and Creoles	230
The critical-threshold hypothesis	233

Simplification and simplicity   234
The diagnosis of prior creolization   236
Pidgin and Creole speech communities   241
Conclusions   242

7 The sociology of Pidgin and Creoles

Introduction   244
Language attitude studies   244
Language planning and engineering   255
The social status of Pidgins and Creoles   260
Bilingualism, diglossia and code-shifting   265
Language decline and death   269
Pidgins, Creoles and international politics   274

8 Pidgins and Creoles in education

Introduction   279
Issues and policies of the past   281
Pidgins and Creoles and educational policies   284
Social factors   291
The teaching of Pidgins and Creoles   293
"Transported" Pidgins and Creoles and education   298
University level courses in and on Pidgins and Creoles   300
Conclusions   302

9 Pidgin and Creole literature

Introduction   303
Pidgins as literary stereotypes   304
Some literary functions of Pidgins and Creoles   309
The use of literary Pidgins and Creoles as linguistic evidence   311
Literature written in Pidgins and Creoles   313
Motives for writing in Pidgins and Creoles   324
Bible translation and religious writings   327
Pidgins and Creoles in the mass media   330
Summary and conclusions   335

10 Conclusions and outlook

Two key conclusions   336
The metalanguage of Pidgin and Creole linguistics   337
Understanding naturalness   339
Non-expatriate Pidgin and Creole studies   340
Linguistic experiments   341
On funding Pidgin and Creole studies   342
Outlook   343

Bibliography   344

Index   377

This book is dedicated to
Jackie, Beverly and Tim

Preface

to the first edition

Writers on Pidgins and Creoles find it difficult to escape from two limitations imposed on them by the very nature of their work. The first involves what Bickerton (1981:83) has called the First Law of Creole Studies, which reads: *Every creolist's analysis can be directly contradicted by that creolist's own texts and citations.* Despite my efforts, this law may well be found to apply at some point in this book. A second limitation is what I would like to call the Second Law of Creole Studies: *Given the choice between neat and untidy data, creolists feel compelled to deal with the latter.* In addition, and this is what makes them invidious to their publishers, Creolists tend to insist that whatever argument they put forward should be illustrated with an extensive list of examples. The book you hold in your hands is no exception. Such was its size when the first draft was completed that it was no longer an economically viable proposition. Of the two remedies suggested to me, either to condense the volume as a whole or to drop a few chapters, I have opted for the second strategy as the less painful one. As a consequence, the chapters on the sociology of language, Pidgin and Creole literature, and education have disappeared. What remains is a detailed description of the processes of pidginization, creolization, and Pidgin and Creole development, and a discussion of the major theoretical issues related to these languages. I have not given up hope of publishing my findings in sociolinguistics and applied linguistics, and I would not wish to argue for a strict separation of theoretical and applied creolistics. However, the greatest need I perceived in Pidgin and Creole studies is to clarify what constitutes their dynamic character and to isolate the most important forces underlying it.

The cut-off point for writings considered in this book is about October 1984. Since then some quite significant work has appeared, particularly in the area of substratum grammar and language and identity. However, at the time of writing this introduction, I do not feel that my arguments stand in need of major revision. Since creolistics is almost as dynamic and changing as its subject matter, some such revision will no doubt become necessary eventually and I hope that this book will stimulate such changes.

Preface

to the second, expanded and revised edition

Since completing the draft of the first edition in 1984, a great deal has been written about Pidgins and Creoles and a much larger body of observationally and descriptively satisfactory accounts now exists of a far wider range of these languages, including those that do not result from European expansionism. Whilst having tried to keep up with developments and having found out a great deal through my research for Wurm et al.'s (1996) *Atlas of languages of intercultural communication in the Pacific, Asia, and the Americas*, it has become impossible for me to take note of everything that is published even on Tok Pisin (the Pidgin/Creole I have worked on most), let alone the entire field of Pidgin and Creole studies. The reader will not fail to note omissions in the revised text.

Coping with a large quantity of new information has been difficult enough; treading the fine line between revision and total rewrite has been more difficult. Since 1984 I have changed many of my views on Pidgin and Creole linguistics. The extent of my rethinking became evident to me when I auto-reviewed my first book on this topic (1974; Muhlhausler 1992c). Since writing the latter I have continued rethinking Pidgin and Creole linguistics. It has not been possible totally to reframe the questions I asked in 1984, though I have tried to be critical of my earlier views wherever possible. I remain convinced that Pidgin and Creole linguistics has not as yet realized its full potential as a counter-example to mainstream linguistic orthodoxy and that its practitioners have remained too ready to accept the role assigned to them by the mainstream.

I have tried to incorporate many of the suggestions made by my reviewers and critics, in particular C-J N Bailey, Alan Kaye, Alain Kihm and R B Le Page. My greatest debt, however, is to Philip Baker whose influence will be evident in improvements to the presentation of, and discussion in, this revised edition. During the hot Adelaide January of 1997, Philip and I spent many hours going through the text, discussing new ideas and getting the manuscript ready for publication. Chris Corne also generously gave me many pages of comments on the pre-final draft. His knowledge of New Caledonian Tayo in particular has been a great help. The final decision of what to incorporate and what to ignore has been mine, however, and I alone am responsible for any errors and omissions.

Acknowledgements

This book is the product of many years of involvement with Pidgin and Creole languages and it is not possible to mention all those who have influenced my thinking during these years. However, I would like to give particular thanks to Stephen Wurm of the Australian National University, who first provided me with the opportunity to carry out fieldwork on Pidgins and Creoles, and who has encouraged my work in this area ever since. I am grateful to those who influenced my linguistics as teachers and colleagues: Rudie Botha at Stellenbosch, Peter Trudgill at Reading, the late Don Laycock and Tom Dutton at the Australian National University, C-J N Bailey at the Technische Universität Berlin, and Roy Harris, Tony Bladon and Suzanne Romaine at Oxford. I am indebted to those who have over the years regularly supplied me with their data and writings, in particular Derek Bickerton, Annegret Bollée, Michael Clyne, Manfred Görlach, John Holm, the late Roger Keesing, Jurgen Meisel, John Rickford, Bruce Rigsby, John Sandefur, Gillian Sankoff, Anna Shnukal, Jeff Siegel among many others. I would also like to thank my mother for supplying me with many hard-to-obtain archival materials on Pidgins and Creoles, and my wife Jackie for a great deal of advice and editorial help with the first edition of this book. Thanks are also due to John Evans for proofreading the entire second edition.

The revision of this book was supported by a small University research grant of the University of Adelaide which is gratefully acknowledged.

The author and publishers would like to express thanks for permission to use the following tables and figures: those on pages 16 and 113 are from R A Hall, 'How Pidgin English has evolved', which first appeared in 1961 in the *New Scientist*, London, the weekly review of science and technology; the figure on page 19 is from Ross Clark, 'In search of Beach-la-Mar', *Te Reo*, 1979; while the table on page 42 is taken from D DeCamp, 'Analysis of a post-creole speech continuum', in D Hymes (ed.) *Pidginization and Creolization of Languages*, Cambridge University Press, 1971.

Above all, I am indebted to my informants in various parts of the Pacific and Australia for their patience and for letting me study their languages. It is my hope that this book will be of help to them.

1 Names and definitions

> *To a Creolist, almost everyone else's definition of a Creole sounds absurd and arbitrary; yet Creolists communicate and collaborate with their colleagues just as Slavicists and Amerindianists do.* (DeCamp 1977:4)

The term 'Pidgin'

When telling a new acquaintance that I have spent most of my academic career "studying Pidgin English", this statement is met either with an outburst of laughter or else the question "Where does the word *Pidgin* originate?" I hope that this book will dispel any notion that the study of Pidgin and Creole languages is a frivolous waste of time, although I may need several chapters to convince the more sceptical of my readers. My reply to the second reaction is much more straightforward. There have been a number of proposals as to the etymology of the term 'Pidgin'. The more widespread of these include:[1]

1. The definition given by the OED of "a Chinese corruption of English 'business'";
2. A Chinese corruption of the Portuguese word *ocupação* 'business';
3. Hebrew *pidjom*: 'exchange, trade, redemption';
4. South Seas pronunciation of English 'beach' (*beachee*) from the location where the language was typically used.

I have come to the conclusion that all of these etymologies may at some point have been real to Pidgin users, the reason being that such interpretations are very characteristic of Pidgin languages. Some of my Tok Pisin informants, for instance, will derive this from **pisin** 'bird', believing that Tok Pisin, like other languages, was given to humans by birds. However, the historical evidence examined by Baker & Mühlhäusler (1990) suggests otherwise and reveals the following:

(a) The word *pigeon* is first attested in the sense of 'business' in Canton:

Ting-qua led me into... a temple of Poo Saat. "This Jos", pointing to the idol,... "take care of fire 'pigeon'", fire 'business' (unpaginated diary of Robert Morrison, entry dated 21 September 1807).

(b) The earliest-known glossary of Chinese Pidgin English (Chinese PE), written by Robert Morrison's son, includes:

Pigeon or *pidginess* 'a corruption of the English word business' (Morrison 1834:3).

(c) The earliest attestation of *pidgin* with exactly that spelling (but with the meaning 'business') is found in Tilden (1831:787).

---

[1] A few others are discussed in Hancock (1979).

1

(d) In the 18th and early 19th century, Chinese PE is referred to by a variety of names of which 'Canton English' is found most often. The three earliest indications that it was also known as 'Pidgin English' (but not in that spelling) were all published in 1859: "pigeon English" (Anon. 1859:20; relating to a visit to Macau in 1857), "Pigeon Englese" (Wood 1859:296) and "pigeon-English" (Smith 1859:29).

(e) The earliest attestation of "Pidgin English", in precisely that spelling, is found in Mayers, Dennys & King (1867:24).

The above information allows us to rule out all but the first two of the possible etyma listed above. Portuguese *ocupação* is a serious contender on both phonological and semantic grounds, and because Portuguese presence in the area predates that of Anglophones. Against this, it has to be said that, without any known exception, all Anglophones with first-hand experience of the Canton/Macau/Hong Kong area in the 19th century and who comment on the origin of the word Pidgin (in any spelling) derive this from 'business' – and that many of these people had no hesitation in identifying the Portuguese origin of other words such as *savvy* and *joss*. Thus, unless a word resembling both *pidgin* and *ocupação* – phonetically and semantically – can be shown to have existed in pidginized Portuguese from Canton and/or Macau prior to 1807, English *business* must be considered by far the most likely etymon.

Such a linguistically accurate account needs to take into consideration that etymologizing for mixed languages brings with it special problems. It should be noted that, because they emerge as vehicles of intercommunication between speakers of many different languages, coincidence of form and similarity of meaning across languages will give a word a high survival rate. I have found, for instance, that in the early formative years of Tok Pisin (New Guinea PE), up to 50% of the lexicon could be traced back to more than one language (Mühlhäusler 1985b:181ff), including the following examples of lexical encounter between Tolai or German and English:

Tolai	German	English	Tok Pisin
atip 'thatched roof'		on top	antap 'on top, roof'
bala 'belly, bowels'		belly	bel 'belly, seat of emotions'
ikilik 'small'		little	liklik 'small, little bit'
	Eis	ice	ais 'ice'
	Arsch	arse	as 'posterior, origin'
	Hammer	hammer	hama 'hammer'
	Bett	bed	bet 'bed, shelf'
	Garten	garden	gaten 'garden'

More than two sources appear to have been involved in some instances. A particularly intriguing case of lexical conflation is that of **sanga** 'pliers, hand of crayfish, forked post, slingshot', which appears to be related to German *Zange* 'pliers', Malay *tiang* 'forked branch' and Australian English *Shanghai* 'slingshot'. Lexical encounters in other Pidgins are probably equally numerous, although they have not always been identified. The earliest reports of this phenomenon are by Schuchardt (1909) for the Lingua Franca, where he observes that "many [Arabic loans] give the impression that they were introduced due to similarity with corresponding Romance forms"

2

(1979:30).[2] For Eskimo Trade Jargon, Stefánsson (1909:227) observes in the same year on the entry for **miluk**:

This is in a way, an interesting form. The whites who use it consider it a corruption of the English 'milk', while to the Eskimo it is their own word 'mi'-luk', which refers to any milk (human, caribou, etc.).

Other well-known examples include Jamaican Creole **doti** 'dirty', which can be traced back to both English *dirty* and Twi *doti* 'dirty'; and Australian Kriol **kan** 'can't' has recently been traced to both English *can't* and Walmajarri *kaya*, a negative used to express inability and many similar cases have become known. Sometimes Pidgins also develop compounds of dual origin, such as Fanakalo **tshisa-stik** 'fuse lighter' from Zulu (Z) *shisa* 'set alight, burn' and English (E) *stick*; **makaza-mbitshan** 'cool' and **tshisa-mbitshan** 'warm' from Z *amakhaja* 'cold' and Z **shisa** 'burn', respectively, with Afrikaans *bietjie* 'slightly; **sokismude** 'stocking' from E **socks** and Z **omude** 'long'. Such compounds are reminiscent of those produced by some bilingual children.[3]

Lexical encounters and mutual reinforcement may continue throughout the history of a Pidgin.

A name, as we shall see shortly, is not in itself a reliable indicator of the existence of a language, language form or any other linguistic entity. Pidgin languages were used long before the label 'Pidgin' was invented. Examples of such early Pidgins include Sabir or Lingua Franca, Pidgin Portuguese of West Africa, and an as yet ill-documented plantation Pidgin spoken in medieval Cyprus. Indeed, little is known about the many contact Pidgins in use in the countries of the Third World before the arrival of the European colonizers. As regards the label 'Pidgin', even today it is not used with consistency. In the speech of non-specialists, it overlaps with terms such as 'lingua franca', 'argot', 'sabir', 'patois' or 'koiné', and the definitions and delimitations given by professional linguists also differ. This, I feel, should not upset us, for it is the common fate of everyday expressions which assume a more specialist meaning within a field of scientific inquiry. The vagueness of the term 'Pidgin' is thus no different from that of other metalinguistic labels, such as 'text', 'sentence', 'construction' or 'topic', as can easily be ascertained by consulting one of the numerous lexicons or encyclopedias of linguistics. For the time being, however, I suggest we accept the popular view of a Pidgin as a structurally reduced trade language. How this popular definition is elaborated in the scholarly discussion of Pidgin languages will be the topic of the next section.

Terminological issues: 'Pidgin'

Pidgin studies have suffered for a long time from terminological and definitional problems, as has been discussed by Mühlhäusler (1974:11-25), Samarin (1975), and Baker (1995a). Since definitions often determine the

---

2   Quotations from Schuchardt's works, originally published between 1882 and 1909, will be generally given in Markey's English translation, listed in the Bibliography as Schuchardt 1979.

3   For a considerable time my bilingual daughter used **tummy-bauch** (English 'tummy' plus German **Bauch** 'stomach') to refer to 'stomach, belly'.

direction of research, it would seem profitable to look at some of them in more detail. The term 'Pidgin' has been defined, among other things, as:

> [Pidgin English] is a corrupted form of English, mixed with many morsels from other languages and it is adapted to the mentality of the natives; therefore words tend to be simply concatenated and conjunction and declension are avoided. (Baessler 1895:23-24, my translation)

> ...the grammatical structure [of Pidgins] has been simplified very much beyond what we find in any of the languages involved in their making. (Jesperson 1922:227)

> A variety whose grammar and vocabulary are very much reduced... The resultant language must be native to no one. (Bloomfield 1933:474)

> A language which has arisen as the result of contact between peoples of different languages, usually formed from mixing of the languages. (Unesco 1963:46)

> Two or more people use a language in a variety whose grammar and vocabulary are very much reduced in extent and which is native to neither side. Such a language is a 'Pidgin'. (Hall 1966:xii)

> The vocabulary is mainly provided by the language spoken by the upper stratum of a mixed society, adapted by the lower stratum to the grammar and morphology of their original language. (Adler 1977:12)

> *Pidgin.* A language with a markedly reduced grammatical structure, lexicon, and stylistic range. The native language of no one, it emerges when members of two mutually unintelligible speech communities attempt to communicate; often called a *trade language*, when seen in the context of the expansionist era of colonial economies. Pidgins contrast with Creoles, which are created when Pidgins acquire native speakers. Many Pidgins are based on European languages, reflecting the history of colonialism, but there are undoubtedly a large number of unstudied Pidgins in the many situations of language contact in Africa, South-East Asia, and South America. Some Pidgins have become so useful that they have developed a role as auxiliary languages, and been given official status by the community (e.g. Tok Pisin). These cases are called *expanded Pidgins* because of the way they have added extra forms to cope with the needs of the users. (Crystal 1992:302)

Note that there are a number of problems with such definitions. First, those who stress the makeshift character of Pidgins – a "supplementary tongue for special forms of intercourse" (Reinecke 1964:537) – ignore the fact that Pidgins can develop to a considerable degree of stability and complexity.

Second, there is a tendency to confuse simplification (greater grammatical regularity) with impoverishment (lack of referential and non-referential power) or reduction. There is also considerable uncertainty as to whether simplification is greatest in incipient or extended Pidgins. Studies in the area of interlanguage (e.g. Corder 1976; Traugott 1976) have drawn attention to the insufficiency of the notion of simplification (or simplicity) in some Pidgin and Creole studies. The complex problem as to the relationship

4

between simplification in the sense of rule generalization, on the one hand, and naturalness and markedness, on the other, cannot be solved here. However, data from developing Pidgins support the view that impoverishment and simplification are inversely related: as the referential and non-referential power of a language increases, so its content must become more structured. A basic jargon used to exchange information in a limited contextual domain does not need structure. In its initial phase it is little more than a list of phrases or lexical irregularities. We thus get the following picture:

Incipient Pidgin: maximally impoverished   minimally simple

          $\downarrow$ $\downarrow$

Developed Pidgin: fully expanded   maximally simple (regular)

One can therefore no longer uphold Agheyisi's (1971:24) view that:

> It is possible that most of the factors which contribute to the development of the simplified variety known as the Pidgin are most active during the pidginization process. This process is said to extend chronologically from the period of initial language contact through the stage when the resulting pidginized speech becomes sufficiently regularised and stabilized.

The third problem to note is that Pidgins are not mixed languages in the sense most often intended. It appears that the most mixed area is the lexicon, where syncretisms of various types are common, and not syntax. Pidgins vary greatly in this respect: whilst Chinese PE relied overwhelmingly on English for its lexicon,[4] some indigenous Pidgins of the Sepik region of Papua New Guinea have highly mixed lexicons. In addition, mixing at the syntactic and morphological levels is virtually absent in the formative phase of Pidgins and becomes more important only after stabilization and considerable expansion have taken place. It is most pronounced in the post-Pidgin phase, that is when a Pidgin comes into renewed contact with its original lexifier language.

Finally, Pidgins are classified and often defined as being based on a principal lexifier language, typically the language spoken by the socially dominant group. Two objections can be levelled against this view (for a more detailed discussion of this issue, see Walsh 1984 and Baker 1990). As pointed out by Dennis & Scott (1975:2), "we will avoid calling the Creoles "English-based" or "Portuguese-based" etc., since we can see no grounds for deciding that the lexicon is the base of the language, as opposed to the semantic-syntactic framework of the language". The second objection is that the mixed or compromise character of some Pidgin lexicons is typically ignored. A third objection is spelled out by Hymes (1971:81) and Baker (1990:109-10), the lack of consideration given to human creativity (in the sense of rule-changing and rule-making, not rule-governed creativity).

---

4   Cantonese influence on the grammar of CPE is apparent only about 100 years after the first use of this language.

5

In view of the above considerations, I would like to propose a new definition of Pidgin:

> Pidgins are examples of partially targeted second language learning and second language creation, developing from simpler to more complex systems as communicative requirements become more demanding. Pidgin languages by definition have no native speakers – they are social rather than individual solutions – and hence are characterized by norms of acceptability.

Implicit in this definition is the assumption that there are qualitatively different stages in the development of a Pidgin. These have been given labels by a number of scholars. Here follow my own preferred labels, side by side with others commonly in use:

Jargon	Pre-Pidgin, multilingual idiolect, secondary hybrid
↓	
Stable Pidgin	Pidgin, basilectal Pidgin, tertiary hybrid
↓	
Expanded Pidgin	Extended Pidgin
↓	
Creole	

The term 'Creole'

The origins of the term 'Creole' are not much less complex than those of 'Pidgin'. According to Valkhoff (1966:38-46), it is widely held that the word originated in one of Portugal's colonies in the 16th century. Both form and meaning suggest an etymology **criar** 'to nurse, breed, nourish', but there may also have been reinforcement from another, as yet unknown, source language. Originally the meaning of **crioulo** was 'white man or woman originating from the colonies', but the word has since adopted a number of additional meanings including 'slave born in a colony' and 'locally-bred, non-indigenous animal'. Its most common meaning in English, according to the *Concise Oxford Dictionary*, is '(descendant of) European or Negro settler in W. Indies, or stemming from these areas' and is used with nouns referring to something like 'exotic' or 'spicy'.

Perhaps the linguistic layman's most common association with the term Creole is that of mixture of culture and race, and it is commonly assumed that linguistic mixture goes hand in hand with these.

The terminological debate in Creole linguistics

Problems with the linguistic definition of Creoles are legion and many of the central issues remain unresolved. The uninitiated reader will probably agree with Givón's (1979:4) characterization of Creole studies as something like a "mythological safari across the equally mythological African jungle of lore" and will find them "liberally strewn with booby-traps and quicksands of idiosyncratic linguistic features". Still, it would seem that the numerous

6

characterizations and definitions of Creole can be reduced to four major types:

1. Creoles are regarded as mixed languages typically associated with cultural and often racial mixture;
2. Creoles are defined as Pidgin languages (second languages) that have become the first language of a new generation of speakers;
3. Creoles are reflections of a natural bioprogram for human language which is activated in cases of imperfect language transmission (cf Bickerton 1981);
4. "Advanced" forms of regional/popular varieties of the metropolitan language.

As in the case of the definition of 'Pidgin', both social and linguistic aspects tend to be found in the above categories. Let us now consider each type in more detail.

Creoles as mixed languages

In discussing the question whether English is a Creole language, Bailey & Maroldt (1977:21) state: "by creolization the authors wish to indicate gradient mixture of two or more languages; in a narrow sense, a Creole is the result of mixing which is substantial enough to result in a new system, a system that is separate from its antecedent parent system". A number of researchers, including Bailey & Maroldt, have concluded from their assessment of the role of mixing in the emergence of Middle English from Anglo-Saxon that English is indeed a Creole. Very similar arguments have been put forward in the case of both Italian, as spoken in the USA (Haller 1981:181-94), and Dutch-derived Afrikaans, spoken in Southern Africa. Valkhoff (1966:26) increased the controversiality of the debate on the latter by declaring that there is "an ancient relation between miscegenation and creolization", implying that Afrikaans developed in the context of intense racial mixture in the early years of Dutch colonization of the Cape. This view was understandably unpopular with the large group of white pro-apartheid speakers of Afrikaans, who preferred to regard their language as a continuation of white dialects of Dutch (cf Jordaan 1974, Raidt 1983). In the context of post-apartheid South Africa the topic of racial mixture in the history of Afrikaans is no longer taboo, and the ideological bias of white "diachronic purists" has been demonstrated by writers such as Roberge (1990). However, in discussing issues such as these, we should heed Schuchardt's cautionary remarks on the relationship between linguistic and racial mixture:

> Linguistic mixture tends to be connected with a more or less pronounced mixture of culture. With the crossing of races, which at least has no influence upon the latter, it coincides only externally; or, to express myself more cautiously, it is not associated in any demonstrable degree with it. (Schuchardt 1889b:508; Markey's (1979) translation)

Indeed, in as much as Pidgins and Creoles develop as indicators and insulators of social distance between members of two different races (as they have done over and over again), one is tempted to suspect that large-scale

7

racial mixture in some contexts tends to discourage the development of Creoles.

Leaving aside the problem of correlating linguistic with social factors, there is another issue which has not as yet been addressed by the proponents of the equation creolization equals language mixing: that is, the possibility that not every linguistic consequence of linguistic encounters is alike. Indeed, there is mounting evidence that one is dealing with many different types of language mixing, some increasing and some decreasing the naturalness of the affected linguistic systems.[5]

Creoles as nativized Pidgins

A Creole, according to the second definition, is a Pidgin that has been adopted by a community of native speakers. This occurs, for instance, when parents from different linguistic backgrounds communicate among themselves and with their offspring in a makeshift Pidgin, which is elaborated and used as a means of intercommunication by the next generation. Thus the children in this situation are exposed to imperfect, reduced language input; elaborate this input using new grammatical devices gleaned from internal resources, that is, by appealing to their 'innate' linguistic knowledge; and eventually speak a language that is both quantitatively and qualitatively different from that spoken by their parents and, in many cases, not intelligible to them.

Creolization in this sense thus appears to be an ideal test case for claims about the nature of the human language acquisition device and universal linguistic knowledge. It can be represented schematically as follows:

Parents' input: Mother's idiolectal Pidgin Father's idiolectal Pidgin
                     (reduced language)   (reduced language)
                                    ↓
Universal knowledge: Language acquisition device
                                    ↓
Children's output: Creole (full language)

Although numerous Creole languages are in existence today, there are a number of problems when it comes to testing the nativization hypothesis. Observations concerning the differences between the second-language Pidgin and the ensuing first-language Creole should preferably be made with first-generation speakers, as Creoles may change through borrowing and for internal reasons, like any other language, once they have come into being. I shall not discuss, at this point, the mounting evidence that the process of Creoles 'being creoled or coming into being' is not necessarily instantaneous and may require several generations of first language speakers (see Ehrhart (1992, 1993) for Tayo and Le Page & Tabouret-Keller (1985) for Belize Creole). A comparison of a present-day Creole with a Pidgin that was spoken centuries ago is unlikely to yield satisfactory evidence. Further, the Pidgin input may vary considerably. Thus, creolization can occur: (a) with Pidgins that are altogether rudimentary and unstable, that is, so-called

---

5   Categorical statements such as mixing leads to greater unnaturalness (as in Bailey 1973) or that mixing merely accelerates the developmental tendencies of single linguistic systems (as in Aitchison 1981) are not borne out by empirical evidence.

jargons; (b) with elementary stable Pidgins; and (c) with expanded Pidgins. Consequently three main sociolinguistic types of Creoles can be distinguished according to their developmental history:

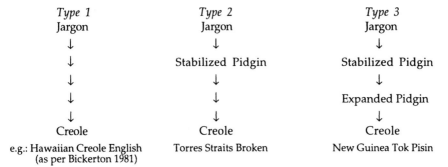

Type 1	Type 2	Type 3
Jargon	Jargon	Jargon
↓	↓	↓
↓	Stabilized Pidgin	Stabilized Pidgin
↓	↓	↓
↓	↓	Expanded Pidgin
↓	↓	↓
Creole	Creole	Creole
e.g.: Hawaiian Creole English (as per Bickerton 1981)	Torres Straits Broken	New Guinea Tok Pisin

If any second language becomes the first language of a speech community, its deficiencies need to be repaired. The nature of this repair will depend on the developmental stage at which creolization sets in.

Of the cases of creolization that can be observed *in situ* today, most belong to type 3 (others include Vanuatu Bislama and West African PE) and a smaller number to type 2 (e.g. North Australian Kriol). There are yet few known instances of type 1, the most interesting type from the point of view of psycholinguistic evidence, all apparently from the Pacific area (Tayo of New Caledonia and Unserdeutsch of former German New Guinea being two possible candidates). Even this subcategorization of Creole types is very abstract and should be supplemented with additional types, such as sheltered/unsheltered Creoles as suggested by Bailey (p c), a difference depending on the presence or absence of a Creole's original lexifier language. The need to differentiate between a number of different types of nativized Pidgins, and to regard the term Creole, in the sense of the second definition (p 7), as a gradient term, springs from the difficulty of distinguishing between first and second languages. In his introduction to the perhaps best known reader on these languages (Hymes 1971), DeCamp (1971a:16) expresses this by saying that a Creole is "a native language for most of its speakers". However, Nigerian PE, Solomons Pijin, Bislama and Tok Pisin have viable Creole communities, while continuing to serve as second languages for most of their speakers. Thus, Mafeni points out:

> While this is a useful distinction [between a Pidgin and a Creole language], it does not always prove possible to make such a neat separation... West African Pidgin ... runs the gamut all the way from true Creole - as a mother tongue and home language - to what one might call 'minimal Pidgin', the exiguous jargon often used between Europeans and their domestic servants.   (Mafeni 1971:95-96)

It is important to remember at this point that a speaker's dominant language may not be his or her first language in the sense of order of acquisition. Therefore, to avoid confusion, one may adopt the term 'primary language' to designate the language that is best mastered. This is not necessarily the mother tongue. All other languages of a bilingual individual are secondary languages. The functional and structural differences between a primary Pidgin and its corresponding Creole may thus be minimal.

A further complication encountered in distinguishing between Pidgins and Creoles and first and second languages is the fact that first-language Creoles can become either partially or totally repidginized. An instance of partial repidginization of a Creole are plantation Creoles, where first-generation Creole speakers are supplemented with raw recruits from elsewhere. Thus, in the case of Sranan, the English- and Portuguese-derived Creole of Surinam, mortality on the plantations was so high during the first hundred years of its existence that the majority of plantation workers had to be recruited from overseas. Thus, Creole speakers of Sranan were outnumbered by second- language speakers of the language for a large part of its existence. Total repidginization is documented in the case of Tok Pisin on Rambutyo Island in the Admiralties (see Mühlhäusler 1979:176). A group of plantation workers from many parts of New Guinea founded a new village on this island, where children began to speak creolized Tok Pisin within a generation. However, because of the very limited usefulness of this language, the second generation of children grew up speaking Rambutyo as their first and Tok Pisin as their second language.

From such observations, it emerges that it is difficult to study Pidgins and Creoles as separate phenomena rather than two aspects of the same linguistic process.

Creoles as reflections of a natural "bioprogram"

Before giving the third definition of 'Creole', it may be of interest to explore briefly why such a definition should have emerged. The existence of so many different manifestations of Creole appears to have led linguists to search for an "ideal" Creole, a search which would seem comparable to that for the invariant idiolect of latter-day American structuralists or the ideal speaker-hearer of transformational generative grammar. The method adopted is to discard all superficial and incidental properties (whatever these may be) and retain the essential core. Thus the purest types of Creole, as defined by Bickerton (1981:4), are those that meet the following conditions:

1. they arose out of a prior pidgin, which had not existed for more than a generation;
2. they arose in a population where not more than 20 per cent were native speakers of the dominant language and where the remaining 80 per cent was composed of diverse language groups.

Bickerton argues that in this narrowly defined social context only one type of linguistic development is possible: that which is governed by an innate "bioprogram". An extensive survey of this hypothesis has been given by Romaine (1988:236-310) and a recent cautionary reassessment can be found in Aitchison (1995). We will explore this hypothesis below.

Creoles as advanced forms of metropolitan languages

The idea that Creoles are advanced forms of a metropolitan language draws on a number of traditions, particularly research on the levelling of colonists' dialects (e.g. German in the Balkans) and Sapirian ideas of "drift" in language development. Whether such concepts can be transferred to situations that involve the encounter of unrelated languages rather than closely related dialects must be doubted. Valkhoff (1966) provides a highly critical analysis of attempts to portray Afrikaans as an advanced form of Dutch. Nevertheless, in the climate of apartheid South Africa the same message could be respected by Raidt (1983). Diachronic purism may not be the motif that prompted Bollée (e.g. 1977a), Chaudenson (1979, 1992) and Valdman (1977c) to make similar remarks about Creole French. However, there is no general agreement as to precisely what "advanced stage of language"[6] means, nor is it clear what should make such advanced stages so impervious to other influences.

Creoloids, the post-Creole continuum, and koinés

If I have suggested, in the discussion of the various definitions of the term 'Creole', a trend towards narrower and more idealized types of language, this was not meant to exclude the numerous attempts by linguists to identify and classify the non-ideal types. For the purposes of this introductory chapter, only the two additional principal non-ideal types will be mentioned, the creoloid and the post-Creole continuum.

The need for the concept of 'creoloid', sometimes also referred to as a semi-Creole, arose out of a number of observations, made from the late 1960s onwards, including the following:

1. Whereas true Creoles develop where there is a radical break in language transmission, many languages appear to have developed with only a partial break.
2. A number of languages with no known Pidgin ancestor nevertheless exhibit many of the alleged typological properties of Creole languages.
3. Next to mixing between fully developed linguistic systems one also finds mixing between full systems and developing systems, such as Pidgins. The results of this second type of mixture tend to be structurally similar to established Creoles.

The term 'creoloid' (semi-Creole or quasi-Creole) has been applied to a motley collection of languages, including Singlish (a form of English spoken in Singapore, see Platt 1975), Afrikaans (see Markey 1975 and Kotzé 1989), Pitcairnese (see Ross 1964) and County Tyrone Irish English (see Todd 1975), as well as old languages such as Marathi, which is said to exhibit signs of intensive contact between Indo-Aryan and Dravidian languages (Southworth 1971), East African Mbugu, which contains Bantu and Hamitic elements (Goodman 1971), and, in the even more remote past, Egyptian (Zyhlarz 1932-33), Germanic (Feist 1932) or the Melanesian languages (a discussion of the latter is given by Lynch 1981). The usefulness of the term 'creoloid' rapidly declines with increasing time depth, since every language history is characterized by a certain amount of mixing and discontinuity of transmission. It is most useful in those cases where new linguistic systems can be shown to have emerged within a very short timespan, as is the case with Singlish, Taglish and similar New Englishes.

---

6   One possible interpretation, "overall reduction of language-specific markedness" is only of limited use, because markedness conflict (e.g. between phonology and morphology) is rife in language change.

11

The term 'creoloid' reflects gradience of social and linguistic parameters in the formative period of languages; the term 'post-Creole continuum', on the other hand, was coined (by DeCamp 1971b) to cater for differential developments in the subsequent history of Creoles. A distinction needs to be drawn between Creoles like Krio of Sierra Leone, Kriol of Northern Australia and Jamaican Creole, which exist in a community where the related lexifier language is also spoken and is a continuous influence on the Creole, and Creoles that do not coexist with a standard variety of their lexifier language. Examples of the latter are English-derived Sranan of Surinam, a former Dutch colony, and Dutch-based Negerhollands of the former Danish Antilles.

The pressure of standard lexifier languages can result, given the right social circumstances, in the development of a linguistic continuum. Such a continuum is called 'a restructuring continuum' and is characterized by the fact that the different varieties located on it are roughly of the same linguistic complexity. It thus contrasts with the 'developmental continuum', where differential complexity is encountered. This contrast can be depicted as follows:

developmental dimension	jargon		
	stable Pidgin		
	expanded Pidgin	post-Pidgin continuum	lexifier language
	Creole	post-Creole continuum	

restructuring dimension ———————————————————→

The varieties on the left side of the above graph are called *basilect*, the related standard lexifier language *acrolect*, and the varieties intermediate between the two, *mesolects*. The social context in which mesolectal varieties develop is one of increasing social mobility and bilingualism, commonly found in post-colonial societies.

A final term which has created some confusion is that of 'koiné'. Siegel (1993), draws attention to the following points:

1. A koiné is the result of mixing between language subsystems that are either mutually intelligible or share the same superimposed standard language.
2. Koinéization, unlike pidginization, is typically a slow and gradual process.
3. The social correlate of koiné development is sustained by intensive contacts and gradual assimilation of social groups.

Thus, although some of the linguistic consequences of koinéization can be similar to those identified in Pidgin development (for example, simplification of inflectional morphology), koinés do not involve the drastic reduction characteristic of early Pidgin development. Siegel's insistence on a terminological distinction between Pidgin and koiné seems well motivated in the light of recent findings, which suggest that there are differential linguistic

12

consequences of the encounters between separate systems, on the one hand, and subsystems of the same superordinate system on the other. It can be seen that the terminological problems addressed in this section are a reflection of the complexity of the subject matter under investigation. The definition of a Pidgin or a Creole turns out to be comparable to the definition of human language. The uncertainties encountered when defining these languages as types are reflected in our next problem, that of identifying individual Pidgins and Creoles.

The identification of Pidgins and Creoles

In the course of my academic life I have carried out fieldwork on a number of Pidgins and Creoles, one of which was a Pidgin whose speakers' existence was in no doubt, but whose existence as a language was under dispute. This language is Papuan PE, about which Capell, an expert on the linguistic scene in Papua, states:[7]

> In Papua, as against the Territory of New Guinea ... Pidgin had never been introduced. By early Government policy from the days of the first government of British New Guinea right up to very recent times, one native language had been chosen as a means of general inter-communication. (Capell 1969:109)

I managed to demonstrate, however, that PE was widely used in many parts of Papua until fairly recently (Mühlhäusler 1978a), and I had no trouble finding informants who could still speak it.

In another piece of research, I discovered a Pidgin whose existence, together with that of its speakers, was not known. Thus, Samoan Plantation Pidgin, the language spoken by workers imported from former German New Guinea, was forgotten for two reasons: because the New Guineans were officially classified as Solomon Islanders by the New Zealand Administration of Samoa; and both speakers and non-speakers believed the language to be English and not a Pidgin. By discovering that these English-speaking Solomon Islanders were in fact speakers of an early fossilized form of Tok Pisin, I was able to fill many gaps in the social and linguistic history of Tok Pisin.

Next comes the case of a language whose existence was known and which had been reasonably well documented, but whose speakers' existence was until very recently not known, Queensland Kanaka English. Officially, all Melanesian sugar-plantation workers had been repatriated from Queensland by 1906, but unofficially many had stayed on, and they and their descendants continued to use this Pidgin (cf Dutton & Mühlhäusler 1984). Again, it was perfectly easy to locate these speakers and to elicit their language.

Finally, I have also worked on a number of Pidgins where both the existence of the language and its speakers was beyond doubt, the most straightforward case being Tok Pisin of Papua New Guinea.

---

7   Capell (p c) subsequently informed me that he had destroyed all the materials he had collected on Papuan PE.

What emerges from this is that because people at the bottom of the social ladder are frequently pushed aside or ignored, little tends to be known about them or their language, and it is commonly believed that they speak the standard language in a country. Moreover, many of the lower-class Pidgin and Creole speakers are not aware that their language is a separate one. Thus, in the case of Papuan PE, my informants claimed to be speaking English, not Pidgin. The term 'Pidgin' has only recently become known to Pacific islanders and asking older inhabitants whether they speak Pidgin is unlikely to make sense to them. In a similar fashion, I obtained samples of New Guinea Pidgin German by merely asking my informants to speak German, and I have no doubts that many other nameless Pidgins and Creoles could be elicited in this fashion.

Even where speakers may be aware that they speak a separate linguistic system and have their own name for it, they may not wish to admit to the fact, particularly not to fieldworkers from outside. Thus, when Tom Dutton and I started recording Queensland Kanaka English, we visited a house where, on entering, we heard the couple speak in this variety. However, when explaining the purpose of our visit, they vigorously denied having any knowledge of the language and kept using standard language, until the atmosphere was sufficiently relaxed and until we demonstrated our own knowledge of PE. The explanation for this behaviour is that speakers of Queensland Kanaka English follow the widely used convention of non-white speakers of Australian PE or Creole English that these languages are not to be used in the presence of whites. I have come across this problem of invisibility again in my recent fieldwork on "Cattle Station English" in the North West of South Australia.

In addition to such practical problems in identifying Pidgin and Creole languages, there are also a number of theoretical ones. The question as to what constitutes *a language*, as against a dialect, argot or patois, has received considerable attention in the past, and detailed studies of the theoretical issues are found in Harris (1980), Romaine (1982b) and Rhydwen (1995). It is almost a truism that problems which have become blurred in fully developed "old" languages are identified much more neatly in the younger Pidgins and Creoles, and the question of language identification is no exception. Thus, it appears that, in the past, many writers have failed to acknowledge any problem in defining a Pidgin or Creole, and have merely followed the well-known formula of naming Pidgins after their location (1) and their principal "lexifier language" (2),[8] as in:

1	*Pidgin*	2
Chinese	Pidgin	English
Nigerian	Pidgin	English
West African	Pidgin	Portuguese
New Caledonian	Pidgin	French

---

[8]   This formula is found in widely used textbooks such as Hockett (1958:424). "Note the pattern by which 'Pidgin' and 'Creole' are used in the designations of specific languages of the sort: X-Pidgin-Y or X-Creole-Y means a Pidgin or Creole based on Y as the dominant language which has supplied at least the bulk of the vocabulary, with X or the languages of the X region, as most important second contributing factor."

This practice has been of considerable use in the initial phase of identifying and locating Pidgin languages. However, it has a number of serious drawbacks, including the following.

First, speakers of these languages are becoming increasingly aware of the negative connotations of the term 'Pidgin' and have therefore introduced new names. These are either user-based, such as Tok Pisin (New Guinea Pidgin), or Broken (for Torres Straits PE), or else invented by linguists, as with Neo-Melanesian, Neo-Solomonic (Hall's creations) and Cameroonian instead of Cameroons PE (see Todd 1979).

More seriously, Pidgins can "fly": that is, a Pidgin found in one location today may have been transported there only recently. Thus, Fernando Póo PE was spoken by mainland West Africans originating from Nigeria and the Cameroons; Melanesian PE can be traced back to New South Wales from where it spread to a number of secondary centres of innovation (see Baker 1993). Thus, New Guinea PE (Tok Pisin) was imported from Western Samoa (see Mühlhäusler 1978b); and Fijian PE (Siegel 1984) appears to be simply Kanaka English transported from Queensland; and, as has been demonstrated by Baker & Corne (1982), the label Indian Ocean Creole French is a misnomer, as the social and linguistic histories of Mauritian and Réunion Creole French are quite separate. In the light of their high geographic mobility, it appears inadvisable to associate Pidgins and Creoles too closely with a single well-defined location.

It is further known that in the course of their history Pidgins can change their lexical affiliation, a process referred to as relexification. Thus, present-day Hiri Motu may be partially relexified Papuan PE (cf Dutton & Mühlhäusler 1979) and New Caledonian Pidgin French may have resulted from relexification of an earlier PE (but see Hollyman 1976). It should be obvious that ongoing relexification poses special problems of language identity over time.

It is true that the problems raised above have been realized, at least implicitly, by a number of observers, and we thus find a few notational devices which alleviate them. An example is the use of non-localized (or only very generally localized) labels, such as Beach-la-Mar (the lingua franca spoken "between the meridians 140° and 180° and between the Equator and the Tropic of Capricorn", according to Reinecke 1937:727), or West African PE. Another relaxation is the interpretation of 'Chinese' in Chinese PE as indicating, elsewhere in the Pacific, "speakers of Chinese origin" rather than "spoken along the China coast".[9]

Nevertheless, problems remain and continue to slow down the discussion of the complex linguistic and sociolinguistic dimensions of Pidgin and Creole languages. I will now show, with examples from the Pacific, that having a name for an entity is not a sufficient condition for the reality, meaningfulness or usefulness of what is supposed to be referred to. Put differently, many of the available names are rough and ready classification devices, but misleading as descriptions or explanations.

---

[9]   This is a 20th century practice. In the 19th century, the Pidgin spoken in China was simply called 'Pidgin English' (see start of this chapter for details).

15

An illustration: counting Pidgins and Creoles in the Pacific

Even a superficial look at the vast literature on PE and Creole English in the Pacific will soon reveal a general lack of agreement both as to whether PE is spoken in a certain area or not and whether such a Pidgin is the same as or different from other known Pidgins.[10] Since, in the past, studies of Pidgins were at best the by-product of other linguistic studies and at worst anecdotal travellers' tales, disagreement as to the existence of a Pidgin in a certain area is understandable.

Most earlier sources (for example, Churchill 1911; Friederici 1911) speak of only one South Seas PE, referred to by such names as Sandalwood English, Trepang English or Beach-la-Mar. This view is continued in Reinecke (1937:751), and it is only in more recent work that different languages are distinguished. For instance, the family tree given by Hall (1961), recognizes several varieties:

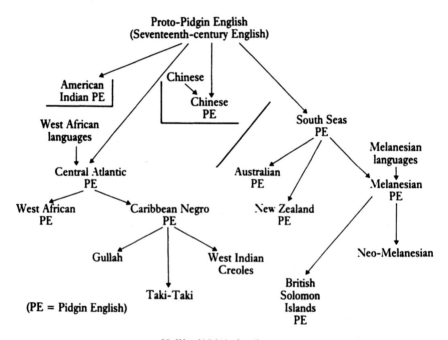

Hall's (1961) family tree

Melanesian PE in this tree roughly corresponds to the former Beach-la-Mar. The reason for the separate development of British Solomon Islands PE is given as follows: "BSI Pidgin is, in its grammatical structure, very close to Neo-Melanesian... In vocabulary, however, BSI Pidgin is distinctly archaic and closer to English than is Neo-Melanesian." (Hall 1955a:68-69). Hall's arguments were not universally accepted and other classifications are given by subsequent authors. Thus, Voegelin & Voegelin (1964:57) state: "Neo-Melanesian, or Pidgin English, is spoken in the Australian Territory of New

---

10   For West Africa a similar observation is made by Mafeni (1971:96).

Guinea (including Bismarck Archipelago), in the Solomon Islands and adjacent islands." The only other variety mentioned by them is 19th century Beach-la-Mar.

Wurm and Hancock separately published more comprehensive accounts in 1971. Their classifications can be arranged in the form of family trees, as is done below.

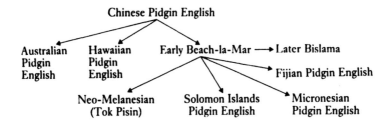

A family tree based on Wurm (1971)

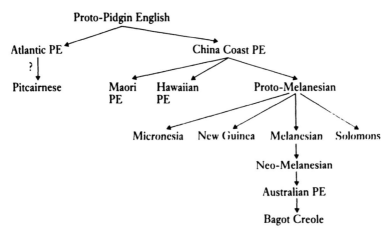

A family tree based on Hancock's (1971) classification

A number of comments need to be made on both these classifications. The principal virtues of Wurm's lie in the fact that it is based on first-hand observation, that it lists a reasonably large number of Pidgins, and that it contains a number of valuable details, such as that Beach-la-Mar is still known in Fiji (Wurm 1971:1008), as has been confirmed subsequently by Siegel (1984). Wurm is also correct in stressing that Australian PE varieties cannot be regarded as direct descendants of Beach-la-Mar (p 1013). There are two problems in his account, however. The first is that he underrates the differences between 19th century Beach-la-Mar and present-day Bislama (p 1008); and the second, that he may, like Hall (1961) have given Chinese PE too important a role in the formation of Pacific PEs (cf Baker 1987).

Hancock's often-quoted classifications (1971, 1977a, 1987) suffer from different shortcomings. Hancock (1971) not only assigns a very different

17

place to Australian PE; he also suggests that "a Neo-Melanesian-like substratum seems to be discernible" (p 509) in Hawaiian PE, a fact which is difficult to establish and even more difficult to accommodate in a family tree. More serious is the confusion between Tok Pisin (Neo-Melanesian) and Papuan PE. It is repeated on the accompanying map, where the locations for "New Guinea or Papuan PE" and "Melanesian PE" (p 575) are given as the New Guinea mainland (New Guinea or Papuan variety) and the Bismarck Archipelago (Neo-Melanesian = Tok Pisin), respectively.

That Australian PE is not a direct development from Neo-Melanesian, as claimed by Hancock, should be evident from the fact that the former antedates the latter, as has since been clearly demonstrated by Baker (1993). The problems of the 1971 classification are not resolved in Hancock's later proposals (1977a). The decision to group all geographic and temporal varieties of Melanesian PE together (1977a:368, entry 115) seems particularly difficult to justify.

In contrast, a number of very closely related Australian varieties of PE receive separate entries; the distinction between entry 107 (creolized English on the Bagot Aboriginal Reserve near Darwin, Australian Northern Territory) and entry 108 (Northern Territory Pidgin) is particularly puzzling. In actual fact, it would be more appropriate to regard these two varieties as different developmental stages of the same language, Northern Australian Kriol. Equally puzzling is Hancock's decision to provide two separate entries for the historically and structurally closely linked Norfolk Island and Pitcairn Island Creoles.

The main excuse for the shortcomings of the classifications discussed so far is the absence of reliable data on many varieties and the lack of any consistent criteria for separating or grouping different Pidgins. These problems are partly overcome in two more accounts of PE in the Pacific. Both Clark (1979) and Wurm et al. (1981) take into account fieldwork and archival work carried out on a number of lesser-known Pacific Pidgins and Creoles, including Samoan Plantation PE, New Caledonian Pidgin, Queensland Kanaka English, Ngatik Men's language and Papuan PE. The principal virtue of Clark is his awareness of changes over time in the relationships between different Pidgins (and derived Creoles). His family tree (1979:48; reproduced opposite) clearly shows that what was one language at one point may be two or more at a later period.

It would seem that Clark's account demonstrates the limits of what a family-tree model may reveal about the relationships between the various Pacific Pidgins. Although it results from a careful assessment of many sources and observation of comparative methodology, it still suffers from a number of shortcomings, including the following:

1. A continuous development is assumed, where in reality there may have been many historical breaks, caused by non-optimal patterns of transmission.

2. Geographical location is relied upon even in those cases where there have been considerable population movements between Pidgin-speaking areas.

3. As in all family trees, the role of convergence and mergers of Pidgins is ignored.

4.   Shared substratal influence is not depicted.

These points will be raised again later in this book.

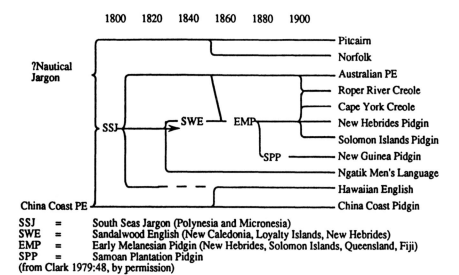

SSJ   =   South Seas Jargon (Polynesia and Micronesia)
SWE   =   Sandalwood English (New Caledonia, Loyalty Islands, New Hebrides)
EMP   =   Early Melanesian Pidgin (New Hebrides, Solomon Islands, Queensland, Fiji)
SPP   =   Samoan Plantation Pidgin
(from Clark 1979:48, by permission)

Historical relations indicated by comparative and documentary evidence

A later attempt at "counting" and mapping Pidgin Englishes (PEs) in the Pacific is made in a map (designed by Wurm et al.) in the *Language Atlas of the Pacific* (1981). The authors of this map have paid considerable attention to overcoming the limitations of a purely geographically based classification. In particular, they have distinguished typographically between flourishing, dying and dead varieties; and mapped areas of (putative) origin as well as areas where the languages were later spoken.

The most important aspect of their classification is the distinction between the *linguistically ill-defined* Pacific PE, whose spread and appearance in many different parts of the Pacific (Loyalties, Tahiti, Samoa, etc.) is documented, and *linguistically distinct* varieties such as Tok Pisin, Papuan PE, Bislama and Solomons PE. Although such a distinction would seem to be a sound basis for counting and classifying Pidgin in the Pacific, a number of problems remain unsolved, the first of which is the fact, mentioned in the text, that a number of regional dialect forms persisted in the New Hebrides until fairly recently. This may be indicative either of the lack of stabilization of the language or the fact that indigenes from different parts of the archipelago traditionally went to work on different plantations. A second problem is that it is not clear whether Micronesian Pidgin is a separate unitary phenomenon. Apart from its origin in general Pacific Pidgin, it was also influenced by Melanesian Pidgin, which was imported by labourers from German New Guinea, and the employment of Micronesians in the Samoan plantations in the 1860s and early 1870s. None the less, the compilers of the map have made significant progress in sorting out the complex picture of

19

Australian Pidgins, by stressing the basic unity of the northern Australian Creole varieties, the complexities of the preceding Pidgin situation, and the presence of a number of imported Pidgins. To conclude, when one looks back on the many attempts to classify and list English-based Pidgins and Creoles in the Pacific, a rather desolate picture emerges. The contradictory and haphazard nature of all but the most recent accounts renders them almost useless as a basis for historical or comparative work. Furthermore, an extremely complex network of relationships is hidden by misleadingly simplistic descriptive accounts.

Since I wrote the above for the first edition of this book, significant progress has been made. Excellent accounts have become available for a number of languages including Bislama (Crowley 1990a), Hawaiian PE (Roberts 1991) and several Australian PEs and Creole Englishes (e.g. Troy 1992). At the same time, the *Atlas of languages for intercultural communication in the Pacific hemisphere* (Wurm, Mühlhäusler & Tryon (eds) 1996) and its companion text volumes contain detailed information about many hitherto undescribed varieties, including Palmerston Island English, PEs of Tasmania, Victoria and South Australia, and Milne Bay English.

The message contained in the discussion of Pacific Pidgins and Creoles should be well heeded by those who wish to use these languages as examples or test cases in theoretical linguistics. In particular, one should avoid deducing general principles of historical development from a comparison of earlier and later stages of different languages, and also one should refrain from postulating universals on the basis of Pidgins which are in fact historically linked. Both sins have been committed in the past and will continue to be committed as long as solid knowledge of the socio-historical context in which these languages developed is lacking.

Increased sensitivity to the matters just raised is certainly very much in evidence in recent Pidginist/Creolist writings and at conferences. As the number of linguists working in this area increases, new Pidgins and Creoles are discovered and described, and general statements about these languages are revised in accordance. It might be interesting to list briefly just a few languages that have been added to the list of Pidgins and Creoles over the last twenty years (many of these are listed by Smith, 1995):

Pidgins	*Creoles*
Tarzanca (Foreigner Talk Turkish, Tourist Turkish)	Ngatik Men's language (English-based, Micronesia)
Dani Police Talk (West Srian)	Unserdeutsch (German-based, New Guinea)
Pidgin Koriki (Papua)	
Pidgin Afrikaans (South Africa)	Palanquero (Spanish-based, Columbia)
Samoan Plantation PE	Sri Lankan Creole Malay
Chinese Pidgin German (Kiautschou)	Berbice Creole Dutch (Guyana)
Chukotka Pidgin Chukchee (Siberia)	Karipuna (French-based, Brazil)
Singapore Bahasa Rojak	Tayo (French-based, New Caledonia)
Labrador Inuit Pidgin French	Lumbee Creole English (North Carolina)
Icelandic-Breton Pidgin	

Often, new discoveries are first announced in the *Carrier Pidgin*, the newsletter for workers in this area. Whether or not such new discoveries constitute separate languages and traditions is not always clear at first, nor do we have information, in many cases, as to the extent of their stabilization and institutionalization. However, initial data collection remains an important part of Pidgin/Creole studies and in many cases time is running out. I personally wish I had the time and opportunity to follow up the as yet undescribed languages mentioned to me in informal conversations: the Pidgin Spanish/English of Melilla (Spanish North Africa), the simplified Manam (New Guinea) used by nut collectors from this island, and the French/English Pidgin allegedly spoken in some Canadian coalmines. The social and geographical marginality of such languages does not mean that they could not be of considerable importance to our theoretical developments.

Conclusions

The field of Pidgin and Creole linguistics in more than one way illustrates the predicament of anyone engaged in pre-theoretical inquiry whilst seeking for deeper explanations. This predicament is compounded by the fact that, for many, Pidgin and Creole studies are supposed to deliver insights into the nature of abstract autonomous language systems, while at the same time such languages can be studied only in their socio-historical context. In fact, Pidgins and Creoles not only illustrate the adage that all linguistic systems leak, but are counter-examples to the notion that such independent systems exist.

As regards the two principal questions addressed in this chapter, the definition of Pidgins and Creoles; and their identification as separate languages, no unequivocal answers can be given, as is only to be expected at this phase of inquiry. It is hoped, however, that the discussion has been helpful to the development of a future explicit theory of these languages. Fortunately, one can learn much about a phenomenon without having agreed on definitions, as is suggested by the quotation at the beginning of this chapter. An awareness of the uncertainties and disagreements is certainly of greater benefit to the field than consensus about something which turns out to be a myth.

2 The study of Pidgins and Creoles

> *The Creole dialects which have grown out of different European languages grafted on African stock, though inferior in general interest to even the rudest languages of native growth, are in some respects well worth attention.*
> (Van Name 1869:123)

Introduction

When the history of linguistics in the 20th century comes to be written, a separate chapter should be devoted to the question "What did linguists regard as legitimate topics of investigation?" For a long time only a few languages were thought worthy of attention; the remainder were given labels such as "ungrammatical" or "deviant".

Grammarians in earlier centuries regarded the classical languages – Hebrew, Latin and Greek – as the only ones deserving of grammatical study, and it was commonly accepted that all other languages fell short of this ideal. Languages with little or no inflection, such as English, were said to be "grammarless". This view is found in Sir William Temple's *An essay upon ancient and modern learning*, first published in 1690:

> The three modern tongues most esteemed are Italian, Spanish, and French, all imperfect dialects of the noble Roman; first mingled and corrupted with the harsh words and terminations of those many different and barbarous nations, by whose invasions and excursions the Roman empire was long infested; they were afterwards made up into these several languages, by long and popular use, out of those ruins and corruptions of Latin.

The rise of European nationalism brought a major reorientation, in that languages such as German, French and English were now regarded as systems on a par with the classical languages. At the same time, the belief that primitive peoples from other parts of the world communicated by means of barbarous tongues remained firmly established. In fact, it was hoped by 18th century linguists that the study of languages spoken by "culturally primitive" and illiterate people could throw light upon the origin of human language.

It is not very long ago that the Reverend Farrar could publish a long list of language freaks including the following (1899:36-37):

> What shall we say, for instance... Of the Yamparico, "who speaks a sort of gibberish like the growling of a dog", and who "lives on roots, crickets, and several bug-like insects of different species?' Of the aborigines of Victoria, among whom new-born babes are killed and eaten by their parents and brothers, and who have no numerals beyond three? Of the Puris of Brazil, who have to eke out their scanty language by a large use of signs, and who have no words for even such simple conceptions as 'tomorrow', and 'yesterday'? (...) Of the Fuegians, "whose language is an inarticulate clucking", and who kill and eat their old women before their dogs, because as a Fuegian boy naively and candidly expressed it,

"Doggies catch otters, old women no?" (...) Of the negroes of New Guinea, who were seen springing from branch to branch of the trees like monkeys, gesticulating, screaming, and laughing?

When observers began to take a closer look at the so-called "primitive" languages, however, they often met with intricacies of grammatical organization that were unfamiliar to them. Thus, the notion that there were developed and underdeveloped languages began to make way, in the late 19th century, to the now widely accepted view that all human languages are of comparable complexity

The question as to what constitutes equality when comparing languages has not as yet been settled, and claims in this area tend to be made on emotional rather than empirical grounds. The earlier view of a close link between grammar and culture has now given way to one in which all languages are regarded as "natural". It would seem that both views are mistaken, however: the former in believing that "primitive man" reveals himself as ignorant and "natural" in matters of language, the latter in ignoring that what seems "natural" to the uninitiated observer turns out to be to a large extent man-made and cultural. This criticism implies that there may be differences in the extent to which human languages can be said to be "natural", and it is suggested that Pidgins and Creoles play a key role in this debate (see Mühlhäusler 1989a). This question, together with that of evaluating linguistic systems, will be taken up again later in this book.

It is interesting that the very data relevant to the question of equality were for so long ignored, and that the status of true languages has continued to be denied to a number of linguistic phenomena, namely child language, Pidgins (and Creoles), and second-language learners' approximative systems. What is common to these languages is that they are linguistic systems in development.

The view that such developmental systems were deviant in some way was dominant prior to 1970, and linguists lacked the conceptual paradigm to describe the dynamics of language development in time and space. Thus, the utterances made by a child were regarded as faulty imitations of the parents' mode, and PE was labelled "bad" or "broken" English. Modern child language studies, however, show that, far from being faulty imitations, the utterances made by a child reflect a separate language system.

In spite of some pioneering attempts by scholars such as Schuchardt and Hall in the field of Pidgin and Creole studies, the view that these are parasitic rather than independent language systems is still widely found. However, a close study of Pidgins reveals that they are systems in their own right. Like child language, Pidgins are highly dynamic, becoming more complex as the communicative demands of their users increase. As with child language, a Pidgin illustrates the capacity of human beings to create efficient communication systems, the principal difference between the two being that children are communicating in an established language community, whereas Pidgins develop to serve new language communities.

Since Pidgins illustrate how adults learn and create new languages, their study has become a major research area in second language teaching and learning. It is now becoming clear that the errors committed by, say, a second language learner of English are to a large extent systematic and can be described in terms of natural developmental processes. In contrast to the development of Pidgins, which takes place without formal tuition or pressure to conform to a pre-existing standard, a formal second-language-learning context introduces elements that may run counter to the "natural" learning order. A close study of Pidgins as examples of "naturally" learnt languages may well result in more efficient second-language teaching.

Today, there are few areas of human communication that are not regarded as a legitimate field of investigation. What is more, developmental systems such as child language and Pidgins are increasingly regarded as central to the study of human language and language-learning capacity.

The reasons why Pidgins and Creoles have been regarded in the past as marginal are not just sociocultural; their neglect also sprang from the lack of both adequate recording facilities and the availability of descriptive models capable of dealing with variability, rapid change and context-dependency. The motives underlying the few studies of these languages that were undertaken in spite of the unattractiveness of the topic will be explored shortly.

Grammar as a gentleman's pastime

Many of the early accounts of Pidgins and Creoles come from the pen of gentleman travellers and administrators whose attention they had attracted because they appeared to them as caricatures of the civilized European tongues. Thus, in the preface to one of the first accounts of Jamaican Creole (Russell 1868), we read: "This little work was never intended originally to meet the eye of the Public; the writer merely prepared it as a source of social amusement to such of his friends as are of a literary turn". A similar sentiment is expressed by Churchill, sometime consul-general of the United States in Samoa and Tonga, in his remarks on Beach-la-Mar, the cover term for the various Pidgin and Creole Englishes of the western Pacific: "Beach-la-mar is an amusing speech; in this brief treatise we have studied it with gaiety of enjoyment which it would be a shame to have repressed" (1911:31).

We can thus see the establishment of a tradition which survives in present-day journalism, where expert and non-expert alike could agree, and where dilettantes could achieve easy recognition and acknowledgment of their own superiority. Pidgins and Creoles, at the lowest levels, have become an after-dinner joke or, to borrow an expression widely used in expatriate circles, a "tropicism", a typical example being this newspaper extract:

> *Those Esses and Tees*
>
> We all know how the New Britain native – around Rabaul more especially – mixes up his esses and tees. He calls a cup of tea "cup sea" and the Post Office "Hout Pote".
>
> Had a puzzling illustration of this other evening. Driving along from Kokopo in one of Tex Roberts' cars the lad suddenly brought the six cylindered juggernaut to a standstill.
>
> "Why the thusness?" I enquired, somewhat bewildered, in my pidginese.
>
> "Me like pus him sail lice", came the response, as he switched on the red light at the rear. – Joy Rider.   (*The Rabaul Times*, 21 July 1933)

It is only a small step from such light-hearted abuse to outright racist nastiness. Thus, a comment on West African PE (by Buchner (1885) in the

24

Deutsche Kolonialzeitung) begins with the statement: "One likes the negro because of his droleness; at the same time one hates him because of his infamy" (my translation). PE is seen by Buchner as the result of such ambivalent attitudes, the funny side being illustrated by the names given by Europeans to their servants, including Bloody Fool, Dirty Fellow, Peasoup, Brandy, Empty Bottle, Mustard and the like (for more on name giving, see Foster, Mühlhäusler & Clarke *forthcoming*).

How the giving of European names reflects both European power and the namer's contempt for Aboriginal people can be seen in the following description of a scene at Milne Point on the Yorke Peninsula in 1850:

> After dinner, I paid a visit to the blacks at their worleys and fraternized with them over some of their fish - they corroboree'd after a fashion and I sung them lots of English songs with which they appeared much pleased and they tried to imitate them. I requested [sic] to give 'white fellow' names to the children and I christened them according to their appearance, 'Belly ache', 'Potbelly', 'Spindle Shanks', 'Duck legs', 'Flat nose', 'Goggle eyes' and so forth. The lubras were some of them very good-looking and they wanted names too so I gave them 'Morning Star', 'Queen of Beauty', 'Water Lilly', 'Snowball', etc.   (Snell's diary, 12 July 1850)

Observations on the lack of linguistic sophistication of Pidgin speakers are often handed down from one generation of amateur linguists to the next. Typical examples are the numerous reports on the name for 'Pidgin' in Pacific PE. In 1902, Baron von Hesse-Wartegg (1902:53) reports the form *big fellow box spose whiteman fight him he cry too much*; and Daiber writes in the same year (1902:255): "It was a Papuan who, horrified, told of *big fellow box white fellow master fight him plenty too much, he cry* (of the big box which the white man beats so much that it screams)". Later, one finds *big fellow bokkes, suppose missis he fight him, he cry too much* (Friederici 1911:100), *big fellow box, stop house, suppose you fight him, him cry* (reported for Samoan Plantation PE by Neffgen in the *Samoan Times* of 27 March 1915); Shelton-Smith (1929) mentions the more likely version of *fight im bokis moosik* for 'to play the piano'; more recently, Mihalic (1969:39) mentions the form *him big fella box, suppose you fight him, he cry* without claiming the authenticity of the version; Balint in his 1969 dictionary lists the entry *bikpela bokis bilong krai taim yu paitim na kikim em*, and lastly (but perhaps not finally), Rushton (1983:82) gives *wan bigfella bokis inside he got plenty tiit all - same sark, an time missus he hitim an kickim he cry out too much*. It may be noted that none of the sources quoted has the same "name" for the piano. Crowley (1990a:37) provides a similar list of this "dreary old joke" for Bislama.

Very little has changed over the years; perhaps, the most important shift is that new technologies are reflected in equally dubious circumlocutions, such as *mixmaster bilong Jesus Christ* for 'helicopter'. Whereas such expressions serve to illustrate the perceived "brighter side" of the colonized peoples, the absence of grammatical distinctions present in related European lexifier languages is frequently appealed to illustrate their mental inferiority, unreliability or brutishness. Only a few of the many examples can be mentioned here. Thus, Adam (1883, quoted from Hesseling 1905:52) opines that "Creoles are adaptions of French or English to the phonetic and grammatical mentality. . . of a linguistically inferior race" (my translation).

25

Linguistic examples often accompany such statements. Very prominent are comments on the absence of the copula, which is also included in this statement by Churchill (1911:23): "In our system of formal grammar the only thing which at all approximates this idea is the verbal noun. The savage of our study, like many another primitive thinker, has no conception of being in the absolute; his speech has no true verb 'to be'.

Overt racism is found in the following lexicon entries in a booklet on Fanakalo (Pidgin Bantu of Southern Africa):

> **AS, adv....sa.** Unbelievable but true. Proves that the native mind works in the opposite direction to ours ...
> **BEAT, vb... chaiya.** "I'll beat you." "Mena chaiya wena." If you are going to get any effect do it first and talk later.
> **GO, vb. int.....hamba** (hortative-footsack).
> **LIE, vb.....** It is extraordinary that there are so few words to describe this national pastime of the native Africans...
> (Aitken-Cade 1951, as quoted in Cole 1953:553)

Contempt for Pidgins and Creoles and their speakers sometimes goes hand in hand with a different emotion, that of pride that the Pidgin or Creole concerned was derived from the writer's own superior native tongue. Thus, while complaining that the "natives" have rendered the European language a "debased mongrel jargon", "a crude macaronic lingo", "a perversion" or one of many similar expressions found in the relevant literature, even in its debased form the European language remains superior to what the "primitive natives" had before. Thus Grimshaw writes on the adoption of Papuan PE by the inhabitants of Rossel Island:

> To be addressed in reasonably good English of the 'Pidgin' variety, by hideous savages who made murder a profession, and had never come into actual contact with civilisation, is an experience perplexing enough to make the observer wonder if he is awake. Yet this is what happens on Rossel Island. English is the 'lingua franca' of the place, filling up the gaps – and there are many – in the hideous snapping, barking dialect that passes for speech along the coast, and making communication possible among the tribes of the interior, who vary so much in language that many of them cannot understand one another. How did this come about? I fancy, through the unsatisfactory nature of the Rossel dialects. Any that we heard were scarcely like human speech in sound, and were evidently very poor and restricted in expression. Noises like sneezes, snarls, and the preliminary stages of choking – impossible to reproduce on paper – represented the names of villages, people, and things.
> (Grimshaw 1912:191-92)

The folk views expressed by the gentlemanly and not so gentlemanly writers of the passages quoted here have influenced professional linguists, educators and administrators for a long time and often still do.

Studies in defence of Pidgins and Creoles

The distorted characterizations and attacks on Pidgins and Creoles were effective for a number of reasons, not least because the speakers of these languages could not defend themselves, being illiterates at the bottom of the colonial hierarchy. Their voice could be heard only through the mediation of a small number of understanding outsiders and, in a very few cases, members of their own community who had risen to a position of respect within their society. One of the earliest defenders of a Creole was the philologist and superintendent of the editorial department of the British and Foreign Bible Society, William Greenfield. The full background to his *A defence of the Surinam Negro-English version of the New Testament* (1830) is given by Reinecke (1980). Greenfield's defence followed an attack in the *Edinburgh Christian Instructor* on the Sranan translation of the New Testament by the Moravian Brothers (Unitas Fratrum) in 1829. The translators were taken to task for being "at pains to embody their barbarous, mixed, imperfect phrase in the pages of schoolbooks, and to perpetuate all its disadvantages and evil consequences by shutting them up to it as the vehicle of God's word". The attacker concludes that, with a little birching and patience, broken English could be replaced by good English in Surinam.

Greenfield's defence includes many points that have come to make up the standard repertoire of those protecting a Pidgin or Creole from its detractors. For instance:

1. Creoles and related lexifier languages are mutually unintelligible.
2. The Creole is a mixed language, (that is, a separate system) comparable to Middle English which had developed out of Anglo-Saxon and French and which, in earlier times, had similarly been accused of being "a barbarous jargon, neither good French nor good Saxon".
3. Etymological spelling can give a totally distorted view of a Pidgin and Creole.
4. Creoles may be more simple in the sense of more regular than their source languages, but not necessarily less developed in expressive power. They are as systematic as any other language.
5. Creoles are not inherently suppressive, but represent a medium through which people can express their own feelings and bring about their own liberation.

Greenfield was far ahead of his time, however, and his spirited defence of Sranan did little to convince those in charge of mission language policies. Similar cycles of attack and defence were to be repeated with languages such as Afrikaans (see Valkhoff 1972), Haitian Creole French (Fleischmann 1978) and Tok Pisin (Mühlhäusler 1979). Many of Greenfield's arguments are also found in the later history of Sranan, for instance in the defence of the language by the missionary Wullschlaegel in his 1858 dictionary.

The fact that the poverty of expression in Creoles is mainly in the minds of those with insufficient knowledge of the language is also a main theme in Thomas' (1869) defence of Trinidad Creole French. Born the son of freed slaves, John Jacob Thomas became a highly respected teacher and a vocal defender of the rights of the members of his race. His realization that misunderstandings of the language were at the root of many social problems resulted in his publication of his *Creole Grammar*. Closer to our own time, Robert A Hall began to defend a number of Pidgins and Creoles in Oceania and the Caribbean, his best-known defence being *Hands off Pidgin English* (1955b), a staunch piece of writing. The book was written in direct reaction to a United Nations pronouncement in 1953 deploring the use of Tok Pisin in the Australian-administered Trust Territory of New Guinea.

Hall's involvement in the politics of Pidgins and Creoles has had considerable impact on this field of study. It can be seen to be causally related to two recent developments: first, the widespread support of professional linguists for many Pidgin and Creole languages and the rights of their speakers, often in the face of continued public animosity; and second, the fact that most of the defence of these languages remains in the hands of expatriate experts, although a small number of Pidgin and Creole speakers from the countries concerned have now also taken up these issues. This situation can lead to conflict, as it has indeed done in a number of instances. Interesting comments are given by Eades (1982:62ff).

Early missionary and pedagogical grammars

We have already noted conflicting views of mission bodies on Pidgin and Creole languages. On the one hand, missionaries aimed at quick and efficient communication with the peoples they were trying to convert but, on the other hand, there appears to have been a widespread feeling that the word of God would be debased by being written or preached in an "inferior" language. It is in this situation of conflict between everyday preoccupation and long-term goals that most of mission grammar writing and lexicography for Pidgins was done. The best results were obtained in those areas where the Pidgin and Creole and its related lexifier language did not co-exist, or where missionaries were not native speakers of the lexifier language. How different missions dealt with their communicative problems will now be illustrated with a few case studies.

Negerhollands (Virgin Islands Creole Dutch)
The islands of St Thomas, St John and St Croix were settled in the early 18th century by Dutch planters and their slaves. Soon after they were taken over by the Danes, who eventually sold them to the United States in 1915. A Dutch-based Creole appears to have sprung up within a very short time, and this language was used by both Danish and German missionaries operating on these islands (for details, see Stein 1989, and van Rossem & van der Voort 1996). Magens in 1770 produced *Grammatica over det Creolske sprog*, based on a Latin model. It is the first systematic account of any Creole. This was followed by a burst of publishing activity, and another grammar for the use of German missionaries appeared around 1802. As the language has very severely declined since – the last speaker died in 1987 – it might well have remained unrecorded without such missionary activities.

Annobón Creole Portuguese
The island of Annobón in the Gulf of West Africa was settled by the Portuguese planters and their slaves at the beginning of the 16th century. It was ceded to Spain 1777, but proper Spanish control does not predate 1850. The first priest was also installed at about that time, and a mission station was opened in 1882 to serve the 1800 inhabitants of the island. Two of the first Spanish missionaries wrote grammars of Annobonese, both modelled on traditional classical grammars (Barrena 1957 (2nd edition) and Vila 1891). A catechism and other religious writings followed, although both missionaries

28

made it perfectly clear that this was an interim measure only and that a mastery of standard Spanish by the entire population was the ultimate aim.

Chinook Jargon

This language, based on Chinook spoken at the mouth of the Columbia River, was an important trade language in pre-European times,[1] but spread and developed considerably with the advent of European fur traders and settlers. Most of the important grammar and dictionary writing for this language is due to the efforts of the Catholic and, to a lesser extent, assorted Protestant missions, in particular Le Jeune's practical vocabulary (1886). Its large body of religious writings is also due to missionary influence. As observed by Reinecke (1937:640): "In so far as the Jargon has a literary form it is due to the missionaries, chiefly Roman Catholics." Such early graphization and standardization incidentally pose a considerable problem for those who would like to regard Chinook Jargon as a paradigm case of a non-European-derived Pidgin. What initially seemed a natural language again turns out to be one that is heavily influenced by culture, not least European culture.

Sango

Sango is the Pidgin version of a small vernacular (c. 5,000 speakers) in the Central African Republic. Since its modest beginnings as a riverine lingua franca in the 1890s, it has experienced considerable linguistic and social expansion in the wake of European penetration of the area (see Samarin 1982). It is today the most important language of this African nation. A number of smallish vocabularies were in currency at the turn of the century, but genuine descriptive work does not predate 1953, when Samarin's pedagogical grammar appeared.

Vanuatu Bislama

The French priest Pionnier who lived on the island of Malakula between 1893 and 1899, like the German missionaries who worked on Tok Pisin, is of particular interest because "his knowledge of English was minimal, so he cannot be accused of anglicizing his data, a suspicion that we can never escape with most other sources" (Crowley 1990a:39). His grammatical description and lexicon (Pionnier 1913) remain one of the most important sources for historians of this Pidgin, as both Keesing (1988) and Crowley (1990) have demonstrated. A second important missionary description of this language is that by Camden (1977).

We have so far considered cases where missionaries, for reasons best known to themselves, have been the initiators and promoters of Pidgins and Creoles and their study. However, missionaries did not always favour the use of these languages and, in some cases, were instrumental in suppressing their study, as the following examples illustrate.

Papuan Pidgin English

In spite of the fact that Papuan PE was at one time probably the most widely understood language of Papua, its existence was played down and denied by both government and missionaries. Arguably the missionaries who controlled

---

[1] This view is not shared by everybody working on this language. For a comprehensive discussion, see Thomason (1981).

most teaching as well as other important areas of communication, are to be held responsible for the decline of this language. Newton appears to reflect the prevalent attitudes of the missionaries towards Papuan PE when he deplores its use in religious services in Samarai prison:

> It would approach blasphemy were one to put in print the form in which truths of religion appear in 'Pidgin' English, as for instance the way in which the Almighty is spoken of, or the relation of our Blessed Lord to the Eternal Father, even though the close connection of the sublime and the ridiculous has elements of humour ... For my own part, when I have taken a gaol service I could never bring myself to use 'Pidgin' English, and not simply because I am not familiar with it.   (Newton 1914:26-27)

No dictionaries or grammars were ever compiled, and none of the scriptures ever translated into this language. Instead, the missionaries developed a number of indigenous languages as mission lingue franche for restricted areas and, for the remainder, lent their support to Hiri Motu, the Motu-based Pidgin (see Dutton 1985a). The legacy of such policies is a Papua New Guinean nation that is split into two: PE-speaking (Tok Pisin) former German New Guinea and Hiri Motu-speaking former British/ Australian Papua. The political and financial disadvantages of this are very considerable. Further details on this language can be found in Mühlhäusler (1996:128-37).

Mauritian Creole
The case of Mauritius illustrates the more general principle that speakers of a superimposed European language frequently find it difficult to accept a lexically related Pidgin or Creole. Thus, in Mauritius extensive passages of the bible were translated into Creole by an Anglophone Protestant missionary while the French-speaking Catholic missionaries tended not to encourage this language. An illustration of the latter is the title of a paper written by Father Louis Ducrocq in 1902: *L'idiome enfantin d'une race enfantine* (the childish language of a childish race).

Town Bemba
Town Bemba, a partially pidginized and creolized language spoken in the Zambian copperbelt, appears to have been discouraged by European missionaries until the very recent past. Heine reports:

> Amongst the Europeans, 'Town BEMBA' up to today has not much been in vogue. In comparison with BEMBA of the rural districts it is designated as "slang", "broken BEMBA", "English with BEMBA grammar", or "mixed gibberish". This also applies to the missionaries, who had declared against the use of 'Town BEMBA', but had on the other hand significantly promoted the tribal language of BEMBA as language of education in the schools.   (Richardson 1961:27, quoted in Heine 1970:59)

The reason for these mission attitudes may be related to the widespread mission aversion to urban modes of life and speech.[2]

---

[2]   The basis for most standard Pidgins and Creoles developed by missionaries tends to be a conservative rural form of the language, as is illustrated with Tok Pisin (see Freyberg 1975) or Sranan (Voorhoeve 1971).

Other languges
Further examples of missionary activities leading to the decline of lingue franche are cases where an existing language was associated with Islam, such as Bazaar Malay in German New Guinea (cf Seiler 1982) and Swahili in some parts of East Africa. In sum, missionary work on Pidgins and Creoles, in spite of all its shortcomings, constitutes one of the major sources of information on earlier stages of these languages. Missionaries were involved insiders in language and communication matters, and were often forced to develop communicative solutions on the basis of limited information and resources. Although most missionary writings are of a descriptive type, some comparative and theoretical material is available. A contribution illustrating this point is Markey (1983:110-13).

Pidgins and Creoles in philology

Linguistics in the 19th century was dominated by the comparative and historical paradigm. Among the opinions widely held by the scholarly establishment of the day were the following:

1. that it was possible to reconstruct family trees for languages and to trace back contemporary languages to an original ancestral language;
2. the idea of linguistic evolution: highly inflected languages were often regarded as developmentally more advanced;
3. that languages change from within, following natural laws: both language mixing and "man-made" changes were regarded as marginal, and sound changes, in particular, were regarded as mechanical exceptionless processes;
4. scientific treatment of language is seen as historical study.

It is easy to see why Pidgins and Creoles were not popular within this paradigm. In particular:

a) They apparently resulted from convergent (mixture) rather than divergent processes;
b) They had few inflectional properties;
c) Regular sound changes and correspondences were difficult to establish: even more frequently than in the case of the older languages studied by the philologist, exceptionless sound laws turn out to be a myth;
d) as Pidgins and Creoles were short lived, their study must have seemed unlikely to throw any light on the question of an ancestral human language.

It is for reasons such as these that the father of Pidgin and Creole studies, Hugo Schuchardt (1842-1927), was regarded as a rebel against the established neo-grammarian doctrine. Although Schuchardt set out to disprove the notion of regularity of sound change with Pidgin and Creole data, he soon became interested in other aspects of these languages, particularly the interaction between typologically and historically different grammars, and in his late writings the operation of language-independent universal forces in their formation. This latter interest links him to some of his lesser-known predecessors, such as the Portuguese scholar Coelho.

31

Schuchardt remains a source of inspiration for present-day scholars for a number of reasons, notably his highly detailed descriptions of many of the world's lesser-known Pidgins and Creoles, in particular those related to Portuguese, and because he advanced ideas far ahead of his times, such as the post-Creole continuum, species-specific language, and the relationship of Black American English to its Creole predecessors.

Schuchardt's considerable creativity and originality of thought are balanced, unfortunately, by a number of shortcomings. He appears to have been unable to construct a coherent model out of his numerous observations, and he often mixes irrelevant details with pertinent theoretical remarks. This, together with his lack of skills in academic politics, accounts for the fact that his writings remained relatively unknown until recently. The appearance of two edited translations of his major writings on Pidgins and Creoles by Markey (Schuchardt 1979) and Gilbert (1980) have brought a new era of appreciation (see also Gilbert 1983).

In addition to his topic being regarded as marginal by his colleagues, the Dutch scholar Hesseling (1859-1941) faced the problem of writing in a minority language. Like Schuchardt, he had gone through the mill of Indo-European studies and subsequently held the chair of Byzantine and Modern Greek at Leiden University. His principal interest, koiné Greek, appears to have led him to the study of contemporary languages of a similar nature, in particular Afrikaans and Negerhollands. In later life he also looked at Creoles based on languages other than Dutch and worked on generalities in the construction of these languages. Unlike Schuchardt, whose major concern was that of substratum grammar, Hesseling regarded language-independent modes of second-language acquisition as the most powerful agents of Pidgin and Creole formation. Like Schuchardt, Hesseling was regarded as a minor figure, even in his home country. A revaluation of his work began with Valkoff's writings on Afrikaans (1966, 1972) and an English translation of some of Hesseling's creolist writings (Markey et al. 1979).

Pidgin and Creole studies continued to be discussed within the framework of comparative and historical linguistics. On the whole, existing methodology was adopted, and their overall impact on philological studies has been almost negligible. We can only single out a few later studies in our brief survey.

Around 1925, a number of scholars suggested pidginization and/or creolization as a major factor in the development of language families. One example is Ray (1926) in which the so-called "pidginization hypothesis of Melanesian languages" was proposed. According to this (p 597), Melanesian languages were regarded as a mixture of Papuan and Indonesian languages:

> The IN [Indonesian] in MN [Melanesian] is a foreign element, introduced by colonists from the west. These settled on some of the smaller islands which became centres of trade and influence in the sea round about, the Pidgin-IN of the settlement eventually modifying and introducing a certain amount of likeness into the originally different dialects ... The IN words found in Melanesia have the characteristics of a Pidgin-tongue.

It is not clear whether the present-day Melanesian languages should be seen as continuations of contact Pidgins or whether they are more in the nature of mixtures of two full systems. Neither Ray nor any of his successors (discussed in Lynch 1981) have a sufficiently powerful model of mixing and pidginization to come up with genuine explanations. Similar problems are also found with Feist's (1932) suggestion that the origin of the Germanic family of languages involved pidginization, and with a later study by Politzer (1949) making similar claims for the Romance languages. Finally, one should mention later work on the emergence of Middle English (Bailey & Maroldt 1977) and Domingue (1977). Again, as was the case with explanations of the origin of Melanesian languages, the distinction between creolization, pidginization and mixing tends to be insufficiently precise, and questions as to whether Middle English can be regarded as a continuation of a medieval French-Anglo-Saxon contact jargon (Albert 1922) cannot be meaningfully asked. For further cautionary notes, see Mufwene (1989).

The role of Pidgin and Creole research as a corrective against overly dogmatic models of linguistic relationship and change thus remained minimal. In contrast, the influence of established comparative historical methodology on the study of these languages has been considerable. In spite of the unsuitability of this model, it has been applied over and over again to Pidgin and Creole data. We can discern two motifs in such studies: the older one of relating Pidgins and Creoles to their European "parent" languages; the more recent of determining interrelationships among Pidgins and Creoles. A staunch defender of the validity of this genetic model is Hall, and it may be this linguistic conservatism which, more than anything else, made Pidgin and Creole linguistics acceptable in North America and elsewhere. Hall regards both Schuchardt's claims that the existence of mixed languages invalidates the genetic model and Meillet's counterclaims that Creoles are direct descendants of languages such as French (for example, Meillet 1921:85) as pseudo arguments based on too stringent criteria for linguistic continuity.[3] Instead, he proposes that by genetic relationship we simply mean: "when we find systematic correspondences in all aspects of language structure ... between two languages .. we conclude that one must be a later stage of the other, or else that they must have come from a common source" (1958:369).

Although such a view enabled Hall to reconcile historical comparative linguistics with American structuralism, it had two damaging consequences. First, it removed sociolinguistic considerations from the analysis of Pidgins and Creoles; and second, it gave respectability to static comparison, a method hardly suited to highly variable and rapidly changing linguistic entities. It is by dint of such simplifications and assumptions that Hall managed to establish the fundamental structural identity of Pidgins and Creoles and their related lexifier languages.

Partly in reaction to Hall's claims, Taylor, one of the most active Creolists of the 1950s, pointed to a number of unacceptable consequences of the traditional model of genetic relationships. In particular, he raised the question of apparently changing genetic relationships that appear to alter over the history of a Creole. He illustrated his arguments with languages such as Papiamentu, spoken in the Dutch Antilles, which allegedly changed from a Portuguese- to a Spanish-based Creole, and Sranan of Surinam, which may have changed from a Portuguese Creole to an English one (but see both Arends and Ladhams *forthcoming*). Taylor's argument was subsequently

---

3   Hall and others take discontinuity to be an annoying detail rather than a central question
     of Pidgin and Creole studies. How a different view could affect the field is discussed by
     Hockett (1950) and, more recently, by Mühlhäusler (1984a).

developed and named *relexification theory* by scholars such as Thompson (1961), and it was studied in great detail for the Surinamese Creoles (Sranan, Saramaccan, Djuka) by Voorhoeve (1973) and a range of other languages by Bakker & Muysken (1995). These studies indicate not only that shifts in genetic relationships can occur in Creoles, but also that, in most parts of grammar, there are considerable differences between European languages and their Creole "daughters", casting doubts upon claims as to genetic link. One needs to keep in mind that processes similar to those labelled 'relexification' are also encountered in non-Creole languages. The practice in many Melanesian islands actively to employ a smaller endolexicon and passively know the exolexicon of a range of structurally very similar neighbouring languages, together with the exchange of lexical items for taboo reasons again can promote outcomes such as the ones focussed on by relexificationist studies such as those by Thurston (1987) for New Britain or Gumperz & Wilson (1971) for Kupwar village in India.

A second application of comparative and historical linguistics to the study of Pidgins and Creoles is the reconstruction of their genetic relationship, sometimes with the additional aim of isolating ancestral proto-Pidgins. A first major attempt was made by Goodman (1964) who, after a detailed study of some forty lexical and grammatical features, concluded that there must be a common origin for all French Creoles and that the most likely place of origin was West Africa. A similar conclusion for the English-based Creoles of the New World is reached by Hancock (1969), where a single proto-PE with some local variants is identified as occurring on the West African coast in the 16th century. (Neither Goodman's nor Hancock's conclusions have won universal acceptance.) In a later paper (1983), Hancock supplements structural and lexical evidence with sociocultural information, paying attention to factors such as migrations, labour recruitment, shift of political boundaries and nature of contacts. That such information is an essential rather than a dispensable constituent of historical work on Pidgins and Creoles has yet to become widely accepted. Thus, in spite of the excellent models provided by Clark (1979) and Hancock, so-called "extralinguistic" factors continue to be ignored in many comparative studies. An example of how this practice affects results is a study by Gilman (1978). The author suggests that Jamaican Creole English and Cameroonian PE both derive from the same language, Proto-PE, and he implies a family tree of the type set out below.

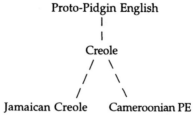

Proto-Pidgin English
|
|
Creole
/ \
/ \
/ \
Jamaican Creole   Cameroonian PE

[family tree implied by Gilman (1978)]

However, the available historical evidence suggests that Cameroonian PE as spoken today is not a continuation of earlier West African coastal PE, but a more recent import from Sierra Leone Krio (see Todd 1979), and that Krio, in turn, may be either a direct descendant of, or heavily influenced by, Jamaican Creole and possibly other West Indian Creole Englishes. The resulting family relationships would consequently be considerably less tree-like and would more closely resemble the following figure:

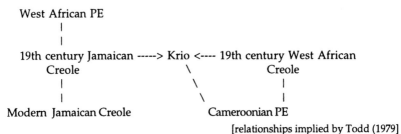

West African PE

19th century Jamaican -----> Krio <---- 19th century West African
Creole   \   Creole

Modern Jamaican Creole   Cameroonian PE

[relationships implied by Todd (1979]

Two views of the relationship between Krio, Cameroonian PE and Jamaican Creole

Thus linguistic comparisons should not be made in an *ad hoc* fashion between contemporary systems. A comparison between modern Jamaican Creole and Cameroonian PE would certainly not seem to be a sound procedure for establishing a proto-language.

A major revaluation of the significance of pidginization and creolization in reconstructing past stages of languages has been attempted by Thomason & Kaufman (1988). Their conclusion is, somewhat surprisingly, that language development without significant contact is normal and that established comparative philology can be beefed up to cope with the abnormal cases of pidginization and creolization. Thomason & Kaufman's book is a complex one and no justice can be done to it in a short paragraph. My own objections include its virtual exclusion of Australian and Pacific data, and the implicit belief that developments can be reconstructed by comparing (arbitrarily chosen) abstract states. Because Thomason & Kaufman do not challenge many of the assumptions of philology that have been challenged by, for instance, Schuchardt and C-J Bailey, their arguments will be received with some relief by many historical linguists. In my own view, Pidgins and Creoles provide radical counter-examples to comparative linguistics rather than superficial little problems.

Anthropological linguistics and sociolinguistics

In a review of the field of Pidgin and Creole studies, Bickerton (1976:169-93) expresses astonishment at the fact that it has consistently been classified as part of sociolinguistics. I have personally experienced the same reaction from many of my linguistic colleagues (i.e., a readiness to label me a sociolinguist simply because most of my work is concerned with Pidgins and Creoles). On closer inspection, one finds that genuine sociolinguistic work on these languages is a relatively recent phenomenon. Symptomatic of this is the absence, within classical anthropological linguistics in the United States (i.e. Boas and Sapir), of any attempt to analyse the linguistic and social dimensions of the many American Indian-European contact languages found in North America, a point discussed in more detail by Silverstein (1972b). It is further symptomatic that Reinecke's monumental doctoral thesis of 1937,

35

Marginal Languages, has remained unpublished and virtually unknown to anthropologists and sociologists, in spite of the fact that it summarizes and critically discusses virtually the entire body of sociological and anthropological writings on Pidgins and Creoles before 1935. A similar fate overtook the often misquoted article by Schultze (1933), which was the first attempt to provide a systematic classification of Pidgins and Creoles according to sociological criteria.

If an integrated view of Pidgins and Creoles has been lacking within anthropological linguistics and sociology until very recently, studies of individual languages, with or without critical remarks on their ethnography of speaking, have been made by numerous anthropologists. Indeed, our knowledge of the early stages of many Pidgins and Creoles would be very deficient without such studies. Let me illustrate this point with the example of Papuan PE. The most extensive reports on this language are remarks by Ray in 1907, following the Cambridge Anthropological Expedition to Torres Straits. In 1918, the Scandinavian anthropologist Landtman published *The Pidgin English of the British New Guinea*, accompanying a volume containing a vast collection of traditional stories in this language (1917). A similarly valuable collection of texts covering the Torres Straits as well as the Papuan coast is given by the Swiss anthropologist Laade (1968). In the last couple of decades things have begun to change and whilst much anthropology remains language-free, some major contributions to Pidgin and Creole linguistics have been made by anthropologists, as is evidenced by the reception Keesing's (1988) monograph on the Oceanic substrate of Melanesian PE received (cf Mühlhäusler 1989b). That the *Annual Review of Anthropology* for the year 1991 contains a detailed discussion of work in this area (Jourdan 1991) is a very positive sign.

Much of the recent upsurge in Pidgin and Creole studies again is due to the interest paid to these languages by anthropologists and anthropological linguists such as Hymes, Silverstein, Sankoff, Rigsby, Jourdan and Keesing, and by sociolinguists such as Labov, Bailey and Trudgill.

Structuralist studies

The period of structuralism in linguistics extends from the early 1920s to the 1960s. It is impossible to do justice to the many developments of structuralism but it seems worth while to single out a few areas which affected Pidgin and Creole studies. These include:

1. the emphasis on description;
2. the association with behaviourist learning theories;
3. the tendency to regard languages as self-contained systems..

The belief that linguists should describe and not prescribe, combined with the strong insistence on the inherent equality of all human languages, undoubtedly created an atmosphere wherein it was possible to produce scholarly descriptions of these once-despised languages. The most productive figure in this enterprise is Hall, who attempted comprehensive descriptions of Tok Pisin (1943), Chinese PE (1944), Sranan (1948), Haitian Creole (1953) as well as grammatical sketches of a number of other Pidgins and Creoles. Also of interest are the descriptive writings of those working on non-European-based languages, such as Samarin's work on Sango (1953) and Wurm & Harris's early writings (1963) on Hiri Motu (then called Police Motu). Common to most of the descriptive work of this kind is the relatively uncritical adherence to established structuralist methods. The legacy of this is a large body of data arranged in a very similar manner and thus well suited to comparative work (if indeed structuralism did allow the comparison of elements across systems).

Perhaps the greatest impact of structuralism on Pidgin and Creole linguistics was the promotion of a particular model of language acquisition, based on behaviourist learning theories. Since languages were thought to be learned by imitation, Pidgins were said to reflect the foreigner-talk register used by speakers of the superordinate language when addressing uneducated foreigners. In addition to imitation, interference (or substratum influence) was considered a second force in the development of Pidgins. According to Bloomfield:

> Speakers of a lower language may make so little progress in learning the dominant speech, that the masters, in communicating with them resort to 'baby-talk'. This 'baby-talk' is the masters' imitation of the subjects' speech. There is reason to believe that it is by no means an exact imitation, and that some of its features are based not upon the subjects' mistakes but upon grammatical relations that exist within the upper language itself. The subject, in turn, deprived of the correct model, can do no better now than to acquire the simplified 'baby-talk' version of the upper language (1933:472).

Such a model could provide plausible explanations for the early development phase of Pidgins and, in conjunction with the notions of interference from a learner's first language, for some of their subsequent development, but it was certainly not an adequate model for creolization, since the qualitative differences between the second-language Pidgin and the following generation's first-language Creole exclude imitation as the primary explanation. The only explanation consonant with behaviourism is the appeal to substratum influence, which is parallel to interference in the learning models appealed to at the time. In fact, Hall states:

> creolization is simply one manifestation of a broader process which, for want of a better term, we can call 'nativization'. A language is nativized when it is taken over by a group of speakers who have previously used some other languages, so that the new language becomes the native language of the group (1966:xiii).

It is interesting to observe how the role of children and their rule-changing creativity is played down in this explanation.

The view of Pidgins and Creoles as self-contained systems can be seen like the two views just discussed, as an attempt to ignore possible 'leaks' in the grammars, in particular the element of time. Hall has justified this as a useful abstraction (1975:138): "a purely descriptive analysis... is... dependent simply on a convenient fiction of the complete removal of the time element from a description". Also ignored are those areas of grammar that

37

are notoriously gradient: that is, phonetics and semantics, and the social forces shaping the creation of variation. Instead, we are given abstract common core or overall pattern accounts. Their neatness and symmetry are achieved at high cost, however. With many Pidgins and Creoles exhibiting greater variability and a faster rate of change than most older established languages, idealized descriptions are even more remote from the goal of observational adequacy. They also reinforce the social myth that Pidgin and Creole users live in static societies and are dependent for the improvement of their lot upon the crumbs that fall from their colonizers' tables.

Transformational generative grammar

In his *Selective chronology of Creole studies* (1981), Reinecke observes that transformational generative grammar (TGG), first widely publicized in 1957, has been "immensely influential in the field of Creole studies as in all linguistic theory". What he did not say is that it has been for many Creolists an almost constant love-hate relationship, resulting in eventual divorce.

In many ways TGG theory and practice remained at the very centre of structuralism. This can be seen in the following features, which are of particular importance for our present discussion.

1. Transformationalist practice is minilectal, that is, it is concerned with single idiolects or varieties at a single point in time.
2. Strict separation is made between structure and use.
3. Linguistic systems are kept separate, with a consequent aversion to fusion and mergers.
4. Synchronic and diachronic grammar are separate.

Such considerations apart, TGG has succeeded in motivating a sizeable number of scholars to do work on previously investigated aspects of Pidgins and Creoles. Thus, on the positive side, the availability of a more refined model of description led to considerable progress in the understanding of the syntax of Pidgin and Creole languages. Whereas in the early days of TGG writers attempted global descriptions of individual languages (the paradigm case being Bailey's (1966) grammar of Jamaican Creole), later writers increasingly restricted themselves to smaller subgrammars and carried out in-depth studies of constructions such as focus (e.g. Byrne & Winford 1993) or verb chaining (eg. Sebba 1987, Escure 1991, Byrne 1991, Muysken & Veenstra 1995, and Corne et al. 1996). A problem with such studies is that identification, description and explanation is focussed on decontextualized sentence-length syntactic structures, and that suprasegmental and situational clues are not considered.

A second area of research which was greatly promoted by TGG was the quest for linguistic universals and/or universals of language.[4] It is no coincidence that a number of scholars (Agheyisi 1971; Givón 1979; Kay & Sankoff 1974; Mühlhäusler 1974) should come up independently with the

---

4   Whereas by *linguistic universals* one understands the formal properties of the descriptive systems needed to account for human languages, *universals of language* refers to observable (surface) properties shared by human languages. The difference is discussed im more detail by Comrie (1981).

suggestion that Pidgins are probably the universal base from which other languages can be derived by means of language-specific transformations. Whatever the limitations of this view, it certainly directed researchers to an inquiry into the common features of Pidgins, and thus indirectly promoted the study of non-European-based Pidgins and Creoles.

The debate about the relative role of Universals and other forces in Pidgin and Creole genesis continues both at the level of general theory and at the one of studies of grammatical detail. Bickerton's (1981) bioprogram hypothesis puts forwards rather concrete proposals as to what such universals might be, particularly in the area of tense modality and aspect (TMA). For a critical survey of TMA in Creoles around the world see Singler (ed. 1990) and the even more critical remarks by Ehrhart (1992), based on her studies of New Caledonian Tayo. Again, excluding sentence-external and situational considerations from the study of modality is unlikely to resolve the many questions that remain unsolved in the TMA debate.

A third innovation of TGG of interest to Pidgin/Creole scholars was its mentalism. Language learning in this approach was not seen as imitation, but as a productive process reflecting innate mental structures. As the operation of the language acquisition device (LAD) was said to be encountered mainly before puberty, and as it was generally held that grammars of adult speakers change, if at all, by minor alteration, TGG was, strictly speaking, not suited to explaining the formation of Pidgins by adults, but only Creole formation. In spite of this, the mentalist learning model was applied to Pidgins; moreover, some traditional explanations that smacked of behaviourism, such as baby talk or substratum influence (mixing), were discarded. It is only very recently that a growing number of scholars have come to acknowledge that Pidgin formation involves a number of strategies, including universals, substratum influence and imitation, and that these factors often conspire to give a result which cannot be traced to any single factor.[5] It is also now more widely accepted, mainly as a result of numerous studies in the area of second-language acquisition (interlanguage), that adults retain the capacity to restructure and drastically change linguistic systems (cf Corder & Roulet 1976). They are true creators of language, not poor imitators of an unobtainable "target".

In addition to these shortcomings, one can identify three areas of TGG which have become particularly bothersome to Pidgin and Creole linguists, and which have led some of them to propose alternative models. These are:

1. Methodological problems with the use of intuitions;
2. Conceptual problems involving the notions of linguistic competence and ideal speaker-hearer.
3. The notion of Pidgins and Creoles as independent entities.

The use of intuitions in Pidgin and Creole linguistics, rather than a corpus of observed data as the basis of analysis, causes problems beyond the more general ones outlined by Labov (1972). This is particularly true of Pidgins that are second languages acquired and spoken by adults with wide-ranging

---

5   The consequence for arguments about Pidgin and Creole origins should be clear: the ability to relate a construction to any single factor's substratum influence, simplified model and universals, is a necessary, but not a sufficient demonstration of the influence of this factor.

differences in proficiency. As pointed out independently in a number of publications (Ardener 1971; Mühlhäusler 1974; Silverstein 1972a), it is simply impossible to obtain reliable answers about acceptability, let alone grammaticality, from Pidgin speakers. When I first set out to undertake linguistic fieldwork in Tok Pisin, I had carefully prepared a questionnaire designed to test speakers' intuitions about a number of constructions. These questionnaires ended up as a fire over which a billy of tea was made. I had come to realize that asking questions about decontextualized isolated sentences was no more regarded as a meaningful activity by my informants than asking random speakers in a Western speech community what colour skunks prefer.[6] The main difference is that Western people feel obliged to answer questions, whereas most Papua New Guineans do not, unless they be where question-answering is socially mandatory, in which case they tend to provide those answers they expect the researcher to want to hear. In addition, it should be noted that many of the metalinguistic labels linguists would wish to employ in such questions (for example, sentence, word) have no counterpart in the language under investigation. Heavy reliance on a corpus is thus unavoidable, and great care must be taken to obtain a representative sample of the language.

The question of representative data is also of importance in establishing how far Pidgins and Creoles can be related to a Chomskyan notion of grammatical competence (that is, the system of rules that an ideal speaker-hearer has internalized and that determines the relationship between the sound and meaning of sentences). The problems are greatest with two developmental stages: namely, incipient Pidgins and decreolizing Creoles.

Both Bickerton (1977) and Silverstein (1972a) hold that there is no such thing as grammatical competence in an incipient Pidgin or jargon. Rather, speakers use a number of strategies, most prominently that of calquing the grammars of their own first languages with the addition of shallow adjustment rules, which creates superficially similar surface structures. Deeper levels of grammars of different speakers would not be affected. An illustration is given in the following surface structure of Tok Pisin:

man ya i haisim ap plak   'this man hoists up the flag'

This may be analysed as either:

    noun – determiner – predicate marker – verb – particle – noun
or: noun – determiner – predicate marker – verb – verb – noun

The verb-particle analysis is preferred by European speakers (and European analysts such as Hall 1943), whereas the verb-chain interpretation is common among Papua New Guineans. Examples of similar equivocal structures in Gullah are given by Mufwene (1989).

The problem of grammatical competence in Creoles (Le Page 1973) and post-Creole situations again involves inter-speaker differences. Let me illustrate the latter situation with an example given by Bickerton (1977:31), who asked twenty undergraduate students of the University of Guyana to

---

6   The colours most commonly given are black and white, red and yellow (presumably reflecting some natural colour hierarchy), mostly with explanations why this should be so. Any Western person can be pushed into providing an explanation, which again is a quite unreasonable request.

translate the English sentence "I was sitting" into their native Guyanese Creole English. He recorded the following thirteen answers:

1	a woz sitin	2	ai de sidong	3	mi bin sidong
4	a de sitin	5	a bin sitin	6	a did sidong
7	ai biin sitin	8	mi bina sidong	9	ai bin sitin dong
10	a bina sidong	11	a woz sitin dong	12	a did sitin
13	mi bina sit				

To describe the kind of variations encountered along the post-Creole continuum as optional or free variation leads to two major problems:

1. that of selecting the obligatory forms/rules of which the remaining forms are said to be expansions or derivations;
2. the fact that the selection of 'optional' rules in many instances is not free, but severely restrained by superimposed implicational rule patterns.

Thus a transformational grammar without optional rules will under-describe the language, whereas one with such optional rules will generate numerous forms which are in clear violation of the rules of the Creole concerned. It is thus understandable that most serious scholars specializing in Pidgin/Creole studies have found the TGG paradigm inadequate or, at best, have adopted it as an interim makeshift solution. As pointed out by Muysken (1981) in the introduction to a volume entitled *Generative studies on Creole languages*, "most generativists ... have shied away from Pidgin and Creole languages because of the variability hinted at or described in the literature". Indeed, of those who have reviewed this volume, two (Markey 1981, Romaine 1984) have pointed out that the title was a contradiction in terms and that some of its papers were anti-TGG in content and aim.

The independency hypothesis of grammar, central to TGG theorizing, has been widely accepted but rarely subjected to a test. As I have tried to argue (Mühlhäusler 1992a), Pidgins and Creoles offer a particularly suitable testing ground for claims to the effect that there are or are not non-linguistic prerequisites to grammatical analysis (see Silverstein 1977). On the one hand, the dependency of Pidgins and Creoles is manifested in the continuing or recurring influence of their lexifier language. A language such as Northern Australian Kriol for many of its speakers remains substandard English whilst others regard it as a separate language. On the other hand, and in common with preliterate languages, the interpretation of many Pidgin and Creole utterances is very much dependent on contextual factors.

It could be argued that generativists have probably lost more by ignoring Pidgin and Creole evidence than Pidgin and Creole scholars have lost by ignoring ongoing theoretical work in TGG. The reason for this suspicion is that Pidgins and Creoles would seem to provide the best test cases for the central question within the generative paradigm: how can one account for the acquisition of human language?

Post-generative models

In his introduction to Bailey's *Jamaican Creole Syntax* (1966), Le Page commented:

The descriptive analysis of an idiolect at any given moment may reveal a great many overlapping systems, some of which are coming to the end of a period of change, others just beginning. The descriptive analyst freezes for a moment what is in fact a highly dynamic system, and describes it in static terms. The quantum mechanics era in linguistics has not yet arrived, but I believe that the study of Creole languages will help it forward, since it appears generally true that the kinetic energy within Creole systems is greater than that within older systems (pp xi-xii).

It is not by chance that this quantum linguistics should emerge first within the description of highly fluid Pidgins and Creoles. The first writer to point out ordered patterning in an apparently messy instance of a post-Creole language was DeCamp (1971b). He observed that basilectal, mesolectal and acrolectal features or rules cannot be combined in any order, but that the possible combinations are highly constrained. These constraints are such that the presence of the most acrolectal feature implies the presence of all other acrolectal features, but not vice versa. DeCamp illustrated this with data from Jamaican Creole English:

Acrolectal features	*Basilectal features*
+A child	–A pikni
+B eat	–B nyam
+C /θ ~ t/	–C /t/
+D /ð ~ d/	–D /d/
+E granny	–E nana
+F didn't	–F no ben

He then established that only seven of the numerous mathematically possible combinations could actually be observed or elicited, as follows:

Observed feature distribution
Speakers

1	+A	+B	+C	–D	+E	+F
2	–A	+B	–C	–D	+E	+F
3	–A	+B	–C	–D	–E	–F
4	–A	–B	–C	–D	–E	–F
5	+A	+B	+C	+D	+E	+F
6	+A	+B	–C	–D	+E	+F
7	–A	+B	–C	–D	+E	–F

These seven permitted combinations can then be arranged in such a way that each speaker differs from the next one by just one feature,[7] to yield the arrangement opposite. Such an arrangement can tell us that feature D is the most acrolectal one, in that its presence in a given speech event implies the simultaneous presence of all other acrolectal features. It excludes combinations such as **no ben** for 'didn't' and [ð] in the same speech event.

---

7   The entire continuum is called a panlectal continuum or grid. The continuum consists of a number of isolects, which differ from the one immediately above or under them by a single feature.

Rearranged data
Speaker

5	+A	+B	+C	+D	+E	+F
1	+A	+B	+C	-D	+E	+F
6	+A	+B	-C	-D	+E	+F

etc.

In its most abstract form, the panlectal grid will look as follows:

The panlectal grid

Speaker/lect	Features:				→ *more acrolectal*	
	B	E	F	A	C	D
5	+	+	+	+	+	+
1	+	+	+	+	+	-
6	+	+	+	+	-	-
2	+	+	+	-	-	-
7	+	+	-	-	-	-
3	+	-	-	-	-	-
4	-	-	-	-	-	-

This rearrangement clearly demonstrates what implicational patterns can occur. A plus implies pluses only to its left, and a minus implies minuses only to its right. The presence of a plus makes no predictions of what is found to its right; the implications are unidirectional. Instead of associating each horizontal line of pluses and minuses with a single speaker, we can make the more realistic assumption that all speakers are polylectal and hence proficient over a greater or lesser span of a polylectal grid. Although the implicational patterns are constant for all speakers of a post-Creole-speaking community in this model, individual competences can differ, as can the perceptive and productive competence of single individuals.

The model suggested by DeCamp was subsequently developed by Bailey, Bickerton and others and has become widely used not only by pidginists and Creolists, but also by sociolinguists and theoretical linguists. A large number of Guyanese Creole texts have been analysed by Rickford (1987), for instance. As the model will be referred to in several places in this volume, it would seem advisable to consider briefly some of its advantages and drawbacks here.

On the positive side, we find that it is capable of displaying, in an orderly fashion, highly variable data; that it can map differences between perception and production which tend to be particularly strong in the rapidly changing Pidgins and Creoles; and that breaks in implicational patterns can be used as indicators of breaks in continuity of transmission.

A number of limitations must be noted, however. First, the model is a way of presenting rather than explaining data. Second, although it is highly useful for displaying variation in a small area of grammar (local variation) , it is extremely cumbersome for mapping all dependencies such as might hold in a language This leads to the following, more serious, deficiencies. In the absence of any procedures for identifying dependencies for the entire grammar and lexicon, the distinction between linguistically motivated implications, historically motivated implications and accidents of the descriptivists' selection cannot be made. Implicational scales of the type A < B < C map, first and foremost, the addition of linguistic features/rules over time,[8] C being added after B, which in turn is added to the grammar after A. In an ideal world, the same implications would hold for all speakers of a speech "community". In actual fact, because of discontinuities of transmission, prestige borrowing, hypercorrection and the non-homogeneity of so-called speech communities, an implicational grid is an idealization, though admittedly considerably less so than a static monostylistic model such as TGG.

Later writers have seen the limitations of the original model and have suggested various ways of overcoming these The repairs suggested depend on the problem different critics have identified. For those who argued that implicational scales simply represent arbitrary historical events, perhaps the most important innovation is the appeal to linguistic naturalness and markedness. What it means is that the least cost for language development is where language changes from more marked to less marked,[9] and that compelling external factors are held responsible for all other changes.

Adding naturalness considerations does not address the problems other critics have identified, in particular the binary (+/−) nature of the features examined and the mono-directional nature of the post-Pidgin/post-Creole continuum. Earlier objections raised by Le Page & Tabouret-Keller (1985) have been expanded by Carrington whose concept of a multi-dimensional Creole space (1992:98) avoids a number of the shortcomings of the continuum model. The approach of Le Page & Tabouret-Keller differs from the lectological one in significant respects:

a. Linguistic variation is seen as multidimensional rather than arrangeable along a single continuum.

b. Parameters that were taken as given in earlier views, such as "language" or "speech community", are treated as explananda.

c. Language performance rather than abstract "polylectal" competence is seen as the focus of linguistic investigation.

Le Page & Tabouret-Keller differ in a number of other regards as well. Most differences relate to their view that language is not a closed, self-contained system capable of rigorous testing and scientific hypothesizing. Instead, these authors point out:

> Our conviction remains that it is extremely hard to carry out sociolinguistic work in a rigorously hypothesis-testing manner when one comes to a society as an outsider and tries, as we have tried, to make no prior assumptions about the social divisions within that society (1985:4).

Le Page & Tabouret-Keller's question, "How do languages come into being?", is answered by appealing to the concept of "acts of identity", i.e. acts by which speakers reveal both their own personal identity and their search for social roles. Languages and their derived grammatical regularities are thus regarded as social constructs, the result of choices that speakers make from

---

8   It is for this reason that the model is referred to as a time incorporating developmental or quantum model.

9   Some Creolists might prefer to regard this as from less natural to more natural. For up-to-date remarks on markedness in creolistics, see Mufwene (1991).

time to time in order to fulfil certain social and personal needs. This view differs dramatically from both that presented by the practitioners of transformational grammar who regard entities such as English as "natural languages" as well as that expressed by Bickerton (e.g. 1981) that Creole genesis is regulated by an innate bioprogram.

The acts of identity approach has triggered off healthy research activity on a range of languages, including Creoles. Studies such as that by Rhydwen (1993) suggest that, as well as voluntary acts of identity, there are also forced ones, such as missionary attempts to make Kriol the language of identity in the North of Australia.

Pidgin and Creole studies as a separate field of inquiry

Having commented on the status of Pidgin/Creole studies *vis-à-vis* the main directions within modern linguistics,[10] I will now examine their emergence as a separate subdiscipline of linguistics.

The first international conference on Creole studies, attracting a total of thirteen participants, was held in Jamaica in 1959. Many of the questions which were subsequently to dominate the field, such as monogenesis, the use of TGG and the status of abstract descriptions, were postulated at this gathering. DeCamp (1971a:14) contends that: "the birth of the field of Pidgin-Creole studies may be dated from that April afternoon in Jamaica, when Jack Berry suddenly remarked 'All of us are talking about the same thing'". At the conclusion of the 1959 conference a considerable amount of agreement had been reached both as to the questions to be asked within a separate subdiscipline of Pidgin and Creole studies, and as to the methodology to be used, in particular field recordings. Last, but not least, there was also consensus as to the social role of Creole studies – that is, that of promoting an understanding of these languages and their speakers, in particular in defending them against the claims of cultural imperialists and colonialist/racist policies.

The second international conference was again held in Jamaica, in 1968, attracting more than 50 specialists. It demonstrated the significant quantitative and qualitative growth of the new field. Of particular importance was the re-establishment of strong links with anthropology and sociology, and the beginnings of alternatives to TGG.

By 1975, the venue of the third international conference on Pidgins and Creoles had been shifted to Hawaii, a shift signalling the growing awareness of the role of the Pacific in the formation and development of these languages. It was, incidentally, the first such conference I attended, and left lasting impressions of conversations with John Reinecke, David DeCamp and many future colleagues. This conference signalled the beginning of specialization within Pidgin and Creole studies. The expressed aim of the conference organizers was to solicit papers from the following three areas: universals in Pidgins and Creoles; challenges to linguistic theory; uniqueness and specificity in individual Pidgins and Creoles. The largest number of contributions fell into the second category, illustrating the fact that Pidgin and Creole research had begun to shake off the limitations of pre-existing

---

[10] I have ignored models within which the description and the use of Pidgins and Creoles as evidence has been minimal, such as systemic, tagmemic and stratificational grammar.

models of description and explanation. Instead, the focus was on the explanation of linguistic variability. In linking synchronic variability to diachronic development, for a number of participants, the traditional division into synchronic and diachronic linguistics became blurred. The most influential development in the first category was Bickerton's remarks on linguistic universals and his arguments, against Sankoff, Givón and myself, that natural (i.e. corresponding with the basic neurological equipment of the species) universals do not occur in Pidgins, but only in first-generation Creole speakers. This argument is still being debated, as will be made clear later in this book.

Further specialization of the field is suggested by the title of the 1979 conference, *Theoretical Orientations in Creole Studies*, held at St Thomas in the Caribbean. In his incisive introductory remarks to the proceedings of this conference, Alleyne (1980) gave a highly self-critical appraisal of the field and its practitioners, pointing, in particular, to the continued dominance of an outmoded and inappropriate (Eurocentric) conceptual bias. At the same time, he drew attention to two particularly strong points of the field: the wide range of questions discussed makes it come closest to an integrated theory of language; and a high level of social consciousness is paired with active academic interest. Another important development at this conference was the link-up between studies of second-language acquisition and Pidgin/Creole studies.

An international conference with a narrower focus was held at York in 1983 under the title *Urban Pidgins and Creoles*. This choice of topic suggests a move away from the conservative basilectal varieties to the rapidly restructuring ones of acculturating urban communities. It also provided an avenue for the study of the rapid stylistic diversification of urban Creoles, enabling them to fulfil the ever-changing stylistic needs of unstable urban communities.

From the 1970s onwards, conferences on Pidgin and Creole topics were regularly held by a number of organizations, including the Society for Caribbean Linguistics, le Comité International des Etudes Créoles, the Society for Pidgin and Creole Languages, the universities of Amsterdam, Essen, Duisburg and, most recently, Westminster. A consequence of such activities has been a huge increase in publishing in this field. The newsletter *Carrier Pidgin* began publication in the early 1970s and has since been joined by *Gazèt sifon blé/Lavwa ka bay* and *Boletim de Estudos Crioulos*, destined for readers of French and Iberian languages respectively, as well as the *Pidgins and Creoles in Education* newsletter. Journals and series include the *Journal of Pidgin and Creole Studies, Etudes Créoles, Amsterdam Creole Studies, Papers in Pidgin and Creole Linguistics* (Pacific Linguistics), *Papia, Kreolische Bibliothek, Creole Language Library* and *Westminster Creolistics*. This list is far from exhaustive. In addition, other journals including *English World-Wide, International Journal for the Sociology of Language, Language in Society*, and *World Englishes* among many others, frequently include articles on Pidgins and Creoles. Using e-mail, up-to-date news can be obtained from CreoLIST@ling.su.se while various search programs provide access to a growing body of information on Pidgins and Creoles.

It is evident from this brief survey that a rather short period of unity is being followed by a new diversity. This is apparent in the growing gap between theoretical and applied studies, as well as in the often heard debates between those who subscribe to genetically-transmitted Creole structures and those who see them as a result of social interaction. Furthermore, the tendency towards regionalization has remained and even increased, with conferences dealing with a geographically limited area or a special group of languages such as Tok Pisin (1969, 1973), Pidgins and Creoles of Melanesia (1987), Papiamentu (1981), Romance languages in contact with other languages (1976), St Kitts Creole (1996), and the publication of a series *Travaux de recherche sur le créole haïtien*.

It is hard to see how things could be otherwise in the light of the flood of new information relating to the field. Whereas a couple of decades ago I could manage to read virtually all publications in the field, I now find it increasingly difficult to keep up with recent developments. I hope that future international conferences will retain a wide scope, in order to give scholars the opportunity to familiarize themselves with the research activities outside their immediate regional and theoretical area of interest.

Outlook

In the business of making predictions, the likelihood that one will be proved wrong is an unavoidable hazard, and my having been involved in Pidgin and Creole linguistics for some time is of little advantage. However, it certainly has helped me to determine those developments which, from my own point of view, would seem to be beneficial to the field. In assessing his own predictions, made on the occasion of the second international conference on Pidgins and Creoles in 1968, Dell Hymes remarked:

> In 1968 ... it seemed inevitable that attention to pidginization and creolization would unite the linguistic and social in a specially revealing way. How we underestimated the resourcefulness and creativity of linguists and psychologists. After a decade, the inescapable embedding of Pidgin and Creole languages in social history remains a theme to be argued for, a topic to be rediscovered (Hymes 1980:389).

Before presenting my own views, I would like briefly to consider two other earlier predictions regarding the Pidgin/Creole field, namely those of Figueroa (1971:503-06) and Bickerton (1974), as they appear to represent two opposite poles.

Figueroa's principal concern is for the political, social and educational applications of the field: that is, how being a Pidgin or Creole speaker affects one's life. He also makes an implicit plea against too much reliance on expatriate white analyses. At the time of his writing, the extent to which cultural factors can influence the analyses of and views on a Pidgin or Creole was ill understood. That they are indeed of very considerable importance has been demonstrated in an article of mine on indigenous and expatriate approaches to Tok Pisin (Mühlhäusler 1984c). However, such factors will remain of marginal interest as long as the wider question of how culture-bound metalinguistic systems affect linguistic argumentation and analysis remains unexplored (cf Lyons 1981). Figueroa hopes that sympathetic research will demonstrate the equality of Creoles *vis-à-vis* their source languages. However, linguists appear unprepared to address seriously the qualitative differences, and study of this kind could well produce results which Figueroa might find unacceptable. In Pidgin and Creole studies, as in other fields of enquiry, premature and socially undesirable findings tend to meet with little enthusiasm, and, in the present social and intellectual climate, some questions, regarded as important by the writer of this article, are perhaps best left alone.

Bickerton (1974), unlike Figueroa, considers the most urgent priority in Creole studies to be the provision of answers to a number of questions in the area of theoretical and historical linguistics asked by Schuchardt, in particular:

1. How do languages get mixed?
2. What is the nature of linguistic continua?

He has since added to these questions (in particular, in Bickerton 1981), relating to questions of general linguistic interest:

3. What is the relationship between first-language acquisition, phylogenetic development of human language and Creole development (in first-generation speakers)?

Because of the importance attached to Bickerton's *Roots of Language* (1981), where this last question is examined, the issues raised therein are likely to be discussed for some time to come. One hopes that the long-overdue question of the relationship between child language acquisition and Pidgin and Creole formation will receive more attention as a result. The narrow focus on the acquisition of abstract grammar in the work of Bickerton (1981, 1989) has hampered progress. Few Creolists have heeded Klein's (1986) critical comments on SLA (second language acquisition) theory, in particular his insistence that any such theory will have to consider that language acquisition is dependent on, and interacts with, the acquisition of parallel information. More critical remarks on the state of language acquisition and creolization research can be found in Aitchison (1995).

Bickerton's proposals are also likely to promote the study of links between the sign languages of deaf people and Pidgins and Creoles (cf Edwards & Ladd 1984, Washabaugh 1986), as it is expected that the same natural patterns of encoding will emerge in all communication systems that have been developed without sufficient input. Although such a development would advance the frontiers of knowledge in the area of linguistic naturalness, there is a danger that the cultural forces instrumental in shaping Pidgins and Creoles will be neglected (see Mühlhäusler 1989a, Washabaugh 1986). Moreover, many aspects of Pidgins and Creoles only appear to be natural; in reality, they are cultural products, the results of conceptual frameworks that are so familiar to us as to pass unnoticed. I thus sympathize with Hymes' fears that an integrative view of Pidgin and Creole communication will yet again be postponed, and that questions which I would regard as important will be regarded as marginal, including the following:

1. Does ontogenetic, phylogenetic and Creole development take place in a smooth continuous fashion[11] or what Figueroa (1971:503) terms "sudden Lamarckian jumps"? These matters are correctly being addressed by those who take a gradualist view of the development of Creole grammar (for a survey, see Arends & Bruyn 1995).

2. What is the extent of social influence on structural development, and how far are we dealing, when discussing Pidgin and Creole structures, with man-made cultural products? What is the relationship between such cultural and biological/genetic factors?

3. What can abstract deductive models of Creole development tell us about the actual historical process? Should we study the emergence of grammar in preference to the emergence of social communicative abilities?

4. How do we best link up phylogenetic and Pidgin/Creole development? There is still a tendency to accept Chomsky's statement (1968:59) that: "It is quite senseless to raise the problem of explaining the evolution of human language from more primitive systems of communication that appear at lower levels of intellectual capacity." Undue concentration on the denotative-predicative aspects of language and arbitrary signs appear to have led to the above statement. However, in explaining the development of connotative/emotive dimensions of Creoles and their indexical and iconic aspects, a link with ethology could well turn out to be necessary. To analyse, for instance, patterns of verbal aggression without reference to wider aspects of the development of human aggression would seem to be a rather limiting enterprise.

My view of future priorities for Creole studies, then, is that they should remain broadly based and that, next to questions of linguistic theory, links should be retained with ethology, sociology, anthropology and communication sciences.

I regard the growing number of younger Pidgin and Creole specialists from a non-Anglophone background, especially in Germany, the Netherlands and Scandinavia, as a positive sign and am looking forward to the revival of creolistics in Eastern Europe.

I have recently made an attempt to use Pidgin and Creole evidence to shed light on the question of linguistic adaptation to changed environmental conditions, exploring the fact that the new inhabitants of desert islands such as Norfolk Island, St Helena and Pitcairn not only had to create a language of intercommunication but also a language suited to talking about an unfamiliar natural environment. My preliminary findings (Mühlhäusler 1996b) suggest that much can be learnt from the development of names and classification systems in the Creoles of such islands.

To gain a better understanding of Pidgin and Creole languages as cultural production and cultural products in my view is of particular importance. There are at least two reasons for this wish. First, if Pidgins and Creoles

---

11 Indeed, it is difficult to see why, in the case of Creoles, the result of a long history of population displacement, social upheavals and cultural mixing should be a smooth linguistic continuum.

should turn out to be maximally natural and culture-neutral, they may represent the level of structure at which human beings could most easily be manipulated.[12] If, on the other hand, Pidgins and Creoles are significantly shaped by human actions, one should take a closer look at the agencies that have shaped them. Thus, a language influenced by colonial attitudes, missionary policies and other authoritarian bodies may not be an ideal instrument for political liberation. One can expect that the development of Pidgins and Creoles, like that of other languages, will lag behind social and technological development in some of the rapidly changing societies where they are spoken. In sum, then, I would like to advocate that the study of the grammatical properties of these languages be integrated with the study of their sociohistorical dimensions, and that, in particular, the communicative factors which gave birth to them be studied more seriously.

---

[12] Thus Creole structures of a natural type could be exploited in advertising and political indoctrination, if the view that the most basic (natural) lingustic structures are the ones that have the greatest persuasive force should turn out to be correct.

3. The sociohistorical context of Pidgin/Creole development

It is becoming more and more difficult to distinguish Pidgins and Creoles on a typological basis, and demographics and social history are better guides as to whether a language is a Pidgin or a Creole.

(Jennings 1995:79)

Introduction

In this chapter I shall investigate the external factors constitutive of, and contributing to, the development of Pidgin and Creole languages.[1] Languages, be they first or second ones, do not arise in a social vacuum. Wolf children who grow up in conditions of severe social deprivation, such as Genie (see Curtis 1977), do not develop language. There are two conditions which have to be met before languages can come into being: first, a need for verbal communication, i.e. communicative pressure; and second, access to a model. These two factors will determine the relative complexity of the evolving language as well as its genetic and typological affiliation.

Non-verbal communication and Pidgin development

In view of the frequency of silent bartering, it is somewhat surprising how little attention has been paid to it in the literature on Pidgins and Creoles. A major summary is given by Dutton (1987). In the absence of any detailed records, and with reliance on sporadic indirect evidence, it is difficult to assess the stability and success of such early non-verbal attempts to communicate across linguistic boundaries. It seems certain, however, that the number of culture-free signs which were available to the interacting parties was extremely limited (cf Morris et al. 1979). Possible candidates for "natural" signs include gestures for cutting, killing, eating and location. It also seems certain that communication was impaired by frequent misunderstandings, even in the small domain of topics needed.

Let me illustrate this with examples relating to the recruiting of indigenous labourers in the Pacific for the plantations of Queensland, New Caledonia, Fiji and Samoa. Holthouse describes a typical early encounter:

> Lacking interpreters for the countless native languages of Melanesia, the recruiters resorted to pantomime, often of the sketchiest kind. To indicate to the kanakas that they were being engaged to work for three years, the expression 'three yam' was used – supposed to be the time taken to grow three crops of yams. Reduced to pantomime it often came down to showing the native a yam and holding up three fingers.
>
> (Holthouse 1969:22)

---

[1]   The division between language-internal (structural forces) and language-external factors (social, psychological forces, etc.) appears a somewhat arbitrary one and is accepted only for the purposes of pre-theoretical discussion.

Even at such a basic level, cultural factors can severely impair communication. For instance, for many Melanesians the show of three fingers means the number two, as they work with a subtractive rather than an additive-counting system. Further, the limitations of the yam symbol to represent the time-span of a year are pointed out, with no mincing of words, in the report of a Royal Commission into Labour recruiting for Queensland:

> The edible tuberous root which we call 'yam' has a different name in nearly every island, and *quá* root does not suggest a period of time. No dependence can accordingly be placed on the use of the word 'yam', or its equivalent as an edible root, or of the words employed for season or feast, as conveying to the minds of natives from numerous and widely separate islands a fixed term which they would at once understand as a period of service. The employment of the word 'yam' at the port of arrival, in explaining a three years' engagement, was, therefore, altogether illusory. (Royal Commission into Labour 1885:xxi)

In the south–west Pacific, silent bartering apparently never developed, as it did in other parts of the world, into a fully developed sign Pidgin.[2] Instead, under the growing pressure for verbal communication, it was added to and eventually replaced by a verbal code, Jargon English. At first, this involved the use of single words and holophrases. Later, grammar covering longer utterances was added.

The complementary nature of non-verbal and verbal means of communication in incipient Pidgins has often been remarked upon. An example is Hale's observations on Chinook Jargon:

> Finally, in the Jargon, as in the spoken Chinese, a good deal is expressed by the tone of voice, the look and the gesture of the speaker. The Indians in general – contrary to what seems to be a common opinion – are very sparing of their gesticulations. No languages, probably, require less assistance from this source than theirs. Every circumstance and qualification of their thought are expressed in their speech with a minuteness which, to those accustomed to the languages of Europe, appears exaggerated and idle - as much as the forms of the German and Latin may seem to the Chinese. We frequently had occasion to observe the sudden change produced when a party of natives, who had been conversing in their own tongue, were joined by a foreigner, with whom it was necessary to speak in the Jargon. The countenances which had before been grave, inexpressive, were instantly lighted up with animation; the low, monotonous tone became lively and modulated; every feature was active; the head, arms and the whole body were in motion, and every look and gesture became instinct with meaning. One who knows merely the subject of the discourse might often have comprehended, from this source alone, the general purport of the conversation. (Hale 1890:18-19)

More recently, similar observations have been made for Japanese PE after the Second World War:

---

2   Bibliographical references on such sign languages are found in Reinecke et al. (1975).

Although it is very difficult to analyze these non–verbal systems componentially, individuals from different cultural backgrounds seem to develop instinct for them early and quickly, and a few of the terms of these systems should be mentioned here. The meaning of the smile, for example, in English and Japanese symbolizes several of the same things. Both peoples tend to use the smile in moments of social uncertainty and as a means of suggesting vague good will. Although the Japanese see the smile also as a mask of much greater kinds of distress, the smile easily becomes a working diamorph of non–verbal Pidgin. Similarly, the giggle is used by both peoples in moments of embarrassment, astonishment, and indecision. In the realm of gestures, both peoples touch each other to indicate reassurance and friendliness, and the slap on the shoulder is almost immediately understood on both sides. (This slapping borders on another and broader inter-cultural similarity, that of a love for joking and mild horseplay.) This process is, more broadly, probably one of the discovery of a set of gestural diamorphs followed by a sorting out of one or the other in social context. (Goodman 1967:48)

However, other studies on Japanese-English communication have demonstrated (e.g. Neustúpny 1983) that many of the non-verbal patterns of communication that emerge cannot be explained in terms of the rules of either culture in contact. Rather, both parties appear to undergo a considerable degree of behavioural regression.

Sometimes, the very early heavily contextualized stages of a Pidgin can still be recovered by looking at socially or geographically marginal varieties of otherwise more developed Pidgins. Thus a pronounced reliance on extralinguistic signals can be observed in Bush Pidgin (the bush varieties of Tok Pisin, see Mühlhäusler 1979), while Todd has found, in contemporary West Africa, "a very basic sort of English (often associated with market mammies) consisting of little more than lexical strings augmented by gesture: buy okra, okra fine, bring money, what of banana?" (1982:286). A promising area of research and of incipient pidginization are migrant or guestworker Pidgins. Harding's (1984) study of the discourse of health visitors and immigrant mothers from the Indian subcontinent in Britain emphasises the role of gestures, accommodation and context in incipient Pidgin development.

Pidgin and Creole research has, in the past, paid relatively little attention to such phenomena, assuming that the development of a linguistic means of intercommunication can be studied in isolation from its gestural predecessors. This, I feel, is a great shortcoming, as there appears to be an interesting relationship between the complexity of a sign language and that of the simultaneously employed verbal means of communication.

Verbal means of communication: general remarks

Although there are many studies on the verbal aspects of Pidgins, relatively few of them pertain to the very early unstable stages of development. The reasons for this are not hard to find: neither the people involved in initial jargon contacts nor the situations in which communication took place lent themselves to systematic observation or recording. Moreover, in the absence of modern recording technology, a considerable amount of filtering out and distortion must have occurred. Major victims of this were instances of unsuccessful or partially successful communication: development all too often is seen as a sequence of successful stages, rather than a process involving regression, discontinuity and failure.

In the absence of reliable information on situational and other external factors, it is difficult to be confident about their role in Pidgin and Creole formation. However, it would seem that at least some claims can be made with relative confidence. Before putting them forward, however, I would like to remind the reader of an important distinction, that between formation and development. I would suggest that the main difference between these two processes can be characterized as follows:

> The formative period of Pidgins and Creoles embraces their development up to the point where a socially accepted grammar emerges, that is, a grammar which is transmitted without significant restructuring, to a subsequent group of speakers. As a rule, formation occurs within a single generation of speakers. By development I mean the subsequent history of the language over a number of generations.

By this definition, the formative period for Tok Pisin of New Guinea falls between 1865 and 1890, whereas its subsequent development, after initial stabilization, begins around 1890. For a Pidgin, the formative phase ends with stabilization. For a Creole, it ends once the first generation of speakers have attained adulthood.

Although such a distinction helps us to distinguish language-formation processes without a model from others where a model has been transmitted by a previous generation, it is not without its problems, the main one being discontinuities arising out of subsequent breaks in transmission. Thus a Creole may be acquired as a second language by a group of non–native adult speakers and thus become repidginized: instances of this are the fate of Jamaican Creole in Sierra Leone and possibly Black American English in Nigeria following the manumission of New World slaves and their resettlement in Africa where pidginized forms of their Creole spread among the local population (cf Todd 1986). Similarly, an already stable Pidgin may become rejargonized, that is, subject to individual language learning strategies, if it is acquired by no socially viable group of speakers. An interesting example is provided by Tok Pisin which, 50 years after its initial stabilization in the coastal areas of Papua New Guinea, was adopted and destabilized by New Guinea Highlanders (see Salisbury 1967).

Consequently, in order to understand what happens at a particular stage in the formation and development of a Pidgin or Creole, we can appeal to the uniformitarian principle,[3] that is, observe the phenomena of the past synchronically by moving along the geographical and stylistic dimensions of the language.[4] I have done this for Tok Pisin when reconstructing the early

---

3 The uniformitarian principle relies on smooth continuous change. It needs to be supplemented, particularly in the case of Pidgins and Creoles, with the catastrophic principle, which accounts for qualitative changes resulting from sudden discontinuous events.

4 Developmentally earlier stages are a frequent source of stylistic diversification in Pidgins and Creoles, a phenomenon referred to by some as backsliding.

unstable varieties of the language. The relationship between geographic remoteness and stabilization in this language can be represented as follows:

The relationship between geographic remoteness and stabilization in Tok Pisin

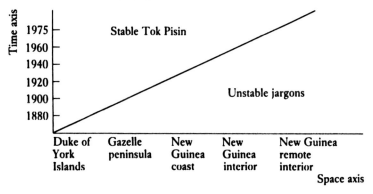

Although this figure is an idealization, there can be no doubt that significant insights into language history can be gained from the uniformitarian method.

Social forces as constitutive factors in Pidgin formation

As already mentioned in the previous chapter, a major source of disagreement in Pidgin and Creole studies has been the role of external or social factors in Pidgin/Creole formation and structural development. The opposing views include that:

1. A distinction between social (external) and structural (internal) factors must be made:[5] internal development proceeds of its own accord, with external factors determining the speed of this development;

2. External factors crucially shape and determine grammatical and lexical structuring. As suggested by Turner (1966:208):

   The structure of Neo–Melanesian [Tok Pisin] derives from the social situation in which the intermediary language was used. Some grammatically important morphemes and some more general details of syntactic structure may derive from one or another of the 'terminal' languages, but it is doubtful whether the importance of these is equal to the importance of the social setting in determining Neo-Melanesian structure.

One must not be led to believe, however, that these are the only explanations. An as yet not fully developed integrationist view (cf Harris 1980, 1981) would deny the possibility of separating linguistic codes from their use in social situations. I have discussed some implications of this view for Pidgin and Creole linguistics in Mühlhäusler (1992b). Again, even if the separability of these factors is subscribed to, it seems legitimate to assume that only some

---

5   In the most catholic view, internal factors relate to a single linguistic system only. Contact between languages is seen as external influence. It is argued (for example, in Aitchison 1981:123) that: "Foreign elements do not of themselves disrupt the basic structure of a language. They merely make use of the tendencies already in the language."

structures are directly caused by social/external factors, whereas others are independent developments. The latter view is the one that is adopted here.

Let us proceed to considering some instances of socially caused linguistic structures. At the jargon stage, in the absence of social norms of linguistic interaction, individuals are free to adopt a number of different strategies for cross-linguistic communication (see Meisel 1983). This choice appears to be very much determined by personality factors, educational background and cultural-group membership. Thus speakers concerned with grammatical correctness are more likely to make use of the grammatical structures of their first language, that is, their strategy is transfer or use of substratum. Other speakers who simply want to be understood tend to regress to earlier stages in their own language development or universals of grammar. A speaker's previous exposure to other Pidgins and Creoles is also likely to be reflected in his or her grammar. In the early developmental stages of many Pidgins, one party in the linguistic exchange was a member of the geographically highly mobile group of sailors, traders and plantation overseers.[6] In some extreme cases, this may have led to relexification (that is, the replacement of the lexicon of an existing Pidgin or Creole with that from another source language). The role of geographical diffusion certainly cannot be easily overrated with Pidgins and Creoles.

Equally important is the role of certain culture-derived stereotypes, typically associated with foreigner talk registers, in early jargon formation. Reduplication and repetition, the use of special word order, and grammatical elements and special lexical items are documented for speakers of such widely different lexifier languages as German, English and Motu. The acceptance of foreigner talk input depends both on the already mentioned individual learning strategies, and the next factor, the nature of the social relationships between groups in contact. Such relationships are mirrored not only in the relative percentage of lexical items in the resulting contact language, but also in its composition and parts of grammar. Thus the asymmetrical social relationship in many culture-contact situations tends to be mirrored in pronoun and address systems. Members of the socially subordinate group are addressed with T rather than V pronouns (from French *tu* and *vous*), as in Vietnamese Pidgin French or New Guinea Pidgin German:

Toi donner moi cadeaux	'(you) give me present'
Du geben mir Geschenk	'(you) give me present'

These contrast with the special forms of address signalling deference used when indigenes address their colonizers, as in:

Monsieur donner moi cadeau	'Sir give me present'
Herr geben mir Geschenk	'Sir give me present'

---

6   This goes for both European and non-European overseers. Thus, in the case of the Queensland sugar plantations, some of the Europeans had previously served in Ceylon, Natal and the Caribbean. In turn, some of the Melanesian workers were employed as overseers on plantations in other parts of the Pacific, such as Fiji and Papua. Because of their social position, their language must have served as a model for Pidgin development. At present, the full extent of the regional mobility of plantation overseers and workers remains unknown. However, there is no doubt that the pattern began with Cyprus and the Atlantic Creoles (cf Washabaugh & Greenfield 1983) was continued in most other plantation areas.

Similar discriminatory speech habits are also found in non-address forms in many Pidgins and Creoles that developed in stratified colonial societies. Thus Tok Pisin distinguishes between **boi** 'male indigene' and **masta** 'male European adult' as well as between **meri** 'indigenous woman' and **misis** 'expatriate woman'.[7] Similar distinctions were also made in Hiri Motu, where the items **taubada** 'male European' and **sinabada** 'female European' had special status in both reference and address. Such asymmetrical pairs tend to be less pronounced in the later developmental stages of Pidgins and Creoles, that is, when horizontal rather than vertical communication becomes their dominant mode. However, we note that Bahasa Indonesia, which began as a language of an egalitarian society, has developed a non-egalitarian address system in recent years.

Another example of external factors promoting structural developments is that of accessibility to and the wish to acquire a target/lexifier language. The two terms, widely used by Creolists, are not unproblematic (see Baker 1990) because they simplistically suggest:

(a) that Pidgin creators aim at speaking a standard language (something which certainly was not the case with Chinese PE).

(b) that the structures of a target language provide the norm from which Pidgins and Creoles deviate.

Nevertheless, the very presence of a standard language (particularly one that is lexically "related"), invited targeted learning and the stability of a Pidgin is greatly promoted by the absence of an imposed or voluntarily accepted target, as there is then little scope for system-destroying hypercorrection. A good illustration is afforded by contrasting the two PEs found in the New Guinea area. Whereas in British/Australian Papua, Papuan PE remained at a very low level of stabilization throughout its existence (cf Mühlhäusler 1978a), in German-controlled New Guinea a stable PE (Tok Pisin) emerged within a few years. In fact, the German administration indirectly contributed to the stabilization of Tok Pisin in two ways: by removing English as a lexifier language; and by creating social conditions in which communication between members of many different linguistic backgrounds became established, giving rise to what Whinnom (1971) refers to as a 'tertiary hybrid'. Whereas the constitutive role of external factors in the formation of Pidgins is relatively clear, for Creoles it is much less so. One reason for this is that adults are much more capable of choice and active manipulation of language than young children.

The extent of external influence in the formation of Creoles appears to be linked primarily to one factor: the linguistic input that children are exposed to. A subsidiary factor is the size and composition of the community in which Creoles emerge. To take this second point first, it appears that for a Creole to develop at all there must be a viable community in which it can be used. By this I mean there must be a large enough number of children whose only means of communication is the Creole. Thus, in the case of a nuclear family where two parents communicate in Pidgin, no creolization is likely to

---

7   More precisely, distinguished, as the use of special forms for Europeans was banned in official language in the last days of the Australian administration and has declined considerably since independence.

occur; instead children will speak one or both of their parents' languages and/or end up being linguistically deprived,[8] as in the instance of mixed-race children in former German New Guinea:

> The mission could not remain indifferent to the sad plight of these children. It began to collect them and when their numbers continued to grow it founded its own institution in 1897 where they were to be educated by the sisters. Now that was a really difficult enterprise. The whites are generally ignorant of the natives' language and in conversation with them make use of Pidgin English, the workers' language, which is a mixture of corrupted English and native dialects. The halfcastes mostly speak only this Pidgin English with a few bits of native language heard from their mother, which of course differs according to the home. On their arrival at the mission station they are therefore hardly able to make themselves understood. (Janssen 1932:150)

As soon as a larger community of children is established, however, a qualitative change sets in. Thus the very same children that spoke little broken German or Tok Pisin (in the above quotation) developed a sophisticated Creole, Unserdeutsch, within a single generation.[9] This language is structurally very different from its potential models of Tok Pisin, Pidgin German and standard German (cf Mühlhäusler 1984b). That the structural viability of a Creole is dependent on its social viability is also seen elsewhere. Thus, Samoan Plantation PE (see Mühlhäusler 1978b) was the first language of many children on the German plantations of Samoa but proved of little use to their later life because the plantation society remained dominated by linguistically less progressive adults; and the language was spoken only within a small ghetto and not outside these plantations. Consequently these Creole speakers adopted the more useful Samoan language as their exclusive means of communication.[10]

When it was brought to Papua New Guinea by returning labourers, however, the language (now Tok Pisin) was in a much better situation. Viable Creole communities developed here around two types of settlements: the non-traditional rural settlements, such as the government palm oil project at Hoskins, which attracted families from many parts of the country; and the large urban centres with frequent intermarriage between speakers from different linguistic backgrounds and no dominant local language.

Detailed studies of a number of Creole communities in New Guinea have been made by Sankoff (e.g. 1975a, 1975b), Mühlhäusler (1979) and Romaine (1987, 1992) confirming the fragility of Creole innovations under adverse social conditions. Thus, those grammatical innovations that deviate most

---

8   The pre-theoretical term 'semi-lingual' is often used in the characterization of such speakers. However, as has been pointed by Martyn-Jones & Romaine (1984), there are considerable problems with this notion.

9   Similar rapid development of a Creole also occurred in other educational institutions (e.g. St Louis, New Caledonia for Tayo, St Paul's, Torres Straits for Broken, and a number of Hawaiian schools in the case of Hawaiian Creole English). The role of schools – particularly boarding schools – in accelerated Creole development is a topic deserving further attention.

10   Some of them also learned English as a second language in later life. I found that the informants who claimed to have grown up speaking creolized Samoan Plantation PE remembered only small fragments of this language.

from established second-language norms tend to be given up by Creole speakers once they begin to communicate as adults. In other instances, a Creole is replaced by a more useful local lingua franca, and in yet other cases heavy reliance is placed on English for structural and lexical innovations.

A number of conclusions can be drawn from such case studies. First, the development of viable Creoles (with socially sanctioned grammars) depends on their functional usefulness and social viability. Children's innovations have little chance of survival in an adverse social environment. Further, creolization is not the only solution for children whose parents provide them with insufficient linguistic input. The solutions eventually adopted may include bilingualism, language shift, and dual-lingualism.[11]

The second way in which external factors can influence Creoles is in the nature and availability of linguistic input from the lexifier language. Many writers draw the simple distinction between access to lexical structures and access to grammatical ones. Whereas lexical borrowing is regarded as a relatively unconstrained process, borrowing of grammar is regarded as exceptional by many. It must be borne in mind, however, that the boundary between lexicon and grammar is language-specific rather than universally motivated, since what is done by means of grammar in one language may be lexicalized in the next. Consequently even lexical borrowing can predetermine much of a Creole grammar in the formative years and change the course of subsequent development. An interesting case is the borrowing of lexicalized causatives such as *kill*, which might block the development of grammaticalized morphological or periphrastic causatives.

Access to lexical and structural resources of the lexifier language (and substratum languages) can be related to a number of other external factors, including the numerical relationship between speakers of each language, whether or not the socializers (caretakers, not necessarily parents) of creolizing children had access to the lexifier language, whether there was any formal teaching, and prevailing linguistic attitudes. Linguists investigating Creoles must constantly keep in mind that access does not necessarily mean acceptance of the model. Pidgin and Creole speakers are not passive recipients of the crumbs that fall from the linguistic tables of speakers of "more civilized" tongues, but active makers and users of languages.[12] Differences from the "model" may well reflect the wish to be linguistically different, that is, it could refer to the indexical rather than the referential /grammatical functions of these languages.

The effects of the institutionalization of and access to the lexifier language of a Creole can be illustrated with a few examples. The island of Reunion was first settled in 1663 mainly by *petits blancs* (lower–class French settlers), Malagasies and Indo-Portuguese women, with the French

---

11   Dual-lingualism (see Lincoln 1975) was probably fairly common in the Creole context: children could understand their parents' vernaculars, but never acquired any skills in it because of its limited use. Another interesting case is that of Queensland Kanaka English, where Pidgin-speaking parents encouraged their children to learn and speak standard English even at home (cf Dutton & Mühlhäusler 1984). Examples involving Northern Australian Kriol are provided by Sandefur (1984:83).

12   The study of Pidgins and Creoles is closely concerned with rule-making and rule-changing creativity. Any model of grammatical description catering for rule-governed creativity only would seem inadequate for the purposes of Pidgin and Creole linguistics.

outnumbering all other races during the formative years of Reunion Creole (that is, until about 1720). As observed by Corne, "At the end of the first period R[eunion] C[reole] has emerged in a situation of linguistic diversity wherein French, in various guises, was the dominant factor" (1982:107). As a consequence, RC has remained structurally close to French such that it might even be called a creoloid.

The reasons why Afrikaans remained linguistically close to Dutch was similar. In the Western Cape Province where it originated, Dutch-speaking whites were numerically dominant and Dutch remained an official language for more than 150 years after a distinct "Cape Dutch" Afrikaans had crystallized. By contrast, the status of Dutch as an official language in the Virgin Islands was tenuous and speakers of Dutch were outnumbered by speakers of other languages. As a consequence, Negerhollands exhibits a much greater structural distance from Dutch than Afrikaans.

Nature and nurture

The concept of "naturalness" is widely found in linguistic writings, although it is often used in an ill-defined way. In a loose sense, the label "natural language" is used to contrast vernaculars such as English, Hindi or Quechua with artificially created languages such as Volapük, Esperanto or computer languages. The naturalness of the former systems is related to the fact that their rules and conventions are mainly unconscious and, it is argued, are not directly amenable to human interference. This argument seems unconvincing, however, in the light of recent work on the socio-historical context of language development, which highlights the importance of conscious interference with language development. To take the example of English, the use of *you* as both singular and plural pronoun (rather than a *thou* / *you* or *you* / *ye* distinction), or the rule which selects *he* as the pronoun in utterances such as "mind the child - he may be deaf" can be traced back to historical events (cf Mühlhäusler & Harré 1990). Again, the morphological complexity of many languages of Melanesia appears to be man-made (cf Wurm 1983). Cultural games such as backslang, rhyming slang and pig-Latin have left traces in the grammar of many languages. It would thus seem more realistic to admit that most of the so-called "natural languages" are in fact a mixture of nature and culture.[13]

The question whether Pidgins and Creoles are natural languages in this first sense has been debated, and it is not by chance that they have often been grouped together with artificial languages in linguistic bibliographies. Reasons for believing them not to be natural languages include the fact that some non-expert observers believe that Pidgins are invented languages. Reed (1943:271) reports the view that Tok Pisin "was invented and introduced by the Germans in order that they might speak before the natives in their own

---

13 Work in semiotics has done a lot to dispel simplistic notions of nature. Thus Culler, in his discussion of Barthes (1983:17), comments: "His writings attempt to show us how we do it and what we are doing: the meanings that seem natural to us are cultural products, the results of conceptual frameworks that are so familiar as to pass unnoticed." In Mühlhäusler (1989a) I have examined the social forces underlying of naturalness in Pidgin and Creole studies.

tongue without being understood".[14] Also, a number of professional linguists regard Pidgins as reduced parasitic systems, rather than "full" languages (that is, systems that can be explained only by reference to a full "natural" language). The first view has no empirical support, and the second can be dismissed on the grounds that Pidgins exhibit constructions and developmental tendencies which cannot be related to their lexifier language or to their substratum languages. It could further be argued that "structural complexity" or "fullness" of a language is a rather shaky concept, as there is little empirical support for the widely held assumption that all natively spoken languages are of equal complexity.

The reader of this book will by now have got used to the idea that for most views on Pidgins and Creoles there is also an opposite view. Thus it is not surprising that, applying roughly the same meaning of naturalness, Pidgin languages have been characterized as maximally natural. In support of this view, the following arguments have been adduced. First, since Pidgins are used as a means of communication between members of different cultures, they have to be culture-neutral. Second, Pidgins are very young languages, that is, they have not been exposed to cultural forces for long enough to have absorbed cultural conventions. In spite of the initial plausibility of such arguments, one must not overstate the case: the imperviousness of Pidgins to cultural forces appears to be restricted to the very early period of formation and development; at later levels they are influenced by their social context.[15]

As regards Creoles, these have been denied the status of natural languages on very much the same grounds given for Pidgins, that is, their being parasitic degenerate systems. However, this view is not heard in linguistic circles, as it is generally admitted that, without a knowledge of the history of a language, one cannot determine whether one is dealing with a Creole. They are thus assigned the status of "full" natural languages.[16]

The term 'naturalness' is also used in a second, more technical sense, and again Pidgins and Creoles are included in the ongoing discussions. Indicators of naturalness are both system-internal and system-external. Language-internal natural rules are characterized as being more resistant to change; more frequent (token frequency); more frequent cross-linguistically; more likely to be the basis of neutralization; and more likely to be the model in analogical change than an abnatural category. Language-external parameters of naturalness are acquired earlier; less subject to speech errors; lost later in language death; or lost later in aphasia. A more detailed discussion is given by Edmondson (1984). Some writers (e.g. Thomason & Kaufman 1988:26ff) have conflated the concepts of (universal) naturalness and (language specific) markedness. For Creoles the two would appear largely to coincide, though this impression may change once in depth studies of a wider range of Creoles become available.

---

14 Although this is certainly untrue for Tok Pisin, there was at least one concrete proposal to introduce an artificial Pidgin language into the German colonies, Kolonial-Deutsch (Schwörer 1916, discussed in Chapter 7).

15 This context includes, among other things, missionary attempts to purify the language, the inclusion of the indices signalling differential power of language users, and certain trappings of polite (in the Western sense) speech such as lexical forms for 'thank you' and 'please'.

16 The possibility that incipient Creoles are lacking in the referential and expressive power associated with older languages is discussed by Whinnom (1971).

Ever since the technical notion of naturalness was introduced into linguistics, observers have been quick to point out the prolificity of natural rules and categories in Pidgins and Creoles. Thus one of the principal syntactic characteristics of Pidgins, their derivational shallowness, was seen to reflect the more general principle that natural rules do not produce intermediate forms that are not also acceptable surface structures. In preparing for Mühlhäusler (1974), I examined the following categories: predilection for a syllable structure CVCV; the absence of highly marked sounds, such as rounded front vowels, clicks, the replacement of voiced sibilants by voiceless ones, etc.; the loss of tonal distinctions; the loss of the passive; the infinitive present form for verbs; a preference for continuous constituents; that the use of masculine for both genders is a language specific markedness convention is supported by data from Buin (Bougainville Island) where the feminine pronoun is selected for mixed groups (see Mühlhäusler & Harré 1990:247), when languages with a gender system become simplified; the use of singular in all cases; and relational words. For each of these categories, it was found that Pidgins prefer the more natural alternative. More about the theoretical implications of this finding will be said below.

The view that Pidgins are maximally natural languages has been attacked by Bickerton (e.g. 1975c), who points to language mixing, structural inconsistencies and similar abnatural phenomena in his data relating to late 19th-/early 20th-century Hawaiian PE. He further points out that subsequent creolized varieties of this language are better candidates for natural linguistic systems.

This apparent conflict can be resolved by considering developmental and gradient aspects of Pidgins and the notion of naturalness. Naturalness must be regarded as a scale ranging from more to less natural phenomena, the latter being referred to as abnatural.[17] Further, naturalness must be related to the individual as well as the social character of Pidgins and Creoles. Individual Pidgin developers have at their disposal a number of strategies, only one of which is that of selecting the most natural solution. A mixture of different strategies can thus be expected in early jargons such as Hawaiian PE, referred to by Bickerton. Once a Pidgin stabilizes as a result of the encounter of numerous unstable jargons, natural solutions have an edge over others, because they tend to optimalize production and/or perception. Again, if a Pidgin expands as the language of an otherwise multilingual community, the cost of adding natural rules is less than adding others, so that – all things being equal – expanding Pidgins will prefer natural solutions.

It can be argued that naturalness goes hand in hand with unconscious language developments, such as those found in children acquiring a first language or adults under great pressure for communication.[18] As soon as the language begins to be used for social purposes such as group identification, stylistic aims and so forth, less natural solutions are inevitably added. In the case of Pidgins and Creoles, there is one prime source of abnatural

---

17 This is to be distinguished form *unnatural*, a term which is best reserved for the results of such wilful external interference as the stretching of the neck, manipulation of the nasal cavities or the enlargement of the lips. Unnatural aspects of language cannot be transmitted, but have to be borrowed or reinvented.

18 Such pressure occurs both in a monolingual context where adults are found to regress linguistically to more natural language, and in multilingual contact situations such as the formative period of a stable Pidgin.

constructions and rules: linguistic borrowing from the superimposed related language. In many instances, such borrowing serves the primary function of enhancing a speaker's prestige. Human beings seem to be prepared to accept a considerable cost in linguistic simplicity and communicative efficiency in order that their language should promote their social standing. In sum, natural solutions tend to be sensitive to external social pressure, and consequently are differentially realized at different points in the developmental and restructuring Pidgin-Creole continua. This can be portrayed as follows:

Nature and nurture in the development of Pidgins and Creoles

Stage	Natural solution preferred	Socially sanctioned grammars	Access to superstrata
Jargon	+/-	-	limited
Stabilization	+	+	minimal
Expansion	+	+	minimal
Creolization	+	+	minimal
Post–Pidgin	-	+/-	considerable
Post–Creole	-	+/-	considerable

These findings can be summarized as follows:

1. Natural categories emerge most readily in socially sanctioned grammars.[19]
2. Natural solutions are favoured by the absence of a particular target language.
3. Natural solutions are found with both children and adults.
4. The cost of linguistic and social prominence is reduced inter-intelligibility and greater cognitive load.

Finally, languages seem gradually to move away from their natural basis and become cultural artefacts. This is happening, or has already happened, with many of the older Pidgins and Creoles. Consequently, to rely on naturalness criteria to set these languages apart typologically, in the absence of a good knowledge of their socio-cultural context, may turn out to be unreliable.

Variability of contextual factors

It has been emphasized repeatedly in this book that, in order to understand Pidgins and Creoles, one also has to understand variability and change. In this section, the main stress will fall on variability of the social factors promoting or causing the linguistic diversification of these languages. The dimensions along which such variation is commonly located are social,

---

[19] This finding does not reflect directly on the various solutions to the questions as to the locus of language. It certainly should not be taken as support for De Saussure's view of language as located in the mind of society. Rather, the table suggests that there is a continued interchange between social and individual forces. For more on this point, see DeCamp (1974).

geographical and stylistic.[20] In discussing them, I will be concerned with linguistic markers and indicators, rather than individual free variation and fluctuations such as are found with jargon speakers. This would serve to demonstrate that even Pidgins are rarely the monostylistic languages they are sometimes said to be, but rather that they share the important design feature of human language of serving in a number of indexical functions above and beyond their referential one.

Sociolectal variation

For most of the history of the better-known Pidgins and Creoles, sociolectal variation has been a relatively unimportant factor. Typically, a distinction could be drawn between the language of the colonized (a basilectal Pidgin or Creole) and the language of the colonizers (the acrolect or its foreigner talk register), although some other dimensions of variation could occasionally be found. Thus, in many Pidgin- and Creole-speaking areas, the domestic servants' language was considerably more acrolectal than that of the plantation workers and villagers. Again, among the colonizers there tends to be a small group of people who need to communicate in the basilect, including missionaries, administrative officers and plantation owners. The effects of a rigid colonial system are nicely illustrated in the following quotation relating to Tok Pisin in the 1920s:

> "Pidgin" is such a language that there are only two white masters of it in the Mandated Territory of New Guinea. That is, there are only two who speak it so fluently that if they were out of sight they would be mistaken for kanakas. The ordinary resident of the islands is far from being an expert. (Shelton-Smith 1929:1)

Almost half a century later, the situation had not changed very dramatically. Bell (1971:38) expresses the opinion that "A rough and hopeful guess is that one in fifty can understand Pidgin as spoken by the indigenes to each other."

Once the original asymmetrical power relations begin to disappear and once social mobility sets in, new language forms, intermediate between the basilect and the acrolect, can develop[21] and often signal newly emerging social groups. The development of such a mesolectal continuum can be illustrated by Nigerian PE, on which Bickerton reports:

> In Nigeria, in the early years of the present century, there was a small handful of educated Nigerians who spoke English, a fair number of uneducated Nigerians, particularly along the coast, who spoke Nigerian Pidgin, and nothing in between. The situation there was much more similar to that of Papua New Guinea than was the Guyanese one, since in Nigeria, as distinct from Guyana, the vast bulk of the population retained

---

20 I am well aware of the difficulties surrounding correlationalism (Taylor & Mühlhäusler 1982). However, in view of the paucity of reliable statements on sociolinguistic factors in Pidgin and Creole formation, the above pre-theoretical classification is the only available basis for comparative statements.

21 The stress here is on *can*. Continued bilingualism or diglossia is another possibility found, for instance, with Northern Australian Kriol (cf Sandefur 1984). Bickerton (1980:109) certainly overstates the case when claiming: "Decreolization is a phenomenon which is found whenever a Creole language is in direct contact with its associated superstrate language."

its vernacular languages; moreover, the situation persisted until the end of colonial rule came in sight.

Over the last twenty years, however, there have been very considerable changes. Both English and Pidgin have spread widely, the former through education, the latter both through the growing geographic mobility of the working class, as here, and through the utility of a contact language in a country divided between many language communities. The result, once again, was the birth of a wide spectrum of varieties intermediate between Nigerian Pidgin and English   (Bickerton 1975a:25-26)

Initially, speakers of the more targeted (anglicized) varieties may not be aware of the differences between their speech and that of basilectal speakers. However, after a while such awareness begins to emerge, as reflected in metalinguistic labels such as Tok Pisin **Tok Bilong Bus** 'Bush Pidgin', **Tok (Pisin) Bilong Asples** 'Village (rural) Pidgin' and **Tok Skul** 'School Pidgin' or **Tok (Pisin) Bilong Taun** 'Urban Pidgin'.

The nature of linguistic variation is often taken as an indicator of types of social change. Thus, in those cases where there remains a clear division between the majority of the population and a small urban post-colonial elite (as, for instance, in the cases of Haiti and Guinea Bissau), the co-existent systems show few signs of merging or being linked by a linguistic continuum. However, to what extent a linguistic continuum can be taken as a direct reflection of certain social conditions remains to be seen. Observers of languages such Hawaiian English or Haitian French Creole differ in their assessment of the linguistic situation.[22]

Next to the correlation between social class and linguistic structures, one also finds special forms of language associated with other types of social groups. Thus, as Pidgins and Creoles are often standardized by expatriate missionaries and used for evangelizing purposes, special church varieties are common: for example, different varieties of Virgin Islands Negerhollands used to be associated with different mission groups, and in the case of Sranan a special archaic church register has been reported (Voorhoeve 1971). Linguistic differences are often the result of accidental factors, but in at least some instances missionaries have exploited existing differences for their own purposes. Thus, language standardization of Tok Pisin in the 1920s was implemented in a number of different ways by different missions, making it difficult, for instance, for a Catholic to follow a Methodist service or vice versa. The table overleaf shows the differences that could be observed in the area of doctrinal terminology.

An even more drastic step is the alleged policy of the Seventh Day Adventist Missionaries in New Hanover to make use of Solomons PE instead of Tok Pisin, thus setting believers and non-believers linguistically apart. Deliberate acts of language creation in Tok Pisin are also reported of the

---

[22] This is partly due to the fact that although an implicational grid with a continuum of lects can be constructed, it may be found that speakers are clustered around the two extremes of such a continuum. The existence of a few individual mesolectal speakers may reflect linguistic principles, but not necessarily social ones. Again, there can be a considerable discrepancy between the perception of speakers (which favours a dichotomous view) and objectively recordable patterns. It is a point on which Lawrence (1964) elaborates.

numerous cargo movements found in Papua New Guinea.[23] Backslang, changes in meaning, and new coinings in secret Tok Pisin serve to exclude certain groups, particularly Europeans, missionaries and mission helpers, women, children and strangers, from gaining knowledge of a particular cargo cult. The use of secret meanings for a number of doctrinal terms, for instance, has often prevented European missionaries from noticing significant differences between their own interpretation of utterances and that intended by members of the community in which they were working. Thus, in the 1920s, shortly after the introduction of Tok Pisin as a mission language, the situation in the Madang area was such that "relations between natives and missionaries, although on the whole extremely amicable, were nevertheless based on complete mutual misunderstanding" (Lawrence 1964:85). Such examples raise the interesting theoretical point of the role of shared grammar in achieving successful communication.

Some doctrinal terms of Tok Pisin

Gloss	Terms used by different missions		
'acolyte'	ministran (G)	altaboi (CP)	kundar (L)
'incense'	wairau (G)	insens (E)	smel smok (CP) / smok smel (PH)
'church'	kirke(G)	sios (E)	haus lotu (PH)
'cross'	diwai kros (PH)	kruse (LA)	bolo (L)
'to believe'	bilip (E)	numur (L)	to i tru (PH)
'heart'	bel (Ex)	hat (E)	liva (Ex)
'procession'	prosesio (LA)	varvaliu (L)	
'rosary'	roseri (E)	kurkurua (L)	corona (LA)
'holy'	holi (E)	santu (LA)	takondo (L)
'to pray'	pre (E)	beten (G)	raring (L)
'sin'	sin (E)	pekato (LA)	
'hell'	hel (E)	imperno (LA)	bikpaia (CP)
'to forgive'	pogivim (E)	larim (Ex)	lusim (Ex)
'virgin'	vetsin (E)	virgo (LA)	meri i stap tambu (PH)
'ascension'	goap bilong Jesus (PH)		asensio (LA)

E = English; G = German; L = local languages; CP = compounding; Ex = extension of meaning; LA = Latin; PH = phrase formation.

A second reason for the use of secret vocabulary in the cargo movements was the belief that words were vested with power of the kind needed to obtain the desired cargo. Brash writes:

> It is significant that some recent cult leaders have used Pidgin, and that they and their followers have imbued certain Pidgin words with supernatural power from other sources. For example, Yali's cult in the Madang District was conducted primarily in Pidgin, and used expressions like **lo bos** (law boss) for assistant leaders of the cult, and **rum tambu** (forbidden room) for Yali's holy room. Yali would often speak in symbolic language - **tok bokis** (story with a spiritual meaning like a parable) or **tok antap** (public statement with spiritual meaning and force) (1975:326).

---

[23] These are millenarian-type religious movements centring around the belief that European goods (cargo) are not man-made, but have been obtained from a divine source. An excellent account is given by Lawrence (1964)..

Particularly fertile environments for the development of new subvarieties of Pidgins and Creoles are towns. The impact of urban modes of living on these languages was the topic of the 1983 York Conference on Pidgins and Creoles, and a number of substantial studies have since appeared (e.g. Jourdan 1985 for Solomons PE, Romaine 1992 for Tok Pisin). I would like to draw attention to two of the cases discussed at that conference: Afrikaans of Sophiatown and Rastafarian varieties of West Indian Creole English.

Sophiatown Afrikaans or Tsotsi Taal (see Janson 1984) is interesting in showing that urbanization can have the opposite effect from that commonly postulated for a post-Creole situation. In the absence of any incentives to merge with white Afrikaans speakers, Sophiatown Afrikaans developed away from the acrolectal norms as the language of an anti-group living in a black ghetto. The enforced move of many speakers to the new township of Soweto brought about a further move away from Afrikaans towards local Bantu languages. In spite of close historical links between standard and Sophiatown Afrikaans, mutual intelligibility is low. As pointed out by Janson: "My main informant G remarked that Taal was popular precisely because it was not understandable to white Afrikaaners" (1984:176).

Rastafarian varieties of West Indian Creole English (cf Pollard 1984, Pütz 1989) are associated with a religious movement found mainly in the urban areas of the West Indies and many British towns.[24] They illustrate the role of active human interference in language development. As with some of the cargo varieties of Tok Pisin above, one aspect of Rastafarian language change is the replacement of seemingly misencoded lexical items by others which, from the viewpoint of their ideology, appear to be in a more iconic relationship with what they stand for. Thus, because of the positive value attached to seeing, 'cigarettes' are referred to as *blind-garettes*. Since to 'oppress' means 'to keep someone down', *downpress* is used, and for similar reasons 'informer' becomes *outformer*.

Geographical variation

Perhaps the most important finding of dialectology is that correlations between linguistic systems or subsystems and geographic entities can rarely be satisfactorily established. The fundamental rationale of dialectology, that geographic isolation leads to the development of new subvarieties, is difficult to apply to Pidgins, as one of their principal functions has been to promote cross-linguistic and inter-regional communication. Isolation is found in the case of self-sufficient plantation settlements on large islands such as Jamaica and New Guinea, although geographic isolation was often neutralized by workforce mobility. Many incipient Creole communities also were too small to be liable to splitting-up processes. There are, however, a number of cases where regional differences have been observed in Pidgins and Creoles.[25] They tend to be associated with certain external factors.

---

24 Pollard (1984) suggests that the roots of the Rastafarian movement lie in the predisposition of the oppressed black poor to accept an ideology that offers a reversion of the social order and a positive self-image. As for Sophiatown Afrikaans, to describe their language purely as an anti-language (cf Halliday 1976) would be far too simplistic.

25 We should be aware of the problems of defining the notion of regional dialect of a Pidgin or Creole. For discussion, refer back to Chapter 1. For purposes of the present discussion, some of these problems will have to be ignored.

As a first factor, different colonial powers may come to control a previously united communication area. Thus, PE-speaking German Kamerun was divided between France and Britain after the First World War, with consequent differences in lexical borrowing and structural stability.[26] Another example is Indo-Portuguese, where one can observe differences between varieties spoken in territories such as Goa, Diu and Damão that remained Portuguese until the recent past and varieties spoken elsewhere which were under the control of other colonial powers such as England (Calcutta), France (Pondicherry) or Denmark (Tranquebar) in the more remote past (Baxter, p c).

A second factor is the differences in the social and functional uses of the language. Thus the dividing line between a Pidgin and a Creole form of the same language may well be a geographic one, as in the case of Northern Australian Kriol (Sandefur 1984). An interesting case is that of Swahili, which gets significantly reduced in form and function as one travels from the East African coast inland to places such as Katanga (see de Rooij 1995). Moreover, in areas where this language is spoken side by side with vernacular Swahili, as in Mombasa, Pidgin Swahili tends to become depidginized. Similar observations have also been made for Hiri Motu, which exists in two main, geographically defined varieties: one is spoken in the vicinity of Motu-speaking Port Moresby, which is heavily influenced by Motu foreigner talk and simplified learners' Motu; the other is a much more structurally independent Pidgin Hiri Motu, spoken in the more outlying areas to the east and west (see Taylor 1978).

A third factor is the different foci of innovation, mainly larger urban centres. Thus, with Tok Pisin, the principal regional varieties are those influenced by the former capital Rabaul and the coastal town Madang. These two centres are also the centre of Catholic and Lutheran mission activities respectively, and mission language-planning efforts are partly responsible for observed regional differences. A comparable situation obtains with Northern Australian Kriol, where different varieties, according to Sandefur (1984), are associated with urban centres such as Bamyili, Fitzroy Crossing and Halls Creek. However, because of the complex history of Pidgin and Creole development in all these cases, convergent developments (merging of different Pidgin and Creole traditions) as well as divergent processes (splitting up of a single tradition) have probably been involved.

Finally, Pidgins or Creoles can be transported to new areas far from their original focus of development. Thus, Samoan Plantation PE was taken back to Papua New Guinea by returning plantation workers. For many years (1880-1914) there were continuous population movements between these two areas, but after 1914 the contacts ceased. Other similar cases involve Black American English transported to the Bahamas and guest-worker Pidgin German transported to Australia (Clyne 1975). The Portuguese Pidgin / Creole of Bidau, East Timor (see Baxter 1990) again shows significant similarities with the varieties spoken in Malacca and Macau.

We still have insufficient knowledge of the regional and geographical factors in Pidgins and Creoles, although for the Pacific region, parts of Asia and the Americas some aspects of their geographic dynamics is captured in a

---

[26] Renewed contact with its original lexifier language destablized Cameroonian in the British-controlled areas more than in the French one.

major atlas (Wurm, Mühlhäusler & Tryon 1996). Most available studies have concentrated on synchronic analysis of varieties spoken in a single place, but this appears to be the least profitable way of approaching the phenomenon. What is needed is the study of the regional distribution and diffusion of Pidgins and Creoles using sophisticated geographic models such as the ones suggested by Trudgill (1983) and paying attention to the metaphor of "Creole space" introduced by Carrington (1992).

Stylistic variation

There are many uses of the term 'style'. For the purposes of this chapter, I shall accept something close to Labov's (1972) meaning, that is, I shall examine the influence of varying degrees of formality and monitoring of speech, rather than the development of poetic traditions. It should also be noted that under this approach style is determined by factors present in the immediate situation of an utterance, but not by factors internal to a speaker such as his or her sex or age.

The isolation of a unidimensional notion of style is not without its problems, and its precarious theoretical status has been pointed out by a number of observers (e.g. Traugott & Romaine 1982). However, because it facilitates the comparison of existing source materials, it would seem best to discuss contextual style separately for Pidgins and Creoles. Pidgins have often been labelled monostylistic, as can be seen from the following observation by Samarin:

> a speaker of a Pidgin, as a *normal* human being in a normal society, can be expected to have more than one code-variety for different uses. The Pidgin, on the other hand, is not normal, and when a person is speaking a Pidgin he is limited to the use of a code with but one level or style or key or register, to cite some terms used for this aspect of the organization of language. (Samarin 1971:122)

However, whereas this may be true for the very first stages in their development, it is well documented that stylistic diversification can set in well before creolization. Unfortunately, very few studies of this phenomenon exist and what will be said about Tok Pisin may not apply to other Pidgins. The two principal sources for diversification in a Pidgin (and probably all other languages as well) are backsliding (that is, recourse to developmentally earlier stages) and borrowing from other systems. In addition, one finds internally motivated development of new stylistic variants, mainly as a result of the introduction of new media such as broadcasting or printing.

In a rapidly developing system such as Tok Pisin (there have been at least three systems over the last hundred years of development which are almost mutually unintelligible, referred to as Nambawan Tok Pisin, Nambatu Tok Pisin and Nambatri Tok Pisin in the metalanguage of some speakers), there is ample scope for backsliding. Developmentally earlier, less grammaticalized stages are used not only in more informal unmonitored speech, but also to achieve certain deliberate effects. Thus, among Tolai speakers of Tok Pisin, the distinction between [s] and [t] is given up on occasions in unmonitored speech, but it is also used in monitored speech to portray a hillbilly mentality or childishness, as in English 'putty cat'.

Because Tok Pisin remains a second language for the majority of its speakers, backsliding is common in situations of stress, with advancing age and when discussing complex topics. For the same reason, the stylistic range of younger speakers tends to be greater than that of their fathers. A well-known example of development in Tok Pisin is the gradual reduction of the original 'future marker' **baimbai** (< *by and by*) to the shorter forms **bambai, babai, bai, ba** and **b'** (cf Sankoff & Laberge 1973).[27] Whereas very old speakers only have **baimbai** at their disposal, younger speakers are proficient along a shorter or longer span of the continuum between **baimbai** and **b'**. Similar choice is found with other prominent grammatical markers such as the adjective ending **pela**, which can be shortened **pla**, and the preposition **bilong**, which is also realized as **bolong, blong** and **blo** or even **ble**.

Although such changes promote optimalization of production, especially in allegro speech, there is a considerable price to pay, namely that of decodability. Therefore such stylistic variants can only emerge once the majority of Pidgin speakers are reasonably proficient. As soon as a Pidgin is used to communicate with less sophisticated speakers, such phonological condensation will be abandoned again.

The effects of borrowing are in many ways opposite to those of backsliding, that is, the result is often less natural and hence more difficult to articulate. Thus, whereas rural Tok Pisin has **sekan** 'shake hands, make peace' with variants such as **seken, skan** and **sken**, in anglicized urban varieties renewed contact with English has led to the restoration of the final cluster to yield **sekand** or even **shekand**. Such pronunciations are common only in carefully monitored styles.

So far, the examples chosen have related to phonological properties. Stylistic variation is equally manifest at other levels of grammar. Thus, to return to **baimbai**, developmentally later varieties tend to have this "future marker" closer to the verb and, for some speakers, the shortened **ba** has become a verbal prefix. In sliding back and forth along the developmental continuum, speakers can fluctuate between synthetic and analytic constructions to express the same grammatical meaning.

The same is true for word formation. Many speakers have at their disposal three different methods of causative encoding: lexicalization, circumlocution and morphological affixation. Thus, in the same speech event one may find **kilim** 'to hit or kill', and **mekim i dai** 'to make die, kill', or **mekim i bagarap** 'to destroy' and **bagarapim** 'to destroy'. These and many other examples point to the conclusion that earlier stages of language development are not simply replaced, but remain accessible to speakers and are used for stylistic purposes.[28]

An excellent theoretical discussion of the forces that promote stylistic flexibility in Creoles is given by Labov (1990). His paper examines why

---

[27] Unlike the situation in most European languages and unlike the analyses proposed by speakers of these languages, Tok Pisin **baimbai** actually stands for 'event taking place after another event', that is, it refers to aspect, not to tense.

[28] I do not wish to claim that all earlier material is preserved. As well as cumulative processes, there is probably replacement and as yet ill-understood mixing, which leads to partial restructuring of earlier material. The fact that such developmentally founded polystylism exists is one of the reasons why communication between less and more progressive speakers of the language can occur. It also accounts for the fact that understanding the latter varieties implies understanding the former, but not vice versa.

Creoles develop a highly redundant tense system, instead of perpetuating the redundancy-free encoding of some of their Pidgin predecessors. More precisely, he studies the transition of tense/time encoding by means of optional adverbs as against encoding by affixation. He concludes that Creoles develop affixes for stylistic reasons:

> in tracing the development of tense so far, it appears that the *essence* is *a stylstic one*. There is no basis for arguing that tense markers express the concepts of temporal relations more clearly than adverbs of time. What then is the advantage that they offer to native speakers, the advantage which native speakers seem to demand? *The most important property which tense markers possess, which adverbs of time do not, is their stylistic flexibility.* They can be expanded or contracted to fit in with the prosodic requirements of allegro or lento style (1990:61).

He could have added a second consideration, had natural morphology been developed at the time. (His paper was written in 1971.) According to the proponents of this theory (e.g. Mayerthaler 1978), there is a tendency towards greater naturalness in morphological development, which manifests itself in constructional iconicity: those aspects of the message that are central should be perceptually more prominent than marginal ones. Thus, the lexical meaning of a word should be encoded by means of a fully stressed word, whereas its grammatical "accidents" are best encoded by means of unstressed affixes.

As in the case of Pidgins, Creole-speakers also have to pay the price of increased complexity in decoding for their stylistic flexibility. Thus, instead of the relative derivational shallowness of early Pidgins, there can be a considerable distance between surface and deeper structures in Creoles. An example of this depth is the variable pronunciation of Hawaiian Creole auxiliary **wen**. Whereas rules of morphophonemic condensation are virtually absent with older Pidgin speakers, Creole-speaking members of the young generation produce numerous variants of this form, including the reduced forms **wen, wn, en, n, we** and **w**. Labov (1990:36) illustrates some of these in the following sample sentences:

45a	So they wen walk [dewːɔk] pas' the bridge
45b	We wen looking [wːnlʊkɪn] for the guy
46	I wen go [ɑ° ŋgo] kick one of 'em
47	So I went look [alʷː ʊk] by the door

He points out that the reductions are due to the operation of a number of phonological rules, whose application appears to depend on stylistic factors.

Again, in addition to such phonological condensation, which can be thought of as reflecting internal development, speakers of Hawaiian Creole English also have the option of borrowing from the superimposed English language and producing the form *went*. This last example illustrates the fact that Creoles exhibit a stylistic distinction to which their speakers refer by expressions such as heavy, deep (basilectal) and light (acrolectal like). Typically, the light Creole is influenced by and mixed with the related superimposed language, but by no means identical with it. Sandefur's data on heavy and light Northern Australian Kriol suggest that this distinction is not just a matter of different varieties linked by ordered phonological or other

71

rules, but a much more complex phenomenon involving lexicalization and lexical diffusion. Thus **dog**, which can mean 'dog' and 'talk' in heavy Kriol, becomes **dog** 'dog' and **tok** 'talk' in the light variety, suggesting that the English model rather than a phonological rule is responsible (cf Sandefur 1984:132). Variability, finally, is a reflection of an absence of focussing. Le Page & Tabouret-Keller's study of Belizean Creole (1985) shows how unfocussed Creoles with great internal variation can become more constrained focussed languages through acts of identiity.

These last examples illustrate the complex interplay between the many factors underlying variation in Pidgins and Creoles. At the same time they also suggest why they should often be more variable than most other languages. Their condensed developmental history and the ready access to a model from which lexicon and structures can be borrowed provide an enormous pool of stylistic and other sources of variability. As they develop from mere media for the exchange of information to carriers of indexical and personal dimensions of meaning, more and more of these potential variants are exploited.

The social typology of Pidgins and Creoles

After our discussion of the major social forces shaping the formation and development of Pidgins and Creoles, one may wish to ask whether such factors and their combinations define subclasses of these languages. A number of attempts have indeed been made, the best known being that of Schultze (1933), who distinguishes four main types:

1. Colonial jargon:	Afrikaans, Pennsylvania Dutch
2. Trade jargon:	Chinook Jargon, Lingua Geral Brasilica[29]
3. Languages of the study table:	Esperanto
4. Slaves' and servants' languages:	Pidgin English

Schultze's classification is of little help for our purposes, as the languages of the first and third category, strictly speaking, fall outside the scope of this book. A critical discussion of his classificatory attempt is found in Reinecke (1937:34ff), as is Reinecke's own classification:

Type	*Example*
Immigrant's mixed dialects	Imperfect acquisition of a new language by immigrants
Trade Pidgins	Chinese Pidgin English
Plantation Creole dialects	Jamaican Creole

Since Reinecke's proposals were first put forward, various comments about criteria to be used in classification have been made, but no attempt, to my knowledge at least, has ever been undertaken to pull all these criteria together into a comprehensive sociology of Pidgins and Creoles. In the following

---

[29] This label relates to a number of former and present-day contact varieties of Brazilian Indian languages and Portuguese spoken in the interior as well as by migrant groups. A full analysis of the various types of language involved here is still outstanding (see Holm 1988-89:299ff). However, it seems clear that one is not dealing with a unitary linguistic or social phenomenon.

pages, I shall discuss a number of parameters useful in this area. I have to insist, however, that the resulting classification is quite preliminary, and that no claims about any direct correlations between a linguistic and a social typology are implied. A much more recent classication of Creoles is that by Bickerton (1989:16) which relies on two parameters only:

Bickerton's distinguishing features of contact situations

	Plantation	Fort	Maritime
Permanent population displacement	+	–	–
First generation nativization	+	+	–

Subsequent writers have pointed to difficulties with the classification (first generation nativization is not widely found on plantations) and the need to add other parameters. As Baker (1995a:10) observes, "one major difference between the children on Hawaiian plantations and those on plantations in the Caribbean and Indian Ocean was that children in Hawaii attended schools where they were taught English". There is of course a difference between second-language input and second-language intake and the Creoles that developed in boarding school environments (Unserdeutsch, Tayo, Broken) exhibit numerous signs of independent development.

Indigenous versus European Pidgins and Creoles

A prominent distinction made by many Creolists is that between indigenous and European-derived (or based) Pidgins and Creoles. This distinction, it should be noted, is usually made on linguistic grounds and is often inapplicable to a sociology of language.

The principal problem with a linguistic distinction is that Pidgins or Creoles based on non-European languages often developed in response to European colonial expansion. Thus both Pidgin Fijian (Siegel 1982) and Fijian Pidgin Hindi emerged in the context of the sugar plantation system brought to Fiji by British colonizers; Hiri Motu or Police Motu, unlike a number of other Pidgins used by the Motuans,[30] developed in the police force, prisons and government patrols introduced by the British and Australian administrations; and many African lingue franche such as Lingala and Sango can again be regarded as the results of colonial social structures.

In contrast, a number of Pidgins and Creoles associated with European languages arose with only minimal contact with European colonizers. Thus the spread of Tok Pisin into the interior of New Guinea often preceded the advent of expatriate missionaries and administrators, and the social conventions governing the use of this language tend to reflect local New Guinean patterns. The notion of English being a "target" language in such instances is quite infelicitous. The same appears to be true of some Australian Pidgins derived from English. The Creoles used in some early maroon communities are similarly spoken by peoples who, with the exception of a period of forced displacement, had little access to the social and linguistic models of their colonizers (e.g. Saramaccan).

---

30 Dutton (1976, 1983b, 1985a), has demonstrated that the languages used by the Motuans on the occasion of their hiris (trade expeditions) were Pidgins based on Koriki and Eleman, rather than any predecessor of Hiri Motu (Police Motu).

The principal criteria for determining whether a language is indeed indigenous should therefore be as follows:

1. Has the language resulted from European colonial expansion?
2. Has the language been used, to a significant degree, in communication between indigenes and Europeans?
3. Is the language indigenous to an area or has it been transported?

Even this classification leaves certain problems unresolved. It is not obvious, for instance, why European colonial expansion should be singled out as a special case. The Malay expansion across Indonesia to New Guinea, for example, has had similar results to Portuguese or English expansion in the area. Again, one may ask why the little-known trade languages used between Arab traders and their partners in Africa (Versteegh 1984), India and China should be labelled indigenous. In some cases there may even have been a gradual transition, involving relexification over a considerable period of time, from a pre-existing indigenous Pidgin to a subsequent European-based one. Pidgin Macassarese, spoken in the North of Australia before it was relexified and/or replaced with an English-derived Pidgin, is a possible example.[31]

The problem of finding objective criteria for distinguishing between indigenous and European Pidgins and Creoles is aggravated by attitudinal factors. Those who speak them may differ considerably in their view as to whether their language is a European or an indigenous phenomenon. Thus recent surveys of attitudes towards Kriol discussed by Sandefur (1984) suggest that the majority of its second-language speakers and first-generation Creole speakers regard it as a European phenomenon. Second-generation Creole speakers, on the other hand, often consider it an Aboriginal language and do not use it in the presence of whites. A recent study by Rhydwen (1993) confirms that such ambiguous views about Kriol persist. I have experienced something similar with Tok Pisin. Older speakers report that the language was brought to them by the whites and they often do not even distinguish it from proper English, whereas the younger generation typically maintain that it was handed down to them by their ancestors, by God, or by speaking animals (reinforced by the fact that **pisin** translates as 'bird').

In conclusion, a European linguistic classification of Pidgins and Creoles is hardly adequate. We need to consider two factors. First, Pidgins and Creoles can change both their structural/linguistic and pragmatic/linguistic affiliation over time. Second, European influence is of importance in the formative years of many Pidgins and Creoles, but is often absent later; in such cases we should refer to later stages as nativized Pidgins or Creoles.

Classification according to domain

It has often been suggested that the linguistic and social character of Pidgin is linked to their narrow domain of communication, thus distinguishing them from full languages. It is also suggested that qualitative differences between Pidgins may reflect the type of domain they are employed in,[32] the following

---

[31] Unfortunately, virtually no linguistic documentation of this language exists. Some notes are given by Urry & Walsh (1981) and in Wurm, Mühlhäusler & Tryon (1996).

[32] Very often such qualitative differences vary from speaker to speaker and region to region within the same Pidgin.

types being frequently singled out as prominent: trade; military purposes; migrant labour; tourism; domestic purposes; and so on. Most of the older Pidgins belong to the trade category, although more recently overseas military involvement and tourism have become increasingly common. Thus American involvement in Asia has given rise to varieties such as Japanese PE (Goodman 1967), Thai PE (Gebhard 1979), Korean Bamboo English, and Vietnamese PE. The impact of mass tourism on Pidgin development has not been studied in most areas.[33] However, Hinnenkamp's (1982) account of a Turkish-derived Pidgin suggests that many insights can be gained from such systems.

Perhaps the best-studied Pidgins are those involving migrant labour. Many regard the plantation system with its large displacement of populations as *the* most important context for the development of Pidgins and Creoles. Whether recruitment of forced labour for plantations results in a Pidgin or a Creole depends on a number of factors. First and foremost, one should distinguish between those plantation areas where labour was employed permanently and those where employment was for limited periods, as in the Pacific – the usual duration for employment in Queensland, Samoa, New Caledonia and Fiji was from three to five years, with an annual turnover of about one third of the labourers This system meant that a number of functionally restricted stable Pidgins were handed down from one group of second-language speakers to the next in a narrowly defined social context.

A similar situation, until recently, was found with the numerous workers from Eastern and Southern Europe who came to work in the industrial centres of Germany, the Netherlands or Scandinavia. Again, the so-called guest-worker Pidgins were employed in a relatively narrow social context and were passed on from one generation of second-language speakers to the next.[34] It has gradually become apparent that many of the guest workers have become permanent migrants. Some of the linguistic consequences of this change in social environment have been that children do not develop a Creole or speak their parents' vernacular, but become integrated linguistically into the host community. The same thing happened with the small number of plantation workers who remained in Queensland after termination of their labour contract: thus, we find a community of about 10,000 Melanesians who have become speakers of Australian English.

Temporary employment abroad often promotes the spread of Pidgins. The spread of Pacific PEs to the Solomons, Papua New Guinea and Vanuatu is largely the result of tens of thousands of ex-workers taking their newly acquired linguistic skills home. It is interesting to note that such was the usefulness of PE in their home areas that it soon expanded socially and linguistically beyond its plantation past. In the past, centres of employment tended to be controlled by speakers of European languages, but we now find speakers of English, German and French employed in the oil industry of the Gulf states where they employ Gulf Arabic Pidgin (see Smart 1990).

---

33 Mass tourism is not an entirely new phenomenon. Apparently, some form of Pidgin Italian was used by medieval pilgrims making for Rome, and it seems conceivable that other religious centres such as Mecca have similar languages (see Coates 1969).

34 In contrast to the plantation system, modern guest workers can move more freely, both geographically and socially, in their host community and thus can have considerably more access to the target language. Instead of a stable Pidgin, one thus mostly finds unstable interlanguage continua (cf Meisel 1975).

Where we are dealing with permanent population displacements, the role of the plantations is even more important, as observed by Sankoff:

> The plantation system is crucial because it was unique in creating a catastrophic break in linguistic tradition that is unparalleled. It is difficult to conceive of another situation where people arrived with such a variety of native languages; where they were so cut off from their native language groups; where the size of no one language group was sufficient to insure its survival; where no second language was shared by enough people to serve as a useful vehicle of intercommunication; and where the legitimate language was inaccessible to almost everyone (1979:24).

One should not forget, however, that in spite of the many discontinuities caused by plantation slavery, some continuities of linguistic and cultural transmission remained. Thus the import of new slaves may occur over a prolonged period of time, particularly where local mortality on the plantations was high, as, for instance, in Surinam. Thus the relative importance of natural human reproduction and replenishment of human resources from the outside would seem to be useful parameters in a social classification of Creoles. Continuity was also provided by the relative homogeneity of origin in some plantations and the consequent survival of many linguistic and cultural habits. Contrary to the often expressed belief that plantation societies were a totally new start, links with the homeland were sometimes maintained over a long period. It is dangerous to generalize here and it seems advisable to carry out a detailed study of the local conditions to avoid unwarranted conclusions.

The geographical mobility of slaves was, for obvious reasons, considerably less than that of indentured workers, and the spread of plantation Creoles was less than that of plantation Pidgins for many years. It was only with the manumission of slaves and their resettlement in places such as Liberia or Sierra Leone that the Creoles of the New World were returned to the Old World. One may wish to conclude that the label 'plantation Creole' does not characterize a uniform phenomenon sociologically.

Pidgins and Creoles that developed out of trade contacts are documented for many different areas, and it is certain that they refute Sankoff's claim that "we know of no cases where a 'Pidgin' has developed in conditions other than those of modern European colonial expansion" (1979:24). Counter-examples are very often not well documented, mainly because those speaking such trade Pidgins were hardly in the business of recording them and in most cases were probably illiterate. Among such lost languages one can mention Pidgin Macassarese in Northern Australia, Arabic Chinese Pidgin of Canton,[35] Pidgin Siassi of New Guinea, and American Indian trade languages spoken in pre-Columbian days (see Silverstein 1972b). Numerous additional examples have been mapped and described in Wurm, Mühlhäusler & Tryon (1996).

---

[35] Relexification theory usually traces contact languages with a European lexicon back to other contact languages with a European lexicon. However, it seems plausible that Cantonese Pidgin Arabic (cf Van Gulik 1966) may have some links with the Pidgin Portuguese subsequently spoken in this area.

Among the pre-colonial trade Pidgins that have become better known, I would like to draw attention to Mobilian (Haas 1975) and the two trade Pidgins employed by the Motuans of Papua (Dutton 1983b, 1985a). Early reports on Mobilian (spoken at Mobile, the trade centre of the Gulf region of the Mississippi) suggest that this language was spoken in addition to their native language by most of the Indians from the east side of the Mississippi, that is, it was widely used as a trade language by numerous groups before Europeans arrived. Linguistically, the language was derived from Choctaw. Its structures exhibit most of the simplifications one has come to expect with European-derived Pidgins, such as the drastic simplification of its morphology. Its lexical composition appears to have differed from area to area, probably in reflection of the relative power of the partners in trade. A fairly mixed lexicon, something which is often associated with trade between equals, is found in the variety among the Alabama (Haas 1975:259):

	Alabama	*Choctaw*	*Mobilian*
fish:	łało	nani	slasu
squirrel:	ipło	fani	fani
horse:	čičoba	(is)suba	suba
dog:	ifa	ofi	ofi
eat:	ipa	apa	apa
fire:	tikba	lowak	lowak
water:	oki	oka	oki
rain:	oyba	omba	hoyba

Traces of this language still survive and have been documented in a detailed analysis (Crawford 1978).

In contrast to the wide geographic spread of Mobilian, the two trade languages used by the Motuans on one of their annual trading expeditions to the Gulf of Papua were highly restricted: an Eleman Hiri Trade Language was used with the Eleman people west of Cape Possession (Papua), and a Koriki Hiri Trade Language was spoken with the Koriki, who lived further west in the delta area of the Puari River. The existence of two trade languages rather than one, which could have been transported as trade spread further west, suggests the precarious position of the Motu traders *vis-à-vis* their hosts: in order to be accepted, they had to accept the languages of their host communities as their linguistic models and, moreover, they also had to observe the strict social conditions attached to their use, such as not addressing women.[36]

The desire of the Motuans' trade partners to maintain non-intimacy is reflected in the highly restricted vocabulary of both trade Pidgins, containing perhaps not more than 300 words relating to the immediate context of the exchange of goods. Their grammatical structures, as far as they are known, again exhibit many of the simplifications of morphology, the absence of derivational depth and an avoidance of embedding. However, there are some important differences between the two varieties, indicating that different strategies of Pidgin formation and development must have been

---

[36] It is interesting to note, as described in much detail in Dutton (1985a), that in trading with their immediate neighbours the Motuans availed themselves of a simplified (foreigner talk) version of Motu. They appear to have been in no position (unlike the Australian administration and its police force) to impose this language in more remote areas.

operative. As the trade relations typically involved speakers of only two different languages, we are dealing with secondary hybrids (in the sense of Whinnom 1971) and thus can expect a higher degree of mixing than in multilingual environments.

Other trade languages that have become better known include Russonorsk (e.g. Neumann 1965), the Chinese-Russian Trade Jargon (Neumann 1966) and Chinook Jargon in its various forms (Thomason 1981). Chinese-Russian Trade Jargon and other trade Pidgins of the Siberian area have been discussed by Wurm (1992a). Further comparative work on the social and linguistic nature of trade jargons and Pidgins would be an enterprise well worth undertaking.

The duration and nature of trade in the above cases differed considerably and in most contexts the preconditions for the development of a Creole out of a trade Pidgin were not met: that is, there was insufficient permanency, no intermarriage and clearly defined social roles. In some instances, however – notably with some Portuguese-based Creoles – a trade language was probably the origin of a Creole.

One example which has been studied in more detail (Kihm 1984, 1994) is Bissau Crioulo,[37] a language brought to former Portuguese Guinea by so-called *lançados*, i.e., adventurers and other marginal characters from the Cape Verde Islands, who settled in order to trade slaves with other overseas territories. The version of Portuguese they brought with them (probably a Pidgin) became a stable Creole in the small mixed-race community that subsequently sprang up around Cacheu and other fortified places. The development of Portuguese-based Pidgins into fully-fledged Creoles depended crucially on the relative absence of Portuguese as a target language. Whereas creolization was interfered with in areas that remained under Portuguese control for a long time after the establishment of an initial trading post (e.g. Goa, Macau and Timor), it could develop unconstrained in other places such as Ceylon (see Schuchardt 1889b), Malacca (see Baxter 1985), or the Moluccas. Macanese, the Portuguese Creole that had developed in Macau, has become virtually absorbed by Portuguese there (see Charpentier 1995), but has remained a separate language in nearby Hong Kong (Thompson 1967). A particularly interesting fate is that of the trade Portuguese of Ternate in the Moluccas in the 17th century. It is suggested (e.g. by Molony 1973) that after the language became a Creole in this small trading post, it was brought to the Philippines towards the end of the 17th century by about 200 migrants, all of them Christians, led by their priest who did not want them to be open to attacks by Muslims and heathens after the termination of European control of Ternate. Subsequently this language and its offspring partly relexified under Spanish influence.

For details of the recent fate of the Portuguese Creoles in India, see Clements (1991).

All the trade Pidgins and Creoles known to me underwent creolization following the prolonged stabilization and expansion of a Pidgin. Thus, whatever their sociological interest, these languages will have little appeal to linguists looking for bioprogram universals. They should, however, afford interesting insights into the impact of social conditions on the lexicon.

---

[37] In spite of its name, the language is a Pidgin for many of its speakers.

Military Pidgins, unlike trade Pidgins, tend to reflect unequal power relations. The best-known cases relate to the recent past, in particular American involvement in South-East Asia, although it is likely that many existed long before. The well-known – but not so well documented – case is the *français tiraillou* (or *tirailleur*) used by African regiments in the French colonial forces in the 19th and 20th centuries (Chris Corne, p c). Military influence manifests itself both in the formation of new Pidgins and in the spread and structural expansion of existing Pidgins. Military and paramilitary forces were instrumental, for instance, in spreading Police Motu (later Hiri Motu) throughout Papua, particularly during the Second World War, and the extensive use of Tok Pisin during the propaganda campaigns of the Japanese and American/Australian forces in New Guinea and other parts of Melanesia provided a tremendous boost to the Pidgins of this area.

A case where military operations triggered off the large-scale creolization of a Pidgin is that of Northern Australia. During the Second World War, in reaction to the threat of a Japanese invasion, large numbers of Australian troops were moved to the Northern Territory and parts of northern Queensland. To facilitate the control and use for military purposes of the local Aboriginal population, Aborigines of different regional and tribal affiliations were brought together in large camps. This had a twofold effect: (1) it weakened the social position of the indigenous vernaculars; and (2) it provided a tremendous boost to Aboriginal PE (cf Sandefur 1984) and koinés based on indigenous languages (see Wurm, Mühlhäusler & Tryon 1996).

It is also interesting, in this connection, to observe that the first structural descriptions and language teaching programmes of the various Melanesian PEs were commissioned by military agencies during the Second World War. Such indirect military involvement may have similarly influenced the development of quite a few other Pidgins and Creoles.

Pidgins that are restricted to the domestic domain are rare, but the domestic context is an important force in their formation and development. A Pidgin that remained restricted is Indian Butler English, first discussed by Schuchardt (1891). He predicted its early demise, but, in spite of the passing of British colonial control in India, certain of its characteristics live on (cf Hosali 1984). In other areas, the gradual disappearance of the domestic servant system has dealt a severe blow to the numerous kitchen Pidgins that were in use in colonial times; many of these were very much *ad hoc* inventions, such as the Pidgin German of the missionary kitchens of Alexishafen in New Guinea, but others were more institutionalized. Often, because of the reluctance of white colonizers to acquire an indigenous vernacular, Pidgin or Creole proper, kitchen jargons survive in a fossilized condition at a much lower developmental stage than the varieties spoken outside. Thus, although on the plantations and goldmines of Papua a relatively sophisticated Pidgin had developed, and although most government agencies had begun to use pidginized Motu (Police Motu, later Hiri Motu), unstable English-derived kitchen jargons survived in colonial households.[38] Examples of these, recorded in 1976, are given in Mühlhäusler (1978a).

---

[38] Note, for instance, the variable use of **I** and **me** as first-person subject pronoun, variable word order in interrogatives, as in **We i go?** as against **Ai go we?**, and the variable absence of prepositions.

An interesting kitchen jargon is pidginized Afrikaans spoken by African servants in white households in South Africa. Although such varieties are often marginal, some at least perform important roles. In many colonial societies, it was customary for white children to be brought up by a black nanny. This may account for the minimal differences between black and white Southern States American English, the many black constructions in white Bahamian English (Shilling 1980), and the development of a creoloid Afrikaans. Domestic personnel had greater access to standard forms of the superimposed language and thus transmitted these to black outsiders. This, however, was not universally so. In most colonial societies, there was an ongoing debate as to the desirability of servants who were sufficiently fluent in their masters' language to overhear conversations at table. Thus the domestic Pidgin or Creole favoured was often lexically unrelated to the whites' language. Much early debate as to whether German or Pidgin German should replace Tok Pisin as the lingua franca of German New Guinea centred around such an argument. Friederici discusses this point and remarks on "the inconvenience of not having a language at the disposal of the master race once German had become generally known, a language in which one could not be understood or overheard by unauthorized natives" (1911:97).

Similar attitudes probably prevented the development of other Pidgins. Thus the policy in the Dutch East Indies (now Indonesia) until the mid-19th century was to prevent indigenes from learning any form of Dutch, by which time a pidginized form of Malay, the precursor of modern Bahasa Indonesia, had become the language of dealings between colonizers and colonized.

We have now examined some of the domains of human inter-communication that particularly favour the development of jargons and Pidgins. What is common to them is the original geographic, social and linguistic distance of parties involved. In most cases, there remains a desire to maintain the social distance, and it is this desire that keeps jargons and Pidgins alive. We have also seen how a jargon or Pidgin depends on its social usefulness for its viability. Survival chances are enhanced considerably if it is used in a number of domains or if it becomes creolized, the most favourable conditions for the latter being created by slavery and the plantation system. As we have seen, however, other social uses of a jargon or Pidgin can also lead to the development of a Creole.

Classification according to function

By function, I mean the communicative purpose to which language is put in a particular utterance. Just as there is no utterance without style, there is no utterance without function, although in both instances attempts have been made to portray decontextualized statements as the reference point for both style and function. These problems cannot all be discussed here. Remarks pertaining to the discussion of linguistic functions can be found in Bell (1976), Halliday (1974), Robinson (1974) and Silverstein (1977).

For present purposes, two assumptions will be made:

1. that Pidgins and Creoles should be regarded as developing entities at structural and functional levels;

2 that there is no reason for the assumption that the propositional (cognitive representational, communicative, referential) function is primary in human communication.[39]
We will further assume, while being aware of the fundamental difficulties, that one can isolate a finite number of linguistic functions and we shall draw these functions from the lists compiled by Halliday (1974) and Jakobson (1960). The most important ones for our purposes are:

Functions	*Role in communication*
Propositional (referential)	The message itself, the information exchanged, information whose truth value can be established
Directive	Getting things achieved, manipulation of others
Integrative	Creation of social bonds, use of language as an index of group membership
Expressive	Expression of own personal feelings towards the message or interlocutors
Phatic	Keeping open channels of communication, counteracting socially undesirable silence, creation of rituals
Metalinguistic	Use of language to discuss language
Poetic	Use of language to focus on the message for its own sake, to play with verbal material
Heuristic	Use of language for obtaining information

Remember again that this is a pre-theoretical classification and that different observers have used different labels and/or different characterizations of individual functions.

Pidgins have long been described as functionally reduced, that is, they are not used in all the above functions. As pointed out, for instance, by Smith (1972:50), the primary function of a Pidgin is the propositional one. In this article, Smith arrives at this and related important insights. Unfortunately his views are based on a rather undifferentiated three-function model and are still within the static paradigm (that is, he ignores the possibility that even a Pidgin with no native speakers can undergo functional expansion). It seems that at least some functions are added relatively early in the Pidgin-Creole life-cycle. Using the above functions, and applying them to a number of Pidgins, I have tentatively concluded that their hierarchy of development is as listed with the important exception that the heuristic function immediately follows the propositional one.

We can project these onto the developmental stages of Pidgins discussed earlier in this book. Thus early jargons serve the purpose of exchanging simple information in a restricted domain, simple statements and questions (propositional and heuristic functions) being sufficient. At this stage, equitable power relations prevail. Even in situations of contact between colonizers and colonized, the numerical proportions are such that power cannot be exercised by the former. Instead, and this purpose is served well

---

[39] Arguments against this assumption include the facts that in child language the propositional function emerges last, and that in multifunctional adult discourse one often encounters utterances with no propositional content, but rarely propositions with no functional connotations.

by a jargon, individual attempts at cross-communication emphasize non-intimacy and non-involvement.

This situation changes once expatriate domination becomes consolidated. At this point, white foreigner talk becomes the dominant model, although pressure for more efficient communication may also result in some stabilization of rules not found in the white input. The principal direction of communication is now vertical, between master and servant, and the directive function of the language is emphasized. Many Pidgins have remained associated with giving orders in a colonial context; this has promoted a negative attitude towards them by language planners and educators in newly independent countries. However, Pidgins can develop considerably beyond this mainly directive function, as pointed out by Wurm:

> The fact that the use of Pidgin as opposed to English may at times in the past have been indicative of social distinctions is not something that can sensibly be held against any language: very much the same situation prevailed with regard to English versus French in Norman days (1969:39).

However, in accordance with the retentionist view of Pidgin development adopted in this book, one suspects that traces of earlier functions continue to survive at later stages, and that the earlier a function emerges, the more dominant it is later. Sankoff (1976:302) has made some pertinent observations about Tok Pisin in rural areas and its continued association with power and non-solidarity:

> Though... Tok Pisin is now a common denominator, even a language of equality among urban New Guineans from diverse linguistic groups, it has retained its associations with and connotations of power and authority at the village level, learned by each new generation in the context of giving orders and shouting at people, as well as playful imitation of such contexts.

As Sankoff further demonstrates, it is used predominantly where forced regimentation plays a role (such as village meetings where people line up to receive orders about the work for the day) and by persons in a position of authority (such as village leaders, the big men, etc.). It may be an awareness of this which accounts for the widely found rule in expanded Pidgins and even Creoles that the language is not to be used in the company of or towards whites and also for the related objection of many of their speakers at being addressed in these languages by an expatriate. One should not ignore the indexical value of language choice in Pidgin- and Creole-using societies.

The change from vertical to horizontal (between indigenes of comparable power in the communication process) communication is the principal reason for stabilization of a Pidgin. In the absence of prestige norms, language universals rather than language or speaker-specific solutions emerge in lexicon and grammar. Language-internal word formation begins to replace borrowing from prestige languages, and natural structures supplement or replace those borrowed from the previously dominant language. The function most closely associated with this process is the integrative one. Speakers now identify with a new type of society, which is neither traditional nor that of the colonizer, within its own social and linguistic norms. The plantation is a typical context for this development, and some Pidgins of this type include

Pidgin Bantu (Fanakalo) of the Natal sugar plantations, Pidgin Fijian and the PE spoken on some West African islands such as Fernando Póo.[40]

A vivid picture of the functional limitations of such a stabilized Pidgin is given by Bateson describing early Tok Pisin:

> The language and its tones of voice and the things that are said in it are a rudimentary third culture, neither native nor white, and within the conventions of this third culture the white man and the native can meet happily, though the culture is germane to neither of them... But neither the white man's philosophy of life, nor that of the native, crops up in the neutral and special fields of Pidgin English conversation. It is not that democracy and private enterprise could not be described in Pidgin, it is just that, in fact they are not (1944:139).

Continued use of a stable Pidgin by speakers from many different language backgrounds, particularly when transported from the plantation to a larger multilingual society such as that of Papua New Guinea or Vanuatu, led to further functional and structural expansion. On the one hand, the permanency of contacts required the encoding of personal feelings; on the other, social norms of politeness such as small talk were needed. The addition of the expressive function typically goes hand in hand with a widening of domain. In many instances, the use of a Pidgin for religious purposes triggered this new functional use. Phatic communion (a term introduced by Malinowski 1923) is associated with new domains (meetings, social gatherings, etc.) as well as new media. In using a Pidgin for telephone conversations, for instance, certain devices referring to this channel of communication and its functioning are required.

It has to be kept in mind, at all times, that Pidgins are second languages and that any new functions have to be seen in relation to the functional use of a speaker's first language. The use of a jargon – a language for propositional and heuristic functions only – typically has little effect on a speaker's vernacular. It is simply added to it. The same is true with Pidgins that are beginning to stabilize and many older stable Pidgins: they are additional to traditional vernaculars, which continue to remain intact and to be used in all functions relevant to the traditional society in which they are spoken.

With the ongoing functional and structural expansion of a Pidgin, however, its relationship with the speaker's first language tends to become changed. Instead of being added to, traditional languages tend to be replaced in an increasing number of domains and functions. This has been documented for the gradual replacement of Taiap (Kulick 1990) by Tok Pisin (for a summary of relevant studies, see Mühlhäusler 1993). This is particularly striking with the expressive function in the domains of religion and abuse. Thus the religious experiences transmitted by expatriate mission bodies to the indigenous population tend to be incompatible with traditional modes of religious expression and Pidgins, or mission lingue franche are preferred.[41] Prayer, services and discussion of religious matters thus are

---

40 Since Fernando Póo was a Spanish possession and its economy only partially controlled by English interests, the PE spoken there underwent a fair amount of relexification in the direction of Spanish, as pointed out by Schuchardt (1979:60).

41 The numerous mission lingue franche in use in Melanesia are discussed by Wurm (1979). For their African counterparts, see Heine (1973).

associated with speakers' second languages. The same is true of insults, expletives and other forms of strong language. For Tok Pisin among the Kwoma, Reed observed:

> We found that youngsters not only counted and sang in Pidgin but also used it in the new game of football – especially in angry altercations. Their own language was not lacking in terms of abuse, but those in Pidgin were preferred (1943:286).

Conventions for talking about talking differ from society to society. For some languages, such as Gbeya in the Central African Republic (Samarin 1969), only two metalinguistic labels – translated as 'good' and 'bad' – are reported. In other cases such as Central American Tzeltal (Stross 1974), a profusion of labels is in use. It thus seems that metalinguistic conventions are very much culture-specific and culture-dependent and to be expected late, if at all, in the development of Pidgin. With the exception of scattered remarks on metalinguistic systems in various Pidgins and Creoles (e.g. Sandefur 1984 on Kriol), no comparative or developmental studies are at hand and the following brief case study of Tok Pisin may turn out to be quite atypical. In a pilot paper on this question (1984c), I distinguished a number of stages:

1. awareness of Tok Pisin as a language separate from English;
2. awareness of distinct varieties within Tok Pisin:
   a) indigenous versus non-indigenous varieties;
   b) socially determined varieties;
   c) diachronic varieties (developmental stages);
   d) stylistic varieties;
3. awareness of grammatical units such as sense group, word classes and word-formation processes.

Labels referring to these categories emerged over a period of more than one hundred years. It took roughly 50 years for the difference between English and Tok Pisin to be expressed, another 25 years before socially determined varieties were labelled, and it is only recently that one can talk about diachronic and stylistic varieties and grammar. This, incidentally, causes a major problem for the fieldworker, since the absence of metalinguistic labels signals not only Pidgin speakers' difficulties in talking about their language, but also their lack of interest in this matter. Most Pidgins are not languages that reflect on themselves.

This lack of self-reflection also means that the poetic function of language is late to emerge. The poetic use of language means that attention is drawn to the language itself as used in a message. Examples include word plays, puns, rhymes, artistic metaphors and other tropes. Such stylistic devices were conspicuous by their absence in Tok Pisin. As observed by Mead (1931:149): "To the unaccustomed ear, Pidgin has a terrific monotony because of the constant repetition of three words, *belong*, *along* and *fellow*." The use of Tok Pisin in the poetic function has emerged only recently and is restricted to younger urban speakers.[42] Examples of contexts in which the

---

42 My attempts to pun in this language, for instance, were perfectly acceptable to young speakers, but either misunderstood or discouraged by older ones, particularly those living in traditional villages.

poetic function is dominant and the linguistic devices used for poetic purposes are discussed by Wurm & Mühlhäusler (1983). Again, the poetic use of Tok Pisin typically implies the reduction of a speaker's use of his or her first language in this function.

Summing up my remarks on the functional expansion of Tok Pisin, it seems obvious that it can occur with second-language speakers and that, as it were, the process of creolization of a language can take place over a prolonged period of time with widespread bilingualism. The functional range that individual speakers occupy can be distributed over a number of languages, and one typically finds a change from initial compound to later coordinate bilingualism, followed again by compound bilingualism with the growing importance of English. Schematically, a highly idealized picture could be drawn up as shown below:

Functional expansion of Tok Pisin

The development outlined above is from a monostylistic, monofunctional language to a polyfunctional one. It is likely that other expanding Pidgins, as well as second languages learned in a more formal context, may follow a similar development. This functional expansion of a Pidgin differs dramatically from the functional development found with first-language acquisition. For instance, Halliday's investigations (1974) of the development of language function in first-language acquisition suggest the following hierarchy:

Halliday (1974)	*Other common terms*
instrumental	
regulative	(directive, social control)
interactional	(phatic)
personal	(expressive)
heuristic	
metalinguistic	
imaginative	(poetic)
representational	(referential, propositional)

The endpoint of first-language acquisition, if the hierarchies developed by Halliday and myself are correct, is thus the point of departure for Pidgin development. Whereas a first language develops in the social security of parent-child interaction and eventually enables the child to correlate to the world outside, Pidgin speakers are faced first with a hostile and dangerous outside world and only gradually develop the structural and functional means to make this world a home. One is tempted to do two things:

1. To correlate the functional expansion of a Pidgin to its structural growth;
2. To explain the differences in the development of first languages and Pidgins as being derived from differences in functional development.

At this point, however, correlations can be only very rough guidelines indeed, principally because we simply lack comparative data and, secondly, because single structures can be used in a number of different functions and vice versa. It is in this light that one has to see the following table.

Correlation of the functional expansion of a Pidgin to its structural growth

Functions	Structure
Cognitive (propositional)	Simple sentence structures, but no grammar beyond the sentence, list-like lexicon
Directive and integrative	Development of systematic aspects in the lexicon, e.g., address system forms that mark politeness, emergence of socially determined lexicon and grammar, some syntactic variants for requests
Expressive	Additions to lexical inventory, beginnings of word formation, emergence of devices for focalization, grammar beyond sentence
Phatic	Increase in stylistic variation at the lexical and syntactic levels
Metalinguistic	Emergence of lexical items for speaking about language, hypercorrection
Poetic	Socially determined variation of earlier stages of a developmental continuum can become stylistic devices, productive word-formation providing lexical synonyms, stylistic syntactic transformations, development of conventions for metaphorical expansion

Our discussion of functional development has been restricted to Pidgins. As regards Creoles, it is usually assumed that they exhibit the same functional potential as any other language, although the continued presence of lexifier languages and associated diglossia may invalidate such a claim for certain groups of speakers.

No studies of the sequence in which such functions emerge in a first-generation Creole, or indeed in child language in older Creoles, have yet been made, although they would form highly desirable complements to Bickerton's claims about bioprogram grammar (1981, 1984). If, as he claims, language ontogeny recapitulates language phylogeny, a study of the likely early non-cognitive dimensions of Creole development may be of considerable importance.

Other bases for the classification of Pidgins and Creoles
The number of parameters proposed in the social classification of Pidgins and Creoles is large and it does not seem profitable to consider them all here.

However, to conclude this chapter a few will be discussed, mainly because they have been influential in the development of the field, in spite of their limited usefulness in empirical testing and theory formation. First, a few words have to be said about an oft-quoted suggestion by Stewart (1962) designed to set Pidgin and Creoles apart from other languages by appeal to social factors alone. Stewart suggests the following criteria:

	Pidgin	*Creole*
Standardization	–	–
Historicity	–	–
Vitality	–	+
Autonomy	–	–

On closer inspection, such criteria turn out to be of very limited diagnostic value. Thus standardization (particularly planned standardization) has been observed in many Pidgins and Creoles; in some cases, such as in Tok Pisin or the Surinam Creole of Sranan, more than 50 per cent of their total life-span is characterized by direct human interference with their development. Other Pidgins and Creoles have become the object of standardization more recently, including Haitian (cf Hall 1972), Bahasa Indonesia, Bislama, Northern Australian Kriol, Seychellois and Papiamentu. Proposals for language standardization exist for other Pidgins and Creoles, including indigenous ones such as Naga Pidgin described by Sreedhar (1977). Recent discussion of standardization in Pidgins and Creoles can be found in a number of the contributions in Le Page et al. (1997).

As regards historicity, Stewart would seem to place too much emphasis on absolute time. Because of this rapid development, one might argue that change that take a 1,000 years in old languages may only take 100 years in a Pidgin or Creole. Note that historicity in relative time is manifested in the present-day variability of these languages, allowing the analyst to recover a considerable portion of their development by means of internal reconstruction. Historicity is also found when one considers them as products of human social history: their development in times of rapid social change again means that many past social forces are reflected in present-day structures. Pidgins and Creoles are not spoken by people without a history, unless one argues that only uniformitarian changes are genuine history.

The criterion of vitality is used to set apart Pidgins from Creoles. This idea is related to Hall's concept of a life-cycle, which implies that:

> normal languages do not have life cycles. A language is not an organism, but a set of habits, handed down from one generation of speakers to another ... To this general principle, however, there is one exception. Pidginized languages normally come into existence for a specific reason, last just as long as the situation which called them into being, and then go quickly out of use. (Hall 1962:152-53)

This view, again, is quite problematic. As studies on language death have shown (for example, those in Dressler 1977b), all languages depend for their continued existence on certain numbers of speakers and certain social purposes. The grammar of a dying language, as Trudgill (1977) has pointed out, can in many ways be regarded as the mirror image of the grammatical enrichment processes occurring in creolization or in the development of expanded Pidgins. Again, first languages need not be primary languages, and, to make things even more confused, pidginized and creolized varieties, vital and dying forms of one and the same language, are often found within a single speech community.

Finally, the criterion of autonomy seems to imply the need for an external language for purposes of structural and lexical development. We already know that access to a lexifier language varies considerably at different points in Pidgin and Creoles development. Many studies of structural development suggest that much of the enrichment is not due to borrowing. Instead, through restructuring and possible borrowing from universals of grammar, Pidgins and Creole can develop powerful mechanisms of growth and perhaps they borrow no more than other languages. One consideration which seems relevant here is Whinnom's (1971) barriers to mixing. As a general rule, the more tightly structured a system, the more likely it is that borrowing will lead to dramatic restructuring or destruction of the system. Pidgins (particularly expanded ones) and first-generation Creoles have highly systematic grammars and hence a drastically reduced syncretic capacity. Borrowing occurs only when there are no drastic linguistic consequences, and when the social gain is greater than the communicative cost incurred. The fact that many post-Pidgins and post-Creoles are found must not be taken as an indicator of lexical and structural dependency.

Although Stewart's criteria thus seem incapable of differentiating between Pidgins, Creoles and other languages, they are of some use in subclassifying the first two. Thus a distinction could be drawn between planned and unplanned, vital (stable or expanding) and non-vital (unstable and contracting), and autonomous versus non-autonomous Pidgins and Creoles. Linguists have tended to prefer the vital, autonomous and unplanned kind for purposes of structural analysis, but there is no reason why the other varieties should not also be given serious attention.

A last dimension I want to mention is that of oral versus literate modes of speaking. Such a distinction has been known for a long time, some interesting early sources being Churchill's (1911) study of Beach-la-Mar and Bloomfield (1933). However, detailed investigations are rare and were probably discouraged by some of the assumptions prevailing in structuralist and transformationalist grammar, including the following:

1. that of the primacy of speech, a view under which written and indeed literate language are often regarded as derivatives;
2. the preoccupation with 'natural' language and the belief that the most informal style is the one most deserving analysis.[43]

The distinction between oral and literate mode is not simply one between spoken and written forms (see Ong's (1982) discussion of this point).

The evidence I have surveyed suggests that in their formative years all Pidgins and Creoles are very much oral languages and many of them remain so until very late in their development. In the case of Pidgins, the reasons are obvious. Until well into their expansion phase, the structural devices needed

---

[43] This view is also found in many sociolinguistic studies. However, it is difficult to see, particularly if one recognizes the role of human involvement in linguistic structures, why more formal styles should be regarded as less desirable objects of sociolinguistic analysis than informal ones.

for subordination and logical discourse patterning are absent.[44] Even their presence or potential presence in expanded varieties and Creoles does not mean that a literate mode will develop or become dominant. No exhaustive study of the factors contributing to its development has been made,[45] but, in the case of Pidgins and Creoles, the following are of importance:

1. There has to be a social function for such a use of language, e.g., public speaking and verbal skills may be seen as the symbol of leadership, as is the case in many Melanesian societies. The ability to address an audience in a Melanesian PE as well as in one or more native vernaculars was regarded as a highly desirable skill for big men (see Salisbury 1972).
2. A literary mode is promoted by non-egalitarian and socially mobile societies, in particular post-colonial ones.
3. The presence of language-standardization agencies, such as missions and language academies, which engage in grammar and dictionary making.
4. The use of the language in the media: newspapers, radio and television.
5. The absence of restrictions on public use of the language, and, in particular, the absence of a diglossic situation where the related lexifier language continues to serve as that of public discourse.
6. The speech community must be of sufficient size to ensure that its members have differential access to information and thus need to use the language in a cognitive function on many occasions. Open communication networks rather than closed ones (see Milroy 1980) again appear to favour a literate mode.

For most Pidgins and many Creoles such favourable conditions do not appear to exist. In the case of Creoles, this indeed raises the question of qualitative differences between languages. Thus, if the literate mode should turn out always to emerge after the oral mode, one may be justified in assigning the status of more elaborate languages to the former. Note that nothing has been said about their speakers at present; in many instances where Creoles have remained oral languages these speakers are bi- or multilingual (cf Mühlhäusler 1995a).

We have now surveyed a large number of factors to be used in the social classification of Pidgins and Creoles, and we have seen how these factors contribute to the considerable social typological differences found within these languages. In as much as these factors influence their formation and development, we can expect an equally large field of linguistic types. With regard to Pidgins and Creoles, we are indeed faced with a situation characterized by Bollée as follows:

> The more the investigation of Pidgins and Creoles advances, the more difficult it appears to become to find generally valid characterizations for the languages traditionally described by these labels (1977b:48, my translation).

---

[44] It could be objected that Pidgins are used to discuss issues that do not involve shared knowledge. This is indeed frequently the case However, it should not be assumed that communication between speakers of different cultural backgrounds using a Pidgin is always successful. Rather, partial or total communicative breakdown has often been observed, and certain domains and/or functions simply cannot be discussed at all.

[45] A preliminary account of literacy in Melanesian PEs is given by Mühlhäusler (1995a).

There are a number of possible responses to this realization:

1. As already indicated, one can justify the unity of Pidgins and Creoles in developmental (diachronic) terms: individual languages may be more or less advanced in terms of a universally valid developmental continuum. This presupposes the possibility of separating linguistic from non-linguistic factors, as well as the primacy of the former.
2. One can observe a number of cases and arrive at certain inductive generalizations, the method implicit in much early research.
3. One can attempt to isolate the ideal social environment for Pidgin and/or Creole development and study. I shall refer to this latter approach as the "desert-island" approach.

The desert-island approach

Sociologists and linguists have often speculated upon the social and linguistic consequences of the development of new societies and languages when shipwrecked individuals are thrown together on a desert island. One of the principal insights derived from such speculations is that only the essential and not the accidental aspects of society and/or language would emerge in the first generation. In view of the multitude of social factors and linguistic consequences noted in Pidgin and Creole development, it would seem reasonable to concentrate on at least some cases where the number of variables is drastically reduced.

The search for such cases can take two forms: first, the scrutiny of actual desert-island speech communities; and second, the setting up of an artificial experiment on such a desert island.

Although most Pidgins and Creoles developed in a context with access to established languages, at least in theory,[46] some were indeed established on a desert island. These include:[47]

1. Pitcairnese on Pitcairn Island;
2. Tristan da Cunha English;
3. Portuguese Creole of Annobón;
4. Portuguese Creole of the Cape Verde Islands;
5. French Creoles of the Indian Ocean;
6. Creole English of Providence Island in the Caribbean.

On closer inspection, however, it appears that even these languages may not be ideal test cases. In the cases of Annobón and probably the Cape Verdes, slaves could already have had considerable knowledge of Pidgin Portuguese when a more developed form of this was brought along by the first settlers and *lançados* from the African mainland, together with some standard Portuguese. Similar objections can be raised against Creole English of Providence Island, and perhaps even the French Creoles of the Indian Ocean where linguistic development may not have been unconnected with developments in French India (see Mühlhäusler 1984d). The relevance of the

---

46 By this I mean that PE speakers on Samoan plantations had access to Samoan, speakers of Fanakalo in South Africa had access to Afrikaans and Bantu languages, and so forth. This access can result in borrowing, bilingualism and change of language affiliation.

47 A recent article by Ehrhart-Kneher (1996) suggests that Palmerston Island might be added to this list.

Tristan da Cunha data (Zettersten 1969) is diminished greatly by the fact that speakers of standard English have been dominant throughout its history; thus this leaves, as the only genuinely interesting case, that of Pitcairn Island.

Pitcairn Island was settled by the mutineers of the *Bounty*, led by Fletcher Christian in 1790. Christian brought with him eight English-speaking sailors, their Tahitian and Tubuaian spouses, and nine others from Tahiti or Tubuai. Most of the male inhabitants succeeded in killing one another off in the next few years, mainly due to disputes over women, and by 1808 only one first-generation male, John Adam, had survived.

The language which developed in the first 20 years of total isolation was thus determined mainly by the linguistic input of mothers (possibly pidginized varieties of Tahitian and Tubuaian, as well as some English), male caretakers (English, some broken Tahitian), and the linguistic inventions of children themselves. At this time hardly any PE had become established in the Pacific; as a consequence, scarcely any of the diagnostic Pidgin features for this area (cf Clark 1979, Baker 1993) are to be found in the language.

The absence of a prior Pidgin model, the almost total isolation in the formative years, and the mixed composition of the island's population thus seem to make Pitcairnese an ideal test case. Its relevance for the so-called bioprogram theory is discussed by Le Page (1983b). Subsequent research by Laycock (e.g. 1989) points to a very different characterization of Pitcairnese: that of an invented cant used alongside acrolectal English.

The scarcity of "pure" cases of Pidgin and Creole development and the difficulties in perceiving the parameters operative in the "impure" cases led Bickerton and Givón to propose a controlled experiment. A description of this is found in Bickerton (1979:17-22). It involves the following procedures:

1. Take sixteen subjects from four different language backgrounds to an uninhabited Pacific island. Their languages should be historically unrelated and typologically maximally divergent.
2. Ensure that you recruit couples with children, so that both adult and child linguistic adaption can be studied.
3. Provide all the necessary social and medical facilities.
4. Give them a highly restricted (about 200 words) lexicon containing names of the most useful objects and activities in this social context.

Bickerton and Givón expected that, within a year, a simple Pidgin would have evolved, and that later a Creole would develop among the children. As the project was rejected by the bodies to which they applied for funding, we can only speculate as to its outcome.

The two weakest points of the experiment appear to be the possibility that individual culture-dependent second-language-learning strategies might have prevailed, if the personality of a leader had been strong enough; and even more problematic is the decision to make English vocabulary available. The boundary between lexicon and syntax is very much a culture and language-specific matter, and the provision of certain lexical resources is likely to prevent the emergence of certain circumlocutory and other syntactic devices. Again, a totally culture-neutral natural communication system is probably unrealizable, although experiments of the kind devised by Bickerton and Givón are certainly useful in that they help us control some of the numerous variables in Pidgin and Creole formation and development.

Summary

The principal aim of this chapter has been to demonstrate that Pidgins and Creoles can be understood only if they are seen as social solutions to the discontinuities in social and linguistic traditions and to the communicative pressures developing in cross-linguistic intercourse. Although the social forces differ from language to language, making it very difficult to establish a coherent social definition of either Pidgins or Creoles, a number of prominent factors are found again and again. My own assessment is that discontinuity of transmission is probably the most powerful factor. This discontinuity manifests itself in the imperfect transmission and reinvention of Pidgin languages, and in the break between one generation's Pidgin and the next generation's Creole in many Creole situations.[48]

A second finding is that those who invent Pidgins and Creoles are not necessarily powerless victims or clean slates ready to be imprinted with the categories of universal grammar. Instead, one should seek for a view in which deliberate human actions determine the degree to which "natural" linguistic categories are used in the formation of such new linguistic systems.

It has been accepted for methodological reasons that a distinction can be made between linguistic and extralinguistic (social) factors in the development of Pidgins and Creoles. It is further acknowledged that the linguistic development can be characterized as possessing its own internal dynamics, governed by considerations such as naturalness. The language that is determined entirely by a natural developmental programme is the one that is least costly in terms of perception and production.[49] In the first instance, its very uniformity makes it useless as a signifying device for different social identities. Thus speakers will invent deviations from natural grammar in order to increase its indexicality. Second, it is not certain, at this point, how powerful natural grammar is. It may well fall short of the communicative requirement encountered even in limited Pidgin contexts. Consequently, language in a number of domains and functions will require human inventions. Third, certain units and constructions may be endowed with special prestige, regardless of their status on a naturalness hierarchy. Prestige forms can develop from within or be introduced from other systems. It is because of such considerations that social factors are seen as both triggering and constitutive of certain (by no means all) aspects of Pidgin and Creole development.

A number of case studies have been presented here and more are needed for a fuller understanding of the complex inter-relationship between linguistic and social factors. As Sankoff states "to understand what happened in any particular case, we must become better historians" (1979:25).

---

[48] A number of the questions to be raised in connection with discontinuity of Pidgins and Creoles are discussed in an important article by Hockett (1950, particularly pp 455-56). These questions have yet to be investigated in great detail (cf Mühlhäusler 1984a).

[49] However, it must not be ignored that there can be irreconcilable conflict between the two, in which case the preference for productive or perceptive modes of optimalization depends on social factors. Generally speaking, second-language Pidgins favour perception-oriented solutions, whereas first-language Creoles favour production-oriented ones.

4. Theories of origin

The real creole is always in the process of receding over the horizon...
and creole grammars tend to be normalized descriptions of an earlier
phase of the language that no one is quite sure was ever spoken by
anyone.   (Labov 1990:25)

Introduction

In this and the following chapter, I will address the linguistic and structural characteristics of Pidgins and Creoles. This will be done in two parts: first, by concentrating on the question of their origin and formation; and second, by examining the nature of their development. One can phrase the first question, one which has dominated the Pidgin/Creole field for many years, as follows: "Why do Pidgins and Creoles exhibit structural affinities among themselves which are often closer than their affinities with perceived lexifier languages?" Underlying this question is the assumption that there are certain typological similarities. This assumption obviously raises a number of questions, particularly that of identifying constructions across languages and between different stages of the same language. Furthermore, it also brings into question the level of linguistic abstraction at which such samenesses are identified. Opinions as to how the structural similarities came about differ greatly and, as already discussed in Chapter 2, tend to be related to current views of language and language relationship. Since the various theories of origin have been discussed in detail elsewhere (for example, in Bollée 1977b, Todd 1974, and Arends, Muysken & Smith 1995), my discussion of them will be rather short. However, as frequent reference is made to them, the reader should be reminded of what is at issue here.

With regard to the origin of Pidgins, the following theories have been proposed:

1. language specific theories:
   (a) nautical language theory;
   (b) foreigner talk/baby talk theory;
2. general theories:
   (c) relexification theory;
   (d) universalist theories.

In addition, we find theories that stress observed differences between Pidgins. They include:

(e) common-core theories;
(f) substratum theories.

In the past, a distinction between Pidgin and Creole formation often was not made, and virtually all of the above explanations have also been applied to Creoles. The only theory that specifically solely addresses the formation of Creoles is Bickerton's bioprogram theory (1981).

I shall start by discussing each of these theories in isolation, although it seems unlikely that any single cause will be sufficient to explain the complex processes which call these languages into being.

Nautical jargon theories

The importance of nautical speech in the formation of Pidgins and Creoles was realized early and can be traced back to the popular view expressed, for instance, by F Robertson:

> The recipe for the language is interesting: Take one sea full of British sailormen, hardy, daring, very British and profane, and leave it in a cool place for two days; extract their speech; then bring to boil and extract what speech remains. Add a coconut shell each of Chinese, Malay, German and Kanaka and bring to boil a hundred or so times, then season with a little war or two; add a few drops of Mission sauce and sprinkle with blackbirder pepper and recruiter salt. Strain through Kanaka lips and serve with beer on boat days, or with undiluted Australian any other time. (Robertson 1971:13-14)

This folkview is usually restricted to individual source languages and, accordingly, I shall look at two such languages – English and French – separately. The first comprehensive account of South Seas Beach-la-Mar (Melanesian PE of the 19th century) is given by Churchill (1911), who emphasizes the contributions of sailors. The alleged lack of grammar in Beach-la-Mar is traced back to the speech habits of this class of people:

> I have already commented upon the fact that the white man, who is without particular intention or principle of philology dominating the production of the mongrel speech for his own greater convenience, is a man of little or no education. The categories of grammar are far above his experience; the few rules and the many exceptions which form the science of our speech have never been feruled into his intelligence - perhaps it was in avoidance of them that he ran away off to sea and became a part of a life of dingy adventure. (Churchill 1911:13)

Unfortunately, little actual information as to the peculiar dialect of these sailors is given by Churchill and direct evidence is restricted to anecdotal material such as that given by Schellong:

> The tribe that happens to have the numerical superiority in the encounter of people from several island groups is likely to gain linguistic superiority as well. Captains and mates are amused by this confusion of languages. They hear this or that strange word and occasionally employ it instead of the English equivalent. Thus, on our cutter **quillequille** is always used for 'quick', **kaikai** instead of 'eat', **bulmakau** instead of 'meat' and so forth. (Schellong 1934:97-98, my translation)

The nautical jargon theory was developed subsequently by Reinecke, who points out that:

> One of the most favourable situations for the formation of such dialects is found aboard merchant vessels which ply the seven seas and ship large

numbers of foreign sailors - and indeed the seaman is a figure of the greatest importance in the creation of the more permanent makeshift tongues.   (Reinecke 1937:434)

The role of nautical English also features prominently in the work of Hall. He claims that by applying the comparative method to PE data, one will find:

> If we have to assign a specific locality to our proto-pidgin-English, it will have to be somewhere in the lower reaches of the Thames, on either bank of the river, in the docks and settlements in such parts of London as Bermondsey, Rotherhithe, Wapping, Shadwell and Limehouse, and in other English seaports such as Plymouth (1966:120).

Although much of these earlier statements were based on informed guesswork, Hancock (1976:23-36) actually undertook extensive comparative work between the Atlantic Creoles and what is known of nautical English of the 17th century. There remain problems with such an approach, however. First, nautical English is not a stable monolithic language, but a highly variable and developing one. Second, there is very considerable overlap between nautical English and other forms of non-standard English. Finally, even if nautical English was the model, it was not imitated in full, but acquired by the non-British interlocutors of these sailors in a more or less modified form. The precise learning contexts, the time of exposure and other social variables remain unknown.

Parallel to a nautical origin for PE are attempts to relate Pidgin and Creole French to maritime varieties of French. On the linguistic side, Faine (1939) and Alexander Hull (1968) have attempted "to reconstruct a hypothetical maritime French... a form of language which might have been used on French ships engaged in the slave trade and in commerce with American ports" (1968:255). In his discussion of this theory, Baker sums up:

> The former existence of a patois such as Faine envisaged appears to be less than an established fact, but it would be unreasonable not to allow both that sailing, as an occupation, must have required its own rather specialized terminology, and that the conditions of living in the restricted environment of a ship must have been particularly favourable to dialect leveling. If something not totally different from Faine's 'composite patois' had indeed existed, it would have been readily available to the extent that there would have been speakers of this on board every French ship which visited the various French trading posts and colonies overseas. But wherever settlers from different parts of France were brought together, one would expect a certain amount of dialect leveling to result... common elements in geographically distant French Creoles are not necessarily attributable to a specifically *nautical* 'composite patois'.
> (Baker 1982:243)

More important, Baker supplements his arguments with a highly detailed study of the verbal contacts that could have occurred both on board recruiting vessels sailing to Mauritius and in ports. His social data indicate that "numerically speaking, sailors are clearly a statistically significant factor". He continues to point out, however, that "there is nothing to indicate that just one 'nautical patois' existed, or that the collective expertise of sailors in communicating with non-Francophones would have equipped them all with a single uniform Pidgin".

The criticisms made against a uniform English and French nautical jargon also appear to hold for other Creoles and creoloids which have, at one time or other, been regarded as continuations of sailor's speech,[1] including Afrikaans (e.g. Hesseling 1979:8). A tentative conclusion to this is that although sailors were instrumental in diffusing language material over vast distances,[2] their role in shaping the lexicon and grammars of the languages thus diffused remains to be proved.

Baby talk and foreigner talk theories

There is some terminological confusion with 'baby talk' and 'foreigner talk', because, in everyday speech, they tend to be associated with both the language used by babies and/or foreigners and the language used by adult native speakers addressing these groups. This latter meaning, however, is the only one used in modern linguistics. In older writings on the origins of Pidgins and Creoles, confusion is often found. Thus Leland (1876) writes of Chinese PE: "What remains can present no difficulty to anyone who can understand negro minstrelsy or baby talk."

Support for a foreigner talk origin is found in some of Schuchardt's writings, in particular in his article of 1909 on the Lingua Franca. Thus, in Markey's (1979) translation, we read:

> All atrocities performed on language derive from its inherent possessors in the same manner as child language depends on the speech of the wet nurse. Or to use another image: it is not the foreigners who break away single stones from a splendid, well-appointed edifice in order to construct meagre huts, but the owners themselves who put them to such ends.
> (Schuchardt 1979:28)

However, in his later article on Saramaccan (1914), Schuchardt offers a more cautious assessment:

> The White was teacher to the Black; the latter repeated the former. And the White always used the most emphatic expressions, exaggerations as they occasionally occurred to him too, in communication with his compatriots. He did not say: "you are very dirty," but "you are too dirty," and thus it may be explained that 'very' in Pacific Beach-la-mar is *too much* and *tumussi* in Sranan Black English (SBE). It is difficult for us to appraise such relationships correctly. We involuntarily regard our language as the model, and we have no feeling for the fusions and obfuscations, the inconsistencies and eccentricities, by which they excel all other languages; we perceive the splinter in the stranger's eye, but not the beam in our own. (Schuchardt 1979:74)

---

1   There is no evidence that today's mixed crews on international shipping routes speak anything approaching a focussed nautical English.

2   Samarin (p c, 1984) brought to my attention that large numbers of West African sailors were employed in other parts of the world, thus acting as possible agents of diffusion of a West African type of Pidgin. We thus appear to have reasons for combining a nautical origin with a relexification theory. This point deserves further attention.

This last quotation affirms the learner's productive role in Pidgin formation as well as the possibility of inconsistencies in the input. Such caution was not always exercised within structuralist linguistics, particularly in the writings of Bloomfield, who, in 1933, wrote the following famous passage:

> Speakers of a lower language may make so little progress in learning the dominant speech, that the masters, in communicating with them resort to 'baby-talk'. This 'baby-talk' is the master's imitation of the subjects' incorrect speech. There is reason to believe that it is by no means an exact imitation, and that some of its features are based not upon the subjects' mistakes but upon grammatical relations that exist within the upper language itself. The subject, in turn, deprived of the correct model, can do no better now than to acquire the simplified 'baby-talk' version of the upper language (p 472).

At the time, his behaviourist views compelled him to assume a virtual equivalence between the baby- or foreigner-talk input and the learner's Pidgin. Bloomfield's views were taken over by a number of influential scholars, such as Hockett, although virtually no empirical support for the claims implicit in the above quotation were ever sought. Such support has appeared more recently in three forms:

1. Experiments involving the elicitation of foreigner and baby talk in formal settings;

2. Observation of contextualized behaviour;

3. Archival research.

Considerable insight has also been achieved through studies in the area of second language acquisition. It has become common practice to see both learning and the provision of a model for the learner as active processes, and to combine both behaviourist and mentalist views of Pidgin formation, as in Clyne (1978) or Ferguson & DeBose (1977).

Experimental elicitation of foreigner talk was pioneered by Ferguson (1975) for English, and has since been carried out for some other languages such as Dutch (Werkgroep 1978) and German (Hinnenkamp 1982), though not, to my knowledge, for any non-Indo-European language. The results of such tests are that a number of morphological, syntactic and phonological simplifications promoting greater naturalness are found for all languages tested; and that such foreigner talk simplifications are variable rather than categorical.

The input given to foreigners in many cases is quite inconsistent. Let me illustrate these points using results obtained applying Ferguson's test to Australian adults with no previous experience of a Pidgin or Creole: individual speakers differ markedly in the application of the various simplificatory devices, as can be seen from the following versions of the sentence *I haven't seen the man you're talking about*:

(a) I no see this man.
(b) Me no see man you talk about.
(c) No see man. (head shaking)
(d) Me no look him man you say.
(e) No seeum man you say.
(f) Man you talk about, I not see.
(g) No seen man you talk.
(h) You talk man. I not seen.
(i) Me [point] no see [eyes] man you [point] talk about. [wild gestures]

The following strategies deserve particular mention:

1. The avoidance of embedded constructions is in evidence in most responses. It either takes the form of loss (as in *a* and *c*) or replacement by parataxis (as in *h*).
2. The expressed feeling that the linguistic message needs to be reinforced by gestures.
3. The avoidance of *do* support in negative clauses. *No* is used as a negator in most responses. This is probably the result of a strong tendency towards one form – one meaning in simplified registers.
4. The avoidance of tensed verb forms.

Apart from these tendencies, which seem to reflect natural categories, there are a number of other changes of a clearly cultural type. They include:

5. The addition of *-um* or *him* to verb forms.
6. Lexical replacement: *talk* 'to say' or *see* 'to look'.
7. The selection of the *me* rather than *I* form of the pronoun as the basic pronominal form.

A number of other processes appear to be difficult to fit into the natural-cultural dimensions and may be random. Most notable here are changes in word order. The tentative conclusion from these and similar experimental data is that baby- or foreigner-talk is governed by cultural conventions as well as natural tendencies towards input simplification. Consequently it does not provide an optimal model for second-language learners, although it does offer one which is considerably easier to acquire than the full standard target language.

A second source of foreigner talk data is actual observations. Because of the lack of recording techniques, and indeed interest in this matter, in the past, one has to rely on secondary evidence such as literary varieties of foreigner speech,[3] for traces of foreigner talk dating back more than ten years. I have recently investigated German foreigner talk (Mühlhäusler 1984b) and traced back its history to the early 19th century, although its use in literature obviously does not reflect actual usage. The earliest passage is found in the speech of a German servant who poses as a Russian traveller in Kotzebue's play *Pagenstreiche* (first performed in about 1810; see von Wiese 1972):

> *Das sein der reichste Mann in ganz   Russland. Er   haben Gueter von*
> He is   the richest man in whole   Russia.   He has   land   from
>
> *Wolga bis   Irtich.*
> Volga to   Irtich [river].
>
> *Braut kann warten.   Der Fuerst schicken kostbare   Diamanten.   So   is.*
> Bride can   wait.   The duke   send   precious diamonds.   So [it] is.
>
> *Peterburch sein   Hauptstadt in   Ukrain.*
> Petersburg is   capital   in   Ukraine (my translation).

The writer of this passage employs a number of strategies that are also documented in later foreigner talk and Pidgin varieties of German, including:

---

3   Secondary foreigner talk in the terminology employed by Ferguson (1975:2).

1.   use of the infinitive instead of inflected verb forms;
2.   variable absence of the definite article;
3.   omission of surface dummy es 'it'.

An interesting feature of this, and indeed many later texts, is the presence of the copula (here in its uninflected form); according to Ferguson (1971) the absence of the copula is one of the most widespread properties of foreigner talk varieties. Note that its presence in the input does not mean that it will be acquired by a learner. However, it again indicated that foreigner talk is in part a cultural form of language.

Perhaps no better illustration of this claim can be given than the reduced forms of German employed by Karl May. The importance of this writer of adventure stories in shaping a German tradition of foreigner talk was first mentioned by Clyne (1975:3), who quotes a number of Pidgin German passages from *Winnetou*, the most widely read of Karl May's works. Clyne observes that although the syntax exhibits a number of Pidgin characteristics such as the use of the infinitive instead of inflected verb forms, there is no loss of copula and the lexicon has not undergone a similar simplification.

It is interesting to note that Karl May portrayed different degrees of simplification with different characters in his stories. Thus, whereas an Italian artist in *Der Peitschenmueller* (originally published in 1886) approximates the syntax and lexicon of Standard German in many of his utterances, the Basuto in *Das Kafferngrab* (originally published in 1879) uses a considerably more pidginized form of German. Let me illustrate this with some text material from *Der Peitschenmueller*:

Ein Koenig? Welch Entzuecken! Was   fuer ein Koenig wird er sein? ...
A   king.   What delight!   What for a   king   will it be? ...

Unmoeglich! Koenig Luigi   kommen nie in Bad, sondern sein sehr einsam,
Impossible! King   Ludwig come   not in spa, but   be   very lonely,

sehr ... Nicht? Oh, ich glauben daran, sehr, sehr.   Ich wissen genau,
very... No?   I   believe in it   very very . I   know for-sure

dass wahr sein. Sie sein da   oben   begraben   und spiel in der Nacht Violin
that true is . She be   there up buried   and play in the night violin

in Grab. Nein, es sein Wahrheit.
in grave. No,   it be   truth.

Foreigner talk features reflecting genuine use of more natural grammar include:

1.   (variable) omission of verb inflections;
2.   omission of surface dummy es;
3.   variable absence of subject pronouns.

On the other hand, one encounters fairly complex features such as the passive construction and (variably) inverted word order in the appropriate grammatical context. Note also the presence of coordination and subordination. Some German lexemes are replaced and/or are followed by Italian ones. However one misses the stereotyped Pidgin German lexemes such as **capito** 'savvy?' and **avanti** 'quick, come on'.

Compare this text with the following passages from *Das Kafferngrab*:

Mynheer rett   Quimbo. Mynheer helf   arm   Quimbo.   Quimbo will nicht   gut
Mynheer save   Quimbo.   Mynheer   help   poor Quimbo.

schmeck Strauss, oh, oh, Mynheer, aber Mynheer nicht treff Quimbo, denn
taste   ostrich, oh, oh, Mynheer,   but   Mynheer   not   hit   Quimbo, for

Quimbo bin sonst   tot.
Quimbo am otherwise   dead.

Quimbo lass liegen Sau? Oh, oh, Mynheer Quimbo ess viel   schoen   Sau.
Quimbo let   lie   pig?   Oh, oh, Mynheer Quimbo eat   much beautiful pig.

Quimbo kenn Tschemba; Quimbo hab red schon gross viel mit Tschemba.
Quimbo know Tschemba; Quimbo have talk already big   much with Tschemba.

I have only selected a very small portion of many relevant passages in this story. However, it should be clear that we are dealing with a much more drastically reduced form of German than in the previous sample. This is obvious from the following features:

1. Consistent use of verb stem (rather than infinitive) instead of inflected verb forms, the only exceptions being the inflected copula. This usage may have been modelled on the Cape Dutch spoken when this story was written.
2. Absence of articles and other determiners. This is unlike Cape Dutch (Afrikaans) and in contrast with the variable presence of articles in the previous text.
3. Uninflected attributive adjectives, similar to Cape Dutch. The Italian speaker uses mainly inflected adjectives, though often with an inappropriate ending.
4. The use of *viel* 'much' instead of *sehr* 'very', unlike Cape Dutch. The Italian speaker uses *sehr*.
5. The use of proper nouns instead of pronouns gives this passage a particularly childish quality. Again, the Italian in the previous text uses the appropriate pronouns.
6. There are few examples of passives and they differ from that used by the Italian through the use of a verb stem instead of a past participle, as in *Quimbo darf nicht werd fress von Loewe* 'Quimbo must not be eaten by a lion'.
7. Logical order is frequently expressed by sequential order, as in *Pferd lauf viel schnell Quimbo verlier Arm* 'if the horse runs very fast, Quimbo will lose his arm'.

The differential use of such features by literary Italians and Africans relates to an important rule for the use of foreigner talk: most of its cultural features (such as lexical replacement) and some of its natural features are employed more readily when the addressee is perceived to belong to an inferior culture, to be dressed accordingly, and where there is power differential.

I have stressed repeatedly that a distinction has to be drawn between culture-specific and universal or natural conventions for foreigner talk. A comparison of the various foreigner talk conventions found with Indo-European languages and those of a number of non-Indo-European languages would make a fascinating study indeed. An excellent basis for an initial comparison would be simplified Motu (of Papua New Guinea). The first missionaries who settled around Port Moresby in the latter half of the 19th century were addressed by the Motuans in a highly simplified foreigner talk version of their language,[4] although for a long time they were under the impression they had been taught genuine Motu. They even began to translate the scriptures into this foreigner talk, until the difference was pointed out to them by their own children, who had grown up in a Motu-speaking environment (cf Taylor 1978).

Another task for the future is the analysis of variability in the literary foreigner talk registers of individual common lexifier languages such as English and French. Some real-life situations have been studied in recent years, notably for Melanesian varieties of PE, Pidgin German and Pidgin Turkish.

Some of the main findings derived from a study of English Foreigner Talk and its role in the formation and development of Tok Pisin (see Mühlhäusler 1981a) are as follows. First, the use of foreigner talk can carry on a long time after its functional usefulness has disappeared. In the case of Tok Pisin, a special foreigner talk register of English – called Tok Masta by the indigenes – continued to be used, in spite of the fact that it was badly understood and that indigenous Tok Pisin had developed along totally different lines. A conclusion is that the importance of foreigner talk is restricted to the very early stages of Pidgin formation, but of little relevance for later development.[5] Second, in later stages of Tok Pisin's life, Tok Masta assumes the role of an index of social superiority. The desire not to mix with perceived inferiors finds its linguistic expression in the growing gap between Tok Masta and the indigenous varieties of Tok Pisin. Third, only indigenes in close contact with Europeans or those with a knowledge of English know foreigner talk. Finally, both structurally and lexically, Tok Masta is highly variable and not a systematic simplification of English. Apart from fairly stable lexical conventions, no normative tendencies have been observed.

A more positive assessment of the social role of foreigner talk is found in studies by Hinnenkamp (1982, 1984) on German and Turkish varieties. As regards Pidgin German and German foreigner talk, Hinnenkamp's research, which is based largely on anonymously taped conversations between speakers of German and Turkish, suggests that there is a very large amount of inconsistency in German foreigner talk input.[6] He also reports that the use of foreigner talk is not necessarily regarded as bad: a number of informants perceive its role in simplifying communication between speakers of different languages; and that simplification has to be regarded as a continuum. These findings agree with earlier ones, such as those of Bodemann & Ostow (1975) or Amsler (1952).

Hinnenkamp goes on to explore affinities with Tarzanca, the foreigner talk variety of Turkish. His data comprise exchanges between Turkish villagers and German tourists in a tourist resort. The types of deviations

---

4   This simplified Motu is not identical with the various trade pidgins (discussed above) used by the Motuans in their annual *hiris* (trade expeditions).

5   In the words of Whinnom (1971), it plays a role in the emergence of unstable secondary hybrids, but not in that of stable tertiary ones.

6   Hinnenkamp's observations confirm my own tests, based on Ferguson (1975), as to German speakers' intuitions. Although most of the expected simplifications turn up at one time or another, they appear side by side with ill-motivated lexical or word-order changes and "normal" German.

from the standard language closely parallel those in German foreigner talk and include (1984:157):

1. loss of pre- and post-positions;
2. loss of nominal inflection and agreement;
3. deletion of the copula;
4. generalization of the infinitive;
5. change in word order;
6. loss of overt question marking;
7. external placement of propositional qualifiers;
8. juxtaposition of subordinating clauses;
9. lexical and grammatical multifunctionality;
10. periphrasis.

Hinnenkamp notes that, although the particular linguistic processes found in German and Turkish foreigner talk and language development differ, their outcome is pretty well the same. This view is also supported by initial observations on simplified Motu (Dutton 1985a).

The importance of the last source of our knowledge of foreigner talk, archival research, is underlined by Naro's investigations into Pidgin Portuguese. His conclusion, reached on the basis of close scrutiny of historical chronicles, missionaries' accounts and other documents, is that: "Portuguese pidgin ... had its origin in EUROPE, not in Africa, beginning with the officially instituted training of translators. Its basic structural peculiarities resulted primarily from conscious modificators of their speech by the Portuguese" (1978:341). Subsequent work by Clements (1992) has pointed to problems with some of Naro's conclusions, however.

We have now surveyed some studies of foreigner talk. Although the database available at present is small and the criterion of observational adequacy has hardly been met (this last point is particularly true for actually employed or primary foreigner talk), a number of conclusions still appear to be warranted. First, foreigner talk tends to be a mixture of cultural conventions and genuine natural intuitions on language simplification. It probably involves a good deal of speakers' regression to developmentally early stages of their own language. Second, because of its mixed nature and considerable inconsistency in its use, foreigner talk is not the ideal simple model some structuralist linguists imagined it to be. Finally, the importance of foreigner talk in Pidgin formation appears to be restricted to relatively early stages of development.

It is difficult to assess the relative importance of foreigner talk in the formation of different Pidgins, but considerable differences can be expected. Foreigner talk is an input in the formative years of Pidgins and thus should be considered. However, it would be wrong to conclude that imitation and rote learning has been established as a major factor in this process.

Relexification theory

In its strongest form, relexification theory claims that most "European-based"[7] Pidgins and Creoles are related via a special process involving the

---

7   Having more than 80% of their lexicon derived from a particular European language.

maintenance of grammar and the replacement of lexical units. The grammar is said to be that of 16th-century Pidgin Portuguese or possibly a Mediterranean contact language. The possibility of relexification, or, as Hall puts it, "the substitution of vocabulary items for others, with the maintenance of a stable syntactic base" (1975:183), was first suggested by Thompson (1961). He surmises that the West African slavers' jargon (Pidgin Portuguese) "may have been the pattern for all the West Indian Creoles just as, in the Eastern and Pacific Portuguese Creole dialects, well known to Europeans of many nationalities, may have provided the model for the two great branches of Pidgin English, China Coast Pidgin and Neo-Melanesian" (p 113).

Other writers have put forward arguments to the effect that the Mediterranean Lingua Franca is the ancestral language underlying most Pidgins and Creoles. Yet others make much weaker claims as to the continuity of the transmission of Pidgin or Creole grammar. Thus Laycock (1970a:ix) merely considers the possibility that relexification of Pidgin Portuguese may have played some part in the development of Melanesian PE.

It is interesting that with most writers who support relexification:

1. The possibility of non-European predecessor languages to European-based Pidgins and Creoles is never raised;
2. No proper distinction is drawn between its role in the formation of Pidgins and Creoles and in their subsequent history;
3. The question of discontinuity in development is not considered.

As regards the first point, it is not impossible that some Pidgins and Creoles which have strong lexical affinities with English may in fact have been modelled on pre-existing indigenous lingue franche. Thus, Kriol of North Australia could be a relexified version of a Pidgin Macassarese, which was widely used in trade with outsiders and as an intertribal lingua franca until the beginning of this century (see Urry & Walsh 1981), and many of the Portuguese Creoles in Asia may have been continuations of earlier Arabic-based trade languages. As regards the second point, it should be noted that relexification is a timeless concept and ignores the fact that Pidgins are developing entities. It is not made clear at what point relexification occurred.

Since the very early stages of a Pidgin lack stable grammar, relexification is not plausible for those Pidgins with unstable jargon predecessors. As regards the relexification of stable Pidgins, there are two possible scenarios, depending on whether a given instance of relexification constitutes an abrupt break in linguistic tradition or not. For this, the analyst requires information as to the absolute length of time needed for relexification, communicative problems, and changes in the composition of the Pidgin-using community.

The difference between the two types of relexification can be illustrated by the examples from Tok Pisin set out below:

	Gradual change (a)		Abrupt change (b)	
Stage 1	**beten**	'to pray'	**binen**	'bee'
Stage 2	**beten o prea**	'to pray'		
Stage 3	**prea**	'to pray'	**bi**	' bee'

In case (a), continuity is maintained by the joint use of both lexical items in a synonym pair. In case (b), the word for 'bee' was introduced twice at different stages in the development of Tok Pisin by different speakers. The external explanation for this difference is that the discussion of non-traditional religion has been one of the central functions of Tok Pisin for most of its existence. On the other hand, there is no such tradition for bee-keeping. A comparison of arbitrary stages of the language, as practised in diachronic analyses, would not capture this difference, although no descriptive problems would arise within a developmental framework such as that proposed by Bailey (1980).

Gradual relexification is associated with a prolonged period of bilingualism and the simultaneous presence of more than one prestige lexifier language. Thus, in the case of German New Guinea, although the relative status of English and German changed over time, both languages were partially accessible for lexical borrowing for a considerable part of its development. At the height of German colonial control, a number of New Guineans who already spoke English-based Tok Pisin introduced more and more lexical items of German origin, creating mixed German-English and predominantly German forms of Pidgin. The close parallelism between Tok Pisin (TP) and the Pidgin German (PG) of Fritz from Ali Island (West Sepik, Papua New Guinea) can be seen in the following text:

PG *Ja frueher wir bleiben, Und dann Siapan kommen.*
TP **Yes bipo mipela stap. Na bihain Siapan kam.**
Eng. Yes, at first we remained. Then the Japanese came.

PG *Wir muss gehen unsere Boot. Wir bleiben und bikples, a, festland gehen.*
TP **Mipela mas go bot bilong mipela. Mipela stap na go bikples.**
Eng. We must go to our boat. We stayed there and then we went to the mainland.

A similar process could be observed in a second German colony, Kiautschou in north-east China. Again, both English and German were important languages, and PE was common among those Chinese involved in trade with Europeans. The growing importance of German appears to have led to the gradual change-over to a Pidgin German via intermediate mixed varieties. One example of such an intermediate Pidgin in the process of changing lexical affiliation is discussed by von Hesse-Wartegg in his comments on the proprietor of the Hotel Kaiser:

> The proprietor with his friendly smile had already learned German. "Ik sabe Deutsch," he addressed me while making deep bows. "Gobenol at gebene pamischu open Otel, Kommen Sie, luksi, no hebe pisi man, no habe dima, bei an bei." Since this Spanish-English-German-Chinese dialect differs from native to native, I want to add the German translation: "Ich kann Deutsch, der Gouverneur hat mir Erlaubnis gegeben, ein Hotel zu eroeffnen, kommen Sie, besehen Sie es; ich habe noch keinen Gast, weil ich keine Zimmer habe, aber nach und nach." The words **pamischu luksi, pisi,** and **bei an bei** are not German, but belong to the lingua franca used between the Chinese and the Europeans, the so-called Pidgin English. **Pamischu** is 'permission', **luksi** means 'look see', **pisi** stands for 'piece', for the Chinese do not say 'one man, two men' but 'one piece man, two piece man'; **bei an bei** is English 'by an by' (1898:10, my translation)

104

No such bilingualism was found in other German colonies. Official attempts to replace Swahili with a kind of Pidgin German by means of gradual relexification miscarried and, in the absence of any important role of German in Samoa, the local PE remained immune to its influences.

Relexification can occur not only in the case of competing prestige languages but also between "indigenous" and imported lingue franche. An as yet not fully understood case is that of Hiri Motu and its relationship to Papuan PE (see Dutton 1985a). Although mission and government in the central districts of Papua favoured the use of a simplified Motu (Police Motu), PE appears to have been the most common language for expatriate-indigenous contacts in the eastern and western parts of this colony. Because of the high regional mobility of the government agents and the developing plantation and mining economies, a significant number of Papuans were exposed to two prestige lingue franche. Indications are that for a long time both co-existed and that only after the Second World War, with the growing importance of the Motu-speaking capital Port Moresby and adverse reactions against PE by educators and officials, did Police (Hiri) Motu eventually take over. It appears that, in at least some cases, this transition occurred in the form of relexification, as is evidenced by a small body of mixed PE/Pidgin Motu texts, particularly those of a recording of a Papuan, Nanai Gogovi, from the Gulf of Papua, made during the Second World War. They include (data from Dutton 1985a):

ai	faia traim traim	dina lau stati
we (excl.)	fire try try	day I start
'we kept trying to fire [the guns]'		'I started (to go) in the daytime'

memero matamata ia	sikulu dekenai ia	aut, ia	gaukaraia
boys new	they school at	they out, they	manufacture
'New boys who were at school had to leave and go out into the workforce'			

namba wan be Taunisvolo	wadaeni seken, Bulesben
number one is Townsville	okay second Brisbane
'Townsville is first'	'Brisbane was second'

The case studies just discussed appear to lend support to the classical version of the relexification theory, which traces other European Pidgins to Pidgin Portuguese of West Africa. Circumstantial sociohistorical evidence suggests that relexification is most likely to have occurred in Whydah (also known as Ouidah, Juda or Ajuda) in Benin (former Dahomey), where for several centuries a Portuguese, French and English fortress and slave depot coexisted.[8] The full socio-linguistic context is not yet known. However, we do know that at least some slaves were kept for a considerable period and that there was some exchange between the different depots. Slaves from Whydah were sent to many parts of the world, including the West Indies and the French plantations in the Indian Ocean. Some of these slaves probably already spoke a partially relexified Pidgin Portuguese; others may have

---

[8]   The Portuguese enclave São João Batista de Ayudá survived until 1961, when it was occupied by Dahomey. It is worth mentioning that a considerable number of slaves were shipped to Brazil via this depot until the second half of the 19th century. The relationship between Brazilian Portuguese and Pidgin Portuguese and African Pidgin Portuguese remains ill understood.

shifted their linguistic allegiance after deportation. Yet others may have understood little, if any, "European-derived" Pidgin. The picture that emerges here is a complicated one. Relexification in many cases may have been an individual strategy for learning a more useful Pidgin. It is not clear to what extent it was a social strategy, nor what its relative contribution was in the formative years of various Pidgins.

Added to this is the problem, identified by Ladhams (*forthcoming*), that "one cannot propose linguistic theories based purely on linguistic speculation". Yet this is what appears to have happened in a number of accounts of "relexification" in Surinam Creoles. As both Ladhams and Arends (*forthcoming*) show, previous writers' accounts of relexification in Surinam (e.g. Voorhoeve 1973, Hancock 1987) constructed hypothetical sociohistorical scenarios such as the relocation of slaves from Brazil to Surinam which, on close inspection, turn out to be quite implausible.[9]

What remains is the synchronic linguistic picture of Surinam Creoles having different proportions of words of English and Portuguese origin. A lexico-statistical comparison of the Surinam Creoles by Huttar (1972) provided the following figures:[10]

A lexico-statistical comparison of Surinam Creoles

Origin:	English	Portuguese	Dutch	African	Total
Sranan	118	7	25	4	154
Ndjuka	116	5	20	3	144
Saramaccan	72	50	6	6	134

(*Source:* Huttar 1972)

Voorhoeve (1973) adduced evidence from synonyms, pointing out that there were hardly any of different lexical origin in Sranan, but a substantial number in Saramaccan. They include:

---

9 Their investigations were stimulated by the observation that the Creoles of Surinam shared most of their grammatical structures, but differed considerably in lexical composition. The similarity in function and encoding of tense aspect and modality in the Surinam and other Creoles was stressed in Thompson's seminal article on relexification (1961) and his representation is shown below.

Thompson's representation of the similarity in function and encoding of tense, aspect and modality in Surinam and other Creoles

markers:	durative	perfective	contingent or future
Cape Verde	ta	ja	lo
Indo-Portuguese	ta, te	ja	lo, di, had (*neg.* nad)
Macau/Malacca/Java	ta	ja	logo (*neg.* nadin)
Philippine Creoles	ta	ya	de, ay
Papiamentu	ta	taba	lo
Saramaccan	ta	bi	sa
Sranan Tongo	de	ben	sa
Jamaican	a, da	ben, min, mi	
Haitian	ap	te	a
Dominican	ka	te	ke

(*Source:* Thompson 1961:110).

10 For a more comprehensive account of the Portuguese vocabulary in the Surinam Creoles, readers should consult Ladhams (*forthcoming*).

Saramaccan	English and Portuguese etymologies	Sranan
bee / baika	E *belly* / P *barriga*	bére
buuu / sangá	E *blood* / P *sangrar, sangue*	brudu
diíngi / bebé	E *drink* / P *beber*	dríi
hói / panjá	E *hold* / P *apanhar*	panjá
lósu / piójo	E *louse* / P *piolholóso*	pói
póri / lot / pondi	E *spoil* (and P *podri?*) / E *rotten* / P *podri*	-
piíti / latjá	E *split* / P *rachar*	príti

Voorhoeve concludes that Saramaccan and Sranan have the same linguistic origin, West African Pidgin Portuguese.[11] The Saramaccan or Bush Negro Language retained much of this Portuguese heritage, since it was removed from English influence at an early stage of relexification by escaping maroons. As I read Voorhoeve's arguments, it is not clear to me whether we are dealing with a split at a Pidgin or a Creole stage but, from the sociolinguistic history given, it would seem to be the former. If this is so, it would provide the needed explanation for the lexical differences between the two languages and the many synonym pairs in Saramaccan.[12] It would not account, however, for many of the grammatical similarities of Sranan and Saramaccan, as creolization and hence large-scale grammaticalization presumably only occurred after the split. It would also fail to account for grammatical similarities between the two Creoles and Ndjuka, which developed, according to Voorhoeve, out of a later, possibly unrelated, PE. That matters are a great deal more complex in evident from recent findings by Ladhams (*forthcoming*) and Arends (*forthcoming*).

Change in lexical affiliation after creolization may have occurred in a number of other instances, such as Papiamentu, a Spanish-based Creole with an alleged Portuguese Creole ancestor, or the Spanish Creoles of the Philippines, where it is still an ongoing process (see Molony 1973 and Lipski 1988). The study of such cases, though irrelevant to an understanding of the creolization process in a narrow sense, may help us to see certain language-mixing processes in a clearer perspective, as is also argued by Thomason & Kaufman 1988). The kind of relexification processes occurring in present-day Philippine Spanish Creoles such as Chabacano are gradual, partial and involve a number of lexifier languages, in particular English and Tagalog. It also appears that they affect marginal (in the sense of less frequently used, as against a basic Swadesh list-type core) areas more than central ones. In the words of Frake (1971:232), these refer to dimensions such as "lesser magnitude, shorter distance, worse evaluation, female sex, younger generation or plurality". The same type of relexification is also found in numerous Creoles. It appears, although hard data are somewhat difficult to come by, that the kind of relexification operating in the transition from one Pidgin to another typically affects the central areas of the lexicon as well.[13]

---

11   The indications from Ladhams (*forthcoming*) are that, in the early years of Surinam plantations, more slaves were recruited from Angola than from West Africa.

12   For a discussion of the systematic use of synonym pairs during relexification, see Mühlhäusler (1978c).

13   A good illustration is the above-quoted incipient Pidgin German of Kiautschau.

To sum up the discussion on the relexification hypothesis, the following tentative conclusions are proposed:

1. Relexification can occur at different stages in the development of Pidgins and Creoles.
2. Both gradual and abrupt relexification appears to have been involved in the history of many Pidgins and Creoles. However, there is no indication that *all* these languages are related in this way.
3. Relexifications appear to account for a number of cases where Pidgins developed from other stable Pidgins without a significant preceding jargon stage. Relexification cannot account for all instances of Pidgin formation, however.
4. The process of relexification appears to be of minimal relevance to Creole formation, although it is often found in subsequent later Creole development.

This means that, in its "classical" form,[14] the relexification hypothesis is insufficient as an all-embracing explanatory parameter for Pidgin and Creole formation. However, because it can create similarities between apparently unrelated languages, a detailed knowledge of its role in the history of individual Pidgins and Creoles is essential, if they are to be used for the study of linguistic universals.

Universalist theories

The view that the linguistic nature of Pidgins and Creoles is universally motivated is not a recent one. It was inherent in Coelho's work on Portuguese Creoles as well as in that of Lenz on Papiamentu (1928). After many years of intensive study, Schuchardt, in his late writings, also appears to favour universalist explanations. Discussing the development of plurals in Saramaccan and other Creoles, he comments:

> Creole dialects have not yet been fully appreciated for their general linguistic significance. They are customarily regarded as products of very peculiar or extreme mixture, but what distinguishes them is, rather, if I dare say so, their universal linguistic features. (Schuchardt 1979:73)

Such initiatives remained unexplored for a long time and resurfaced only with renewed interest in linguistic universals in the wake of transformational generative grammar. Perhaps the most exciting development was Heine's demonstration (1973, 1975) that African Pidgins that were quite unrelated to those based on European languages shared many of their structural properties. The discussion of universals has been hampered by insufficient attention to two questions:

1. The crucial question at what point in the development from jargon to Creole universal forces will have been most likely to have occurred.

---

14 Since the 1980s, Lefebvre has investigated the possibility that Haitian Creole is relexified Fon (cf Lefebvre 1986) and, in recent years, this has often been termed 'the relexification hypothesis'. The weaknesses of this approach are essentially the same as those of the "classical" relexification hypothesis.

2. The identification of universals at surface and deeper levels of grammatical organization.

The first point involves two separate issues: the ability to resort to linguistic universals; and the susceptibility of emerging or developing languages to such forces. With regard to the former, there has been considerable disagreement. In the wake of assumptions and findings during the early days of transformational generative grammar, it was usually assumed that access to linguistic universals was restricted to children before the critical threshold of puberty and hence of no importance in the formation of Pidgins by adults. This is expressed thus by Naro: "the speakers involved in the process of pidginization on both sides do not have inward access to the *faculté du langage*, that is to either the heuristic procedures of grammar construction or the innate theory of linguistic structure" (1975:48-49). This argument is also employed by Bickerton (1976), who rejects claims by scholars such as Kay & Sankoff (1974) that Pidgin speakers are able to use their *faculté du langage* to select a universally motivated base grammar. Bickerton (1976:176) points to a considerable body of evidence from a number of jargons to support his view that "obviously, if pidgin speakers did have the power to reduce their language to some kind of universal base, this power would have to be exercised at the beginning, rather than the middle or end, of the pidginization process". This assumed hypothesis is not supported by data from early Hawaiian PE, which, according to Bickerton (ibid.), "showed internal differences so gross that it is possible to determine the ethnicity of the speaker from written texts and on grounds of syntax alone. The theory that pidgin-speakers have access to universals cannot, therefore, derive any support from empirical studies".[15]

As noted earlier, unstable jargons are very much subject to individual communication strategies, including transfer, resort to linguistic universals and others discussed by Meisel (1983). For relatively homogeneous groups, such as Japanese plantation workers in Hawaii in the 1920s (cf Nagara 1972, Roberts 1995), transfer would seem to have been perfectly viable, as universal solutions become necessary mainly in heterogeneous communities. The fact that adult speakers have access to universal strategies does not imply that they must make use of them.[16]

Bickerton, however, who does not agree with this, sees universals as appearing principally in one context: that of creolization of a jargon or undeveloped Pidgin. Thus he explains the already mentioned similarity of grammatical systems in Creoles the world over in terms of an innate blueprint which surfaced intact whenever the child's language acquisition device failed to find adequate data (cf Bickerton 1981). Inadequate input is associated with early Pidgin-speaking plantation communities, where the data consist of the unstable and communicationally inadequate Pidgin and a large number of different vernaculars such as are spoken by members of the older generation. Without wishing to commit myself with regard to the unlearnability of pre-

---

15 When Bickerton interviewed these speakers they were very old and had not used the Pidgin actively in some instances. The differences thus could also reflect language attrition.

16 The principal difference between adult and child language acquisition thus would seem to be that adults have a number of options, a childlike acquisition strategy being just one of them.

existing parental vernaculars, I agree that there is likely to be resort to universal strategies in such a situation.

Progress in the area of Pidgin and Creole universals has long been hampered by the assumption that universals must necessarily be of a static type ("unrestricted independent" in Greenberg's terminology). Thus the universal that no Pidgin has a copula was regarded as disconfirmed by the discovery that some Pidgins had a copula. The limitations of this view were first made explicit by Heine, who dynamically characterized linguistic universals in African Pidgins. Speaking of their shared properties, he observes:

> The common denominator in all these changes seems to be a shift from language-specific to what we feel justified in calling 'universal' grammar: the process of pidginization tends to eliminate all the features by which languages are distinguished and to replace them by features that can be assumed to be present in all languages - either implicitly or explicitly. Operations like the 'stripping' of late syntactic rules and the establishment of one-to-one correspondences between underlying and surface structure items are manifestations of this process.
>
> The extent to which languages have been affected by this process varies considerably. (Heine 1975:13-14)

It is not quite clear from this quotation whether Heine conceives of universals as a static endpoint to which individual Pidgins approximate to a greater or lesser extent, or whether he is referring to an implicationally ordered dynamic development. It is this latter view which has emerged as the most favoured hypothesis in recent years.[17] In this model, it would be claimed for a construction such as plural marking that its presence or absence does not define a language as a Pidgin or Creole, but that, if it emerges at all, it will always appear with nouns in subject position that refer to human beings, then be extended to other grammatical positions (direct object, indirect object, after prepositions, in that order) and degrees of animateness.[18] We are thus arguing in terms of Greenberg's implicational universals.

The assumption at this point, although necessary empirical confirmation is not available for many areas of grammar, is that the implicational hierarchies underlying Pidgin and Creole development are the same. In the case of an emerging Creole, the endpoint of development would be reached much faster, however, than in an expanded Pidgin, where the process can go on over many generations of speakers.

The identification of universal processes and units also needs to be considered in the light of differing theoretical stances. There are two principal approaches to the study of linguistic universals. The first is the Greenbergian approach (cf Greenberg 1963), which is based on the comparison of surface characteristics of a large number of languages. Examples (from Greenberg 1963) are:

---

17 The argument is that following this developmental hierarchy is the least costly solution in terms of productive and perceptive effort. However, this natural development can be overruled by pragmatic and cultural considerations.

18 Similar study on the development of pronoun systems can be found in Mühlhäusler & Harré (1990).

Universal 34: No language has a trial number, unless it has a dual. No language has a dual, unless it has a plural. (This is an unrestricted implicational universal.)

Universal 42: All languages have pronominal categories involving at least three pronouns and two numbers. (This is an unrestricted independent universal.)

Universals of the Greenbergian type can be easily falsified with evidence from new languages, as has been done for universal 42 by Laycock (1977a:33-41).

A second approach to linguistic universals is that of Chomsky (e.g. 1965) and other transformationalists. It consists of postulating a small number of abstract universal principles, which are said to enable children to learn any language. Examples include the following:

1. The grammars of all languages have a category VP (verb phrase). (This is a substantive universal.)
2. The semantic component interprets syntactic deep structure. (This is an organizational universal.)
3. If the phrase X of category A is embedded within a larger phrase ZXW, which is also of the category A, then no rule applying to the category A applies to X, but only to ZXW. (This is the A-over-A principle, a formal universal discussed by Chomsky 1968:27-47.)

It should be noted that these are universals of formalization and that their alleged status as mental realities is largely removed from empirical verification. The approaches to universals of both Greenberg and Chomsky are deficient in a number of ways:

1. As suggested by Bickerton (1981), they compare languages consisting of mixtures between cultural and (biologically founded) natural grammar, that is, systems which are strictly speaking not comparable. At best, one will obtain a mix between natural universals and others based on cultural and other factors.[19]
2. Both types of universals are static, that is, based on fully developed adult grammars. They are therefore difficult to relate to findings from Pidgin, Creole and child language development.

To consider the first point, genuine natural universals would be expected in one instance: that of rapid creolization of an unstable jargon, the context considered by Bickerton (1981). The fact that older Creoles and adult Pidgins violate a number of such universals can be regarded as irrelevant to our understanding of the natural roots of human language. Genuine counter-examples are found in young Creoles, however, an instance being Bickerton's claim (1981:52-53) that they have no category VP. In turn, other young Creoles such as Tayo (Ehrhart 1993) do not conform to Bickerton's views on universals.

---

[19] A study of such possible factors in Pidgin and Creole development is made by Koefoed (1975), who adduces the following two additional sources for language universals: universal factors of performance, and general laws or trends of language evolution.

Such an argument raises a number of serious questions, in particular that of the ability of young children to acquire languages that have deviated considerably from the postulated natural basis.[20] Sranan, for instance, violates Greenberg's near universal number 18:[21] "When the descriptive adjective preceded the noun, the demonstrative and the numeral, with overwhelmingly more than chance frequency, does likewise". In Sranan, however, as pointed out by Koefoed (1975:8ff), the descriptive adjective precedes the noun, whereas the demonstrative pronoun follows it. Sranan is an old Creole and its present-day grammar may have been preceded by one where universal no.18 was not violated. The source of the violation could have been language mixing that resulted from continued substratum influence on this language. Again, it would be interesting to see if Sranan-learning children start off with both adjectives and demonstratives before the noun.

The initial hope, then, that because of their relatively young age, Creoles would not have developed far enough away from their natural base to make them useless for surface comparisons of the Greenbergian kind, is not fully justified. Creoles, and in all likelihood Pidgins as well, may be closer to such a universal base, but they do not provide direct access.

The argument just given implies that direct access is barred because of the historical changes undergone since these languages came into being. There is also a second reason: that the development leading to a Pidgin or Creole, rather than the endpoint of such a development, should be taken as the basis for comparison in universals research. It can be expected that the change from a less to a more complex system of verbal communication will progress along universally motivated lines, particularly in those situations where the target language is relatively inaccessible and where there are great pressures for communication. As yet, only partial studies of the internal development of Pidgins have been made (see summary by Sankoff 1979) and no direct studies of the development of a first-generation Creole out of a jargon are available. Those who have put forward claims in this area, such as Bickerton (1981), have had to rely on indirect evidence.

Comparative evidence on Pidgin and Creole development remains scarce and the hypothesis of a single, language-independent expansion programme is too restrictive. However, it would seem wise to put forward a strong claim and revise it as needed, and the evidence suggests that linguistic universals to date are the most satisfactory explanation of the origin of Pidgin/Creole structures. A developmental universalist hypothesis has no difficulty in accounting for observed differences between "synchronic" grammars of different Pidgins: they are seen as reflecting different stages in linguistic development. However, before the emergence of developmental models, such differences strongly militated against universalist proposals and enhanced the plausibility of two major theories of Pidgin and Creole formation, which will now be discussed.

---

[20] Bickerton, in this case, would argue that natural Creoles are acquired with greater ease and without the many wrong starts and deviations from target grammar characteristic of the acquisition of older languages. While much research on child language acquisition does not seem to bear out this hypothesis (cf Aitchison 1983), Adone's (1994) study of the acquisition of Mauritian Creole provides some support for Bickerton's position.

[21] The notions of 'near universal' or 'statistical universal' have often been attacked because they are empirically vacuous. However, they can be used as initial discovery procedures.

Common-core theories

Among the various explanations of Pidgin and Creole formation put forward by Robert A Hall in various places, the idea that Pidgin grammar is the core common to the grammars of the languages in contact attracted the largest number of followers. The structural resources of a Pidgin language as seen by Hall are:

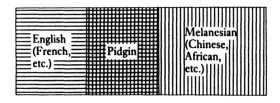

Structural resources of a Pidgin (from Hall 1961:414)

Hall's view appeared highly plausible at the time, especially in a climate where behaviourist learning theories prevailed. The intersecting hachured area can be interpreted as that of learning facilitation in a contrastive view of second-language learning. It is not easy to see how it could relate to first-language development, however. Thus Pidgin learners take the easiest way out by concentrating on those structures that are learnt with the least effort. However, there are some very serious objections to such an explanation. First, the areas of facilitation may turn out to be those parts of grammar that have least communicative relevance. Second, the common-core model is totally static and ignores the fact that at different points of linguistic development a different core would obtain. As pointed out by Posner (1983), there is an unfortunate tendency to compare the present-day standard variety of the lexifier language rather than earlier dialectal stages and/or informal varieties. Indigenous languages are equally bound to change over time. Thus, in the case of the formation of Tok Pisin, English has undergone only minor changes, whereas one of its major indigenous parent languages, Tolai, has changed dramatically over the last few decades. Third, this view assumes that the speakers of the Pidgin resulting from such language contacts are perfect bilinguals (that is, have equal access to all systems involved), as what is common to two languages can only be established once they are fully known. In fact, at the time that Pidgin grammars come into being, access to the lexifier language often is very limited. Finally, there is a growing body of factual counter-evidence. The available literature on Pidgins and Creoles abounds with examples of constructions that cannot be assigned to any identified parent language.[22]

Thus, the pursuit of the common-denominator model does not appear to be a very promising one, although identification of grammar across systems, just like the identification of lexical items across languages, may have been one component in their grammatical development. As regards Creoles, the fact of withdrawal of model languages excludes a common-denominator

---

[22] One such example is the development in Tayo of a subject-indexing (or referencing) pronoun unmarked for number or person (Chris Corne, p c).

113

explanation for their grammatical structures during their formative years. Again, identification of structures across languages may be a factor in their subsequent linguistic development.

Substratum theories

The idea that Pidgins and Creoles combine the lexicon of one language (typically the superstratum – that is, the socially dominant one) with the grammar of another (typically the substratum or socially subordinate one) has been around for a very considerable time. In the field of early Creole studies, it is associated with names such as Lucien Adam (writing on French Creoles), Herskovits (writing mainly on English-based Caribbean Creoles) and Schuchardt in his early writings. The reasons for appealing to substratum explanations are varied. They include:

1. The desire to demonstrate that there are mixed languages and that *Stammbaum* (family-tree) models of language relationship therefore stand in need of revision;
2. The desire to demonstrate linguistic and cultural continuity for Americans of African origin;
3. The study of changes in naturalness and internal consistency under conditions of language contact and borrowing.

Although each of these goals is worthwhile in itself, amazingly little progress has been made in the area of substratum studies over a long period of time, the main reason being the almost total absence of a well-designed model for language mixture. I have discussed the issues involved in a number of places (e.g. Mühlhäusler 1980a, 1982a, 1985, 1989a) and I will only mention some arguments here. A refutation of Keesing's (1988) claims can also be found in Baker (1993).

Mechanical mixture versus linguistic compounds
One of the most common exercises in substratum research has been to identify lexical items or grammatical constructions directly with those of a source language. Thus the lexical item **kavale** 'car, carriage' in Samoan Plantation PE would be traced to Samoan **ta-avale** 'carriage'; Jamaican Creole **nyaka-nyaka** 'very pretty' would be traced to an African substratum; or **happy-happy** for 'very happy' in the same language to the English item 'happy' and an African construction of iteration. In all these examples, substratum and superstratum features can be separated in a mechanical way. Indeed, the very use of the word 'stratum' suggests that geological rock strata provide the basis for substratum theory, as illustrated in the upper figure opposite.

However, there is no reason to expect that substratum elements can be isolated in an easy mechanical way in all instances. To return to our geological metaphor, there is a second possibility: metamorphosis of pre-existing material as a result of a volcanic intrusion, as illustrated in the lower figure below. In this instance, only some of the original and some of the intrusive material can be directly identified. The remainder, the metamorphic material, is very much in the nature of a chemical compound: that is, it is unlike any of the contributing elements. Linguists have progressed very little in their understanding of such material and, until they do so, claims as to substratum influence will remain restricted to a subset of potential cases.

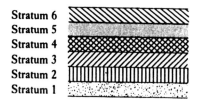

Stratum 6
Stratum 5
Stratum 4
Stratum 3
Stratum 2
Stratum 1

The stratum view of language mixing

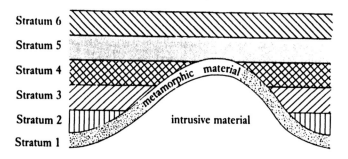

Stratum 6

Stratum 5

Stratum 4

Stratum 3

Stratum 2   intrusive material

Stratum 1

The metamorphic view of language mixing

"Borrowing grammatical rules"

Whereas borrowing in the area of the lexicon, including cases of lexical syncretism, appears to be relatively easy to describe, the same is not true of the area of grammar. Let me illustrate these problems of establishing substratum influence with a practical example. Most attributive adjectives in Tok Pisin appear before the noun. A small group, however, appear after the noun (so-called postmodifiers), including:

Tok Pisin	English gloss	Tok Pisin	English gloss
botol bruk	broken bottle	tok giaman	untrue talk
banana mau	ripe banana	han kais	left hand
het kela	bald head	graun malumalu	swampy ground
ples nogut	bad place	wil pas	stuck wheel
tok tru	true talk	buk tambu	holy book

Wurm suggests that Tok Pisin postmodifiers reflect substratum influence from Tolai:

> The appearance of adjectives of different classes preceding or following the nouns which they determine attributively is a typical feature of the Austronesian Tolai which shows the phenomenon uniquely amongst New Guinea Austronesian languages. It may well have entered Pidgin from this source.
> (Wurm 1977b:515)

115

There are a number of problems with this suggestion. First, it is not clear what grammatical rule is involved here. If it was simply the rule that "some, but not all, attributive adjectives appear postnominally", then one could point to a similar rule in English, manifested in, for instance, *money galore, president elect, court martial,* etc. This rule would support a superstratum grammar view as well as a substratum and a common-core view. We must go on to examine adjectives affected in both English and Tolai, and it then becomes clear that those adjectives that appear postnominally in English do not do so in Tok Pisin.

Influence from Tolai could manifest itself in two ways: either in the form of a different word order with a newly borrowed item of Tolai origin (thus conforming to the often held principle that "ordering of syntactic constituents can be borrowed only if the phonetic form of at least one member has also been borrowed"); or in the form of calquing. Let us examine both possibilities against the historical evidence available.

The only items of Tolai origin in the list of postmodifiers are **mau** 'ripe' and **malumalu** 'swampy'.[23] The former word is documented long before the latter, and thus seems to be the best candidate for triggering off a new word-order rule in Tok Pisin. However, as pointed out by Mosel (1980), "Tolai **mao** 'ripe' appears before the noun and not after it as in Tok Pisin". As regards **malumalu**, it does not belong to the group of Tolai adjectives that can appear postnominally, and furthermore seems to be an intransitive verb for most Tolai speakers.

The explanation that the new word order is a result of direct substratum influence is thus disconfirmed by the data. The second possibility is indirect influence or calquing. This possibility is alluded to by Mosel (1980), who points out that both Tolai **tuna** 'true' and Tok Pisin **tru** are postmodifiers. (Tok Pisin has a variant premodifier **trupela**, however). The available historical evidence suggests that **tru** was not the first adjective to appear postnominally. The only postnominal attributive adjective mentioned in Brenninkmeyer's grammar is **nogut** 'bad'. He writes:

> If the adjective appears after the noun, it becomes predicative and is linked to the subject by means of *he = he is,* as in:
> **Pig he fat, boy he nice...banana he 'mao' kaikai he no tan**
>
> Exceptions: No good which followed the noun without the **he** and **save** 'intelligent, wise'.
>
> Man no good   Man save   Boat no good
>
> (This appears to have developed in the defective pidgin of beginning learners of the language.) (1924:10, my translation).

The corresponding Tolai adjective **kaina** 'bad' is only found before nouns, however. This clearly indicates that the rule emerged in Tok Pisin without any direct or indirect support from either Tolai or English. The fact that further adjectives were subjected to it subsequently may have something to

---

23   I will ignore **tambu** 'sacred, taboo', as in **buk tambu** 'holy book, bible', because of its phonological properties and the fact that the word is widely found in other Oceanic languages and Pacific Pidgins. Moreover, it is not listed as a postmodifier in Brenninkmeyer's grammar (1924).

do with substratum influence. What is important, however, is that in most cases there are very significant differences between Tolai and Tok Pisin adjective ordering, as documented in detail by Mosel (1980).

One is reminded of Bickerton's more general statement on the role of substratum influence in Pidgins and Creoles (1979:3): "Although there are here and there some sweeping similarities which tease you and provoke you to go on with the search, you never find any language which has quite the same kinds of structures as the Creole language does."

The location of substratum influence

A recurrent argument in this book has been that Pidgins and Creoles must be seen as dynamically developing and changing entities rather than as systems. As regards the determination of substratum influences, nothing is more misleading than a simple static comparison between two languages. Let me illustrate this point with the example of reduplication, a construction seldom found in European lexifier languages and therefore typically assigned to substratum influence. In his thesis on Miskito Coast Creole English, Holm (1978) considers a number of semantic shifts brought about/associated with reduplication, including:

1. Continuation of action, as in **krai-krai** 'constantly crying';
2. Intensification of meaning, as in **big-big** 'very big';
3. Accumulation (of small things), as in **bomp-bomp** 'a skin rash'.

For all of these, he cites numerous parallels in African languages spoken in the areas from where Miskito Creole speakers originated. At the same time, he dismisses the idea that English baby talk might have been involved.

Steffensen notes that reduplication is associated with children's speech in languages as diverse as Zuni, Arabic, Marathi, Spanish and Japanese:

It is precisely because reduplicated forms are *not* associated with children's speech in ... many African languages that the latter would seem more likely sources for the phenomenon in creoles than would English. The European association is likely to have contributed to the old, simple-minded characterization of creoles as a kind of baby-talk.

(Steffensen 1979:120)

In spite of the initial plausibility of Holm's arguments, there are some serious problems. First, he operates with a purely synchronic analysis. He does not indicate whether reduplication developed in the Creole's Pidgin predecessor, during creolization itself or later, perhaps even under the influence of American Indian languages. His argument also leaves another question unanswered: it is that precisely the same type of reduplication is found in Tok Pisin of New Guinea. An initial explanation in agreement with West African substratum influence is that Tok Pisin, like Misquito Coast Creole, may have developed out of an older Pidgin Portuguese, heavily influenced by West African languages. This explanation is excluded on empirical grounds, since the development of productive patterns of reduplication in Tok Pisin only occurred in the 1950s, many years after its formation and stabilization. Moreover, a detailed comparison between Tolai (the main substratum language during formation and stabilization) and Tok Pisin carried out by Mosel is rather sobering:

> The divergences between Tolai and Tok Pisin suggest that the general idea underlying reduplication in Tolai on the one hand and in Tok Pisin on the other is different. Apart from intensifying reduplication, in Tolai all instances of the second type of reduplication have in common that they express some kind of imperfective aspect, while in Tok Pisin the only function of word level reduplication is to signal some notion of plurality ... Thus substratum influence of Tolai upon Tok Pisin can be excluded as far as verbal reduplication is concerned. (Mosel 1980:114)

A type that appears to be a good candidate for substratum influence is reduplication to signal plurality and/or distribution, as in **makmak** 'many spots or rash' or **talinga talinga** 'lots of mushrooms (in different places)'. This construction is found in a number of other Creoles (see the index to Arends, Muysken & Smith 1995), but commenting on reduplicated plurals and Chinese substratum influence in Macanese (Portuguese Creole of Macau and Hong Kong), Coelho cautions:

> The facts accumulated by us show clearly that the essential characteristics of these dialects are everywhere the same regardless of differences of race, climate, distance, or time. It is in vain to seek in Indo-Portuguese, for example, any influence of the Tamil or Sinhalese. The formation of the plural by reduplication of the singular in the Macao dialect can be attributed to Chinese influence, but this process is such an elementary one that little can be established by it.
> (Translation quoted from Reinecke 1937:18)

A developmental comparison of Tolai and Tok Pisin echoes these remarks. The use of reduplication for plural marking is highly productive in Tolai, and during intensive contacts between Tolai and Tok Pisin around 1910, two lexical items appear to have been formed in Tok Pisin under Tolai influence: **sipsip** 'sheep' and **meme** 'goat'.[24] However, in spite of access to Tolai, no more plural reduplicatives appeared, and it is only in some very recent creolized varieties of Tok Pisin far removed from Tolai influence that reduplication as a productive process of plural formation re-emerged. A static synchronic comparison between such advanced forms and Tok Pisin and Tolai indeed suggests close parallelisms. However, to postulate substratum influence on the basis of such evidence would be quite misleading.

We can now return to the question: at what point in their formation are Pidgins and Creoles susceptible to substratum evidence? Let us discuss this stage by stage.

The jargon stage. Individual strategies for cross-language communication are dominant at this stage and they include transfer of structures belonging to the speaker's first language. However, the very nature of unstable jargons restricts the usefulness of the transfer strategy. As pointed out by Meisel:

---

[24] The forms **me** and **sip** are documented in some very early texts.

if Bickerton is right and at the time of HCE [Hawaiian Creole English] development, HPE [Hawaiian Pidgin English] was still a jargon, this would mean that it was little more than a list of lexical items and irregularities, lacking systematicness and structural regularities . And in this case, quite logically, it does not make much sense to talk about transfer of L1 syntax. Instead - and this would partly apply to stabilized pidgins too - what looks like syntax (substratum or superstratum or creatively generated) is rather the result of pragmatic principles, e.g topic-comment order, initialization of information which is useful to 'set the stage' for the following proposition, and so forth. This is in accordance with claims to the effect that the 'pragmatic mode' precedes the 'syntactic mode', ontogenetically as well as phylogenetically.

(Meisel 1983:31)

It would seem desirable to examine the data discussed by Bickerton (1981) and Labov (1990) to determine whether transfer from substratum languages is indeed as prominent as they claim.

The presence of substratum influence at the jargon stage is unconnected with a second point, that of the continuity of transmission of jargon grammar, which is low, as jargons are to a significant part invented and reinvented by individuals. Consequently, however strong substratum influence is at the jargon stage, it is unlikely to be of great import for subsequent stabilization.

The stabilization stage. Stabilization, or tertiary hybridization, involves the gradual elimination of individual solutions and the establishment of social norms. At the same time, it is the beginning of a transition from a pragmatic to a syntactic mode of verbal intercourse.

The first aspect means that speakers from a number of different substratum languages are involved. In some cases these may be typologically similar or indeed belong to a single Sprachbund, influencing the emerging Pidgin. This fact may account for some of the structural differences between developmentally comparable Pidgins such as Chinese PE, West African PE or Melanesian PE. The more different their areal linguistic background, the less likely is substratum influence, and the more speakers rely on universal strategies.

As regards the second aspect, we are faced with the general principle that only those constructions that fit into the developing grammar of a Pidgin can be borrowed.[25] Let me illustrate this with data from the development of causatives in Tok Pisin.

Early Tok Pisin used either lexicalized causatives, such as **kill** 'to kill' or zero derivation as in:

masta raus mi	'the European threw me out'
mi raus	'I was thrown out'

The first morphological causatives in Tok Pisin, documented around 1910, are calques from Tolai, an instance of substratum influence. Compare the examples overleaf.

---

[25] This is true for any developmental system (that is, one that develops from lesser to greater complexity), including child language and second-language acquisition.

Tolai		Tok Pisin	
mat	'to die'	save	'to know'
vamat	'to kill'	meksave	'to inform'
maranga	'to be dry'	pas	'to be stuck'
vamaranga	'to dry'	mekpas	'to fasten'
		nois	'to shake, quiver'
		meknois	'to shake something'

The examples illustrate that Tolai **va-** is identified with Tok Pisin **mek-** but the Tolai construction, in spite of its great productivity, simply did not catch on.   Instead, Tok Pisin speakers developed their own convention for morphological causative marking.   They used the transitivity marker **-im** (which had become firmly established in the language) to signal causatives, in the following order: with intransitive stative verbs; with intransitive non-stative verbs; with adjectives; and with transitive verbs.   Morphological causatives calqued from Tolai appear to have become lexicalized because they conflict with a natural developmental hierarchy underlying causativization.

One is led to conclude from this and similar evidence that the chance of constructions from a substratum language being available at the right time and fitting into an independently given programme of Pidgin expansion is relatively low.[26]   Consequently one would not expect great substratum influence at the stabilization stage.

The expansion phase.   What goes for stabilization also appears to go for subsequent expansion.   What can be borrowed from other sources is determined by the independently operating developmental programme.   In fact, as grammaticalization increases, the syncretic capacity of an expanding Pidgin decreases: the more tightly structured and systematic the Pidgin becomes, the more likely it is that borrowing will lead to dysfunctional development.   Expanded Pidgins are particularly vulnerable when exposed to their former lexifier language.   The cost of borrowing from a prestige superimposed variety thus is high.

Creolization.   We have distinguished earlier between different types of creolization, according to whether a first language is developed out of a jargon, a stable Pidgin or an expanded Pidgin.   As regards the latter two cases, little carry-over of substratum influence can be expected in the formative years of a Creole, because little was encountered in the models.

When it comes to the formation of a Creole out of a jargon, two obstacles – one social and one linguistic – are encountered.   Bickerton (1981) and some other researchers are confident that, in this type of creolization, access to a substratum vernacular must have been very limited, mainly because of the profusion of different first languages spoken by the creolizing children's parents.   However, we can suspect that, in at least some cases, children also acquired a second language side by side with their creation of a Creole, and

---

[26] This developmental programme, or innate syllabus as it is sometimes called in second-language-learning research, appears to be universally motivated. At least, this strong hypothesis is assumed to provide a useful empirical framework for the discussion of Pidgin development. It is left open whether the source of these universals is pragmatics or biology.

that, particularly if typologically similar languages were involved, carry-over of substratum grammar cannot be excluded. However, in the absence of a proper theory of language mixing, this is difficult to confirm.

Bickerton also stresses the limitations of borrowing for a developing system, in this case a first-language Creole:[27]

> at any given stage in that development, the language could only incorporate rules of a certain type, and would have to reject others. Indeed presence in the input may not even be a necessary, let alone a sufficient, condition since the first creole generation could well have devised such a rule for itself. (Bickerton 1981:50)

Note that this feature of Creole development is very similar to first-language development in children: parental input is ignored or accepted only when it can be accommodated in their developing grammar.[28] Eventually, in "normal" language learning, children must deviate from their natural tendencies and acquire the caretakers' model. Because of the absence of socially or linguistically viable models, creolizing children have considerably more freedom to impose their solutions.

We do not yet have enough observational data to test claims in this area. Particularly serious is the absence of data on the change from pragmatic to grammatical modes of communication in data from first-generation Creole speakers concerning the influence of the first generation on the second.

Subsequent Creole development. The discussion of substratum influence at different stages of Pidgin/Creole development suggests a more general principle: mixing is disfavoured when languages develop from less to more complex systems, at least it is constrained in that only those elements that fit the expanding grammar can be borrowed from outside. It would appear that the obstacles to mixing are greatest after the transition from pragmatic to grammatical modes of verbal communication, that is, greater with expanded Pidgins than stabilizing ones.

Contrary to what has often been said, from Sapir onwards, about language mixing with fully developed systems, that they only borrow what is in agreement with their internally motivated drift and that borrowing thus merely accelerates developments that would occur without outside contacts, it appears that "finished" systems are much more open to outside influence than developing ones. One of the reasons for this may be that they are typically used by adults, who employ mixing for indexical (particularly social) purposes. In adult speech, the system-destroying abnatural results of mixing are tolerated because of their social benefits. Cultural solutions thus take over from natural ones.

As regards Creoles, the natural solutions developed by the first generation of children often lead a very precarious existence. They are replaced by abnatural solutions as well as by further natural developments as in any other language. I will return to this in the next chapter.

---

27 Note that Bickerton only speaks for first languages; he appears happy to admit any kind of borrowing for second-language development.

28 At least as far as production grammar is concerned.

In summary, then, it would seem that the role of substratum influence has often been overestimated because of:

1. deficient methodology, such as the lack of developmental perspective and the readiness to classify any similarity between a Pidgin or Creole and an indigenous language as substratum influence;
2. no proper distinction between the formation and subsequent development of Pidgins and Creoles.

It can be meaningfully discussed only with regard to individual developmental stages. An important explanatory parameter is also the social benefits and linguistic disbenefits of borrowing and mixing.

Substratum influence and components of grammar
The idea that different parts of grammar are not all equally susceptible to borrowing and mixing is an old one (see discussion in Mühlhäusler 1985a and Appel & Muysken 1987). In Creole and Pidgin studies, it is already implicit, for instance, in the following quotation from Schuchardt's Saramaccan studies:

> However, we must consider that, if initially the influence of African languages on Black English was only able to exert itself within the framework indicated thus far (the syntax), then this restriction was subsequently voided: namely, at the point when the slaves not only spoke creole with the Whites, but also when they spoke it among themselves, though without having lost their mother tongue, which was readily refreshed by constant importation from Africa. It is during this period that we have transfer of African words. (Schuchardt 1979:75)

As a general principle, it can be postulated that the more arbitrary an area of grammar, the more readily can languages borrow from one another. With regard to the formation of developmental continua such as the Pidgin–Creole continuum, this implies that substratum influence will be most pronounced in the areas of lexical semantics, prosodic phonetology, some segmental phonetology, and pragmatics. On the other hand, superstratum influence will be strongest in lexical form and segmental phonetology.[29] Syntax, inflectional morphology and derivational morphology are relatively independent of substratum or superstratum influences.

This means that findings to the effect that substratum languages are the principal source of Creole semantic structures (Huttar 1975) cannot be extended to the syntactic component and that, in the areas of syntax and morphology, linguistic universals will be the main source of structural expansion, irrespective of whether this expansion takes place with second-language Pidgin speakers or first-generation Creole speakers.

This hierarchy is confirmed by recent research in second-language learning (interlanguage). With regard to syntax and morphology, Meisel (1983:30 ff) suggests that even within these components there are areas of greater and lesser susceptibility to transfer. He observes that:

---

[29] It is assumed here that the superstrata language typically becomes the lexifier language. I have not considered relexification, as this is dealt with separately in this chapter.

1. omission of normally obligatory elements (verbs, subject pronouns, articles, etc.) cannot be explained with transfer, or at least not with transfer alone;

2. bound morphology is never transferred; in the case of free morphology, it is concerned with instances of lexical transfer;

3. syntactic transfer is most likely to occur in areas where syntax and semantics are interwoven, for example, relative ordering of two elements where one modifies the other (examples would be adjective-noun sequences, compound nominals expressing possession, part-of-relationships, etc.).

Finally, the reader needs to be reminded that the selectively small amount of transfer (whose status, moreover, is not always well established) is overshadowed by a much larger number of instances of non-transfer. Identifying such non-events will provide correctives against some of the most inflated substratist claims.[30]

It is hoped that further research will expose additional constraints on borrowing and that consequently the role of substratum influences, at least during Pidgin and Creole formation, will be shown to be quite restricted. There would seem to be strong ideological reasons, however, why such research is not popular at present.

Some notes on superstratum influence

The model of the lexifier language available to the developers of Pidgins and Creoles, as already mentioned in the discussion of nautical jargon and baby theories, may indeed have been quite different from the standard languages of today and even those of their times. Some very pertinent remarks are found in Posner's review of books dealing with French Creoles (1983). In discussing the analysis of Haitian Creole of Lefèbvre and her colleagues (1982), she writes:

> What is surprising, in a work hailing from Montreal, is that modern standard French is usually contrasted with creole, rather than the non-standard varieties that more plausibly formed the basis on which Haitian creole developed. For instance the deictic particle **la**, postposed not only to nouns and noun phrases but also to clauses, prepositions and adverbs is seen by Claire Lefebvre as a noun determiner that has been reanalyzed as a clause determiner, possibly under the influence of West African languages like Ewe or Yoruba. Yet it may be only a step from documented Canadian usage, in which an unaccented phatic **là** 'there' appears in a whole set of contexts, including at the end of subordinate clauses not introduced by the **que** complementiser that is obligatory in modern Standard French... A historical linguist is more interested in the process by which what seems to be discourse usage in Canada, may have become a syntactic rule in Haiti, rather than whether **la** is dominated by X or $\overline{X}$ or $\overline{\overline{X}}$. (Posner 1983:195)

---

[30] In my review of Keesing's (1988) claims concerning substrate influence in Melanesian PE, I list a number of constructions that were never borrowed from Melanesian languages (Mühlhäusler 1989b:473ff).

123

Posner's example raises the more general problem of observational and descriptive adequacy in Pidgin and Creole studies. Usually the grammars used as the basis of comparison between Pidgins or Creoles, on the one hand, and sub- or superstratum languages, on the other, are believed to be descriptive. Creolists are generally aware that many older grammars are highly prescriptive and they tend to make allowances for this fact. However, I feel that the extent of prescriptivism in grammar making is very much underrated. Pronouns provide an interesting example, because the pronoun systems of many Pidgins and Creoles differ markedly from those found in the descriptions of their European lexifier languages. A grammar of English with clearly descriptive aims is Leech & Svartvik (1975). The table below shows their account of English personal pronouns. However, this table hardly represents the ways in which present-day native speakers of English use personal pronouns, or indeed as they would have been used when speakers of other languages were exposed to the English model in the formative years of Pidgins and Creoles (see Mühlhäusler & Harré 1990).

English personal pronouns

			subjective case	objective case
1st person	singular		I	me
	plural		we	us
2nd person	singular		you	you
	plural		you	you
3rd person	singular	masculine	he	him
		feminine	she	her
		non-personal	it	it
	plural		they	them

Source: Leech & Svartvik 1975:260.

With regard to the pronoun **we**, the following observation is made in an empirical study by Wales:

> the general flexibility of personal pronouns, often over-lapping with one another, to express a wide range of references, with varying degrees of generalization, (ii) the tendency for even generalized references to be discourse-oriented, and speaker-oriented in particular, (iii) the frequent conflict, as a result, between surface form and ostensible reference on the one hand, and deeper reference, heavily biased towards egocentricity, on the other. (Wales 1980:25)

What this implies, among other things, is that **we** is frequently used to address second persons in both singular and plural, as in:

| we want to eat our food now | (e.g. nurse to patient) |
| we heard in our last lecture | (lecturer to students) |

We certainly cannot be sure that **we** or its counterpart in other European lexifier languages was not used in this second-person function, particularly at a time when the directive function of the language was a dominant one.

Consider Taylor's statement on first and second-person plural pronouns in some West Indian Creoles:

> The pronouns of 1st and 2nd persons plural are both **nu** (or **n'**) in Haitian Creole, **unu** (**un** or **u**) in Sranan; and while French *nous* and Dutch *ons* offer plausible models for 1st plural, extension of meaning to 2nd plural cannot be regarded as 'gradual modification'. (Taylor 1963:811)

However, in the light of my previous observations, we certainly cannot be confident that the non-distinction of pronouns was not already in the line input to creolization. What is claimed to have been introduced from substratum languages, as a result of faulty learning or internal development, thus may have been in the input. It certainly should not come as a surprise that certain pragmatically governed regularities of lexifier languages eventually became grammaticalized in later Pidgins and Creoles.

Conclusions

We have now examined the most prominent theories of Pidgin and Creole origins, and must return to the question of their explanatory power. Disregarding questions of detail, such as the precise nature of the superstratum model, the formation as well as the subsequent development of Pidgins and Creoles was determined most strongly by the following three forces: universals of development; substratum influences; and superstratum influences. We have reason to believe that their respective influence is dependent on the developmental stage of a Pidgin and Creole as well as on a number of social factors. The problem as to how to portray the interplay of factors during the formative years of Pidgins and Creoles is comparable to what Sato (1993:138) argued for decreolization:

> How best to accommodate the social–psychological dimensions of linguistic varieties to the study of decreolization remains a problem..., but not an insurmountable one.

It is for such reasons that purely structure-oriented single–cause explanations will not suffice, if we look at a Pidgin or Creole as occupying a stretch rather than a point in time. Even if one wants to exclude social factors, single-cause theories are inadequate because they ignore the important possibility of a conspiracy between different forces. Most notably, one can expect combinations of:

1. superstratum and universal tendencies;
2. substratum and universal tendencies;
3. substratum and superstratum;
4. all three factors.

Such combinations can occur at all levels of grammar.

With regard to borrowed vocabulary, it is not sufficient to establish cognates; one must also analyse the possible sources of the various kinds of lexical information (cf Fillmore 1971:370-91). This point can be illustrated using the Tok Pisin item **bel** 'belly, pregnant, seat of emotions'. The phonological shape of this item can be related to both Tolai **bala** 'belly, seat of emotions' and English **belly**. It is strange that the Tok Pisin form does not have a CVCV structure; the reasons for this are not known at present.

The semantic information 'belly' can be traced to both English and Tolai, whereas the meaning 'seat of emotions' can be traced to Tolai and the semantics of numerous languages spoken in the area of New Guinea. The meaning 'pregnant' appears late in the development of Tok Pisin as a metaphorical expansion.

At the level of grammar, let us consider the claim by Dalphinis that the absence of a copula in West Indian Creoles demonstrates their African roots:

> In the deletion (ø) of the 'copula', we again find extreme similarity between the West Indian Creole Languages and African Languages of West Africa. For example:
>
> | | |
> |---|---|
> | Jamaican Creole: | [im ø dred] - he *is* a Rasta |
> | St Lucian Patwa: | [i ø fu] - he *is* mad |
> | Yoruba: | [omi ø tutu] - the water *is* cold |
> | | [ejawɔmi ø atata] - my wife *is* beautiful |
> | Twi: | [o ø bɔdam] - he *is* mad |
> | | [insjo ø aw] - the water *is* cold |
> | | [eje ø fefefe/ejefe] - she *is* beautiful |
> | Central Ibo: | [wagnjim ø maramma] - my wife *is* beautiful |
> | | [mmiri ø ɔji] - the water *is* cold |
> | | [ɔ ø baraba] - he/she/it *is* rich |
>
> It is therefore not surprising that a literal word-to-word translation of many West African Languages would give close approximations to West Indian Creole Languages. (Dalphinis 1982:10-11)

This explanation ignores the much more likely explanation of a conspiracy between universal processes, simplified input and substratum factors (cf Ferguson 1971 for the former two factors). Where these factors coincide, the cognitive cost for those developing a Pidgin or Creole is least. It is for such reasons that Pidginists and Creolists should be on a constant look-out for developmental conspiracies and the linguistic syncretisms resulting from them.

5 The linguistic development of Pidgins and Creoles

I think it can easily be argued that the fundamental problem for linguistic theory is to understand ... how linguistic structures evolve, come into being and change into new (sub) systems and thereby to learn what the true nature of language is. (C-J N Bailey 1982:25)

Introduction

Development is of supreme importance, as has been emphasized repeatedly in this book. Pidgins and Creoles should be regarded as dynamically evolving and changing systems, not as states or a sequence of states. When it comes to applying such desiderata to real linguistic description, however, a number of problems are encountered. First and foremost, there is still a lack of systematic longitudinal studies for any span of the Pidgin-Creole continuum although considerable progress has been made in recent years with the search for – and exploitation of – historical records, particularly with regard to Surinam, the western Indian Ocean, and the southwestern Pacific. Where there is a complete absence of such research, the need has arisen to reconstruct non-documented or ill-documented aspects of language development from what-ever data are to hand. Such reconstruction is usually based on the idea that language development is uniformitarian, that is, a steady development in one direction, rather than a sequence of discontinuous developments alternating between progressive and regressive phases.[1] The suspicion that traditional methods of linguistic reconstruction may be less than optimal for Pidgins and Creoles has been expressed by a number of scholars (for example, Dutton 1980; Hoenigswald 1971) and should constantly be kept in mind when reading this chapter. Second, to make the description of Creole and Pidgin development possible, a number of concessions have to be made. These include separating the dimensions of restructuring and development, in spite of the fact that actual developments are probably more realistically described as a product of these two (and possibly additional) factors. Finally, although I have attempted to do justice to inter- and intra-individual variability, none of my observations is based on controlled sampling and therefore they may not always be representative. All these limitations are unavoidable, given the enormous amount of data to be considered and the small number of researchers working in the field.

Unlike Bickerton (1981), I am not convinced that there are any ideal paradigm cases of Pidgins and Creoles, and that a great deal of labour can be saved by simply considering those.[2] Although acknowledging the need for deductive theorizing in our field, I have chosen to offer mainly inductive generalizations on the basis of as extensive and representative a body of data as possible.

---

[1] By this I mean that development achieved at an earlier stage may be erased subsequently only to reappear later.

[2] Note that even for Bickerton's paradigm language, Hawaiian Creole English, little or no developmental descriptions are available.

In outlining the development of Pidgins and Creoles, I will refer to the following key notions. *Structural expansion* is defined as those additions to a system of verbal communication that increase its referential or non-referential potential. It is roughly synonymous with the processes of grammaticalization and addition of lexical resources. Its counterpart, *reduction* in structure, or *impoverishment*, comprises those processes that lead to a decrease in the referential or non-referential potential of a language. *Simplification* means certain areas of language are made more regular, in the sense that rules apply to greater numbers of items or structures. The notion of simplification is a problematic one (see Mühlhäusler 1974, Meisel 1983), because we can determine local, but rarely global simplification of grammar, and also because it is not synonymous with naturalness.[3] It remains to be investigated how greater regularity contributes to greater learnability of Pidgins. *Complication* means the opposite of simplification; that is, the loss of rule generality. Again, no obvious link with loss in naturalness of a language has been established. *Restructuring* means the use of different devices to achieve the same referential and non-referential effects. Note that these devices refer to lexical and grammatical properties of Pidgins and Creoles, but not to paralinguistic or pragmatic ones.

The last point takes us to another problem: the assumption that grammaticalization processes can be studied in isolation from pragmatic and cultural information. In the absence of sufficient information, this assumption will have to be taken as the basis for our present discussion. However, I shall attempt to point out areas where pragmatic considerations determine the direction of grammaticalization. The organization of this chapter is determined by the following parameters:

1. Developments at separate developmental stages in the life of Pidgins and Creoles;
2. Developments in different components of grammar.

The jargon stage

Jargons, as we have already said, are individual solutions to the problem of cross-linguistic communication and hence subject to individual strategies, the principal ones being lexicalization or holophrastic talking; pragmatic structuring; grammaticalization by transfer; and universals. In most documented cases, combinations of these strategies have been observed. Cultural and personality factors appear to determine which strategy is favoured. An interesting observation regarding holophrastic talking is found in Zöller (1891:419; my translation):

> There are three stages in penetrating foreign languages. The first and lowest stage which we in educated Europe hardly know, but which is observed more often than the second stage in communication between the white man and the members of the coloured races, merely comprises a more or less limited knowledge of the vocabulary.

---

[3] In an earlier article (1980c:21), I suggested that simplification would usually lead to an increase in naturalness. This, it seems, is an unwarranted view, as has been pointed out to me by C-J N Bailey (p c). Rule generalization often implies its extension to less natural environments of application and/or rule output of a less natural type.

It seems that this strategy is limited to the very earliest period of interlingual contact and is viable only in an extremely limited domain. A possible example is that of labour recruiting in the Pacific in the 19th century,[4] as exemplified in the following conversation reported by Ribbe (1903:223; my translation):

> *Me like boys* the white man says to the black man, *plenty kaikai (food). No fight* (corporal punishment)? asks the black. *Yes, plenty kaikai and no fight,* the white replies. *What you pay me?* the owner of a slave or a village chief asks. *One fellow anikow* (an axe) the recruiter replies.

In this exchange, at least some of the utterances used by the indigenous speakers are probably remembered in toto. Candidates are *What you pay me?* in the above text and phrases such as **aidono** 'I do not know', **orait** 'it is all right', or **gutwan** 'this is good' in others. In another trade jargon, the Sino-Russian mixed language of Manchuria (Jablonska 1969), Chinese **tuo-shao Ch'ien** 'what is the price' is reduced to **doscen**.

The fact that rudimentary communication in terms of holophrastic and very basic grammar (mainly two-word utterances) also occurs nearer home was documented by Harding (1984), in her analysis of the language used between health visitors and mothers from Asian countries who now live in the Birmingham area. Two examples of such conversations are:

Health visitor	Asian mother's response
HUSBAND WORK/	yes
FACTORY/	factory yes
ALL DAY/	yes all day so:
SO YOU ON YOUR OWN\	yes
BABY. ALL RIGHT/	all right
MILK. ALL RIGHT/	all right

(/ = rising intonation; \ = falling intonation)　　　　(Harding 1984:145)

Harding demonstrates the operation of numerous discourse structuring devices (such as the provision of the most likely answer in the above example). Thus, although most of the linguistic norms of standard English are replaced by a very different foreigner talk version, the majority of the conversational conventions are upheld. This suggests that one should look at the communicative effects of such jargons as well as their lexical and grammatical inventories. Thus particular attention has to be paid to Ferguson's (1977:30ff) categories of "clarification processes" and "expressive and identification processes". Without these, mechanical rule simplification and shedding of morphological complexities will not result in a communicatively efficient jargon.

The context-dependency of jargons has been known for a long time, as is illustrated in the following discussion of an Eskimo trade jargon:

> Take as an instance the jargon sentence **Kim-mĭk-ka'i-li pi-cū'k-tŭ** (...). If it were in answer to "Why are you whistling?" it would mean "Because I

4　The situation referred to is that of "pulling" raw recruits, that is labour trade in newly opened up areas. The labour trade in Melanesia shifted, at a rapid pace, from the Loyalties and New Hebrides in the south to the Solomons and New Guinea in the north.

want the dog [e.g., my dog, his dog, the dogs, your dogs] to come". If it were in answer to "Why do you want Jim?" it might mean "Because I want him to bring a dog [his dog, my dog, etc.] to me." If it were in answer to "Why are you locking the door?" it might mean "Because the dogs keep trying to get into the house." If in answer to "Why did Jim go to Fort Macpherson?" it might mean "Because he wants to get dogs there" - and so on, world without end. It will therefore be understood that the translations given for the illustrative sentences in the body of the vocabulary are but a few among the many possible meanings of the word combinations used.

(Stefánsson 1909:221-22)

The contribution of pragmatic context is particularly easy to see in the areas of tense and iconic word order. Labov (1990)[5] has presented a well-argued scheme for the development of tense in Pidgins. He points out that, in the initial stages, particularly those where no communal grammar exists, there is a very strong tendency to give the overall time reference paragraph-initially. The following passage of Hawaiian PE, spoken by Max, a native speaker of the Philippino language Ilocano, illustrates this:

Well... in the Filippine, this now... you see, he die in three hours ... and then he come back a--*live* again ... Three hours die, after three hours, come back live, he talk--tell the story about (1990:16).

This text also illustrates the second aspect, that narrative sequencing rules are iconic of the sequence of real events reported. It is assumed that this is the most natural strategy and therefore favoured. Thus English 'if' clauses, which can appear either initially or in second place, are typically rendered by juxtaposed sentences of the following type (examples from Dutton 1983b:90):

Samoan Plantation PE: **no mani, no kam** 'If I have no money I won't come'

Hiri Trade Language (Kerema): **Aie, na nava pene na navai. Rae imo.**
Gee, I fish some I eat. Insides good
'If I could only eat some fish I'd feel a lot better'

In later stages of Pidgin development, grammatical markers tend to be introduced, thus reducing the need for strict clause ordering.

Substratum influence appears most likely when only two languages are involved (secondary hybridization); when these two languages are related, thus inviting cross-linguistic identification; and when individuals are not concerned with correctness in the target language. Both Cocoliche, the Spanish-Italian jargon used by Italian migrants in Argentina (see Bauer 1975:78-83; Whinnom 1971), and the Italian-Portuguese contact language of Brazil (cf Hall 1966:18) meet these requirements.

Cocoliche and congeners differ from other jargons in that they are not substantially simplified in lexicon and grammar (a consequence of the similarity of the contact languages and the strong social integration between their speakers), and that many of the transfer processes appear to have no

---

5   Written in 1971 and widely distributed in ms form, this was cited as Labov (1971a) in the first edition of this book. The text was later published in Singler (ed.) (1990:1-58) and all page references in this edition will be to the latter printed version.

communicative function. Compare the following Cocoliche examples from Whinnom (1971):

1. The treatment of grammatical number: the singular form *il pantalone* 'trousers' rather than standard Italian plural is chosen, because of Spanish *el pantalon;*
2. Spanish gender is used with Italian nouns, as in *la latte* 'milk' and *la miele* 'honey' (in both cases instead of standard Italian masculine).

As there are no social norms, and as individuals change their grammars with growing integration into the Spanish-speaking host community, one can only point to salient interference phenomena found with "typical" migrants. It remains to be seen what insights can be gained from the study of such targeted interlanguages of closely related languages.

Substratum influence in makeshift jargons involving unrelated or distantly related languages appears to be more revealing for our purposes. We shall look briefly at the ways it is manifested at different levels of grammar.

Pronunciation has often been singled out as that area where substratum influences can make themselves felt most freely. However, in the case of jargons one must distinguish between departures from the lexifier language due to substratum influence in production; mishearing and other perceptual difficulties; and universal (natural) tendencies in pronunciation. Often, variant pronunciations are found in single texts, indicating that different strategies are used by the same speaker. The extent of such variation can be seen from statements relating to two South-East Asian varieties of jargon English: varieties spoken in Hong Kong and American Japanese Military Jargon. Regarding the phonology of the former, Kang-Kwong Luke observes:

> The phonetic values of segments show a great deal of variation from those which resemble the external norms of British and American English to those which show clear signs of influence from the Cantonese phonological system. 'Sorry', for instance, may be variably realized as [sɔri], [sɔwi] and [sɔ:li:], and possibly some other shapes (1984:194).

Similar observations were made by Goodman about English-Japanese Jargon:

> A rather simplified but essentially accurate statement of the phonological process of EJ-Pidgin would be that it contained a nearly perfect set of diaphonic correspondences and a few diaphonic compromises. The English speaker using the Pidgin employed English phones almost entirely and occasionally modified them slightly in what he considered the direction of corresponding Japanese phones. The Japanese speaker of the Pidgin employed Japanese phones in the same way. Where the corresponding phones of the two languages exhibited a close phonetic similarity, little difficulty existed. But where corresponding phones were phonetically very dissimilar, both speakers seemed to learn quickly the correspondences (1967:51).

Examples given include the changes in the pronunciation of 'baseball': It is:

> an English loan-word completely assimilated in Japanese; phonemically, its diamorphs are English /beysbol/ and Japanese /besuboru/. In EJ-

131

Pidgin, either of these is an acceptable and comprehensible pronunciation, and the two words illustrate certain basic diaphonic correspondences. English /r,l/ correspond to Japanese /ř/ which is a retroflex flap vibrant with occasional lateral release. English /ey/ corresponds to Japanese /e/.

(Goodman 1967:51)

Both statements are reduced in their theoretical importance by the application of a phonemic basis for cross-linguistic comparison. Although it is obvious that jargon-speaking individuals develop strategies for identifying sound systems, we do not know whether this is done for phonological reasons or for the more likely (though difficult to define) reasons of phonetic similarity. The view that jargon pronunciation merely constitutes the most simple or natural way of pronouncing another language certainly is not borne out, for instance, by data from Chinook Jargon where Thomason (1981) observes that we have considerable evidence pointing to the fact that English speakers of the Jargon recognized its complex phonology, including glottalized stops and dorsal fricatives, and in at least some cases made a considerable effort to learn them. In 1882, one contemporary observer, Gill, explicitly states that "the pronunciation of these words can only be thoroughly learned by conversation with the Indians, whose deep gutturals and long-drawn vowels are beyond the power of our alphabet to represent" (Thomason 1981:311). At the same time, some English speakers considerably distorted the pronunciation of Chinook Jargon forms. It appears that mutual understanding between whites and Indians could be attained, however, once the latter had become accustomed to the mispronunciations of the former, a situation comparable to many other jargon contexts.

Reliable recordings of jargon texts are hard to come by, but the following text, written by a Rarotongan missionary in the New Hebrides in the 1880s, can be taken to be a good representation of the processes under discussion here (from Schuchardt 1979:10-11):

> Misi kamesi Arelu Jou no kamu ruki mi Mi no ruki iou Jou ruku Mai Poti i ko Mae tete Vakaromala mi raiki i tiripi Ausi parogi iou i rukauti Mai Poti mi nomoa kaikai mi angikele nau Poti mani Mae i kivi iou Jamu Vari koti iou kivi tamu te pako paraogi mi i penesi nomoa te Pako Oleraiti
>
> Ta. Mataso.
>
> 'Mr Comins, (How) are you? You no come look me; me no look you; you look my boat, he go Mae today. Vakaromala me like he sleep house belong you, he look out my boat. Me no more kaikai, me hungry now, boat man Mae he give you yam very good; you give some tobacco belong me [dative], he finish, no more tobacco. All right. Ta, Mataso.'

Note the following points. First, substratum influence is most likely in cluster simplification by means of epenthetic vowels, the "confusion" of l and r, and the avoidance of final consonants. Second, perceptual difficulties are reflected in the loss of unstressed syllables, as in **arelu** for 'how are you'.[6] Finally universal factors, or more likely a conspiracy between universal factors and substratum influence, are evidenced by the predilection for CVCV word structure and phonological reduplications, such as **tete** for today.

---

[6]   This expression, incidentally, is a good example of holophrastic expressions in jargons.

In all the examples discussed so far, the simplification of word structure by means of vowel epenthesis has figured prominently, and this phenomenon has long been regarded as an excellent candidate for substratum language influence. Thus, speaking of the early Beach-la-Mar varieties of New Caledonia in 1883, Schuchardt writes:

> I will not go into the phonetic details, but the following forms are readily explicable as derivations from Polynesian or Melanesian phonological structure: **esterrong** = strong, **esseppoon** = spoon, **essaucepen** = saucepan, **pellate** = plate, **coverra** = cover, **millit** = milk, **bock-kiss** = box, etc. It is well-known fact that the New Zealanders particularly reshape foreign words beyond recognition. (Schuchardt 1979:24)

However, these may be only partial similarities. Comparisons of English loanwords in Tok Pisin's principal substratum language Tolai with their cognates in early Tok Pisin reveals some surprising differences. The following is adapted from Mosel (1980:19)

Tolai	*Early Tok Pisin*	*English source*
palet	plet, pelet	plate
tarautete	trausis, tarausis	trousers
galat	glas, galas	glass
tito	stua, situa	store
bulititon	buluston, bluston	bluestone
torong	sitirong, strong	strong
ˈpatiket	bisket	biscuit

Even more surprising is the absence of cluster simplification by means of epenthetic vowels in Pitcairnese. Although consonant groups do not occur in its substratum language, Tahitian, in Pitcairnese "there is no aversion to – or rather an abundance of consonant groups" (Ross 1964:143). Ross expected to find forms such as Tahitian **totoni** (< *stocking*), but found none. Does this mean that vowel epenthesis was not employed in the English-Tahitian jargon which preceded Pitcairnese?

Epenthesis has been associated with increasing the naturalness and simplicity (preferably both) of a jargon. However, lexical evidence from languages developed out of earlier jargons, particularly a survey of the Surinam Creoles (Smith 1977a), suggests that highly complex rules are needed to convert, for example, English lexical items into the corresponding epenthesized items of Sranan. They may indeed reflect different strategies by different groups of speakers, and can thus be seen as a continuation of the unsystematic processes of language simplification and adaption of the jargon phase. Vowel epenthesis has received renewed interest in the comparison of first-language acquisition and pidginization, in connection with the hypothesis that adults begin to develop their second language in the same way that they developed their first. This view is attacked by Aitchison (1983, 1995), who claims that, although cluster reduction is found in both child language and early Pidgins, the former achieve this by means of consonant deletion, the latter by means of epenthesis. Aitchison's view is supported mainly with evidence from well-established stable Pidgins, which moreover have remained in contact with their lexifier language. For the earlier jargon stage, it can be observed that next to forms with epenthetic vowels,

133

which are easier to perceive for speakers of the target language and therefore reinforced, one finds some evidence of language-learning strategies that parallel those of young children. Thus, in the Sino-Russian mixed language of Manchuria, "when Chinese pronounce words of foreign origin, the consonant clusters found in such words are eliminated either by means of inserting a vocalic element between the consonants or through the simplification of the consonant cluster itself" (Jablonska 1969:139). Again, in a number of early texts in Melanesian varieties of PE, examples of cluster simplification by means of omission such as **tesen** 'station', **tima** 'steamer' or **sos** 'church' are widely found. Very much the same point can be made by comparing Boni, one of the eastern maroon Creoles of Surinam, with Sranan. Whereas the former contains numerous examples of cluster simplification by means of omission, the latter, probably because of longer contact with English, appears to prefer the retention of clusters, or epenthesis. Compare the following words (data culled from Smith 1977a):

Boni	Sranan	English
toosi	trusu	thrust
dingi	dringi	drink
feele	frede	afraid
koosi	krosi	clothes
beeni	breni	blind
goon	gron	ground

There are, without doubt, many more such cases of natural universal phonological strategies. The identification of cognates after such processes have occurred constitutes a considerable problem, however. Let me illustrate this with the example of Tok Pisin **abus** 'animal, edible meat'. For this form, until recently, no etymology had been established. However, on hearing my own daughter refer to her soft toy animals as **abus**, it occurred to me that the Tok Pisin form had probably been derived from the English one by means of a number of straightforward phonological processes, including:

1. the identification, because of perceptual similarity, of [l] and [u], *animals* thus becoming **animus**;
2. the loss of the least-stressed syllable, resulting in **amus**;
3. the replacement of a nasal consonant by a homorganic stop, resulting in **abus**.

The form **abus** probably survived in Tok Pisin because it looked like an item borrowed from a native vernacular. Had it looked more like English, its chances of survival would have been diminutive.

In this survey of jargon grammar, most attention has been paid to phonology. The syntax of such languages is typically governed by pragmatic principles and some transfer of substratum grammar. The widespread absence of syntactic rules and an almost total lack of morphology account for the frequently used attribute "grammarless" when referring to such languages. Jargons certainly afford interesting insights into the role of syntactic patterns in the communicative process.[7] This leaves us to investigate the lexical and

---

7   The role of syntax in this process is commonly overestimated. Some more recent observers are inclined to believe that syntax is like the spare wheel on a car, that is, it is used for communication only if other "wheels of communication" are punctured.

semantic properties of jargons. Much has been written about the composition of jargon lexicons. One view is that there appear random macaronic mixtures of two or more languages; a second view holds that the lexicon of a jargon is typically derived from one language only. Actual empirical support can be found for both views, although the latter is much better documented.

Genuinely mixed lexicons appear to be restricted to the very first stage of contact between two partners, in particular situations where neither is socially dominant. In 1883, Schuchardt (1979:19) referred to trade languages on New Caledonia and other Pacific Islands consisting of "a mixture of New Caledonian, Chinese, English, and French words, e.g.: *tayos lookout belong faya* 'friend, look out for the fire', *bonjour tayo* 'good day, friend'". Sino-Russian of Manchuria is said to consist of approximately two-thirds Russian and one-third Chinese lexical material, and in Russonorsk we find considerable lexical variation. Neumann (1965:222) reports that both Russian *drugoi* and Norwegian *ander* can be used for the ordinal number 'second', and that for 'good' we find two Norwegian-derived (*god* and *bra*) and two Russian-derived (*dobr* and *xoros*) forms. More recently, Clark (1979:30ff) presented a long list of examples from mixed jargons found in the Pacific in the early years of European contact. They include:

Ah, karhowree *sabbee* lee-lee, ena arva tee maitai!
    'Ah, the white man knows little, this **ti**-liquor is good!'

me, tamaree... *plenty* kanaka Martair
    'When I was a boy, there were people at Ma'atea'

Why you no like to stay? Plenty moee-moee – *plenty* ki-ki – *plenty* whihenee – *Oh, very good place* Typee.

Mixture was also found within individual lexical items, particularly in the form of lexical encounters of hybrids. Thus, in the ad-hoc jargons developed in the dealings of US soldiers stationed in the American sector of Germany with the local population following the Second World War, a clear preference for words that can be identified across both languages is identified (Amsler 1952). Examples include:

Item	Form
guest	English *guest*, German *Gaest(e)* (plural)
wine	English *wine*, German *Wein*
beer	English *beer*, German *Bier*
drink	English *drink*, German *Trink*

It appears that the usefulness of such mixed jargons is very limited when one of the partners is mobile, and after a while such mixed jargons become replaced by varieties based on the dominant language, with the occasional substratum word thrown in. In fact, it is in the lexicon that stable conventions begin to develop first. To take jargon English as an example, we can distinguish different regional conventions, following Clark (1979):

1. **Worldwide lexical conventions:** for example, *along* (comitative), *been* (past anterior), *by and by* (future, posterior), *him* (third-person pronoun), *piccanninny* (child), *plenty* (plural, quantifier), *savvy* (to know), *suppose* (if), *too much* (much, many);

135

2. **Sino-Pacific features:** *allsame* (like, as if), *catch* (to get), *fellow* (adjective marker or noun classifier), *got* (have), and *stop* (to be located, exist).

Such lexical features were spread by the highly mobile traders, whalers and sandalwood cutters. In addition, members of this group used whatever other words of their own language appeared useful for establishing contact with new groups. In cases of multiple contacts of one group with many others, the most mobile language naturally became the lexifier language of a jargon.[8]

In the case of trade jargon in border areas between groups that are not mobile, the change-over from a lexically mixed to a more lexically uniform language appears to be associated with factors such as the relative cultural or political dominance, and in whose territory the language is predominantly used. To illustrate the former factor, we find, for instance, that in the Russian-Chinese contact language of Kjachta (described by Neumann 1966), the lexicon was almost exclusively composed of Russian items, or that the military Pidgins developed between American troops and the Japanese (see Goodman 1967) or the Thai (see Gebhard 1979) are lexically entirely English.

The second factor is particularly strong in so-called tourist jargons. Thus the rudimentary language developed between German tourists and Turkish peasants described by Hinnenkamp (1982, 1983), the medieval pilgrim's jargon spoken in Rome, and the many individual jargons spoken by early missionaries and travellers in exotic countries typically exhibit the lexical dominance of the language spoken by the host community. With modern mass tourism and Coca-Colonization of the Third World, this picture has changed: English- and German-derived jargons are found in many places.

Often things are not as simple as just outlined. There are many documented cases of a number of different jargons co-existing in a very small geographic area. Thus, in Fiji, English-based, Fijian-based and Hindi-based rudimentary jargons coexisted for a considerable time (see Siegel 1982), as did Motu-based and English-based jargons in Papua (see Dutton 1985a).

Turning to the size of the jargon lexicon, we find a very low type-token ratio and also a very low number of lexical types. Thus Dutton estimates that for the two Hiri trade languages, a lexicon with about 300 entries appeared to have been sufficient (1983b:94), but he points out that individual variation had to be expected. The dominance of individual strategies and the non-permanence of a jargon's lexicon outside its small core are also emphasized in the following observations on English-Japanese Jargon:

> it seems that the lexicon of a reasonably well established pidgin is particularly characterized by its capability for temporary extension. Americans and Japanese, both proficient in the pidgin to the extent of possessing a sense of diaphonic correspondences and a basic grasp of vocabulary and syntax, time and again stipulated new vocabulary items according to the needs of very specific situations. These items did not remain in the permanent lexicon. (Goodman 1967:54)

---

8 There is one notable exception to this principle, namely the different trade languages used by the Motuans of Papua: simplified Motu is used with their immediate neighbours, a trade language with considerable Elema components in dealing with the Elema peoples, and one with a considerable Koriki component for their dealings with this group (see Dutton 1983b:94ff).

The difficulties of accurately determining the size of the lexical inventory are illustrated by the case of Jargon English in the Pacific. All observers appear to agree that, compared with the lexical resources of its principal lexifier language, the inventory of lexical bases found in Jargon English was diminutive. Churchill's remark that "we find the irreducible minimum which is felt to underlie all the refinements of vocabulary" (1911:12) may be regarded as representative of many similar statements. Estimates as to the precise number of lexical items have been made only for the early stabilized Pacific PEs, although they may be taken as an indication of the number of lexical bases found in Jargon English as spoken by the Pacific Islanders. The lowest estimates are those for the New Hebrides. Speiser claims that the "mutilated English" spoken there contained hardly more than 50 words (1913:9), while Jacomb puts the figure at "no more than a hundred words" (1914:91). Genthe suggests around 300 lexical bases for Samoan Plantation PE spoken in the 1880s (1908:10), whereas Churchill (1911), "who unfortunately drew his vocabulary from various sources instead of setting down the words he had actually heard used" (Reinecke 1937:764), gives about 300 words.

The very small lexical inventory should be seen in conjunction with the very general meaning of most lexical items, a consequence of the context-dependency of jargons, and their being governed by pragmatic rather than grammatical rules. The generality is expressed, more than anything else, by the use of the same form in numerous grammatical classes and functions. This freedom from lexical specification, as Silverstein (1972a:381) refers to it in his discussion of Chinook Jargon, "can increase the 'information' of each unit. A great part of the lexicon of Chinook Jargon is in fact made up of 'words' both semantically and grammatically ambiguous, in a far less systematic way than e.g. English, with its zero deverbative and denominative formations." The tendency towards categorial multifunctionality is also encountered in all the jargons I have examined to date. A long list of relevant quotations is given in Mühlhäusler (1974:104ff).

Next to generality of meaning, the small set of lexical items in jargons is recycled to serve a wider field of reference by means of rudimentary circumlocution. Because of the absence of fixed rules of syntax and word formation, such circumlocutions are often very unstable. Six examples from three different jargons are given below.

Examples of circumlocutions

Chinese-Russian	uma konecaijlo	'mad'	(sanity + finished)
jargon of Kjachta	ruka sapogi	'gloves'	(hand + boots)
	jazyka meda	'skilful orator'	(tongue + honey)
Chinese PE	top-side-piecee-heaven-pidgin-man		'bishop'
Beach-la-Mar	coconut belong him grass not stop		'he is bald'
			(i.e. there is no grass on his coconut)
	pickaninny stop along him fellow	'egg'	(i.e. little one is inside)

Such examples of the linguistic nature of jargons underline their un-satisfactory character as means of verbal communication. In the absence of stable shared codes between interlocutors, messages frequently got distorted and one can only guess at the degree of understanding found in jargon situations. It certainly cannot be assumed that non-verbal aids employed at the same time eliminated all ambiguities.

Jargons are unstable both linguistically and socially. Moreover, they are not transmitted in any consistent way from speaker to speaker or generation to generation, but invented in an ad-hoc fashion. I hesitate to use Hymes' term 'pre-pidgin continuum' (1970:70) since what preceded the crystallization of Pidgins is by no means a continuous process of grammaticalization and conventionalization. The tertiary hybrids that emerge from the encounter of secondary jargons are qualitatively different languages.

Stabilization

Stabilization of a Pidgin is the result of the development of socially accepted language norms. Such norms develop when none of the languages in contact serves as a target language. Whinnom suggests (1971:91-115) that stable Pidgins are unlikely ever to have arisen out of a simple bilingual situation. Instead, they owe their stability to the fact that a jargon (secondary hybrid) is used as a medium of intercommunication by people who are not speakers of the original lexifier language.

The social conditions under which Pidgins acquire stability are outlined in Chapters 3 and 4; we shall now concentrate on their linguistic/structural properties. Generally speaking, stabilization implies the gradual replacement of free variation and inconsistencies by more regular syntactic lexical structures. In the former area, a pragmatic mode of speaking begins to give way to a grammatical one, whereas in the latter lexical dependency on outside resources is supplemented with internal means of lexical expansion. Most important, the new grammatical devices are independent of a speaker's first language or other individual language-learning strategies. Thus a stable Pidgin acquires a stable language community and social norms to which its members conform. Grammatical stability develops gradually and is achieved at different times in different parts of grammar.

As regards the linguistic forces shaping stabilization, language-independent solutions appear to be favoured. This is understandable, because the lexifier language tends to be socially or otherwise remote, and the very fact that stabilization occurs in a highly heterogeneous linguistic environment prevents the adoption of solutions characteristic of any single group of speakers. Put differently, in the absence of sufficient overlap and agreement among the speakers of the various jargons in such a situation, universally motivated solutions need to be adopted. The two facts, that there is a qualitative difference between an earlier and a later stage in the development of a language, and that there is a prevalence of universals in the later stage, would seem to be sufficient reason for studying this process in great detail. In reality, very little has been done, and some Pidginists /Creolists have not regarded the distinction between jargon and stable Pidgin as one deserving great attention: the two stages are often lumped together and compared jointly with Creoles, which develop at a later stage.

The phonological component

Of all parts of grammar, those of pronunciation and phonology remain the least stable in stabilized Pidgins. The different processes of restructuring the superstratum and substratum systems are carried out only to the extent that communication is not impaired. As long as there is sufficient structural and contextual redundancy, pronunciation and phonological rules can differ quite significantly from group to group and speaker to speaker. Within such a general setting, I have tried to isolate those properties that are most salient in stabilized Pidgins. They include the small inventory of sounds, the effect of phonological distinctions in substratum languages, tonal distinctions, phonotactics, derivational shallowness and tempo.

Small inventory of sounds.[9]   The small size of the sound inventory of Pidgins, particularly when compared to their lexifier and substratum languages, is caused by the elimination of many marked sounds and also by the reduction in the number of phonological contrasts. The former process typically involves the grouping together of a number of marked sounds in the lexifier language under a single sound in the Pidgin. For instance, in the Pidgin Zulu (Fanakalo) used between Zulus and speakers of non-Bantu languages, the three Zulu clicks are usually replaced by [k]. In the various Pidgin Germans I have studied, there is a very strong tendency to replace both [ç] and [x] by [k], and in Pidgin French, the abnatural rounded front vowels are generally replaced by their unmarked, more natural unrounded counterparts.

Typical of the relationship between English and various PEs is the realization of [s], [ʃ] and [tʃ] as [s], as in Tok Pisin **san** 'sun', **sem** 'shame' and **sok** 'chalk', or the replacement of [ð] and [θ] by [d] and [t] respectively, as in Cameroonian PE **den oto** 'their car' (<*them*). These observations pertain to a widely scattered set of Pidgins, many of them apparently unrelated. Thus, in a survey of African Pidgins, Heine (1975:3) observed:

1. The number of vowels tends to be reduced to five. None of these pidgins, however, has less than five vowel phonemes.
2. Distinctive vowel length tends to be lost.
3. Palato-alveolar fricatives tend to be replaced by alveolar fricatives.
4. Voiced fricatives tend to be replaced by voiceless fricatives.

This general picture is also confirmed by data from indigenous Pidgins spoken in the Pacific. Chinook Jargon, however, appears to provide counter-evidence against the claim that Pidgins exhibit maximally unmarked phonologies (see Thomason 1981:305). Different groups of speakers appear to have proceeded different distances along the path of "naturalization", and variability persists even after many years of use.

Effect of phonological distinctions in substratum languages. The analysis of the phonologies of stabilized Pidgins soon disperses the notion that they are simply the lowest common denominator of the phonologies of the languages in contact, judging from the small body of comparative work available (in particular, a study of Tolai and Tok Pisin by Mosel 1980). During the very

---

9   This heading relates to both the actual sound segments (phones) and form-distinguishing sounds (phonemes). Because of the lack of derivational depth in the phonological component of Pidgins, the relationship between phones and phonemes comes close to that postulated within structuralist phoneme theory. I do not accept the "phoneme" as a theoretical construct, however.

139

first years of Tolai involvement with Tok Pisin, substratum influence was found. Commenting on the Blanche Bay Tolai, Schnee remarks:

> One and the same Pidgin-English word is pronounced quite differently by natives from different regions, depending on whether the consonants of a word are found in the kanaka language in question or not. In the dialects spoken in the Blanche Bay (near Herbertshöhe) the consonants **c, f, h, s, z** as well as the English **th** are missing. Since, in addition, most of the natives find it difficult to pronounce consonants in sequence, many words are mutilated to a degree that they become unintelligible (1904:304; my translation).

A few years later, however, social norms for pronunciation had developed in Tok Pisin that overruled substratum influence.

Mosel mentions that "the phoneme /s/ which is absent in Tolai, has been introduced as a separate phoneme in the Tolais' Pidgin. Secondly, Tok Pisin exhibits the distinction between lax and tense vowels which is absent in Patpatar Tolai languages" (1980:24).

The fact that both production and perception of Tok Pisin sounds cannot be explained just in terms of substratum influence is also borne out by Bee's (1972) investigation of the Tok Pisin spoken by native speakers of Usarufa.

Tonal distinctions. Surveying African Pidgins and Creoles, Berry writes:

> Peculiar to the African pidgins would appear to be the simplification of tonal systems. The extreme of simplification in this respect (which only occurs perhaps when large numbers of non-Africans have had a significant role in the formation of the pidgins) is the replacement of tone systems by one of stress (1971:527).

Implicit in the above quotation is the view that tone will survive whenever the majority of users are speakers of a tone language. Thus Manessy (1977:133f) mentions that in Sango the three punctual tones of Ngbandi-Sango-Nyakoma have been preserved, since this language is used virtually exclusively by speakers of tone languages. Confirmatory evidence for this principle comes also from Vietnamese Pidgin French (Liem 1979), where five tones are encountered.[10] Liem does not mention whether or not native speakers of French have also adopted these conventions. Presumably, they emerge only among speakers of different local languages. The situation is probably comparable to Chinese PE where, among native speakers of European languages, no tonal distinctions were made.

Phonotactics. There appears to be a strong tendency in most stable Pidgins, whatever their sub- and superstrata languages and whatever their jargon predecessors, to favour open syllables and words of the canonical shape CVCV. Double obstruent clusters, in particular, are rarely encountered. The two morpheme structure rules postulated by Johnson (for English Proto-Creole) may well be "universals of pidginization" (1974:128).

---

10 This is also one of the few instances where a common denominator view makes the correct predictions.

There is a second tendency, independently observed by a number of researchers, that of having a bisyllabic word structure:

> African-based pidgins tend to have a syllable-per-word ratio of around 2.00. Fanagalo, for example, has been found to have a ratio of 2.01 whereas Zulu, its source language, has 3.09. Kenya Pidgin Swahili has a ratio of 2.32 as opposed to 3.01 of Standard Swahili. In the texts examined, 53.0 per cent of the Fanagalo words and 53.6 per cent of the Kenya Pidgin Swahili words are bisyllabic whereas the percentages of bisyllabic words in Zulu and Standard Swahili are 27.7 and 30.4, respectively. (Heine 1975:4-5)

I have made similar observations for Tok Pisin (Mühlhäusler 1979). The restriction on word length is one of the main reasons why word-formation processes such as compounding and derivation are relatively rare in early stabilized Pidgins.

Derivational shallowness. Although stable Pidgins exhibit a great deal of free variation in their pronunciation, conditioned variation and phonological rules are rare. We can explain this by referring to the two principal causes for phonological rules in language:

1. They reflect language change and diversification over time;
2. They reflect strategies for the optimalization of production (sometimes referred to as "natural" phonological processes).

Because of the relatively shallow time depth, time-related linguistic changes (such as emerge in transmission from one generation to another) do not play a major role. Their role is further diminished by speakers strongly favouring strategies optimalizing perception, aiming at the invariance of linguistic forms and a one-to-one relationship between meaning and form.

> In fact, it seems a useful working hypothesis, doubtless overstated, that phonology in pidgin languages consists only in a set of systematic phonemes which provide underlying representations that are the same as their surface representations. There are no phonological rules that accomplish deep alternations such as those in *good, better, best*, or the less deep alternations such as those between the first vowels in *nation*, *national*; that is, there are no such alternations to be accounted for. (Kay & Sankoff 1974:62)

One should remember, however, that Pidgin speakers have the ability to communicate across varieties, which probably involves some structured phonological rules.[11] In sum, then, the phonological systems of Pidgins exhibit strong tendencies towards simplification and increase in naturalness, the principle of one form, one meaning being dominant. Ease of decoding is also promoted by one last factor to be mentioned here, the tempo at which Pidgin discourse proceeds.

---

[11] As well as such rules there will be guesswork, dependence on contextual factors and, in many cases, misunderstandings. For a detailed discussion of cross-lectal communication, see Trudgill (1983:8-30).

Tempo. Related to the absence of phonological rules is the matter of tempo. An interesting case study involving the comparison of a vernacular (Buang) and a Pidgin (Tok Pisin) is that by Labov. Using Sankoff's field data, he established some significant differences between fluent Buang and fluent Tok Pisin. In the following text involving language shift, the seven Tok Pisin lexical words took as long to articulate as the preceding eleven Buang phonological ones:

> Am uukwàmin vo ken, alòk, kek ukwang in vo gángk ungwe:
> yú yét sìndáun, bái yu páinim sìk.
> 'You think about it, but now I've thought of something else:
> you're the only one sitting down, you will take sick' (1990:15).

At present, comparative material on this point is not available, but one can expect to find that Pidgins are generally articulated at a slower rate of delivery than vernaculars.

Generally speaking, it would seem that the more basic a Pidgin, the more important is its decodability and the more likely its speakers will resort to strategies that allow for the maximum amount of naturalness of encoding, without affecting the more important need for ease of decoding. Wherever there is conflict between the former and the latter, considerations of decodability will carry the day.

Loss of inflectional morphology

The claim of universality of this phenomenon (Goodman 1971:253) is supported by evidence from many, often unrelated, Pidgins. A few quotations will illustrate how widespread the phenomenon is:

> That inflection is the commonest casualty in the contact situation seems true of both European and African pidgins. The massive reduction of the Bantu nominal prefix system in Fanagalo and other indigenous African pidgins parallels the less striking losses of gender, case and number distinctions in European pidgins. (Berry 1971:527)

Berry also writes that "Pidgin Sango can best be described as a dialect of vernacular Sango, simplified by the loss of most of its morphology" (p 521). Reinecke, on Vietnamese Pidgin French, states that "Except for a few isolated forms standard French inflection has been dropped and has not been replaced by new formations as in many creole dialects" (1971:51). Further examples, as well as some critical remarks on this phenomenon, are given by Samarin (1971:125ff).

The loss of inflectional morphology can be accounted for by two factors. First and foremost is the principle of ease of decoding, or one form = one meaning. Inflectional complexities such as are found in the lexifier languages of many Pidgins would make them virtually unlearnable in the situational context they are acquired. Some simplifications of inflections may have been present in the model given to Pidgin-speakers; one consistent property of foreigner talk registers is the reduction of inflectional variants.[12] A second

---

[12] Some writers, for instance Coates (1969) in his discussion of German-Italian, have appealed to contrastive factors as a further source of interference. Recent work in the area of interlanguage appears to rule out such an explanation, however.

factor is the relatively low level of grammaticalization in early stabilized Pidgins. In particular, grammatical categories peripheral to a message tend to disappear: tense, number and aspect are typical victims. Where these categories are expressed, this is usually done by separate free forms rather than affixes.

The principal functions of inflectional morphology across languages are:

1. to signal relationships between words in utterances;
2. to add "accidental" information such as tense, case, number, etc. to words;
3. to signal word-class membership.

Are such functions necessary in a Pidgin? As regards the first function, word-order conventions typically take order from morphological signalling. Additional morphological encoding thus would increase the linguistic complexity of a Pidgin, reducing its learnability.

A second reason for the absence of morphological signalling of grammatical relationships is that Pidgins are only weakly grammaticalized in their early stages of development. Instead, syntactic relationships are derived from pragmatics. As fixed grammatical relations are rare, one cannot expect a significant degree of morphological encoding of such relations.

As regards the second function, in Pidgins the traditional grammatical categories (accidents) are typically signalled by free forms such as paragraph or sentence-initial adverbials for tense and aspect. Affixes thus would merely express redundantly what is already expressed by means of free adverbials and again increase complexity.

With regard to the third function, most observers seem to agree that there is little fixity of word classes and, in view of the ease with which words can be functionally shifted from one environment to another, overt marking of grammatical (rather than pragmatic) class membership does not appear to increase the communicative efficiency of the language. There are, however, some exceptions to this general principle. Nouns that can be agents are considered less susceptible to categorial shift. They are also much more likely to become morphologically signalled, as can be seen from the presence of special affix-like agent classifiers in a number of Pidgins, for example, **tauna** 'person' in Hiri Motu or reflexes of 'man' or 'fellow' in various PEs. In Australian and Pacific jargon English, the use of *fellow* was found variably in a number of positions in surface structure of sentences, such as following nouns, preceding nouns and following adjectives.

Because of its central role in understanding grammaticalization of Pidgins, a number of detailed studies of *-fellow* were made in recent years (e.g. Baker 1996a, 1996b and Mühlhäusler 1996d) and its diffusion has been documented on a map in Wurm et al. (1996). Whilst there remain a number of puzzles, the analysis of a very large body of representative data from around the Pacific demonstrates:

(a) that some previously held views, such as Keesing's (1988) claim that the uses of *fellow* could be traced back to the grammar of Melanesian languages, are inaccurate. Keesing ignores the fact that most uses of *fellow* were documented in Australian PE some considerable time before Melanesians adopted the language.

143

(b) that the development of grammatical regularities governing the use of *fellow* was gradual and relatively slow. Simplicity appears to be a late development in the history of Pidgins.

(c) that the diffusion of *fellow* resembles lexical diffusion much more than the spread of large chunks of grammar; new uses for *fellow* are continually (re)created in different parts of the Pacific.

(d) that in many Pidgins *fellow* competes with other affixes and zero-marking, resulting in considerable variability in Pidgins such as South Australian PE (Mühlhäusler 1996d).

(e) that sources of the different uses of *fellow* include the superstrate English (as in *you fellow(s)*, second person plural pronoun), substratum influence (as in the incipient tendency in South Australian PE to signal pronominal ergativity), overgeneralization, reanalysis, and others.

In view of such findings, abstract simplistic notions such as substratum grammar would seem problematic.

A last category which is widely signalled in Pidgins is the distinction between transitive and intransitive verbs.[13] Signalling transitive verbs by means of an affixed -m, -im or -it appears to have developed independently in a large number of English-derived Pidgins.[14] As in the case of **-pela**, fixed conventions emerge after much fluctuation in earlier stages. The distinction between transitive and intransitive verbs is also siguelled in several Romance Pidgins as well as in some "indigenous" ones. A comparative longitudinal study of this phenomenon would seem to be an urgent priority, given the interest of scholars in acquisition studies and theoretical linguistics.

To sum up, the absence of morphology can be seen as the result of promoting greater ease of decoding, simplification of the target (lexifier) language and impoverishment. It also relates to the low level of grammaticalization found in early stabilized Pidgins. Yet another factor is the wider problem of borrowing inflectional morphology; because inflections tend to be weakly stressed, they are often filtered out or ignored during borrowing.

Pidgins, as we have seen, can develop inflectional morphology again. It appears that the marking of grammatical word classes is one of the first functions of emerging morphological conventions. As Pidgins develop further, many other categories can be added, as will be demonstrated below.

Syntax
The functions of inflectional morphology and syntax (word order) are seen by many linguists to be complementary: what is expressed by word order in one language may be expressed by inflections in the next. This view has led many Pidginists to the belief that the scarcity of inflectional morphology in Pidgins is compensated by firm-word order conventions and other syntactic devices.

---

13   Some interesting parallels with first-language acquisition can be observed here. For details, see Clahsen (1984).

14   Ms M Vincent (p c, 1984) of the University of Hamburg has pointed out to me that the encoding of transitivity is also common in her data on West African *Petit-Nègre* (Pidgin French), as in *je l'allume le feu* 'I light the fire'.

In real spoken Pidgins, the alleged fixity of word order is much less in evidence, and the loss of information resulting from word-order fluctuations is made up by pragmatic and textual information. Nevertheless, when compared with their source languages, Pidgins tend to have a considerably reduced number of basic utterance structures. Let us now consider some of the syntactic properties that have figured prominently in recent discussion of Pidgin universals.

SVO word order. Linguists tend to distinguish between sequence of surface elements and order at deeper levels of syntactic patterning. In most languages, transformational processes of deletion, addition and permutation are seen as accounting for the difference between sequence and order. In Pidgins, where transformations are rare, a much more direct link between the two levels is occasionally postulated and the most basic word order is identified as SVO. It is certainly remarkable how widespread this SVO word order is in apparently quite unrelated Pidgins. Heine (1975:9) remarks:

> In most Bantu languages, the object pronoun precedes the verb whereas all known Bantu pidgins have the opposite order. Thus, Standard Swahili:
>
> **ni-ta-m-piga** (I-Future-him-hit) 'I shall hit him' becomes in
> Kenya Pidgin Swahili: **mimi na-piga ye** (I-Aorist-hit he).

For Pidgin Fijian, Siegel (1983b:11) notes that the variable word order of standard Fijian, with its alleged preference for VSO, is reduced to a single SVO order in Pidgin Fijian. In contrast to Turkish, where the direct object precedes the verb, it is found after the verb in the pidginized Turkish described by Hinnenkamp (1984:158-59). A clear predilection for SVO order is also observed in all PEs I have had the opportunity to study. A particularly interesting case is that of Chinook Jargon:

> When we turn to the syntax we find at once a consistent feature in all the Indian sources that is hard to account for unless we assume the existence of a grammatical norm for CJ. This is the regular SVO sentential word order pattern, which, as was mentioned above, is not found as a statistically dominant word order in any Indian languages in the Northwest.
> Many of the languages, like Chinook, have SV word order as a stylistic possibility, but the dominant, basic word order in most of the languages is VSO. (Thomason 1981:333)

However, in spite of the wide distribution of SVO word order, there are a number of counter-examples in "indigenous" Pidgins and more may be discovered as these languages become better known. There seems to be a preference for OSV in Hiri Motu,[15] and Sreedhar's data on Naga Pidgin (1977) suggest an SOV basic word order. There is need for more empirical research, especially using larger samples of naturally occurring speech. My own suspicion, based on the observation of a large body of data on Pacific PEs, is that the notion of fixed word order would be weakened by such research. Nevertheless, the apparent tendency towards SVO word order certainly deserves closer investigation.

---

15 Some very early texts of Hiri Motu contain examples of SVO word order, however.

Invariant word order for questions, commands and statements. The relationship between word order, on the one hand, and questions, commands and statements, on the other, is by no means a straightforward one, even in languages such as English, where interrogative order is typically paired with questions, declarative order with statements, etc. (see Schegloff 1978). In fact, as can be seen from child language studies and conversational analysis, the job of asking questions is, on the whole, quite separate from that of producing interrogative patterns. It is therefore not surprising that in Pidgins the "luxury" of different word orders is seldom found.[16] Compare the following utterances in Tok Pisin and Hiri Motu:

Tok Pisin (SVO)	Hiri Motu (OSV)	Gloss
yu klinim pis	gwarume oi huria	'you are cleaning the fish'
yu klinim pis[17]	gwarume oi huria[17]	'are you cleaning the fish?'
yu klinim pis	gwarume oi huria	'clean the fish!'

Similar findings pertain to all the Pidgins I have investigated to date.

Grammatical categories (qualifiers of propositions). The need to express possibilities, contingencies and similar ideas is met by qualifiers. Kay & Sankoff's statement that in a Pidgin such "propositional qualifiers will appear in surface structure exterior to the propositions they qualify, or not at all" (1974:64) is confirmed by the data available for a sizeable number of stable Pidgins. Not all sentence qualifiers are equally likely to appear at the periphery, however. Thus, only very few Pidgins exhibit sentence-external negators, one such being South-East Australian Aboriginal PE as spoken in the early days of contact (between 1788 and 1850). Examples of the use of the negator *bail* include:

> *Bail Saturday tumble down white fellow, bail Jingulo tumble down white fellow, bail me tumble down white man fellow.*
> 'It wasn't Saturday who killed the white man, nor Jingulo nor I myself'
> (*Sydney Gazette*, 2 January 1828; adapted from Dixon 1980:70)

In many other Pidgins, the negator usually comes before the verb phrase, as in the following PEs:

Chinese PE:	man no can stop	'the man cannot stop'
Bislama:	oli no save mekem	'they do not do it'
Cameroons PE:	dem no bi lak dat	'they're not like that'
Nigerian PE:	im no de sing	'she does not sing'

A grammatical category that typically occurs sentence-externally is that of tense/time. In fact, some linguists have argued that the grammatical category of tense is lost, and that its semantic notions are best described as being expressed lexically by means of adverbials, which typically occur at the beginning or end of sentences or texts. Examples illustrating this point

---

[16] This can also be seen as relating to the nature of linguistic input. Although word order in foreigner talk tends to be more restricted than in full languages, there is no clear correspondence between different word orders and different main sentence types.
[17] Usually with rising intonation.

include some from the south-west Pacific. Thus, in Pidgin Fijian, "time relationships are indicated either by context or by... temporal adverbs which come either sentence initially or before the VP marker **sa**" (Siegel 1983b:7). In Samoan Plantation PE, in contrast to its successor Tok Pisin, the signalling of tense and time is fairly undeveloped (Mühlhäusler 1978b:67ff). In many instances, the lack of linguistic information must be made up by reference to contextual factors. Most typically, however, tense and aspect can be expressed optionally by means of adverbs or aspect markers. Adverbs used for this purpose are generally found at the beginning of a paragraph and not repeated with every instance of the verb.

> Mi stap long Fiji wan faiv yia PIPO. Mi go long ples mekim suga bilong as. Plenti Indian fella wokim de. Plenti Yuropin i wokim long suga... 'I was in Fiji five years ago. I went to this place to cut sugar for us. Many Indians were working there. Many Europeans were employed in the sugar industry'

The best-known example of tense encoding in a Pidgin is the use of **baimbai** in Tok Pisin. The dramatic changes occurring in this part of grammar during expansion of Tok Pisin will be discussed below.

Lack of number distinction in nouns. There is a widespread absence of number distinctions in nouns in the majority of Pidgins surveyed. However, in some of them optional number distinctions (mainly between singular and plural) can be expressed by quantifiers or numerals, and there is also a strong tendency for nouns referring to animates and humans to be marked for number in a redundant fashion. Let us consider how number is expressed in selected Pidgins.

According to Heine, in Kenyan Pidgin Swahili: "In those cases where the number distinction singular/plural is retained with human (or animate) concepts but not with non-human (or inanimate) concepts [sic]. This holds for both nominal as well as pronominal expression of number" (1975:8). In Chinese PE, no formal means of indicating noun plurals other than optional use of quantifiers is found. In the Lingua Franca, according to Schuchardt, the "substantive has one form for the singular and plural" (1979:28-29). Finally, Manessy states for Pidgin Hausa:

> In vernacular Hausa, the formation of the plural of nouns is a very complex process involving a dozen suffixes and diverse modifications of the noun stem: partial or total reduplication, vowel alternations; furthermore, several plural forms may correspond to the same singular form. In the vehicular variety the plural is obtained by the adjunction of **dryawa** 'much' to the singular form (1977:130).

Pronoun systems. The pronoun systems of stabilized Pidgins in all likelihood illustrate the minimal requirements for pronoun systems in human language. When contrasted with the preceding jargon stage, they further illustrate the crystallization of an ordered part of grammar out of chaos. With regard to the English jargons of the Pacific, for instance, the following observations characterize their early beginnings:

1　Many utterances appear without any overt pronoun, where such a pronoun would be expected in standard English. An 1840 example is:

Now got plenty money; no good work
'now I have lots of money so I do not need to work'.

2.　Proper nouns or nouns are used instead of pronouns:

Kanaka work plenty 'we shall work hard'.

3.　There is considerable variation in the forms standing for the same concept. Thus 'I' appears as *me, my* and *I*; 'we' as *us, we, me, my* and *I*, and so on.

4.　No consistent norms are found for distinguishing between singular and plural pronouns.

Stabilization involved different solutions in different Pidgins. The system of Samoan Plantation PE has eliminated most of the fluctuations found in its Pacific predecessors, with the exception of variation in third person singular. The difference between subject and object forms in the plural, but not the singular is an interesting violation of a universal principle that marked categories make fewer distinctions than unmarked ones. However, such abnatural solutions appear to be tolerated in several Pidgins (Koefoed 1975), and this is not the place to discuss their implications for linguistic theory.

The Samoan system is also interesting in that we can observe a solution for marking plural pronouns which was not borrowed from either its substratum or superstratum language: the use of the quantifier **ol** (< *all*) as plural marker in pronouns. The stabilized pronoun system is as follows.

	Subject forms	
Person	*Singular*	*Plural*
First	mi	mi ol
Second	yu	yu ol
Third	em, him, hi	emol, himol

	Object forms	
Person	*Singular*	*Plural*
First	(bilong) mi	(bilong) as
Second	(bilong) yu	(bilong) yu ol
Third	(bilong) em (him)	(bilong) dem

In addition to these forms, a number of fossilized forms of English pronouns are found in expressions such as **aiting** 'it seems to me' (< *I think*), **aidono** 'I don't know', **yes aidu** 'yes', and **maiwot** 'my word!' Such forms indicate that the Melanesian plantation workers were exposed to some kind of standard English during the formative period of this language.

In Tok Pisin, where pressure from standard English was subsequently greatly reduced, the distinction between subject and object forms of pronouns was abandoned. At the same time, the plural marker **-ol** was restricted to the third person, and the form **-pela** (< *fellow*) was adopted as a plural marker instead. Again, this possibility was already inherent in the highly variable jargons preceding Samoan Plantation PE and Tok Pisin. The resulting system in early Tok Pisin thus looked like this:

Person	Singular	Plural
First	mi	mi-pela
Second	yu	yu-pela
Third	em	em ol

Stabilization once more is manifested as the restriction of variability[18] and approximation to paradigmatic univocity.

Prepositions. There appears to be a major typological difference (discussed, for instance, by Givón 1979) between languages that make use of prepositions and others that express the same relations by means of verb chaining. In the case of "European-derived" Pidgins, a large repertoire of prepositions is found in the lexifier languages; however, very few of them get adopted in the stable Pidgins derived from them. The reason for this appears to be twofold. On the one hand, the rules governing the choice between different prepositions can be extremely complex. On the other hand, the semantic or functional load of many prepositions is negligible. Consequently, in accordance with the more general principle that in Pidgins semantically full lexemes tend to be more important than grammatical words, the number of prepositions encountered in most Pidgins is diminutive. Let me illustrate this with a few examples.

Taking the case of Pidgin German (guest-worker German), Clyne remarks: "the choice of preposition causes considerable difficulties for both bilinguals and learners of German as a second language ... Those few guestworkers who used prepositions at all, tended to select the wrong ones" (1968:136ff). The lack of prepositions is also in evidence in the pidginized varieties of German spoken on Ali Island in New Guinea (examples from Mühlhäusler 1977a):

Früher ich war Alexishafen.	'Earlier, I worked *in* Alexishafen'
Wir muss gehen unsere Boot.	'We must go *to* our boat'

Hollyman (1976) provides examples from New Caledonian Pidgin French:

la nuit, moi porter kai-kai	'At night, I shall bring food'
lui a'iver son village	'He arrived at his village'

Likewise, in Vietnamese Pidgin French (Liem 1979):

battre lui moi	'beat him for me'
monsieur couper couteau	'he uses the knife to cut'
madame aller autobus	'she went by bus'
monsieur aller Nha-Trang	'he went to Nha-Trang'

The principal stable Pidgins of the Pacific are characterized by a one- or two-preposition system of grammatical relations, although some of them acquired additional marginal prepositions by means of borrowing. In the one-preposition systems, *long* (<English *along*) is the most common form; in the two-preposition systems, a reflex of *belong* meaning 'for, possessive or purpose' is added. The choice of *belong* is of particular interest, since it is not

---

[18] This expression, coined by Hjelmslev, is used frequently by Pidginists and Creolists to refer to a constant relationship between a unit at the content level and one at the expression level.

149

a preposition, but a verb in English. As pointed out by Clark (1979:16), Chinese and South Seas PE reanalysed English sentences containing *belong* in quite different ways. The data discussed in Wurm, Mühlhäusler & Tryon (eds) confirm that in general *belong* is added to PEs which earlier had but a single preposition, *long*.

So far we have considered the more superficial aspects of prepositions in stabilized Pidgins. There are a number of important principles involved here, some of which have been discussed by Traugott (1976). Most noticeable is that the splitting up of the semantic space covered by prepositions proceeds in an unitary fashion in both first-language and Pidgin development. It is hoped that Traugott's important hypothesis is examined with further longitudinal data from Pidgin development in order to establish the universality or otherwise of this phenomenon.

Lack of derivational depth. The distance between surface and deep structures is defined by a number of grammatical operations. For single (simple) sentences these include: rearrangement, deletion, addition and agreement. In the Pidgins surveyed, such operations are either absent or only minimally present. Thus the same word order is used for statements, questions and commands; the second person singular is not deleted (as in many lexifier languages) in the imperative forms (typical PE for *go!* is 'you go'); special grammatical additions such as dummy verbs are not added; and inflectional morphology promoting grammatical agreement is absent. Rules of grammar tend to be few, and those that are found are context-independent rather than context-sensitive. Lack of derivational depth is also seen from a second property, the scarcity of complex sentences in Pidgins. Again, in most Pidgins surveyed, the only complex sentences permitted are those that do not impinge on the direct mapability of deep structures onto surface structures, that is, conjoining. Embedding, on the other hand, is extremely rare and, in most Pidgins, emerges only during the later stages of grammatical expansion. This is true of Pidgins with no apparent historical links.

Consider the Elema and Koriki trade languages. Dutton (1983b:90-91) observes: "Complex ideas are expressed in both [Elema] and [Koriki] by juxtaposing simple sentences or by introducing the second sentence with the word for 'okay' in each language".

The absence of embedding in pidginized varieties of Swahili is commented upon by Scotton as follows:

> What is actually missing are the relative constructions and other forms of subordination which mark complex sentences in the Standard dialect. The result is an 'abbreviated' syntax consisting mainly of content words, with the listener left to make the connections (1969:101).

The data from Papuan PE are typical for the range of functions covered by simple juxtaposition in early stabilized Pidgins. They include the following (data from Mühlhäusler 1978a):

1. Simple conjoining of sentences or parts of sentences, with the actions occurring in the following sequence:

   He take knife, he go fight Otapeg, another boy, run up, he throw knife away.
   or: *you watch, me fellow go bush, I leave you inside house.*

2. Concatenation can also express the conditional conveyed in English by 'if', for example:

   patrol no longwe, very good, patrol longwe tumas, no very good
   'if the patrol is not far away that's good, if the patrol is far away that's bad'

3. Temporal relationship ('when') between two statements can be conveyed as follows:

   (mi)sik, mi sindaun   'when I was sick I stayed at home'

4. Concatenation can also express a causative relationship, as in:

   Kiwai man no kill him two boy belong you, I big man.

5 Relativization:

   one fellow name Mat he go burn down my house
   people stop along Sydney go look see picture
   that pigeon he been sing out my name, I plant him.

It will be demonstrated later how such conjoined constructions can be reinterpreted and become the point of departure for embedding in more fully developed Pidgins.

The form taken by WH-*question words.* In most lexifier languages of Pidgins, the forms corresponding to English *who?*, *where?*, *when?*, etc. are expressed by single words. However, in Pidgins across the world, analytic expressions are favoured. Consider the small sample in the table below.

The form taken by WH-question word in various Pidgins

Language	Form	Gloss	English
Kenyan Pidgin	**saa gani**	hour which?	'when?'
Swahili	**siku gani**	day which?	'when?'
	titu gani	thing which?	'what?'
	namna gani	kind which?	'how?'
	sababu gani	reason which?	'why?'
Fanakalo	**ipi-skati**	where-time?	'when?'
	yini-ndaba	what-matter?	'why?'
Samoan	**wat man**	what man?	'who?'
Plantation PE	**wat nem**	what name?	'what?'
	wat taim	what time?	'when?'
	wat ples	what place?	'where?'
			('whence?', 'whither?')
Chinese PE	**hu man**	who man?	'who?'
	hot fo	what for?	'why?'
	hot ting.	what thing?	'what?'
	hot say	what side?	'where?'
	hot fasan	what fashion?	'how?'
	hot tim	what time?	'when?'

A number of Creoles contain similar question pronouns, presumably reflecting a carry-over from a previous Pidgin stage (see Bickerton 1981:70-71). Note, however, that in at least some Pidgins (for example, the Lingua Franca) no complex question pronouns were found.

Anaphoric pronouns. A construction that is extremely widespread across Pidgins is the use of anaphoric pronouns that may eventually become generalized predicate introducers. Thomason (1981) notes that a construction involving a pleonastic pronoun is absent in most of the languages spoken by users of Chinook Jargon, but found with most speakers of the Jargon, as in:

t'alap'as	pi	lilú	łaska	məłayt	iht-iht	łaska	haws
coyote	and	wolf	they	live	one-one	they	house (p 336)

In the various English-based jargons preceding stabilization of plantation Pidgins in the Pacific, an anaphoric pronoun was variably present in most areas, although there was very considerable inter-individual and intra-individual variation. Examples from Samoa and New Caledonia, recorded by Schuchardt's informants in the 1880s, include:

boat he capsize, water he kaikai him	'the boat capsized and sank'
plenty bullamacow he stop	'there were lots of cattle'
coconut belong mi too much sore	'my head is sore'

At the time, there was an almost categorical absence of anaphoric pronouns when the subject was a pronoun, reflecting a similar restriction in English. As stabilization occurred, a number of new conventions emerged: there was a movement away from English grammar, and partial incorporation of the grammatical conventions of the substratum languages. An interesting example is afforded by the data on early Tok Pisin (some such observations have also been made in Sankoff 1977).

The movement away from English grammar is exemplified by two features: first, the generalization of *he* to referents which are female or neuter (Schuchardt still had examples such as *woman she finish thing me speak him*); and second, the fact that i (rather than *he*) very gradually begins to appear after the third-person pronoun **em** and in a very few cases after other pronouns as well.

The use of **i** in Tok Pisin appears to have been reinforced by the fact that Tolai had a similar construction.[19] As in English, Tolai used different forms of the pronoun for different kinds of subjects. However, with third-person singular subjects, the anaphoric pronoun i was used and it is this accidental encounter with English **he** which may have promoted the rapid stabilization of **i**, first as a generalized anaphoric pronoun for singular and plural subjects, and subsequently as a predicate marker.

We have surveyed nine syntactic constructions that have been identified as salient for stabilized Pidgins. In a number of cases, it was specifically noted that there was no apparent input model for such constructions and that, moreover, very much the same solutions appear to emerge wherever pidginization occurs and whatever the lexifier languages. Although we do not have full knowledge of the psychological and neurolinguistic processes underlying pidginization, it certainly seems that adults have retained the

---

[19] Keesing (n d) attempts to demonstrate that in Solomons PE this construction is due to substratum influence. In the light of the other evidence just considered, this explanation is not fully satisfactory. The question can only be settled once comparative data, similar in scope and quality to those used by Keesing, are considered.

capacity to develop consistent grammatical structures out of rather inconsistent input, a claim frequently denied by those who operate in terms of a critical threshold model of language acquisition.

Stabilization in syntax, as indeed in other components of grammar, first and foremost implies a reduction of variants. The solutions found tend to conform to the general principles of syntagmatic and paradigmatic univocity and derivational shallowness. Of the many solutions that appear consistent with such requirements, only a small subset is actually encountered, suggesting universal limitations on the possible form of Pidgins at this stage.[20]

The lexicon

Stabilization in the lexicon manifests itself in a number of ways, including the emergence of norms as to what constitutes a lexical item of the language, the crystallization of preferred norms of lexical variants, and the developments of lexical field structures. Apart from such general traits, there are a number of more specific similarities in the lexicons of stable Pidgins.

The lexicon of a stable Pidgin is further shaped by a number of constraints, including considerable pressure for one form = one meaning encoding; pressure to maximize the usefulness of a very limited lexical inventory; and the absence of processes of derivational morphology. We shall now consider these factors.

Emergence of norms. Jargon lexicons have a very small stable core and a large variable area, as any item of the lexifier language and most items of the substratum languages are potential words. This freedom of lexical choice is restricted considerably in a stable Pidgin. First, only a very small part of the lexicon of the lexifier language is selected as the basis of the derived Pidgin. Consider Fijian, where more than 80 different words for different kinds of cutting exist. Siegel observes that in Pidgin Fijian "there are only two words for cutting: **ta** and **musu**" (1983b:12). This one-to-many relationship between a single lexical item in the Pidgin and several synonyms and near-synonyms in the lexifier language is equally characteristic of other Pidgins. Compare:

Pidgin German of New Guinea	Standard German
kaput	*zerrissen, zerbrochen, zeplatzt, zerschlenzt, zerfetzt, schadhaft, durchlöchert,* etc. 'broken'

Trade Spanish of the Piñaguero Panare	Standard Spanish
matándo 'to kill, die'	*matar* 'to kill'
parándo 'to stop, stay, live at, bed with'	*parar* 'to stop, stay'
kitándo 'to remove, discard, abduct'	*kitar* 'to remove' (Riley 1952)

Not only is the number of actual Pidgin items highly restricted, but there are also conventions as to the lexical information found with each such item, namely:

1. a standard pronunciation (with some latitude in acceptable variants);

---

[20] It is suggested that the notion "possible grammar" is a variable one, depending on the developmental stage a first or second language has reached.

2. a standard range of meanings;
3. conventions regarding the grammatical status of a word;
4. conventions as to its social acceptability.

The lexical information that is acceptable in a Pidgin can be very different from that associated with its cognate in a lexifier or substratum language. Let us consider examples for each of the above categories. First, we will consider conventions for pronunciation:

Language	Lexical item	Source	Gloss
Tok Pisin	**kisim**	English *catch* + im	'to catch, obtain'
Tok Pisin	**bruk**	English *broke, broken*	'to break, broken'
Tok Pisin	**umben**	Tolai [ubene]	'net'
Fanakalo	**bulughwe**	Afrikaans [brøx]	'bridge'
Fanakalo	**sikwelet**	Afrikaans [skølt]	'debt'
Fanakalo	**tshisha**	Zulu [isa]	'to burn'

Somewhat special are cases where two words of the lexifier language have become one in the related Pidgin. Examples are reported from a wide range of languages. In Pidgin Fijian, for instance, inalienable nouns are typically borrowed from Fijian, together with the third-person singular possessive pronoun affix -na, as in the examples given by Siegel (1983b:13):

tamana 'father'   **tinana** 'mother'   **ligana** 'hand'

The agglutination of French articles has received the attention of a number of scholars (e g, Bollée 1980, Baker 1984), mainly because the various French Creoles exhibit very different degrees of agglutination. Such variation, it has been argued, can provide important clues to the history and development of the French Creoles. The following table is adapted from Baker (1984:90).

Number of nouns having an initial syllable wholly derived from a French article attested in Haitian and three Indian Ocean Creoles

French articles	Creole forms	Number of agglutinated forms attested in the Creoles of:			
		Haiti	Mauritius	Reunion	Seychelles
du	*di-*)				
de l'	*dil-/del-*)	4	34	8	29
des	*diz-/dez-*)				
le	*li-/le-/*				
les	*le-/lez-/liz-*	10	62	1	45
la	*la-*	98	375	3	370
	Total	112	471	12	444

Baker has identified the presence of speakers of noun-classifying Bantu languages in Mauritius in the formative years as a likely cause of the far more numerous cases of agglutination in Mauritian and Seychellois than in Haitian or Reunion Creole. A detailed analysis is not yet available for New Caledonian Tayo where similar cases of agglutination are found but those listed by Ehrhart (1993) include:

dife 'fire' (< *du feu*)   **dolo** 'water' (< *de l'eau*)
lafore 'forest' (< *la forêt*)   **lakrwa** 'cross' (< *la croix*)

The same phenomenon is observed in Vanuatu English-derived Bislama, which borrowed extensively from French during the years of the French-

English condominium. Examples include **lafet** 'feast'(<French *la fête*) and **lasup** 'soup' (<French *la soupe*).

That word and morpheme boundaries of the lexifier language are often ignored in the derived Pidgin is finally illustrated by a sample from Tok Pisin:

Tok Pisin	From English	Gloss
baimbai	*by and by*	'soon'
nambis	*on the beach*	'beach'
tudir	*too dear*	'expensive'
sekan	*shake hands*	'to make peace'
trausel	*tortoise shell*	'tortoise'

Second, whereas in the jargon phase conventions for the meaning of lexical items were often lacking and miscommunication was rife as a result, there is far more agreement about meaning in a stable Pidgin, particularly in the core areas of the lexicon. These meanings can differ considerably from those of the lexifier language, as is illustrated in the following examples:

Language etyma	Item	Meaning in Pidgin	English
Samoan PPE	**holimpas**	'to rape, hold tightly'	*hold fast*
	pisup	'tinned food, bully beef'	*pea soup*
Cameroons PE	**kontri**	'home area, maternal village'	*country*
	stik	'tree, stick, guava'	*stick*
Fanakalo	**stronmani**	'circus'	*strong man*

Words from substratum languages can equally be changed, as can be seen with the following Tolai loan-words in Tok Pisin:

Tolai		TokPisin	
mao	'ripe banana'	**mau**	'ripe, mature'
tubuan	'old woman, mask of old woman'	**tubuan**	'wooden mask, carving'
ubene	'fishing net'	**umben**	'net (in general)'
virua	'victim, human flesh'	**birua**	'enemy, warrior'
kabag	'white lime'	**kambang**	'lime'
pagagar	'to be open'	**pangangar**	'to be in position for copulation (of female)'

A tendency, observed in many Pidgins, is that of more powerful words from the lexifier language to acquire an attenuated meaning in the corresponding Pidgin. Typical of this is the widespread use of *too much* in the meaning of 'much', or the choice in Lingua Franca of *cunciar* 'to tackle, perpetrate' instead of *fasir* 'to do' to convey the latter. Another example comes from Chinese Pidgin Russian of Kjachta, where the word for 'to hit, beat' is derived from Russian *pokolotit* 'to give a sound beating', rather than *bit* 'to beat'.

Third, the grammatical class membership of words of the lexifier language is often changed in the Pidgin. Examples of this phenomenon include Beach-la-Mar **hariap** 'quickly' and **tasol** 'but' (< *that's all*); the use of the Elema adjective **eka** 'bad, poor' to mean 'sickness' or 'to be unhappy' in the Elema Trade Language; and the use of the English noun *heap* as a quantifier 'many, plenty' in American Indian PE.

Finally, as regards the social appropriateness of words, considerable differences may exist between a Pidgin and its lexifier language. Many words that are rude in the latter are perfectly acceptable in the former. Consider the following examples from Tok Pisin:

Tok Pisin	From English	Meaning in Tok Pisin
bagarap	*buggered up*	'tired, ruined'
sit	*shit*	'leftovers, faeces'
kan	*cunt*	'female genitals'
as	*arse*	'seat, buttocks, origin, cause'

In these and other instances, the norms of Pidgin lexicons differ from those of the lexifier language, thus demonstrating their linguistic independence.

Lexical field structures. So far we have described the lexicon as a socially sanctioned list of irregularities, and for most Pidgins this list-like nature is indeed a dominant characteristic. However, there are signs in some areas of the lexicon of some tighter field-like organization of lexical material, particularly in domains that are dominant for the users of a Pidgin. Such lexical fields are typically neither a calque from substratum languages nor directly borrowed from the lexifier language, but an amalgam developed out of the special communicative needs of Pidgin-speakers. Unfortunately, little research has been carried out on this topic, and I must draw on my own studies of Tok Pisin.

An example of such a developing semantic field is that of enumeration. Many number systems are found in the geographic area of Papua New Guinea, and decimal systems are widespread in the Melanesian languages spoken in the area where Tok Pisin stabilized. This facilitated the adoption of the English system of counting, though not without certain changes:

> The system of enumeration in pidgin is a clear example of linguistic syncretism under the impact of culture contact. And we may also observe herein significant cultural adjustments by the natives toward European institutions of economics and finance. The cardinal numbers from one to ten are patently of English derivation: won, tu, tri, for, faif, sikis, sefen, et, nain, and ten; but with numbers above ten, the native pattern of grouping numbers more frequently occurs. Thus eleven is wonfela ten won, twelve wonfela ten tu, and so on to twenty, which is tufela ten.   (Reed 1943:282)

A second example is that of kinship terms. It appears, however, that stable conventions existed only for central kinship terms, whereas considerable latitude was - and still is - found with the more peripheral ones. Although a number of items appearing in this field have English cognates, their semantic information has been restructured:

Tok Pisin	*central meaning*	*Tok Pisin*	*central meaning*
tumbuna	'grandparent, grandchild'	**papa**	'father'
kandare	'maternal uncle or aunt'	**mama**	'mother'
brata	'sibling of the same sex'	**smolmama**	'paternal aunt'
susa	'sibling of the opposite sex'	**smolpapa**	'paternal uncle'

One form = one meaning. The requirement that there should be one form for one meaning is one that is frequently violated in the older languages. Reasons for this include the borrowing of incompatible suppletive items, pressure for stylistic flexibility, and conflict between strategies promoting optimalization of production and others optimalizing perception. The requirement that one form should express one meaning and vice versa is violated in two ways: (a) one form stands for a number of meanings (homophony); or (b) one and the same meaning is expressed by a number of forms (synonymy). Whereas the former is found frequently in stable Pidgins, synonymy or near-synonymy is rare. The reason would seem to be that some homophony is of little consequence, since disambiguation can occur by means of textual and contextual information. Thus the fact that **sip** in Tok Pisin can mean 'sheep', 'ship', 'jeep' and 'jib' is unlikely to result in any major communicative disasters. The presence of synonyms, on the other hand, constitutes a considerable cost, particularly at a stage where propositional rather than connotative dimensions of meaning are dominant.

The requirement of one form = one meaning also relates to recurrent semantic components.[21] One example of such recurrent elements is the negative in antonym pairs. There are many examples of Pidgins encoding antonyms by adding an equivalent of 'no' to the base form, including:

Tok Pisin	Gloss	From English
no kamap	'to be absent'	*come up*
no inap	'deficient'	*enough*
no hatwok	'easy'	*hard work*

Fanakalo	Gloss	Literal translation
hayi figile	'absent'	*has not come*
hayi muhle	'bad'	*not good*
hayi bona	'blind'	*not see*
hayi saba	'brave'	*not fear*

Another recurrent element is the male and female animates expressed by putting an equivalent of 'man' or 'woman' before the base noun. Examples are documented for a number of Pidgins including:

Samoan Plantation PE	Gloss	Translation
man hos	male horse	'stallion'
wumen hos	female horse	'mare'
man pik	male pig	'boar'
wuman pik	female pig	'sow'
Cameroons PE		
man fawul	man fowl	'rooster'
wuman fawul	woman fowl	'hen'
man got	man goat	'billy goat'
wuman got	woman goat	'nanny goat'
Hiri Motu		
boroma tau	pig man	'boar'
boroma hahine	pig woman	'sow'
boromakau tau	cattle man	'bull'
boromakau hahine	cattle woman	'cow'

---

21 Meisel (1983:14) refers to this as the "factorization principle". A discussion of some of the issues involved is given by Dixon (1971).

As a final example, the semantic feature (+ human) is very frequently expressed by means of an affix translating as 'man'. Although some suppletion is encountered with the most frequently used words for persons, more peripheral terrns tend to be morphologically perspicuous, usually considerably more so than in the related lexifier language. Examples include:

HiriMotu	Gloss	Translation
diba tauna	know person	'expert'
hadibaia tauna	teach person	'teacher'
hereva tauna	say person	'subject of conversation'

Tok Pisin	Gloss	Translation
kaisman	left man	'left-handed person'
kamman	come man	'new arrival'
loman	law man	'generous person'
masman	march man	'marcher'

Similar examples were found in virtually all the Pidgins I have examined.

Maximum use of a minimum lexicon. Although Pidgins are considerably less powerful in terms of their referential potential than their lexifier languages, nevertheless they have developed mechanisms to extend a highly restricted lexical inventory. This is done primarily by letting the syntactic component do some of the work of the morphological and lexical components in related lexifier languages. The principal mechanisms are the use of syntactic paraphrases and circumlocutions; use of grammatical categories such as aspect to distinguish between meanings; the use of multifunctionality, that is, the use of the same word in a multitude of grammatical functions; and the generation of verbs from nouns.

In contrast to the long-winded jargon circumlocutions, stable Pidgins often have phrase-like formulas for the description of new concepts. An interesting case is Hiri Motu, which has a formula of the type O - V - **gauna** 'a thing doing something to an object' as in:

Hiri Motu	Gloss	Translation
kuku ania gauna	smoke eat thing	'pipe'
lahi gabua gauna	fire burn thing	'match'
traka abiaisi gauna	truck raise thing	'jack'
godo abia gauna	voice take thing	'tape recorder'

The use of grammatical categories to distinguish between meanings can be illustrated by the Tok Pisin aspect markers **pinis** (completion) and **nating** (frustrative):

painim	'to search'	**painim pinis**	'to find'
rere	'to prepare'	**rere pinis**	'to be ready'
indai	'to be unconscious'	**indai pinis**	'to be dead'
bagarapim	'to damage'	**bagarapim pinis**	'to destroy'
hukim	'allure'	**hukim pinis**	'catch with a hook'

A very similar picture is found in Hiri Motu with *vadaena* 'completion':

Hiri Motu	Gloss	Translation
bada/bada vadaeni	big/big completion	'big'/'grown up'
kaukau/kaukau vadaeni	dry/dry completion	'drying'/'dry'
dika/dika vadaeni	bad/bad completion	'bad'/'rotten'
mase/mase vadaeni	die/die completion	'about to die'/'dead'

Nating can be found in a number of collocations. Its meaning is more difficult to recover and some contextual information is usually needed. Depending on the context, **pusi nating** can mean (inter alia) 'a desexed cat', 'a stray cat', 'a very weak cat' or 'a cat without a pedigree'. Other examples include:

bun nating	'very thin, skinny'
kuk nating	'to cook vegetarian food (no meat)'
sik nating	'a minor disease'

Jargons feature looseness of grammatical class membership but, because of the lack of grammatical conventions, this cannot be exploited in a systematic fashion. Once grammatical class membership can be deduced from an item's position in a sentence, however, considerable savings can be made. The widespread use of the third mechanism, multifunctionality, in Pidgins can be seen from the following quotes for a large number of diverse languages:

> It should be remembered that in [Chinook] Jargon elements are indiscriminately verbs, nouns, adjectives, or adverbs depending on their meanmg and the ability an element of a given meaning has to serve as another form of word. (Jacobs 1932:40)

> Another key process in the syntax of English-Japanese Pidgin is the use of many words in a variety of grammatical functions. This process is closely related to and probably inseparable from the semantic tendency towards abstraction. (Goodman 1967:53)

> The predicates of such simple sentences [in Hiri Motu] often consist of words which we have called bases, and which can be translated by English verbs, adjectives or nouns. (Wurm & Harris 1963:3)

The prominence of this phenomenon has been remarked on by a number of Pidginists; for example, Wurm writes: "A characteristic feature of Pidgin is the presence of many universal bases, i.e. words which can function as nouns, noun and verb adjuncts, intransitive verbs and transitive verbs ... The functional possibilities of pidgin bases are fundamental to the grammar of Pidgin" (1970:8).

Voorhoeve (1962), went so far as to calculate the actual savings derived from the multifunctional use of lexical items:[22] "there exists a certain relationship between the size of the vocabulary and the complexity of the grammar"(p 241) which is optimal in Pidgins and Creoles. "Now, if we introduce two grammatical rules into our hypothetical language, to distinguish, for example, between verbs and non-verbal words, then this means that the number of words can be reduced by a half". He goes on to claim that "compared with a model language containing X words and X rules,

---

22 Voorhoeve originally based his calculations on a Creole (Sranan), but appears to be generalizing to Pidgins. In a later article (1981), Voorhoeve revises some of his earlier views on the matter. He also considers data from a wide range of Pidgins and Creoles.

Creole languages have X/p (X divided by p) words and Y + p (Y plus p) rules. The reduction in the number of words is far greater than the increase in the number of rules"(p 242). In reality, the saving achieved is much less, particularly in stable as against expanded or creolized Pidgins. Contrary to the idea that early Pidgins are characterized by overgeneralization and optimal application of grammatical rules, such rules as shifting lexical items from one grammatical category to another are often under-utilized and restricted by constraints. When considering multifunctionality in early Tok Pisin, for instance, one is struck not only by the absence of numerous mathematically possible forms, but also by the fact that restrictions on productivity appear to have been inherited from substratum sources.

Although use of one and the same lexical item in a number of functions may constitute a considerable gain in simplicity, one of the less desirable consequences is a violation of the principle of one form = one meaning.

Finally, most Pidgins surveyed exhibit a considerable shortage of verbs. One way of obtaining new verbs is the generation of verbs from nouns. A second way, and one which involves explicit signalling of the category verb, is to employ a phrase of the type 'to make' + N. Examples of this construction are documented for a number of unrelated Pidgins, for example:

1. Pidgin German (Hinnenkamp 1984:159):

foto machen	photo make	'to take a photograph'

2. Hiri Motu:

laulau karaia	picture make	'to take a photograph'
durua karaia	assistance make	'to help'
hera karaia	decoration make	'to adorn'

3. Tok Pisin: The construction is widely found in Tok Pisin of the 1920s, but appears to have virtually disappeared by 1930. Examples include:

mekim hos	make horse	'to saddle'
mekim krismas	make Christmas	'to celebrate'
mekim pepa	make paper	'to write, sign a labour contract'
mekim man	make man	'to marry a man'

Examples for Chinook Jargon, as well as a more general discussion, are given by Silverstein (1972a:602ff).

We have now surveyed the principal internal means by which stable Pidgins expand their lexical resources. It should have become obvious that word formation at this stage is very restricted and Pidgins therefore have to rely on external borrowing for most of their lexical expansion.

Sources of lexical borrowing. Pidgins at an early stage of development are constrained in two ways: their internal word-formation mechanisms are still underdeveloped, and borrowing from outside systems is made difficult by a number of linguistic and social factors.

As regards the linguistic factors, there is an oft-expressed belief that any word of the lexifier language is also a potential word in the related Pidgin (this view was expressed, for instance, by Mafeni 1971:103). This, however, is not quite the case, because:

1. Pidgins tend to have a marked preference for bisyllabic or at least short words;
2. Pidgins have more rigid phonotactic restrictions on consonant clusters than their lexifier languages;
3. The boundary between lexicon and syntax is different in the two languages.

Thus, Pidgins have fairly tight internal structures, which make borrowing difficult. Long and morphologically complex words of English, such as *uneducated, specialization, information, select committee, citizenship, archbishop,* etc. will tend to violate these conditions for optimal word length, particularly after clusters have been split up by means of epenthetic vowels. **Sitisensip or sipesialaisesen** ('specialization') – both documented as recent loans in urban Tok Pisin – are very strange-sounding items in a Pidgin and a potential source of misunderstanding.[23] Moreover, they are unacceptable bases for further word-formation processes, such as compounding or derivation.

Without wishing to go into detail, it should be conceded that there are principled linguistic barriers to borrowing in Pidgins. Generally speaking, the less complex and/or the more regular a system, the less it is susceptible to outside influence.

Apart from such internal barriers to borrowing, there is the question of access to potential sources of new vocabulary. Stabilization (or tertiary hybridization) takes place at a time when the lexifier language is relatively withdrawn. In fact, the most clear-cut examples are those where it was almost fully withdrawn, as with Cameroons PE and Tok Pisin under a German colonial administration. At the same time, it typically occurs in the context of considerable linguistic diversity among the speakers of substratum languages, diminishing the chance of any single language becoming the obvious source of innovations. It may be for this reason that Pidgins are typically lexified from the languages of socially dominant groups.[24]

Differential social status is also reflected in a second way: typically, the core vocabulary is borrowed from a single main source, whereas more marginal (statistically less frequent, more specialized) items tend to be borrowed from substratum languages. Let me illustrate these general observations with examples.

According to Cole (1953:4ff), the lexicon of Fanakalo consists of about 70% Zulu vocabulary; the remainder is borrowed from Afrikaans or English. The core vocabulary is almost exclusively derived from Zulu.

More than 90 per cent of the lexicon of Samoan Plantation PE and virtually all its central lexical bases are derived from English. A few words are borrowed from Samoan and, in its later years, a handful of lexical items of New Guinea origin were added by plantation workers recruited from there.

Tok Pisin differs from its Samoan predecessor in two regards: first, the considerable element of local languages in non-central domains of communication, and second, the heavy reliance, in its early years, on German

---

23 There appears to be an as yet uninvestigated principle that longer words tend to invite more communication errors than bisyllabic ones.
24 An example of a Pidgin that developed in the context of social equality between European colonists and Australian Aboriginals at Port Essington is discussed by Harris (1984). Its lexical composition appears to have been an even mix between the contact languages.

as a lexifier language. Again, the lexical core of the language remains uniformly derived from English.

The vast majority of lexical items in present-day Hiri Motu are derived from Motu, with a significant borrowed element in the more marginal areas of the lexicon from English and Tok Pisin. However, there are indications of a more lexically mixed earlier stage (discussed in Dutton 1985a), signalling the close contacts between the semi-official Papuan PE and Police Motu which existed in the 1920s and 1930s.

Reinecke writes that "remarkably few Vietnamese words are used in [Vietnamese] Pidgin French. Not a single Vietnamese word appears in Swadesh's 200 word list ... Most of the Vietnamese words in Pidgin French are names of foods and plants" (1971:50).

The above data illustrate the very strong tendency of present-day Pidgins to be lexically affiliated to one main language. However, such synchronic evidence must not be taken to mean that more mixed lexical systems were not found at earlier stages of stable Pidgins.

Stabilization - a summary

Although I am fully aware that stabilization and the crystallization of stable Pidgins are dynamic processes, the data at hand make a description in dynamic terms difficult. We often find ourselves in the unenviable position of having to argue about developments from the perspective of a plateau or endpoint reached. None the less, I hope that the following general characteristics are truly salient, if not universal elements of the development of stable Pidgins:

1. The reduction of variability found in preceding jargon stages;
2. The establishment of relatively firm lexical and grammatical conventions;
3. The development of grammatical structures independent from possible source languages.

Moreover, when compared to their lexifier languages, one finds that:

4. Subsequent to their stabilization, Pidgins are unintelligible to speakers of the lexifier languages;
5. When compared, Pidgins are partially characterizable as reduced and simplified versions of their lexifier languages;
6. The reduction in form is accompanied by a reduction in function: the most immediate victim of such functional reduction is stylistic flexibility.

Stable Pidgins are thus in many ways quite restrictive systems, incapable of filling the needs of first-language communicators and inadequate even for some of the requirements of their second-language users. Although they have acquired some linguistic autonomy, their potential for internal growth remains restricted, as is borrowing from outside sources. However, in the narrow social context, in which they tend to be institutionalized, Pidgins are a highly efficient means of communication.

It has been noted over and over again that Pidgins with no shared history exhibit amazing similarities in their structural make-up. Such evidence provides necessary, but by no means sufficient support for the view that people appeal to innate linguistic universals when under pressure for communication, such as is found in a Pidgin situation. An alternative view would seek to relate Pidgins to more general pragmatic and problem-solving capacities found with human beings. In the absence of more detailed observations, particularly longitudinal studies, we shall have to postpone judgement on this matter.

The expansion stage

The notion of expanded or extended Pidgin was formally introduced by Todd, although it was implicit far earlier.

> Clearly distinguishable from this type of pidgin is what I call an 'expanded' or 'extended' pidgin. This is one which develops in a multilingual area, which proves extremely useful in inter-group communication and which, because of its usefulness, is extended and utilized outside the range of its original use... They differ from restricted pidgins in that, in them, we see the emergence of new languages with the potential to grow and spread or to disappear if their usefulness as a means of communication comes to an end (Todd 1974:4).

The underlying assumption is that adult second languages can be elaborated to the extent that they become comparable with Creoles and other vernaculars. The notion of expansion relates to increases both in the communicative functions and domains and a Pidgin's referential and non-referential power.

Since it takes place only in special external circumstances, the number of expanded Pidgins is relatively small. Clusters of expanded Pidgins are located mainly in the linguistically highly heterogeneous areas of West Africa and Melanesia. Typically, they accompany increased geographic mobility and inter-tribal contacts, generally as a result of colonial policies. The best-known expanded Pidgins are Tok Pisin and West African PE (particularly the Cameroon variety). Others include recent varieties of Hiri Motu, Bislama, Solomons PE, Sango and some varieties of Torres Straits Broken. Longitudinal studies of these languages are becoming available (e.g. Keesing (1988) for Solomons PE and Crowley (1990) for Bislama, while several maps and articles in Wurm et al. (1996) portray developments and changes in the expanded Pidgins of the Pacific area).

The importance of expanded Pidgins to linguistic research is twofold. First, they illustrate the capacity of adults to drastically restructure existing linguistic systems. Secondly, they call into question such dichotomies as first and second, primary and secondary, native and non-native language. The structural changes to be discussed in the following sections highlight not only the considerable complexity of expanded Pidgins, but also the ordered fashion in which new constructions are added to existing simpler grammars.

The phonological component

The phonology of expanded Pidgins has attracted relatively little attention, especially concerning development. However, some generalizations are still possible. Phonological expansion is manifested in the following areas:

1. A steady increase in phonological distinctions;
2. The emergence of phonological rules;
3. The increasing use of former free pronunciation variants for stylistic purposes.

I will now illustrate these points with data from Nigerian PE, Torres Strait Broken and Tok Pisin.

The increase in phonological distinctions. Stable Pidgins were characterized by a small inventory of distinctive vowels and consonants, as a rule considerably reduced in comparison with their lexifier language, and also smaller than the speaker's substratum phonological inventory. Additions to this inventory typically involve taking over distinctions from the lexifier language (and it is therefore difficult to draw a clear-cut distinction between development and restructuring at the phonological level), although substratum and adstratum languages may provide additional material.

West African PE, Torres Straits Broken and Tok Pisin all appear to have had a five-vowel system during early stabilization, in all cases:

After some time, this was replaced by seven-vowel systems; in the case of Nigerian PE (Mafeni 1971:107-08) and Tok Pisin, the inventory was:

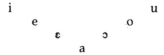

Torres Straits Broken had distinctive vowels in the central area (Dutton 1970:145). Vowel length was not distinctive in any of the three Pidgins. More recent varieties of coastal Tok Pisin have replaced the seven-vowel system by a ten-vowel system, which is being restructured by some speakers to include contrasts in vowel length. Torres Strait Broken, where contact with English appears to have been more intensive, has a twelve-vowel system, involving both quality and length contrasts, as demonstrated by Dutton (1970:145).

The consonant systems of the three Pidgins under discussion are again considerably more extensive than those found at earlier developmental stages. They still differ from their lexifier language in the exclusion of certain highly marked sounds (in particular, certain sibilants and forms of *th*). Nigerian PE has some sounds not found in English (including labiovelar [kp] and [gb], and also palatal [ɲ]). The consonants of both Tok Pisin and Torres Strait Broken at first sight appear to be a subset of the English consonant system. However, their phonotactic properties, as will be shown shortly, can differ.

When comparing earlier stages of Tok Pisin with expanded varieties, we find that, irrespective of a Tok Pisin user's native language, a number of distinctions absent from earlier Tok Pisin are now widely made. These include a distinction between [s] and [t], [p] and [f], and [l] and [r], in that order. For further details, see Wurm & Mühlhäusler (1985).

The emergence of phonological rules. Pidgins, and second languages in general, are governed by strategies for the optimalization of perception, i.e. strategies promoting the ideal of one form = one meaning and one meaning = one form. Thus rules that promote the ease of production tend to be suppressed in the early stages of development. It is only in a community of fluent second language speakers that such rules have a chance of gaining wider acceptance.

There are two types of phenomena subsumed under the label of 'phonological rules': phonotactic restrictions; and rules that delete, permutate or supplement phonological information of base forms. As regards the former, a highly limited set of possible syllable and word structures was found with stable Pidgins. Of particular interest are consonant clusters. Mafeni (1971:108) states that "'The generalised formula for Nigerian Pidgin syllable structure is: /C$_{S0-2}$VC$_{0-2}$/ and /N/ where the subscript figures indicate the possibilities in terms of number of elements, for that place of syllable structure". Speakers of more developed varieties, on the other hand, admit the following syllable structures: "Conservative speakers tend to avoid clusters altogether, however, either by dropping one member of the cluster as in **pún** - one pronunciation of the word **spún** (spoon) - or by vocalic intrusion, as in the case of **sìpik** instead of the more anglicized pronunciation **spik**" (Mafeni ibid.) Clusters with three consonants are found only with speakers of restructured anglicized varieties of the language. Very much the same observations can be made for Tok Pisin. In early forms of this language, we find a very strong preference for a CVCV word structure. Words containing three or more syllables and syllables containing consonant clusters are very rare. However, a longitudinal study of the Tok Pisin lexicon clearly shows a recent quite dramatic increase in lexical items that violate these conditions. Thus early records suggest that English *straight* became either **tiret** or **sitiret** in Tok Pisin. Records around 1930 report **steret**, whereas in most recent times **stret** is found. The role of epenthetic vowels in such forms is discussed by Pawley (1975).

In sum, it appears that development in the area of phonotactics is manifested as a gradual relaxation of the many restrictions so characteristic of earlier Pidgins. As regards other phonological processes, very little is known at present. However, it seems evident that the relaxation of phonotactic restrictions must be seen as a precondition for the existence of phonological processes that result in a phonologically more complex output. In most cases, phonological rules result in variants and thus increase the load of the decoder. As long as the majority of them are second-language speakers, the degree of phonologically conditioned variation can be expected to remain small.

Later developments in the phonology of Tok Pisin illustrate the operation of rules separating underlying from surficial forms.[25] A first example is the rule reducing vowels in unstressed syllables. Thus the adjective ending **-pela** of earlier developmental stages of the language is reduced to [pəla] or [fəla] in allegro varieties of present-day expanded Tok Pisin (cf Lynch 1979), and

---

25   C-J N Bailey coined the word *surficial* to avoid the negative connotations of 'superficial'.

the earlier future marker **baimbai** is frequently reduced to **babai, bai** or **ba** (see Sankoff & Laberge 1973).

A second example concerns voiced plosives. Whereas older varieties of Tok Pisin reflect the Melanesian practice of pronouncing the sounds [b], [d] and [g] with a strongly nasalized onset (i.e. [mb], [nd] and [ng] respectively), Tetaga (1971) demonstrates the decline of this among younger speakers. He observes that the use of prenasalization is now regarded as a marker of social backwardness and employed mainly as a stylistic device by younger speakers. This, then, takes us to a third aspect of phonological development.

The use of variants for stylistic purposes. There are two principal sources for the emergence of registers of style in a developing Pidgin: borrowing from external sources; and backsliding, that is, the use of developmentally earlier forms in special stylistic functions. A comprehensive picture of these processes is given by Wurm & Mühlhäusler (1983), and only some brief comments on the second aspect will be made here.

For instance, in addition to the above-mentioned stylistic use of prenasalized consonants in Tok Pisin, proficient younger speakers also can be observed to ignore their usual distinction between [s] and [t], [p] and [f], and [l] and [r], and to insert epenthetic vowels when speaking to less advanced speakers or when portraying a hillbilly mentality. No systematic observations on phonological backsliding in any expanded Pidgin are available at present, however.

Inflectional morphology
Although all the expanded Pidgins examined here remain fundamentally analytic languages, there are signs in at least one of them, namely Tok Pisin, that inflectional devices are beginning to make an appearance.[26] For most speakers, the transition from free morphemes to affixes has not been completed and there remains a considerable amount of variability. Let us consider some of the developments encountered.

First, the full stress-bearing **hia** 'here' of earlier Tok Pisin, in constructions such as **dispela man hia** 'this man here', has been changed to unstressed **ya**. This form has come to convey either emphasis or 'noun previously referred to in a text' (that is, it has moved in the direction of a definite article as in **man ya** 'this man, the man') (see Sankoff & Brown 1976 for more details).

Second, one of the best-documented instances of developing inflectional morphology is the transition from sentential adverb to verbal prefix in the case of the so-called future marker **bai** (discussed, for instance, in Sankoff 1979, Sankoff & Laberge 1973).[27] In Tok Pisin, the earlier form of **baimbai** was not only gradually reduced phonologically, but also has come to be used redundantly, has moved from sentence-initial to preverbal position, and in some instances has become a prefix (but see more recent work by Romaine, e.g. 1992, chapter 8). Although this appears to have begun with second-language speakers, it is particularly common in creolized varieties of Tok Pisin. Compare the first sentence, spoken by a middle-aged speaker from a

---

[26] This constitutes a counterexample to Todd's view that "it seems unlikely that modern varieties of English will become increasingly synthetic" (1984: 251).

[27] The Tok Pisin future marker, unlike English **will**, signals action taking place after another reported action as well as action taking place after the speech event. It is thus better described as an irrealis or posterior marker.

remote rural area, with the second, recorded by Sankoff of a young speaker in an urban area:

> *Bai* em kam bek na i stap na kaikai na kisim wara.
> 'She will come back and stay and eat and fetch water'

> Pes pikini ia *bai* yu go long wok, - *bai* yu stap ia na. bai yu stap long banis kau bilong mi na *bai* taim mi dai *bai* yu lukautim.
> 'You, first son, will go and work in, you'll remain here and you'll stay on my cattle farm and when I die you'll look after it'

A further example illustrates both redundancy and shift to a preverbal position:

> Bihain ol man *bai* stap wantaim hetman bilong ol.
> 'Afterwards the people will stay with their leader.'

A third form in Tok Pisin that has undergone phonological condensation is the habitual marker **save** (to **sa** or **se**) and this is now being prefixed to verbs. Again, affixation is a variable feature and encountered principally in informal allegro speech of younger speakers. A longitudinal study of yet another example of affixation, the clitization of anaphoric pronouns, has been discussed by Sankoff (1977).

It is likely that similar examples of morphological expansion occurred in other Pidgins, although unfortunately it is often not possible to determine at which stage. For example, in the case of Sri Lankan Portuguese Creole (discussed by Smith 1984), the development of a number of affixes may have occurred prior to creolization. As in the case of Tok Pisin, the data discussed by Smith suggest a dual process of phonological reduction of stress-bearing full words and their gradual shift into a position close to the verb. Thus the verbal prefix **lo-** 'future' is derived from the Portuguese adverb **logo** 'soon', **ta-** 'present progressive' derived from the auxiliary **esta** 'present progressive', and the **ja-** 'past' prefix relates to **ja** 'already' in the lexifier language. Although it is difficult to reconstruct developments in Sri Lankan Portuguese Creole, the ongoing expansion of languages such as Bislama, Hiri Motu and Solomons PE may provide interesting data for generalizations on morphological expansion.

The syntactic component

The three most important aspects of expansion in the syntactic component are the sources of grammatical innovation; the ability of adult second-language speakers to drastically restructure their grammar; and parallels between Pidgin expansion and other forms of language development. Observations of many Pidgins suggest the following general properties of syntactic expansion:

1. Syntactic innovation appears to be language-internal and derived from universal principles of language development. Borrowing is a minor factor and restricted by general principles.
2. Dramatic growth can take place in the absence of creolizing children.
3. There are significant parallels between Pidgin expansion and other kinds of second-language and, to a lesser degree, first-language development.

Observations on the longitudinal development of number encoding in Tok Pisin will illustrate these points. In Tok Pisin, number marking for nominals emerged as follows. In the jargon stage, there was no formal means of marking plurality. In the stabilization stage, ol (< *all*) is used as a plural pronoun. In the following text, spoken by a very old speaker near Dagua, plural is indicated only with the first pronoun of a sentence, otherwise the third-person singular pronoun i is used. With some nouns, plurality is implied by the context:

> Siaman i kamap. Nambawan samting bipo dispela graun no gat masta. I no gat masta. Ol i raun nating i kamap long Wallis, i kamap.
>
> 'The Germans arrived. At first this land had no Europeans. It had no Europeans. **They** (predicate marker) sailed about and **they** arrived on Wallis, **they** arrived'

It is significant that this method of plural marking is not found in either Tok Pisin's lexifier languages or its principal substratum language, Tolai.

In the early expansion stage, plural was redundant with pronouns and animate nominals, indicated by means of ol or various quantifiers, as in the following text spoken by a middle-aged speaker from near Maprik:

> Mi toktok long ol pipol insait long ples, toktok long rot o long skul samting... Ol i no bin wok long helt, nogat, ol i save sindaun nating. Na ol i no save troimwe pekpek long bus. Ol i save sindaun wantaim ol pekpek.
>
> 'I speak to the people in the villages, I talk about the roads and... schools and so on... **They** didn't do anything about their health, **they** ... just sat around. And **they** used not to throw away their excrement(s) in the bush. **They** used to live with their excrement(s)'

The forms **pekpek** and **ol pekpek** illustrate the variable use of plural ol with inanimates. This feature, and the redundant use of ol with other quantifiers, characterizes the following stage. In the late expansion stage, the following examples were recorded with young second-language Tok Pisin speakers:

> olgeta mipela ol man, ol wanwan tasol ol i stap na ol Erima ol sampela ol man tu ol i dai na planti ol bikpela ol man ol i dai olgeta.
>
> 'all we [inclusive] (pl.) man [= all us men] (pl.) a few only they stayed and (pl.) Erima people (pl.) man also they died, and many (pl.) big (pl.) man they died entirely [= and only a few Erimas were left and some of them also died, and a large number of "big men" were lost]'

As regards point (3) above – parallels with second-language development in more structured (targeted) teaching contexts – my own non-representative collection of data from German learners of English suggest a comparable development. Thus, in spite of the fact that both languages have plural marking in all grammatical environments, learners appear to be inclined to omit English plural markers with inanimate and abstract nouns, particularly in oblique case and after prepositions. My data on Torres Straits Broken again suggest that the emergence of plural marking takes the path outlined for Tok Pisin. Whether this is due to some innate developmental programme or the result of more general pragmatic factors – what is pragmatically important is more likely to attract morphological markers than what is not –

cannot be decided here. The absence of substratum and superstratum influence in the development remains significant, however.

A second construction illustrating grammatical expansion is that of causatives. This example also illustrates the transition from a lexical to a syntactic and eventually morphological way of encoding the same message.[28] The development of causative encoding in Tok Pisin and its immediate predecessor occurred as follows. During the jargon stage only a few lexicalized causatives, such as *kill* 'to kill' and *break* 'to break', are found. The absence of periphrastic and morphological causatives can be accounted for by developmental factors. The fact that one is dealing with a one-word or two-word grammar at this stage means that constructions of the type **mekim NV** 'to cause N to do what is expressed by V' are automatically excluded, in spite of the fact that such periphrastic causatives were found in most, if not all, of the linguistic systems in contact. The lack of morphological causatives can be explained in terms of the general principle that inflectional and derivational morphology are late developments; that is, they are the first victims of language contact and the last features to be restored. As the language develops, more lexicalized causatives such as *cut* 'to cut', 'to cause to be cut' and *move* 'to cause something to move' are added. The first instances of periphrastic causatives are found in Tok Pisin's direct predecessor, Samoan Plantation PE (Mühlhäusler 1978b). Examples include:

yu mekim sam wara i boil 'bring some water to the boil'
mi mekim kabora ia drai 'I dried the copra'

As sentences with simple embeddings become increasingly common, so the use of periphrastic causatives becomes more widespread. By around 1900, the idea of causativity could be unambiguously encoded and, assuming that simplicity of expression and optimal decodability were the main forces in the development of Pidgins and Creoles, one would expect the development to have ended here, as it appears to have done in other expanded Pidgins examined, such as West African PE and Torres Straits Creole.[29]

The structural expansion during the expansion phase is characterized by a drastic increase in referential potential during its first half and by a significant increase of non-referential potential in later years. The development of morphological causatives is an instance of the latter type of expansion, for, as we have seen, the referential demands of Tok Pisin speakers were fully met by the periphrastic construction. This is rather similar to the development of tense marking discussed by Labov (1990). In present-day Tok Pisin, morphological causatives are stylistic variants of the equally widespread periphrastic causatives.

The first morphological causatives made their appearance in the late 1910s and early 1920s, at a time when contact with Tolai was intensive. A result of this contact was morphological causatives of the type: prefix **mek** + V. This must be regarded as a direct calque of Tolai **va** + V. Compare:

---

28 This transition from lexicalization to morphological encoding appears to be a general trend in Pidgin expansion. It reflects the move away from optimalization of perception to a state where perception and production are more balanced. It also suggests that the boundary between the different components of grammar is not universally determined.

29 A possible exception is Hiri Motu where morphological encoding of causatives is common(see Dutton & Voorhoeve 1974:138). However, we may be dealing with a special case of post-Pidgin development caused by pressure from the lexifier language.

Tolai		Tok Pisin around 1920	
mat	'to die'	save	'to know'
vamat	'to kill'	meksave	'to make know, inform'
maranga	'dry'	pas	'fast, obstructed'
vamaranga	'to make dry'	mekpas	'to fasten, tie up'
		nois	'to shake, tremble'
		meknois	'to make tremble, shake'

In spite of the productivity of this pattern in Tolai, it did not catch on in Tok Pisin, and the above examples are the only ones found today. Their status is that of lexicalizations. The reasons for this absence of carry-over from Tolai seem obvious. In the development of morphological causatives, non-statlve verbs (**nois**), adjectives (**pas**) and transitive verbs (**save**) should occur later than with + stative verbs. The new calques are premature, since they do not fit in with the developmental tendencies of Pidgins.

The use of the same lexical base in a number of grammatical functions (zero derivation) is a widespread phenomenon in Pidgins and Creoles (cf Mühlhäusler 1978d) and is also used for causativization in English, as in:

to walk a horse	=	to make a horse walk
to burp a baby	=	to make a baby burp
to start a car	=	to make a car start

Although this method is used in some related Pacific Pidgins and Creoles (e.g. Torres Straits Pidgin),[30] it is not found in Tok Pisin. Instead, transitivity marker -**im** is used to signal causativization.

The first morphological causative ending in -**im** is found around 1910, **rausim** 'to throw out' derived from raus 'to be outside' (from German **raus**). By 1927 we get a number of additional lexicon entries pertaining to the context of giving and receiving orders in a colonial setting. They include:

bek	'to be back'	bekim	'to return something'
boil	'to boil'	boilim	'to boil something'
hariap	'to be in a hurry'	hariapim	'to make someone hurry'
lait	'to be bright'	laitim	'to light something'

The above four items violate the postulated developmental hierarchy. In the mid- 1930s, a number of stative intransitive verbs underwent morphological causativization:

slip	'to sleep, be horizontal'	slipim	'to make lie down'
stret	'straight'	stretim	'to straighten'
orait	'all right'	oraitim	'to mend, repair'
pinis	'finished'	pinisim	'to finish'

Shortly afterwards, the first morphological causatives are derived from true adjectives (that is, those belonging to the small set that can appear in attributive position). They appear in the following order:

---

30   See Shnukal (1991:183) on the transition from Pidgin to Creole in the language now known as Torres Straits Broken.

bikim	'to make big, enlarge'
kolim	'to make cool'
sotim	'to shorten'
switim	'to make feel pleasant'
truim	'to make come true'
raunim	'to make round'
stretim	'to straighten'

From the early 1960s onwards, more and more non-stative verb bases underwent causativization. The pattern appears to be on its way towards full productivity.

noisim	'to make noise'
sanapim	'to make stand up, erect'
pundaunim	'to make fall down'
wokabautim	'to make walk'
pairapim	'to make belch'
gohetim	'to make advance'

The first causative derived from a transitive verb base was found in 1973:

dokta i dringim sikman	'the doctor makes the patient drink'

The outcome of such expansion must be seen against the wider grammar of which it is part. Thus, after the development of a number of tense and aspect categories, the distinctions one can make in languages such as West African PE and Tok Pisin are very much comparable to those of English. Consider:

English	Cameroons PE[31]	TokPisin
she goes to market	i go maket	em i go long maket[32]
she is going to market	i di go maket	em i wok long go long maket
she has gone to market	i don go maket	em i go long maket pinis
she went to market	i bin go maket	em i bin go long maket
she will go to market	i go go maket	em bai go long maket

In addition, Tok Pisin can express aspectual distinctions that are not grammaticalized in English.

In addition to the development of compulsory encoding of grammatical categories, syntactic mechanisms of embedding are also introduced during Pidgin expansion. In many cases, reanalysis of conjoined construction leads to the establishment of conventions for embedding. Again, data of a longitudinal type from languages other than Tok Pisin are not available. However, the endpoint of development reached in languages such as West African PE, Torres Straits Broken or Hiri Motu is usually comparable to stages identified during the expansion of Tok Pisin, suggesting that this process is highly constrained. More details can be taken from a useful overview of this phenomenon by Sankoff (1979). Generally speaking, one finds that:

---

[31] Data adapted from Todd (1979: 283).
[32] There are a number of competing constructions, including **em i go long maket i stap** and **em i go long maket i go**.

1. With increasing age, expanding Pidgins become grammatically more complex in that embedding and even multiple embedding are commonly encountered in the speech of younger speakers;
2. There is a growing tendency to mark embedded sentences by such means as relativizers and complementizers;
3. Markers of embedded structures originate by means of reinterpreting existing forms;
4. There appears to be a natural order in which complex sentences emerge in a developing Pidgin; however, many details remain ill understood.

I will illustrate these points with data on the development of complementation in Tok Pisin. This construction was not borrowed or calqued from either substratum or superstratum languages, but instead developed internally by means of reanalysing or expanding the use of existing material. The principal sources for complementizers were:

1. sentence adverbials **olsem** and **baimbai**;
2. prepositions, that is, **long** and **bilong**;
3. verbal concatenation as in **se**.

Two of these, **baimbai** and **olsem**, were found in a letter written in 1913:

mi laik *pabai* **iu givemi log en**   'I want you to give it to me'

mi tokiu *olsem* **mi laik save tok bolog iu**
        'I am telling you that I want to know your opinion'

Subsequent to the reanalysis of sentence adverbials as complementizers, we find that prepositions are also used for this purpose. The data to be discussed shortly lend support to the 'localist hypothesis' that "the extension of the use of cases from marking local and concrete relationships to their use in marking abstract or syntactic relationships" (Washabaugh 1975:6) is a regular universal process.[33]

The historical development of this particular type of complementation appears to be one in which the formal marking of the embedded sentence has developed very gradually. In the earliest grammar of Tok Pisin (Brennink-meyer 1924), only complementation without complementizers is documented, as in:

gut yumi go   'It is good for us to go, let us go'

As late as 1970, Wurm (p 77) wrote that "noun clauses in Pidgin have no distinguishing characteristics, and precede (as subject) or follow (as object) other clauses without a conjunction". It must be taken into consideration, however, that Wurm is referring to Highlands Tok Pisin, which in some ways is less developed than the corresponding coastal varieties.

The earliest example of the use of the preposition **long** as complementizer that has come to my attention is found in Hall (1943:62):

kiap i no laik long mi long mekim taim
        'the patrol officer does not want me to get myself indentured'

---

33   The knowledge that prepositions often develop into complementizers is old, and a thorough discussion of some cases can be found, for instance, in Paul (1970:370ff; first published in 1880).

It would be a gross over-simplification, however, to state that more and more instances of the **long** complementizer are encountered as the language develops. In actual fact, a large number of intervening factors, some of which are discussed by Woolford (1979), are also operative. First, **long** is used differentially after different verbs, as the data in the following table indicate (from Woolford 1979:115) .

*Percentage use of **long** preceding the complements of* laik, laikim, giaman *and* tokim

speaker	age	laik	laikim	giaman	tokim
		'want (intr.)'	'want (tr.)'	'pretend'	'tell'
G	50	0 (0/17)	0 (0/4)	100 (3/3)	50 (1/2)
P	35-40	0(0/13)	100 (1/1)	100 (1/1)	50 (1/2)

Second, there may be social and sex-preferential differences. Third, the range of **long** is encroached upon by other competing complementizers in the speech of some users of Tok Pisin. The technical aspects of **long** grammaticalization are discussed by Woolford (1979) and will not be repeated here.

A last Tok Pisin complementizer, **se**, is of particular interest, as it has parallels in numerous other Pidgins and Creoles. The development of English **say** into **se**, a "complementizer following verbs of saying, believing etc.", appears to have taken place in the following stages. First, **se** becomes collocationally restricted, that is, it is used only together with other verbs of similar semantic content, as in:

em i tok i se	'he said, was saying'

Second, the **i** joining the two verbs is dropped, because of the semantic similarity of the concatenated verbs:

em i tok se: mi laik kam	'he said: I want to come'

Third, sentences in which the speaker is non-coreferential with the agent of the reported event neutralize the distinction between direct and indirect speech:

em i tok se papa i gat sik	'he said: the father is ill'
	'he said, that the father was ill'

Finally, **se** is reinterpreted as a complementizer following certain verbs, rather than as an independent verb in concatenation. Conventions for the treatment of pronouns in the embedded sentence are introduced at the same time:

em i tok se em i laik kam	'he said that he'd like to come'

In Tok Pisin, **se** is only found after a very small number of verbs. However, in Cameroons PE, its use has been extended to such a degree that "la proposition introduite par **se** peut se trouver après n'importe quel verbe" (Féral 1980:279).[34]

A solution paralleling that of Tok Pisin and West African PE is also in evidence in pidginized varieties of Quechua. Whereas the particle *ñispa* is used to introduce quotations in standard varieties of Quecha, in pidginized

---

[34] A number of writers, mentioned in Rickford (1977:212), have postulated an African origin (Akan **se**) for this complementizer. The evidence presented here suggests a conspiracy between substratum and universal forces in Pidgin development.

forms of this language the related particle *nisha* "is used to complement verbs of saying and asking, but moreover, verbs of believing, wondering, wanting" (Muysken 1975:13). The fact that Pidgins often develop strikingly similar solutions to the same problem of grammatical expansion has led observers to postulate historical relationships between them, where in fact we are dealing with independent development. An interesting example is the case of the relativizer **we** (< *where?*), which is found in, among others, West African PE, Bislama, Solomons PE, Tok Pisin, Queensland Kanaka English, Krio, Torres Straits Broken and Kriol.

With present-day evidence only, applying the criteria of comparative linguistics would suggest that a relativizer **we** was already present in some as yet ill-described proto-PE. However, data of a longitudinal kind do not support such a hypothesis. Thus, when Dutton carried out fieldwork in the late 1960s in the Torres Straits, he failed to elicit relativizers (cf Dutton 1970:146), whereas in 1978 I had few problems in obtaining a relativizer **we** used not only for spatial and temporal relative clauses, but also to refer to animates. In Tok Pisin, **we** was not documented until the early 1970s, that is, many years after contacts between German West Africa and German New Guinea had come to an end. An implicational analysis of my own data suggests a development of the type:

1. **ples we em i stap longen**   'the place where he lived'
2. **taim we em ikam (longen)**   'the point in time at which he arrived'
3. **man we i stap long ples**   'the people who live in the village'
4. **samting we mi bin lusim tingting longen**   'something which I forgot'

Speakers who use the fourth version will also use **we** in the preceding contexts, but not vice versa. It would seem that a similar development accounts for the emergence of the relativizer **we** in other PEs. This case clearly serves as a warning against reliance on the traditional comparative method in Pidgin linguistics.

The case of West African PE **we** may have a different story, that is, its origin may well be traceable back to Krio constructions such as the following (Jones 1971:82):

Da kau we no get tel, na God go dreb in flai.   (literally: 'That cow which does not have a tail, it is God who will drive away its flies')

Da buk we yu bin gi mi, a don los am.
(literally: 'The book which you gave me, I have lost it')

The development of relativizers again illustrates that there are only a very small number of sources for this construction. Next to a reanalysis of a form of 'where',[35] we find a form corresponding to 'who', as in English, or a form corresponding to 'that'. All these solutions are found, incidentally, in the development of Tok Pisin, although some of them have not been successful. Whereas these examples illustrate the development of grammar through the reanalysis of existing grammar, some observers have also pointed to a second source for new grammar, namely pragmatic factors. An example, again

---

35   This is also found in numerous non-Pidgins, for example, Alemannic *wo* in *Dr Ma wo kumme isch* 'the man who arrived'.

relating to relativization in Tok Pisin, is the development of the emphatic marker **ya** (< *here*) from a locative adverbial to a bracketing device at the beginning and end of relative clauses (Sankoff & Brown 1976).

In surveying these and other aspects of the syntactic development of Pidgins, one can clearly see the movement away from a stage where surface sequence was determined by pragmatic factors to one of considerable discrepancy between surface sequence and grammatical order. Grammaticalization of this type certainly increases the overall complexity of a Pidgin. However, at the same time it allows for stylistic variation, for devices which emphasize and de-emphasize aspects of meaning and structures beyond those found within simple sentences. It seems remarkable that such complexities appear to be the necessary accompaniment of functional expansion and that, moreover, the sources of functional expansion are very similar across languages. Unfortunately, the data base discussed here is rather limited, and it is hoped that more comparative longitudinal studies will become available soon.

The lexical component

It was argued that syntactic development served the principal function of increasing the stylistic flexibility of a developing Pidgin. One suspects that lexical expansion is geared towards increasing the referential potential of a Pidgin as it is used in new domains or functions. Although much of lexical expansion is related to this aim, a surprising amount of lexical development appears to serve mainly stylistic requirements.

Lexical expansion is manifested in two ways: either as borrowing from external sources, typically indigenous languages in the absence of the lexifier model, or as the development of language-internal devices of word formation. The reliance on these mechanisms appears to be unevenly spread among expanding Pidgins. Although some Pidgins (such as Hiri Motu) have a fairly limited word-formation power, others (such as Tok Pisin) have developed a considerable array of derivational devices. An example of an expanding Pidgin that relies almost exclusively on borrowing is Sango (described by Samarin 1961 and Taber 1979). The process of lexical modernization of this language is seen by Taber as follows:

> But it obviously is in desperate need of new vocabulary. We have already seen that the few morphological processes known to tribal Sango have been lost in pidgin/creole Sango, so that the usual processes of derivation and compounding are unavailable. Some terms can be created syntactically in the form of phrases, especially noun-plus-modifier phrases, which are common in the language. But for many concepts and cultural items, Sango must look beyond its own limited resources. Whenever someone wants to talk about a republic, or a hypodermic needle, or school, or a truck, or politics, he quite automatically turns to French (1979:192).

As a consequence, in a large collection of text samples, more than 51% of the lexical types in Sango were found to be of French provenance. It is interesting to note that a token count gives quite different results:

> The 508 French types account for only 6.8% of the tokens, that is 6.8% of the running text. The Sango types account for 91.3% of the tokens (1.9% are

175

proper words, which are ignored in this study, even though they would be an interesting subject for study themselves). Sango types occur on an average 69 times each, while French words occur only 5 times each. Of the 508 French types, 205, or 40%, occur only once each in the corpus (1979:192).

Equally interesting is the observation that a large number of recent loans are not needed to increase the referential power of Sango, but merely add to its stylistic flexibility. On average, 17% of all French loans had perfectly good Sango synonyms (Taber 1979:194). Similarly heavy reliance on French is also found in other African Pidgins, such as pidginized Fula (cf Noss 1979).

The reverse case, that of "European-derived" Pidgins borrowing from local vernaculars during their expansion, is illustrated with data from Pacific PEs. Such borrowings are often found in the more peripheral areas of the lexicon, and furthermore tend to refer to marked rather than neutral or unmarked meanings. Unlike borrowing from prestige superimposed languages, which is dependent on social factors, borrowing from indigenous sources often depends on regional preferences.[36] Thus, during the expansion of Tok Pisin in the 1930s, a number of lexical items were borrowed by different regional varieties, including:

	Tok Pisin	*Gloss*
1. New Ireland region	pudel, pudelim	'heap, to heap'
	tapak	'leprosy'
	talambar	'picture'
	ramitim	'to kiss, to lick'
	palar	'flat'
	pirpir, pir	'story'
2. Manus Island	bulukai	'sago boiled with water'
	burukin	'dish'
	burumbut	'to tread on'
	kaur	'bamboo'
	kauvas	'friend, gift'
3. New Britain	varkurai	'court case, debate'
	vinamut	'silence, peace, retreat'
	kukuvai	'umbrella'
	kulkulup	'cup, drinking vessel'
	vivingul	'flute, to play the flute'

Few of these have survived. The relatively low status of indigenous forms is seen from the following estimates of their proportion in a number of contemporary Pacific PEs:

Bislama:	90% English, 5% indigenous, 3% French, 2% other
Tok Pisin:	77% English, 16% indigenous, 7% German and other
Solomons Pijin:	89% English, 6% indigenous, 5% other

As indicated above, the pressure for new lexical material is lessened by the development of word-formation devices in a number of Pidgins. Generally speaking, this proceeds along the following lines:

---

[36] For Nigerian PE, this is illustrated by Mafeni (1971:105).

1. Jargon stage: there is no productive word formation.
2. Stabilization stage: circumlocution is used to express new ideas; there are a very small number of compounds at word level.
3. Early expansion stage: there is an increase of word-level compounds. As a rule the surface structure of derived lexical items is relatively close to their putative deep structure.
4. Late expansion stage: there is a strong tendency to derive word-level rather than phrase-level lexical items. There is also an increasing discrepancy between lexical surface structures and related deep structures, and lexical programmes become increasingly productive.

As regards the origin of new lexical patterns of word formation, two views can be noted. One, which was proposed, for instance, by Camden (1979) for Bislama, and by Sreedhar (1984) for Naga Pidgin, suggests that calquing of indigenous word-formation patterns is the principal source. Another view which I have proposed (Mühlhäusler 1979) suggests development independent of external sources. This latter view is supported by the observations that many Pidgins develop no word-formation devices where numerous such devices are found in contact languages, and that the emergence of word-formation appears to follow certain universal lines. Thus, as the expansion of a Pidgin proceeds, we observe:

1. The development of more and more abstract patterns of word formation;
2. A development from phrase-level to word-level derived lexical items;
3. A tendency towards greater derivational depth.

The endpoint of this development may well be a word-formation component that looks similar to one found in a substratum language or, indeed, looks like a common core of substratum and superstratum word formation, as in Bislama: "while the Bislama lexical structure looks basically English to a native speaker of English, it also looks basically Tangoan to a native speaker of Tangoan" (Camden 1979:54). However, during the stages leading up to this endpoint, considerable discrepancies may have existed, as can be seen in Mosel's detailed comparison of Tok Pisin and Tolai word formation (1980). The three tendencies mentioned above can be illustrated with some longitudinal data from Tok Pisin.

The emergence of more abstract patterns. The emergence of compounds is a good illustration of this principle. In the initial phases, syntactic compounds (in Bloomfield's (1933:233) terminology) – i.e., compounds that reflect syntactic surface structures – are the only ones permitted. Examples include the type adj. + N (for example, **blakboi**) related to a syntactic phrase adj. + N. The emergence of fixed collocations of this type can be observed as early as the jargon phase, where we find:

big food	feast
white man	European

although an increasing number of such examples are recorded after 1900 in both Tok Pisin and the closely related variety of Samoan Plantation PE. The most common word-level compounds in use at the time include:

blakboi	black indentured labourer
nuboi	freshly indentured labourer
olboi	labourer having served a three-year term
waitman	European

A great increase of compounds of this kind is found in Borchardt (1926), who lists the following five and several others:

biknem	fame
bikples	mainland
blakboi	native labourer
bluston	antiseptic
haiwara	flood, tide

Many more words following this pattern have been added since. It is interesting to observe that this type of compound does not exist in Tok Pisin's principal substratum language, Tolai, and that, moreover, most of the Tok Pisin compounds have no English cognate, which suggests development from internal resources. It is also interesting that Pidgins with only limited word-formation powers, such as West African PE or Naga Pidgin, have comparable compounds; for example, Naga Pidgin **kala borol** 'black bee' and **ori poka** 'white ant'; Torres Straits Broken **waitpis** 'white fish', and **bikfist** 'celebration, big feast'; or West African PE **deiklin** (< *day clean*) 'dawn'.

Adjective and noun compounds are also found as exocentric compounds, and it is with these that substratum influence is often cited as the major factor in their emergence. Thus Mafeni, in commenting on the two principal ways of word formation in Nigerian PE, remarks:

> The second important method of word-formation is the kind of compounding known as calquing, utilising English loan-words in combination according to the pattern of compounds to be found in Nigerian languages; stròng-héd or tròng-héd (stubborn), big áy (greedy), lòngà-trót (i.e. 'long throat') and bòtòm-bèlé (vagina), òpùn-áy (boldness, wisdom, or to browbeat) are a few examples which spring readily to mind.
>
> Briefly, therefore, although English has supplied the vast majority of the items that make up the Nigerian Pidgin lexicon, the various substrates also supply vocabulary items (however few) as well as the more important processes by which the English loan-words are made to acquire new or additional meanings (1971:106).

Similarly, Camden, in discussing the word-formation component of Bislama and comparing it with Tangoan, a Vanuatu vernacular, points to close parallelisms between the two languages: e.g.:

> In Tangoan, a noun phrase occurs consisting of a head noun followed by a second noun which modifies it. The second noun may indicate purpose or characteristic of the head noun, particularly its species or the type of materials used in its construction.
>
> In Bislama, a noun phrase occurs consisting of a head noun followed by a second noun which modifies it. The second noun may indicate purpose or characteristic of the head noun, particularly its species, or the type of material used in its construction.

Thus **haos prea** 'house prayer' ('a house for prayer'), **boks tul** 'box tool' ('a tool box') where the second noun indicates purpose, **lif kokonas** 'leaf coconut' ('a coconut leaf'), **lif aranis** 'leaf orange' ('an orange leaf') where the second noun indicates species, **haos kava** 'house sheet metal' ('a house with a galvanised iron roof') where the second noun indicates material (1979:85).

Compounds exhibiting such a word order are not found in other expanding Pidgins, such as Naga Pidgin (Sreedhar 1984), but they do occur in Tok Pisin, where Tangoan influence was certainly never experienced. As pointed out by Mosel (1980), compounds of this type in Tok Pisin were found before contact with Tolai and, on the basis of my own data, appear to have become highly productive only after contact with Tolai had come to a virtual end. A substratum language may thus have reinforced an ongoing development, but certainly cannot be regarded as its only source.

Greater restraint with regard to deducing origins from rough parallelism is found in Hancock's studies of lexical expansion (1975, 1980). In the latter study, in particular, Hancock points to the relatively large set of language-internal sources of lexical innovation, when compared to external borrowing (1980:67). Compounding, it is concluded, is a language-internal process. The best argument against the substratum view of the origin of new compounds is developmental/longitudinal; thus, although a comparison of a developed Pidgin with substratum languages may reveal many similarities, the word-formation patterns of the substratum languages were not readily borrowed by the Pidgin at earlier stages, when they were maximally accessible. Hancock's (1975) remark that "Calquing, or adoption-translation, was probably not widely employed as a method of augmenting the lexicon during the early period" is explained by the fact that no transfer of lexical structures is possible unless a developing Pidgin is ready for them. That is, abstract asyntactic or exocentric types of compounding cannot be borrowed in the early stages of Pidgin development.

This argument also relates to a second form of word formation, reduplication, which, in the view of many, though not Hancock, is the paradigm case of substratum influence. Thus Mafeni, writing on the expansion of Nigerian PE, observes:

> The contribution of African languages to the lexicon of Nigerian Pidgin may, however, not be fully appreciated if we consider only direct borrowings from these languages; of far greater importance are the various processes of word-formation which it has adopted from the substrates. There are two principal ways in which Nigerian Pidgin increases its lexicon apart from the direct borrowing of lexical items. The first, which we have mentioned above, involves the phenomenon of reduplication as a method of word-derivation. In this way new words may be formed either as intensives of the words from which they have been derived, or with completely different meanings from them (1971:106).

Data from several Pidgins contradict this view, which has been expounded, for example, by Thompson (1961). Although there are a number of reduplicated forms in many Pidgins, in almost all instances these are fully lexicalized rather than members of a productive word-formation paradigm.

The role of reduplication in Pidgins such as Papuan PE, Chinese PE, Pidgin German of New Guinea or Japanese PE is minimal, and Reinecke, discussing Vietnamese Pidgin French, observes that "Reduplication, prominent in many pidgin and creole languages, is lacking in Tay Boi, even though it is virtually the only morphological feature of Vietnamese" (1971:51), thus providing interesting evidence against the substratum view of origin. A comparison between reduplication in Tok Pisin and Tolai, carried out by Mosel concludes:

> Tolai and Tok Pisin have only a very few types of reduplication in common. Since we have already found out, that the types of verbal reduplication shared by both languages result from two different though related and partly overlapping concepts, there are only three other types of reduplication left which correspond to each other:
> 1. the reduplication of nouns denoting plurality,
> 2. the reduplication of cardinal numbers by which distributional numbers are derived,
> 3. the reduplication of adverbs denoting intensity.
> But these types of reduplication are too common to prove substratum influence.   (Mosel 1980:11)

To this, it must be added that those instances of parallels between the two languages were late to emerge (that is, they did not emerge before the 1950s), a long time after close contacts with Tolai had come to an end. It is true that there are some cases of reduplication calqued from Tolai, but such calques tend to be restricted to individual lexical items and have not resulted in productive morphological patterns. Much of the argument about substratum influence would become unnecessary if the distinction between isolated calques and borrowed patterns were made. As regards the latter, we appear to be unable to relate their development to any external source.

From the available evidence, it can thus be tentatively concluded that expansion of derivational morphology follows language-independent lines: that there is a gradual change from patterns closely related to syntactic surface structures to others which are less transparent, a development also reflected in the change-over from phrase-level to word-level formation of new lexical items.

Change in size level. The formation of new lexical items during the stabilization phase of Pidgins often takes the form of lengthy circumlocutions, and for a long time phrase-level lexical items were preferred to word-level ones. The reasons for this general tendency are, among others, limitation on word length in less developed Pidgins and their general derivational shallowness. The replacement of older phrase-level items with phonologically shorter word-level ones with a single stress is illustrated with some examples from Tok Pisin. For example:

Form recorded before1975	Form recorded in 1975	Gloss
lam wokabaut	wokabautlam	'hurricane lantern'
manki bilong masta	mankimasta	'servant (male)'
mekim hariap	hariapim	'to speed someone up'
hatpela wara	hatwara	'soup, hot water'
mani pepa	pepamani	'paper money'
wara bilong skin	skinwara	'sweat'

It is quite clear from these examples that English influence was only marginally involved here, if at all. It is also noteworthy that the downward shift in size level occurred many years after the cessation of contacts with Tok Pisin's principal substratum language, Tolai. We are thus dealing with language-internal development. A detailed case study will illustrate the gradualness of process, proceeding by way of lexical diffusion rather than generalization or overgeneralization. Thus, in Tok Pisin, lexical phrases of the form **man bilong V$_{int}$** expressing 'someone who usually does what is referred to by the verb' documented in reasonable numbers for the mid-1920s, including **man bilong singaut** 'noisy person, beggar' and **man bilong slip** 'sleepy, lazy person'. The only word-level items at this point are **sutman** 'policeman' and **sutboi** 'indigenous hunter'.

For the mid-1930s, the authors of the *Wörterbuch mit Redewendungen* remark (Anon. ca 1935:53) that "-man as the suffix of verbs forms agent nouns" (my translation). However, only a few word-level items are listed, including **wasman** 'watchman' and **stilman** 'thief'. Phrase-level items listed in the *Wörterbuch* include: **man bilong save** 'wise person', **man bilong pait** 'warrior, fighter' and **man bilong pret** 'fearful person'. No additional word-level items are documented until Mihalic (1957), who adds **saveman** 'wise person' and a few others. A few more are found in Mihalic (1971), including **holiman** 'a saint'. My own observations confirm that the trend towards word-level derivations continues and that a number of items which were earlier recorded only as phrase-level items are now being supplemented by word-level items, such as **paitman** 'fighter, warrior' and **pretman** 'easily frightened person'. For a more detailed account, see Mühlhäusler (1983b).

Increased depth of lexical derivation. In the lexicon, as in other components of grammar, expansion increases the distance between surface structures and related deep structures. In the lexicon, this is associated both with the above mentioned tendency towards asyntactic compounds and with the relaxation of a convention barring recursive application of word-formation rules. Let me illustrate this point briefly.

Although a number of different ways of word formation are encountered in expanded Tok Pisin, there is one powerful restriction to their use: only one lexical programme can be applied to a lexical base at any given time. This means, among other things, that:

1. No instrumental verbs can be derived from nominal compounds. Thus although there is a form **saripim** 'to cut with a grassknife' derived from **sarip** 'grassknife', no form ***grasnaipim** can be derived from **grasnaip** 'grassknife'.
2. No intensifying reduplications can be formed from denominalized verbs. Thus, whereas **kilkilim** 'to hit with force' can be derived from **kilim** 'to hit', no form ***brumbrumim** can be derived from **brumim** 'to sweep', since this is a complex lexical item (that is, a verb derived from the lexical base **brum** 'broom').
3. No compounds involving more than two components are found. Thus, whereas **man** 'man' plus **meri** 'woman' can be combined to form **manmeri** or **meriman** 'people' and whereas **sikman** or **sikmeri** 'patient' are documented no form ***sikmanmeri** 'sickpeople' is permitted.

A number of progressive second-language speakers of Tok Pisin have begun to ignore these limitations and now produce some of the above-listed asterisked forms. Unfortunately, I have no comparative data for other expanding Pidgins, but it is hoped that one is dealing with a general tendency.

One can conclude from the evidence presented here that new methods of extending the lexicon from internal resources can emerge within expanding Pidgins without substratum or superstratum influence. Moreover, we have seen that influence from or borrowing of substratum material is restricted to those items that can be accommodated in the developing patterns of lexical enrichment: as the initial creativity of Pidgins increases, so does their syncretic capacity.

The development of stylistic flexibility

Implicit in much of what has been said so far is the observation that the grammatical expansion process observable in Pidgins is not aimed primarily at increasing their referential power, but at providing stylistic choice. This is achieved through reduction rules in the phonological component, the parallel development of morphological and syntactic devices encoding the same meaning, or through the emergence of extensive synonymy or near-synonymy in the lexicon.

The sources of this increase in stylistic flexibility are a complex mixture of language-internal and -external factors. First and foremost, they reflect a development of expanding Pidgins away from being a mere medium of communicating denotational information to one for expressing a number of personal emotions. Put differently, there is a growing need for encoding the indexical dimensions of language, such as group membership, politeness or sex. Next to this, we find an expansion of the language resulting from its use in new media (radio, print) and its use as a form of art.

In discussing emergent stylistic differences, it should be remembered that there is no easy one-to-one correspondence between form and stylistic application; the same formal means can be used to achieve different stylistic effects and different forms may be employed for the same effect.

The effect of a Pidgin's use in a new function – in this case that of playing a verbal game – is illustrated by the use of riddles in Cameroons PE. Todd (n d) points out that the reason for the emergence of riddles in this Pidgin is the lower age at which it is learned, for riddles are seldom asked by adults. Riddles, like PE proverbs, jokes and folktales, are very much an urban phenomenon, associated with the growing number of intertribal marriages. In spite of this ongoing detribalization, urban riddles preserve the fundamental insights of a pre-urban society. This is reflected in the fact that many of them are calqued on a vernacular model. The following examples are given first in Cameroons PE, then as a morpheme-by-morpheme gloss, and finally in Todd's translation:

Tɔri wei mek man krai ivɛn fɔ i   mama i   haus
story rel. make man cry   even for he mama he house
'something that can make one cry even when one is perfectly safe'

Smok fɔ faia   Pua bɔi wei i di   go skul
smoke for fire   poor boy rel. he prog. go school
'smoke from the fire'   'educated poor boy'

Tudei nɔting no dei fɔ haus, tumɔrɔ haus di fulɔp
today nothing no loc. for house, tomorrow house prog. full + up
'Today the house may be empty but tomorrow it will want for nothing'

A second type of linguistic play found in expanding Pidgins is the use of poetic metaphors. The reader should be reminded that, in earlier developmental stages, the distinction between metaphor and literal meaning was not well defined and that social conventions for literal meaning emerge only late in Pidgin development. Thus the use of such expressions as:

bel bilong mi i hevi	my belly is heavy	'I am sad'
bel bilong mi i isi	my belly is easy	'I am contented'

in Tok Pisin are metaphorical expressions from the point of view of target language speakers, but not for indigenes. Distinct from such phenomena is the deliberate creation of metaphors to achieve certain poetic effects. This activity, named **tok piksa** 'picture talk' or **tok pilai** 'play talk', is found in a number of domains: for instance, in connection with drinking. This act is referred to by **tok piksa** terms such as **botomapim** (to turn bottoms up = to empty a glass), **kapsaitim** (to turn over, upside down = to drink hurriedly), **drink paia** (to drink fire = to drink alcoholic beverages). **Tok piksa** references to some drinks on offer in Papua New Guinea include **meri buka** ('Buka girl'), a type of rum so called because of the black (Buka people are very black) girl on the label; **grinpela man** (green man = beer in a green bottle); and **braunpela man** (brown man = beer in a brown bottle). A term sometimes used to refer to intoxicating liquor in general is **spesel mailo** 'a special type of Milo (a malt drink)'.

A similar drinking vocabulary, involving considerable use of metaphorical speech, is found in Cameroons PE. Todd's (1979) analysis of a narrative concerned with drinking isolates a number of deliberate metaphors:

mi a bi smɔl man we di tek kɔp literally: 'I'm a little man who habitually takes a cup' but implying: 'I'm very fond of a drink'. (Todd 1979:285)

Realizing this, the listeners are prepared for other references to drinking and for the idiosyncratic code associated with it. Taken out of context:

i nak bɔtu fɔ ma hed

could imply 'he hit me on the head with a bottle', but here it means 'he put a bottle in front of me, implying that I could help myself'. In the text, we have three terms for a large bottle of beer:

kiŋ sai <English *kingsize* **ɔdine** <French *ordinaire*
ŋgɔŋgi probably in many of the vernaculars, certainly used in Lamso, often in the form **ŋgaŋgi**

On seeing the bottle, the speaker tells us: **a di krai....... a krai ɔntɔp i finiʃ** which, out of context, would mean 'I'm crying... I cry on top (over) it until it is finished', but here it implies 'I drank very slowly, savouring the delights of every mouthful until it was finished'.

Yet another example of emerging verbal poetry are proverbs. Whereas proverbial expressions are only now emerging in Tok Pisin, they appear to be firmly established in West African (particularly Cameroons) PE. Todd (1979:289) not only demonstrates the viability of proverbs in this language, but also shows the close similarities between proverbial expressions in Krio (K) and Cameroons PE (C), thereby supporting an argument that the latter is a continuation of Krio. Examples illustrating these two points include:

> K: bad bus nɔ de fɔ, trowe bad pikin
> C: bad buʃ no de fɔ, trowe bad pikin
> 'no matter how bad a child is his parents will not want to get rid of him'

> K: we ɛleja mit mɔnki i jit pɛpɛ, i se na dʒakato
> C: dʒam pas dai mɔnki tʃɔp pepe tɔk se na ndʒakato
> 'when a monkey is hungry he eats pepper and calls it garden eggs'

Language games are not just related to the structural properties of a particular Pidgin, but also to the very choice of the Pidgin in the first place. Thus, in a discussion of Cameroons PE in urban Douala, Pradelles de Latour (1984) observes that two linguistic games of 'making fun' and 'making secret' are typically performed in Pidgin, mainly because compulsory marking of honorifics and certain indexical rules of speech use found in local African languages do not exist in Cameroons PE. Thus, for the function of 'making fun':

> there is a voluntary obliteration of the differences between generations, statuses and sometimes even sexes (a father can address his daughter as he would his son): "Jean-Marc, yu kam tchop?" (b), (meaning: with me) a father asks his 8 year-old son, as he would a person his own age. "How papa, yu tchop ol di tin, yu no lif mi som tin?" (c), says a son in Pidgin, and the father laughs. It would be absolutely unthinkable for this young boy to say such a phrase in Bangwa or for the father to accept such a comment in his language.

The same relaxation of traditional bonds of obligation is encountered in the use of Cameroons PE as a language for 'making secret':

> "If your father is there and you don't want him to hear, it's O.K. to use Pidgin", says a young man. In this example among others, Pidgin appears as the means of telling something to someone in such a way, that those not involved will not understand what it is all about. But, contrary to a certain logic that would advise both partners concerned by the message to step aside from the group, it seems that it is precisely in the midst of family members or friends that one feels the urge to transmit a confidential message: one must add that the harmless and far from urgent nature of such exchanges is striking to the observer.

In Tok Pisin, comparable uses of language are expressed in terms of special stylistic registers of the language itself. Thus secret varieties of Tok Pisin exhibit a number of structural devices not found in everyday language. Backslang or **tok mainus** is used to refer to taboo areas in communication and exclude outsiders from access to a conversation between initiates. So, for instance, **kepkep** is used as a euphemism for **pekpek** 'to defecate' and **supsup** for **puspus** 'to have sexual intercourse'. Aufinger (1948-49) reports from a plantation context the warning **alapui wok, atsam i mak** standing for

iupala (in standard orthography: **yupela) wok, masta i kam** 'you (pl.) work, the master is coming'. Aufinger suggests that the practice of Pidgin backslang developed as a result of the introduction of writing.

Substitution of lexical items is also widespread in secret varieties. **Tok bokis** describes a linguistic register which involves the replacement of lexical items by others whose meaning and/or form are conventionalized within a large or small group of speakers, rather than being predictable from lexical conventions concerning metaphorical shift or lexical derivation.

A particularly rich field for the study of **tok bokis** are the various Melanesian cargo movements. For example, according to Schwartz (1957), some **tok bokis** items used by the followers of the Paliau cargo movement on Manus Island were **kastem haus** (custom house), referring to a shed for receiving and handling goods in trade with other villages; **mep** (map = graveyard); **orait** (all healthy = to be equal to the white man in terms of knowledge, goods, etc.); **star** (star = turnstile in the village [having reference to heaven]).

I recorded some **tok bokis** terms from members of the Pele cargo movement in the Yangoru-Dreikikir area of the East Sepik Province. For example, **gaten memore** (memorial garden = cemetery); **kandere** (maternal uncle = someone who has died and will give money to the living); **wok** (work = the Pea movement); **rot bilong kandere i pus** (the uncle's road is obstructed = the dead body fails to provide money).

The use of Tok Pisin backslang illustrates an important point in the discussion of stylistic diversification: the dependence of linguistic structures on the medium in which they are used. Spelling and pronouncing words backwards appears to be crucially related to the institutionalization of Tok Pisin as written medium. The use of Pidgins in the media can also be related to the emergence of numerous other phenomena. One of the main effects of writing Pidgins is that they have been, wittingly or unwittingly, moved close to their lexifier language. Thus spelling often approximates to standard English usage in Tok Pisin:

Phonetic spelling	Written convention	Gloss
go kwap	**go goap**	go go up
daun tampilo	**daun daunbilo**	down down under
torowe	**troimwe**	to throw away

Deliberate policies of the editors of influential Tok Pisin newspapers have had other effects. In the *Rabaul News*, many loans from English were introduced in the late 1940s, and in the largest present-day publication, *Wantok*, certain syntactic constructions, such as the use of subordinate-clause bracketing in relative embedding, are encouraged. Many idiomatic expressions for beginning and concluding letters have also emerged. Broadcasting has led to yet other innovations. In Tok Pisin, the past marker **bin**, and the use of the pronoun **yumipela** 'we' (inclusive or exclusive) (discussed by Siegel 1985:81ff) have been significantly promoted by radio announcers, as have many new lexical items such as **stopwok** 'strike' or **raneweman** 'refugee'.

Our understanding of the stylistic resources of Pidgins is far from complete, and registers such as baby talk, public speaking or family interaction remain unexplored. It is hoped that there will be more studies of Pidgin registers and their origin and use, and that modern techniques such as video-recording will be employed to gain a fuller understanding of the great communicative potential of expanded Pidgins.

The expansion stage: a summary

The study of expanding Pidgins suggests that the differences between first and second languages may be very tenuous. Innovations such as are produced by second-language speakers, principally adults, have been shown to be comparable both to the linguistic changes and elaborations produced ontogenetically by children acquiring a first language, and to the processes found in historical changes of 'normal' languages. What distinguishes expanding Pidgins is the enormous speed at which such qualitative changes occur. West African or Melanesian varieties of PE today are very different from varieties spoken fifty years ago, and intelligibility between expanded Pidgins and their related lexifier languages seems to be generally absent.

The study of Pidgin expansion often seems to suggest a unidimensional progression from less complex to more complex systems. This, as the evidence presented here shows, is an oversimplistic view. Different Pidgin-speakers introduce competing solutions to certain communicative problems and as a consequence, we find considerable variability, including inter-individual variation. In addition, a detailed study of expansion often reveals unsuccessful innovations by individuals and subgroups. The general impression gained, although this needs to be corroborated by more comparative studies, is that the overall process of expansion is narrowly constrained by a number of developmental principles (such as the one which says that less marked constructions should precede more marked ones). As a result, borrowing from external sources, be they of the substratum or superstratum type, is relatively limited, particularly in the earlier stages of expansion.

The study of expansion also suggests that repair of referential deficiencies is not a major factor in language growth, particularly not towards the end of expansion. Much more important is the introduction of stylistic flexibility, variation and choice. As the requirement for ease of perception becomes less important, more choice and greater distance between superficial and underlying structures is introduced.

Creolization

Creoles, as was pointed out in Chapter 1, are commonly regarded as Pidgins have become the first language of a new generation of speakers. It should by now be abundantly clear, however, that there are numerous difficulties with this simple formula. However, work which has followed in the wake of Bickerton's *Roots of Language* (1981) has done little to clarify the problem.

A major distinction, though one not always made, is that between the linguistic innovations accompanying the first-generation creation of a Creole and subsequent changes over a longer time-span. Whatever the latter may tell us about general properties of linguistic change, it is unlikely to shed light on the former. One should thus distinguish two types of questions:

1. What are the linguistic correlates of initial creolization?
2. What are the sources for subsequent structural expansion?

Regarding the former, Valdman has observed:

> The expansion of linguistic functions served by a creole is accompanied by a set of processes subsumed under the term creolization: (1) relative stabilization of variation; (2) expansion of inner form; (3) complexification of outer form. While the corresponding mirror-image process, pidginization, has received detailed attention, creolization has remained by and large ill described (1977a:155).

Regarding the latter, different views are found, falling roughly into the universalist and substratum camps, which were discussed above.

The linguistic documentation of creolization is extremely sketchy. Particularly distressing is the lack of longitudinal studies. Most Creolists rely on the comparison of the endpoints of creolization rather than the ongoing processes. Although this methodology has resulted in some highly interesting insights into common Creole grammar, it is methodologically suspect. One fact, which is becoming more widely acknowledged, is the lack of any reliable documentation of the transition from a rudimentary Pidgin to a first-generation Creole, and there are now voices that maintain that any creolization will draw on the resources of earlier elaborated Pidgins.

The study of the actual process of creolization only began a few years ago (with Sankoff & Laberge 1973) and has concentrated mainly on syntax and semantics. Other aspects of grammar still await study, as does the area of pragmatics. The picture of creolization presented here is therefore an abstraction and in need of further substantiation.

The phonological component
The fact that Pidgins were second languages and learnt, in most instances, by adults imposed considerable restrictions on their phonological flexibility. Generally speaking, all phonological processes favouring production at the cost of perception were discouraged. At the same time, segments and sequences that were difficult to produce were avoided. Both phenomena are reflected in the phonological systems of many Creoles. Their relative phonological shallowness, when compared with languages such as English, appears to be due mainly to two factors: first, the need to communicate with second-language speakers for some time after initial creolization, and second, the short life-span of these languages. The most comprehensive case study of the sound system of a Creole that arose out of an undeveloped jargon is that of Pitcairnese. Useful information on Hawaiian Creole English is given in Bickerton & Odo (1976). The Pitcairnese data are particularly useful in testing two of the main claims as to the origins of the phonological systems of Creoles: namely the retention of earlier Pidgin forms, and substratum influence. According to the hypothesis of the retention of earlier Pidgin forms, one would expect a highly simplified shallow phonology, characterized by the absence of difficult sounds and sound sequences. This does not hold for Pitcairnese, although occasional lexicalized exceptions such as **mema** 'mainmast' or **ko** 'because' suggest the existence of an earlier Pidgin.

Substratum influence in the phonologies of Creoles has been a second favourite explanation. Thus Le Page (1960:18) appeals to the "process of translation by West African ears" when discussing cluster simplification in Jamaican, and Holm (1980:56) traces a number of Bahamian pronunciations to West African origins. A study of the Pitcairnese data, however, does not suggest such close parallelisms, even if we heed Ross's caution that "In Pitcairnese philology, it is always necessary to keep in mind the possibility of a linguistic feature existing at the Settlement being replaced, partially or entirely, under later English influence" (1964:142).

Counter-evidence against substratum influence comes from four sources. First, regarding the evidence from consonant clusters, Ross states:

> In Tahitian, consonant-groups do not occur, and all words end in a vowel. It might, perhaps, have been expected that Tahitian influence would have been strong enough to modify English words in Pitcairnese to make them conform with these rules. In fact, this has not happened.
>
> In Pitcaimese, there is no aversion to – rather an abundance of – consonant groups (1964:143).

Second, vowel length is distinctive in both English and Tahitian; however Ross's data seem to suggest that it is non-distinctive in Pitcairnese. Third, the voiced stops [b], [d] and [g] are absent in Tahitian, whereas they are widespread in Pitcairnese. Finally, with regard to voiceless stops, in Tahitian [k] appears as a variant of [t] only, whereas in Pitcairnese the two sounds distinguish forms. It appears that the presence or absence of sound or sound combinations in the substratum language was not a very powerful factor in the formation of Pitcairnese.

In discussing the phonological processes leading to the establishment of another Creole, Krio, we are hampered by two factors: first, inadequate knowledge of the external history of the language (it would seem to be over-simplistic to describe it as a simple continuation of a pre-existing Pidgin); and second, the lack of very early documentation of pronunciation. Jones (1971: 70-71) points out that "it may very well be that many words reverted to their English forms because of the continuing and increasing contact between the two languages, in a situation where its exclusive use in education confers a superior status on English". Jones appears to suggest that the phonology of Krio is best understood by appealing to African substratum languages spoken in the same area. As with Pitcairnese, Krio does not distinguish long and short vowels. Compare:

English:	mill	teeth	wool	move
Krio:	**mil**	**tit**	**wul**	**muf**

Jones (1971:72) remarks: "The Krio vowel system is thus more akin to that of many African languages than to English." With consonants, cluster simplification again is an outstanding trait of Krio. Some examples illustrating this phenomenon include:

English:	straight	strength	scratch	ground
Krio:	**tret**	**trenk**	**krach**	**gran**

However, cluster reduction is far from categorical, and in at least one case the Krio cluster is more complex than the corresponding English one. Compare (Jones ibid.):

English:	beans	ants	fence	rinse
Krio:	**binch**	**anch**	**fench**	**rench**

188

Rickford discusses the problem of clusters and substratum influence in more detail in the context of tracing Black American English to its Creole roots. He dismisses claims that Creoles are direct continuations of earlier simplified Pidgins, by drawing attention to the systematic variability found with phonological phenomena in Creole. Thus:

> While consonant cluster simplification by itself might be considered 'simpler' in some articulatory sense, it is difficult to see how a system which in its application is contingent on a host of subtle factors could be considered 'simpler' than one in which simplification is either categorically present for all final clusters (the case in some West African creoles?) or categorically absent (more nearly the case in Standard English) (1977:199-200).

He further points out that there are few neat parallelisms between cluster presence and deletion in English-based Creoles and West African languages and that:

> in any case, in view of the widespread occurrence of some form of consonant cluster simplification in other dialects of English (both in the United States and elsewhere), arguments for substratal influence in this case might seem very strained (ibid.).

The various English-based Creoles of Surinam illustrate how complex cluster "simplification" can be. As regards the English word-final clusters -nd and -nt alone, the variants shown in the table below have been recorded by Smith (1977a:27) for these languages.

Variants of English word-final clusters -nd and -nt in Surinam Creoles

English	Sranan	Older Sranan	Boni	Djuka	Saramaccan	PSC[37]
bend	béni		béni		béndi	béndi
send	séni	sendie (1798)	seni	sende	(*sendi* 1778)	séndi
find	féni	*finde* (1780)	féni	fénde	fén(d)i	féndi
blind	bréni		béeni			beléndi
want	wáni	*wandi* (1780)	wáni	wani		wánti
		wan(1780)	wã			wán
hand	ánu	*hanoe*(1798)	ana	ána		hán(d)a/u
			anu			
stand	tan	*tan* (1780)	tã		tán	tán
ground	gron	*gron* (1780)	goon	goón	goón	gorón
hunt	ónti	*hoendi* (1780)	hónti	hónti	hóndi	hónti

Source: Smith 1977a: 27.

The first observation to be made about the data in the table is that it is virtually impossible to argue about Creole origins on the basis of synchronic comparison of present-day Creoles. Second, both the starting points and development of cluster treatment can be different for different Creoles based on the same language. Third, in the case of Sranan, cluster simplification appears to be a more recent process, that is, one that took place after

---

37 "Proto-Surinam Creole". I remain doubtful as to the feasibility of reconstructing proto-Creoles. In this particular case, the appearance of more complex clusters appears not to be a case of retention of proto-forms, but the result of convergence with the lexifier language.

contacts with the substratum languages were severed. Modern Sranan appears to exhibit more similarities with West African languages than Sranan spoken at the time of the slave trade. In conclusion, in the absence of longitudinal data, as well as very good socio-historical information, claims as to strong substratum influence in Creole phonologies appear to be dangerous.

If the notion of substratum influence seems problematical with sound sequence and phonotactic restrictions, it becomes almost impossible to prove in the case of phonological rules. All we can say is that rules of phonological condensation that are not found in an earlier Pidgin can appear in the Creole of the following generation. An example is the condensation of Hawaiian PE **wen**. Pidgin speakers of this language, according to Labov (1990), only have two variant pronunciations whereas, for Creole speakers, considerably more variability exists:

> Alternating with the full form [wɛn] are reduced forms [wən] and [wn], [ɛn], [n] and [ŋ], [wa] and [w]. The lone nasal consonant usually assimilates its point of articulation to a following consonant. The lone glide can be particularly difficult to hear: it may be reduced to a feature of rounding on a vowel or consonant (Labov 1990:36).

Examples given include:

> So they wen walk [dewɔk] pas' the bridge.
> We wen looking [w:nlukin] for the guy Malcolm, eh.
> I wen go [a°ŋgo] kick one of 'em.
> So I went look [al:uk] by the door.

Next to such reduction of full lexical items, phonological reduction processes are particularly common with grammatical markers such as tense, aspect, number or category markers. The most detailed studies of this phenomenon relate to Creoles that developed from expanded Pidgins, such as Tok Pisin and Guinea Bissau Crioulo (Kriol). This is understandable, as there would have been few forms to condense in a tenseless, aspectless and number-less jargon. The phonological condensation of the Tok Pisin irrealis (or future) marker **baimbai** to **bai** (discussed above) is paralleled by a similar development in Bissau Kriol:

> There is in Kriol a complex TA [Tense-Aspect] marker *or* combination TA marker auxiliary, **na bin**, where **na** is punctual and **bin** is homophonous (identical?) with **bin** 'to come', meaning 'punctual future', i.e. that such and such a thing will take place at such and such a time, explicitly stated or part of shared knowledge:
>
> (9) **amañan n na bin kunpra arus** 'tomorrow I will buy some rice'
>
> For (9) children quite often say:
>
> (10) **amañan n nin kunpra arus** 'id.'
>
> where **nin** can be pronounced either [nʌiŋ] or [niŋ]. The phonological derivation is clear: deletion through fricativization of intervocalic /b/ is a fairly regular process in BK in 'small' atonic words. The grammatical result is the creation of a new, fully grammaticalized TA marker which, having no link to any other lexical item, can now enter into the speakers' competence with nothing but its grammatical "meaning" (Kihm 1984:209).

Developments such as these appear to have their beginnings with adults, but are accelerated in communities of first-generation Creole-speaking children. A major reason for this kind of contraction seems to be the pressure for a more natural morphological system (in the sense of Mayerthaler 1978), where semantically less important information is signalled by means of phonologically less prominent forms.

In summing up what little we know about the role of phonological restructuring in creolization, it appears that there is a strong tendency towards both phonological and morphological naturalness. As regards the former, my own observations on Tok Pisin creolization suggest that the pronunciation of children can indeed be very different from that of second-language adults. Recordings made of children playing were virtually unintelligible to their parents, primarily, it would seem, because of their more "advanced" phonology. However, older children typically conformed more closely to the norms of adult second-language speakers. This means that many of the expected introductions of natural phonological processes actually occur in creolization, but are later filtered out for communicative reasons. This process is comparable to children in other societies learning to conform to adult standards by suppressing many of the natural processes encountered in early child phonology.

Many questions concerning creolization of the phonological component remain unanswered. Of particular interest, and undocumented to date, would seem to be the question whether new words are spontaneously created by children to make up for the numerous lexical gaps allegedly found in their Pidgin or jargon model. If this indeed occurred, it could provide badly needed evidence in the area of universals of sound symbolism (cf Taylor 1976).

Once creolization has occurred, Creole phonologies can continue to change, due to internal pressures or outside borrowing. Although such subsequent changes do not help us to understand the nature of creolization, their study is important in determining what is genuinely universal in Creole formation. All too often universals are derived from the comparison of arbitrarily chosen later stages of Creole development.

This point can be illustrated with two examples, one from Surinam and one from the Indian Ocean. Smith (1977b) gives a detailed survey of the fate of the English **liquids** subsequent to creolization in Sranan, Djuka, Boni and Saramaccan. For words of the structure C liquid V(C), the complex picture of development is summarized in this table:

Development of words of structure C Liquid V(c) in four Surinam Creoles

English	Saramaccan		Boni	Djuka	Sranan			
	mod.	1778			mod.	1844-56	1798	1765-81
split	piíti	plitti	piíti	príti	príti	priti	prietie	plitti
sleep	---		siibi	siíbi	sríbi	sríbi/slíbi	sliebie	sliepe /slibi
play	pεε	pre	peé	peé	prej	pleh	pley	pree
fly (n)	(feéi)		fée	feefée	frejfrej			vly
fly (v)	bɔɔ	blo/bro	boo	boó	bro	blo/bro	bloo	
clothes	koósu	krossu klossu	koóʃi	koósi	krósi	klósi	kloosie	klossi
black	baaka	blakka brakka	baáka	baáka	bláka bráka	blákka brákka	blaka	blakke blaka

(source: Smith 1977b:33).

Of particular interest in Smith's paper is the observation that tonal distinctions in Djuka are not so much a take-over from African substratum languages, but apparently the result of a historical development:

> In Djuka however there took place a sort of tone-spreading when the unstressed/low toned syllable followed the stressed/high toned syllable and the subsequent syllable began with a liquid:
>
> bátala   bátara   bátala   bátála   bátáa
>
> This preserved the original structure of the word, or at least the memory of the original structure of the word (1977b:33).

The complexity of Surinam Creole treatment of liquids is surpassed by the problems facing the linguists studying final-vowel truncation in the French Creoles of the Indian Ocean (Corne 1982:49-78). Both Reunion and Mauritian Creole lose their final vowels in certain conditions: that is, they sometimes have a long form ending in [-e], sometimes not: for example, kon ~ kone 'to know'. Originally, it was assumed (Corne 1982:70ff) that the phonological and syntactic, though not semantic environments for the final-vowel truncation rule were similar, but not identical, in both Creoles. However, Baker (p c) has pointed out to me that the choice of long vs short form in Mauritian is always sensitive to syntactic transitivity whereas this is not the case in Reunion, yet another instance of a Pidgin or Creole formally signalling the distinction transitive – intransitive.

Corne concludes his investigation of this phenomenon as follows:

> Although the evidence is not conclusive, there is a clear implication that the FVT [final-vowel truncation] rule appeared initially in 'slave' Creole, while 'master' Creole used long forms. This is obviously an oversimplified view, since Whites had at all times access to French morphology and syntax... while the exposure of non-Whites to French would have been highly variable. The picture then is that of a morphosyntactic rule being gradually adopted and gaining a semantic value quite absent from any variety of French (1982:72).

To this it must be added that the development of the various semantic regularities governing final-vowel truncation occurred long after contacts between Mauritius and Réunion had become insignificant and contacts with other French Creole-speaking areas in the New World had been severed.

Inflectional and derivational morphology

The only studies of the ongoing appearance of inflectional morphology in a Creole are those of Tok Pisin. Generally speaking, there appears to be no qualitative difference between the developments in expanded second-language Tok Pisin and creolized Tok Pisin. Instead, creolization merely continues and generalizes ongoing changes. Comparative data from other Creoles would be particularly welcome.

Let me illustrate these observations with the example of plural marking in creolized Tok Pisin.[38] Arguing from what is widely maintained in the theoretical literature on creolization, I set up the following hypotheses:

---

[38] Remarks on plural marking at earlier stages are given on p 168 above.

1. Plural marking will become categorical in all environments, that is, it is semantically determined;
2. The position of the plural marker in the noun phrase will become fixed;
3. Differences in surface form will always be associated with differences in meaning;
4. Semantic plural will be marked in parts of the sentence other than the noun phrase.

None of these predictions was borne out in full. Moreover, it appears that different solutions to the problems of plural marking are found in the three creolized varieties of Tok Pisin examined: that is, those of Malabang (Manus Island), Yip (on the Keram River) and urban Lae (data recorded by Sankoff and Laberge in 1971). Unfortunately, the texts examined were not of sufficient length for a detailed syntactic analysis such as the one undertaken here, and elicitation and formal interviews were only used in Malabang. However, the following generalizations can be made with confidence.

First, plural marking remains variable for all creolized varieties examined; the only instance of categorical plural marking was that of animate subjects in Malabang Tok Pisin. None the less, plurals without **ol** are in the minority in all semantic environments of the varieties examined. My own feeling is that the trend towards a categorical marking of the semantic plural is blocked by the fact that **ol** is a relatively stressed free-standing formative and not an unstressed affix.

Second, my data suggest that the position of **ol** in the noun phrase is not fixed in creolized Tok Pisin and that variation is found not only across creolized varieties in different localities, but also within the speech of individual speakers. However, the favourite form is the one in which ol appears at the beginning of a noun phrase. Compare the following data:

1. Speakers from Yip aged between 8 and 12 years:

ol adj. N	*adj. ol N*	*ol adj. ol N*
ol dispela lain	**dispela liklik ol tumbuna**	**ol narapela ol tumbuna**
'this group'	'those little grandchildren'	'the other grandchildren'
ol planti dok	**olgeta ol pis**	
'many dogs'	'all the fish'	

2. Speakers from Malabang (first-generation Tok Pisin speakers, aged 25-35):

ol dispela lain	**dispela ol man**
'this group'	'these people'
ol faivhandet masalai	**bikpela ol man**
'five hundred spirits'	'big men'
ol lokal pipel	
'the local people'	

3. Speakers from Lae (children recorded by Sankoff in 1971):

ol dispela man	**ol dispela ol man**
'these men'	'these men'
ol sampela man	**sampela ol man**
'some men'	'some men'

More fixity is found with some prenominal modifiers such as **olgeta** 'all', always followed by **ol**, and **lokal** 'local', always preceded by **ol**. It is not clear to me to what extent the position of **ol** is linked to certain lexical items.

Third, although the principle of one form, one meaning is realized to a greater degree in creolized Tok Pisin than in other varieties, I have not been able to find any consistent difference in meaning between, for instance **ol sampela man** 'some men' and **sampela ol man** 'some men'. I would predict, however, that unless speakers settle for one of these alternatives, a difference in meaning will develop in creolized Tok Pisin.

Finally, the prediction that plurality will be marked in parts of the sentence other than the noun phrase is partly fulfilled in Malabang Creole Tok Pisin, where a kind of agreement between plural noun subjects and reduplicated verbs is developing. Examples of this construction are:

ol pikinini i pilaipilai	'the children are playing'

as against:

wanpela pikinini i pilai	'a child is playing'
(*wanpela pikinini i pilaipilai)	
planti man i lainlain	'many men were lined up'
ol manmeri i bungbung	'the people gathered'

In conclusion, the following generalizations can be made about morphological developments in Tok Pisin's creolization phase:

1. The differences between non-creolized and creolized Tok Pisin are slight rather than drastic;
2. Although there is a definite tendency for rules to become more productive (and less restricted by environmental conditions), the endpoint of maximum simplification has not yet been reached;
3. The amount of redundancy found in creolized Tok Pisin is not greater than that found in late expanded Tok Pisin.

Most Creoles, it appears, still have not acquired any significant inflectional categories and those that have, like some Portuguese-based ones, may have acquired them some time after creolization, in which case their change from isolating to inflectional languages is comparable with that in other full languages. Creoles for which the absence of inflectional morphology has been explicitly stated include Guyanais of French Guiana (St Jacques Fauquenoy 1974), Krio, the English-based Creoles of the Caribbean, and many more. In those cases where inflectional categories have developed, this typically involves condensation of pre-existing fully stressed markers of grammatical categories, as in Tok Pisin. Thus:

> where Mauricien Creole has *Mo té apré manzé* for 'I was eating', the usual representation of the Haitian equivalent is *M tap manjé* (Faine 1939). In the French Creole of the Antilles, we have a future marker **ke**, which seems to have been derived from the durative marker **ka** with **ale**; **ka + ale - kale - kae - ke**. (Labov 1990:38)

The problem with Labov's account is his use of linguistic data from two different periods, in that the Mauritian example dates from 1880. A comparison between the forms of the Mauritian sentence current in 1880,

194

1939 and the present day would have been a more secure basis for claims about developmental trends. As these condensations are often optional and characteristic of fast-spoken language, their representation in available grammars of Creoles is often sketchy. Therefore the emergence of inflectional morphology does not appear to be a necessary feature of creolization, although the fact that it subsequently emerges in many Creole studies suggests considerable inter-speaker variation in the use of condensed and affixed grammatical markers, thus casting doubt on the idea that the transition from isolating to inflectional Creoles follows any universally pre-programmed path.

As regards the development of derivational morphology or word formation, more information was particularly forthcoming in the 1980s, notably on English-based Creoles such as Krio (Jones 1984), Sranan (Sebba 1981, Voorhoeve 1981), and the Australian Creoles (for example Steffensen 1979). More comprehensive surveys were made by Hancock (1980) and Allsopp (1980). We must again distinguish between cases where some word-formation processes are found in the preceding Pidgins and those where the Pidgin is lacking in derivational morphology. We must also distinguish developments accompanying creolization with first-generation speakers from subsequent developments.

The only documented case of a Creole that has developed from an expanded Pidgin which already had word formation worth mentioning is that of Tok Pisin. The principal difference between second-language expanded and first language creolized Tok Pisin was found to lie in the following areas:

1. Existing derivational rules are generalized (i.e, made fully productive);
2. Derivational processes can apply recursively;
3. Some derivational morphology is borrowed from local vernaculars.

The following examples will serve as illustrations. First, we will consider the derivation of causative verbs from intransitive verbs and adjectives. Only a small number of forms are encountered in most second-language varieties of the language. In creolized Tok Pisin of Malabang, this rule has become virtually exceptionless; new forms encountered include:

Malabang Tok Pisin	*Gloss*
wara i STINGIM ol plang	'the water makes the planks rot'
dispela kaikai i SWITIM maus bilong mi	
	'this food gives my mouth a pleasant taste'
meri i BONIM pikinini	'the woman gave birth to a child'
em i wok long RAUNIM diwai	'he is busy making a piece of wood round'
meri i SMATIM em yet	'the girl dolled herself up'

It is interesting to note that Malabang Tok Pisin now exhibits the same lexical productivity in this area as Tok Pisin's original principal substratum language, Tolai. A static comparison of the two languages would suggest direct substratum influence.

Second, a major increase in Tok Pisin's lexical power is caused by the relaxation or abolition, in the creolized varieties I studied, of the constraint on multiple derivation. Instead, recursive application of derivational rules yields numerous new forms such as:

1. The derivation of abstract nouns from derived verbals:

huk	huk	huk
'hook'	'to go fishing'	'fishing'
kuk	kukim	ol Hailans i gat narapela KUKIM
		bilong saksak
'to boil, cook'	'to cook something'	'the Highlanders have a different
		COOKING METHOD for sage'

2. The derivation of abstract nouns from reduplicated verbs:

holim	holholim	paip i gut long HOLHOLIM bilongen
'to hold'	'to grasp, hold fast'	'the pipe is good with regard to its
		HANDLING QUALITIES'
lukim	luklukim	meri i gut long LUKLUKIM bilongen
'to look, watch'	'to gaze, stare'	'the girl is really very good looking'

3. The reduplication of derived verbals:

smok	smokim	smoksmokim
'to smoke'	'to smoke (coconuts)'	'to smoke thoroughly'
sak	sakim	saksakim
'bag'	'to fill in bags'	'to fill many bags'
krugut	krugutim	krukrugutim
'crooked'	'to crush'	'to crush to little pieces'

It is important to note that many of the changes in the lexicon do not relate to an increase in referential power of the language, but provide new linguistic styles.

Finally, borrowing of derivational affixes from a local language is illustrated with the following set: creolized Tok Pisin of Manus Island has developed a new variant way for expressing concepts, previously expressed by complex lexical items in the second-language varieties:

Second-language Tok Pisin	Malabang-creolized Tok Pisin	Gloss
Manusman	pomanus	'a true Manus man'
Manusmeri	pimanus	'a true Manus woman'
man bilong smokim paip	popaip	'a pipe smoker'
man bilong smokim brus	pobrus	'a cigar smoker'
spakman	pospak	'a habitual drinker'

(po = 'man' and pi = 'woman' in local coastal Melanesian languages)

Other studies of derivational morphology in Creoles are not developmental. To date there is no evidence that a powerful derivational lexicon develops within a single generation of children to make up for the numerous lexical deficiencies of their input language. However, it is possible to make a number of observations. These relate to the origin of word-formation processes in preceding Pidgins; the role of substratum languages; and the overall power and regularity of Creole lexicons. Many writers have asked whether there are any aspects of Creole derivational morphology that set them apart typologically from other languages. The two areas singled out most frequently are multifunctionallty and reduplication, which are both said to be present in Creoles to a greater extent than in other languages, due to the fact that Creoles continue a trend already noticeable in their Pidgin predecessors. With regard to multifunctionality, Voorhoeve (1981:26) explicitly states: "subsequent grammatical expansion in a creolization process does not offer incentives to create semantically empty affixes. This may explain why multifunctionality seems to be more frequent and more regular in Pidgins and Creoles than in the model language." Unfortunately, he does not illustrate the actual process of expansion. A study of multifunctionality in Sranan (Sebba 1981) suggests that, although this process is extremely common, it is also subject to a number of fairly complex restrictions: for example, no nouns can be derived from benefactive or position verbs. The presence of such restrictions, as well as differences from restrictions in the lexifier language, make the suggestion of direct Pidgin ancestry less attractive. However, only a longitudinal analysis could answer the question.

Reduplication in Creoles again has often been traced back to preceding Pidgins. Thus, Thompson argues:

> The amount of iteration which takes place in Creole languages is striking. We must, however, guard against according this phenomenon too much importance. Not everyone who says 'sí, sí, señor', 'ay, ay, sir' or 'oh, la la' is a Creole speaker. Iteration is common to many languages and the part it plays in the formation of pidgins could, alone, explain its vigorous presence in the Creoles (1961:111).

However, as already pointed out, productive reduplicative processes are not widespread in Pidgins, and indeed are neither a necessary nor sufficient typological property of Creoles. The data presented in studies on Northern Australian Kriol, for instance, suggest no direct link with a Pidgin antecedent, although Steffensen suggests:

> It will be claimed that semantically-motivated reduplication in the Australian creole is similar to that found in other English-based creoles, including Jamaican, Krio and Pidgin English of West Cameroon, a fact providing some support for the genetic relationship of these languages. In the case of adjectivals, the process is similar to that which has been described for an Aboriginal language, showing a syntactic influence of the substratum languages. These two sources of reduplication clearly parallel the two sources of the language (1977:603).

In sum, then, Creoles are qualitatively different from documented Pidgins spoken previously. Lack of longitudinal studies prevents us from determining whether there has been an abrupt break or whether these differences reflect a gradual drifting apart.

The influence of substratum languages on Creole word formation has often been advocated. Again, with the data we have, it is difficult to draw any firm conclusions. Where more detailed studies exist, such as with reduplication in Seychellois and Australian Creoles, direct substratum influence is seen as a very minor factor. It is true that many Creoles exhibit a certain amount of transparent calques such as the ones given by Hancock (1980:81). These include five calques of African origin from Trinidad and Tobago: ha:d-e:z 'stubborn' (*hard* + *ears*), kʌt-ai 'to turn away one's glance' (*cut* + *eye*), lɔŋ-ai 'to be covetous' (*long* + *eye*), da:k-ai 'poor vision' (*dark* +

197

eye), mɔːtə-pɛsl 'pestle' (*mortar* + *pestle*); and three of Malay origin in Papia Kristang Creole Portuguese: kumi-bɛntu 'stroll' (lit. *eat* + *wind*), mai-pai 'parents'(lit. *mother* + *father*), olu-di-pɛu 'ankle'(lit. *eye* + *of* + *foot*). However, such calques typically are lexicalizations rather than the basis of productive processes of word formation. In fact, I have yet to see hard evidence to convince me that substratum languages have played an important role in the development of word formation in any Creole. I should add that younger Creoles appear to be even less affected than older ones, suggesting that similarity of the derivational lexicons of languages such as Krio and West African vernaculars is the result of prolonged language contacts rather than the process of creolization or even Creole development over time.

A cursory examination of the lexicons of a number of Creoles suggests that they are neither very regular nor very powerful. The cumulative impression is one of numerous competing developments, a high degree of lexicalizations or semi-productive processes, and a continued reliance on borrowing from outside sources. This, however, can only be a tentative conclusion, and I am well aware of DeCamp's brilliant demonstration (1974) that the full extent of productivity in a Creole language cannot be recovered by conventional methods of fieldwork.

As yet, the change-over to a system with a derivational lexicon has been described only for an expanding Pidgin (Tok Pisin in Mühlhäusler 1979). How first-generation Creole-speakers in instances of more abrupt creolization cope with their lexical needs remains ill understood. With regard to the potential sources for new word-formation patterns, we should keep two things in mind. First, the discontinuities in the transition from Pidgin to Creole make direct expansion of a pre-existing Pidgin an unlikely explanation for many Creole languages. Second, it is by no means clear that Creoles have the syncretic capacity to borrow derivational morphology from substratum or other outside systems.

In the light of these observations, a gradual development out of internal resources, comparable to that encountered in Tok Pisin, seems more likely. In this view, new derivational regularities would result from surface analogy, reanalysis of pre-existing structures and rule generalization. Linguistic evidence from a number of present-day Creoles suggests that these processes take place over many generations and that, in most instances, they remain a long distance away from the theoretically possible optimal endpoint.[39] It is only in those cases that have been subject to active language engineering (as, for instance, Bahasa Indonesia, Swahili or Afrikaans) that anything like full productivity has been reached.

Syntax

Almost all recent discussion of creolization has centred around syntactic observations. Most important are Bickerton's suggestions that a number of widely found aspects of Creole syntax are indeed innate or bioprogrammatic. This issue is still being hotly debated and cannot be dealt with in full here.

It again seems best to distinguish between Creoles that have arisen out of expanded Pidgins and others that have developed out of unstable jargons, and between developments accompanying creolization and those occurring

---

[39] This endpoint is to be understood as full productivity and absence of suppletive patterns (cf Markey 1985).

later. Studies of Tok Pisin and Australian Aboriginal Kriol, both of which developed out of expanded Pidgins, have suggested considerable syntactic variation within even small groups of Creole speakers, or indeed individuals. Thus Koch (1984) found that relative clauses in Central Australian Aboriginal Creole were introduced by a number of different relative markers, including **we** (< *where*), **wanim** < *what name*), **who** and **what** as in (data from Koch 1984):

we just got a lot of kurtungurlus *who* work for them	(Peter J 95)
and some of them kurtungurlu been pass away	(Peter T 75)
pewelerrenge *what* 'im talk kurrkurr kurrkurr nighttime	(Sam 5.30a)
etenetene *where* him jump (an insect)	(Sam 5.32)
alpalhe ('fur string') *where* they cut'm from rabbits	(Sam 5.32)
Euro they *where* they live along hill	(Peter T 101)
nytveypere *wanim* flying, nighttime	(Sam 5.31)

These forms appear to have coexisted for some time without streamlining of relative marking. Similar findings for Tok Pisin were arrived at by Aitchison (1983). Differences were found within a small group of females living at a hostel in Lae, the second largest town in Papua New Guinea, and these differences did not disappear even with members of the same family. In addition to different language-internal solutions to the problem of relative markers, some group members had also borrowed grammar from Tok Pisin's lexifier language English, rendering the distinction between creolization and decreolization a difficult one to maintain.

Supporters of the bioprogram theory of Creole syntax would argue that such variation in the Pidgin-Creole complexes is symptomatic of the gradual transition from second to first language. Children who are exposed to minimal jargon input would presumably have fewer structures to reanalyse, and hence would have to appeal to innate solutions. However, this theory leaves several unexplained points:

1. The obvious qualitative differences between Creoles such as Hawaiian Creole English and their jargon or Pidgin predecessors;
2. The syntactic similarities between Creoles world-wide;
3. The fact that such similarities arose without apparent historical links and without shared substratum languages.

I will deal with these points in turn.

First, Bickerton's Hawaiian Pidgin and Hawaiian Creole English show numerous documented qualitative differences. Speakers of the former appear to have at their disposal an extremely rudimentary syntax, idiosyncratic and generally devoid of grammatical markers. Speakers of the latter have acquired, within a very brief time, a relatively complex Creole syntax. Bickerton argued that "such structures can only have been acquired by processes inaccessible to pidgin speakers" (1984:177). Why second-language Pidgin-speakers never learnt the more sophisticated language of their offspring seems strange, particularly as no such aversion to learning is found with Tok Pisin or the Australian Aboriginal Creoles. The reasons would seem to be social (having to do with their bilingualism, the social networks they operate in and so forth), rather than a mental inability to learn more complex structures as adults. If indeed the Creole of the children is such a "natural" system, it should surely be one that is highly learnable. Another consideration with regard to the generational language differences is that Bickerton does not have data to show at what age and in what order the Creole constructions were acquired.

Second, there is considerable disagreement as to the world-wide similarities of Creole structures, although "the hypothesis of the structural interdependence of Creoles with different lexical components" (Hellinger 1979:332) remains popular. I have had the privilege of examining data from a hitherto virtually unknown Creole, Unserdeutsch, a German-based Creole of Papua New Guinea, which appears to be a case of an insufficient jargon turning into a Creole within one generation. A comparison of this Creole and Tok Pisin, which was also used by Unserdeutsch-speakers, with Bickerton's bioprogram features reveals some major discrepancies, however. Using the features singled out by Bickerton (1981) as diagnostic of biogrammar, the following observations were made.

1. *Movement.* Rules move focused constituents to sentence-initial position. Such rules are found both in Tok Pisin and Unserdeutsch, for example:

    Nur ein Name i konnte ni finden 'Only one name I could not find'

2. *Article.* The definite article is used for presupposed-specific NP; an indefinite article for asserted-specific NP; and zero for non-specific NP. Unserdeutsch does not appear to follow this system (nor does Tok Pisin), as can be seen from the following utterance:

    I lesen Buch 'I read a (particular) book'

    According to Volker, "reflecting perhaps the lack of articles in Tok Pisin, the use of either article is optional and in many sentences, Vunapope Germans omitted an article where this would not have been possible in English or Standard German" (1982:37).

3. *Tense-modality-aspect system.* Neither Tok Pisin nor Unserdeutsch appear to fit into Bickerton's suggested universal framework for Creole languages. Like southern dialects of German (spoken by the majority of the German mission workers), Unserdeutsch has only one past tense, in addition to present and future tenses. Like Tok Pisin and English, but unlike High German, it signals the distinction between durative and non-durative aspect. The important distinction in Tok Pisin between inception and completion, on the other hand, is not found in Unserdeutsch.

4. *Realized and unrealized complements.* The data available to me do not permit any definite statements on this point.

5. *Relativization and subject copying.* Whereas Tok Pisin conforms to the universals postulated by Bickerton in this area of grammar, Unserdeutsch does not. The most common relative pronoun appears to be **wo**, as in:

    Der Mensch, wo is am bauen de Haus, hat gehauen sein Finger.
    'The man who was building a house hurt his finger(s)'

6. *Negation.* Neither Tok Pisin nor Unserdeutsch conform to the conditions for negation in Creoles laid down by Bickerton.

7. *Existential and possessive.* Whereas the same lexical item is used to express existentials (there is) and possessives (have) in many Creoles

and in Tok Pisin, Unserdeutsch does not have this construction. This is surprising since the Tok Pisin model (**mi gat mani** = 'I have money', compared with **i gat mani** = 'there is money') was available and southern German dialects have this feature (**es hat Geld** = 'it (e.g. the child) has money' or 'there is money').

8. *Copula.* In Unserdeutsch, the copula is conspicuous by its presence and, what is more, it is inflected for person and tense.

9. *Adjectives as verbs.* Adjectives are used as verbs in many Creoles and in Tok Pisin, but not in Unserdeutsch. Other changes of grammatical category are observed in this language, however: in particular, abstract nouns may become verbs or adjectives. It would seem that the presence of a verb-adjective distinction is closely connected with the presence of a copula in Unserdeutsch.

10. *Question forms.* Like Tok Pisin and all other Creoles, Unserdeutsch shows no difference in syntactic order between questions and statements, e.g.:

Du will drinken Kaffee 'Do you want to drink coffee?/You want to drink coffee'

In spoken discourse, differential intonation patterns are often used to distinguish questions from statements.

11. *Question words.* Whereas question words are typically polymorphemic in the Creoles considered by Bickerton as well as in Tok Pisin, Unserdeutsch has a mixed system. Compare:

Standard German	Unserdeutsch	Tok Pisin	Etymon gloss
warum	**was, warum**	**wa(t)nem**	why?
welche	**was fuer**	**wa(t)nem**	what (e.g. time)?
wieviel	**wieviel**	**hamas**	how many?
wer	**wer**	**husat**	who?

12. *Passive equivalents.* Unlike virtually all other known Creoles, including Tok Pisin, Unserdeutsch has a fully developed passive construction. It is basically the same as that found in English, using the formula copula + past participle + *bei*, as in:

Der Chicken war gestohlen bei alle Rascal.
'The chicken was stolen by the rascals'

The above information has to be considered in the light of available linguistic models at the time when Unserdeutsch came into being. The models in question are standard German (taught to the speakers at school), (New Guinea) Pidgin German (a very rudimentary Pidgin) and a newly stabilized Tok Pisin. The table overleaf indicates the presence or absence of Bickerton's features for these languages. This clearly demonstrates that Unserdeutsch differs drastically from Bickerton's ideal Creole, whereas Tok Pisin, as used by second-language speakers, exhibits considerable overlay with his diagnostic features. At the same time, it reveals major structural differences between Unserdeutsch and the two input languages – Pidgin and "standard" German. Similar differences are also found in Pitcairnese (cf Le Page 1983b). Finally, in the light of such findings, the question of origins for Creole syntactic structures must be asked again. The fact that both Pitcairnese and Unserdeutsch developed out of Pidgins unrelated to those that have been the base of most other Creoles could be taken as an indication that the structure of a Creole is linked, in an as yet ill-understood fashion, to its Pidgin precursor. However, some qualitative differences remain to be explained.

Presence or absence of various features in available linguistic models at the time when Unserdeutsch came into being

Feature	Hawaiian Creole	New Guinea Pidgin German	Tok Pisin	German	English	Unserdeutsch
1. Movement	+	–	+	+	+	+
2. Definite article	+	–	–	–	–	–
3. Tense, etc.	+	–	–	–	–	–
4. Complements	+	n.a.	–	–	–	?
5. Relativization	+	–	+	–	?	–
6. Negation	+	–	–	–	–	–
7. Existential	+	+	+	+	–	–
8. Copula	+	0	+	–	–	–
9. Adjectives	+	–	+	–	–	–
10. Questions	+	n.a.	+	–	–	+
11. Question words	+	–	+	+/–	+/–	+/–
12. Passive equivalent	+	n.a.	+	–	–	–

n.a Not applicable, no evidence;   0 Variable presence;   + Categorical presence;   – Absence

More historical research is needed into the diffusion of Creole grammar. The fact that some of the Portuguese speakers working on the Hawaiian plantations in the 19th century had been recruited from the Creole-speaking Cape Verde Islands may well account for the wide distribution of some of Bickerton's Creole features.

The degree of access to the target language must also be further researched. The fact that the lexicon of most Creoles appears to have been drawn largely from the socially superordinate language suggests that this access cannot have been as limited as is often made out. Lexical borrowing can be expected to have considerable repercussions in the syntactic component. If, for instance, the difference between causative and non-causative verbs is fully lexicalized in the lexifier language, then the emergence of productive rules for causative formation is likely to be slowed down or prevented. Many Creole-speakers have been exposed to standard forms of its European lexifier language in the classroom or on mission stations.

Access to substratum languages is another area of dispute. Supporters of the bioprogram generally admit the availability of substratum languages as potential models, but are quick to point out the various factors that make them unattractive to children. In the absence of any first-hand data on creolization of jargons, I would prefer to postpone judgement on this.

Even if it should turn out that first-generation Creole-speakers were maximally cut off from syntactic input – and no evidence to support this has since come to light – such conditions would be necessary rather than sufficient components of a bioprogram explanation. In his review of Bickerton (1981), Foley (1984) spelt out the functionalist alternative. In discussing the alleged bioprogrammatic nature of the SVO word order of Creoles, Foley pointed out that this is the most likely solution to the problem of variable word order in the Pidgin stage for simple functionalist reasons. Since Creole-speaking children do not develop inflectional morphology:

> without inflections to mark the subject or object of a sentence, word orders like SOV or VSO are problematic because the order of the subject and object may not be altered without changing the meaning of the sentence, but such languages tend in fact to use such rearrangements heavily to signal the relative importance of the subject or object. The word order SVO avoids this problem by using the positions on either side of the verb to indicate subject and object, and movement of the object before the subject, as in *John, I saw yesterday*, causes no interpretation problems because the subject is the immediately preverbal noun. Note that in this explanation there is no need to appeal to an innate bioprogram which specifies SVO word order. The restricted input plus the constraints imposed by human communicative needs determine this preference (Foley 1984:337).

These matters remain unresolved, but it seems obvious that a great deal more has to be learnt about Creole syntax before a final judgement can be made.

I have already mentioned the paucity of longitudinal studies of Creole syntactic development, and there are few reliable guidelines for distinguishing between developments during and subsequent to creolization. That such subsequent development has played a major role in many of the present-day Creoles is well known. The relative isolation in which some of them have developed does not appear to have slowed down their rate of internal change. A detailed discussion is beyond the scope of this book, but a few cases will serve to highlight the strong parallels between Pidgin expansion and changes in later Creole development.

As pointed out by Voorhoeve & Kramp (1982), Bickerton hardly acknowledges the possibility of syntactic change in Creoles other than for change motivated by decreolization under the influence of a dominant language. If it is true, however, that many internal developments subsequent to creolization spring from the "need to differentiate basic concepts" (1982:12), then they are well worth considering.[40] Voorhoeve & Kramp follow up a number of developments in Sranan, including the creation of a future marker, changes from an aspect-centred to a tense-centred system of verbal modification, and the development of new prepositions. A particularly interesting case is the development of three-place verbs. Sranan, as recorded in the late 18th century, had the following phrase structure (PS) rules (Voorhoeve & Kramp 1982:3):

1. S -> NP AUX VP
2. VP -> V (NP) PP
3. PP -> **na** NP

These rules provide for a maximum of two arguments per verb.[41] In later texts, however, strategies for adding a further argument to verbs are encountered, among them the use of the all-purpose preposition **na**, as in:

---

[40] Such evidence would be of particular interest to the question of qualitative differences between languages, as it suggests the possibility that the first-generation Creoles (those created by children only) may be lacking in important areas of grammar.

[41] Cases of verbs chaining are ignored for the sake of this argument.

ju gi assranti na Bakkra?   'Did you give brutality to a white man?'

It appears that the development of **gi** into a three-place verb proceeded in stages. In the early texts it can only be a three-place verb, if the third argument is pronominal. Later any NP is permitted. This kind of change is difficult to categorize and certainly involves more than a reanalysis of existing linguistic structures.

A similarly "spontaneous" development involves the Jamaican interrogative form **duont** (Roberts 1977:101-08), meaning 'isn't that so?'; this is a relatively recent form. It is unusual because of its phonological shape (final-consonant cluster); its not being used as a social marker; and its functional differences with pre-existing tags in both Jamaican Creole and standard English. Thus it is not simply a new form used in an old function,[42] but a sign with new form and function.

Other documented examples of Creole development most frequently take the form of syntactic reanalysis. A very common example is the emergence of complementizers out of prepositions (Nichols 1976; Washabaugh 1975). Nichols notes the close parallel of this development in the expanded Pidgin Tok Pisin and the Creole Gullah.

A number of changes in the history of French-based Creoles are discussed by Valdman (1977a:155-89), including phonological condensation of grammatical markers and changes with verbal and nominal modifiers. Among the latter, Valdman discusses the development of an older system, illustrated in Mauritian Creole for **lisjĕ** 'dog':

Singular		Plural
en lisjĕ	Indefinite	**lisjĕ**
lisjĕ-la	Definite	**ban lisjĕ-l a**
mo lisjĕ	Possessive 1sg	**mo ban lisjĕ**
sa lisjĕ-la	Demonstrative	**sa ban lisjĕ-l a**

into a new one, which adds a plural marker identical with the third-person plural pronoun. A further development is the shift of the demonstrative from a preposed to a post-nominal position in some French-based Creoles; this is summarized, for instance, in Haitian Creole (ibid.: 168) as follows:

Singular		Plural
ju liv	Indefinite	**liv**
liv-la	Definite	**liv-jo**
liv-sa-a	Demonstrative	**liv-sa-jo**
liv-li	Possessive 3sg	**liv-li-jo**
liv-la-a	Deictic	**liv-la-jo**
liv-li-a	Possessive +Deictic	**liv-li-a-jo**

Valdman arrives at his conclusions primarily by comparing different French Creoles and only occasionally relying on longitudinal evidence for individual Creoles. In view of the above-mentioned unsuitability of the comparative paradigm for Creole studies, his conclusions must be interpreted with care. In fact, Baker (1982:210-11) clearly disconfirms Valdman's suggestion that the Mauritian system is a conservative one. A detailed longitudinal examination of the plural marker **ban** (< Fr. *bande* 'bunch') makes this abundantly clear.

---

[42] This, as will be shown shortly, is the typical property of decreolization processs.

The fact that **ban** is found in Mauritian and Reunion, as well as the minor Indian Ocean Creoles, does not warrant the conclusion that these Creoles all derived from an ancestral language containing this form. Although the count noun **ban** 'group, shoal' is attested in Mauritian Creole from the middle of the 19th century, it was not used as a pluralizer until about 1880. As regards Reunion Creole, Baker remarks: "The earliest examples of /ban/ as a plural marker I have yet found in RC are in Fourcade (1930). In that text, /ban/ occurs with some frequency and thus can scarcely then have been a new feature of RC" (p 211). One can therefore only agree with his conclusions:

> It seems clear from the above that /ban/ alone did not function as the plural marker at the beginning of the 19th century in any Indian Ocean Creole but had acquired this status in MC by 1885 at the latest. Whether this was a Mauritian innovation - a distinct possibility on the available evidence - or not, remains to be determined. However, one can at least conclude that the presence of a grammatical (or lexical) item in all the Indian Ocean Creoles does *not* prove that this was a feature of eighteenth-century RC (p 211).

In conclusion, longitudinal accounts of Creole expansion – both for the process of creolization itself and for subsequent developments – would seem essential. The short-cuts taken by many scholars in the past appear not to lead to the insights they had hoped for and have often produced a quite unrealistic picture.

Lexicon and lexical semantics
Although much has been said about the lexicon of individual Creoles, comparative studies and those using up-to-date lexicological techniques are rare, as is reliable information as to the point in time at which lexical items entered a Creole. Many of the traditional studies only consider the relative proportion of substratum and other "foreign" lexical material, concluding mainly that the European element is dominant. Thus, Sylvain refers to Haitian Creole as "une langue éwé à vocabulaire français" (1936:136). Aub-Buscher (1984) similarly concludes that, after considering all foreign loans, "a solid residue of 90% of entries in a Trinidad French Creole glossary has its origin in the central or dialectal French of past centuries".

Aub-Buscher categorizes foreign loans in Trinidadian French Creole according to semantic domains. These loans include:

1. Magic and traditional religion:
   obja   'magic'   (Efik, Twi)
   wãga   'magic spell' (Douala, Mbondu, Bolo, Songo, Sama)
   dẽge   'sorcerer's sleight of hand'   (Ngombe)

2. Traditional ways of food preparation:
   akra   'fritter'   (Yoruba, Igbo)
   tõtõ banan 'mashed green bananas'   (Twi)
   kuku   'corn'   (Ewe)

3. Polite names for body parts:
   pumpum   'female genitals' (Twi)
   lolo   'penis'   (Ewe ?)
   bõda   'buttocks'   (Bambara, Kikongo)

205

4. Local fauna:

tiktak	'large ant'	(Bulu)
kōgowi	'sort of millipede'	(Kikongo)
kulu (bwa)	'termite'	(Kanuri)
kungala	'frog'	(Kikongo)
zēglētē	'sea bird'	(Ewe, Kikongo)

Other domains, such as local flora, fish names and diseases, are typically of Amerindian origin.

Regarding the European part of the lexicon, a number of Creolists have painstakingly traced its elements back to regional or social varieties of lexifier language. One example is Holm's (1978) analysis of the Miskito Creole English vocabulary. Examples of the numerous British English words that Holm identified in this Creole include:

British dialect origin of some Miskito Coast Creole English words

Dialect words	Gloss	Regions							
arm-hole	'armpit'		1			4	5	6		8	
atween	'between'	G	1		3						
bawl	'shout, cry'		1			4				8	9
bro	'male peer'								7		
drownded	'drown'		1			4	5	6			
evening	'afternoon'		1				5		7		
first	'immediately'					4	5				9
frowzy	'musty'	G	1		3						
gal	'girl'	G							7	8	

G General, 1 Ireland, 2 Wales, 3 Scotland, 4 North England, 5 West Midlands, 6 East Midlands, 7 East Anglia, 8 Home Counties, 9 West of England (adapted from Holm 1978:47).

There have been a number of innovative attempts to gain a better understanding of the contribution of non-European languages to the vocabulary of the so-called European-based ones. An important consideration is that of Edwards: "The factors which determine that the phonological form from one heritage will be adopted by Pidgin-speakers are sometimes distinct from the factors which determine the origins of the semantic, symbolic, emotional content for any given lexeme" (1974:5). Thus lexical items should not be regarded as undividable wholes, but as capable of accommodating different types of lexical information from different sources. In the case of many "multi-level syncretisms", the shape of a lexical item is similar to that of the related European language, whereas semantic or syntactic-categorical information may be traced back to substratum languages. This idea was taken up by Givón (1979) and Mühlhäusler (1979), among others, and tested against data from various Creoles. It appears that the extent of non-European influence on lexical semantics is fairly extensive and that the traditional method of comparing undivided cognates for lexical comparison is insufficient. A major attempt to determine the extent of substratum semantics across a wide range of Creoles was made by Huttar (1975). He examined the degree of correspondence of lexical semantics between the Surinamese Creole Djuka and 43 other languages with respect to 20 lexical roots. His findings (1975:694) were:

1. The major factor we may call 'linguistic substratum'. This label subsumes the total linguistic background (genetic, areal, and contact phenomena) of the native speakers of non-European languages involved in the initial contact situation that produced a pidgin. It does not include extralinguistic cultural background.
2. A second factor that appears important enough to merit further investigation is the role played by language contact after the original pidginization period.
3. The nature of creoles themselves - arising from pidgins not only by expansion of vocabulary, but also by extension in meaning of existing vocabulary items - plays at most a minor role. (Extension of meaning occurs in pidgins as well.) This pidgin-creole factor is clearly less significant than factors 1 and 2.

This suggests that the lexical semantics of the source language are modified to a considerable extent in related Pidgins and Creoles, and that resulting differences are due principally to substratum influence; that language mixing is particularly common at the lexical level (disconfirming earlier views as to the relative lexical purity of Pidgins and Creoles); and that, moreover, substratum structures must have been available both during and subsequent to the creolization process.

That substratum influence is not haphazard and restricted to single lexical items is seen by the apparent continuation of lexical field structures from substratum languages in later Creoles. This is obviously what can be expected in the case of a gradual transition from a Pidgin to a Creole, as, for instance, in the case of Australian Kriol. Sandefur (1981:256) illustrates this with Kriol kinship terms, where the lexical forms of English have been paired with meanings typical of Aboriginal kinship systems:

dedi	< *daddy*	'father and father's brothers'
mami	< *mummy*	'mother and mother's sisters'
anggul	< *uncle*	'mother's brothers'
andi	< *aunty*	'father's sisters'
greni	< *granny*	'mother's mother and her brothers and sisters' as well as 'sister's daughter's sons and daughters'
meit	< *mate*	'spouse and spouse's brothers and sisters'
gajin	< *cousin*	'mother-in-law and her brothers and sisters'

Lexical field structures of substratum languages are also encountered in Creoles that allegedly emerged over a much shorter period, such as Jamaican Creole and Djuka. Both these languages formerly had a West African system of day-names, i.e. names given to children according to the day of the week on which they were born born. Kahn (1931:171) presents the following table demonstrating the similarity of such names in Djuka and Twi (of Ghana):

Day of birth	*Male* Djuka	Twi	*Female* Djuka	Twi
Sun.	Kwassi	Kwassi	Akwasiba	Asi/Akwasiba
Mon.	Kodjo	Kwadjo	Adoea/Adjoba	Adua
Tue.	Kwamina/Kwabina	Kobina/Kwabina	Abena/Akoba	Abena/Arabat
Wed.	Kwakoe/Quakoe	Kwaku	Akoea	Akua
Thu.	Jaw/Akhor	Know/Yow/Yawa	Jaba	Awbah/Awybah
Fri.	Koffi/Koffay	Kwaffi	Afida	Yah-awfua
Sat.	Kwassi	Kwassi	Aruba	Anenimwah

207

DeCamp (1967) reports the same phenomenon for Jamaica and other Creole-speaking areas of the New World. This West African system of name-giving appears to have gradually died out and was obsolete by the end of the 19th century. The reasons given by DeCamp include social changes as well as the fact that most of these names underwent semantic deterioration. For example, **quashie**, which originally meant 'male person born on a Sunday' (see **Kwassi** above) had come to mean, among other derogatory things, 'fool', 'irresponsible ne'er-do-well' and 'pig-headed man' (1967:145).

An area where retention of substratum language is particularly intense is that of exclamations, interjections and related phenomena. Cassidy remarks:

> the great majority of interjections in the Creole are of African origin. In use by slaves these were not necessary to communication, however natural they might be to expression of feelings or emotions. They did not require translation or relexification; their meaning was evident in context, and could even, in different contexts, serve for such related emotions as fear and anger (1975).

Examples from Jamaican Creole English mentioned by Cassidy include:

aóo, aóa	(< Twi *áò*)	'what! why! hey! ay! fie!'
bábwá	(< Twi *bóbŭóo*)	'exclamation of astonishment'.

With the advent of theories of linguistic naturalness and markedness, a new instrument for determining the "foreign" element in European-based Creoles became available. An early paper in this category is Frake's (1971) analysis of the Spanish-based Creoles of the Philippines; his initial findings have since been confirmed by data from other Creoles.

As a general principle, in a marked-unmarked pair of the same set, the indigenous forms tend to occur in the marked category. Thus, for Zamboangueño we find that the less marked singular pronouns are derived from Spanish, and the more marked plural ones are derived from indigenous Philippine languages:

	Spanish-derived	Derived from Philippine languages
person	singular	plural
1	*yó*	**kami**
1+2		**kitá**
2	*tú*	**kamó**
3	*ʔéle*	**silá**

Frake also found similar contrasts in other lexical domains, including:

1. Adjectives contrasting magnitude:

Spanish-derived		Derived from Philippine languages	
grande	'large'	**dyútay**	'small'
lihéro	'fast'	**mahínay**	'slow'
mapwérso	'strong'	**malúya**	'weak'

2. Nouns contrasting sex or age, such as:

byého/a	'old man/woman'	**báta?**	'child'
plóres	'blossom'	**putput**	'bud'
soltéro	'bachelor'	**dalága**	'unmarried girl'

3. General versus specific names for food items, such as:

komida	'food'	kanon	'main dish'
pwerko	'pork'	lecon	'suckling pig'
peskao	'fish'	tulinan	'tuna'

Different origins for cardinal numbers are documented for a number of Creoles. Ferraz provides the following example for Angolar (spoken by the descendants of maroons on São Tomé):

> The only cardinal numbers in Angolar which are of Portuguese origin are those for 1, 2, and 3 ('ūa, 'dosu, 'tesi), which occur also in compounds with these numerals. For the rest, the Angolar numerals are of Bantu origin, and are very similar to those of Kimbundu, for example:
>
> | | Angolar | Kimbundu |
> |-------|---------|----------|
> | four | 'kwana | kwana |
> | six | sa'mano | samanu |
> | sixty | ma'kyɛ sa'mano | makwi a samanu |
>
> The Angolar numbering system suggests that when the Angolares left the main community, São Tomense may not yet have had more Portuguese numerals than Angolar has (1974:185).

Unfortunately, it is not reliably known whether the Angolares took to the interior of the island subsequent to creolization. Evidence on this point could throw light on the question of differential complexity of Creoles. In any case, data now available suggest that the indigenous forms were borrowed late (that is, possibly subsequent to creolization), and that substratum influence may not have played a major role during creolization itself. We certainly are again alerted to the fact that static comparisons are not reliable in determining the affiliations of Creoles with their numerous contact languages.

Studies that give information as to the precise timing of loans from languages other than the lexifier language are not numerous, but they confirm the principle just mentioned. An example is Shnukal (1984) who notes the growing tendency of Torres Straits Broken to adopt grammatical markers and lexical items from the Western Islands language as in:

1. Aspect markers: **lak, kainɛ, mata, kasa.**

ɛm i go baik gɛn / lak ɛm go baik (gɛn) / kainɛ ɛm go baik (gɛn)	
	'She went back again'
ɛm pɔ jan / ɛm mata jan	'She can't stop talking'
ɛm i giaman wagbaut / ɛm i kasa wagbaut	'She's just walking around'

2. Intensifiers: **mata, mina.**

ɛm i prapa gud man / ɛm i mata gud man / ɛm i mina gud man	
	'He's a very/truly kind man'

3. Emotives: **gar, jagar.**

ɛm i gud mɛt blo mi / ɛm mai prɛn gar	'She's my good friend'
wai, ju go nau / jagar, ju go nau	'I'm sorry you're going'

4. Kin terms: **atɛ, aka.**

pop / ata / atɛ	'grandfather'	aka 'grandmother'

These kinds of lexical replacements occur side by side with the increase of referential power of this Creole by adding indigenous forms such as:

nazir / kabar	'trochus'	nasɛm / natam	'namesake'
kipro / kɛkei	'seagull'	ketai / kutai	'wild yam'
goi / pɛdauk	'bald head'	abal / kausar	'pandanus'

Another Creole that has undergone significant changes in its later history is Javanese Creole Portuguese, described by Hancock (1972). Here, as in Papiamentu (Netherlands Antilles) and the English-based Creoles of Surinam, Dutch has made considerable inroads. However, whereas in the latter two Dutch vocabulary is more marginal, in Javanese Creole Portuguese it is found more at the centre of the lexicon, perhaps reflecting its relative weakness *vis-à-vis* other languages spoken in Java in the later years of its life. Lexical replacement in language death situations does not appear to follow the same principles as with viable vernaculars (see Dressler 1977a).

Changes in the lexicon, particularly lexical semantics, are not only of the unconscious type largely in evidence so far, but may also be due to deliberate human interference. The development of a special Rastafarian lexicon of Jamaican Creole is a good example, as are the numerous lexical innovations introduced by mission bodies, or some aspects of the Shelta lexicon (cf Hancock 1974).

Although much remains to be done in the area of lexical studies, there can be little doubt about the insufficiency of the notion that Creoles are a lexical continuation of their European ancestral language.

Conclusions

Studies of creolization have concentrated on what is sometimes called "hard-core" grammar. Consequently many aspects of these languages remain ill described. Examples of serious gaps in our knowledge include ideophones, discourse grammar, speech acts and many other areas of "higher-level grammar" and language use. Even if descriptive work in these areas becomes available, we will still have to face the more basic issue of the degree of dependence of Creole structures on external contextual conditions.

Work in linguistic functionalism, such as Duranti (1981), has provided interesting support for the idea that the speech situation can crucially influence the language associated with it, and there can be little doubt that environmental/external factors interact with historical and/or biological factors in shaping the nature of Creoles. Differences in the referential and non-referential power of Creoles, should these become more firmly established, may well turn out to be the result of the special conditions in which they developed. Thus, to name one example, the establishment of turn-taking conventions may be crucially determined by the frequency and quality of caretaker-child interaction (Bruner 1981:161ff), and its absence in a number of West Indian Creoles (cf Reisman 1974) may reflect disruptions in earlier transmission patterns.

The absence of certain sounds in Creole phonologies may also be due to similar environmental conditions. As Edmundson has pointed out, different linguistic features are affected at very different times in phonology. Thus "the neutral detector for prevoicing will not survive until the thirtieth day of life, whereas the voiced-voiceless detector is more tenacious" (1985:120ff).

Further studies of creolization and Creoles offer one of the best opportunities to solve a number of the fundamental issues of the linguistic sciences.

Post-Pidgin and post-Creole continua

The notion of a post-Creole continuum was introduced first by DeCamp (1971b) and has subsequently been extended to cover post-Pidgin situations. In general terms, by a post-Pidgin or post-Creole variety we understand a Pidgin or Creole which, after a period of relative linguistic independence, has come under renewed vigorous influence from its original lexifier language, involving the restructuring and/or replacement of earlier lexicon and grammar in favour of patterns from the superimposd "target" language.

Work in this area by, e.g. Aitchison (1983) and Rickford (1983a) highlights several problems, notably the locus of post-Pidgin and post-Creole grammar. Whereas the grammatical structures of stabilized and expanded Pidgins and Creoles are widely acceptable, post-Pidgin and post-Creole varieties are often individual solutions, reflecting the speaker's social mobility and social aspirations rather than shared social norms. Depending on one's standpoint, the post-Pidgin and post-Creole continuum can be interpreted quite differently, as observed by Rickford:

> Note, however, that while the community's 'decreolization' between time 1 and 4 would undoubtedly involve language acquisition, each new lect serves as an *addition* to the community's linguistic repertoire rather than a *replacement* of any earlier lect. In individual second language acquisition, however, progress along the continuum seems to involve replacement of one interlanguage grammar with another, rather than addition to or expansion.   (Rickford 1983a:5)

It is only in the first sense that one can speak of "elaboration", as Valdman (1977a) does, when looking at post-Creole development. From a different perspective, there are merely changes in individual grammars. Mesolectal speakers, it appears, can be proficient in more lects than basilectal speakers, however, particularly if movement along the social and linguistic continuum involves social or financial benefits.

Further problems with the notion of decreolization include the separation of untargeted and targeted growth of Creoles (a point raised by Aitchison 1983, Kihm 1984, and Meisel 1983), discontinuities in the continuum, and the question of whether such continua reflect any general linguistic principles, such as the development from less to more marked constructions in a fixed sequential order. The principal aim of this section is to present data which may throw light on such questions, rather than proposing final answers. These will be forthcoming only once a more comprehensive theory of language mixing is available.

A last point is of a more terminological nature. Some linguists would like to reserve the notions of depidginization and decreolization for the transition of a Pidgin or Creole to its original lexifier language. Others have suggested that continua can develop with lexically different target languages, such that, for instance, a former English-based Creole may gradually be turned into a Dutch-based one. I believe that there are good reasons for keeping such processes separate, and I shall therefore only consider examples of depidginization and decreolization in the more limited sense. I shall again look at the developments in individual components of grammar. I should remind the reader, however, that in DeCamp's original model (1971b) the continuum embraced constructions from different levels simultaneously and that the separation into different levels is particularly problematic in continuum situations. The reason for this is that mixing between systems whose components of grammar do not neatly correspond can lead to the disruption of the original organization of a grammar.

Phonology
The separation of internal change from decreolization is particularly difficult in the phonological component, where one cannot apply Bickerton's (1981:113) formula: "In spontaneous change, an already existing form or structure acquires a new meaning, function or distribution. In decreolization, an already existing function or meaning acquires a new form or structure", as we are concerned with forms only. As a general rule, phonological changes appear to be triggered off by lexical borrowing and innovations restricted to recently borrowed lexical material. In some instances, rule generalization and hypercorrection is also found.

A case study of phonological developments in a post-Pidgin situation is that of Tok Pisin, where, among other things, the following changes have been observed. First, Laycock (1970a:xii) reports that "some Pidgin speakers who have learnt English add an eleventh (vowel), as a third pronunciation of **o**. This is [ɔ], as in English *court* (Pidgin **kot**)". I have found little evidence for a spread of this pronunciation, however.

Second, whereas Laycock (1970a:xv) states that English [dʒ], as in June, is usually pronounced [s], the English pronunciation is becoming increasingly common, as in **joinim** 'to join', **jeles** 'jealous', **jem** 'germ'.

More dramatic than the addition of such marginal sounds to the sound inventory of Tok Pisin is the ongoing restructuring of a large number of words in the direction of their English etyma, a process which is greatly facilitated by the addition of new consonant combinations, in particular medial consonant clusters. Since medial clusters tend to be restored before final clusters, however, we find new irregularity in Tok Pisin's derivational lexicon as a result. Consider:

Lexical item		Derived form in:		Gloss
		expanded Tok Pisin	*post-Pidgin Tok Pisin*	
bihain	'behind'	bihainim	bihaindim	'to follow'
poin	'point'	poinim	pointim	'to point at'

Limited access to the English model has meant that cluster restoration occasionally takes the form of hypercorrection, as in **kistim** instead of **kisim** 'to catch', or **iustim** instead of **iusim** 'to use'. Changes in the treatment of clusters are also felt in the morphophonemic area of the language. Thus there are now exceptions to the general rule of expanded Tok Pisin that a transitive verb is formed simply by adding -im to the intransitive stem. Note that there is as yet no new simple rule in anglicized Tok Pisin, for at least some intransitive verbs can end in a consonant cluster, for example, **rifand** 'to refund' and **koment** 'to comment'. The presence of such consonant clusters affects yet another rule, that of reduplication. Instead of the former **holim** 'to hold', **holholim** 'to hold tightly', we now have **holdim** 'to hold' and **holholdim** 'to hold tightly'.

Another far-reaching consequence of restructuring under the impact of an English model is described by Hall (1956:95-96). Following Australian pronunciation, Tok Pisin [e] is variably replaced by [aj] in words such as **longwe** 'far' and **nem** 'name'. Because of the frequency of this replacement, a number of back-formations have arisen, including **keke** for **kaikai** 'food', **lek** for **laik** 'to like' and **tulet** for **tulait** 'dawn'. Note that, as a result, a number of potentially annoying homophones have emerged, as **lek** already means 'leg' and **tulet** 'too late'.

For post-Creole situations, a number of detailed studies of phonological changes have been made, concentrating again on cluster restoration and the addition of 'hard' sounds to the phonological inventory of Creoles. The final vowel truncation in the Indian Ocean French-based Creoles was, as pointed out in the section on creolization (pp. 212-13), a case of independent development. On the other hand, its apparent tendency to disappear in Reunion Creole could be seen as being related to the influence of French in various guises. The table below, compiled by Corne, illustrates the gradual decrease in truncated forms as one moves from basilectal to more acrolectal varieties of Reunion Creole.

Decrease in truncated forms, from basilectal to more acrolectal varieties

Region	Infinitives Short (no.)	(%)	Long	Past Participles Short (no.)	(%)	Long	Total	Total short	Approximate percentage short
Dos-d'Ane	62	100	0	17	94.5	1	80	79	99
Ste Suzanne	104	85	18	40	81.5	9	171	144	84
Grand Coude	24	68.5	11	28	78	8	71	52	73
Etang Sale	18	64	10	7	35	13	48	25	52
Grand-Ilet	10	33.5	20	17	63	10	57	27	47.5

Source: Corne 1982:59.

A similarly extensive data analysis is presented in Akers's paper on consonant cluster restoration in Jamaican Creole (1981). Although Akers succeeds in demonstrating a fairly neat transition from basilectal to acrolectal Creole, it is not clear to me that his continuum maps more than a lexical diffusion process.[43] Comparisons with similar processes in other Creoles would seem desirable to settle this point.

As regards the increase of the meaning distinguishing sounds or phonemes, it appears that, by and large, highly marked sounds appear late in decreolization. For example, DeCamp (1971b) found that the ability to produce interdental fricatives in Jamaican Creole implied the ability to produce all other mesolectal forms.

It is important to keep in mind that mesolectal forms can be unlike either the basilect or their acrolectal target. In many instances, the transition proceeds via a large number of separate pronunciations. Thus Sandefur

---

43 To me, his data do not seem to suggest a restoration of clusters starting from the most natural to increasingly less natural phonological environments.

213

(1984:121) reports that the following series is common in decreolizing Northern Australian Kriol:

jineg – jinek – sinek – sineik – sneik	'snake'
buludang – bludang – blutang	'bluetongue lizard'

Kriol speakers regard the middle forms as Kriol proper and those on the left and right as heavy and light respectively. These data also illustrate the enormous task involved in establishing regularities in the ordering of different phonological processes (e.g., cluster restoration *vis-a-vis* final voicing).

Inflectional and derivational morphology

An important claim as to the nature of decreolization is that of Bickerton, that there is a concept of "possible change to grammatical state G1" which governs the sequence of grammars intermediate between basilect and acrolect. He claims:

> This point is worth stressing insofar as at least some generativists (Lightfoot 1979:385) appear to believe that there may be "no formal constraints on the ways in which a grammar may differ from that of the preceding generation, beyond constraints imposed by the theory of grammar, i.e., both grammars must satisfy the limits on a possible grammar of natural language." This view is almost certainly incorrect, given the facts of decreolization (Bickerton 1981:110).

We shall look at this claim, and the related one that new forms appear first in old functions, using data on plural marking in post-Pidgin and post-Creole Tok Pisin. If Bickerton is correct, then:

1. English -s would have first become attached to those Tok Pisin words that could freely appear with the plural marker -ol;
2. -s, the acrolectal form, would replace -ol in roughly the same sequence that -ol developed during the expansion of this language. This process has been discussed in the section on Pidgin expansion (pp 214-15).

However, the data on plural marking in urban Tok Pisin do not bear out these hypotheses. Instead, they indicate, as has been suggested by Bailey (1977), that mixing of systems of comparable complexity leads to unnaturalness. The first person to draw attention to this phenomenon was Hall (1956:99-100). Hall documents plural -s for the following lexical items in Tok Pisin:

bepis 'babies'	des 'days'	traktas 'directors'	yams 'yams'
yias 'years'	kreps 'crabs'	mails 'miles'	pauns 'pounds'
praisis 'prices'	silings 'shillings'	taims 'times'	wiks 'weeks'

Although Hall does not provide information on the grammatical environment in which these forms were found, it seems clear that the presence of the plural -s is not determined by the degree of animacy of a noun. My own data suggest that the presence or absence of plural -s is neither determined by the animacy hierarchy, nor by the grammatical environment, nor, in the case of written Tok Pisin, by spelling. The following examples are taken from letters written in anglicized Tok Pisin. Sentences by the same writer are grouped together:

bilong mipela ol meri 'of us women'; planti meri wok olsem taipis, *post office clerk, nurses, radio announcer* na sampela wok moa 'many women work as typists, post office clerks, nurses, radio announcers and in other jobs'; ol *Pacific Island* 'Pacific Islanders'.

sampela boys [subject] 'some boys'; ol meri skulmanki go long haiskuls 'the schoolgirls go to the high schools'; long ol boys 'to the boys'; olgeta kantris ol i laikim man na meri *citisens* 'all countries appreciate both their male and female citizens'; ol pipol bilong narafelo kantris 'people from other countries'; bilong dispela tupela stejes 'of these two stages'; bipo yu givim kain points 'earlier on you gave a number of arguments'; ol skulmeri i save pulimapim spes bilong ol boys 'the schoolgirls take up the places for the boys'; putim boys wantaim meri 'put the boys with the girls'; hevim seperet haiskuls long boys 'have separate high schools for the boys'.

ol gels [subject] 'girls'; mipela ol girl [subject] 'we girls'; pilai long ol girl 'have sexual intercourse with girls'.

Comparable data are also found in urban Bislama (Charpentier 1983:8), particularly in official discourse. Again, the data given do not suggest any implicational hierarchy for plural -s affixation.[44]

No detailed study of developing plural marking for a Creole has come to my attention. However, data on the appearance of a plural -s in Krio (Jones 1984) again suggest that it enters the language in a random rather than well-ordered manner.

Data such as these would seem to disconfirm Bickerton's view that decreolization is constrained by factors comparable to those that constrain the expansion of a language.[45] Again, although often the functions are old and the forms new (as in gavamen 'government officials', stafs bilong haiskul 'the staff of the high school' or ol bisnisgrups 'a business group'), there are cases where both form and function are new in mesolectal Tok Pisin. Even then, English grammar may not be the only source.

In summary, one can say that the kind of mixing processes found when two linguistic systems of comparable complexity are in contact are quite different from those resulting from contact between a developing Pidgin and other languages. In the former case, borrowing appears to be largely free to increase the unnaturalness of the developing mesolect, whereas in the latter case borrowing is highly selective and restricted by universal principles of language development.

---

[44] An interesting case of decreolization is mentioned by Eersel (1971:322):

In December 1967 a young Surinamese poet published a collection of poetry with a subtitle containing puwemas 'poems', that is, with an -s suffix for the plural. In a interview with one of his colleagues he declared that he wanted to start a discussion on the need for a plural in Sranan. That is why he introduced it on the title page of his book! [The book is: *Sibioesi, Powemas foe Jozef Slagveer*, Paramaribo, 1967]

[45] Bickerton (1980:112) proposes that "a decreolization change is a natural development when a creole is in prolonged and initmate contact with its related superstrate". What duration and type of contact would make decreolization natural is not clear to me.

The influence of English on the derivational lexicon of Krio has been studied by Jones. As with other languages in the post-Creole stage, extensive lexical borrowing from the lexifier language is encountered in Krio and "one of the largest categories of words modern Krio seems susceptible to are, in fact, English words with derivational affixes" (Jones 1984:183). This is of interest for two reasons. First, although Pidgins, especially in the early stages of development, tend to discourage the take-over of long or morphologically complex forms, similar constraints do not appear to exist for extended Pidgins or Creoles. This again weakens Bickerton's view on the matter. Second, unlike at earlier developmental stages, derivational affixes borrowed along with lexical loans tend to become rapidly productive.

Some of Jones' examples of this type of borrowing include the affix -a from English -er (as in *runner, killer, teacher*). It appears that this affix is gradually encroaching on the traditional method of forming agent nouns from verbs (that is, adding the noun *man* 'person').[46] This agentive suffix has become productive, as illustrated in the following forms:

bada (< English *bad* + -er)   'a very evil person'
bɛla (< Temne *bɛl* + English -er)
                        'hypocrite, person who destroys others by evil gossip'
chaka (< Fulfulde and Arabic *chak* + English -er)   'drunkard'

A second set of examples given by Jones includes the prefix **ova**:

ovaplɔs (< English *over* + *plus*)   'more than the mark, too much'
ovajaye (< English *over* + Yoruba *jaye*   'too much happiness'

The affix -ebul (< English -able) provides a third set of examples:

ajayebul (< Yoruba *ajay*)   'exaggerated, fantastic, out of the ordinary'
ejebul (< English *age(d)*))   'aged, advanced in years (of a person)'
masmasebul (< Krio **masmas** 'bribe' (< English *mash*, reduplicated))
                        'fertile for shady deals'

Similar processes are probably found in Creoles elsewhere. The widely held view that derivational morphology is particularly unborrowable will thus need to be revised in the light of Creole evidence.

Syntax

The most detailed studies of post-Creole developments are in the area of syntax. One language in particular, Guyanese Creole English, has been described in considerable detail (Bickerton 1975b). Data on other Creoles have also become available in recent years and some simple case studies will illustrate the kinds of phenomena and descriptive solutions presented.

The nominative shift in Hawaiian Creole pronouns. In basilectal Hawaiian Creole as well as in child varieties, there is no formal difference between nominative and accusative pronouns. However, as pointed out by Peet (1979:151), there is a strong "nominative shift" gradually replacing

---

[46]   Precisely the same process can be observed in Tok Pisin, where forms such as **woka** and **draiwa** are replacing **wokman** 'worker' and **draivman** 'driver'. However, the -a has not yet become productive in Tok Pisin.

accusative subject pronouns with their nominative counterparts. The 'nominative shift' has at least one apparent constraint: subjects of copula sentences retain the accusative form longest. Accusative subject pronouns are representative of basilectal Hawaiian Creole, child Hawaiian Creole and "plantation" Pidgin.

Peet obtained much of his data by means of hypno-elicitation, involving hypnotic age regression of Hawaii Creole speakers. The nominative shift takes the form of a gradual replacement over a number of years. Moreover, it is sensitive to the syntactic environment, in that subjects of copular sentences retain the accusative form longer and appear to progress at a different rate for different pronouns. Generalizations should not be made on the basis of a small sample, but the data are certainly suggestive. An example is the transition from the **as** to the **wi** first-person plural pronoun:

Transition from the **as** *to the* **wi** *first-person plural pronoun*

Session	Suggested age	As (no.)	Wi (no.)	W i (%)
1	3	1	1	50
2	4	4	5	56
3	4+	4	39	91
4	5	0	2	100

Source. Peet 1979:153.

Negation in Guyanese Creole. Rickford (1983a) discusses some interesting aspects of decreolization, using, among other data, information about verbal negation. His summary displays the differential use of the main variants of the negator by three different informants in both spontaneous conversation and formal interviews by an expatriate. Rickford's data suggest that the mesolectal form differs from both basilect and acrolect forms. The first informant appears to operate in terms of two discrete systems rather than a continuum, indicating that mesolectal competence cannot simply be associated with either individuals or society. The presence of an expatriate interviewer, or indeed the formal interview situation, tends to favour the incidence of acrolectal over basilectal forms.[47] Rickford's view that "speakers in a creole continuum move upwards to higher lects by expanding their linguistic repertoires rather than by replacing one lect by another" is borne out.

Relative markers in Tok Pisin and Australian Kriol. In the section on Pidgin expansion earlier, a number of language-internal methods of relative marking were discussed, involving various types of reanalysis. The presence of a viable method of relative encoding has not prevented languages such as Tok Pisin from changing these yet again in the direction of their superimposed lexifier language. It appears that the relativizer **husat** 'who' began as a calque from English in written Tok Pisin, particularly in direct translations by both European and indigenous translators. The case of **husat** appears to differ from Bickerton's postulated normal path for decreolization in two ways. First, a new form is not used in an existing function; rather, a pre-

---

47 This message should be heeded by those creolists who are under the impression that external factors do not influence grammatical behaviour. A more detailed rejection of this independence hypothesis is given by Duranti (1981).

existing **husat** 'question pronoun who?' begins to be used in an English function, as in:

opisa em i man husat i gat gutpela trenin
　　　　　'an officer is a man who has good training'
Mister Paul Langro **husat i bin askim sapos gavman i ken rausim tupela bisnisman**　　　　　'Mr Paul Langro who asked whether the
　　　　　government could deport two businessmen'

Second, it appears that in the course of further development **husat** was no longer restricted to human beings, but extended to grammatical contexts where relativizers such as **we** 'which, that' were previously found. Siegel (1985:88-89) gives examples, recorded around 1980,[48] for this phenomenon:

Dispela liklik sik bilong Melbon Kap tasol i paulim planti wok manmeri insait long biktaun bilong PNG husat gat haus bet
　　　　　'This "Melbourne Cup fever" has fouled up many working
　　　　　people in the cities of PNG which have horse racing betting shops'

Thus we have a development of a type in which Tok Pisin calques an English function and subsequently reverts to a previous Pidgin function. Although it is not necessarily a counter-example to a unilinear view of post-Creole development, it certainly underlines the fact that internal and external developments interact in a fairly complex manner.

The Central Australian Aboriginal Creole data discussed by Koch (1984) differ from Tok Pisin in that here both the English form and the English function were borrowed simultaneously. The same apparently is true for the complementizer *that* in this language.

Verb serialization and prepositions. Most Pidgins and Creoles have a very small inventory of prepositions. Relationships that are encoded in prepositional phrases in languages such as English typically take the form of verbal chains (cf Givón 1979), or else are covered by the few existing general prepositions. The addition of new prepositions from the superstratum lexifier language thus will have two effects: first, to reduce the importance of verb serialization, and second, to delimit the areas of meaning of pre-existing prepositions.

The emergence of new prepositions has been documented for many Creoles. In Central Australian Aboriginal Creole, for instance, the existing general preposition **long ~ longa** and the use of a verb chain of the type V + **got'm** 'with' are both replaced by forms borrowed from English, as in the following examples given by Koch (1984):

Some here **at** Warrabri... some **along** Tennant Creek...
My father sitting **in** this shade ... **long** this shade.
You fella go back **longa** camp **with** you father.
I b'n come back from camp **long** my brother.
With a spear? ... "Goin' back, that man, **long** 'is camp, **got'm** spear".

As with borrowed relativizers, the development of prepositions appears to be less neat than one would have hoped for. With Tok Pisin, for instance,

---

[48]　Examples of **husat** with (+human) antecedents date back to at least the 1960s.

borrowed prepositions can follow English in both form and function, as in **ten tu tri**, instead of **ten minit i painim tri klok** ('ten to three'). They can also take English forms used in a Tok Pisin function, as in **I no stret long laik bilong pipol ov Papua Nu Gini** ('This is not correct in the view of the people of Papua New Guinea'). In addition, borrowed prepositions can be open to multiple interpretation, as in **ol i pait egens long enimi**, in which either both **egens** and **long** are interpreted as prepositions (i.e., a complex prepositional phrase as found in traditional Tok Pisin), or **egens** is interpreted as a verb ('to oppose') followed by the preposition **long**. The new form is thus found in two functions simultaneously. Similar cases must be expected for other Pidgins and Creoles, as the lack of inflectional morphology tends to increase the ambiguity of surface structures.

An investigation of my data on new prepositions in Tok Pisin suggests that their addition does not follow the natural hierarchy for prepositional development postulated by Traugott (1977). This, in turn, suggests a qualitative difference between the ordered grammaticalization of Pidgin expansion and initial creolization and the rather unsystematic appearance of new constructions in the post-Creole situation.

Our discussion of post-Creole developments has been restricted to local phenomena. Little is known about the relative sequence in which such new constructions enter the grammar of depidginizing or decreolizing languages, although in DeCamp's original sketch of a post-Creole continuum this was a central idea. There can be little doubt, however, that developments at one level of analysis have repercussions at other levels, as will become obvious in the discussion of lexical borrowing.

The lexicon

Although earlier writers such as Todd (1974:59-60) have suggested that Pidgins and Creoles can borrow freely from their lexifier languages without structural penalties, more recent observers have found that lexical borrowing can have considerable repercussions on systematic aspects of grammar, and that borrowing involves more than taking over a linguistic sign.

Again, as with syntactic developments, the bioprogram theory provides a strong hypothesis: borrowing is constrained by the principle that borrowed lexical forms first appear in indigenous meanings. Thus Bickerton writes:

> This tinkertoy concept of decreolisation is a radical misconstrual of the processes involved. In fact, creole and superstrate differ, in their structure, at every linguistic level and in every linguistic component, in such a way that simple feature-substitution is out of the question even in such relatively unstructured areas as the lexicon. (Bickerton 1981:111)

This view is almost certainly too restrictive. Among data I have scrutinized, there appear to be numerous instances in which new lexical borrowings are introduced in toto or where a new meaning is attached to an existing form. An instance of the latter is the common tendency in Pidgins and Creoles to impose the etymological meaning onto existing forms. Thus educated urban Papua New Guineans are now found either to avoid items that resemble English expletives such as **bagarap** 'ruined' and **bulsitim** 'to deceive', or to use them in the full awareness of their English connotations. The number of lexical items thus affected is significant, some important examples being:

Lexical item	Interpretation in urban Tok Pisin	Interpretation in rural Tok Pisin
rabis	poor, destitute	rubbish, worthless
baksait	back	backside
pisop	to depart quickly	to piss off
sarap	to be silent, quiet	to shut up

More important than linguistic or language-internal constraints on lexical borrowing in post-Pidgin and post-Creole situations are social ones, in particular access to the target language (which often remains limited) and the social functions of prestige borrowing. Some interesting general observations on these two points are made in Samarin's paper on lexical developments in Sango (1966). For many speakers, access to the lexically related prestige vernacular Sango is very restricted. This incomplete knowledge of the prestige system has led to two self-defeating strategies. First, second-language Sango speakers reject a Sango word, if it happens to be a close cognate with a form in their first language. Also, second-language speakers enrich their Sango lexicon by borrowing anything that does not bear resemblance to forms of their first language; for instance, a Banda speaker may use a Gbaya word and a Gbaya speaker may use a Banda word (p 200).

Incomplete access to the prestige model can also manifest itself in fluctuations in the meanings of recently borrowed forms. Thus the following meanings of **jeles** (< *jealous*) were given to me by speakers of urban Tok Pisin in the early 1970s: 'to fight with', 'to have sexual intercourse with', 'to tell a secret' as well as 'to be jealous'. Only the last meaning could not be expressed adequately in earlier forms of Tok Pisin. Note also that the new form replaces a number of established lexical phrases (such as **eramautim tok hait** 'tell a secret') and stems (such as **puspus** 'to have sexual intercourse'). Similar examples could be adduced for other depidginizing and decreolizing systems.

Lexical borrowing, it has been suggested, can have repercussions in other components of grammar. This is most apparent in pronunciation, where new sounds are typically borrowed. New lexical items are often suppletive to existing ones, that is, an older solution involving a regular grammatical process is replaced by a borrowed lexical solution. For example, Tok Pisin distinguishes between verbs signalling inception and completion of an action by means of the grammatical markers **laik** 'inception' and **pinis** 'completion', as in:

mi (laik) rere 'I am preparing myself'   **mi rere pinis** 'I am ready'

em laik dai 'she fainted'   **em dai pinis** 'she is dead'

ol i laik painim 'they are beginning to look for it'

     ol i painim pinis 'they found it'

This regular grammatical process is being replaced by lexicalization as a result of borrowing the verbs **priperim** 'to prepare', **ankonses** 'to be unconscious, faint' and **luk po** 'to look for' in urban varieties of the language.

Because many of the processes that are encoded lexically in their target languages are encoded by means of regular grammatical processes in Pidgins and Creoles, extensive lexical borrowing can have far-reaching grammatical consequences.

Conclusions

The concepts of depidginization and decreolization remain insufficiently understood. The data do not suggest a simple unidimensional continuum between a Pidgin or a Creole and a related target language, even if it was possible to separate neatly internal and external factors of development. It also appears that the formula of new forms in old functions is insufficient as a characterization of the total process.

Decreolization, it appears, required catastrophic as well as uniformitarian explanations. Bickerton has done a great deal to illuminate the nature of the latter, but an account of depidginization is still needed.

Linguistic development of Pidgins and Creoles: summary

I have attempted to come to grips with the complex phenomenon of linguistic flux and change characterizing Pidgins and Creoles. The account has been rather uneven in coverage, both as regards the languages considered and the grammatical components for which data were provided. Further problems relate to the conversion of fundamentally static data into information suitable for dynamic description.

The following provisional findings are worth emphasizing, however. First, the changes that can be observed in the development of Pidgins and Creoles are ascribable to three major factors: internal expansion with changes in complexity, which appears to be governed by universal forces; internal changes with no change in complexity, which, though using processes found across a large number of languages, do not appear to follow any single universal programme; and externally caused restructuring. Second, the structural changes described can, but need not, proceed in a neat linear fashion. In most documented cases, such linearity is replaced by discontinuous developments and other catastrophic events. Third, the shape of Pidgin and Creole grammars appears to be crucially related to a number of external factors, in particular the influence that individual linguistic strategies can bring to bear on these developments. Fourth, it would seem desirable to distinguish between local developments (taking place without affecting other parts of grammar) and more global ones that affect other areas of grammar. Most available studies only concern themselves with local effects. Finally, given the numerous gaps in observation and description, no explanation for the processes of Pidgin and Creole development is available at present. For the most part, the data discussed in this chapter are in the process of being explained.

The achievement of a developmental dynamic account of Pidgins and Creoles is a worthwhile task. I hope, in particular, that detailed descriptions of the development of many more of these languages will become available soon and that a true predictive theory of Pidgin and Creole development will be possible one day.

6 The relevance of Pidgins and Creoles to linguistic theory

At the present, creole studies has a unique opportunity of contributing to, perhaps even decisively influencing, the development of general linguistics - an opportunity foreseen by Schuchardt nearly a century ago. (Bickerton 1974:85)

Introduction

It is often hoped that Pidgin and Creole linguistics will provide new insights for theoretical linguistics, although these hopes are not universal. Kihm (1983), for instance, argues that linguists have failed to demonstrate that Creoles develop differently from other languages, and that consequently the term 'Creole' has no meaning in linguistic typology.[1] Although this is an issue that remains to be settled, Pidgins must be regarded as a special case in that they are quantitatively and qualitatively reduced human communication systems, spoken as second languages and acquired by adults. One can therefore expect some significant differences from other languages, including Creoles.

However, even if the differences between Pidgins and Creoles, and between them and other languages or types of language learning (see Wode 1986), should turn out to be negligible, there remain a number of reasons for studying them and relating one's findings to linguistic theory. First, factors that are peripheral or less noticeable in other languages, and hence seem to be irrelevant to linguistic theorizing, are quantitatively prominent in Pidgins and Creoles. Examples include linguistic variability and rapid change over time. Second, because of their short life-span, developments that can only be postulated for the prehistory of other languages can be retrieved by a careful study of historical sources or even by contemporary fieldwork. Third, because Pidgins and Creoles arise in a maximally culture-neutral environment, they are paradigm cases of 'natural' languages. Their subsequent development can illustrate the gradual impact of cultural forces on such natural objects. Fourth, an understanding of Pidgins and Creoles can lead to a more realistic reconstruction of earlier stages of languages and human language. Finally, the study of Pidgins and Creoles poses special methodological problems, whose solution may enrich linguistic methodology in general.

In the following sections, I shall single out a few areas where Pidgin and Creole studies have provided particular challenges to linguistic theory. No attempt at an exhaustive statement will be made, nor will theoretical points made elsewhere in this book be repeated in any detail. Fuller details can also be found in Mühlhäusler (1996c).

---

[1] Similar arguments have since been advanced by Mufwene (1986), Kihm (1991), Manfredi (1993) and Corne (1995:121n1).

The comparative method and the family-tree model of historical relationships

One of the earliest reasons for the scientific study of Pidgins and Creoles was, as pointed out in Chapter 2, their challenge to certain views of language history and relationships, in particular the view that languages are genetically related to a single ancestral language. This relationship, it was argued, could be studied by systematically comparing linguistic material from two or more systems. It seems best, in my discussion, to distinguish between the underlying assumptions and the method itself. As regards the former, it is held, in the words of Hall:

(i) That among languages related through having come from a common source, the process of differentiation has always been gradual; and

(ii) That, among such languages, the relationship has always been 'pure', that is, there has been little or no introduction of structural patterns... from any source outside the language family concerned (1966:115).

It is only under those conditions of uniformitarianism and linguistic parthenogenesis that family-tree-like relationships can be postulated. The metaphor of a family tree is a powerful one, but there are a number of obvious limitations to it. For instance, family trees in everyday life have one surprising property: they allow one to trace back only one of the two sexes of ancestors. Thus, whereas it is perfectly possible to trace one's grandfather's grandfather's great grandfather, it is very difficult, if not impossible, to do the same for one's grandmother's grandmother's great grandmother. In other words, family trees are cultural interpretations or artefacts, rather than objective mirrors of reality (particularly since biological fatherhood is much more difficult to prove than biological motherhood).

Family-tree models of languages are similarly selective. It is assumed that languages typically develop by diffusion, more particularly inheritance, which means diffusion from one generation to another. Accordingly, later languages are traced back to one single earlier language, which is positioned directly above it in a family tree; this language, in turn, is traced back to a single node, until the presumed ancestral language is reached. The familiar form of the family-tree model is thus as shown here:

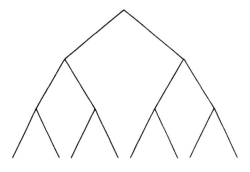

The form of the family tree model

The initial aim of Schuchardt, and other scholars sympathetic to his ideas, was to demonstrate that Pidgins and Creoles are mixed to such an extent that a single-ancestor model was incapable of accounting for observable data. The matter remained unresolved for many years, mainly because of the inconclusive nature of the data appealed to. Thus, as recently as 1966, Hall dismisses Schuchardt's arguments and defends the family tree as a suitable model for Pidgins and Creoles:

> But even though all languages are 'mixed', some - to paraphrase Orwell's famous expression - are more 'mixed' than others. We are left with the question whether, in fact, the more mixed languages are so mixed as to invalidate the assumption of genetic relationship, particularly as applied to a language of whose history we have no detailed knowledge. In theory, a language might conceivably combine elements from two or more sources so that they were perfectly evenly balanced and so that they would be, therefore, unclassifiable according to our customary assumption. Yet, in practice, such a condition of perfect balance is never found - not even in any of the pidgins and creoles that have been investigated in more detail than say, Schuchardt or Jespersen were able to do, and not even with their (admittedly extensive) carryovers, in structure as well as vocabulary, from Chinese, Melanesian, African, or other substrata. In Haitian Creole, the proportion of French structure is both greater and more fundamental than that of African-type structure; and the same is true of Chinese Pidgin English, Neo-Melanesian, Sranan, Gullah, etc., in relation to English and the various substrata involved (1966:117).

A similar sentiment is found in Meillet's assertion (1921:85) that "what little grammar Creole has is French grammar" (my translation).[2] Hall argues that empirical evidence suggests the feasibility of his approach:

> Even with the data available at present, it is evident that the ancestral form of any given group of related pidgins and creoles can be reconstructed, using the accepted techniques of comparative linguistics, and that the 'proto-pidgin' which we reconstruct in this way shows a reasonable correspondence to certain features of the 'source' language which we already know from other materials (1966:118).

An actual tree illustrating Hall's views is given in Chapter 1 (p 16). In Chapters 4 and 5, however, I have tried to provide data which make Hall's position quite untenable. They include the observation that, even among lexical items, different aspects of lexical information are derived from different external sources; and also the fact that at least some Pidgins and Creoles have a highly mixed lexicon, even in the area of basic vocabulary, particularly in their early stages of development. These two points suggest that family-tree construction on the basis of lexical cognation is not feasible. As regards mixing at other levels, I have adduced data to suggest that lexifier languages, generally speaking, do not play an important part in the grammaticalization of Pidgins and Creoles; and that chance similarities do not warrant any conclusions of genetic affiliation.

---

[2]   This is discussed in more detail in Kihm (1983:76ff).

224

More detailed studies of grammatical development in Pidgins and Creoles have demonstrated that grammar can also be derived by language-internal means, through reanalysis and possibly from universal sources. A simple dichotomy, either superstratum or substratum, thus is not sufficient. A major problem with Hall's view is the simplistic idea that language mixing must be of a mechanical type rather than in the nature of chemical compounding. As yet, we have no reliable identification procedure for linguistic systems resulting from mixture, but we certainly do have enough examples of non-mechanical mixing.

What is perhaps the most serious flaw of the genetic-tree model as applied to Pidgins and Creoles is that it presupposes identity of languages over time which they simply do not possess. Whether or not a Pidgin is a highly mixed system can be determined only by reference to a particular developmental stage. Language mixing is a successful strategy in some stages, but not in others. Its success is further dependent on a large number of external factors. Again, mixing is not an instantaneous phenomenon, but in many instances is a prolonged process constrained by the linguistic nature of the systems in contact.[3]

These last remarks lead me to consider the comparative method appealed to in establishing family trees. The usual comparison of arbitrarily chosen language states cannot, as has been illustrated with numerous data, provide any reliable information about historical links. In particular, a comparison of a Pidgin and Creole with a contemporary form of either a substratum or superstratum language can be totally misleading; a more reasonable basis for comparison would be non-standard varieties spoken at the time when Pidgins and Creoles came into being (as Chaudenson (1974) has done for Reunion Creole). Also, it often turns out (as in the previously discussed cases of causative encoding, relativization and plural marking) that Pidgins and Creoles become more similar to alleged source languages after a long period of internal development and after all contacts with those source languages have been severed. Consequently, the only way of identifying even plausible areas of borrowing is the comparison of developing systems rather than static ones.

The factual and philosophical reasons why the comparative method is inapplicable to the study of Pidgins and Creoles will also apply to other languages, and the evidence from Pidgins and Creoles is thus very much supplementary in nature. Its main importance lies in its promise to lead to new ways of unravelling complex language relationships. Many illustrations are given in Wurm et al. (1996).

Continuity and discontinuity in language development

A second important question of historical linguistics is: "In what sense is it possible for a language to undergo changes of the kind familiar from the historical grammars, and yet remain the same language?" (Harris 1977:17). Historical linguists working with "normal" languages have chosen either to ignore this problem or to propose a number of *ad hoc* solutions, including the appeal to continuity of speech communities, intelligibility and geographic

---

3   How these constraints operate in the case of Guinea Bissau Portuguese Creole pronouns
     has been demonstrated by Kihm (1984).

boundedness. More recently, linguists working on the description of linguistic continua have been able to show that historical continuity involves the addition of low-level rules to a grammar, and that the development from internal resources can be pictured as a continuum composed of implicationally patterned rules.

Occasional mention is made of discontinuities between grammars, but most of these discontinuities are seen to be the result of minor discrepancies between the grammars of successive generations rather than sudden breaks in a linguistic tradition. Very little has been written about this topic since Hockett's important introductory survey (1950), and the assumption that uniformitarian change and gradualness are a precondition for doing historical linguistics continues to prevail (for example, in Lass 1979:53ff).

That discontinuities cannot be theorized away in the case of Pidgins and Creoles is becoming more widely accepted. Hoenigswald, for instance, has pointed out that:

> More than in the case of natural languages one expects to run into problems of identity from stage to stage. It is difficult enough to be quite sure, both in theory and in practice, when a given ordinary language is a descendant (under change) rather than a collateral relative of a given older language. It has been said that to discover a line of descent is to discriminate what has gotten handed down from mother to infant over the generations from what has passed through other channels. If this is true, the pidgins, with their special mechanism of exclusively secondary transmittal (?) should indeed be troublesome to place on a family tree. And if it is further the case that pidgins are typically born and then again dropped from use in shortlived bursts of activity, the whole linear notion of 'gradual' change is not even a superficially useful approximation to the truth (1971:476).

These sentiments are echoed in Markey's statement that "pidginization/ stratified creolization signals a virtually complete disruption of continuity" (1980:1). Apart from providing further problems for the adherents of a family-tree model of language relationships, this discontinuity poses very difficult problems for the historian of Pidgins and Creoles.

The assumption that two documented Pidgins spoken at different times in the same area are part of a continuous development is implicit in many historical accounts. For example, we find that, whereas Carr appears to suggest a continuous development from the early seaport jargons (*hapa haole*) spoken in Hawaii around 1800 to modern varieties of *Da Kine Talk*, she has to admit that "we are without records of the many intermediate stages in this change" (1972:xiv). A very different account is given by Bickerton:

> Over the last few years I've been privileged to be in one of the few places in the world where a pidgin language still survives - Hawaii. It survives there for the very simple reason that the Hawaiian pidgin does not date from the first European contact. The first European contact was strictly between English speakers and Hawaiian speakers and produced a language known as hapa haole which is quite distinct from the subsequent pidgin.
> Pidgin English really only dates from the turn of the century (1979:8ff).

226

On-going research by Roberts (cf 1995) should ultimately settle this question. A second example is that of West African PE of the Cameroons. Whereas Schneider (1974:22) and Feral (1980:11-49) trace modern Cameroonian PE back to the broken English used in the first European trading posts and settlements, Todd (1979:289ff) proposes, supported by some very convincing evidence, that its links with the pidginized forms of English spoken before 1850 are very slight or non-existent, and that instead we are dealing with a second-language version of Krio (and hence ultimately Caribbean Creole), which was introduced after 1850. In both instances, any attempt to reconstruct missing intermediate stages would seem ill advised.

Discontinuities in the development of Pidgins and Creoles are not restricted to such extreme cases. More often, we find partial discontinuities resulting from factors such as (in the case of Pidgins) changes in established patterns of second-language transmission, sudden shifts in the functions and domains in which a language is used, or dramatic changes in the composition of the Pidgin-speaking population. In the case of Creoles, discontinuities arise through repidginization resulting from the large-scale influx of new second-language speakers, sudden changes in the superstratum language, splitting up of speech communities under conditions of marooning or manumission, and so on. Most of these factors are encountered with Tok Pisin, the language whose history I have studied in most detail. In the hundred years of its history, we find a number of significant breaks in the composition of the speech community, including the decline in the importance of European speakers, the severing of the links with Samoa, the decline of the plantations and compartmentalization into regional and social varieties; several changes in the substratum and superstratum languages, including the change from English to German and back to English again, the decline of Tolai, and the growing importance of speakers of non-Melanesian languages, in particular Highlanders; and a number of changes in social functions, mainly a development from a master-servant language to an indigenous lingua franca to either a regional lingua franca or Creole. All these external factors have left traces in the linguistic development of Tok Pisin. It is possible to identify at least three, and possibly five, qualitatively different and mutually only partially intelligible varieties with no discernible transitional varieties linking them.

The discontinuous developments of Pidgins and Creoles are not marginal accidents, but, in all likelihood, constitutive of their nature. If this assessment should turn out to be correct (and I have given many more details in Mühlhäusler 1984a:118-34), then this will provide a considerable challenge to historical linguistics. As in the case of mixed systems, the available uniformitarian models of description will have to be supplemented with catastrophe models of linguistic change.

Systematicity and rule-governedness

Linguistic theory tends to treat languages as closed systems governed by a finite set of grammatical rules. Both notions are applicable to standardized written languages, but, as has often been pointed out, are problematical for the description of everyday spoken discourse. The solution favoured by Creolists is to replace static systems of the conventional type with dynamic implicationally ordered ones such as have been developed by Bailey, Bickerton and DeCamp. However, even if large areas of grammar can be shown to be governed by such implicational scales, the fact remains that an even larger part of grammar will remain impervious to such treatment.

The question of systematicity in Pidgins and Creoles has been dealt with in detail by Labov (1971), in an article that has not yet stimulated sufficient discussion. He points to both the logical possibility of unsystematic areas of language and adduces a considerable body of supportive data from Pidgins and Creoles. He stresses the important role of system-eroding hyper-correction and hyper-creolization, as well as the fact that mixing of linguistic systems can lead to ill-integrated results. Although speakers of all Pidgins and Creoles have considerable skills in repairing their languages, one cannot assume that they are all equals in terms of "systematic adequacy".[4]

In previous chapters, some examples of unsystematic linguistic behaviour were discussed, in particular in connection with jargons. Variability was seen at both the interpersonal and intrapersonal levels. However, communication problems are also encountered at developmentally much later stages.

It would seem that Creolists should give up the notion of an ideal speaker who knows the system of his/her language and that of a linguistic system located in some collective mind. In the case of all the Pidgins I have looked at, and probably with many Creoles, such an assumption would not seem to be a useful abstraction, but a falsification of the nature of the subject matter. What is needed is a serious study of non-ideal Pidgin or Creole speakers and their problems in day-to-day communication. Misunderstandings of this kind, it will be rightly objected, are not unique to Pidgins and Creoles. There have been numerous voices (for example, Harris 1982; Reddy 1979) stating that the conduit metaphor of communication falsely suggests that successful exchange of messages is unproblematic. However, the dangers of such a view may well become much more obvious, if data are selected from communication involving culturally, racially and socially widely different interlocutors, as with Pidgins and Creoles. For up-to-date information on the debate about rules, see Toolan (1996, chapter 7).

Nature and nurture in linguistic structures

One of the main insights of semiotics, but one which is often unheeded, is that the notion of naturalness is extremely problematic. As put by Vico in 1725 in his *The New Science* (quoted from Hawkes 1977:14), "human beings are habituated to and made to acquiesce in a man-made world which they nevertheless perceive as artless and 'natural'". More recently, in writings on the philosophy of science, the claim has been made that "shifts in the notion of what a thing does 'naturally', that is, if left to its own devices, are the stuff of which scientific revolutions are made" (Reddy 1979:296). Consequently, and not surprisingly, there is widespread confusion in linguistic circles between what is "normal" and what is "natural", reinforced in the more recent past by the sloppy use of the term "natural language" within transformational generative grammar.

---

[4] The criterion of systematic adequacy is employed widely in language planning and language engineering (see, for instance, Tauli 1968).

The debate about the naturalness of linguistic systems has recently been revived by Bickerton's (1981, 1984) suggestions that the grammar of Creole languages is maximally natural in that it is shaped by an innate bioprogram rather than historical forces. This hypothesis, if worked out in further detail and if shown to be correct,[5] could have some interesting implications for general linguistic theory. It would suggest that languages can differ qualitatively in their distance from the natural foundations of language.[6] Bickerton's theory suggests an extremely simple solution for determining this distance:

		Endpoint of grammatical		
Language X	minus	development of first-generation Creole	equals	Cultural grammar

The debate as to whether languages are works of man or works of "God", which many linguists believed was settled in favour of the latter, is open again. However, Bickerton's attempts to protect his theory against the increasingly large body of counter-evidence suggests that this window of opportunity is being closed again. This matter has been debated extensively by the contributors to Pütz & Dirven (1989).

Qualitative differences between linguistic systems

The suggestion that languages may differ in their distance from their natural foundations inevitably leads to the problem of equality among linguistic systems. Although this has been a taboo topic for many years, it does not deserve to be one. Whinnom's pertinent remarks (1971:108ff) on this matter certainly deserve to be taken very seriously. In one sense, the topic can easily be diffused: Pidgins are second languages for people who speak another "full" language and therefore need not be of the same complexity or cultural appropriateness as other languages. We have seen that they have the capacity to grow more complex as they are put to new functional uses. In the early stages of their development, it is their very simplicity which makes them so suited to their communicative functions.

The complexity of Creoles is a very different matter. After discussing the relative adequacy of medieval Spanish and Latin, Whinnom concludes that there are similar differences in Creoles:

> There may be some reason to suspect that the creole-speaker is handicapped by his language. Creolists have had a hard enough struggle to justify the respectability of their discipline, and modern linguists are rather more sensitive than 19th-century linguists to patronizing and despective attitudes to creole languages (partly because of a well-intentioned but mistaken failure to distinguish between attitudes to languages and attitudes to speakers of those languages); but, without wishing to spark an emotionally loaded discussion, I feel that someone

---

5 Whether shared Creole grammar is due to an innate bioprogram or shared pragmatic forces, the fact remains that Creoles (and Pidgins) develop in a maximally culture-neutral (free) environment.

6 Similarly, from a developmental point of view, by contrasting, say, Creole development and first-language acquisition of English, one could deduce the increasing importance of cultural learning over biological acquisition as children grow older.

should venture the suggestion that modern linguists may have been dangerously sentimental about creole languages, which, with only a few notable exceptions, constitute in most communities a distinct handicap to the social mobility of the individual, and may also constitute a handicap to the creole speaker's personal intellectual development (1971:109).

At present, we lack the criteria to answer this question. My own work in this area (e.g. Mühlhäusler 1982b) has led to the following tentative conclusions as to what questions might be profitably asked:

1. Why do all languages (including older Creoles) give up most of the postulated bioprogram/natural categories? Is there any disadvantage to a system based closely on such fundamentals of human communication?
2. How can one find culture-free determinants of qualitative language differences? What may be a cognitive advantage in one culture may be a distinct disadvantage in the next one.
3. There is ample evidence that older cultural languages also block or impede cognitive processes. How can the respective "damage" caused by different linguistic systems be assessed?
4. What is the relationship between cognitive and social adequacy?

Answers to these and similar questions should be based on the linguistic skills of polylectal speakers or speech communities, not on grammatical descriptions of abstract competence. Moreover, since the boundary between verbal and non-verbal communication differs from culture to culture, a mere comparison of the verbal repertoire seems futile. What needs to be studied is the full set of communicative skills available to speakers of Creole and other languages.

It would also be dangerous to generalize from the perceived inadequacies of a communicative system to inadequacies of average members of a speech community. I expect that the differences in communicative skills within a language community would outweigh those across languages.

Insights from language planning, philosophy of language, language pathology and the study of what Ullmann (1957:122) has labelled "semantic pathology" should be combined with empirical research to throw light on these matters. The resulting findings are likely to be important in two areas: social and educational planning and historical linguistics. If there are determinable qualitative differences, these are likely to be one of the major causes of linguistic change.

Language learning, Pidgins and Creoles

Qualitative differences between languages have been most reliably demonstrated in the area of learnability. This factor has received considerable attention in recent years for the following three reasons. Research into the nature of second-language learning has revealed the operation of apparently language-independent learning hierarchies. Bickerton (1981) has claimed strong parallels between first-language acquisition and Creole formation. In fact, he regards many early acquisition errors as reflections of a bioprogram. Finally, the question of a critical threshold for language acquisition has received renewed attention.

In view of the vastness of the issues involved, only a small number of points can be covered in this chapter. In particular, I have decided to leave aside the area of interlanguage studies, referring the reader instead to summaries (for example, Corder 1976, Wode 1977 and 1986, Meisel 1983, Aitchison 1995). I do not wish to suggest that there should not be the closest co-operation between Pidginists/Creolists and interlanguage researchers; however, I do consider that pidginization and creolization can be regarded as the unmarked case of language acquisition and should therefore be studied before acquisition in contextually more complex situations.

A question I would like to investigate in more detail is the correspondence between Pidgin development and child language acquisition. Before this question can be answered, one has to locate the areas of grammar and points in time at which such parallelisms are most likely to occur. As regards the former, it is not likely that the emergence of lexical semantics will be parallel, as the first domains and functions of Pidgins differ very significantly from those of child language. As regards the latter, the basis of comparison cannot be arbitrarily isolated states, but oniy dynamic development. Both child language and Pidgin development are maximally culture-free in their initial phases, and a comparison of very early grammatical development is therefore the most promising enterprise.

The search for parallels is further affected by the model of language acquisition employed; this, in turn, depends on whether one regards languages as either static or dynamically developing entities. Most existing models are of the replacement type: that is, earlier developmental stages are replaced by increasingly more complex ones, until at last adult grammar is acquired. That earlier stages are considered lost is manifest in the concept of instantaneous acquisition of language, postulated as a useful abstraction within TGG. The alternative, the retention model, states that earlier stages of acquisition are not lost, but retained, either by a simple addition of developmental strata or else by way of fusion and mixture. A useful discussion is given by Ochs (1979). Support for this view comes from the fact that developmentally earlier stages of language are available.

As regards the relationship of these two models to the question of parallels between child language acquisition and Pidgin development, one should note that, whereas in the replacement model the existence of foreigner talk registers and Pidgins alike is described in terms of deviation from an ideal endpoint, in the retention model the structures of such varieties are related to the ability of adults to regress to developmentally earlier stages. Pidgins in their early stages could then be seen as conspiracies between language-specific regression and universal, possibly bioprogrammatic, tendencies.

The question of alleged parallels has been dealt with by Aitchison (1983). Her strategy is to pick out salient features of Pidgins and to discuss their status in Pidgins and child language respectively. The problem with this is that her Pidgin data are of a static type, typically representing stabilized, mildly standardized varieties. As my own data are developmental and, in general, relate to the earlier jargon phase, my conclusions are quite different from hers. Let us turn to some of her diagnostic constructions.

1. *Reduction in the number of phonological contrasts.* This characteristic, according to Aitchison, is found in both Pidgins and child language, with the important difference that in child language the number of contrasts eliminated is vastly greater, such as seriously to impair comprehension. My own data on jargons suggest that homophony is equally rampant in the earliest stages of Pidgin development, and moreover, that strategies for overcoming its disadvantages appear to be comparable in children and adults. Thus, at the age of two, my bilingual daughter had a word [daks] deriving from both German *Dachs* 'badger' and English *ducks*. It meant any soft cuddly toy animal. A similar extraction of common meaning, or folk etymologizing, is also found in many Pidgin homophones. Thus English *bandage, fence, banish* and *punish* are all realized as Tok Pisin **banis**, meaning 'to put something around something else, thereby constraining someone or something'.

2. *Simplification of consonant clusters.* According to Aitchison, in child language clusters are typically simplified by deletion processes, whereas in Pidgin the same aim is achieved through epenthetic vowels. This, as has been pointed out several times in this book, is simply not supported by the data:[7] for example, in Cameroonian PE **pun** ('spoon') or Vietnamese Pidgin French **sam** ('room' < *chambre*).

3. *Paradigmatic univocity.* This term, introduced by Hjelmslev, means that a stable relationship obtains between a content and an expression-level unit. Such a relationship is reported for many Pidgins: for example, for most African pidgins by Manessy (1977). However, data suggest that this is not a characteristic of initial pidginization. Thus, in early Papuan PE, one finds considerable variation in the encoding of personal pronouns. For the first person singular, for instance, the forms I~me~my for subject and object position coexist. For some speakers, the difference between *me* and *I* is felt to be one between subject of transitive sentence and subject of intransitive or object of transitive sentence (that is, it behaves like an ergative system); for others, it is simply a case of free variation. An example of the latter is a story told in 1976 by Eka Kave, a Papuan domestic servant (Mühlhäusler 1978a:1437). This text also constitutes a counter-example to the next assertion made by Aitchison (1983).

4. *Syntagmatic univocity.* By this we understand two phenomena: first, the replacement of analytic by synthetic constructions; and second, fixed word order. Eka Kave's story, with its variable word order for interrogative structures, is not consistent with the first phenomenon. As regards the second, Aitchison finds that there is little evidence that children impose analytic constructions onto their speech to any great extent, implying that in Pidgins this is common practice. However, although this is generally so for stabilized or expanded Pidgins, this is not the case for earlier phases. The reader will remember that plural encoding in Pacific Jargon English was achieved not by a single analytic device, but by means of a whole array of strategies, including dependence on textual or contextual information, the use of a number of quantifiers such as *plenty, too much, all* or *altogether*, by

---

7   Recent work on cluster simplification in second-language learning suggests that there remain numerous gaps in the area of observational adequacy of this phenomenon.

occasional transfer of superstratum or substratum morphology, and by the iconic process of reduplication. The many competing strategies were eventually streamlined during stabilization.

Aitchison mentions other salient features, none of which in fact characterize the early phases of Pidgin formation. One must conclude, then, that differences between child and adult language acquisition have not been demonstrated for the early stages of Pidgin development,[8] although one must remember that what has been examined are local developments in small areas of grammar rather than the sequence in which such developments occur relative to one another.

The question of parallelisms between child language and pidginization is of interest not only because of the descriptive convenience which would result from its confirmation, but also because it relates to the more general issue of child and adult learning.

The critical-threshold hypothesis

The critical-threshold hypothesis of language learning suggests that the ability to acquire or drastically restructure human languages dramatically declines after puberty, as does the ability to relearn language lost under pathological conditions. This hypothesis suggests fundamental differences between Pidgin development in adults and first-generation creolization in children. This is precisely what is argued by Bickerton (1984:175). Pidgins are seen as haphazard ill-structured systems whose grammar (and lexicon in some cases) closely parallels its users' substratum language. Evidence for this view is indeed found in the language of very old speakers of Hawaiian Pidgin, on which Bickerton bases his views on Pidgins. His data are problematic for two reasons, however. They represent the speech of elderly speakers, whose capacity in a second language can be expected to have deteriorated considerably (cf more general remarks by Clyne 1977). Second, even if no significant deterioration had occurred, Bickerton's data seem to refer to the jargon stage, when a number of individual language acquisition strategies, including transfer, can be expected, as has been pointed out above.

It is difficult to disconfirm conclusively Bickerton's claim that expansion in first-generation children proceeds differently from Pidgin development, as his data only represent the endpoint and not the development itself. However, this endpoint would appear to be perfectly attainable by adults. For instance, of the areas of grammar distinguishing Hawaiian Creole English from its putative Pidgin predecessor, the four where it shows 'substantial identity' with all other Creoles (existential possessive, adjective as verb, questions and passive equivalents) are also shared with Tok Pisin, as is the copula encoding, which is present in *many* Creoles. Bickerton's remark that "the degree of identity is quite remarkable when we consider that HCE shares none of the substratum languages of the other creoles" (1981:72) is not more remarkable than the observation that, in the case of Tok Pisin, such apparent

---

8   At least, it has been demonstrated that adults can, and frequently do, adopt the same strategies of acquisition observed in very young children. This is not to say that they do not have other strategies at their disposal; whether natural or cultural strategies are used would seem to depend primarily on social and socio-psychological factors (see Meisel 1983).

recourse to universal bioprogram grammar was taken by second-language-speaking adults. In fact, adults and children appear to behave very much in the same manner: when there is no input, or highly conflicting input, they will turn to their bioprogram. When there is sufficient input, they will try to incorporate it into their developing system, even if it involves having to commit a large number of unnatural linguistic acts.

The crucial factor therefore is not a speaker's age, but discontinuity of transmission resulting in insufficient access to a pre-existing model. Similar or identical expansion of linguistic systems will be encountered in three situations: first, where the target is maximally remote, that is, in cases of both untargeted first-language acquisition (first-generation Creole) and untargeted second-language acquisition (Pidgin). The second situation is where the resulting system is a social rather than an individual solution. In the case of a pidgin developing in a highly multilingual environment, the strategy of transfer is highly restricted and the developmental sequences thus appear to be the same. It is also interesting to observe that natural interlanguage grammar is most likely to emerge where learners find themselves in a natural discourse setting (rather than in the classroom). The third situation in which similar expansion of linguistic systems will be found is where we are dealing with the early stages of language acquisition.

Discontinuity in transmission has both positive and negative effects, in that it encourages the selection of certain types of solutions, while discouraging or blocking others. If it is the case that certain features and rules can only be acquired if learners are exposed to them during a narrowly defined period of time, the likelihood that such features will figure in a Pidgin or a Creole is remote. However, in order to make sense of this, the global notion of critical threshold will have to be abandoned in favour of a much more detailed account of the critical time for learning individual features and constructions. Pidgins and Creoles can be used as a heuristic tool here, since it is precisely those features that are absent in these languages that are likely to be subject to some time-limit on their learnability.

The notion of critical threshold is also linked to another issue, that of the independence of grammar from external factors. In a model of language that treats grammar as an independent variable (that is, independent of other possible innate cognitive skills), observed surface differences between L1 and Pidgin development are highly significant. However, if grammar is seen as developing to serve a number of functions, such as making requests or establishing social bonds, it can be expected that the sequence in which such functions become important to language learners also influences grammatical development. The order in which children acquire new functions differs quite significantly from that found in adult second-language acquisition and Pidgin formation. All this means is that the activation of certain linguistic developments is dependent on the presence of specific environmental factors, rather than on different cognitive abilities of children and adults.

Simplification and simplicity

Although these two terms often describe the linguistic nature of Pidgins and Creoles, what is meant by them has remained obscure. Three earlier attempts at defining these notions have been made by Agheyisi (1971), Mühlhäusler (1980c) and Meisel (1983).

Studies in the area of interlanguage (for example, Corder 1976, Traugott 1977:132-62) have also drawn attention to the insufficiency of the notion of simplification in some Pidgin and Creole studies. The latter points out that:

> The natural semantax hypothesis suggests that a large number of linguistic phenomena often called 'simplification' do not in fact involve processes of simplification ... The result of acquisition may be an internalized system simpler from a comparative point of view than others' systems, but in itself it is not simplification (p 153ff).

Uncertainty appears to be due to the following reasons:

1. The confusion of second-language learning strategies with the outcome of a structural comparison;
2. The failure to distinguish simplification and impoverishment;
3. The lack of observational data about the first stages in the Pidgin-Creole life-cycle;
4. Discrepancies between folk views and technical description;
5. Confusion of descriptive simplicity with learnability or naturalness.

I would refer the reader to the above-mentioned authors as regards interlanguage and related issues, and begin my discussion of the matter with the second reason.

Although impoverishment involves the loss of referential or non-referential potential of a language, simplification is neutral with regard to a language's expressive power. Simplification only refers to the form of the rules in which a language is encoded, indicating optimalization of existing rules and the development of regularities for formerly irregular aspects, for example, grammaticalization of the lexicon. Simplification is a dynamic concept. It expresses the fact that as one moves along a developmental continuum, more and more regularities appear. Its opposite, complication or increase in irregularity, is basically the result of restructuring following language contact. It is thus found on the restructuring continuum. It appears that impoverishment and simplification are inversely related: as the referential and non-referential power of a language increases, so its content must become more structured. A basic jargon used to exchange information in a limited contextual domain does not need structure. In its initial phase, it is little more than a list of phrases or lexical irregularities. We thus get the picture below.

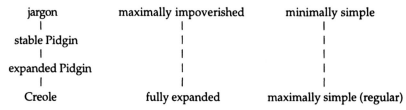

It has been held by a number of authors that simplification is most vigorous during the actual formation of a Pidgin - that is, in its jargon phase. Empirical studies of incipient Pidgin systems (such as Bickerton & Odo 1976, Mühlhäusler 1979 and 1990, Silverstein 1972a) reveal a different picture.

Silverstein (1972a) stresses two aspects of jargon grammars, namely their being drastically reduced and their structure being definable only in terms of a speaker's first language. My (1979) study found less evidence for substratum influence, at least in the derivational lexicon and in syntax, and presented jargon as almost entirely lacking in grammatical regularities. Such evidence suggests that degrammaticalization and impoverishment, though not simplification, are symptomatic of the formative stage of a Pidgin (cf also Labov 1971). This is related to the more general principle that regularities are less necessary to organize a small inventory of items than for a large one. In addition, it reflects the gradual decrease of context-dependency as Pidgins develop into more complex systems.

My use of simplicity in this technical sense has been criticized by Meisel (1983), who, among other things, points to the discrepancy between what learners describe as simple and what counts as simple for the Creolist. Examples mentioned by him include the reduction of morphology and the disappearance of grammatical function words. It would seem that non-linguists apply the term simplification to the overall system of verbal and non-verbal communication, whereas my technical definition considers the generality of rules for the verbal system only. I am prepared to concede that this may be a dangerous abstraction. However, in the absence of descriptive devices capturing the entire communication process, it would seem to be defensible. It certainly seems to be supported by observations that even expanded Pidgins are considerably easier to learn than older languages of comparable expressive and referential power.

It should not be forgotten that the relationship between grammatical description and mental processes is not a simple one and that the use of the term 'grammar' to describe both, as is customary within TGG, is quite misleading. The fact that a grammatical process in one language can be described in simpler terms than a comparable process in another language is only one of the factors that determines its learnability or "simplicity for the learner". Considerations of naturalness, token frequency, and associations outside the system under consideration are equally likely to play a part.

A final point raised by Meisel (1983) relates to the fact that my notion of simplicity is a strictly local one. This, I admit, is a very severe limitation, but one which can only be overcome once the inter-relationship between different parts of developing grammars is better understood and once genuinely developmental accounts of different languages are available.

A satisfactory characterization of simplicity and simplification thus remains wanting, but this should not stop us from discussing this notion in the context of Pidgin and Creole studies.

The diagnosis of prior creolization

Whereas the notions of simplicity and simplification are concerned with synchronic systems, there is an equally lively debate on the next question – whether or not it is possible to diagnose a prior Creole stage on the basis of contemporary (synchronic or shallow diachronic) evidence. This question has been asked of several languages and language families, including the Melanesian group (cf Lynch 1980), English (cf Bailey & Maroldt 1977) and

Black English Vernacular (cf Rickford 1977). A principled discussion of this problem is also given by Cassidy (1971) and Southworth (1971). Unfortunately, in discussing this question, a number of writers do not distinguish between creolization in the sense of 'highly mixed language' and creolization in the sense of 'lexically related, but drastically restructured language, the result of major discontinuity in transmission'. I feel that this distinction is an essential one, as we have ample reason to believe that mixture over a long period of time involving two or more full languages has results that are different from mixture involving complexity-changing systems, such as developing Pidgins.[9] Whereas in the former case abnatural or polysystemic solutions can be expected, the result of the latter tends to be a relatively homogenous, integrated system. The question of prior creolization should therefore be restricted to discovering major discontinuities in earlier language stages.

From the above-mentioned general articles, in particular Rickford (1977), it emerges that the following four identification procedures are most commonly appealed to:

1. information from external history;
2. simplification of grammar;
3. admixture from substratum languages;
4. divergence from the dialects of a lexically related language.

To these another, still much debated, is added either explicitly or implicitly:

5. typological similarities with known "genuine" Creoles.

In most instances, researchers require a conspiracy of three or more of the above factors before seriously considering the possibility of prior creolization. Even then, no absolute certainty can be gained, as can be seen from a brief investigation of the relative merit of the above parameters.

With regard to the first parameter, the best-known case of Creole development is that of the Caribbean and it has been widely accepted as the paradigm case. Three scholars, Alleyne (1971), Grimshaw (1971) and Mintz (1971), have sketched some of the socio-historical conditions that accompanied the development of Pidgins and Creoles in this region. They provide a useful basis for comparison. Thus Southworth argues, with regard to the situation of mixed languages in the Indian subcontinent:

> It seems ... that the co-existence of interdependent but distinct hierarchically arranged social groups was a characteristic of all the Caribbean slave communities, as well as other situations which have given rise to European-based pidgins (e.g. in Melanesia and the Philippines). This characteristic, which would seem to be a crucial one, is also present in the multi-caste towns and villages of contemporary India, and has been a fundamental feature of society throughout the subcontinent from very early times (1971:268).

---

9   A detailed account of these differences is given in Mühlhäusler (1984a).

237

Distinct social groups were also identified as an important factor in creolization by Bailey & Maroldt (1977),[10] and similar discrepancies in power relations were postulated by Dutton (1978) for Austronesian and non-Austronesian "mixed" languages of south-east mainland Papua New Guinea. The presence of two distinct social groups speaking different languages would seem to be a necessary, but not sufficient condition for the development of linguistic discontinuity and creolization. Thus other types of language change have been observed under these conditions: for example, the gradual *rapprochement* of two typologically different languages in the case of Kupwar (Gumperz & Wilson 1971), the death of either the dominant or socially inferior language (cf Aitchison 1981), and prolonged institutionalized bilingualism or dual-lingualism.

The question as to sufficient reasons for assuming prior creolization thus remains to be answered. It would seem that the most promising area of inquiry will lie in establishing discontinuities, catastrophic changes and periods of accelerated change; this will require a knowledge of historical details which is difficult to achieve. What has been said by Rickford about the question of American Black English Vernacular is equally applicable to the more remote processes of the origin of Melanesian, Germanic or "modern" Romance languages:

> If we are to resolve such possibilities, we will need to sift through a great deal of historical and ethnographic evidence and interpret it with great sensitivity. In any case, until we have the required documentation and analysis, there is little more we can say about the extent to which conditions favorable to creolization were present in the United States.
> (Rickford 1977:194)

Concerning the second parameter, simplification has been adduced as one of the main reasons for Ray's hypothesis of the pidginization/creolization of Melanesian languages and Southworth's (1971) account of the linguistic situation in the Indian subcontinent, among others. There are, however, some major difficulties with the notion of simplicity and simplification. Even if an adequate definition could be found, it is not clear whether such simplification would be retained over a long period of language change. We are, at present, not much further than Rickford was in 1977, when pointing out these and related problems. In particular, his warning against making statements about simplification on the basis of arbitrary comparison of isolated synchronic states should not be ignored:

> We also need to confess that in comparing the *present* form of the standard language with the *present* form of the hypothetical creole, we are implicitly assuming that no major changes have taken place in the relevant features being compared in both languages since the periods at which the original pidginization or creolization might have occurred. Where this assumption cannot be verified, our comparisons to determine simplification might well be meaningless. (Rickford 1977:195)

---

10 Bailey & Maroldt do not assume, however, that creolization here involved the development out of a pre-existing Pidgin. Such a Pidgin has been identified by Albert (1922). Its role in the formation of Middle English is not understood at present.

It is clear that simplification is not a sufficient criterion for deducing prior creolization, and it is even doubtful whether it is a necessary one. With regard to the third point, although mixture is regarded by some writers (for example, Bailey & Maroldt 1977; Southworth 1971) as a particularly important criterion, I hope to have made it clear in this book (particularly in the previous chapter) that mixture *per se* cannot be a reliable indicator of creolization. The reasons for this include the facts that mixing can be the result of long and continuous or brief and sudden encounters; that mixing is not consistently found with different stages and types of Pidgins and Creoles; and, given no developmental data, natural (internal) developments and the results of mixing are often indistinguishable.

My major hope is that a combination of substratum research and considerations of linguistic naturalness could give us an instrument for post-dicting creolization. I have tried to demonstrate in the preceding chapter that although Pidgin development and creolization are severely constrained by language-independent developmental "programmes", decreolization or contact between systems of comparable complexity is much less constrained, and also that the principal constraints for developmental programmes appear to be naturalness hierarchies such as the animacy or accessibility hierarchies.[11] My hope thus is that the traces left by rapid creolization are distinct from those left by gradual contacts between full languages. Let me illustrate this with an example. Lexical mixture in the case of creolization would be a linguistically (but not socially) random process, in that lexical replacement of pre-existing terms does not follow any naturalness or marked-ness hierarchies. Thus, in Jamaican Creole, we find *eat* replacing **nyam** and *child* replacing **pikni**. In the case of rapid creolization, we expect all lexically unmarked (most natural) items to come from the lexifier language and a greater or smaller proportion of more marked items from the substratum, as is indeed the case in Philippine Spanish Creoles (see Frake 1971).

The process of gradual replacement in the lexicon is also retrievable from synonyms such as may coexist in present-day varieties, and may be supplemented with information about stages in the development of a language where synonym pairs were used in day-to-day communication. One such case is that of Tok Pisin, where traditional lexical items are gradually being replaced with others that bear a closer resemblance to English. Some instances of the multitude of synonym pairs I have observed include:

Tok Pisin	Gloss
ol ofisa i bin RISAIN o LUSIM WOK BILONG OL	
	'the officers resigned or left their job'
em i wok long planim KASANG o PINAT	'he was busy planting peanuts'
em i kisim gut RES o MALOLO	'he takes a good rest'
yumi mas PREVENTIM o STOPIM	'we have to prevent or stop'

The same phenomenon has been reported for Middle English, particularly for the years 1250-1400, when numerous French loan-words were flooding the

---

[11] I am aware of the fact that these are theoretical constructs rather than directly observed facts. Still, within these limitations they are a useful basis for numerous generalizations on language development.

239

language. Thus Jespersen reports that an understanding of these new loans was promoted by the systematic use of synonymy:

> A greater assistance may perhaps have been derived from the habit which may have been common in conversational speech, and which was at any rate not uncommon in writing, that of using a French word side by side with its native synonym, the latter serving more or less openly as an interpretation of the former for the benefit of those who were not yet familiar with the more refined expression. (Jespersen 1948:89f)

Such evidence would suggest a gradual relexification of Middle English, rather than an abrupt new start following creolization. At present, our understanding of language mixing remains limited and its usefulness to the task of diagnosing previous creolization is limited accordingly.

Fourth, the notion of divergence from the dialects of a lexically related language has been underutilized because of the compartmentalization of linguistics and the resulting splitting off of dialectology in the days of structuralism. However, in more recent models within the developmental framework (cf Bailey 1982), this notion has become important again, especially where there is a break in the implicational pattern governing a linguistic process. If such gaps are numerous when comparing two lexically related systems, a major break in continuity, suggesting creolization at some point in the past, is likely. Some actual examples involving American Black English Vernacular are given by Rickford (1977). This criterion is also discussed with regard to Motu and Hiri Motu by Wurm (1964).

Finally, the view that there are certain typological properties that signal prior creolizations is found, for instance, in Lounsbury:

> There is a possibility that gross typological differences reflect, if not thought or culture, then something of the accidents of the social histories of speech communities, as these have created periods and circumstances in which traditional linguistic structures were, one might say, destroyed, and language rebuilt, putting (as Powell and so many others expressed it) "old materials to new uses". It may be of interest in this connection that the purest 'analytic' and 'isolating' languages known are the Pidgins and Creolized languages. These have long been the unwanted stepchildren of linguistic science. But it is in these that one can see most clearly something like the first principle in the building of grammar that was posited by the evolutionary typologists. One may note that the historical circumstances that gave birth to the Pidgins and Creolized languages were far more drastic and destructive of continuity of tradition in language than were those that gave impetus to change in the modern 'analytic' Romance vernaculars, or in early modern English (1968:205-06).

The use of typological arguments has indeed been common, as has been pointed out by Rickford (1977:198). Again, there are numerous problems here. In the first instance, we still have no general agreement as to the grammatical properties of Creole-type languages. The so-called bioprogram features used by Bickerton, for instance, may be historical accidents rather than genuine inevitable categories. They certainly do not figure prominently in languages such as Unserdeutsch or Pitcairnese, which, by other criteria, count as Creoles. Second, even if Creoles were characterized by a recurring

240

set of grammatical properties, this is at best a necessary condition for the Creole status of a language, for none of the properties appears to be unique to Creoles (cf Kihm 1983). Third, Creoles change like other languages subsequent to creolization. The direction of change may well be away from those features commonly thought of as being characteristic of Creoles. In the absence of typological constancy over time, the criterion of typology is not particularly useful for reconstructing linguistic prehistory.

However, the above statements refer mainly to the local constructions and typological properties commonly used in the Creole identification process. Lounsbury's suggestion that disruptive events in the history of languages can leave long-lasting traces is well worth further investigation.

The question of identifying pidginization and creolization in the history of languages thus remains at best partially answered. However, I am confident that a continued study of the development of these languages will provide insights of value to the historical linguist.

Pidgin and Creole speech communities

The notion of "speech community" was relatively uncontroversial until recently. Concern with its usefulness was voiced by a number of contributors to a volume edited by Romaine (1982b) and in a paper by Rigsby & Sutton (1982). For the field of Pidgin and Creole studies, a critical investigation was made by Labov (1980). The importance of Pidgins and Creoles for the discussion of this concept lies in the following points.

1. The nature of speech communities is dynamic and changing, rather than a given constant parameter.
2. Pidgins, at least in their early developmental stages, illustrate that communication is possible without any well-defined community.
3. As pointed out by Labov, the range of variation encountered in Creole 'communities' is so great "that the tools developed for the analysis of variation elsewhere, dealing with alternate ways of saying 'the same thing' do not apply" (1980:370).
4. As the description of post-Creole phenomena shifts from individual to social grammars, the question of the "locus of language" (see DeCamp 1974) is of renewed interest.

I will briefly expand on these points.

First, the fact that the composition and boundaries of speech communities can change rapidly in Creoles is illustrated by both Le Page & Tabouret-Keller's studies on Belize Creole (e.g. 1985) and Rigsby's studies on the Creole situation in the Cape York area of Queensland (Rigsby 1984). Within a geographically relatively small area, and with a very low number of speakers, we find a highly complex relationship between the social groups interacting and the varieties of speech these people use and identify with. We find Aboriginal Creole-speakers with no fixed norms, others who identify with the norms of immigrant Torres Straits Islanders, others with their own norms for Creole English, and yet others who aspire to the external norms of Aboriginal or white Australian English. To integrate all the linguistic rules into a coherent community grammar seems an impossible undertaking. In conditions where one is dealing with a rapid succession of migration, forced

241

resettlement, culture change and shift in models, no one-dimensional implicational pattern of linguistic structuring can be expected. This, it would seem, is also the message given by the inventor of implicational scaling of linguistic structures, DeCamp, in his discussion of the relationship between language and social networks in Jamaica.[12]

With regard to the second point, one of the reasons why pidgins come into being is the desire of different groups to maintain distance and non-solidarity over a prolonged period of time. The composition of jargon and pidgin-using groups can change rapidly over time, with no continuity of transmission or even grammatical traditions. Although in the very early stages norms for linguistic behaviour are absent, such norms may develop subsequently. Their principal function in languages such as Chinese PE or the Hiri Trade languages was to enable users of a Pidgin to communicate efficiently over a narrow range of topics. It is interesting that in many instances speakers of a Pidgin believe that they are speaking the other party's language, not realizing the separate linguistic nature of their lingua franca.

It is true that Pidgins can change their social status over time and that social norms for the language may develop even in short-lived communities, such as plantation communities in systems operating with indentured labour. This only underlines the changeable relationship between language and communities of speakers. The same problems of defining clear-cut communities are encountered in post-Pidgin and post-Creole situations. The extent of compartmentalization remains to be determined, as does the amount of miscommunication and communication breakdown one finds in such communities.

Third, the impossibility of describing variation as deviations from a single norm or in terms of optional rules poses considerable problems for those who wish to maintain the independence hypothesis of linguistic and social structures, a point forcefully made by Le Page (1980). However, before an alternative to the independence hypothesis gains wider acceptance, Creolists will have to think carefully about the amount of abstraction needed to cope with what otherwise would be too complex to describe.

Finally, linguists have opted variably for locating language either in the individual or in society. It appears that this dichotomy is neither necessary nor useful and that a fresh start should be made, acknowledging the possibility of a gradient between the two poles, at different points on which different grammatical phenomena are located. Progress in this area is unlikely until the conduit metaphor of linguistic communication (see Reddy 1979) is replaced by a more adequate model.

Conclusions

The title of this chapter is perhaps somewhat misleading, since much of what I have discussed here comes under the category 'Is linguistic theory relevant to Pidgin and Creole studies? My conclusion is that many of the assumptions shared by present-day theoreticians are challenged by evidence from these languages, including the uniformitarian principle of change; the possibility of

---

12 The proposition that social networks, rather than the larger speech community, are a likely locus for shared linguistic knowledge has become more widely accepted since Milroy's (1980) research on Belfast English.

atemporal models of description; the separability of linguistic and extralinguistic factors; and assumptions about the nature of the human communication process from Shannon & Weaver (1949) to Jakobson. Pidgin and Creole languages are, more often than not, the extreme counter-example to general claims. This works both ways. On the one hand, linguists have accepted findings triggered off by Pidgin and Creole data and revised their theoretical thinking accordingly; a good example is that of implicational ordering in linguistic continua. On the other hand, however, linguists have remained suspicious of Creole evidence; it is seen as somehow a freak case for whose sake a general theory of human language should not be changed. The main task facing Pidginists and Creolists will be to state why their evidence should be regarded as of central concern. Unless this is done, they will find themselves in the situation outlined by Hymes:

> In 1968, it seemed inevitable that attention to pidginization and creolization would unite the linguistic and the social in a specially revealing way. How we underestimated the resourcefulness and creativity of linguists and psychologists! After a decade, the inescapable embedding of pidgin and creole languages in social history remains a theme to be argued for, a topic to be rediscovered.   (Hymes 1980:389-90)

Although this chapter has summarized a number of arguments proposed earlier by my Creolist colleagues, it differs in its emphasis on historical and developmental processes, and also on non-optimal and disruptive types of communication.

Given the short period of time and small number of workers concerned with the questions raised in this chapter, the impact of creolistics on general linguistics thus far must give one cause for satisfaction. It also promises that further concern for relating findings from Pidgins and Creoles to other areas of linguistic inquiry will continue to yield highly interesting results.

7 The sociology of Pidgins and Creoles

When occasions for the use of a language decline, it appears to follow that the language must decline also. Tok Pisin has nowhere to go but down. (Laycock 1985:667)

Introduction

This chapter will deal with a number of issues in the area of sociology of language, the study of the use, social functions, attitudes and political status of languages, in contrast to sociolinguistics which is concerned more with the embedding of linguistic developments and processes in a social context (see Neustúpny 1983 for a further discussion of differences). The general concern will be for processes observable in the present or the recent past, particularly those which are of relevance to language planners and educators.

The treatment of the various topics to be dealt with in this chapter has been rather uneven, some topics like decline and death of Creoles having attracted wider attention only very recently. Equally uneven is the coverage of the sociology of individual Pidgins and Creoles and, for a number of quite major languages, virtually no information is at hand. As a result, this chapter will be explorative and, it is hoped, an invitation to more detailed studies of social aspects of Pidgins and Creoles.

Language attitude studies

There has been increasing interest in language attitude studies, reflected not only in the volume of output but also in the appearance of a number of principled statements and techniques designed for the specific purpose of measuring attitudes. One example is a collection edited by Shuy & Fasold (1973). It also appears that concern for Pidgins and Creoles has played an important part in this growing interest in language attitudes, e.g. Spitzer (1966), Wurm & Mühlhäusler (1979), Piau & Holzknecht (1985), Rickford & Closs-Traugott (1985), Sato (1991) and Sapinski (forthcoming). Whilst for these languages attitude studies still are at a rather modest level, there are hopes that they will bring a better understanding of the functioning of special communities and of the forces determining the direction of linguistic change (e.g. hypercorrection and hypercreolization).

In an important article, Agheyisi & Fishman (1973) discuss the underlying assumptions and methods of language attitude studies, as well as the problems, notably those of defining the term "attitude" and devising research methods capable of obtaining objective information about linguistic attitudes. Progress in the study of language attitudes towards Pidgins and Creoles has been hampered by two facts:

(a) Neglect of local attitudes; and
(b) Paucity of up-to-date techniques, such as surveying with questionnaires and matched-guise tests.

Studies acknowledging such difficulties remain rare, and far more precise information is needed. Agheyisi & Fishman (1973:141) distinguish the following three types of attitude studies:

1. Those dealing with language-oriented attitudes;
2. Those dealing with stereotyped impressions of language varieties and their speakers;
3. Those dealing with behaviour resulting from certain attitudes.

The present section will be structured around these types. Most language-oriented studies deal with attitudes towards languages as wholes, i.e. they look at how both insiders and outsiders judge the merits of a language. Most studies of Pidgins and Creoles fall into this category. A much smaller group of studies evaluates attitudes towards grammatical constructions or lexical material. The case of Sierra Leone Krio, described by Spitzer (1966) and Jones (1971), illustrates the almost continuous conflict between those who stress the role of a Pidgin or Creole as a means of self-expression and those who regard it as an obstacle to self-advancement. Krio has co-existed throughout its history, beginning with the settling of Sierra Leone by freed slaves at the end of the 18th century, with its related "lexifier" language English. English dominated official life and education right from the start and it is for this reason that negative attitudes towards Krio appear very early. English was regarded as the only way to achieve upward social mobility and Krio consequently was seen as a major obstacle to achieving civilization and enlightenment. Spitzer quotes the principal of the Educational Institute as having stated in 1901:

> The Sierra Leone patois is a kind of invertebrate omnium gatherum of all sorts, a veritable ola podrida collected from many different languages without regard to harmony or precision: it is largely defective and sadly wanting in many of the essentials and details that make up and dignify a language. It is a standing menace and a disgrace hindering not only educational development but also the growth of civilization in the colony.... (1966:41).

At roughly the same time, a counter-movement against foreign influences on Krio society made itself felt. Uncritical acceptance of European ways, including linguistic habits, was seen as a threat to the dignity of Africans and after promoting African dress and surnames, a small but active group began to stress the importance of Krio as a means of expressing a separate African identity. This movement was helped by the First World War, as concepts such as nationalism and national identity gained wider currency. These ideas are most strongly expressed in the writings of some individuals but were not shared by the majority of the elite, and, with independence, the leaders of the new nation opted for English "as a 'neutral' language promoting the interests of national unity" (Spitzer, p 48). According to Spitzer, this decision meant that the debate about Krio had come to an end and that it could now develop freely in those domains that were not reserved for the official language, such as education, national politics and external relations. Ambiguity in attitudes towards Krio was reported by Jones (1971:68) but more recently Shrimpton (1995:217) confirms a significant overall improvement in its status:

With independence the Krios, who previously, as administrators and civil servants, had been so closely linked to the British and to the English language, found that such former affiliations and loyalties were now often more of a disadvantage than an advantage. The result of this seems to have been a greater readiness to accept and identify with their own real native language, Krio, as they sought to establish a new place and a new identity in a changing society. A change in attitudes has also taken place among other sections of the population in Sierra Leone. Antipathies and antagonisms on the part of other groups towards the Krios, because of their earlier role and allegiances, are no longer particularly discernible. A third reason for the general increase in willingness to accept Krio as a fully-fledged language has been the interest shown in it by outsiders.

This situation is also reflected in the linguistic structures of the language. As demonstrated by Jones (1984), borrowing from English is extensive, including in such areas as derivational and inflectional morphology.

Whilst Krio was the language of a large community of native speakers, Papuan PE and Hiri Motu (Police Motu) of Papua were in a much weaker position. In their case, official attitudes rather than speaker's attitudes were paramount. The case of these two Pidgins is of particular interest, as it illustrates how attitudes and policies can lead to the decline of apparently viable Pidgins. As pointed out by Wurm:

> Its [Hiri Motu's] encouragement as a lingua franca and its use by the police force and administration officers led to the elimination of Pidgin in Papua – an effective act of external language planning (1977a:337).

Let us briefly look at some of the attitudes involved in bringing about this replacement of one lingua franca by another.[1]

Pidginised varieties of English are in evidence right from the beginning of the colonization of Papua, first by Britain, then by Australia. The attitudes of most expatriate white settlers were rather unflattering. Thus, Bromilow calls it a "crude jargon of debased English" (1929:74), Cameron "very quaint" (1923:108), and Newton refers to it as "that barbarous perversion of English" (1914:26). The local population at the bottom of the social hierarchy did not share these negative views. The majority of Papuans appear to have been under the impression that they were learning true English and therefore felt no resentment against the language.

Government attitudes were determined by two factors:

(a) The desire to have an effective means of communication in this linguistically highly heterogeneous colony, and
(b) The desire to impose standard English as the universal language of all Australian possessions.

The first motive was the dominant one in the initial years of administration, and whilst lip-service was paid to the promotion of English, the emerging PE seemed a very satisfactory answer to the communicative needs of the administration. The readiness of the Government to accept Papuan PE, at least as an interim solution, can be seen from King's remarks:

---

[1]   A full account is given by Dutton (1985a).

In the report of the same year the Administration said: "The great difficulty of language is becoming less. For in the east end of the Possession the digger and trader are propagating 'pidgin' English. The vocabulary is not always eclectic, but it is very useful". (King 1909:296)

Policies directed against Papuan PE began with the transfer of the administration of the territory from Britain to Australia in 1906. In particular, Governor Murray introduced a number of measures to eradicate this "vile gibberish", as he called it. Butcher remarks on Papuan PE in Daru and the campaign to eradicate it:

> Many had picked up pidgin English but Riley had set his face against this horrible jargon and was training a number of young people in Daru to speak and read correctly in addition to training them in the vernacular Kiwai language. I was in full agreement with him and failed to see why the people could not be taught to use simple English instead of the vile gibberish they had acquired. I therefore set myself to cultivate the habit of using the simplest words possible to express my meaning and found if I did this, the man who spoke pidgin not only understood me but began to copy me. As Colonel Ainsworth said when reporting on the Mandated Territory of New Guinea, "There is no reason why it should be easier for a native to say 'one feller boy' than it would be to say 'one boy', yet the Authorities there have made this horrible jargon the official lingua franca." They were until recently doing all they could to encourage it and what is still worse have, with the aid of certain missionaries who should know better, committed a crime against all decent language by fixing it in writing (1963:50).

These sentiments were shared by the missions operating in Papua, however.

Newton appears to reflect the prevalent attitudes of the missionaries towards Papuan PE when he deplores its use in religious services in Samarai prison:

> It would approach blasphemy were one to put in print the form in which truths of religion appear in "Pidgin" English, as for instance the way in which the Almighty is spoken of, or the relation of our Blessed Lord to the Eternal Father, even though the close connection of the sublime and the ridiculous has elements of humour (1914:26-27).[2]

Other Pidgins, such as Tok Pisin, have survived amidst a barrage of similar negative official and semi-official attitudes. In the case of Papuan PE, its demise was brought about by the simultaneous development of a Pidgin based on the indigenous Motu language, spoken in the capital Port Moresby. To what degree Motu or simplified Motu received official support before the First World War is not clear and requires further investigation. King reflects that "either we must learn pure and dignified Motuan, or the Papuan must learn grammatical English" (1909:302). King does not consider the possibility of using a simplified Motu, and one begins to wonder how much simplified Motu was used between Papuans and expatriates before 1914. There is some

---

2   Similar views, mainly that the translation of the scriptures into a Pidgin or Creole would constitute blasphemy, are documented for many of these languages, including Afrikaans, Haitian Creole French, Tok Pisin, Australian Aboriginal Kriol and Krio.

evidence that some form of Motu was used in various kinds of official business. Thus, Chignell writes: "Government native business at Tufi is carried out in Motuan, which is the tongue of Port Moresby; and when the R[esident] M[agistrate] comes to Wanigera he and his police speak that language in the village" (1915:21). Even as late as the mid-1930s the viability of Police Motu was extremely low:

> Native lingua francas they found ineffective except in limited areas. Thus Motu, which the administrators of Papua once considered making the official language of that Territory, was in 1925 the tongue of only 2000 Motuans, spoken by 3000 other natives and understood by 20,000 out of a quarter of a million. As they have opened up the "bush" of New Guinea and the larger islands, the Europeans and their policy "boys" have carried Pidgin English with them to tribes who have never seen a white man before.
> (Reinecke 1937:738-39)

At the highest levels, negative views of Police Motu persisted as an English-only policy was promoted, as can be seen in the following statement by Governor Murray:

> The advantages of Motu was admitted. It is much more easily learnt than English, particularly by those natives who speak a Melanesian language, it is not very difficult even for the average white man, it spreads rapidly, and, in a corrupted or "pidgin" form is the common language of prisoners, police, and, to some extent, native labourers. But there can be no doubt that the best thing for the native is that he should learn English. It is true that, in the transition state through which we are passing, much of the alleged disobedience of natives is due to the fact that the employer has been unable to make them understand his meaning; but the remedy is to go forward to English, not backward to Motu (1925:35).

At the level of everyday administration of the territory, however, Policy Motu began to get promoted around that time, for instance by the practice of spreading it through the prison system. Hides writes about the experience of an imprisoned Kukukuku warrior:

> One of them Didiam by name was sent to and detained at Port Moresby for seventeen months, where he reluctantly learnt to speak Police Motu, and a little of the ways of the Government. He was "nursed" and "tutored" in the hope that he would be of some use to Government officers as a medium of interpretation (1935:160).

By the end of the Second World War, Police Motu was firmly entrenched as the lingua franca of Papua. Whereas in pre-war years, its survival had, to a great extent, depended on the favourable attitudes of expatriate administrators and missionaries, we now begin to find positive indigenous attitudes towards this language. In the years leading to independence, it became increasingly a vehicle of Papuan self-identity, a process culminating in the renaming of the language as Hiri Motu in 1971, a name recalling its putative origin in the annual trade expeditions of the Motuans to the gulf of Papua. The fact that it originated in the colonial police force and was linguistically closely related to Papua PE became forgotten (cf Dutton & Mühlhäusler 1979).

Indigenous feelings for Hiri Motu grew with the emergence of a movement that wanted to split off Papua from the newly independent state of Papua New Guinea. However, subsequently, the younger generation began to turn away from it. As observed by Dutton & Mühlhäusler:

We have been told that, in the Rigo area just east of Port Moresby where the language was very strong twenty years ago, the younger generation is not learning it in the numbers that one might expect. The reasons for this seem to be threefold:

1. With the switch to local government councils as administrative units years ago the people do not have to know Police Motu to govern themselves; they do perfectly well in their own language, Sinagoro, which is the largest language in the area and which is known as a second language by member language groups in the Rigo Local Government Council;

2. English which has been taught there for many decades is now widely known and serves as the main external language of communication;

3. Young people identify better with Tok Pisin than with Hiri Motu (presumably because it is the language of the towns and of change) and are learning that instead of Hiri Motu (1979:219).

Positive attitudes are likely to remain for a considerable time but whether they will be sufficient to ensure the survival of Hiri Motu in the face of competition from the more "useful" languages of Tok Pisin and English remains to be seen.

Whereas we have so far considered attitudes towards languages as wholes, some information about attitudes towards aspects of grammar has also become available. The case of Tok Pisin, discussed in more detail by Mühlhäusler (1982b), illustrates important differences between European (expatriate) and indigenous attitudes in this area. Expatriate criticism tends to be directed primarily towards lexical items with unacceptable connotations in the lexifier language. The main missionary criticism against Tok Pisin has been that it is full of crudities and obscenities. One expression in particular annoyed the missions, *goddam*, which according to a number of sources was a very frequent vocabulary item before 1930. Thus, Friederici reports:

If a Melanesian exclaims "God dam! He savee too much!" when he refers to another Melanesian who is magnificently decorated as to look like a negro from Washington or Virginia, he will always create amusement. But it made me really sad when I heard a man from Lamassa, while he was building a mon (boat), muttering: "God dam, work belong Kanaka he no good!"　　　　　　　　　　　　　　　　　(McDonald's (1977) translation)

Mead comments on the initial effort of the missions to remove crude expressions from the language:

When the missionaries preach and translate the Bible into pidgin, they make some effort to smooth out the crudities of the language, but in the hands of the boys these all crop up again. Pidgin without continual "goddams" and "bloodys" is inconceivable to the boys (1931:151).

Mission bodies were set up in the 1930s with the expressed aim of "removing the crude or obscene expressions from approved language use and replacing them with others taken from the existing inventory of expressions" (Hoeltker 1945).

A second concern of expatriates has been that the pronunciation of indigenes deviated from that of English. When the first dictionaries of the language were compiled by the (predominantly German) Catholic missionaries in the 1930s, their writers appear to be guided not by local pronunciation, which is described as "vulgar", but by the real or presumed English etymon. Examples include:

vernin	< burn	(vulg.	**boinim**)
boks	< box	(vulg.	**bokis**)
drift	< drift	(vulg.	**drip**)
foldaun	< fall down	(vulg.	**pundaun**)

It is interesting to contrast such views with those of indigenous observers. Their principal criteria for favourable or unfavourable attitudes towards expressions in Tok Pisin are:

(a) Whether they contribute to social harmony; and
(b) Whether they are understood by a reasonable proportion of the speech community.

The following quotations illustrate their concern with socially damaging words.

(i) The use of **kuk** 'cook' instead of **meri** 'wife' to signal the interior status of women.

> **Sampela man em ol i save kolim ol meri bilong ol olsem kuk bilong ol. Ating plenti long yufela i save harim dispela kain tok tu? Sori brata, yu husat man yu save kolim meri bilong yu olsem kuk bilong yu, orait ating yu mas baiim em long olgeta potnait long mani ....**

> 'Some men call their wives "cook". A lot of you have perhaps heard this expression. My dear brother, if you call your wife your cook you'd better pay her fortnightly wages' (Unpublished letter addressed to *Wantok* newspaper in 1974; simplified translation added)

(ii) The insults **graslain** 'grasscutter, hillbilly' and **smelbek** 'someone who shovels copra into bags, a smelly person, hillbilly'.

> **Graslain, smelbek, planti taim me save harim hap tok hia Kolim ol man i no bin i gat gutpela edukesen o ol man i save wok long ol plantesen o ol man i save stap long ples o ol man i save sakim kopra long smal bek na. gras lain ... Dispela kain tok olsem in no pasin bilong bung. Em inap kirapim trabel laka.**

> 'Grasscutter and smelly person. I have heard these expressions many times. This is how they call people with little education or the workers on a plantation or the villagers in their home villages or the people who fill copra in bags, smelly people and grass-cutters. These expressions do not promote unity, they mean trouble, you see?' (Letter to *Wantok*.,15 November 1972; translation added)

(iii) Lack of precision in names for motor vehicles. A saloon car may be referred to as **kar, sip** (< jeep) or **taksi** in different parts of the country. Many speakers do not distinguish between **trak** 'truck' and **trakta** 'tractor'. The following unpublished letter to *Wantok*, written in 1971, deplores the use of **trakta** 'tractor' instead of **taksi** 'small car, taxi' (translation added).

> Mi bin halim planti man na meri ol i save kolim taksi long trakta, tasol mi ting dispela pasin i no stret long tingting bilong mi. Taksi i no save givim mani long yumi. Yumi save spenim mani long taksi... Na trakta i save givim mani long yumi taim em i brukim graun... 'A taxi does not produce wealth for us. I hear many people call taxis 'tractors', but this is not right to my way of thinking. We spend our money on taxis... A tractor gives us money when it is used for ploughing'.

Gradually, under the influence of mission teaching and the spread of English, expatriate attitudes towards Tok Pisin expressions are becoming more common among indigenes. Educated speakers can be observed to avoid expressions associated with unfavourable etymons, and pronunciations reflecting English models are gaining favour. A further development is the desire, on the part of many Papua New Guineans, to remove expressions which reflect outdated power relations, such as the distinction between **meri** 'indigenous woman' and **misis** 'European woman' or **boi** to refer to 'indigenous male in expatriate service'.

The cases studied so far all involve the simultaneous presence of a Pidgin or Creole and its principal lexifier language, and moreover considerable social stratification along language lines. Attitudes towards Pidgins and Creoles appear to be significantly different where such conditions are not met. Thus Wood (1969) points out that Papiamentu, the Spanish/Portuguese-based Creole of the Dutch Antilles, enjoys high prestige and favourable attitudes from all social and racial groups. One main reason appears to be the fact that Europeans (particularly Sephardic Jews) have always been members of the Creole-speaking community.

The next group of attitude studies is concerned with stereotype impressions of language varieties and their speakers. Pidgins and Creoles are often highly variable, such variability being associated with social, racial and geographical factors. The best studies are attitudes towards varieties spoken by expatriates and attitudes found along the post-creole continuum. The case of Tok Masta (Tok Pisin as spoken by expatriates) illustrates how linguistic attitudes can change with changing social relationships between groups. In the first decades of Tok Pisin's development few indigenous speakers realized that their language differed from that spoken by the Europeans. In fact, for a long time Tok Pisin was called **Tok Vaitiman** by the Papua New Guineans. Judgements about correctness can only develop once the speakers of a Pidgin see it as an independent language. Reinecke (1937) remarks:

> But when, owing to closer and more frequent contacts with the other party, a group that has been speaking a trade jargon comes to realize that it has been using a sub-standard dialect, it reacts in accordance with its attitudes regarding 'correct' speech, much as do the speakers of a creole dialect. In this case the change to a recognized language is quicker and easier, because they have no attachment to this supplementary tongue. This stage has been

reached in the Chinese ports: it was being reached among the Russians who traded to northern Norway: it is beginning to be evident in parts of West Africa; but in Melanesia it is barely apparent among a very few natives of the thousands who speak Beach-la-mar.

Commenting on Reinecke's observations a few years later, Reed noted a significant change in the pattern of indigenous attitudes:

> We now find, however, that the terms *tok pijin* and *tok boi* are part of the speech and stand in contrast to *tok ples waitman* and *tok ples bilong Sydney* which designate true English. This distinction implies the general acceptance by natives of pidgin's subordinate position. More direct confirmation was given by a Kwoma informant who, laughing at his own naiveté, told how he had believed pidgin to be the white man's speech "true" before he had been recruited. But even before he had learned pidgin for himself, he had been disabused of the notion that the white *masta* had no other speech of their own (1943:288).

At this point, the fact that Europeans pronounced words differently and used different grammatical constructions in Tok Pisin remained unnoticed. If anything, the expatriate use of Tok Pisin provided the model which helped to bring about a gradual change of Tok Pisin in the direction of English. First reports of indigenes making a distinction between Tok Pisin as spoken by themselves and that spoken by Europeans are found mainly after the Second World War. Mead mentions "... men who have been away at work for a long time and are able to make fine distinctions between Neomelanesian [= Tok Pisin] as the European speaks it and Neomelanesian as spoken among themselves" (1956:376).

The first mention that indigenes actually disapprove of the expatriate variety of Tok Pisin is found in Wurm (1969):

> Indigenes... are becoming increasingly critical of the mistakes made by Europeans speaking the language and of the incorrect pidgin of many Europeans in general (p 37).

The name **Tok Masta** appears to be of quite recent origin. It reflects the growing self-awareness of the Papua New Guineans in the years preceding independence and a more critical attitude towards the ways of the expatriate population. The following statement by Piniau stands representative for the views of many educated Papua New Guineans:

> Expatriates are mistaken if they think that Tok Pisin cannot be used to express everything well. If they find difficulty in expressing themselves, it is because they either do not know Tok Pisin well or they still think and formulate their ideas in their own native language (1975:96).

In present day Papua New Guinea the use of Tok Masta is viewed even less charitably. It is a "bad" form of Tok Pisin because it has come to be a symbol of those Europeans who do not wish to integrate with the Papua New Guinean society:

I cannot help but see the many evidences of bad Pidgin as used by some expatriates as a symptom of their condescending attitude towards people in this country.   (Letter by L Brouwer in the *Post Courier* of 9 July 1973)

The impression gained from Tok Pisin evidence, that attitudes are multi-dimensional, is confirmed by Rickford (1983) investigating attitudes towards basi-, meso- and acrolectal varieties of Guyanese Creole English. Rickford criticises what he calls the "standard view of language attitudes in creole-continua", i.e. the view that the superimposed standard variety is good with non-standard varieties worsening the nearer they are to the basilectal end. This view, he points out, cannot account for the fact that non-standard varieties continue to flourish in spite of a policy of more than 150 years' standing of making English the general language of Guyana.

His own research involves both informal observations and formal interviews of the matched-guise type.[3] The text persons belong to two socio-economic groups: (i) manual plantation labourers and (ii) white collar workers and shopowners. The informants are asked to rate the speakers (a) in terms of their most likely employment, and (b) how they would fit in their own circle of friends. The answers to the first question generally agree with the standard view of attitudes in creole communities. The answers to the second question, however, paint a different picture: basilectal speakers are rated most highly by manual workers:

Here the NEC [= non estate class, i.e. non manual workers] respondents appear to be behaving in accord with the standard view again, at least insofar as they rate the basilectal 'speaker' most negatively (least likely to fit in with their circle of friends) and the mesolectal and acrolectal 'speakers' more positively. The ratings of the EC [= estate class, i.e. manual workers] respondents, however are no longer parallel to those of the NEC, but almost diametrically opposed. On this scale, it is the basilectal 'speaker' who is rated most favourably by the EC, and the mesolectal and acrolectal speakers less so - quite contrary to what the standard view of language attitudes in a creole continuum would have predicated. (Rickford 1983b:8)

We thus have a clear distinction between status-related and solidarity-related language attitudes and, consequently, an explanation of why Creoles persist almost unchanged in spite of the prestige attached to acrolectal systems.
Related to attitudes to socially determined varieties, and sometimes difficult to separate from them, are views on geographically determined varieties. Generally speaking, in the Pidgins and Creoles surveyed, the varieties associated with the political capital and/or important centres of trade and commerce enjoy the highest prestige. There can be changes in the history of individual languages, such as the gradual shift in Tok Pisin from the former prestige varieties spoken around Rabaul to those spoken around Madang and other centres on the New Guinea mainland and where, most recently, the varieties of the big towns in the Highlands are gaining in prestige. A clear differential in prestige between coastal urban and remote rural varieties is seen in the case of Jamaican Creole English where the "bush

---

3   This involves the same speaker recording texts in different language varieties. Informants are then requested to evaluate these recordings in terms of speakers' occupational status, honesty, reliability etc.

talk" or "broken language of Quashie" (DeCamp 1971b:350) is often a target of ridicule.

A rather complex state of affairs is found in the relatively young Australian Creoles, Torres Straits Broken and Roper River Kriol. Australian Aboriginals in contact with Torres Strait Islanders in some mixed communities on the Australian mainland typically regard Torres Strait norms as the best and can be seen to shift their language in this direction (cf Rigsby 1984). Torres Strait Islanders themselves regard the varieties of Darnley and St Paul, the two islands where the arrival of South Sea Islanders from outside triggered off creolization early this century, as the model for Broken, rather than those varieties spoken in the capital of Thursday Island. A number of changes in attitudes towards Australian Kriol as spoken in different communities are reported by Sandefur (1984) and Rhydwen (1993).

Studies dealing with the behaviour resulting from certain attitudes most commonly concentrate on the domains and functions in which Pidgins and Creoles are selected. A typical example is Eersel's (1971) article on language choice in Surinam. Whether Sranan or Dutch is selected is determined by both the absolute and relative status of speaker and addressee. Eersel (1971:318) provides the following scheme:

(1) High – High. Dutch and Sranan, with a preference for Sranan in intimate relations between males. Females belonging to the elite group show a somewhat conservative attitude in language choice. Relations between the sexes linguistically correlate with this conservative attitude.

(2) High – Low. Nearly always Dutch, when speaking to bilinguals. In time of political campaigning, or for some obvious reason, Sranan.

(3) Low – Low. Mostly Sranan.

(4) Low – High. Sranan or Dutch, depending on the nature of the relation and the social distance between speakers. Choice here is not like that when a high status speaker addresses one of low status. In some instances it is considered bad behaviour to speak in Dutch to one's superior, although in other instances the reverse is true.

This scheme is also found within families, particularly those of high social status (ibidem):

Because all parents want their sons and daughters to climb high on the social ladder, they insist that they speak Dutch. Sometimes parents speak Sranan to their children but expect them to answer in Dutch, even when they, the parents, do not completely understand Dutch. Children have to speak Dutch to each other, at least in the presence of their parents. In higher social circles nearly monolingual Dutch-speaking children can thus be found.

Unfortunately, Eersel does not provide much longitudinal information and I do not know of any study concerned with developments in language use in Surinam since independence.

That political changes can have significant repercussions in the use of a Pidgin or Creole is shown by Charpentier & Tryon (1982) for Bislama, spoken in Vanuatu. Most important for these were the favourable attitudes of the new political elite towards Bislama which resulted in its proclamation as a national language.[4]

The shift in the use of Vanuatu's three main languages – English, French and Bislama – is illustrated in the following chart given by Charpentier & Tryon (1982:158). This shows clearly the significant expansion of domain, function and medium that have resulted from the changes in the attitudes towards Bislama.

Language use in Vanuatu pre-1970 and post-1980

pre-1970 post-1980	oral E+F	oral B	oral V	written E+F	written B	written V
1. Orders	1	3 2				
2. Political speeches		3				
3. At home	1 *1*	1 2	3 3			
4. Newspapers				2 *1*	1 2	
5. Radio news	3 2	2 3				
6. Local songs		1 2	3 3			
7. Church hymns	2	2	2 2			
8. Religion	3 2	3	3 2	1 *1*	3	3 2
9. Oral tradition		1	3 3		1	1 *1*
10. Village meetings			3 3			
11. Letter writing				1 *1*	1	2 2
12. Slogans, advertising		*1*	3		*1*	2
13. Education	3 3	(1)*(1)*	(1)	3 3		(1)
14. Foreign communications	3 3	*1*		3 3		

Usage: 3 considerable, 2 frequent, 1 occasional; E: English, F: French, B: Bislama, V: vernacular.

Language planning and engineering

In the previous paragraphs, a gradual change from unfavourable to favourable attitudes towards Pidgins and Creoles was illustrated for a number of languages. It is such factors that create favourable conditions for language planning and engineering. Following Wurm (e.g. 1980), we can distinguish between external and internal language planning – the former being policies and official practices, the latter language engineering in the narrower sense. Language engineering can be further subdivided into graphization (provision of standard spelling), standardization (establishment of a superimposed standard variety), and modernization (adapting the language to meet the requirements of a modern society). Observations on external language planning have already been made in the section on attitudes and will again be provided in the discussion of education policies in the next chapter. I shall therefore concentrate here on the three principal

---

4   Article 3 of Vanuatu's constitution, quoted from Charpentier & Tryon (1982:154) reads:

(1)   The national language of the Republic is Bislama. The official languages are Bislama, English and French. The principal languages of education are English and French.

(2)   The Republic shall protect the different languages which are part of the national heritage, and may declare one of them as a national language.

(Article 3 was simultaneously published in Bislama and English.)

types of internal planning. These are concerned with the following types of adequacy:

(i) Referential adequacy, i.e. "the capacity of the language to meet the needs of its users as an instrument of referential meaning" (Haugen 1966:62);

(ii) Systematic adequacy, i.e. a language should be structured in such a way that its rules are maximally general and natural;

(iii) Acceptability, i.e. a form must be adopted or adoptable by the majority of whatever society or sub-society is involved.

Linguists and educators usually regard the first two criteria as the most important. However, as the history of graphization for Haitian Creole demonstrates, such theoretical considerations are frequency overruled by questions of acceptability.

The controversies surrounding the development of a written form of Haitian Creole have been largely concerned with the differences between what is linguistically and socially acceptable. This case has been extensively discussed in the literature (e.g. Fleischmann 1978, Hall 1972, Stubbs 1980, and Valdman 1968, to mention but a few). Similar tensions between linguistic and socially acceptable solutions are documented for other Pidgins and Creoles.

Winford (1991) discusses the dimensions along which Caribbean Creoles vary and the consequences for their standardization and instrumentalization. Discussion of these topics as they relate to a number of Atlantic, Indian Ocean and Pacific Pidgins and Creoles will also be found in several of the contributions to Tabouret-Keller et al. (1997). While graphization is concerned with providing standards for rendering the spoken word in writing, standardization comprises a much larger area of engineering activities. As observed by Wurm (1975:109):

> The question of standardization of a language arises if it displays a number of diverse parallel forms on one or several levels... and is to serve as the common medium of inter-communication on advanced levels to a community within which several of these diverse parallel forms of the language in question can be encountered.

The first step in standardization is to determine a core variety of the language. In most Pidgin/Creole cases, this has been the variety of the administrative capital, though from a linguistic point of view, other solutions tend to be preferable. Often, the best is the structurally most coherent, most natural and stylistically most flexible variety.[5] How such criteria can be applied to an actual language can be illustrated by Naga Pidgin, spoken in Nagaland and adjacent areas of India. This Pidgin exists in three main varieties:

(a) A southern regional variety (SP), consisting of the speakers of Angami, Kachari, Zemi, Liangmei, Rongmei, Bengma, Sema, Khezha, Chokri and Mao.

(b) A northern regional variety (NP) consisting of the speakers of Konyak, Sangtam, Phom, Chang and Khiamnagan; and

---

5   These three criteria do not always coincide, however, and careful consideration has to be given to their relative weighting.

(c) A central regional variety (CP) consisting of the speakers of Ao, Lotha and Yimchunger. (Sreedhar (1977:158)

The linguistic complexity of these varieties is uneven. Thus, the southern variety shows the greatest number of phonological oppositions. It has the additional advantage of having most of the sounds of the two official languages, English and Hindi, in its sound-inventory and is also spoken around the State's capital. We thus have a conspiracy between a number of factors favouring the choice of one variety as the basis for pronunciation and writing. Differential complexity is also found in the area of plural marking:

> In the Angami variety, the grammatical category of number is available only with the nouns and the personal pronouns. The nouns take /bilak/ and the pronouns take /khan/ as the markers of plurality. However, the nouns referring to non-human class (Nnh class) optionally delete the plural marker when the context gives the clue.
>
> The Zemi, the Rongmei, the Bengma, the Khezha, the Mao and the Chokri belonging to the Southern pidgin (SP), show absence of plurality with the nouns referring to the inanimate being (Nina class) but show its presence with Nh class and the nouns referring to animate non-human beings (Nanh class).
>
> The Sema variety of the pidgin shows the absence of plurality with the Nina class of nouns and is rarely found with the Nanh class of nouns. The Nh class of nouns indicated plurality by the word /log/ 'people' following the nouns concerned. (Sreedhar 1977:159-60)

In essence, the varieties are located at different points of the developmental continuum for plural marking, the principal factor involved being degrees of animacy. Different varieties also encode plurals by means of different markers. The decision Sreedhar arrives at for plural marking is:

> Opposition between the singular and plural, with the optional deletion of the plural marker when plurality is indicated elsewhere, e.g.:
>
> **suali** 'girl'; **sualikhan** 'girls'; **duy suali** 'two girls'
>
> This feature of the optional deletion of the plural marker is found in the Naga languages and also in Indo-Aryan and Dravidian languages (p 166).

From a developmental view this is not the optimal solution. Whilst I agree with the choice of the form -**khan** as the plural marker, it would seem that Naga is developing in the same direction as other Pidgins, i.e. plural marking for nouns lower on the animacy scale and redundant plural marking. An alternative solution, compulsory redundant plural marking with all concrete (though perhaps not abstract) nouns, may be preferable. This solution would have the additional advantage of also being found in the official language, English.

Geographic as well as social factors are involved in the distinction between varieties of Hiri Motu (cf Dutton 1976). A survey carried out in the early 1960s identified a central variety, spoken around the Papuan capital of Port Moresby and sharing many features with pure Motu and a more pidginized non-central variety. Because of the numerical dominance and geographic spread of its speakers, the non-central variety was favoured by

257

many as the basis of standardization. However, as observed by Dutton (1976:107):

> There are arguments in favour of both. As already indicated the Non-Central variety is the largest and most widespread, and therefore may be said to represent in one sense the "true" Hiri Motu. Yet the Central variety is to a certain extent more prestigious than the Non-Central one because of its association with the capital of the country, i.e. with that part of the country where development is most obvious and where new ideas originate. It is also the variety that is more akin to its principal source language "pure" Motu and is in consequence (and by definition) more flexible and better able to tap the resources of the fuller language. Finally, it is the variety that has been most used in mission literature and is therefore presumably already seen as standard in certain areas.

Differences between the two varieties are found mainly in the areas of morphology and syntax. A large number of these are listed by Dutton (pp 112 ff). One such difference concerns the encoding of possessives:

English	"pure" Motu	Central dialect	Non-Central dialect
my father	tama-gu	tama-gu	
		lauegu tamana	lauegu tamana
your father	tama-mu	tama-mu	
		olemu tamana	olemu tamana
his father	tama-na	tama-na	
		iaena tamana	iena tamena
his head	kwara-na	kwara-na	
		iaena kworana	iena kwarana

In deciding the standard, factors such as the following have to be considered:

(i) Ease of decoding; the longer forms are easier to perceive and thus preferable for second-language speakers of Hiri Motu.

(ii) Iconicity: What is semantically marginal should be morphologically marginal. This criterion is met best by the shorter unstressed affixes of vernacular Motu and central Hiri Motu.

(iii) One form-one meaning: the inflected nouns of the central dialect violate this criterion.

(iv) Developmental expectation: one can expect that affixation will replace analytic phrases.

(v) Similarity with the other two principal languages of Papua New Guinea. English, like the Central dialect, uses different forms for personal and possessive pronouns. However, it is similar to the non-Central dialects in that the possessive pronoun precedes the noun it modifies. Tok Pisin possessive marking appears to differ from both English and the two dialects of Hiri Motu.

This case illustrates the complexity of standardization at the level of grammar. When language-internal criteria do not provide an answer, the criterion of acceptability is particularly important.

It is widely held that standardization of the lexicon is an easier task as the lexicon is a basic list of irregularities, i.e. arbitrary linguistic signs. This, however, is not quite the case and the choice between variants of lexical items can be determined by a number of principles, including:

(i) Zipf's law, i.e. items which refer to culturally central concepts should be shorter than those referring to marginal domains. This principle very often excludes borrowing from culturally distant languages.

(ii) The principle (related to (i)) that complex ideas are best encoded in morphologically complex words.

(iii) The boundary between lexicon and syntax may differ from variety to variety; lexical items encode concepts, syntax percepts (singularities).

(iv) Homophones and near-homophones should be avoided when choosing between otherwise equivalent lexical solutions.

To this must be added that certain lexical items may acquire connotations rendering them unsuitable for some speakers. An example is the widely observed avoidance of reduplicated forms for "serious" domains of discourse. Standardization in the lexicon is typically related to the modernization process. As a result of changing technologies and social structures, different groups of a Pidgin- or Creole-speaking area invent or borrow new terms to cater for the new referential needs. Standardization involves the selection of those that are rated most highly on the scales of systematic adequacy and acceptability. How modernization[6] of the lexicon can be achieved is illustrated with the example of political vocabulary in Tok Pisin.

When Tok Pisin was first used as a parliamentary language in the late 1960s, it was hopelessly inadequate from the referential point of view. When I visited the Parliament in 1976, most referential inadequacies had been repaired, but at a cost. Most new expressions were loans from English and thus hard to understand for the occasional visitors to the House and for the voters back in the villages. A workshop was held at the University of Papua New Guinea in September 1976 at which proposals were made which would mean that Tok Pisin could meet all referential requirements of parliamentary transaction. At the same time, parliamentary and political language would become more transparent to the average villager and thus enable a larger part of the population to get involved in national politics. Full details are given in Wurm & Mühlhäusler (1985, sections 6.1 and 6.8).

The success or failure of such acts of linguistic engineering is obviously dependent on political decisions and hence out of the hands of linguists. The extent to which pidgins and congeners have been changed by acts of planning in a politically favourable atmosphere is illustrated by the cases of Afrikaans (e.g. Shaffer 1978), Swahili (Whiteley 1969) and Bahasa Indonesia (see Perez et al. 1978 and Moeliono 1994). The study of such cases has become a semi-autonomous field within sociolinguistics and a discussion of all the issues involved is outside the scope of this book.

---

6   Whilst modernization is often equated with development along Western lines, this is not necessarily so. Changes in both social and technological areas may well occur in very different ways, Iran being an example.

The social status of Pidgins and Creoles

In this section we shall take a brief look at the often heard allegations that these languages are reflections of outmoded social models and therefore likely to perpetuate inequalities. My first response is that social control through Pidgins and Creoles would seem to be little different from that found in "normal" languages.[7] Furthermore, since both linguistic structures and social consciousness change over time, there appear to be no intrinsic reasons why Creoles, like many vernaculars around the world, should not become vehicles of modern thought and social liberation.

Pidgins and Creoles have sometimes been labelled "deliberately invented" systems. Reed discusses and dismisses the claim that Tok Pisin "was invented and introduced by the Germans in order that they might speak before natives in their own tongue without being understood" (1943:271ff). In fact, the only case where a Pidgin was deliberately invented as a means of social control is that of Pidgin German, and it would seem interesting to consider this case as a theoretical extreme of human interference in Pidgin/Creole development. Two attempts to artificially create a simplified German are known, namely Baumann's *Weltdeutsch* (1916) and Schwörer's *Kolonialdeutsch* (1916) which were written during the First World War in expectation of a German victory resulting in large-scale colonial expansion. *Weltdeutsch* was designed primarily for the use of allies and friends, particularly those in Eastern Europe. Since it was meant for the use of "civilized" people, the primary concern of the author was to keep the language as close as possible to High German. Baumann identifies two principal areas for simplification:

1. Simplification of German spelling by introducing a quasi-phonemic orthographic system
2. Elimination of non-functional variation in grammar and lexicon.

Whereas Baumann aimed at maintaining the referential power of the language by eliminating most of its stylistic potential, Schwoerer's planned colonial language is considerably more restricted in structure and function. He acknowledges Baumann's proposal but is quick to point out that a much more drastically reduced language is needed if established colonial lingue franche such as PE, Swahili and Afrikaans are to be replaced. Schwörer sees these languages as an insult to Germany and a source of communication difficulties in a future monolithic German Africa. Schwörer identifies the following functions for *Kolonialdeutsch* (my translation):

1. To provide a unified lingua franca to be used both between Germans and "natives" and among "natives" from different language groups.
2. To increase the geographical mobility of native workers and thus reinforce a divide et impera policy: natives can be transferred from one colony to another... thus increasing their reliability (p 13).

---

[7]   That linguistic structures perpetuate outmoded ways of social behaviour is simply a reflection of the more general principle that linguistic and social change do not proceed at the same pace. Allegations that English is a sexist language are thus comparable to those that Pidgins and Creoles are colonialist. Or, as systemic linguists argue (e.g.Halliday 1992): languages are fossilized theories of experience.

260

3. The language will be a symbol of German authority.
4. It will be a working language for the German masters and colonizers (p 15).
5. It is not meant as a means of communication between speakers of German living in the German colonies.

It is evident that Schwörer is guided by the desire to secure German colonial domination both within her colonies and against attacks from outside. At the same time, the social distance between indigenes and white colonizers is to be institutionalized and perpetuated.

The authoritarian setting for which *Kolonialdeutsch* was intended is illustrated with a putative example of how this language was to be taught to the "natives":

Der Sprachunterricht
Aufseher (Eingeborener, der gut K.D. spricht,): *Ich will nun wieder halten Schule für euch, weil ick habe Zeit an diese Abend für eine halbe Stunde. Aber ihr müßt lernen de deutsche Sprache so schnell wie möglich. Also aufpassen. A, sagen mir, was ist das?* (zeigt seine Hand).
A (Anfänger): *Diese sein Ande.*
Aufseher: *Gut, aber du mußt sagen: Das ist eine Hand. B, sagen mir, was ist diese Sache?* (zeigt eine Grammatik).
B (Anfänger): *Diese Sage ise eine Buge fü leanen de daitse Spage.*
Aufseher: *Ja, ist recht, aber deine Sprache ist noch nicht gut.* (korrigiert B) *So nun will ich wider C fragen. Ich tat gestern fragen de gleiche Sache.* (zeigt ein Kaiser-Bild). *Wer ist das, C? Tust du nun wissen?*
C (Anfänger, schr ungewandt): *No, ise glose Mann, abe ig wissen nit, was ise.*
Aufseher: *C, Du bist immer de gleiche Schafkopf!*

The language lesson
Supervisor (native who speaks good *Kolonialdeutsch*): *I want now again hold school for you, because I have time on this evening for a half hour. But you must good pay attention; for you must learn the German language as fast as possible. O.K., listen. A, tell me, what is this?* (points to his hand).
A (beginner): *This be hand?*
Supervisor: *Good, but you must say "This is a hand". B, tell me, what is this thing?* (shows him a grammar).
B (Beginner): *This thing is a book for learn German language.*
Supervisor: *Yes, that's right, but your language is not good yet.* (corrects B) *O.K. now I want to ask C again. I did ask the same question yesterday?* (shows a picture of the Kaiser). *What is this, C. Do you know it now?*
C (beginner, very clumsy): *No, is big man, but I know not, what is?*
Supervisor: *You are always the same idiot.*

With regard to the linguistic properties of *Weltdeutsch* and *Kolonialdeutsch*, some interesting parallels can be discerned with Newspeak, a literary language for socio-political control in Orwell's *1984*. Newspeak shares a number of salient features of Pidgins and Creoles such as "an almost complete interchangeability between different parts of speech" (Orwell 1949:242), as well as the following characteristics of artificial varieties of simplified German:

Property:	Weltdeutsch	Kolonialdeutsch	Newspeak
Impoverished lexicon	–	+	+
Powerful derivational morphology	–	–	+
Highly regularized inflectional morphology	+	+	+

The absence of derivational morphology in Pidgin German may have been deliberate; it makes it more difficult for its users to invent names for concepts they themselves require, thus increasing its dependence on the outside German model.

One can only speculate about what would have become of *Kolonialdeutsch* had it indeed been institutionalized in the German colonial empire that never was. In all likelihood it would have been modified by its speakers and, like many other Pidgins, changed from an instrument of social control and vertical communication into one of solidarity and horizontal communication. Studies of actual Pidgins and Creoles support the view that social control through these languages is at best partial and typically restricted in time and space. In actual fact, a large number of Pidgins and Creoles developed in an atmosphere of relative equality and, to the best of my knowledge, never were a means of social control. Among these are Russonorsk, the Hiri trade languages, Chinese Pidgin Russian, Japanese PE and the Turkish-based Tarzanca described by Hinnenkamp (1982). In other cases, however, Pidgins did develop in an atmosphere of social inequality and were employed to maintain such inequalities. A typical case is that of Fanakalo of southern Africa. This language probably developed first on the sugar plantations of Natal in the 19th century in the context of white overseers giving orders to Indian and African workers, or in the mouths of Indians attempting to make themselves understood to Africans (see Cole 1953) or, as suggested by Mesthrie (1989), as a medium of intercommunication between Afrikaners, English-speakers and Zulus even before the arrival of indentured Indian labourers. In the course of time, the linguistic characters of this language changed, reflecting changes in its speaker population. Over the years it spread to most parts of southern Africa, mainly due to the formal courses in Fanakalo held in the South African mines, where workers from many different language areas came together. The language was also used in colonial times in the former Southern (Zimbabwe) and Northern Rhodesia (Zambia), but has rapidly declined there since political independence.

The majority of Pidgins and Creoles appear to have changed with political changes from languages of inequality to languages of political liberation. Solomons PE, for instance, originated in a strictly authoritarian atmosphere, young men from many areas learning the language in the context of orders given by either white Europeans or indigenous **bosboi** (native overseers) at the turn of this century. By 1930, it had changed into a lingua franca, extending beyond the original plantation context. Associations with authoritative behaviour remained. Thus, the adoption of Solomons PE by the South Seas Evangelical Mission was part of its general policy of changing the cultural and religious attitudes of the missionized peoples. An even more direct attempt at social control occurred during the Second World War, when millions of leaflets written in PE were dropped by both the Japanese and the Allied Forces all over Melanesia. This use of PE for war propaganda purposes is documented most extensively for Tok Pisin. Clark (1955:11-12) describes the use of such pamphlets by the American forces:

> One effective use of Pidgin by our intelligence force was in compiling warning pamphlets which were printed or mimeographed in that language, and which were dropped from planes over isolated islands in the Japanese-occupied zone. Scores of our fliers had been marooned on these islands by plane failures or by combat disablement. Crews of wrecked bombers would often drift for days on rubber rafts until prevailing ocean currents carried them within sight of such atolls.
>
> The purpose of the pamphlet drops was to convince the natives that they must rescue and care for these men. The language had to be abrupt and forceful, as the islanders have a great respect for military strength and an equal contempt for weakness.
>
> The pamphlets stated that Japanese power was rapidly declining as American troops and planes poured in to reinforce the Australians and British. If the islanders rescued our castaways, fed them, and helped them to reach safety, they would be rewarded. If they helped the Japanese or gave them information regarding our movements, or if our castaways were abused or neglected, bombing planes would come to kill them and to destroy their villages.

An example of one such war pamphlet is given below:[8]

OL LONG LONG KANAKA I STAP ONTAIM LONG JAPAN NAU BALUS
BILOG YUMI KUM TOROMOI BOM NAU KILIM YU PELA ONTAIM.......

---

[8]   An excellent collection of such pamphlets is held in the War Museum in Canberra.

The official English translation reads: 'Our planes will bomb any natives who are foolish and stop with the Japanese and kill them and the Japanese'. A subtle change in the function of the language was signalled by these pamphlets. Solidarity between black Melanesians and white Australians and Americans being stressed in many of them. This finds linguistic expression in the use of the inclusive first person plural marker **yumi** to refer to whites and blacks alike (**soldia bilong yumi i banisim ol Japan** – pamphlet dropped by the Australian Army near Dagua, East Sepik Province), a significant change from the pre-war master-boy pattern. The Australians were dependent on the goodwill of the indigenes and identification with a common cause helped to break down barriers: "Australian troops working and fighting alongside village men treated them generally as equals, and broke down the strict pre-war caste system between black and white" (Ryan 1972:22). This solidarity was aided by two other factors: the New Guineans' awareness of the limited powers of the whites in the face of Japanese aggression and the subsequent American invasion of New Guinea where blacks serving in the US Army were seen to perform duties formerly associated with whites only. In the Solomons too, social relations changed after the war. Not only was the language used more and more to signal solidarity between its speakers, the range of speakers changed from an all-male group of plantation workers to the wider population, including women and children. In the days preceding independence it acquired much the same functions as the Pidgins of neighbouring New Guinea and Vanuatu, expressing social change and political liberation as well as nationalism.

Thus, when the Solomon Islanders gained independence in 1978, Pidgin featured prominently at the independence ceremony, as can be seen from the following newspaper extract:

CEREMONY WILL FEATURE PIDGIN
From GRANIER FORBES in London

The Duke of Gloucester is to talk Pidgin when he formally hands over independence to the Solomon Islands on behalf of the Queen.

The Queen enjoys Pidgin English, and the Duke, who leaves London today, has been practising hard to learn its finer points before the two-week trip.

A spokesman for Kensington Palace said yesterday, "The Duke has been listening to a couple of tapes made for him by two Solomon Islands students who happen to be in England".

"After making a speech in English, including the Queen's message, the Duke will say a few words in Pidgin during the independence ceremony"

(*Canberra Times*, 27 April 1978)

The change-over from a language of colonial domination to one of political and cultural liberation is becoming increasingly important in Pidgin- and Creole-speaking societies. Much of the early history of this aspect of these languages still has to be written, e.g. their use in the war of liberation in Haiti and in newly established nations such as Indonesia, as instruments of opposition to colonial powers.

The difficulties encountered by their promoters have often been discussed, for instance, by Dalphinis (1982) for West Indian Creole, Noel

(1975) for Tok Pisin, and Keesing (1990) for Solomons Pijin. These writers provide arguments against a colonial nostalgia, the view that the only way to achieve a civilized society is by adopting colonial norms of behaviour and language. Dalphinis, like many West Indians, emphasizes the power of Creoles to help their speakers find their lost roots via the African origin of many lexical items and syntactic constructions. This may turn out to be objectively not the case, but at a subjective level, it may help speakers of such formerly despised languages to take a new pride in speaking them and to avoid those schizoglossic attitudes brought about by accepting the norms of a language that is not their own. For an illustration of this, see Cérol (1991).

Once larger numbers of speakers thus change their attitudes, the way for language planning and engineering is open. One of the more immediate benefits will be that participation in public life is no longer reserved for a small group of acrolectal speakers and that the chance to receive a decent education is no longer linked to a child's first language.

Bilingualism, diglossia and code-shifting

Virtually all Pidgins and most Creoles are found in bi- and multilingual societies and this is often seen as one of the principal reasons for their changeability and relative instability. In the past, the problem of bilingualism was often approached from a static descriptive point of view. However, as the distribution and role of the different languages spoken in Pidgin and Creole areas changes as much as the linguistic structures themselves, a historical developmental account would seem more appropriate. Such an account is most economically given by reference to the individual development stages in the life of these languages.

The very early stages of Pidgin development (the jargon stage) are characterized by individual rather than social bilingualism, as can be seen in the case of Tok Pisin. There is no social role for a jargon at this point within a speech community, though such functions are quick to develop. The first functions to appear in the New Guinea Highlands language Usarufa were characterized by Bee. "Within their homes Usarufa speakers speak either their own or one of three neighbouring languages. Pidgin is reserved for strangers, some pseudo-sophisticated court cases, joking, and dogs" (1972:69). Similar roles for Tok Pisin are reported for Papua, where the language is beginning to make inroads into Hiri-Motu-speaking areas. Rew writes:

> In the quarters and among themselves, the Papuan residents used either their vernacular, Police Motu, or English. Occasionally they would call out and joke in basic pidgin. Yet when they addressed the New Guineans they used only English despite the fact that the New Guineans used Pidgin while speaking among themselves (1974:81).

As Tok Pisin became stable, its role vis-à-vis the other languages of Papua new Guinea became better defined. Bateson, for instance, sees its position principally in a kind of cultural no-man's land:

> The language and its tones of voice and the things that are said in it are a rudimentary third culture, neither native nor white, and within the conventions of this third culture the white man and the native can meet

happily, though the culture is germane to neither of them.... But neither the white man's philosophy of life, nor that of the native, crops up in the neutral and special fields of Pidgin English conversation. It is not that democracy and private enterprise could not be described in Pidgin, it is just that, in fact, they are not (1944:139).

Over the years, however, its role became both more defined and more important to local speech communities, though its use was usually restricted to nontraditional topics and settings, e.g. council chambers, baby clinics, mission context. It could also replace the vernacular in some other domains such as counting or swearing, as has been observed, for instance, by Reed among the Kwoma:

> We found that youngsters not only counted and sang in pidgin but also used it in the new game of football - especially in any altercations. Their own language was not lacking in terms of abuse, but those in pidgin were preferred (1943:286).

For most other purposes, the traditional vernacular or lingue franche were used. An example of a society where Tok Pisin functions in such a way is the Buang community described by Sankoff (1972). There, almost all men and younger women are fluent in Tok Pisin, and many are fluent in Yabem, the mission lingua franca which predominates in the Buang area. The constraints on code switching have been represented by Sankoff (1972:39). She confirms that stable Tok Pisin is reserved for non-traditional topics, particularly when discussed in public, as well as in contexts where speakers from different backgrounds meet. Its use has come to be regarded as compulsory in public places, such as markets, by many Papua New Guineans as can be seen from the following letter to *Wantok* (December 18, 1974: 2; translation added):

> **Mi save lukim ol manmeri long Vanimo ol save tok ples planti taim. Long maket na long stua na ol i no save rispek long narapela ol man, nogut tru. Bai ol i tok ples klostu tru long ia bilong yu na bai ia bilong yu i pen...Taun em i ples bilong planti man i bung. Yu go long taun yu mas tok pisin... Gutpela pasin yu mas tok pisin, orait, narapela man i ken harim toktok bilong yu.**
>
> (I noticed that the people in Vanimo talk a lot in their own language. In the market and in the store they do not respect other people. On the contrary. they use their vernacular really close to your ears and your ears ache. The town is a place where lots of people come together. If you go to town you must speak Pidgin.... It's good manners to speak Pidgin, then other people can understand you).

During the stabilization stage Tok Pisin was largely supplementary to the traditional vernaculars in that its use was restricted largely to new topics and situations resulting from the culture contact situation. During expansion, on the other hand, Tok Pisin began to replace the traditional vernaculars, a situation of relatively stable co-ordinate bilingualism giving way to a changeable situation of compound bilingualism,[9] where Tok Pisin was used

---

[9] Whilst there are doubts as to the psychological validity of this distinction, at the level of the sociology of language it is a useful one. The former refers to situations where

266

in more and more traditional domains. The endpoint of this development in rural areas is the gradual decline and eventual death of the traditional vernacular and a monolingual situation where a creolized variety of Tok Pisin is spoken as the sole language. For a detailed account of this process, see Mühlhäusler (1993). Some highly interesting remarks about such structural decline of Melanesian languages have also been made by Wurm (1983, 1992b).

In urban areas, however, the traditional bilingualism is replaced by one involving Tok Pisin and its lexifier language English. Initially, code switching between these two languages is comparable to that between Tok Pisin and local vernaculars during stabilization. However, in this post-Pidgin situation we can observe a two-way process of:

(a) Tok Pisin encroaching upon the functional domains formerly occupied by English, and

(b) English encroaching upon domains previously reserved for Tok Pisin.

The former process can be associated with the democratization of many areas of public life. The second can be associated – although not necessarily – with the development of urban elites.

An example of (a) is the increased use of Tok Pisin in parliamentary transactions. Noel (1975:78) reports the following figures for the use of Tok Pisin in the House of Assembly:

1964-1968	40%
1968-1972	60%
1972-1973	95%

In the first four-year period its use was restricted to certain topics and certain strategies on the part of its users in preference to English or Hiri Motu. Hull remarks: "Matters of intense interest to Indigenous Members such as the Bird of Paradise Bill or the Playing Card Bill are nearly wholly discussed in Pidgin even by those Official Members who participate" (1968:22). He further remarks that "most members use Pidgin to catch votes and sway opinion in the House" (p 23). This has certainly changed since and Tok Pisin has developed from a language for restricted purposes into one for all parliamentary business. To the extent that Tok Pisin has come to be regarded as on a par with English in a wide range of contexts, the choice of one or the other code is no longer strictly regulated, and mixing of the two systems in a public context by bilingual individuals is thus encouraged, particularly in public speaking, and is regarded as enhancing the speaker's prestige.

A comparison between the role of English in traditional villages and on the campus of the University of Papua New Guinea illustrates the changing patterns of code switching. In the village setting we are dealing with coordinate bilingualism, whereas on the Univeristy of Papua New Guinea campus we are confronted with compound bilingualism, the two languages providing interchangeable alternatives.

While English continues to be taught in numerous village schools, its use outside the classroom is restricted to conversation with visiting (white)

---

languages are kept functionally separate, the latter to one where either of the languages can be used in either function or domain.

officials or tourists, perhaps letter-writing, reading, and occasional church services. It is also used when a person is in an exceptional state of mind. Thus Taylor reports about vernacular-English switching in the Motu village of Tubuseria:

> However, when a person is drunk or in some excited emotional state such as anger, pain, or disgust, English is often used even by people who do not speak English in any other speech situation (1968:49).

The situation is very different in a context such as the University of Papua New Guinea or at one of the teacher training colleges where the predominance of Tok Pisin and English over the vernaculars is quite obvious. English is the language not only of the classroom but also of certain recreational pursuits such as cinema-going, reading, and, to some extent, of political debate. However, in recent years, Tok Pisin has also become established in these areas. Personal observations suggest that one is dealing with a transitional stage between a clear diglossic situation and the development of a linguistic continuum characterized by the weakening of the situational and social constraints that previously determined code choice. As a result, one encounters a degree of mixing where code switching cannot easily be explained by either social or linguistic criteria.

A diglossic situation, where two closely related linguistic systems, such as a Pidgin or Creole and its lexifier language, are used side-by-side in different functions and domains, typically occurs in stable hierarchically-ordered societies. In Papua New Guinea, the encounter between English and Tok Pisin in local society only occurred when barriers to upward social mobility were coming down and no stable societal diglossia ever developed as a result. In Haiti, on the other hand, a very different picture is encountered. Here, a large majority of monolingual Creole-speakers (perhaps 90% of the population) and a small class of bilinguals (French and Creole) are found. The latter make up the middle and upper classes and dominate public life. It is among this group that a diglossic situation is encountered. Stewart (1962:156) provides the following scheme for summarizing the conditions for the use of either code:

	Formalized	Unformalized
Public	French	Creole, French
Private	French, Creole	Creole (French)

He draws attention to the fact that shifting from one code to the other is comparable to style shift among monolinguals. However, he does not pursue the question of the relative expressive power of Creole as spoken by monolinguals and bilinguals, thus leaving open the possibility that the repertoire of the former is less elaborate than that of the latter. The study by Stewart and a later one by Valdman (1968), whilst greatly advancing our knowledge of language use in Haiti, still fall short of solving a number of theoretical and descriptive problems, in particular problems of development and linguistic indexicality. As observed by DeCamp (1971a:30):

> Both the creole diglossia and the post-creole continuum require further study. Even in Haiti, which has been the most extensively reported of the French creole areas, the functional distribution of standard and creole

French is so complex that it is by no means understood.... The simple statement that standard French dominates creole in a relation of diglossia does not begin to describe the complex factors which determine which language will be used in a given situation.

A better understanding of bilingualism and diglossia in Creoles is desirable for several reasons, the most prominent being that of historical reconstruction. If it becomes possible to isolate the factors promoting diglossia in the case of French Creoles and continua type situations in the case of the English ones (see DeCamp 1971b:350), such knowledge could be used in reconstructing prehistorical types of language encounters such as those between Indo-Aryan and indigenous languages of India discussed by Southworth (1971) or language contact in prehistoric Europe (cf Ureland 1978). Work in the area of interpersonal communication has also demonstrated that the choice of different codes in Creole-standard situations is determined by a number of subtle factors and that being a competent speaker in a diglossic situation involved a knowledge of these factors in addition to a knowledge of the linguistic codes (see Gumperz 1982). An in-depth study of this phenomenon in black British society was made by Sutcliffe (1984). Finally, a better understanding of bilingualism and diglossia would be an asset in assessing the viability of theories of origin such as the relexification theory, particularly when combined with a study of the next topic, language death.

Language decline and death

A survey of the role of Pidgins and Creoles in the literature on language death reveals two main motifs. The first is the observation that the processes of Pidgin and Creole development are in many ways mirror images of the linguistic processes encountered in language decline. The most elaborate demonstration of this is given for Albanian dialects in Greece by Trudgill (1977). As these issues are of a core-linguistic nature, nothing more will be said about them here. A second motif is mentioned in Hall's famous article on the life-cycle of Pidgins:

> To this general principle, however, there is one exception. Pidginized languages normally come into existence for a specific reason, last just as long as the situation which called them into being, and then go quickly out of use. Only if the situation changes radically does such a language acquire a longer lease of life and, by becoming creolized, pass over to the status of a "normal" language. From this point of view, although even a pidginized language is not a true organism, we can speak of pidgins as having "life-cycles", and of their being "inherently weak" in that, not their linguistic structure, but their social standing is normally not hardy enough to enable them to be used outside of their original context (1962:152).

A useful terminological distinction in the discussion of this issue is given by Aitchison (1981:208ff) and is that between language suicide and language murder. The former occurs when two related systems are in contact and one system gradually merges with the other, such as in the case of decreolization. The latter is the functional encroachment of one language onto another, often accompanied by political or other social pressure. We shall consider this second process first, as this is what Hall had in mind when originally formulating his life-cycle metaphor.

The question of whether a jargon or Pidgin has died is crucially linked to the already mentioned problem of establishing the identity of such a language over time. The fact that linguistic systems called Lingua Franca were spoken in the Mediterranean over a long span of time or that forms of broken English called Beach-la-Mar existed in the Pacific throughout the 19th century does not in itself warrant the conclusion that the same linguistic system survived over a long period. Instead, we must consider the possibility – a very real one in the case of jargons – of a total or partial reinvention of similar systems by different people in the same locality.

Of the different types of languages considered in this book, jargons are the most vulnerable because they are very much individual solutions and because they are heavily dependent on a narrowly defined social context. Such is the brevity of life of many *ad hoc* means of cross-linguistic communication that they go entirely unreported and undocumented. Even some of the better institutionalized jargons, such as the whaler's jargons of the Pacific, the French-American Indian jargons of Canada, or the numerous European-Oceanic contact jargons, have long disappeared. In many cases, the context that called them into being had disappeared, but this is not the only reason. In the study of Pacific jargons, for instance, one can observe a gradual replacement of linguistically highly mixed solutions by those based on a European language, a consequence of a shift in the power relations between the parties in contact. Whilst the topics of discussion may have remained the same, the prestige of the expatriate visitors grew over the years, causing changes in the lexical nature of jargons (cf Clark 1996 for the case of Pidgins in New Zealand in the 19th century).

Language murder in the case of stable Pidgins is widely commented upon, but in-depth studies of this phenomenon are rare, a major exception being Jourdan (1983). Let us consider a few cases of the death of Pidgins:

Vietnamese Pidgin French. A Pidgin French called Tay Boi, developed in Indo-China after the establishment of a French garrison in the 1860s. It was used mainly in vertical communication between Europeans and Vietnamese traders, servants and policemen, though rarely in inter-tribal communication. Thus, in spite of its institutionalization with the colonial system (particularly the army), it rapidly disappeared after French withdrawal in the 1960s. Reinecke also observes that a new Pidgin which has since been established in Vietnam is not a continuation of the former French-based one:

> Tay Boi has not survived in use between Vietnamese and American military personnel, nor has it influenced the Pidgin English that now has its place, apart from a word or two (beaucoup, fini). The Pidgin English of Vietnam derives from Pidgin English used by American forces previously in Japan and Korea (1971:47).

The reasons for the death of Pidgin French lie primarily in the loss of its main *raison d'être*, that of enabling the indigenous population to communicate with their French colonizers. A second reason was its general low esteem and finally, its strong associations with outmoded forms of colonialism.

Pidgin Fijian. Pidgin Fijian first developed between native Fijians and imported Melanesian workers on the Fijian sugar plantations. About 5,000 of the 27,000 Melanesians were recruited from the Solomons, and, on termination of their labour contract, took Pidgin Fijian back with them. For some time it looked as if Pidgin Fijian was to become a general lingua franca of the South-Western Pacific and, in particular, that of the Solomons. However, within a generation it had disappeared from there and been replaced by Solomons PE. The two reasons for its death include the reluctance of English speaking expatriates to adopt a Fijian-based Pidgin in the Solomons and the numerical dominance, in later years, of PE-speaking Solomon Islanders returning from Queensland.

After the termination of Melanesian labour trade, the number of imported labourers in Fiji dwindled. Those who were left behind did not find Pidgin Fijian a viable means of communication, and instead of developing a Creole, adopted a standard form of Fijian. However, as pointed out by Siegel (1983b), the extinction of Pidgin Fijian was prevented by a possibility not considered by Hall, transfer from one group of speakers to another. It was adopted by imported Indian labourers, "either on some of the smaller plantations or from Fijians after the indenture era. It became Indian Pidgin Fijian which differs from P[lantation] P[idgin] F[ijian] mainly in phonology and some phrase level ordering of elements" (Siegel 1983b:38).

This case is comparable to the transfer of Japanese PE to Vietnam by the American Army mentioned above.

Queensland Kanaka English. Aboriginal PE of a mainly NSW origin became the working language on the sugar plantations of Queensland around 1880 and was used both as a means of horizontal communication among the many Melanesian indentured workers (more than 10,000 at the peak in 1886) and in communication between the Melanesians and members of other races (Aboriginals, Chinese and White), often in a vertical function (see Dutton 1980, Dutton & Mühlhäusler 1984). Its linguistic stability and social importance is reflected, for instance, in the fact that it was adopted as a language of evangelization. However, the decision to repatriate all Melanesians between 1904 and 1906 meant that the viability of the Melanesian community was in doubt in spite of the fact that the ratio of males to females was more favourable (about 3 : 1) than at any time in the past. Thus, whilst the parents in many Melanesian families spoke to one another in Kanaka English, thereby providing the preconditions for this language to become a Creole, they discouraged their children from using it. Instead they urged them to learn proper English at school or from their school-going older siblings. The negative attitudes of the parents were reinforced by the fact that most Melanesian children went to white State Schools where both teachers and peers looked down on Kanaka English.

Jourdan (1983) has studied the decline of Kanaka English in Mackay, one of the main centres of the sugar industry. It appears that, after a brief period of bilingualism and bidialectism extending for no more than three generations, a total shift to English monolingualism occurred.

The case of Queensland not only illustrates how changing external conditions lead to the death of a Pidgin, it also shows that creolization does not occur wherever children grow up in Pidgin-speaking families. The same phenomenon was already observed in Fiji and has also been found among

271

third generation speakers of Samoan PPE, where, instead of creolizing their parents' Pidgin, children shift to a more useful language spoken in the wider community. Whilst Kanaka English thus died out in Queensland it continues to be spoken, in a changed and more developed form, in the areas where the labourers were originally recruited. Both Solomons PE and Vanuatu Bislama are in many ways continuations of the Queensland tradition of PE.

The cases surveyed here fall into two types, one the replacement of a Pidgin by a standard language, signalling the absorption of Pidgin speakers by the majority culture and, in the case of Vietnamese Pidgin French and Fijian Pidgin in the Solomons, its replacement by a Pidgin of a different lexical affiliation. It is this latter case which has greatly occupied the minds of those advocating a relexification view of Pidgin development and family history. However, the relexification view seems inapplicable both for the Vietnamese Pidgins and Solomons PE and evidence against relexification has been put forward by Hollyman (1976) in the case of the replacement of an English-based Pidgin by a French-based one in New Caledonia. My own findings for the development of Pidgin German in New Guinea suggest an even more complex picture: for some individuals, one can observe a gradual transition from PE to Pidgin German via intermediate mixed varieties whereas for others, Pidgin German is more in the nature of an independent development, even for those who are also proficient speakers of Tok Pisin.

Hall (1962) regards creolization as the principal mechanism by which Pidgins can escape a fate of extinction. However, Creoles are often vulnerable to both language murder and language suicide. Let us look at a few case studies of the replacement of Creoles.

Some Portuguese Creoles of Asia. Following the establishment of a Portuguese colonial empire in the East, a large number of Creoles came into existence, most of them closely linked structurally and historically. Their subsequent history is one of decline and disappearance, either through language murder or suicide. Whereas the former is encountered in areas which came under the influence of other colonial powers (such as Sri Lanka or Java), the latter is common in other territories that remained Portuguese (such as Goa or Macau). The first Portuguese settled in the area around present-day Jakarta in the late 16th century. However, an important Portuguese Creole speaking community developed only after the Dutch took over and began to import slaves and labourers to Java. The language of this new community was Creole Portuguese:

> While at one point Java Creole Portuguese threatened to oust the Dutch language completely, its speakers were too localized for it to resist the social and political importance of that language, or the numerical importance of Malay; thus its rather rapid decline began about 1800, and by 1816 the distinctly 'Portuguese' section of the community had become one with the Malay population socially, and increasingly, linguistically. The language did, however, survive in Pekan Tugu (now a district within greater Djakarta) into the 20th century. Huet [1909] found Creole Portuguese spoken as a home language in this village in 1906, but no reports have appeared on the state of the language since that time, although Valkhoff's suggestion that it may have become extinct even before World War II may prove to be substantiated. (Hancock 1972:549)

272

From Java, this Malay-Portuguese was spread to other Dutch-controlled areas, particularly South Africa. The importance of this language in the formation of Afrikaans was first pointed out by Hesseling and later elaborated on by Valkhoff (e.g. 1966). Spoken Malay-Portuguese survived in the Cape until the middle of the last century after which time it rapidly disappeared, having no status or functional niche in which it could survive.

The tenacious character of Portuguese Creole is also documented for the Ceylonese variety (cf Hesseling 1910, translation 1979). When the Dutch took over Ceylon from the Portuguese, a number of measures were taken to replace this language by Dutch. Commenting on the rivalry between these two languages, Hesseling (1979:24) writes:

> The government understood the danger and tried to stop it with prohibitions, but the social structure maintained the old speech of the first white settlers. And here the influence of women on the form of daily speech appears to have been of major significance. The following clause occurs in the stipulations of 1656 whereby the Portuguese were to leave the island; I rely on a *Report on the Dutch Records in the Government Archives at Colombo*, edited by R G Anthonisz: "All fathers, mothers, brothers and married sisters must be transported in our ships and thereafter taken wherever they wish to go, be it Goa, St Thomas, Cochin, or other Portuguese settlements, or by it to Holland. The unmarried daughters must, however, remain and become engaged to Dutchmen." This stipulation, barbaric by present-day standards, does not occur in the official redaction of the tracts; but, Anthonisz says, it certainly has not been tampered with.

The result of such adverse policies was that Portuguese and Portuguese Creole gradually receded from public life and from the speech of the ruling classes. Although there was extensive use of Portuguese Creole in religious publications throughout the 19th century (Reinecke et al. 1975:98-103), by the second half of the 20th century it survived only among a group of workers in the east of the island (Smith 1984), long after all traces of Dutch in Ceylon had disappeared.

A third Asian Portuguese Creole, Ternateño, had developed around the important trading post of Ternate in the Moluccas. However, as the Portuguese community came under attack from the local rulers, many of its members fled to the Spanish Catholic Philippines, taking their language with them (see Whinnom 1956). Here, it was apparently relexified into a Spanish Creole, though details of this process are not well documented.

Negerhollands. Dutch Creole of the Virgin Islands is the legacy of Dutch trading activities and brief political control of part of the area. The immediate cause of Dutch being spoken in the Danish-controlled islands was the Dutch and their slaves having been driven from other islands by the British. By 1688, about half the European households in the Danish Antilles were Dutch compared with one fifth which were Danish. At one time, such was the status of Dutch Creole that it was used for bible translations and other religious writings as well as private and semi-official written communication. Its demise is due mainly to changing social conditions. The changeover from a plantation society with closed communication networks to a commercial economy involving numerous contacts with English-speaking

273

outsiders following emancipation in 1848 favoured linguistic change. English rather than the official Danish became the language first of the towns and gradually the rest of the islands. The sale of this territory to the USA in 1916 put an end to any role for Danish. The last surving speaker of the language died as recently as 1987 but the functional death of the language appears to have occurred early this century. For further information, see van Rossem & van der Voort (1996).

We can now turn to cases of language suicide which, as has been pointed out are typically found where a Pidgin or Creole and its lexifier language co-exist over a longish period of time. Thus, whilst the PE of Cameroon is being rapidly restructured in the direction of English in urban areas (see Todd 1984), the same language spoken on former Spanish Fernando Póo has remained structurally and lexically stable. Again, the Portuguese Creole of Macau, Macanese, is said to have merged with Portuguese in Portuguese Macau whilst it still survives in an archaic form in neighbouring Hong Kong, as is also the case of Papia Kristang in Malacca in an English- and Malay-speaking environment. Aitchison (1981:210ff) provides a detailed illustration of depidginization and decreolization as examples of language suicide. Whilst much of the linguistic and social evidence suggest a gradual changeover from a number of Pidgins and Creoles to related lexifier languages, Aitchison ignores the fact that contact between two related systems can have two outcomes:

(i) A new third system, unlike either of the contributing systems
(ii) The total absorption of the Pidgin and Creole by the standard language.

I suggest that the second process is found only where decreolization is accompanied by some modicum of language murder.

The study of language death thus provides interesting insights into the history of Pidgins and Creoles, but its study must advance beyond the present level of ill-defined and pre-theoretical classifications.

Pidgins, Creoles and international politics

The case of Dutch and Portuguese Creole in Ceylon suggests a recurrent theme in linguistic politics, namely the desire to impose one's own language, or at least a Pidgin version thereof, in one's territory. This motive was particularly strong in the late 19th century when a number of European powers competed for colonial domination of the world. Germany, a late-comer on the colonial scene, was particularly sensitive to linguistic issues. In its colonies PE was the most widespread lingua franca, as can be seen from the table opposite.

German opinions of how best to handle this problem differed from colony to colony and also over time. However, both the Berlin government and the colonial home lobby held very strong views on the weak position of German, since they regarded language in the colonies as a means of political control, and to this end it was necessary to enforce the use of the language spoken in the mother country. In German New Guinea, the widespread use of English, particularly PE, was regarded as a direct threat to German control. Thus, Governor Hahl argued in a letter to the Kolonialabteilung of the

Auswaertiges Amt in Berlin (10 August 1903, Reichskolonialamt records, vol. 3133, Potsdam) that "The fight against the English language is a task of self-preservation" (my translation). The same view was taken by the mouthpiece of the colonial lobby:

> ... the spread of Pidgin English politically involves great dangers, especially if, in addition, English is preponderant in communication among the whites as, for example, in German New Guinea, but above all in the Bismarck Archipelago. Isn't it risky to raise English to the status of a lingua franca there when Australia is in the vicinity, looking greedily toward this German colony? (*Deutsche Kolonialzeitung* 30.21.344 (1913); my translation)

Lingue franche in former German colonies	
colony	*established lingua franca*
East Africa (Tanganyika)	Swahili, English (among Indians and some coastal dwellers)
South West Africa (Namibia)	Afrikaans and reduced forms of Afrikaans
Kamerun (Cameroon)	PE
Togo	PE
Samoa	Samoan; English (among elite); PE (on plantations)
New Guinea	some PE in coastal areas; some Bazaar Malay on mainland New Guinea
Kiautschou	some PE
Micronesia	some PE

The aim of replacing PE with German was achieved in only one area, however, German Micronesia. Although they were acquired from Spain, English traders and missionaries had spread both regular and Pidgin varieties of English to many of the islands. Due to the small size of the individual islands and their populations, attempts to replace English and Spanish with German appear to have been relatively successful. In a report on the development of the German colonies in the South Seas (*Denkschrift über die Entwicklung der Schutzgebiete in Afrika und der Südsee im Jahre 1906/7.* Reichstag Aktenstück zu Nr. 622, S. 41 we) we read (in my translation):

> One has to agree with the teachers' complaint that their pupils have had insufficient opportunities to apply their knowledge of German outside the classroom. However, one can observe a change for the better, since the German settlers avoid the use of Pidgin English in their dealings with the natives. In the Marianas, Pidgin English has been eradicated well and truly for some time now. In addition, it must be mentioned that the use of German has become established, particularly among the younger natives, not only in Saipan but also in Palau and Yap.

Solenberger (1962:59-60) reports that German influence was still found in the Marianas in the early 1960s:

> In the short period from 1899 to 1914 a small staff of Germans so impressed those inhabitants of the Northern Marianas who were educated within that period that they still show a marked preference for German speech, literature, music and dances.

It is interesting to see that German fears before the First World War indeed became reality. German West Africa, Samoa and New Guinea all became English-speaking countries, the presence of PE presumably facilitating this process.

The question of language and political control is also illustrated by a number of other cases involving Pidgins and Creoles. Of those which have become newsworthy in the comparatively recent past are Miskito Coast Creole English, the Dutch Creoles of Guyana, Pidgin varieties of Malay, and Belize Creole.

Miskito Coast Creole English developed on the coast of Nicaragua in the first half of the 17th century when "traders from the ill-fated Puritan colony on Providence Island (1630-41) and then.... buccaneers" (Holm 1978:40) settled in the area. A British colony was established in the early 18th century but the settlers and many of their slaves were driven out by Spaniards in 1780. However, some slaves and many Creoles stayed behind, living in virtual isolation from the rest of the country. Occasional attempts to re-establish British control failed. With the establishment of the Sandinista government in Nicaragua, the Creole speakers gained considerable attention, as they opposed attempts by the central government to be integrated into the mainstream Spanish-speaking society. There are reports about forceful deportation and other attempts to destroy the unity of the Creole community as well as renewed appeals to Britain by its members.

A similar conflict between Spanish speakers and Creole English speakers is found in Belize. Again, Belize was settled by British colonists and their slaves in the 17th century, an act which was never recognized by Spain. However, Spanish attacks on this settlement in the 18th century, unlike the Miskito Coast, were successfully repelled and a British colony, British Honduras, was declared in 1862. Neither this colony nor the now independent state of Belize were recognized by neighbouring Guatemala. The three principal linguistic groups are speakers of Spanish, in the provinces bordering on Guatemala, English around the capital and some coastal areas, and Creole in most other areas. Hellinger (1972) and Le Page & Tabouret-Keller (1985) report a shift towards Creole from speakers of both English and Spanish. Le Page refers to:

> Belize, under external threat, and from the starting-point of a wide range of cultural and ethnic identities ("Spanish", "Maya", "Creole", "Carib", "Mestizo" being only the five main labels applied when I first visited the colony in 1952), is now seeking a common "Belizean" identity, one aspect of which is tacit recognition of something called "Creole" as the Belizean language (1980:334).

The survival of Belize as an independent political unit is thus seen by its inhabitants as a condition for the survival of their Creole identity.

A similar, as yet unsettled, conflict is going on between Guyana and Venezuela. Again, its origins can be traced back to a foreign European power, this time the Netherlands encroaching on territory belonging to Spain. The legal and political problems stemming from Venezuela's claim to vast areas of Guyana are discussed in Robertson (n d) which, because of the sensitivity of the issue, is not to be quoted (and is thus excluded from the bibliography). Very briefly, the Spanish position (and that of Spain's successor, Venezuela) has always been that the Dutch could only claim such land as they actually colonized and controlled. Thus, whereas the coastal areas of Guyana were firmly in Dutch hands, and after the British takeover in the 19th century, in British hands, control over parts of the interior is a matter of dispute. However, Robertson's discovery of a Dutch-derived Creole in the area claimed by Venezuela has added considerable weight to Guyana's position, and in fact helped to vindicate it.

Pidgin languages as evidence for former control are also appealed to in the highly sensitive area of Indonesian expansion of the East and South. Whilst Indonesian claims to parts of Papua New Guinea or indeed Northern Australia are not openly made, there are fears that such claims may be made in the future and that linguistic evidence may play a role. As regards Papua New Guinea, there is an old myth, repeated by Rowley (1965) among many others, that a Pidgin form of Malay was firmly established before the arrival of the German colonizers in the 1880s. This myth was exposed by Seiler (1982) who shows that such visits from Indonesia to the coast of Papua New Guinea "had only just started when the Germans arrived" (p 71) and, with the exception of very few places, such as the island Tarawai, were quite insignificant. Again, the influence of Malay bird-of-paradise traders in the Sepik border areas more or less coincides with but hardly predates, the German colonial presence.

The greatest impact of Malay on New Guinea languages such as Tok Pisin comes much later when German plantation owners began to import Malay and Chinese from the former Dutch East Indies. For a while, Malay was used as a semi-official language but with the discontinuation of Malay labour and because of the resistance of the missions who disfavoured a language with strong Muslim connotations, its useful life came to an end soon after 1900. The historical claims of Indonesia to parts of Papua New Guinea would seem to be extremely weak in the light of such new evidence. Stronger trade links and quite considerable linguistic influence is documented for northern Australia, which was visited by trepang fishers from Macassar possibly as early as 1650 (cf MacKnight 1976 and relevant maps in Wurm et al. 1996). The intensity of the contacts between the Macassarese and Aboriginals of the Northern Territory can be seen, for instance, in the fact that Macassarese Pidgin was used not only as a trade language with the foreign visitors but also as an inter-tribal lingua franca (cf Harris 1984). It was replaced only at the beginning of this century when more and more English speakers settled in the Northern Territory and has now disappeared leaving only a few lexical traces in local languages. To what extent Macassarese grammatical structures are preserved in the PE that replaced it is not known at present. The argument that this part of Australia was influenced linguistically and culturally by visits from the area of Indonesia thus is a fairly powerful one. Whether or not it will ever be used to political ends remains to be seen.

The argument of prior established language is a dangerous one and could also work against Indonesia in other areas. Thus, Portuguese Creole probably predates Pidgin Malay in the eastern parts of Indonesia and the presence of a distinct linguistic and cultural tradition of Portuguese and Portuguese Creole may yet become a powerful argument in the East Timor dispute.

A language which has attracted considerable attention in recent years is Afrikaans which, probably a creoloid itself, is spoken as a simplified second language and as a creolized pidgin by numerous mixed-race and black citizens of South Africa and Namibia. However, non-white feelings against this language have been running high for some time. Attempts to make its teaching compulsory in the 1970s in black schools sparked off riots in South Africa and such were the anti-Afrikaans feelings in Namibia that the new SWAPO government has opted for English as the official language (see Phillipson 1992 for details).

8 Pidgins and Creoles in education

To send children to school and encourage them to read Pidgin instead of normal English seems odd in the extreme. (French 1953:60)

Introduction

At the conference which launched the field of Pidgin and Creole linguistics (Jamaica 1959), educational matters dominated the discussion. Linguistic inquiry into Pidgins and Creoles was linked very closely with its perceived justification, the improvement of education for speakers of these languages. This close link has not been maintained, however, and the justification of Pidgin and Creole studies today is often seen as their importance in the area of theoretical linguistics (see Chapter 6). Nonetheless, there remains a widespread feeling among educators and the Creole-speaking public that linguistic studies should contribute to educational questions. Reasons why many Creolists are reluctant to get involved with educational matters include:

i) Their feeling of incompetence in this area
ii) Their not wanting to get involved in social and political issues
iii) The realization that their findings may be in conflict with prevailing expectations and attitudes
iv) Bad experiences in the past.

However, some individuals have continued to explore and have significantly pushed back the horizons in recent years. A considerable body of research and applications is regularly discussed in the *Pidgins and Creoles in Education* (PACE) newsletter. Valuable information can also be found in Siegel (ed., 1992). That Pidgins and Creoles have become important in the education systems of a number of countries is due to both research and the personal commitment of researchers to improving the status of these languages.

Educators have identified similar problems for virtually all Pidgin- and Creole-speaking communities. Severe educational underachievement is manifested most clearly in failure in the standard language, typically the language lexically related to their Pidgin or Creole. The data set out below, illustrate such underachievement in four Creole-speaking communities.

Achievement in London GCE "O"-level in selected subjects, 1962

	Barbados		Guyana		Jamaica		Trinidad	
Subject	*Entry*	*% pass*	*Entry*	*% pass*	*Entry*	*% pass*	*Entry*	*%pass*
English language	150	10.7	2483	19.6	661	19.4	1521	23.1
English literature	91	24.2	1245	21.5	46	13.0	349	12.3
Geography	34	0	409	39.8	51	13.7	366	14.2
History	77	29.9	1167	34.4	41	4.9	145	23.4
French	52	15.4	113	19.5	16	25.0	229	11.4
Biology	13	23.1	344	20.3	103	14.6	140	12.9
Physics	5	60.0	90	31.1	38	18.4	97	20.6

(Le Page 1968:433; table adapted and abbreviated)

279

It would seem that the uneasy relationship between Pidgin and Creoles on the one hand and the (colonial) standard languages on the other contribute significantly to academic underachievement and other socially undesirable side-effects, such as the perpetuation of class distinctions in post-colonial societies. Craig (1980) has devised a classification of educational policies in West Indian Creole communities, which has been adopted for the Seychelles (d'Offay de Rieux 1980) and Northern Australia (Sandefur 1984). It has proved highly useful and forms the basis of this chapter. Craig (1980:247-48), expanding on earlier work by Fishman, distinguishes the following types:

1. Monolingualism in school in the dominant language. In this alternative the home language of the child is completely ignored.
2. Monoliterate bilingualism, in which the home language of the child is used in school only to the extent necessary to allow the child to adjust to school and learn enough of the school language to permit it to become the medium of education.
3. Monoliterate bilingualism, in which both languages are developed for aural-oral skills, but literacy is aimed at only in the one language that happens to be socially dominant in the community.
4. Partial bilingualism, in which aural-oral fluency and literacy are developed in the home language only in relation to certain types of subject-matter that have to do with the immediate society and culture: while aural-oral fluency and literacy in the school language are developed for a wider range of purposes.
5. Full bilingualism, in which the educational aim is for the child to develop all skills in both languages in all domains.
6. Monolingualism in the home language, in which the aim of the school is to develop literacy only in the home language of the child.

Implicit in all of these is the realization that speakers of the Pidgin or Creole must get access to the superimposed standard language at some stage. When and how this can be achieved is what is at issue.

Educational policy is intimately linked to the factors discussed in Chapter 3 on the sociohistorical context and Chapter 7 on the sociology of language. In addition to considerations of a linguistic and psychological learning theory, any educational solution must also take into account the wider ecological context in which Pidgins and Creoles are typically spoken. Educational policies in such places are often articulated against a background of extreme scarcity of financial and skilled human resources. Even when these are available local conditions may prevent the successful implementation of education policies. During my research in the Western Desert interior of South Australia in 1995, I identified a number of problems:

(a) There was a considerable amount of deafness, ill health and malnutrition.
(b) Petrol sniffing and alcoholism was widespread among teenagers.
(c) The informal Aboriginal English used by many children had no prestige either among their relatives or their white school teachers. Its principal function appeared to be that of an anti-language.

There are other factors which make for a very shaky basis for any formal education and altering the status of the local informal English would do little in itself.

Issues and policies of the past

Craig observes that "in most Creole language situations, an educational policy is seldom chosen by explicit and rational processes; rather, communities tend to drift into policy positions under the force of historical and emotional commitments. This has been true in the officially English countries earlier mentioned and is also true for most others" (1980:246). I will illustrate this with the case of Tok Pisin, which is a particularly interesting example because educational policies were shaped not only by successive colonial powers but also by international bodies such as the United Nations. Romaine (1992) contains many complementary references.

From 1884 to 1899 German New Guinea was administered not by the German Empire directly but by private business interests. For understandable reasons, the New Guinea Company did not feel inclined to spend any resources on education, particularly not on the teaching of German. Instead, they indirectly promoted and certainly tolerated the spread of Tok Pisin. As regards the policies of the German administration which took over in 1899, their ambitions to make German the language of instruction as well as of general communication were restricted to rhetoric. Throughout German colonial presence, little progress was made in establishing state schools, their total enrolment in 1912 being about 500 compared with more than 22,000 students enrolled in mission schools. An education ordinance restructuring and expanding existing teaching facilities, particularly those for teaching German, became law in January 1915, and one of its central aims was to eradicate Tok Pisin.

Mission policies at the time were diverse, ranging from the use of English as the medium of instruction, to the development of mission lingue franche, and to the teaching of and in German. As regards the first group, a number of Protestant missions operating from English-speaking countries had established themselves in the area of the Bismarck Archipelago before the declaration of the German protectorate. Though the local vernaculars were used for mission work, the fact that English was taught in mission schools belonging to this group was a continued cause of annoyance to the German government. More influential were the three mission companies operating out of Germany and employing German missionaries. Each was restricted to one area. The Lutheran mission started its activities in the Finschhafen-Sattelberg area and used two local vernaculars (Kâte and Jabêm) as mission languages (see Mühlhaüsler 1996a). The practice of the various Catholic mission bodies differed, but at least one of them, the Divine Word Missionaries, promoted German at all levels. That this did not always meet with great success, can be seen from the following report:

> The Catholic missions educate their pupils in the German language; yet this knowledge, as far as I could ascertain, is restricted to the recitation of verses and songs. It remained quite impossible for me to make myself understood in German with these pupils even on the most elementary topics. This may be rather better in their communication with the teachers where daily recurrent topics are concerned and there are certainly exceptions. But as a lingua franca German is quite unsuited; it is too complicated and besides contains sounds which the native finds hard to pronounce. (Neuhauss 1911:121; my translation)

Educational policies under Australian administration in the Trust Territory of New Guinea in the years after the First World War were characterized by a lack of consistency. As observed by Reed (1943:273):

> Three main courses were open to the territorial administrations with respect to the language problem. They could (a) teach the natives their European language; (b) adopt a native speech as a *lingua franca* and teach it; or (c) accept frankly the local Pidgin, attempt to purify it, and give it official status. Actually, no one of these alternatives has been adopted and carried through in its entirety.

The first policy, monolingualism in the dominant language was proposed by the Australian government for the Kokopo school, the largest in the territory. In its *Annual Report to the League of Nations* (1932:23ff), the Australian government stated:

> After mature consideration it was decided to make an effort to introduce English, purely spoken, as the official language of the school. English is the official and commercial language of the Territory, and one of the objects of the course laid down is to fit a modicum of the pupils for minor positions in the official and commercial activities of the Territory. It is interesting to note the progress made so far. The teacher will dictate to a pupil the sentence "Did you go for a walk?" and the boy will write the words down quite correctly, thoroughly understanding the meaning. The teacher will then ask him "Where did you go?" but the oral answer required to this question is almost invariably given by the boy in "pidgin" English - "Me bin go along Vunapope." There is however, little doubt that the disinclination to speak grammatical English will disappear as time goes on.

Such optimistic prognostications were hardly born out by educational reality and financial support for this enterprise was pretty half-hearted. Lawrence (1964:48) remarks:

> In education, the official aim was to teach English and train natives for the lower grades of the Public Service. But between 1923 and 1937, annual expenditure for the whole Territory fell from £18,000 to £5,000. By 1939-40, there were only six Administration schools with a total of 491 pupils. The failure of native education meant, of course, the retention of Pidgin English as the *lingua franca*.

In view of this, a type four policy (partial bilingualism), involving a gradual transition from Tok Pisin to English, was proposed by the pre-Second World War Director of Education, Groves.[1] Smith reports that this proposal was followed up immediately after the country had been liberated from the Japanese occupying forces:

---

[1] Groves represents the paternalistic type of colonial administrator. His views are expressed in the following lines (quoted from Johnson 1974:9):

. . . . .with native teachers and in a native environment, it will never be possible to teach English even reasonably well in the village schools, even if it were desired to do so. All experience and reason are against it. When English is widespread in New Guinea villages, they will no longer be New Guinea villages. And a sorry day that indeed will be.

Introducing the 1952 Education Bill Groves stated that "one of the main scholastic aims in the administration's school system is the teaching of English." But in the 1950 syllabus, revised 1952, he authorised the use of Pidgin under certain circumstances. "If Pidgin itself represents a successful avenue for teaching those important things which it is considered desirable to teach at this stage in the village environment," he suggested in 1951, "It would not be unwise to give it official approval, standardise its phonetic orthography and use it to the fullest extent". (Smith 1969:17)

Under this policy Tok Pisin was used not only in primary education but also in adult education such as in para-medical training. It was dealt a severe blow, however, in July 1953 when a report from the UN Trusteeship Council stated: "The UN Trusteeship Council today urged Australia to put a stop to the use of Pidgin English in the Trust Territory of New Guinea" (quoted from Hall 1954:85). The Australian administration saw itself compelled to withdraw its support for teaching in Tok Pisin, literacy programmes, and government publications. It also withdrew support from the missions which had increasingly switched to instruction in Tok Pisin.

By 1969, with self-government and independence around the corner, the debate gained new impetus. A conference addressing Tok Pisin and education was held in Port Moresby in 1969. As university education of Papua New Guineans had not progressed much at that time, the discussion took place almost exclusively among expatriate experts. The most vociferous advocate of monolingual English education was the newly appointed vice chancellor of the University of Papua New Guinea, Gunther. Gunther advocated universal primary education in English, something which he felt could be achieved by a moderate financial investment, as much of this money would become available by discontinuing support for Tok Pisin. At the same time he envisaged a number of other measures, particularly in the area of broadcasting and adult education. Gunther's views were based on the perceived desire of Papua New Guineans to obtain a universal education in English. Such a sentiment was indeed widespread at the time, as English was seen as the key to well-paid jobs and life in a prestigious urban environment. As more and more indigenous Papua New Guineans entered the debate a different picture began to emerge, however. The emerging black elite began to realize that:

1. Universal education in English is an extremely costly enterprise with dubious chance of success. The first secretary of Education after independence for instance attacked "the semi-magical belief that speaking and writing English like Europeans means the possession of many goods and power" (Tololo 1975:11) and the first Minister of Education, Olewale, advocated unofficially that every child in Papua New Guinea should receive part of their education in Tok Pisin or Hiri Motu.
2. A knowledge of English is not equivalent to social mobility
3. An English-dominated education system perpetuates expatriate values and views.
4. English education is likely to promote social divisions.

All these issues are debated at great length in the proceedings of the 1973 conference on Tok Pisin (McElhanon 1975), at subsequent meetings of the Linguistic Society of Papua New Guinea, and at a meeting in 1988 at the Divine Word Institute in Madang (see Verhaar (ed) 1990). It is of interest to note that the main advocates for Tok Pisin in the schools were white expatriates (see articles in Wurm (ed.) 1977c), while Dutton (1985b:535-36) points out that "no one in a position to influence government education policy in Papua New Guinea has so far been prepared to press for even a limited education in Tok Pisin as part of that policy.[2] Practically, however, Tok Pisin is used, and is allowed to be used in government schools as an explanatory language in teaching when necessary". Piau, one of the few indigenous writers on this topic feels that "the underlying reason that people give for retaining English as the medium of instruction is... that the only way to have status, wealth and power is through English" (Piau & Holzknecht 1985:489). Dutton (1985b:536) adds that much of education occurs outside the state system and that mission Tok Pisin schools cater for many drop-outs or push-outs from the state system. Romaine (1992:88) comments on a second phenomenon, the increasing trend for the rich elite to send their children to fee-paying English-medium international schools. Recent moves to introduce vernacular education again are not the result of a clear policy, nor is the informal use of Tok Pisin in the tertiary system. However, they do guarantee a relatively conflict-free pragmatic approach to the choice of instructional medium as well as a smooth transition from one policy to another. Moreover, they cater for the diverse conditions prevailing in different parts of the country. Craig's statement at the beginning of this section, rather than characterizing a deplorable state of affairs, may well turn out to have its positive sides too. As we have just seen, even explicitly well-formulated educational theories mean very little in a society that is not ready for them. What makes societies ready for different policies will now be examined in somewhat more detail.

Pidgins and Creoles and educational policies

The suitability and success of the different policies identified by Craig is related to various linguistic and social factors. The haphazard way in which educational policies were established in the past stems largely from not taking such factors into consideration. Let us consider some linguistic factors first.

Whilst Creoles are comparable, in expressive power, to full languages, many Pidgins are not. This functional and structural restriction poses limitations in their usefulness as media of instruction. Moreover, many Pidgins are learnt only by adults and are of little use in teaching young

---

2   However, influential public voices, such as that of the vice chancellor of the University of Papua New Guinea, continued to advocate the use of Tok Pisin:

"There is no reason, for example, why Tok Pisin should not be the major language of instruction in community schools throughout most, if not all, parts of the nation. Far more children know Tok Pisin before they go to school than know English, and most children are much more likely to hear Tok Pisin than English outside the classroom. This gives it a considerable advantage over English as a familiar language through which primary education could proceed more effectively. Its use in schools would in turn not only increase its status but would provide a most effective means of spreading the standard written version of the language" (Lynch 1990:395).

children, the exceptions being expanded Pidgins such as Bislama, Sango, and Tok Pisin, which are learnt relatively early and structurally resemble full languages. In this connection, Sandefur (1984) remarks that, of the numerous Kriol-speaking communities in northern Australia, only very few have been identified by the various state governments as being genuine candidates for a bilingual Kriol/English education. The principal criterion for Sandefur was the extent to which Kriol has become institutionalized as the first language of a community. However, educational practice (see Rhydwen 1993) turned out to be affected by numerous other socio-psychological factors and it now appears as if Kriol-medium education is on its way out.

It has to be realized that Creole languages, whilst being complex forms of communication,[3] may nevertheless be difficult to adapt to syllabuses designed by speakers of the related standard language. Social code-shifting conventions may have reserved the domains which are of greatest relevance to a western type of education for other languages, a reason why English and French are felt to be the proper languages of education in Vanuatu and why the national language, Bislama, was even banned in the high schools and inside the Ministry of Education (Siegel 1989:2). The situation in present-day Vanuatu is comparable to that in Europe up to about the 18th century, where many domains of learning were discussed in Latin only. Crucial in this connection is the linguistic relationship between the Creole and the dominant language. There is a difference between situations without lexical affiliation – e.g. English-based Sranan versus Dutch in Surinam, Spanish-based Papiamentu versus Dutch in the Netherlands Antilles, or the various Spanish-based Creoles versus Tagalog in the Philippines – and cases where much of the lexicon is related, as in Creole English versus English in much of the West Indies, northern Australia, West Africa and the Pacific. Among the latter group, it is also necessary to distinguish situations where linguistic continua are found (e.g. Guyana and Jamaica) from those where basilectal and acrolectal varieties are kept distinct, as for instance in Haiti or Papua New Guinea. Where languages are lexically unrelated, established methods of bilingual teaching would seem appropriate. Where they are not, the close historical relationship between the two languages may necessitate special adjustments in teaching and, in the case of linguistic continua, new methods of teaching will have to be devised, as is currently being explored by Malcolm (1995) for Western Australia. One area which is particularly problematic in this last situation is that of assessing structural and lexical correctness.

With regard to cases where a Pidgin or Creole coexists with a lexically related standard language, the following possibilities have been suggested, often without further examination:

1. That the Pidgin or Creole is simply a non-standard dialect of the superimposed language; this view has been particularly common with heavily decreolized varieties such as African American English.

2. That it is an imperfectly learnt version of the superimposed language.

3. That it is a discrete linguistic system, a view often reinforced by the practice of giving it a separate name such as Ebonic or Kriol.

---

3 Whinnom (1971:110) reminds educators that the question of the adequacy of Creole languages has not as yet been settled.

As regards the identification of dialects, the most useful criteria are:

(a) The dependency principle, which implies that different dialects share the same underlying structures but differ in the number and/or order of rules deriving surface structures; and

(b) the dynamic version of (a), that the different surface manifestations are found along the same implicationally ordered lectal continuum (see Bailey 1996).

These criteria replace reliance on surface similarity, counts of lexical cognation and impressionistic statements about mutual intelligibility.[4] In most instances, the result of applying them to Pidgins or Creoles and their related standard languages will be negative, i.e. they cannot be regarded as related dialects.

The second view, that Pidgins and Creoles are imperfectly learned versions of the target language is a view widely held by educators and, indeed, many Pidgin and Creole speakers themselves. Suggestions that Pidgins and/or Creoles are somehow like learners' interlanguages have probably reinforced it.[5] Much will depend on whether "interlanguage" is taken to mean, as suggested by the term's initiators, a structured system intermediate between two particular languages or, as favoured in much subsequent research, a developing system beginning with a tabula rasa and ending in a target language (see Corder 1976). Under the former assumption, contrastive analysis and study of interference will be important; under the latter, investigators will concentrate on language-independent forces of development.[6] These two interpretations of "interlanguage" stem from the way access to the target language is seen. A view which stresses interference tends to assume that access is no problem but that learning of new knowledge is temporarily impeded by old knowledge; the target is eventually reached by shedding more and more such knowledge and replacing it with the relevant target knowledge. If this model of interlanguage should turn out to be correct one would expect a different type of interlanguage for each group of Pidgin and Creole speakers acquiring the related target language. Moreover, Pidgin speakers from different first-language backgrounds could also be expected to have differential problems. Thus, researching ways of teaching the standard language would be very costly. The problem facing the educator is that of bridging the gap between the endpoint of Pidgin and Creole development and the target language.[7] Schematically, this can be represented as follows:

---

4   The unreliability of cognate counts for the identification of relationships between languages and their Pidgin and Creole relatives has been discussed in the examples of Motu and Hiri Motu, by Wurm (1964). However, despite numerous problems, this criterion is still widely used.

5   Such parallelisms are suggested, for instance, by Schumann (1978). Stauble (1978), on the other hand, suggests a close parallel with decreolization.

6   There is a further dichotomy among interlanguage theoreticians, i.e. between those who regard the development of interlanguages as driven by internal forces of grammar (e.g. contributors to Corder & Roulet 1976) and those who emphasize communicative functions (e.g. Huebner 1983, Sato 1990, Selinker 1991).

7   Implicit in this view is the oft-expressed opinion that Pidgins and Creoles can be taken as the bridge by means of which the target language can be reached. The unidimensional character of the putative transition further encourages the view that one can turn Pidgins and Creoles into their target languages by means of gradual lexical and grammatical adjustment over a period of language engineering.

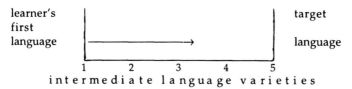

intermediate language varieties

The view of language-independent Pidgin and Creole development affords a very different interpretation. Deviations from the target would be seen as a conspiracy between inadequate access and universally motivated hierarchies of second-language development. This can be represented as follows:

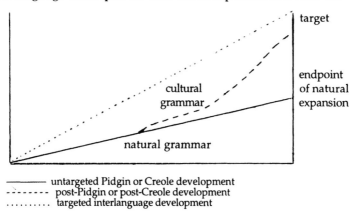

——————— untargeted Pidgin or Creole development
- - - - - - - post-Pidgin or post-Creole development
.... targeted interlanguage development

Thus, in interlanguage learning in a situation with a target both natural and cultural grammar has to be acquired, whereas Pidgin and Creole development occurs in a maximally culture-free learning context.

The above scheme also raises another matter, that of the relative status of post-Pidgin/post-Creole continua and interlanguage. Bickerton (e.g. 1975b, 1981) regards decreolization as a well-ordered natural process. If this were indeed the case, then the stages found in decreolizing systems would provide a perfect syllabus helping students to make the transition from a Pidgin/Creole to the superimposed standard language. As I have tried to demonstrate, there appears to be evidence that depidginization and decreolization are at best a mixture of such natural processes and a number of abnatural ones, such as hyper-correctional. Under this view, the sequence of changes observed outside the classroom would not necessarily provide a good basis for syllabus.

One must conclude that, to regard Pidgins or Creoles as imperfect versions of a target standard language, is to miss important aspects of their linguistic nature. A programme aiming at teaching proficiency in the superimposed standard language should not be based on this assumption. The notion that Pidgins or Creoles and their lexically related superimposed languages are discrete systems is becoming increasingly accepted by linguists, though it often violates the common sense of speakers of both language groups. As observed by Le Page:

> The problem for most West Indian children in the Creole-English-speaking islands is not that of foreign language learners of English or

287

native speakers. Their Creole speech has no literary norm other than that of standard English - but as a spoken language it has its own phonological, grammatical, lexical, and semantic structures, which differ, often quite sharply, from those of the spoken dialects that underlie the standard usage of the textbooks and of the examiners. But neither the teachers nor the children are equipped to recognize the differences (1968:434-35).

Thus, there is a discrepancy between the unconscious norms governing Creole speech and the superimposed standard language. Speakers' behaviour in such a situation will include both random and non-random shifts in the direction of the upper language and similar schizoglossic phenomena (see Haugen 1963). Schizoglossia can manifest itself on both individual and social behaviour. In the case of Northern Australia, there is a division between those users who accept Kriol as the name of a proper language and others who do not. The source of this would appear to be that Kriol identity was engineered by outsiders (missionaries and linguists), a fact not acknowledged by Sandefur (1984).[8]

In his discussion of Australian "Kriol" in education, Sandefur (1982) takes the existence of Kriol for granted and simply distinguishes between *de facto* transitional bilingual programmes and genuine planned ones. Characteristic of the former is that they are not well organized and properly staffed and tend to be "implemented" through force of circumstance (e.g. the presence of Kriol-speaking teachers in the classroom or the need to communicate somehow with younger children who control virtually no English). Sandefur confirms Craig's (1980) observations that "in such situations the teachers tend to remain unaware of the extent to which they themselves resort to the Creole language, and it is only to covert observers that their Creole discourse tendencies are fully revealed" (p 9). What he does not address are the socio-psychological complexities identified by Rhydwen (1993).

Teaching in schools where non-standard Pidgin or Creole forms of English are spoken requires language awareness among teachers, pupils and the wider community. Language awareness programmes should include:

i)   Creation of metalinguistic awareness of and metalinguistic vocabulary for the distinct linguistic systems.
ii) Carefully planned exercises highlighting differences in grammar and lexicon.
iii) An introductory discussion of the sociolinguistic status of Pidgins and Creoles in general.
iv) Remarks on the social and linguistic history of the languages used in the classroom.

English World-Wide and the series of *Occasional papers* on Caribbean language and dialect published by the Society for Caribbean Linguistics have included some pertinent material for teachers preparing language awareness classes. Some relevant hints are also contained in Hudson's (1984) discussion of the

---

8   For ideas on this, see the contributions to the journal *Language Awareness*. For specific suggestions as to how to establish literacy in the desert community of central Australia see Clayton (ed., 1996).

use of Kriol in the Yiyili (Western Australia) Aboriginal Community School and a number of other schools in Australia surveyed in Clayton (ed., 1996). Sharpe (1985) explicitly subscribes to the idea that English should be taught as a foreign language to speakers of Kriol. Prior to receiving formal instruction in English, learners are to attend a communications course consisting of the following components:

1. Identification of appropriate domains for English and Kriol; in order to increase the awareness different classrooms were earmarked for English only and Kriol only.
2. Lexical studies including compilation of a Kriol-English dictionary.
3. Translation exercises.
4. Reading and writing Kriol.
5. Exercises in contrastive grammar.

At the end of the year, some significant changes had taken place. These are characterized by Hudson (1984:4) as follows:

> Whereas these English forms had always been guessed at in the past, the games soon had the children aware of what the equivalent forms are in Kriol. Of course moving from this kind of knowledge to incorporating it into their English speech is another step which needs to be taken this year. After one term of this Communications Course, the English teacher found that the children would often ask for clarification as to which language they were to work in , Kriol or English, and on being told it was to be English would consciously omit features of Kriol which previously they were not able to do.

Such programs are particularly useful where one is dealing with clearly different systems. In the case of post-Creole continua, particularly when most speakers are clustered around the acrolectal end of the continuum, problems arise. Most commonly, language differences and communication difficulties are related to differences in grammatical structures. Whether or not special teaching programmes are required cannot just be decided on linguistic grounds. In the case of Black English Vernacular (BEV), for instance, linguistic criteria suggest that there should be few problems, as it appears to form a single system with standard English. Labov (1973:64) observes:

> Certain parts of the tense and aspect system are clearly separate sub-systems in the sense that they are not shared or recognized by other dialects, and we can isolate other such limited areas. But the gears and axles of English grammatical machinery are available to speakers of all dialects.

Purely linguistic or grammatical differences are of course not the only dimension of difference, nor the most important. Communication difficulties arise more readily in the area of language use (pragmatics) than through grammatical ambiguity or when groups do not wish to communicate. Linguists have little to say about the conflicts between Serbs and Croats or coloured and white Afrikaans-speakers during apartheid days. Thus, in order to determine whether speakers of a late post-Creole need special attention in teaching programmes, their language has to be studied from a sociolinguistic point of view, such as the ethnography of speaking. Let me illustrate this with the example of Aboriginal English in south-east Queensland. Eades (1982, 1991) mentions significant differences between white and Aboriginal English as regards questioning.[9] Whilst both groups share the same grammatical devices for forming interrogative structures, there are significant differences (a) in the type – token relationship of the different structures available to both groups, and (b) in the conventions underlying the asking of questions. This causes numerous misunderstandings. Some such differences are:

a) In south-east Queensland Aboriginal English there is no obligation to reply to questions. School children who fail to give an answer to a teacher's question typically do so because of deference to the teacher or because they are under the impression that the teacher knows the answer and therefore is not soliciting information. This failure to reply is interpreted as obstructiveness or stupidity by many white teachers.

b) Not everyone in a community has the same rights to information. It is thus felt to be appropriate to withhold information from someone who is not entitled to it, for instance a teacher.

c) It is considered inappropriate and rude to ask direct questions when trying to find out information of a significant nature.

Similarly, important difference between many West Indian Creoles and "standard" English is found in the area of turn-taking and pauses. Whereas in standard English interlocutors wait for certain conversational cues before taking their turn, in languages such as Antiguan Creole, "there is no regular requirement for two or more voices not to be going on at the same time" (Reisman 1974:113). Other differences between English and Antiguan ways of speaking include:

i) The virtual absence of silence and pauses in Antiguan.

ii) Repetition "is not only acceptable speech behaviour in Antigua, it appears to have positive value attached" (p 121).

iii) Boasting in Antigua is perfectly acceptable even where there is nothing to back up a claim, and is often resorted to as a defence against criticism.

Expatriate teachers often mistake these culture specific forms of speaking for "a set of meanings which they got when contrasted with the more formal conventions associated with English culture: meanings of rudeness; stubbornness; 'ignorance' in the sense of unruly behaviour, stupidity; 'noise' in the sense of disorder" (p 116).

Language awareness programmes for both teachers and pupils should thus include language use as well as grammar. The implications for bilingual programmes of the types discussed by Craig are that conventional grammar-centered teaching methods, such as the grammar translation or audiolingual

---

9   It is not clear to what extent those differences are due to ethnic background and what social class factors are involved, a common problem as social deprivation and ethnicity are often related.

method, will have to be replaced by situational and communicative competence approaches.

Social factors

Insights from linguistics and the ethnography of communication, when applied to education, are subject to a number of social and economic constraints. Thus, Pidgin- and Creole-speaking societies generally have limited research funding, numerous social problems, and widespread non-literacy. Moreover, having gained political independence, their inhabitants are often reluctant to accept advice from outside experts, an understandable attitude given the inadequacies of earlier colonial education policies.

The most crucial factors in determining the success of educational programmes are the attitudes of the teachers and the parents. A number of case studies of teachers' attitudes have appeared, among them Taylor's study of attitudes towards BEV (1973) and Winford's account of attitudes in Trinidad (1976), Reinecke's study of English in Hawaii (1969) and more recent updates by Sato (1985, 1993).

Taylor's report on about 500 teachers of different geographic, racial and professional origin led to interesting insights into possible effects of teaching policies current at that time, in particular bussing. He found the most favourable attitudes towards BEV in those groups with three to five years teaching experience as well as a widespread tolerance among many teachers towards non-standard varieties but he also established that teachers in exclusively white schools had the least tolerant attitudes. Consequently:

> The data suggest that the bussing of black children into predominantly white schools is likely to cause them to come in to direct contact with teachers who are most likely to have negative attitudes toward their dialect and its use in the schools. However, given experiences with these children, their attitudes might change to conform with those which seem to prevail for teachers in mixed schools. If true, the bussing may be more useful for the educational enrichment of the teacher than for the pupils.
>
> (Taylor 1973:198)

The debate surrounding African American English (Ebonic) continues unabated with many of the arguments failing to distinguish between causes and symptoms and failing to take into consideration decades of sophisticated sociolinguistic research.

Winford (1991), like many other writers on Caribbean matters, points to the ambivalence underlying the linguistic and cultural behaviour of Creole speakers. It would seem that much of this ambivalence could be reduced by making educators more aware of the linguistic and social nature of the languages spoken in their area.

Parents' attitudes and parental pressure are also of prime importance. For example, one of the main reasons for the death of Queensland Kanaka English was the parents' strong desire for their children to learn standard English (see Mühlhäusler 1991:177). The same picture is encountered in numerous other colonial or post-colonial societies. Thus, d'Offay de Rieux states with regard to Creole and French in the Seychelles:

In pre-independence situations linguistic imperialism was so strong that generations have been brainwashed into thinking that Creoles were not only useless, but a handicap to economic development and social mobility (1980:268-69).

A very similar antagonism was encountered in Nigeria, in a community where Nigerian PE is clearly the most widely used language. Shnukal & Marchese summarize their findings as follows:

> It is therefore not surprising that, with the exception of two women, the adults were uniformly opposed to lessons in primary school being taught in Pidgin, believing that it would "harm" their children's acquisition of standard English (1983:21) .

Such attitudes can change over a period of time. Shnukal (1991:193) contrasts the negative attitude of older Torres Straits Islanders with the views of young speakers who have revealed it as "a marker of identity, ethnicity and separation from white Australians". But, as she points out, this revaluation is most common among those who are fluent speakers of standard English as well. This could be taken as an argument for a monoliterate bilingualism approach in education.

Sato (1990:132ff) mentions a similar revaluation for Hawaiian Creole English which manifested itself in widespread community action against a 1987 proposal by the Hawaiian Board of Education to make "standard English.... the mode of communication for student and staff in the classroom setting and all other school related settings".

A common problem of education in Pidgin and Creole settings is the range of varieties in which children are most comfortable. In many classrooms there is a (usually) small group of solely standard-language speaking children, i.e. those of the colonial administrators, overseas advisors and indigenous upper class. For example, in the ABC islands (Aruba, Bonaire, Curaçao) of the Netherlands Antilles in the 1960s:

> only the children of the Dutch expatriates now receive an education in their native language, and the only opportunity for linguistic continuity in education for those Antilleans who wish to proceed to university or technical school is to go to the distant Netherlands, where their training may be inapplicable to the Caribbean environment.   (Wood 1969:78)

In this particular instance, the decision to teach exclusively in the lexically unrelated superordinate standard language was motivated not only by social attitudes but also by economic factors. It enabled the colonial administration to recruit surplus teachers from the mother country and to use teaching materials from there. Together with the practice of using the metropolitan syllabus and training methods for local teachers, this made it possible to set up a sizeable education programme within the provisions of a small budget. Apart from short-term financial savings, an indirect benefit for the colonial power was the acquisition of trained persons. For the colony itself this is an enormous loss. As pointed out by Wood (p. 80) with regard to the Netherlands Antilles:

> this has resulted in a significant drainage of human resources at the highest level of educational attainment, as many Antillians with high

292

educational qualifications, rather than returning to the islands, have remained in the Netherlands.

Meanwhile, significant social and political changes, including the partial separation of Aruba from the other islands, have taken place. In an update on the question of Papiamentu in education, Appel & Verhoeven (1995) mention a number of initiatives, including proposals to "make Papiamentu the language of instruction throughout primary school". Their assessment is that "the lack of sufficient human and financial resources might obstruct or at least seriously delay the implementation and effectuation of such a substantial and educational innovation" (p 73).

Financial considerations indeed continue to be paramount in independent Pidgin- and Creole-speaking countries. The initial investment needed dramatically to improve education, for instance, through the development of training facilities and material for genuine biliterate bilingual programmes, is often lacking. This vicious circle of cheaper solutions today at a greater cost in the long term is found in many areas of life in Third World countries.

Another factor which militates against curriculum changes is centralization. As long as the policies of individual schools are determined by distant (even overseas) administrators and policy-makers, the positions countries have "drifted into" remain difficult to overcome. The solution of initial monolingualism in a Pidgin or Creole has had a chance only in highly decentralized education systems such as that of Papua New Guinea, northern Australia and some adjacent Pacific nations, where education policies were made by groups outside the central government such as missions or local communities.

In sum then, the decentralization (localization) of educational policies and a large-scale promotion of linguistic awareness would seem to be the two major ways of reducing educational problems of Pidgin and Creole speaking countries.

The teaching of Pidgins and Creoles

I shall now turn to the way in which Pidgins and Creoles are taught, learnt and acquired, concentrating on Pidgins as a special case of second-language acquisition. In most documented cases, Pidgins and Creoles were acquired in an informal uncontrolled setting rather than through formal instruction, by teachers or textbooks. The very fact that they were regarded as corruptions of a target, or entirely grammarless, militated against the provision of teaching materials for these languages. The ways in which Pidgins were acquired informally differ from language to language and from period to period. Few studies have been made of this process, though it could provide insights for second-language teaching. The only area of more detailed studies and longitudinal accounts is that of guest-worker Pidgins in central Europe (Meisel 1977, 1983)

Some details are also available for Tok Pisin, whose initiation and stabilization on the plantations of Samoa occurred spontaneously, without any teaching other than that of deliberate transmission of some lexical items.

Its subsequent spread, however, deserves to be discussed in some detail. Since the running of the economy and administration of German New Guinea depended on the availability of a lingua franca, official help in spreading Tok Pisin occurred early. Thus, New Guineans recruited for the Samoan plantations received their first lessons in Tok Pisin in the recruiting depots of Mioko Island and aboard the vessels that took them to Samoa. Once Tok Pisin had become the working language of the Rabaul area, bush dwellers were also forcibly taken there to acquire the language in the local prison (**kalabus**). The painter Nolde gives a vivid description of this procedure:

> "We often encountered some of the wild men who had arrived with us on the steamers... the purpose of their forced stay in Rabaul was to gradually acquire some means of communication, be it gestures, the customary 'Pidgin English' or German concepts and words".
>
> (Nolde 1965:65, my translation)

Firth (1973:168) discusses a similar practice aimed at creating a reliable core of government interpreters (*tultuls*) and village headmen (*luluai*):

> At village after village from Mugil Harbour to Hansa Bay the patrol would arrive, persuade one man to accompany them back to Madang in order to learn Pidgin, or if there were Pidgin speakers already, appoint a *luluai* and a couple of *tultuls*; then all the strong young men might be conscripted for forced labour in Madang and orders given that twenty new coconut palms had to be planted for every able-bodied man in the village.

Once sufficient numbers of Tok Pisin speakers were available, the language – because of its enormous prestige – spread without further government interference. Mead (1931:147) observed:

> Pidgin English, especially a knowledge of the names of the strange objects used by the white man, is the most important key to entrance into this world of adventure. In the back villages where a white man is seen perhaps twice a year, five and six-year old boys go about muttering long pidgin phrases to themselves, learning pronunciation and cadence before they understand the meaning of words. By the time they are well-grown "monkeys" of twelve and thirteen, they can converse easily in this new language, and even have time to school the smaller boys by the hour.

In addition, the language was taught informally by patrol officers and policemen visiting the interior of the country. One of the few available descriptions of this process is given by Ruhen:

> Once in 1949, on an expedition led by Sir Horace up the Sepik River, I had the electrifying experience of watching Pidgin take root for the first time. We made the first European contact with three constantly feuding New Guinea tribes, and, using sign language, persuaded 48 young men, all of warrior status, to come with us to the coast, 900 kilometres away. We hoped they might take jobs for a year or so, learn something about commerce, and become agents for inter-tribal peace when they returned home.
>
> Every morning during our week-long voyage downstream, Sergeant Rovai, a policeman from Bougainville, confronted the naked, suspicious young men. He pointed in turn to his hair, eye, nose and mouth and

294

solemnly intoned their Pidgin names: *gras, ai, nus, maus*. Then he went on to other parts of the body: *han, pinga, bel* (hand, finger, stomach). But even when he got his puzzled pupils to repeat the words and actions, they clearly did so without comprehension.

One day, a small aircraft flew over, and the warriors looked up in fear at their first sight and sound of the monster. Rovai took immediate advantage. "Balus!" he cried, pointing at the aircraft. "Balus! Balus!". With expressions of wonder and growing understanding the warriors tried the new word. Whereupon Rovai pressed his advantage, alternately pointing at the aircraft and pulling his hair, crying, "Balus! Gras!"

Within three days, our primitive passengers were chatting hesitantly in Pidgin with boat crew and policemen - and, most remarkably, with one another, with traditional foes (1976:47).

In more recent years, formal teaching of Tok Pisin to indigenes has become quite widespread, in particular through mission-run Tok Pisin schools in outlying areas (see Zinkel 1977). In 1973 the first course designed to teach Tok Pisin to adult Papua New Guineans (particularly non-literates from newly opened up areas) was made available (Sadler 1973b). The method used is the direct method, i.e. the teacher uses Tok Pisin for instruction from the beginning, moving from words and phrases for actions in the classroom to common situations outside. The book is designed in a way which requires only minimal teaching experience from the instructor.

Written teaching aids for Pidgins are rare and, in many cases, are of very dubious quality. One of the earliest examples is a booklet on the Lingua Franca. Schuchardt comments:

> In 1830 the only extensive source for our knowledge of Lingua Franca saw the light of day, in itself a quite paltry concoction composed for use by the French expeditionary force that took Algiers in the summer of 1830, was entitled *Dictionnaire de la langue franque ou petit mauresque, suivi de quelques dialogues familiers et d'un vocabulaire de mots arabes les plus usuels; à l'usage des Français en Afrique*, Marseille, 1830 (1979:40).

Some of the shortcomings identified by Schuchardt include the carelessness with which phonological matters have been handled and dubious lexical usages.

Chinese PE is exceptional in that teaching aids were prepared not by the speakers of the target language but by the Chinese themselves. Foreign residents in Macau and Canton created a demand for servants able to communicate with them. To assist this, a remarkable booklet (Anon. ca 1830) was produced which has been described by Williams (1837) and Hunter (1882). Baker & Mühlhäusler (1990:95ff) obtained a copy and analysed some of the linguistic properties of this 372-entry vocabulary. This aid to learning Pidgin English certainly found a ready market and was reprinted on several occasions up at least to the end of the 19th century. For further information about this booklet and the social context in which Chinese PE was learnt, see Tryon, Mühlhäusler & Baker (1996).

In spite of its opposition to PE in its African colonies, the German administration in Cameroon made wide use of a dictionary and phrasebook by Hagen (1910) which "was acquired by every official arriving in the country" (Emonts 1922:229). A sample of this learning aid is given below:

German	Cameroon Pidgin	English
Halt!	Halt!	Stop!
Nieder!	Nieder!	Down!
Headman und zwei Mann, ihr geht hier links herum.	Hetmann end tu mann, ju woaker hir for left seit.	Headman and two men, you walk to the left.
Lamina, die Posten werden alle halbe Stunde gewechselt.	Lamina, dem schensch dem posten oal haf auer.	Lamina, the sentries are to be changed every half hour.
Um acht Uhr machst Du alle Feuer aus.	Et oklock ju kill oal feier.	Extinguish all the fires at eight.
Marsch!	Marsch!	Forward!
Passt auf, die Leute haben hier Bambusspitzen in die Erde gesteckt.	Luk aut, dem pipel mek tschugge-tschugge for graund.	Look out, the people have put bamboo spears in the ground.

In the already mentioned German New Guinea, learning of Tok Pisin by expatriates differed from that by indigenes in a number of ways. Thus, although no official teaching aids were at hand, a number of travel writers added appendices teaching the rudiments of the language to their books which were meant to be read during the long journey by sea. Examples are Schnee (1904), who outlines the essentials of its grammar and lexicon and Friederici (1911) who supplements Schnee's sketch. However, Friederici advises (p 95) that proper Tok Pisin should be learnt in one's dealings with "natives" and that grammatical sketches compiled by Europeans could at best supplement real life learning. The first group to learn and teach Tok Pisin systematically were the German missionaries who remained after the Australian take-over. The Catholic Church had adopted Tok Pisin as a mission medium in the 1920s and the first complete course for German missionaries was written by Borchardt in 1930. Borchardt, like many scholars at the time, held that a Pidgin is a combination of native syntax and European vocabulary. Thus his course is based almost entirely on Bley's Tolai grammar (1912). This assumption had two consequences: those rules of Tok Pisin which reflected independent developments or transfer from English were neglected, and both pronunciation and meaning of lexical items was characterized as being closer to English than was actually the case. Borchardt's course was based on the grammar translation method, the grammatical categories used being those of the classical European languages. This decision further weakened his course materials. The use of this and similar books has resulted, in the meantime, in the development of a special mission dialect of Tok Pisin which is at variance with that spoken by the indigenous population, a development reminiscent of that in Surinam discussed by Voorhoeve (1971).

Outside the German speaking mission stations little was done about the often criticized inability of the Australian settlers to communicate with the indigenes. No teaching aids were available to them, a fact which is mentioned and deplored at regular intervals in the colonial press. The call for pedagogical grammars and other teaching materials fell on deaf ears during peacetime and they only became available to speakers of English as a result of the Second World War, i.e. under the pressures for effective communication and propaganda during the war. American soldiers were taught Tok Pisin by the audiolingual method based on Hall's structuralist analysis (Hall et al. 1942), whilst many Australians learnt it from booklets such as those by Helton (1943) and Murphy (1943), two laymen who, whilst providing invaluable sociolinguistic information, often fell short of adequately characterizing the syntax and lexicon of the language. Their booklets are of dubious pedagogical value.

The effects of the war on the teaching of Tok Pisin were not lasting. After 1945 most expatriates did not learn it formally but continued to use their variety of broken English. The situation only changed just before the achievement of Papua New Guinean self-government, when many expatriates showed an interest in attending Tok Pisin courses. The sudden desire for teaching materials resulted in the publication of materials which otherwise might not have seen the light of day, as has been pointed out in a critical survey by Laycock (1970b). Meanwhile demand for more sophisticated teaching materials increased. It was finally met on the eve of Papua New Guinean independence, in 1973, when two courses designed explicitly for the teaching of Tok Pisin to Europeans appeared, those of Dutton (1973) and Sadler (1973a). Dutton's has since become the standard course and is used by such diverse groups as the Australian army, the diplomatic service, university students and Hiri Motu-speaking Papuans. A new totally revised edition meets the demands of post-colonial Papua New Guinea (1995). Smith's (1990) crash course caters for the needs of those who have to speak the language within a minimum of time whilst Franklin (1992) contains lexical exercises supplementary to the other courses. Classes in Tok Pisin are now offered on a regular basis in a number of places in Papua New Guinea.

The acquisition of Papua New Guinea's second lingua franca, Hiri Motu, has, if anything, been even more haphazard. It was informally taught to Papuans on government stations and in prisons but formal teaching aids for Europeans were unavailable until very recently. The first course, Wurm & Harris (1963), was for the use of anthropologists and other fieldworkers rather than the white expatriates. Materials suitable for the latter group first appeared in the 1970s, particularly Dutton & Voorhoeve's (1974) audio-lingual course.

The contrast between the "intellectual laziness" of the dominant group and their desire to have a smooth-running, communicatively competent population of workers as in Papua New Guinea is also found with Fanakalo in southern Africa. Whereas a few whites had a smattering of the language, picked up informally or from phrasebooks of very dubious status such as Bold (1961) and Aitken-Cade (1951), the black mine workers were instructed in a formal way by bodies such as the South African Iron and Steel Corporation or the mining companies. Although this language was concentrated around the mines of Gauteng (Witwatersrand), it was used in the domestic context in most other parts of the country.

Many aspects of the learning and acquisition of Pidgins and Creoles remain ill documented and more research is sorely needed, in particular fieldwork and direct observation of learners' behaviour. Such research will have implications for theoretical understanding of Pidgin and Creole development, in particular the question of the naturalness of these languages. Formal teaching, such as may have occurred at various stages in the history of these languages, may be an important fact in promoting abnatural linguistic developments. There are certainly good reasons to assume that natural learning is only one of the factors underlying Pidgin development. Learning or non-learning of Pidgins and Creoles can also have repercussions in the area of language death. Thus, the demise of Pidgin Fijian in the Solomons is in part related to the unwillingness of European settlers and administrators to learn this language, as was also the case with many other indigenous Pidgins, such as Macassarese and Chinook Jargon.

Once again, the close relationship between linguistic, sociolinguistic and applied linguistic considerations in the study of Pidgins and Creoles has been highlighted.

"Transported" Pidgins and Creoles and education

A "transported" language is one which has been taken from its country of origin or institutionalization to an overseas country following the migration of large numbers of its speakers. Examples include the large-scale migration of speakers of Haitian Creole to North America, Surinamese speakers of Sranan to the Netherlands, West Indians to a number of West European countries and, on a smaller scale, migration between Creole-speaking countries such as that from Surinam to the Netherlands Antilles or Papua New Guineans to the Torres Straits Islands.

Creole-speaking migrants usually settle in the urban areas of their host countries and some of their problems were investigated at the 1983 York Conference on Urban Creoles. Among the transported Creoles, that spoken by people from the Caribbean in contemporary Britain is the best documented case. Since the first major waves of immigration in the 1950s, a number of changes have occurred. Details about these can be found in the writings of Sutcliffe (1982, 1984) and Edwards (1981). The majority of the migrants were speakers of an English-based Creole, though few of them would have been aware of the fact that their language was not English. Initially, there was a widespread desire to assimilate socially and linguistically with the white British community and some assimilation did occur. However, in the wake of unemployment, racial hostility and increasing ghetto development, the trend has been reversed.

Linguistically, these two opposing trends manifested themselves in the early 1980s as (i) the adoption by black speakers of white lower class varieties of English rather than RP or some related norm encouraged by the schools, and (ii) the development of a new type of urban Creole, called "London-based Creole" by Breinburg (1984:32) and "Jamaican"[10] by Le Page who characterized it as follows:

> But very often the language used at home is the language their parents brought from the Caribbean. Some of the children still use this in school too; *and others are beginning to re-invent what is often called "Jamaican"*,[11] just to show solidarity as a group. This is particularly true of young adolescents. What we have at rock-bottom is a question of identity... This "Jamaican" is of course different in many ways from the Caribbean languages (1981:2).

---

[10] This name reflected the view that the linguistic norms of Jamaican Creole were beginning to replace those of the smaller English-based Creoles spoken in the migrant community.

[11] On this point, see Putz (1989).

Consequently, many of the children were bilingual or at least bidialectal, though few of them were able to operate in the prestige variety. Breinburg commented:

> ...there is a linguistic shift in Language (dialect) of young black people in the inner cities of Europe. This shift is *from* the speech pattern of the parents, who are Creole speakers, *to* that of the lower working class indigenous population, and not that of the standard language indigenous population desired by the schools (1984:31).

Le Page had earlier pointed out that teachers were well aware of this and that, in many instances, severe educational disadvantages could result:

> It is very hard for most teachers not to be subconsciously prejudiced in favour of white middle-class children. The chances are that those children *will* do better at school - they have everything going for them, especially if they speak with what is called Received Pronunciation (RP). It is members of their class who set the exams and mark them. We thus have in Britain a tendency towards a self-perpetuating elite (1981:27).

Various solutions to the above problem were discussed in the 1970s and 1980s. At present, most of these solutions remain untested. It is generally agreed that the most desirable state of affairs would be some transitional bilingualism with black children being taught initially through their home vernacular and subsequently in British English. In actual practice, for financial and other reasons, monolingualism in the dominant English language is the norm.

Positive discrimination, such as special coaching, as Le Page has pointed out, tends to be regarded negatively by black children as they "may want to do it on their own merits, not because they are teacher's pet" (1981:27). Dalphinis (1982:12) advocated self-help within the Black community:

> Politically informed Blacks have addressed themselves to this problem, which is essentially one of communication, by creating Supplementary Schools to politicise Black parents and their children how best to cope with the literacy demands of a centralized-capitalist society which, through its own inherent 'ignorance', finds it expedient to exclude and/or destroy what it cannot, or refuses to understand.

Another solution, very much in favour in the early 1970s, was that of compensatory education, the best known examples being the pre-school programme Headstart in the USA and various programmes related to Bernsteins's views on language in the UK (for a critical discussion see Gordon 1981). The underlying assumption of this approach was that sectors of the population are linguistically and consequently culturally deprived. Compensatory programmes typically prepared children from "deprived" backgrounds for participation in the culture of the social mainstream. Apart from the very shaky arguments in support of a deprivation view and the dubious nature of white middle class norms as the linguistic and cultural yardstick, compensatory education could also reinforce the cultural ambivalence of Creole speakers in mainstream society. It also ignored the fact that children may have good reasons for not accepting the dominant culture and choosing to perpetuate ethnic markers in speech and culture (cf Giles 1980). Thus, the deficit hypothesis of Black English and associated compensatory teaching programmes came under severe attack from, e.g. Labov 1973, Dillard 1972 and various authors in Williams (ed., 1970). A kind of mirror image of compensatory education is the suggestion, discussed in Dillard (1972:271), that teachers should have knowledge and awareness of black language and culture. Pioneering experiments by Stewart indicated the viability of such measures and it is becoming increasingly accepted that language awareness programmes for teachers can solve many problems, particularly when combined with the following ideas.

Le Page (1981:29) suggested that teachers in racially mixed schools should set up their own informal research groups to study the causes of differential achievement of black and white students. Attitude studies would be important here, investigating why parents and teachers want to change their students' linguistic behaviour as well as why students are impervious to many of the teachers' attempts.

Evaluation measures also need to be reviewed. It is now accepted that the criteria by which success at school is judged reflect the majority view of the dominant culture. It seems reasonable to expect differences of spelling and grammar between students whose primary language coincides with the target and students whose language does not. Next to the development of more neutral test criteria, teachers should identify those areas of behaviour where children from Creole-speaking backgrounds excel and develop their abilities in them.

The shared underlying message of the above suggestions is that successful education of Creole-speaking children in non-Creole environments requires much effort, in particular, making explicit implicit cultural assumptions, a considerable amount of linguistic and sociolinguistic knowledge by teachers and a social climate in which teachers, students and parents can cooperate. Awareness of the problem is not a solution but a necessary foundation for improvement.

University level courses in and on Pidgins and Creoles

Whilst, at first sight, the heading of this section involves two quite separate questions, there are important links between them which call for unified treatment. The feedback relationship between teaching in and teaching about a language is often seen as when academic interest in Afrikaans leads to its elevation to tertiary use (for a more detailed account see Shaffer 1978) or the teaching of Swahili leading to teaching in Swahili at tertiary institutions in Tanzania.

Teaching university courses in a Pidgin or Creole is constrained by a number of considerations including:
a) The modernity and referential power of the language.
b) Teachers' linguistic proficiency.
c) Teachers' attitudes.
d) Cost of translation and publications.
e) Access to international knowledge and historical information.

300

The first considerations are shared with numerous other languages originally used in traditional societies. Inevitably, such languages will initially be referentially inadequate and hence of limited use in the discussion of advanced academic topics. However, as has been demonstrated again and again (for instance in the cases of Indonesia and Tanzania), traditional languages can be modernized through systematic language planning and engineering. This, particularly the implementation of new linguistic proposals, takes time: for the successful transition from one language to another in higher education, many years may be necessary and the eventual transition is typically preceded by an extended period of bilingualism. The time factor is also important when it comes to the teachers' linguistic background. Many colonial universities in Pidgin- and Creole-speaking areas were staffed, almost exclusively, by expatriates who were speakers of the superordinate standard language. In many instances, locals trained by such expatriates continue to teach in this language and a transition from one teaching medium to another again can take years.

Indonesia, where Bahasa replaced tertiary education in Dutch, is a case in point. Again, the transitional period will be characterized by institutionalized or informal bilingualism. Whilst many educated speakers of Pidgins and Creoles accept that these languages are suitable media for primary and perhaps seconday education, their use at tertiary level has far fewer supporters. Such views are not so much the result of emotional factors but of practical considerations such as (d) and (e) above. The cost of making a traditional language suitable for university teaching can be considerable. Numerous person-hours and scarce resources will be employed for translation rather than the transmission of new knowledge or research. Because of the small number of students, textbooks and other materials will be short runs and will be priced accordingly. My own experience of receiving an undergraduate education in Afrikaans is a good illustration. The inroads the acquisition of Afrikaans textbooks made into my limited financial resources were very severe indeed. Such considerations are of even greater importance in the Third World. Access to knowledge located elsewhere in time and space can also be restricted. Thus, the decision to discontinue the use of Dutch in the Indonesian higher education system cut off students and scholars from a very long tradition of studies published in Dutch. The exclusive use of Swahili in the universities of Tanzania would break a tradition where writings about the country were in English, and students' access to earlier sources might be limited in the same way that access to documents in the earlier colonial language, German, is in present-day Tanzania or Papua New Guinea. Whatever the type of bilingualism chosen for lower levels of education, it would seem that full biliterate bilingualism is essential if such discontinuities in academic tradition are to be avoided. This also goes for links with international knowledge. As long as students are also functional in at least one major international language, the choice of a Pidgin or Creole as the medium of instruction would seem justified.

Conclusions

The debate on the role of Pidgins and Creoles in education has been going on for some considerable time, though relatively little has been achieved in resolving the problems addressed. If any single motive for continuing problems in this area were to be singled out, I would point to the miscommunication between members of different cultures.

The most frequently made observation is that students in Pidgin- and Creole-speaking societies fail to achieve the goals set principally by outsiders to the culture. One of the reasons for this, it is argued, is that they speak a different language. The various policies discussed by Craig and others suggest ways of overcoming the language problem in the education process. The general agreement appears to be that some kind of transitional bilingualism is the best solution given various external constraints.

A more radical approach is the suggestion that power structures, white middle-class views on education and the culture-specific measures of achievement are at issue. Changes in this area can promote educational achievement of Pidgin and Creole speakers.

None of the writers I have had access to addresses another, potentially even more important problem: the fact that learning is a cultural and not a natural process. As pointed out by E T Hall (1959:71):

> People reared in different cultures learn to learn differently. Some do so by memory and rote without reference to "logic" as we think of it, while some learn by demonstration but without the teacher requiring the student to do anything himself while "learning". Some cultures, like the American, stress doing as a principle of learning, while others have very little of the pragmatic. The Japanese even guide the hand of the pupil, while our teachers usually aren't permitted to touch the other person. Education and educational systems are about as laden with emotion and as characteristic of a given culture as its language. It should not come as a surprise that we encounter real opposition to our educational system when we make attempts to transfer it overseas.

To understand how Pidgin- and Creole-speakers are best taught we need to know how they learn.

9 Pidgin and Creole literature

[Creole]..... cannot express that wide range of emotions which we, as sensitive human beings, are capable of. (Keane 1951:105)

Introduction

This chapter addresses a number of topics relating to written forms of Pidgins and Creoles. Here one must distinguish between their use as special registers in the literature of the socially dominant language and independent writing in a Pidgin or Creole. A further distinction is that between the medium of writing (see Mühlhäusler 1995a) and written literary genres. A consideration of genre broadens the discussion to include oral literature.

The discussion of literature raises a number of questions dealt with in earlier chapters such as standardization and graphization, as well as the social functions and the expressive power of Pidgins and Creoles. The debate has been most vociferous in this latter area ever since the first international conference on Creoles in 1959 asked whether these languages are capable of sustaining literature of any merit (Le Page 1961:121ff).

Since then there has been a profusion of writings about Pidgin and Creole literature as well as a veritable explosion of literary activity in a number of Pidgins and Creoles, particularly in the post-independence societies of Central America, Africa and the Pacific. Because of small print runs and problems of communication it is no longer possible to consider even a representative body of evidence. However, I have tried to supplement my own first-hand experience with the Australian and Pacific scene with data from other areas. Meanwhile, a number of major studies concerned with this question have appeared, most notably Voorhoeve & Lichtveld's *Anthology of Surinam Creole literature*, (1975), Laycock's (1977b) study of Tok Pisin writing, a volume edited by Ludwig (1994; especially pp 111-90) and Fleischmann's (1978) chapter on Caribbean Creole French writing, Kloss's (1978) survey of the literature of Pidgins and Creoles having lexical affiliation to Germanic languages, and Braithwaite (1984) for Atlantic English Creoles. Jackson's (1990) study of Indo-Portuguese verse provides interesting perspectives on orality and literacy in Creole studies.

In organizing this chapter, I was guided by the chronological events of the Pacific area. Here, unlike the Caribbean and the Indian Ocean, the use of local Pidgins as means of self-expression occurred quite late in their development, and only after they had been made thoroughly non-respectable through constant white use of them to ridicule or demean their speakers.[1] This may be due to the fact that European colonization in the Americas occurred at a time when recent stereotypes had become established in the Americas and Africa. Still, even for the English Caribbean, literature other

---

[1] A case study of how speakers of South Australian Aboriginal PE were prevented from using this to express their own voice is given by Foster & Mühlhäusler (1996).

than oral is late to emerge. Whilst Winer & Rimmer (1994) demonstrate that Creole writings in Trinidad began in the 1830s rather than the 1920s as had been stated previously, Allsopp's comment on the Jamaican situation is probably more representative of the overall situation:

> Jamaican Creole... is wholly and truly oral and only artificially and experimentally a scribal art of humorous newspapers [sic] columnists, versifiers, and extremely few serious writers apart from novelists who must use it in their dialogue (1983:95).

One needs to add that Creole literature has suffered from a mismatch between production and perception, writer and audience, and that this gap is narrowing only very slowly as these languages become markers of separate identity – to achieve wider acceptance will involve also the disappearance of the negative stereotypes often found in literary Pidgins and Creoles produced in the colonial period.

Pidgins as literary stereotypes

Traditions of the literary use of Pidgins and Creoles have long existed in a number of Western European languages, and they share many similarities. As regards structural properties, their institutionalization is manifested in the availability of manuals for writers and directors as to how to produce instant Pidgins. One such manual is that of Herman & Herman (1943) where recipes for numerous versions of foreigner talk and Pidgins or Creoles are found. Let us consider the example of Beach-la-Mar, or Pacific PE. The authors of this manual provide the following instructions regarding the use of the endings *-um* and *-fella* whose grammatical development is discussed in Chapter 5.

> One of the chief changes comes with the addition of "um" to the verbs used in Beche le Mar. It is added to almost every verb, as in "walkum", "eatum", "callum" and "scratchum".
>
> Another variation from Chinese Pidgin lies in the use of the word "fella" which is usually attached as a modifier, not only of people, but of inanimate things as well, as in "this fella bone him olo". (This bone is old.) It is also used after the person pronoun "me", as in "Me fella me savee talk along white fella man".. (I understand white man's talk) (p 280).

They also provide a small list of stereotype lexical items, including:

mary	'woman'	*sing out*	'to call, holler, talk, etc.'
gammon	'to lie'	*walk about*	'any kind of action'
bokkis	'box'	*long way li'l bit*	'far'
sittor	'store'	*long way big bit*	'very far'
close up	'near'	*cross*	'any type of anger'

An example of how to incorporate such stereotype lexical items into narrative literature is given by Sayer (1944) in his short story *Three Pidgineers* which features speakers of Melanesian, Australian Aboriginal and Chinese PE. Such formalized instructions are the endpoint of a long history of literary use of Pidgins and Creoles in English.

Perhaps the earliest, and without doubt one of the most influential examples of literary PE appears in Defoe's *Robinson Crusoe*, first published in

1719. The story is based not on the writer's first hand experience of the Pacific but on his extensive study of travel literature. The book contains numerous passages of Pidgin as well as observations on how this language is acquired by Friday. The initial context of learning is described on p 170 as follows:

> I understood him in many things, and let him know I was very well pleas'd with him; in a little time I began to speak to him, and teach him to speak to me; and first, I made him know his name should be Friday, which was the day I sav'd his life; I likewise taught him to say Master, and then let him know, that was to be my name; I likewise taught him to say yes and no, and to know the meaning of them.

Considerable progress is made as can be seen from the next quotation, six pages later:

> I had a mind once to try if he had any hankering inclination to his own country again, and having learn'd him English so well that he could answer me almost any questions, I ask'd him whether the nation that he belong'd to never conquer'd in battle; at which he smil'd, and said, "Yes, yes, we always fight the better"; that is, he meant always get the better in fight; and so we began the following discourse: "You always fight the better," said I, "how came you to be taken prisoner then, Friday?"
> Friday. My nation beat much, for all that.
> Master. How beat? if your nation beat them, how came you to be taken?
> Friday. They more many than my nation in the place where me was; they take one, two, three, and me; my nation over-beat them in the yonder place, where me was no; there my nation take one, two, great thousand.

Further exposure to English does not appear to do Friday much good, however. Instead, he continues to speak in a fossilized form of interlanguage, as the experts would call it today.

We can contrast Defoe's work with Melville's various writings (cf Mayoux 1960) relating to a Pacific setting which appeared in the early days of the 19th century. As the writer had travelled extensively in the area he describes and was familiar with reduced forms of English, his language is of more than literary interest. An example is the following passage spoken by an old man in Tahiti when engaging in a tirade against the ships crew:

> Presently we made out the following:- "Ah? you *pemi*, ah! - -you come !– What for you come? -- You be fine for come no pilot. -- I say, you *hear?*-- I say, you *ita maitui* (no good). -- You *hear?*-- You no pilot. -- Yes, you d--- me, you no pilot at all; I d--- you; you *hear?*... You *sabbee* me?... You know me, ah? Well; me *jim*, me *pilot* -- been pilot now long time... Ah! me *sabbee*- - me know -- you *piratee* (pirate) -- see you long time, but no me come --
> (Melville 1847:102-03)

At about the same time, literary attestations of Pidgin and Creole English appeared in North American writing. Thus, Miller (1967) lists a number of examples of American Indian PE, which begin to multiply around the third quarter of the 17th century. A full study of this variety has been made in a PhD thesis by Beverly Flanigan (1981).

A separate tradition of Black English in American literature emerged slightly later. It is discussed, in much detail, by Dillard (1972), who also points out the influence of Defoe on the literary representation of black people. A rapid increase in the number of black Pidgin- or Creole-speaking characters occurred after 1800. For one of the most famous examples, Edgar Allan Poe's *The Gold Bug*, a number of detailed analyses exist, a summary of which is given by Stockton (1971). A passage from this short story follows here (Mabbott (ed.) 1951:253):

> "Well, Jup", said I, "what is the matter now?- how is your master?"
> "Why, to speak de troof, massa, him not so berry well as mought be."
> "Not well! I am truly sorry to hear it. What does he complain of?"
> "Dar! dat's it! - him neber plain of notin- but him berry sick for all dat."
> "Very sick, Jupiter! - why didn't you say so at once? Is he confined to bed?"

The tradition continued in numerous other American stories, novels and plays, including such famous ones as Harriet Beecher Stowe's *Uncle Tom's Cabin* (1852) and Mark Twain's writings. In spite of many predictions to the contrary, literary forms of Black American English are alive and well and have found their way into new media. Thus, in the wake of increasing black awareness, one finds many examples on television (cf Fine et al. 1979).

In British and American writing, an early period of undifferentiated foreigner talk or black talk is followed by a more finely-tuned variety. Thus, from the 1830s onwards, the literary representations of Africans, American Negroes, South Sea islanders and other foreigners follow somewhat different conventions, though writers with little exposure to actual models continue a general undiversified Pidgin/Creole style (as in Schuchardt [n d]).

Among the better known figures of 19th century literature, examples of the English of the Egyptian Arabs are given by Trollope in *The Bertrams*:

> De sahib, him vera respecble man; him kill him cook, Solyman this morning---him want to take all him money to the grave; but no, no, no! devil hab him and money too --- him gib poor Arab one shilling for himself, yes, yes, yes! and then Arab no let him tumble down and break all him legs (1859, 2:231) --- him no kill, him head berry hard (1859,2:249).

R L Stevenson, a long-time resident of Samoa, makes extensive use of a literary form of South Seas PE in his short stories, e.g. in *The Beach of Falesa*:

> – No good. Man he drink, he no good.
> – Why you bring him? Suppose you no want drink, you no bring him, I think.
> – "Now you talk willy" said she. "White man, he come here, I marry him all-e-same Kanaka; very well! he marry me all-e-same white woman. Suppose he no marry, he go 'way. All-e-same thief, empty hand. Tonga-heart - no can love."

Equally extensive use of South Seas PE is encountered in the writings of Jack London, a writer who even contributed a philological analysis of this variety, (1909). The tradition of South Seas English is continued in the writings of Michener (e.g. 1947).

Stereotype foreigner versions and literary Pidgins and Creoles are even more widely encountered in examples of "lesser" literature such as popular and trivial writings or cartoons. For instance, the pseudonymous writer

Dogberry (1894) reports on a "negro case" involving a charge of attempting to strangle his wife with a rope:

> Daniel being called upon for his defence, began thus: "Oh, massa, massa, me am very old. Me live in dis good country dis five years. Me have got money in de bank, and some good tings, but dat wicked, naughty little woman go pawn my shirts to get trink, and, by Cot, me hand no tinner since last Horn-fair."

Because the social value of Pidgins and Creoles is conventionalized in large sections of the community speaking the related superordinate language, its use in popular literature, advertisements and so on can be observed from about 1900 onwards. An example of this is in the Australian advertisement for shirts dating from 1911, reproduced below. Cozzolino et al. (1980:129) comment: "The best known advertising figure in Australia".

In 1906, J K Pearson and J L G Law formed a partnership to manufacture shirts. In 1911 they converted it to a company and combined the first two letters of their surnames to create the corporate name: Pe-La-Co. Mulga Fred, an actual Aboriginal from the Geelong area, and the line *Mine Tinkit They Fit* were adopted as the new company's advertising promotion. Mulga Fred of Pelaco Bill as he became known, was featured on posters, points of sale and in press advertisements.

Mine Tinkit They Fit

All a Boy! Altogether Master 'e savee 'long all something now

Another advertisement illustrating the racist associations of PE is the one reproduced here (left) which appeared in the *Rabaul Times* (New Guinea) of April 24th 1926 . The victims of such jokes were not only black speakers. Sometimes, white society was criticized by presenting the black view of matters in a Pidgin form as in the following passage from the *Western Grazier* (Australia), dealing with the defoliation of Aboriginal country by white settlers. The text appeared in 1901:

307

God bin make um country first time. He bin make um plenty grass, plenty water. He bin have um little fella mob kangaroo, emu, turkey, plenty duck. Then whitefella come. He see um country. He like em, cobbon. He yan, and come back, fetchum monkey and bullocky, big mob. Cobbon, big fella mob. Bullocky and monkey bin tuck out grass, and bin pfiniss um waterhole. Then whitefella bin make um dam an' pfstop um creek. God, he don' like um, but he no bin yabber. Then water he bin go bung more, an' whitefella he bin pfetch um hingin and pfmakem bore. Then God he cobbon saucy, He want kickem up cobbon bluffy row-bullocks and sheep eat up grass-whitefella swear, and God laughs-won't send rain, says "Alright. You bin plurry pflash, makin' dam and makin' bore, yah, yah! Now you makem blurry grass."

Finally, the use of Pidgin- and Creole-type forms is frequent in cartoons such as Tintin, Asterix and Mickey Mouse. All of these make extensive use of stereotyped Pidgin and, as they are available in a wide range of languages, contribute to the spread of such stereotypes.

In many of the writings discussed considerable information is given about the social context of Pidgins and Creoles. The following, quoted from Reinecke (1964:534-35) is a condensation of Traven's (1934) account in the novel *The Death Ship*:

With so many different nationalities aboard, it would have been impossible to sail the Yorikke unless a language had been found that was understood by the whole crew. The lingo of the Yorikke was English. At least that was the name the language was given, to distinguish it from any other language known under the moon. Chinese Pidgin English would be considered elegant compared with the Yorikkian English. A newcomer, even a limey, a cockney, or a Pat, would have quite a lot of trouble during the first two weeks before he could pick up sufficient Yorikkian to make himself understood and understand what was told him.

Such examples from English-speaking literature could be multiplied; particularly important, and as yet hardly tapped, is the use of Aboriginal, Melanesian and Chinese varieties of PE in Australian literature.

Let us consider some more general matters now. First, whilst one can discern separate national traditions, there appears to be a considerable degree of cross-fertilization between writers in different countries, beginning with Defoe. Literature containing Black American English was widely read in Britain and Australia and, in my own studies of old Australian newspapers, I have come across numerous examples of anecdotes in this variety. Literature thus may have served as an important diffusion mechanism of Pidgin and Creole grammar and lexicon.

Secondly, Pidgins and Creoles as literary varieties appear to be a relatively late phenomenon, and one that has remained restricted to a particular type of exotic literature. In an of the languages used in writings about various utopias and dystopias, Laycock (1987) encountered only one case of a Pidgin being spoken in such a setting. This relative shallowness of literary tradition emerges even more clearly in Dutch. An investigation into Dutch translations of *Robinson Crusoe* gave the picture set out below of the perception of the "other" as deviant linguistically.

Dutch translation of Robinson Crusoe	Utterances by Friday	% deviant (Pidgin) utterances
I (1754)	59	0
II (1851)	50	48
III (1880)	44	48
IV (1906)	62	0
V (1925)	60	78
VI (1946)	52	81
VII (1950)	88	77

Table adapted from *Werkgroep Taal* (1978:11)

Very similar results were obtained when I examined the development of literary Pidgin German in the translations and derived works of *Robinson Crusoe* literature, and also in my joint analysis of South Australian writings (Foster & Mühläusler (1996).

Some literary functions of Pidgins and Creoles

In the introduction to his novel *Papuan Epic*, Bushell (1936:9) writes:

> Life in New Guinea is enlivened not a little by the extraordinarily expressive and amusing pidgin-English inevitably used by the semi-civilised native. It has always been the policy of the British pioneer to promote the speaking of English amongst native races. This causes much confusion in their primitive minds when endeavouring to express themselves in the new and difficult language of the white man. How far they cleverly succeed, and amusingly fail, will be evident from my pages.

Bushell merely spells out what, at the time, was a long-established literary convention. In all English-speaking countries until very recently the Pidgin-Creole register signalled the low social status or intelligence of a speaker, the lightheartedness of topic or non-conformity with accepted norms of the superstrate culture. This is particularly obvious in oral folk literature and verbal games of the *Confucius him say* type. In the latter, Pidgin-like sentences are used to promote a double entendre as in:

Confucius him say man who fart in church sit in own pew
Confucius him say seven days honeymoon make one whole week.

That very much the same connotations are encountered in written literature is confirmed, for Nigerian PE, by Tonkin (1979:306):

> More surprising, perhaps, has been its continued literary survival in restricted situations only, e.g. for backward traditionalists or "low-life comedy". In E Caseley-Hayford's *Ethiopia Unbound* (1913) which we could call the first African novel, the Gold Coast Political Officer uses Pidgin to his African-protagonists. In these exchanges the author delineates the hated set of insulting behaviours of which Pidgin was the symbolic register. Although the novel is from a Gold Coast writer, it foreshadows nearly all subsequent uses of Pidgin by both "naive" and "sophisticated" writers in Nigeria...published in England, Pidgin speakers include ignorant, bullying politician-chiefs and university porters, but the protagonists do not normally talk it among themselves.

Very much the same observations have been made for Caribbean writing by O'Callaghan (1981), for Pidgin and Creole Portuguese by Naro (1978) and pidginized or foreigner talk versions of Spanish by Weber de Kurlat (1962). The use of *petit nègre* and foreigner talk French in French novels and plays is governed by comparable social conventions. Similar conventions in literary Pidgin German were discussed in Chapter 4..

The use of literary Pidgins may have consequences beyond those intended by the authors. The permanent association of Pidgin and Creole speech with backwardness, uncivilized or ridiculous behaviour can promote a racist view of the inhabitants of the third world, as has been pointed out, for instance by Dorfmann & Mattelart (1975) in their analysis of Mickey Mouse cartoons and by Hinnenkamp (1982) in a discussion of Herve's Tintin characters. The general idea conveyed to the readers of Mickey Mouse is that most members of exotic races speak some childish primitive jargon. The idea is reinforced by the extravagant clothing and use of ridiculous gestures or postures of these Pidgin speakers. In some instances, similar language is also spoken by monkeys, dogs or dwarfs.

As has been pointed out by Tonkin, writers of neo-African and other new literatures find it difficult to break out of such inherited conventions. One way out is that of adopting a distinction between stereotyped expatriate forms of Pidgins and Creoles which signal traditional literary functions and genuine code switching between the superimposed language and related Pidgin or Creole. Thus, in Tok Pisin writing after independence, stereotype **Tok Masta** – the variety spoken by expatriates – is increasingly employed to ridicule them, as in Michael Mosoro's short story *Caught in Between* (1975) where the white electoral officer addresses his black audience as follows:

> Before you vote, I will call your names from this book and you say, "yes sir", as you go to vote. You go over long this man, em will help you long mark the man you like....

In genuine Tok Pisin the last sentence would have read:

> Yu go long dispela man long hap ya, em bai halpim yu long yu makim man yu laik vot longen.

In modern New Guinea writing, English and Tok Pisin are increasingly used in the functions they serve in actual society, for instance a code switch from Tok Pisin to English signals a sudden shift to non-solidarity as in Namaliu's (1970) play *The good woman of Konedobu*. Burus has just asked Irea to dance with him. Her answer is: "**Yu---u. Nogat, mi no laik. Raus**! Get lost, you bush kanaka. I don't know you. You! No, I don't want to. Get lost! ....."

Similarly, when Shakespeare's plays were performed in Surinam, Dutch was used for urban settings, but Sranan for scenes set in the forest (Pos 1983). Lee (1979) has investigated such language choice in a number of Nigerian novels, in particular switching from English to Nigerian PE. Particular praise is bestowed on the writer Achebe (p 295).

> Among novelists I would like to offer the works of the Nigerian, Chinua Achebe, as an example of astute ethnographic observation of linguistic behaviour. Speech events in his novels and short stories draw on the full range of resources of the speech community, from native African languages to English to Nigerian English to Pidgin.

310

There is a vast difference between these literary conventions of a monolingual audience, where a Pidgin- and Creole-like stereotype is accepted in a limited number of functions, and a bilingual audience, where the employment of two languages reflects their relative social roles in real life. The former usage has probably outlived its usefulness and may in fact cause more damage than good. The latter use, on the other hand opens up quite new perspectives for bilingual literature in bilingual societies.

The use of literary Pidgins and Creoles as linguistic evidence

It should by now be clear that literary Pidgins and Creoles were frequently employed so as to remain intelligible to a non-Pidgin/Creole-speaking audience. Consequently, and in view of the fact that Pidgins and Creoles when used in indigenous communities are usually unintelligible to speakers of related lexifier languages, one can expect a fair degree of selection, if not fabrication, by authors. Linguists have nevertheless used them as evidence, particularly for early linguistic history, where other kinds of data are often absent. A plea for taking literary evidence seriously is made, for instance, by Miller (1967:145) in a paper on American Indian PE.

> Fiction I also consider to be an equally valid source of authentic pidgin speech because of my conviction that language structure cannot be manufactured at the whim of the author. The fact that the same pidgin characteristics are found in fiction as in nonfiction seems to prove this assumption beyond any doubt.

In this case, the absence of a tradition of literary American Indian PE in the early period makes her argument plausible. However, as one moves on in time, the dangers of interference of established stereotypes with actually observed language increase. In many instances, only careful investigation of a number of different sources can decide whether the literary form represents a genuine example or at least a reasonable approximation to the actual language. A case where opinions have changed over time is the assessment of Black English as employed in Edgar Allan Poe's *The gold bug*. As Stockton (1971:194) points out, rather negative feelings were expressed for some time by Poe's critics, though Stockton himself and Dillard (1972) after him, point out that this assessment is hardly warranted. After a thorough examination of Jupiter's syntactic, lexical and phonological peculiarities, Stockton (p 213) concludes that:

> Despite his other traits, Jupiter must stand or fall because of his dialect. He does not commit the worst fault of Negro dialect, speaking like a colonel on the piazze in one paragraph and a fieldhand chopping cotton in the next. Analysis reveals his linguistic inconsistencies as minor: they can lend some verisimilitude, absolute consistence being a blemish in any literary dialect. He speaks a quasi-Gullah, a literary convention which rests on two bases, Negro speech on the Southeastern Coast with some not-unexpected Gullah features, and "the common body of folk-speech which underlies American dialects in all sections of the country".

Dillard also notes that many alleged stereotypes turn out to be genuine examples of Black English, particularly the Gullah variety, spoken in the 1840s (see Dillard 1972:95ff).

Literary representation of speech, whilst containing genuine black constructions, nevertheless does not represent anything approaching actual spoken discourse, and certainly does not give an exhaustive picture of Black English at the time. Discrepancies between literary Pidgins and Creoles and the genuine article have also been discussed for a number of other languages. Schuchardt (1882) mentions inconsistencies in literary Reunion Creole, whilst my own analysis of literary Pidgin German (Mühlhäusler 1984b) clearly demonstrates both (a) different strategies by different writers; and (b) significant differences between literary and actual forms of Pidgin German in the Pacific.

A further example of the discrepancy between actual language and its literary counterpart are television plays featuring Black American speakers. Fine, Anderson & Eckles (1979) investigated the use of the following features of Black American English in a large number of situation comedies (p 25):

> Both the total number of non-standard (BE) variants and their relative frequencies per total turns are low. The mean frequency of BE variants per total turns for all shows is 13. Three categories ("be" for habituation, deletion of -s suffix marking the possessive, and the pleonastic noun construction) contain no variants and two categories (deletion of the past tense marker and deletion of -s suffix marking the plural) show one variant apiece. Four categories (deletion of -s suffix for third person present tense, deletion of the auxiliary verb, deletion of the copula, and negative concord account for 94% of all non-standard variants. Although these categories are far more heavily represented than the others, the frequency of the variant in each relative to the total number of turns in each show is low.

Their findings suggest that "television presents a homogenized version of Black English" (p 25) and that black features are selected only when there is no danger of rendering the language unintelligible to white members of the audience.

The authors' observations that black writers are "caught in the bind of producing comedy shows dealing with black characters for a predominantly white audience" (p 28), is very much the situation that, until very recently, most writers employing Pidgins or Creoles have found themselves to be in.

A particularly clear example of the dangers of accepting literary evidence at its face value is encountered in accounts of Chinese PE (CPE). The American author Charles Leland probably did more than anyone else to draw attention to the existence of CPE by publishing his *Pidgin-English Sing-Song*. However, it is now known that he never visited China and wrote the book in London drawing his information from secondary sources (Baker 1987:200n1). In fact, unaware that CPE had evolved during its already considerable history, Leland mixed features from different periods, overgeneralised others attested only sporadically, and violated existing rules of phonology and word formation for English-derived vocabulary.

Leland's literary fabrications were used as the main, and sometimes exclusive, source of statements about CPE until well into the 1980s.

What has been said about literature in the narrow sense also goes for other forms of written Pidgins and Creoles. Pidginists and Creolists have to rely heavily on such sources for early stages of these languages;[2] in my own research into the history of PE in Australia and the Pacific I have found the following procedures helpful:

(i) To ascertain that writers actually have had first-hand experience with a Pidgin or Creole. By this criterion a writer such as Stevenson is to be taken seriously in the study of PE in Samoa, and Upfield's detective novels (e.g. 1931, 1963), set in central Australia, can be regarded as equally authentic.

(ii) To determine whether the different Pidgin and Creole styles are used when portraying literary characters from different locations. Many writers are quite insensitive to geographically and socially caused variants.

(iii) Quantitative analyses are an excellent aid for discovering inconsistencies.

(iv) Criteria such as naturalness and implicational order provide a guide to the authenticity of literary Pidgins.

(v) It often helps to work out a common core description if material from different writers is at hand.

It is often not realized that in the early days of Pidgins and Creoles, the distinction between expatriate foreigner talk and indigenous versions of a language was considerably less than it is today, the former being perfectly acceptable as a means of communication. Thus the language of early writings is usually the version of the socially dominant group. Genuine data on how the other parties spoke are much rarer.

It is perhaps for this reason that the opinion that Pidgins and Creoles are European-based has persisted so strongly. Once the bias of the data is realized, however, a different view, advocated in earlier chapters of this book, is likely to emerge.

Literature written in Pidgins and Creoles

The discussion so far has centred upon Pidgin and Creole passages in texts written in the superimposed language. The development of a separate literature in these languages must be seen as a virtually independent phenomenon. However, some connections can be made, since the origins of Pidgin and Creole literature are almost always to be found in that of non-native expatriate speakers. The same appears to be true of oral literature. Before going into details, I will briefly summarize the chronological development of Pidgin and Creole literature as given in Reinecke's 1981 *Selective chronology of Creole studies*. The following information was extracted from this non-comprehensive and by no means exhaustive source:[3]

---

2 Stein's (1995) comparison of the Negerhollands bible translation with the language of slave letters deals with a fortunate exception to this and raises some interesting theoretical points.

3 Literary forms of Australian Pidgin English are conspicuous by their absence in this chronology.

1455   First use of Negro-Portuguese in verse, 14 years after importation of first black African slaves.

1520   Encina writes a humorous poem in the Lingua Franca of Jerusalem tour guides.

1671   Molière, using snatches of Lingua Franca, supplies the word *sabir*, a French synonym or near-synonym for *pidgin*.

1774   Psalm-book in Neger-Hollands published by (German) Moravian Brethren, followed in 1823 by (Danish) Lutheran translation. These and other religious writings establish a "high" literary style of the Creole.

1795   First example of written Afrikaans: a humorous poem.

1822   Chrestien, *Les essais d'un bobre africain*, the first more or less intentionally humorous literary use of Mauritian Creole French.

1825   *Declaracion corticu di catecismo*, first printed book and first known religious publication in Papiamentu.

1828   *Fables créoles*, first literary use of Reunion Creole. First known catechism in Mauritian Creole.

1838   *The adventures of a Creole*, written by a Grenada-born white Creole.

1846   Hale, pioneer sketch of Chinook Jargon. Marbot's paraphrase of La Fontaine's *Fables* in Martinican Creole, a genre imitated in other French Creole areas. Jiménez, lexicon and illustrative texts of creolized Spanish Gypsy speech. First Afrikaans edition of *Die betranbare woord*, a volume of Islamic religious texts.

1849   Putman's grammar of Dutch written in Papiamentu. Héry, *Esquisses africaines*, first humorous literary use of Reunion Creole.

1872   Saint-Quentin, grammar of Guyanais Creole; his brothers [sic] publish the first extensive collection of folk literature in creole.

1876   Leland, *Pidgin-English sing-song*, the first and best use of Chinese PE for humorous effect.[4]

1879   Egger first compares infants' speech with pidgins/creoles, Atkinsons' facetious sketch of "Yokohamese" Pidgin Japanese, soon to become extinct.

1883   Harris uses Gullah in literature, the first of a number of writers, notably Gonzales (1922-24). Brinton, *The Güegüence; a comedy ballet in the Nahuatl-Spanish dialect of Nicaragua*.

1885   Pères Blancs publish catechism in Kingwana Swahili, the first known religious writing in that dialect. Parépou, *Atipa, roman guyanais*, the first novel written in a creole.

1885-1900   Anderson's translations of the Gospels and Acts into Mauritian Creole.

1927   Kroon, *Dos novela*, the first substantial literary work in Papiamentu, whose literature "gets rolling" only in the 1940s.

1932   Tavares, *Mornas*, the first major literary use of Cape Verdean creole.

1953-   Voorhoeve's writings on Sranan, putting its study on a scholarly plane and encouraging its use as a literary medium.

1955   Stichting voor Culturele Samenwerking (STICUSA) takes up the task of cultural interchange between the Netherlands and Surinam and the Netherlands Antilles, encouraging literary production in Sranan and Papiamentu.

1957   Trefossa, Trotji, first outstanding literary work in Sranan. Translation of NT into Kituba.

---

4   But see my remarks above.

In spite of some shortcomings, Reinecke brought out the main trends in the development of Pidgin and Creole literature very clearly, these being:

(i)   the dominance of humorous use until very recently.
(ii) the importance of religious writings (including translations of the scriptures) and collections of folk tales.
(iii) most of the early writers are Europeans, visitors or settlers.
(iv) a fair proportion of the early writings have anonymous authors.

One category not mentioned by Reinecke is the oral tradition of songs and storytelling, an important one in some Creoles. It is also one with a long history, a form dating back to the 15th century being the songs by German and Swiss *Landsknechte* (mercenaries) in Italy. Their Pidgin Italian is also found in more formal literature together with other Pidgin Italians such as the varieties used by the Greeks (*gregesche*) and Moorish speakers (*moresche*). An outstanding example is *Matona mia cara* 'My dear Madonna' whose linguistic features are discussed in much detail by Coates (1969), to which a very free and somewhat speculative translation has been added here:

Matona mia cara	*My dear Madonna*
1. Matona mia cara, mi follere canzon	My dear Madonna, I want song,
Cantar sotto finestra, lantze buon compagnon	I want to sing under your window;
	mercenaries are good companions
Refrain: Don, don, don, diri, diri, don	
2. Ti prego m'ascoltare, che mi cantar de bon,	Please listen to me, for I sing of good
E mi ti foller bene, come greco e capon	things, and I desire you as tenaciously
	as the northeast wind
3. Com' andar alle cazze, cazzar con le falcon	As I go hunting, hunting with the falcons
Mi ti portar beccazze, grasse com rognon	I bring you woodcocks, as fat as kidneys
4. Se mi non sapre dire tante belle rason,	I don't know how to make beautiful
Petrarcha mi non saper, ne fonte d'Helicon	speeches. I don't know of Petrarca or
	the springs of Helicon
5. Se ti mi foller bene, mi non esser poltron;	But if you desire me, I'll not be timid;
Mi ficcar tutte notte, urtar come monton	I'll thrust all night, butting like a ram.

Orlando di Lasso (1532-1594)

The use of Pidgin in sea shanties in the Far East and the Pacific may go back to the 16th century. The first documented examples are those sung by sailors of European origin. Two stereotypical examples mentioned by Hugill (1977) are one in Pidgin-English and Swedish, called *Kinakusten* (China coast) and another song sung by German and Scandinavian sailors in the China Coast trade called *Sampan Girl*. Some Chinese words are found in the latter.[5]

1. Me have got a flower boat
   Come sailing Chu-ki-ang
   Sampang girlie play to you
   All the same sing-song.

2. Lao-yeh, you like me?
   Tzia-tzia, velly good
   Foreign man to Canton come,
   Me got plenty chow.

3. Homeside have got pidgin
   Me savvy me can tell,

   Bring me master chicken
   Chia-da velly well.[6]

---

[5] *Tzia-tzia*, flower-boat girl, *Chia-da*, a chicken.
[6] Such songs contrast with those written by Leland in his famous *Pidgin-English sing-song* (1876). The topic of the following example would seem to be one which has no place in the cultural setting in which CPE was used:

Such songs were undoubtedly also common on board the recruiting vessels that sailed the Pacific in the second half of the 19th century and it is possibly in this context that many songs were passed on to the indentured plantation workers. Some early songs also originated on the plantations themselves, e.g. the following one which was sung on the German plantations of Samoa and New Guinea (mentioned by Jacques (1922); I obtained this text during fieldwork in Samoa in 1975):

olo boi i limlimbur tumas	the workers take a lot of time off
kaikai misineri	they eat the missionaries
puspus olo meri	they make love to the girls
olo boi i limlimbur tumas	the workers take a lot of time off

The language of this song, such as its Tolai lexical items, variable presence of the plural marker **olo** and the absence of the transitivity marker **-im** suggest that it dates from around 1900. The second song, recorded by Jacques (1922), refers to an episode where a German vessel, the Roland, has run aground:

I longtaim long Sigismund	The Sigismund and
I longtaim long Sigisan	the Seestern are waiting a long time
putim daum long Roland	for the Roland
i go daun long Rabaul	to go to Rabaul.
ol kevin i no save nating	The cabin-boys know nothing;
kipasim Roland	lockup the Roland,
kipasim Sigismund	lock up the Sigismund,
kipasim Sigisan	lock up the Seestern

A fuller account of the tradition which developed in Tok Pisin from such beginnings is given by Laycock (1977, 1985).

The European tradition of employing stereotypical PE in song-writing continues to the present. An interesting collection of South Seas English poetry and songs is that of McLaren (1926):

I no more like this job of mine
I'm tired alonga schooner and the sea
I no more think-it plenty fine,
Like when as crew-boy I been sign,
To go long way from place belonga me.

My hours for rest they very few;
All-time I scrub-it deck and paint-it rail,
And polish brass till it's like new,
And take-it wheel and help-it crew
Go pull alonga rope belonga sail.

Which makes me think it proper rot
To sing about a cradle longa deep -
My word, I savee I can not,
When sun it come too plenty hot,
Go longa shade and rock myself to sleep!

Littee Jack Horner	He put inside t'um
Makee sit inside corner	Hab catchee one plum,
Chow-chow he Climas pie;	Hai yah! what one good chilo my!

Even more recently, the following song was recorded in Papua New Guinea by Bryant Allen (p c). It is sung by the (mainly expatriate) *didimans* (agricultural officers in pre-independence days),

Mipela mipela didiman	We are the agricultural workers;
husat meri laik i ken	any woman who wants to, may.
ol i kolim mipela nambawan man	They call us the best of men;
o mipela didiman	we are the agricultural workers.
Mipela wok long nait na de	We work night and day,
na mipela no gat dola-de	and do not even receive a dollar a day
mipela no gat gutpela pe	we do not receive good pay,
o mipela didiman	we agricultural workers.
Mipela save go wok bus	We go and work in the bush,
kaikai pinis na mi smok brus	eat our food and smoke,
tingting long olgeta samting i lus	thinking of all the good things we are missing;
o mipela didiman	we are the agricultural workers.
Kiap i ting mi rabisman	The administrative officer thinks we are all worthless
mi holim meri long tupela han	I reach out for women with both hands
sapos em i laik kotim mi i ken	if he wants to prosecute me, he's welcome
o mipela didiman	We are the agricultural workers.
O hapkas pikinini ples pulap	The place is full of half-caste children
inap long go long wanpela trak	enough to fill a truck
maski long moa, ating em inap	to hell with more, I think that's enough
o mipela didiman	We are the agricultural workers

As regards story-telling, a distinction should be made between stories circulated in white expatriate circles illustrating the "primitiveness" of Pidgin and Creole speakers, those following indigenous tradition and those produced in indigenes imitating European stories. A well known example of the first type is the indigenous version of the Garden of Eden story. Here follows extracts from two versions, the first reported by Jack London (1909: 359-64) for the Solomon Islands, the second one by an anonymous writer in the German *Koloniale Rundschau* (1911:567) for German West Africa:

1. Before long time altogether no place he stop. God big fella marster belong white man, him fella he make'm altogether. God big fella marster belong white man, he make'm big fella garden. He good fella too much. Along garden plenty yam he stop, plenty coconut, plenty taro, plenty kumara, altogether good fella kaikai too much. Bimeby God big fella marster belong white man, he make'm one fella man and put'm along garden belong him. He call'm this fella man Adam. He name belong him. He put him this fella man Adam along garden, and he speak, "This fella garden he belong you". And he look'm this fella Adam he walk about too much. Him fella Adam all the same sick: He no savvee kaikai; he walk about all the time. And God he no savvee. God big fella marster belong white man, God say: "What name? Me no savvee what name this fella Adam he want".

2. Them first first time, you save nothing no live, das oll: God he live! no other thing, no ground, no wata for hem self, oll he be mix like su su pota-

pota. Then God he begin, he part him: some place, he put the ground, some place he put them wata, but man no fit look him, becos su su dark.

By and by God he say: "better I make some lantern!" Then he hang him one big one, he col him, say: "moon" and he fix plenty small small one for op, col him, say: "star".

Then he begin, he make oll thing, he make any kind beef, he make bush, he make farm two. After wats he say: "how, I no get peopli?" Then he take some ground for hand, he mass him, he make him turn op like man, he col him, say be: "crooboy!" - Befor he put him for some big big garden; plenty chop live there inside, plenty planten, plenty makaho, plenty fruits, plenty palmoil, eny kind beef two he live, das oll; work no live! so them place be fine too much.

Undoubtedly the most famous examples of black Creole storytelling are the stories involving the spider Anansi.[7] These are found throughout the Caribbean including the Creole-speaking countries of the South American continent such as Surinam and Guyana, as well as the place of Anansi's origin West Africa. A detailed description of the context in which this story-telling occurs is given by an anonymous writer of African literature (*Transactions of the Incorporated Royal Society of Arts and Agriculture* 1868 – original located in the Schuchardt Archives, Graz):

> The exploits of Anansay are transmitted from one generation to another: and one of the pleasantest pictures to be seen in Jamaica, of peasant comfort and enjoyment, is that of a circle of youngsters seated around some village story-teller, as he recounts the cunning, and the exploits of Anansay.
>
> One big hungry time, when nobody can't get nutten fe nyam, Anancey say to Green Lizard, "Bra Green-lizard, me yerry say one rich lady da liba 'lodda side ob de country an' him got one big pen an' plenty of little; meek we go de work fe him...." Green-lizard say "Berry well, Bra Ann.; anyting you say me we' do." De two ob dem set out an' dem walk walk fe tree whole day - tay dem come to de lady pen. When dem come to one ribba dat run before de gate, Ann. say "Tap, Bra Green-lizard, tap! Me got someting fe tell you. When we go to dis lady house you mus' n't name Green-lizard an' me mus' n't name Ann.

The development of Surinamese oral literature and the role of street-singers is discussed by Pos (1983), with additional remarks to be found in Adamson & van Rossem (1995). The latter authors list five genres: riddles, proverbs, tongue twisters, prose narrative, and song, but point out that other analysts have identified more distinctions (p 77).

Whilst in many West Indian Creoles a virtually unbroken tradition of story-telling existed from the days of African slave trade to the present, this is not so pronounced for Pidgins, story-telling being done in the vernaculars rather than Pidgins. Thus Laycock (1977b: 615) writes with regard to Tok Pisin:

> An oral tradition in Pidgin narrative has not yet established itself. Comparatively few Pidgin texts by indigenous speakers have been

---

[7] Other spellings include Anansay, Anansi and Nanzi.

published in any "undoctored" way; some of the major collections to date are to be found in the Pidgin manuals of Laycock (1970a), Dutton (1973) and Wurm (1970). It should be noted, however, that most of these texts are in fact translations of vernacular stories, and are told in Pidgin only for the benefit of the European recorder; situations rarely arise (or, at least, have rarely been observed) where narratives are told in Pidgin to a predominantly indigenous audience.

However, in the more developed varieties of this language, and particularly in its creolized form, the oral narrative has gained greater importance. This can be seen from the numerous conventions for discourse structuring and the fact that the topics covered typically pertain to the Tok Pisin speaking culture intermediate between traditional and Western society. An example is the following extract from Jack and the Beanstalk told to me by Yangol of Yip in 1973:

Olrait dispela stori wanpela lapun	Well, this story..., an old woman lived
meri em i stap long ples na emi karem	in a village and gave birth to a child.
wanpela pikinini, pikinini i kamap	The child grew up like a European
olsem masta na em tokim em yu givem	and told his mother: Give me your
mi dispela kau strait em wokabaut long	cow. Well, he travelled along the
rot i go nau painim wanpela man strait	road and he found a man. Well, sell
yu salim long en na kisim mani long en	it to him and get his money. He took
na em karim igo wanpela man trikim em	the cow with him and a man tricked
na givim bin beg longen nau em givim	him and gave him a bag of beans and
em na karem go pinis em karem i kam	he carried it back home. His mother
na mama i lukim em na hepi nogut tru	saw the bag and was terribly happy.

A similar example, this time for Hawaiian Creole English, is the following version of Goldilocks and the Three Bears, recorded by Stetser (1976:119):

After a while Góldie da *kúmu,*	After a while Goldie became hungry,
hungry, tíred, an sore foots, bin	tired and with sore feet
come along, an spa(r)k da *hale.*	came along and saw the house.
She go by da dóo(r) and téll,	She went to the door and said,
"Hello dea. Anybody stay home?"	"Hello there. Is anybody home?"
(medium voice) Chee! No more	Gee! There wasn't any answer.
da answer. So she peek inside	So she peekedinside and and she
spa(r)k da trée bówl *lúau*	saw the bowls of chicken stew
on tóp datáble. Sóme óno	on the table. The smell was very
da sméll! So she gó inside	appetizing! So she went inside.

We shall now examine how these general characteristics are realised in a number of Pidgin and Creole literatures.

Sranan literature
Sranan, like other Pidgins and Creoles, is characterized by a vigorous growth of religious literature at a relatively early stage and a slow but gradually accelerating growth of secular literature, particularly in the second half of this century.

Religious literature was created first by the Protestant Herrnhuter (Moravian) missionaries. The first handwritten catechism was completed in

1777 and large parts of the New and Old Testaments were translated before 1800. In 1816 the four gospels were published followed by a song book in 1820, the entire New Testament in 1829 and a number of semi-religious story books and tracts since 1853. They also published the world's first Creole monthly, the *Makzien vo Kristen-soema* in 1852 which appeared, with some interruptions, until 1932. The Catholic mission began publishing somewhat later and less extensively. Their bilingual journal *De Katolieke Waarschuwer* only survived from 1894 to 1895. The combined efforts of these missions resulted in relatively stable conventions for a written form of Sranan, thus encouraging secular writings by its speakers.

The first Sranan poem *Een huishoudelijk twist* 'a domestic tiff' appeared in 1786. It was written by Hendrik Schouten, a Dutchman. The poem portrays a domestic argument in which the man shouts at the woman in Dutch and she answers with equal intensity in Sranan.

However, the policy of the churches also to use Dutch in their church services from the second half of the 19th century helped to stabilize a state of affairs in which Sranan writing remained in the hands of expatriate whites, whilst educated black speakers tried to express themselves in their colonizers' language. It effectively prevented the development of an indigenous literature until about 1940. At this point the dissatisfaction with the expatriate domination of Surinamese cultural life was voiced by Koenders, a teacher and government worker. He founded a committee (*Pohama* <*Poti hanu makandra* 'put hands together') with the aim of standardizing the spelling and modernizing the lexicon of Sranan. His aims are discussed in his newspaper *Foetoe-boi* 'messenger' of March 1949:

> To begin with, they tried to make us lose our mother tongue, forget our very own language, turn us into Dutchmen, something which is impossible. Our forefathers, however, didn't know better and thought that that was the best they could do for us. In effect it rang the deathknell for us right up to this very day, because at present there are many who don't understand that a nation without a language can never be anything which is worthy of the name nation.

To prove his point, he wrote a book on a biological topic, a book of songs and other materials. Equally vociferous was a Sranan-centered cultural movement founded by Bruma in Amsterdam in 1952, the *Wie Eegie Sanie* ('Our own things'). Bruma particularly stressed the importance of restoring the bonds between educated Creole speakers and the working classes. Apart from promoting the use of Sranan by others, Bruma himself wrote a number of short stories, poems and plays.

Out of such forerunners grew a new Creole awareness in Surinam, culminating in the work of H F de Ziel, writing under the pen name Trefossa. His poems broke with a tradition of translating literary work from other languages and they not only deal with the everyday concerns of ordinary Surinamese but are written in everyday language too. Here is the beginning of a poem by Trefossa:

mi go – m'e kon	I've gone – I come
te dreeten winti sa trotji	if the dry season wind starts singing
ne Mawnidan:	in Mahogany Street:
– krioro fa?	- Creole, how?

m'sa pitji:	I'll answer:
– dja mi de,	– here am I
– banji fu ba-m 'ma seti keba:	– granny's bench has been set ready
– ertintin... ertintin...	– once upon a time.... once upon a time....

Between 1950 and 1980 about 35 collections of poetry representing 25 writers appeared, best known is that by Voorhoeve & Lichtveld, (eds, 1975).

Of the different genres, the greatest progress occurred with theatrical plays. Koenders created a theatre which stages 20 - 30 performances a year (see Kloss 1978) and which continues to flourish.[8]

On the other hand, non-fictional and technical[9] literature is very much underrepresented no doubt reflecting the continued restrictions on Sranan's use. Its future as a literary language depends very much on official support in both Surinam and the Netherlands, where a very large number of Sranan speakers have settled.

French-based Creoles in the Caribbean

From the point of view of the sociology of language there are three types of French Creoles in the Caribbean:

(a) The Creole of independent Haiti

(b) The Creoles of French overseas territories such as Martinique

(c) French Creoles spoken in British-controlled or English-speaking independent nations such as Dominica and St Lucia.

For this latter group, literary activity appears to be on the increase. As regards French-controlled territories, neglect of, and negative attitudes towards, Creole results in an unfavourable atmosphere for literary activities. Moreover, whatever is produced here is likely to be judged as a regional variety of French literature rather than an independent development. Thus, the most favourable conditions for an independent Creole literature are found in Haiti, though even there a number of severe restrictions are in evidence. A fuller account of French Creole literature has been given by Fleischmann (1978), and more recently by Ludwig (1989).

I will restrict the discussion to the use of Creole in French Caribbean literature before 1980. Unlike other French Creole-speaking territories such as Reunion, Mauritius or French Guiana, the use of Creole in literature came very late in the Caribbean. Until almost 1930 the prevailing view of black writers was that the only possible medium for literary expression was standard French, preferably a variety which equalled or excelled the elegance of the metropolitan one. This view was found in both independent Haiti and the various French dependencies. A change, originating among black writers residing in France occurred in the 1930s when indigenism became an important motive. This manifested itself mainly in the incorporation of Creole, as long as this did not render the work unintelligible to metropolitan French readers. The perceived function of this use of Creoles was:

---

8   Details on these can be found in Pos (1983).

9   One of the few Pidgin/Creole languages that has been used extensively in technical literature is Tok Pisin where a sizable body of instructional materials and technical handbooks have appeared in recent years. More details can be found in Laycock (1977b).

(i)   to give the writings local colour, and

(ii) to portray actors who did not speak anything but Creole in real life.

The subsequent fate of this indigenism was one of rapid disappearance in the French-controlled territories and one of growth and development in Haiti. The reasons for this have to be sought in the fact that the audience for the Martinican novel was the metropolitan reader. To them, any inclusion of Creole material would give a lopsided impression of underdevelopment and drollness, the kind of impression which had been conditioned by years of use of reduced varieties of French in this literary function. Moreover, the use of a standard variety of French is seen as a lever to influence the foreign metropolitan audience, though there is the constant danger that the very adoption of the metropolitan language may be interpreted as a victory of colonial educational and language policies. A way out of this dilemma was suggested by Frantz Fanon: that the individual should take possession of the French language or, as expressed by the Martinican writer Aimé Césaire: *j'ai voulu coloniser la langue française* (in Fleischmann 1978:649).

The need to communicate with a metropolitan audience was not so strong in Haiti, where the principal debate was not whether Creole should be written at all but which genre it should be employed in, more specifically whether it was a suitable medium for "high" literature. Thus, it was generally accepted that Creole had a place in popular theatre, comical writings and folk literature such as story-telling. In fact a reasonably large number of such writings have appeared in print over the years (cf Sylvain 1936, Fleischmann 1978). As with other Creoles, poetry is widely regarded as a domain suited to Haitian Creole. The reason it would seem is that poetry is associated with subjective feelings, lack of precision and emotions, i.e. properties which are also associated with the Creole language itself.

The only unsuitable genre identified by most Haitian writers, even those sympathetic to the language, is the novel, in particular the kind of novel where complex social and philosophical issues are dealt with. As observed by the Haitian writer Coulanges (1967:654): *"le créole ne peut être la langue de la pensée abstraite et cartésienne"*. As observed by Fleischmann, the main problem was not the inherent limitations of Haitian Creole, but the absence of a tradition. In contrast to an old literary language such as French, there are no literary norms, no stylistic conventions, no earlier texts to which reference can or must be made. To create the rules for a literary game would take time and considerable effort. Even if rules could be found, and there are signs that this is happening, there remains the problem of the audience. Writers in Creole-speaking countries have continuously faced the dual problem of having to write either for an overseas audience or for a small indigenous elite. Their real aim, that of reaching the Creole-speaking masses, remains largely unfulfilled due to illiteracy, the pre-occupation with more mundane matters in a degraded environment, and the negative self-view of Creole speakers (with a few exceptions such as the Seychelles).

The problems encountered in Haiti reflect those of ethnic literature in general as discussed by Ostendorf (undated) who suggests that the difficulties of writers for minorities are part of the process of creolization in the wider sense:

This process of simultaneous de- and acculturation, desocialization and assimilation with its sense of instability and fluidity, and the ongoing need to synthesize fragments of the old and the new experience is called by linguists "creolization". Though a term for language change it is quite useful in the discussion of ethnicity.

His remarks on symbolic and real ethnicity can be easily transferred to the discussion of Haitian literature. Whereas the symbolic creoleness, the incorporation of Creole passages into texts written in the standard language, reflects the writer's having learned the literary rules of the dominant culture (and indeed their having become part of such a culture), real Creole literature can be expected only from those who have minimal access to superordinate values, i.e. the group which is least likely to engage in literary production. At the best of times ethnic, and in particular Creole, writers are men or women of two worlds (Ostendorf: ibidem)

> 'Ethnic' refers to a duality in identity which is based on the doubling of social realms. Ethnic writers straddle those two realms, are marginal or liminal men and women, are 'of two worlds'. The split in the social realm is mirrored in a double consciousness (W E B DuBois), in shifting loyalties (Germans in WWI), ambivalent socialization patterns ('defeated victors' A Cahan), and - much later - in ironic vision (Bellow, Ellison).

It is interesting to observe the contrast between Creole literature in divided societies such as Haiti or the French West Indies, and unified societies, such as Papua New Guinea. In this country, the speakers of Tok Pisin have successfully removed its stigma as a colonial language and turned it into a genuine vehicle of cultural expression within a relatively short span of time. In Papua New Guinea, however, the destruction of the substrate culture was very much less than in the case of African slaves brought to Haiti, as was the exposure to superordinate cultural forms. One sees the importance of a positive self-image for the emergence of a separate literature with Afrikaans which acquired in less than a century, a literature as sophisticated as any (cf Dekker 1958 or Antonissen 1960). Both Tok Pisin and Afrikaans benefitted from considerable public funds to promote their literature despite a very small initial audience. Now that support for Afrikaans is declining, it will be interesting to see what will happen to literary production,

To return to Haiti, whilst the debate about the value of Creole for high literature continues, there is agreement that non-literary and technical literature should be promoted, as the immediate social benefits are perceived to be much greater. Thus we find much educational literature dealing with topics such as hygiene, improving agricultural practice or counteracting perceived undesirable behaviour such as drinking or gambling, often written by well-meaning outsiders and of doubtful effectiveness. Similar attempts in Tok Pisin often result in misunderstanding and/or non-action (cf Franklin 1975). Students of mass communication in developing countries are becoming increasingly aware that the simple provision of information is not the best way of promoting desired changes. Instead, many educational programmes have had the effect of widening the gap between rich and poor (cf Rogers (ed.) 1976).

Motives for writing in Pidgins and Creoles

It would seem that writing in Pidgins and Creoles has often been a planned rather than a spontaneous activity. In fact, we can distinguish the following motives:

(i)   Entertainment
(ii)   Educating and uplifting
(iii)   Proving the adequacy of the language
(iv)   Social control
(v)   Promotion of social bonds such as national unity
(vi)   Artistic self-expression.

Historically, these motives emerged in roughly this order, though there are obvious fluctuations with individual Pidgins and Creoles.

Enough has already been said about the first motive earlier and I will therefore continue with my remarks on the educational motive. The prevalent colonial view is found in Hall (1954b) where, "a white man's burden" attitude is expressed in the following terms:

> Clearly there is a vacuum here which it is our duty to fill, in order to bring as much information as possible to the natives of New Guinea and to enable them to share in the aesthetic and intellectual aspects of European culture, as well as its technology. It we do not do so, others hostile to our interests will not fail to step in and fill the vacuum. The present notes constitute merely a tentative discussion of the types of material needed and the means of supplying it (1954b:942).

Desirable for Hall are:

(i) Informative literature of a technical type.

(ii) Creative literature including (p 943):
    (a) Traditional stories both European (ancient, medieval and modern) and Melanesian. A start in this direction has been made by the present writer in re-telling such legends as those of Troy, Roland, Tristan and Isolde, and El Cid: many more are needed (ibidem).
    (b) Original inventions.

(iii) Poetry, of which some has already arisen in Neo-Melanesian (e.g. songs of home-sickness, satirical songs, love-songs, work-songs etc.)

Great care must be taken in the preparation of such materials. Dangers include, in Hall's view (ibidem):

> The level of contents should not be too low, nor should European authors yield to the temptation to write down to their native audience. Obviously, certain taboos imposed by European culture-patterns will have to be observed, such as those against frank mention of excretory and reproductive functions, which often occurs in folk-tales. However, especially in government-sponsored activities, other pressures towards bowdlerisation and emasculation of subject-matter are likely to be exerted by religious, political and other groups. These pressures should be resisted as much as possible, since they tend to constitute an unofficial censorship and to eviscerate any solid intellectual or emotional content.

As long as literature develops in the sheltered atmosphere of mission and government agencies, Hall feels that undesirable trends can be checked. However, additional protective measures such as censorship will have to be introduced, once commercial publishing begins (p 944):

> When publication of Neo-Melanesian literature on a commercial basis does become practicable, we may expect further problems to arise, especially those of the introduction of undesirable types of literature (e.g. "comics", pornography and the like) by unscrupulous commercial interests.

Whilst such considerations may still be heeded by some expatriate missions, they are hardly relevant to writing in the newly independent Pidgin and Creole societies. If the high culture of the dominant outside group continues to be the measure against which indigenous production is judged, cultural colonialism is likely to be perpetuated.

The motive of proving linguistic adequacy is found with both expatriate "pisinophiles" and "creolophiles" and indigenous speakers. With the former, the criterion again appears to be that Pidgins and Creoles are suited to expressing the ideas found in expatriate "high literature". Thus, with regard to Tok Pisin, Laycock (1977b:617-18) writes:

> A few brief translations have been undertaken by Europeans as tours-de-force, or as demonstrations that Pidgin is not an "inadequate" language; noteworthy among these translations are a version of a passage from Sophocles' Oedipus Rex by Gaywood (1951), a myth of Theseus and Ariadne retold by Hall (1959), and Murphy's (1943) translation of Mark Anthony's speech from Shakespeare's *Julius Caesar* (...):
>
> > *Pren, man bilong Rom, wantok, harim nau. Mi kam tasol lang planim Kaesar. Mi no ken beten longen. Sapos sampela wok bilong wanpela man i stret; sampela i no stret; na man i dai; ol i wailes long wok i no stret tasol. Gutpela wok bilongen i slip; i lus nating long graun wantaim long kalapa. Pasin bilong yumi man. Maski Kaesar tu, gutpela wok i slip* [italics added].
>
> Along the same lines, my own translation of *Macbeth* has been completed and will eventually be prepared for publication.

Similar translations exist for other Pidgins and Creoles and it would seem interesting to present them for the sake of comparison. The following Krio version, by Thomas Decker (1988:54-55), was first performed in Sierra Leone in 1964 (Shrimpton 1995:218).

> Padi dem, kohntri, una ohl wey dey na Rom. Meyk una kak una yeys ya!
> A kam ber Siza, a noh kam preyz am.
> Den kin memba bad wey pohsin kin du, lohng tem afta pohsin kin dohn dai.
> Boht plenti tem, di gud wey pohsin du, kim ber wit im bon dem.
> Meyk i bi so wit Siza.

The Early Modern English original reads as follows:

> Friends, Romans, countrymen, lend me your ears;
> I come to bury Caesar, not to praise him.
> The evil, that men do, lives after them;
> The good is oft interred with their bones.
> So let it be with Caesar.   (*Julius Caesar*, Act 1, Scene 2)

A set of translations of this passage into Torres Straits Broken was compiled by Rigsby (1984). He gave the following versions by indigenous speakers of this language in a handout:

> *Torres Straits Creole 11*
>
> Pren, Roman kantriman, tane thalinga blo yu kam po mi pás;
> Ai kam po bere Size, ai no kam po preizem.
> Dha nogub passen man i sabe mekem i matha stap wen dha man i dai;
> A gud pasen blo man wadh i kasa plande taim wantaim berem lo boun blo em
> Mekem olsem dhiskain po Siza gar.

This translation was made and checked by Rodney Mitchell. It displays some features from Kalaw Kawaw Ya, its indigenous substrate language from the top western islands of Torres Straits: Saibai, Duaun, and Beigu islands.

> *Torres Straits Creole 12*
>
> Pren, Roman, kantrimen, yupla lisen po mi;
> Ai kam ya po bere Siza, ai no wande preize em.
> Da nogud ting man i mekem i no stap lo dempla;
> Da gud ting yupla berem lo bon blo dempla.
> Letem diskain lo Siza.

This translation was made and checked by Frank Kaigey and Anna Shnukal. It is the variety of TSC that is spoken by people from the eastern islands of Torres Straits - Darnley, Stephen and Murray islands.

> *Torres Straits Creole 13*
>
> Pren, Roman, kantriman, lisen po mi pas;
> Ai kam po bere Siza, ai no kam po preize em.
> Da nogud ting man i mekem i stil stap ya wen ol man i dai;
> A plande taim dem gud ting blo man i wantaim berem lo bon blo dempla
> Mekem diskain po Siza tu.

This translation was made and checked by George Passi, who is from Murray Island in eastern Torres Straits.

As was observed in Chapter 2, similar translations were made for a number of Creoles by missionaries who wanted to demonstrate the suitability of a Pidgin or Creole for bible translations or religious writings.

A language-specific discussion of the notion of adequacy has been given by Noel (1975) for Tok Pisin. The wider issues involved here have been discussed by Rickford (1984).

The motive of promoting a social bond or indigenous consciousness, such as negritude or roots is relatively recent, emerging mainly in the context of the movement for political and cultural independence. However, it must be remembered that in most Creole societies the desire for political independence took precedence over that for cultural independence and that the need to create an independent national Pidgin or Creole culture is often not realized. Again, the impetus for this development typically comes from individuals or small private groups rather than from governments or other big funding organizations. Greater public support for Pidgin and Creole literature could have significant long-term advantages.

The use of literature, in particular popular literature and the media, for the purpose of social control is widespread in all societies. It is more prominent in societies where information is relatively scarce and controlled by a small number of organizations than in older less centralized societies. An examination of who is in the business of writing, publishing and disseminating literature in Pidgins and Creoles is likely to reveal a concentration in government and mission agencies. Some of the latter, such as the Summer Institute of Linguistics[10] are largely expatriate and multinational organizations. This monopoly manifests itself in the lack of variant interpretations of events and in the difficulty of obtaining any literature that does not carry some implicit or explicit value judgement. Thus, in the case of Tok Pisin, introductory books on topics such as cooking (Lilke 1972), child care (Thamm 1970 and health (Tscharke 1972) contain references to Christian doctrine. Their audience is unable to distinguish between the factual and non-factual statements in these books, and it is little wonder that Christian religion has been repeatedly interpreted as a way of obtaining cargo (cf Lawrence 1964). The same problem is seen in many other Pidgin- or Creole-speaking areas. Such control over written materials typically excludes a large number of people from developments which involve them directly. The establishment of a more heterogeneous press could remedy this, though current trends are against this. Before making too hard a judgement, however, one should remember that such incipient forms of written communication typically follow a situation where most of the population were cut off from virtually all outside information by a small elite.

A full investigation of the social forces involved in the publishing of information in Pidgins and Creoles is still needed. It may reveal a number of hitherto only hypothesised costs of Pidgin and Creole literacy. Perhaps the most difficult literary motive to analyse is that of self-expression. To do it justice one would have to survey a considerable body of literature, examine representative writers,[11] and investigate underlying social conventions. Written self-revelation has only recently come to third-world societies and was often stimulated by white models.

Again there is the problem of how to obtain a dialogue with an audience. The most likely consumers of all types of Creole or creolizing literature have so far been expatriates, both readers and critics. Once this begins to change, and there are signs that this is happening in some countries, new Pidgin and Creole literatures have a chance to develop from within, both for the motives discussed here, as well as in new functions specific to their setting.

Bible translation and religious writings

The importance of religious literature in Pidgin and Creole literature is particularly pronounced in the Pacific region where:

---

[10] SIL is involved in publishing for the following English-based Pidgins and Creoles: Northern Australian Kriol, Tok Pisin, Soloman PE, Djuka, Saramaccan and others.

[11] Some highly pertinent remarks can be found in C W E Bigsby (ed, 1980) and the review of this reader by R A Lee in the *Times Higher Education Supplement* of 20 January 1981). Lee comments on the fact that "black writers have been engaged in a rite of repossession, the freeing of black identity from the oppressor's value-laden, often racist idiom". Such attempts are also seen in the language of the Rastafarians.

(i) it is by far the largest and often the only, body of writing and

(ii) in virtually all instances, it predates non-religious literature.

Thus, religious considerations have influenced not only the form of Pidgins and Creoles (church varieties having been dominant in a number of countries) but also their very choice: Because of its association with Islam, Bazaar Malay was discouraged by missions in Papua New Guinea, as was Swahili for a long time. Changes in mission language policies are closely associated with the ups and downs of these languages (see Mühlhäusler 1995a for details). The various approaches to bible translation can be seen from a comparison of Mark 1:1-5, in a number of Pidgins and Creoles:

(i) *English* (New English Bible)
1. Here begins the Gospel of Jesus Christ the Son of God.
2. In the prophet Isaiah it stands written: "Here is my herald whom I send on ahead of you, and he will prepare your way".
3. A voice crying aloud in the wilderness, "Prepare a way for the Lord; clear a straight path for him".
4. And so it was that John the Baptist appeared in the wilderness proclaiming a baptism in token of repentance, for the forgiveness of sins:
5. And they flocked to him from the whole Judaean countryside and the city of Jerusalem, and were baptized by him in the River Jordan, confessing their sins.

(ii) *Bislama*
1. Hemia gud nyus blong Jisas Kraes, Pikinini blong God.
2. Hem i stat olsem we profet Aeasea i raetem bifo, we God i talem se "Hemia man blong karem tok blong mi. Mi mi sanem hem blong hem i go fastaem, yu liaen Hem bambae i mekemrere ol rod blong yu".
3. Wan man i stap singaot long draw ples, i se "Yufala i mekemrere rod blong Hae God", We hem i Masta blong yumi, Yufala i stretem ol smosmol rod blong hem".
4. Ale hiaen, nao Jon, hem i kamtru long drae ples, i stap baptaesem ol man mo i stap prij. Hem i talem se "Yufala i mas tanem tingting blong yufala from ol sin blong yufala, mo yufala i mas tekem baptaes, nao bambae God i tekemaot ol sin blong yufala.
5. Olgeta man blong ol velej blong Judia wetem olgeta blong Jerusalem oli stap go lesin long hem. Oli stap talemaot ol sin blong olgeta, nao Jon i stap baptaesem olgeta long Jodan Reva.

(iii) *Solomon Islands Pidgin*
1. Hem nao Gud Nius bulong Jisas Krais, Pikinini bulong God.
2. Hem i stat olsem profet Isais hem i raetem taem God hem i tok olsem long hem: "lu lukim desfala man ia. Mi sendem hem fo talemaot olketa toktok bulong mi. Baebae hem i go fastaem long iu, an bae bae hem i kiliarem rod fo iu.
3. Long darae ples wea nating hem i gorou long hem wanfala man baebae hem is singaot olsem: "lufala mas meke rere rod bulong Lod ia. lufala mas mekem steret olketa rod wea baebae hem i wokabaot long hem!"
4. Bihaen, Jon, man hu hem i baptaesem pipol, hem i kam long wanfala darae ples an hem i pris long olketa pipol olsem: "lufala mas lusim olketa ravis

wei an ravis tingting bulong lufala an sensem hat bulong lufala, an lufala mas baptaes, hekem God hem i save tekemaot sin bulong lufala".

5. Olketa pipol long distrik bulong Judea an olketa hu i stap long Jerusalem i go aot to hererr. Jon Olketa ia i talemaot olketa sin bulong olketa an Jon hem i baptaesem olketa long riva Jodan.

(iv) *Tok Pisin*

1. Dispela em i gutnus bilong Jisas Krais, Pikinini Bilong God.
2. Dispela gutnus em i kamap pastaim olsem profet Aisaia i raitim "Harim, mi salim man bilong bringim tok bilong mi, na em i go paslain long yu. Em bai i redim rot bilong yu.
3. Long graun i no gat man, maus bilong wanpela man i singuat, i spik, "Redim rot bilong Bikpela Stretim ol rot bilong en"
4. Jon, man bilong givim baptais, em i kamap long ples i no gat man, na em i telimautim tok long ol manmeri i mas tanim bel na kisim baptais, na bai God i tekewe sin bilong ol.
5. Na olgeta Judia na olgeta manmeri bilong Jerusalem ol i go long Jon Na ol i autim sin bilong ol, na Jon i baptaisim ol long wara Jodan.
6. Na Jon i save putim klos ol i bin wokim long gras bilong kamel, na em i pasim let long bel bilong en. Nam em i save kaikai grasop wantaim hani bilong bus.

(v) *Hiri Motu*

1. Dirava ena Hatuan Iesu Keriso ena Sivarai Namona ia matamaia inai bamona.
2. Peroveta tauna ladana Isaia ia torea, "Dirava ia hereva, ia gwau, 'Oiemu vairana dekenai lauegu hesiai tauna lau siaia. Oiemu dala do ia karaia hegaegae'.
3. Ta is boiboi taunimanima idia noho lasi gabuna dekenai inai bamona, 'Lohiabada ena dala umui karaia hegaegae, iena da'a umui hamaoroimaoroa'.
4. Unai dainai Ioane Baptaiso ia mai, Taunimanima idia noho lasi gabuna dekenai ia haroro. Ena haroro be, taunimanima edia lalona idia giroa, bona bapetiso idia abia, kara dika gwauatao lalona idia giroa, bona bapetiso idia abia, kara dika gwauatao toana.
5. Iudea kahana taudia bona Ierusalema hanua taudia ibounai idia lao Ioane dekenai. Idia gwan, "Ai be kara dika taudia". Vadaeni Ioane ese idia ia bapatisa henia toridane sinavai lalonai.

For each of these Pidgins or Creoles, variations can be found, a fact which is illustrated with a number of versions of the Our Father in Tok Pisin. The first three were published in 1937, 1934 and 1941 respectively whilst the last version is the one currently in use. It first appeared in the Nupela Testament translation of 1969.

Alexishafen

Fader bilong mifelo, yu stop long heven - Ol i santuim nem bilong yu - Kingdom bilong yu i kam - Ol i hirim tok bilong yu long graund olsem long heven. Tude givim mifelo kaikai bilong de - Forgivim rong bilong mifelo - olsem mifelo forgivim rong - ol i mekim long mifelo. Yu no bringun mifelo long traiim - tekewe samting no gud long mifelo. Amen.

Vunapope

Papa bolong mipela i stap antap - naim bolong ju i tambu - lotu bolong ju i
kam - mipela daun olosem ol antap i harim tok bolong ju ju bringim kaikai
tede bolong mipela - ju larim mipela i olosem mipela i larim ol, ol i mekim
nogut mipela - ju no bringim mipela klostu long rot i nogut - ju lusim ol
samting nogut i raus long mipela. Amen.

Rabaul

Papa bilog mi fela, iu stop an top alog peles bilog iu, i qud mi fela sigsig out
tru alog nem bilog iu; i moa beta ol a fasin bilog iu i stop oltuqeta peles. I
qud mi fela mekim tru ol a lo bilog iu, ol a sem oltuqeta man i savi mekim
alog peles bilog iu. I qud iu givim mi fela kaikai inafim mi fela alog tude. I
qud iu no mekim koros alog mi fela alog ol a fasin no qud mi fela mekim, ol
a sem mi fela no qat koros alog ol a man i savi korosim mi fela. Iu no
bringim mi fela alog ol a samtig no qud; i moa beta iu luk outim mi fela so
mi fela no ken mekim ol a fasin no qud. Amen.

Nupela Testament (1969)

Papa bilong mipela, yu i stap long heven, nem bilong yu i mas i stap holi./
Kingdom bilong yu i mas i kam. Laik bilong yu ol i bihainim long heven,
olsem tasol mipela i mas bihainim long graun tu./ Nau yu givim mipela
kaikai inap long dispela de./ Na yu lusim ol sin bilong mipela, olsem
mipela tu i lusim pinis sin bilong ol man i bin rongim mipela./ Na yu no
bringim mipela long samting bilong traim mipela, tasol tekewe mipela long
samting nogut. Tru.

Pidgins and Creoles in the mass media

No survey of literary forms of Pidgins and Creoles would be complete
without at least a cursory survey of their use in the mass media namely
newspapers, television, radio, films, magazines, and recordings of popular
music. Again information is often not readily available and I cannot hope to
make useful generalizations about the limited evidence at hand. However, it
is a useful research area and of considerable interest to students of mass
communications. In contrast to 'high literature', there are few arguments
against the suitability of Pidgins and Creoles for the mass media. Rather, the
chief problems appear to be economic ones, i.e. the cost of disseminating
news to small language groups having educationally and socially
underprivileged speakers, over relatively large geographical areas. In most
Pidgin- and Creole-speaking communities information is spread by
interpersonal communication rather than mass media and attempts to change
this pattern are few.

In this section I will present a brief general survey, followed by a
contrastive study of communication in Papua New Guinea and Jamaica. The
first journal published in any Creole was the religious monthly *Makzien vo
Kristen-soema* in Sranan, which first appeared in 1852, followed by a journal in
Sri Lankan Portuguese Creole in 1868 and two serials in Papiamentu *El
Civilisado* (1871-75) and *Amigoe di Curacao* (1884). Kloss's (1978) survey of
Pidgins and Creoles based on Germanic languages reveals a generally low
level of activity in the mass media. For instance, for West African PE of the
Cameroons, an information sheet was issued by members of the Peace Corps
for a few months in 1963 but little else had appeared by 1978. For Nigerian

PE we find that whilst there are a number of magazines and comics written in a mixture of Pidgin and standard English, support for more written Pidgin is not strong (Shnukal & Marchese 1983). On the other hand, most of their informants favoured its increased use in television.

Recent changes in the status of Vanuatu Bislama have already been mentioned. As regard the area of mass communications, this language was first used in radio transmission in the early 1960s. At roughly the same time, the French administration began to issue a bi-monthly summary in Bislama of their French weekly bulletin. The British Residency followed suit in 1971 when they began to include Bislama texts in their newsletter. From the mid 1970s onward a drastic increase in the Bislama content of official publications and in broadcasting occurred, a trend which has accelerated after independence. Similar trends, although at a slightly more modest level, can be observed with Solomons PE in the neighbouring Solomon Islands Republic. Radio programmes in Bislama, Tok Pisin and Solomon Islands Pidgin are broadcast not only locally but also by the ABC from Australia. Such programmes, or indeed other forms of mass communication, are not available for the various Pidgins and Creoles spoken in Australia itself. Outside the Pacific area, we can point to the cases of Afrikaans, Bahasa Indonesia and Swahili, as well as radio and TV broadcasts for some of the French Creoles in the Caribbean. For an English Creole, Devonish (1984) has proposed to make Creole the language of the mass media in Guyana. He vividly portrays the undesirable relationship between political power and mastery of standard English and the resulting exclusion of the mass of the population from the country's political processes. He sees the change-over to Creole in mass communications as involving two stages (pp 95-96):

> The first stage would be to train those persons within the organisations who are charged with disseminating information to the public. Such persons, be they writers of pamphlets, journalists, public speakers or political organisers, need to be made familiar with the structure of Common Creolese which would have to be prepared for the purpose. The disseminators would need, as well, to be taught a standard writing system for Creole, possibly a modified version of the Cassidy-Le Page orthography which was originally developed for Jamaican Creole.
>
> The next step would be to explain to the public what is being attempted and why. Public education on the language question is not going to be achieved overnight. There is likely to be a long and heated argument, both inside and outside the movement, as to the correctness or otherwise of the langue practices being implemented.

For a survey of the "instrumentalization" of Caribbean Creoles, see Winford (1991:579ff).

The situation in Jamaica in the 1960s is discussed by Alleyne (1963) who deplores the lack of any genuine discussion of political issues by much of the population. As in many other Caribbean nations, the standard language of the former colonizing power continues to dominate all formal and public acts of communication. Alleyne (p 23) points out that:

> This type of linguistic situation prevents the proper functioning of the democratic political system, as it makes the flow of communication between the elite and the masses extremely difficult. The official formal media of

331

communication use, almost exclusively, European languages. And the reasons for this are several:

(i) During the colonial era, particularly at its inception, there was little necessity for communication between the ruling elite and the native population at large and the formal media were directed only to this ruling elite; although the ruling elite has changed ethnically, and formal media continue to use European languages;

(ii) The rationale that the native languages are inadequate as vehicles for highly scientific explanation or intellectual thought;

(iii) The need for opening the doors of the country to the international world, with its economic and cultural implications;

(iv) The usefulness of the European languages as linguae francae to defeat tribalism.

Writers such as Devonish (1986) and Winford (1991) have argued that the language issues in most Caribbean societies are more complex than standard versus Creole and that a better understanding of the overall language ecology will need to precede any attempts of status planning and instrumentalization of stigmatized varieties in official functions. Alleyne (1963:28) mentions the castigation of new notions as one example when Creoles were not used in the Caribbean.. This contrasts with Papua New Guinea where the official version of the castigation is in English, but where the languages used in drafting and debating it were Tok Pisin and Hiri Motu, both Pidgins. The use of standard English in newspapers has another, equally undesirable feature. Because of its prestige, the printed word retains a kind of magic power that has been lost in many other societies as pointed out by Alleyne (ibidem):

> The printed word has in Jamaica, as well as other societies in the world, a great deal of magic power and is often considered the purveyor of truth. There seems to be a correlation between education or "sophistication" and gullibility. The lower the degree of education and "sophistication" the greater the degree of gullibility, would seem to be the general pattern; but precise tests are necessary in order to confirm this. In Jamaica, attitudes such as "How do you know that? Did you see it in the newspaper?" or "Do you think a newspaper would go to the trouble of printing something if it were not true?" may be said to reflect a low degree of education and sophistication; while such an attitude as "Oh! That's only propaganda; you can never believe what you read in the Gleaner" reflects a higher degree.

Moreover, the discussion of matters of general interest in readers' letters is restricted to a small elite, again in striking contrast to Papua New Guinea where contentious issues spark off a flood of letters to the editor of Wantok and other Tok Pisin publications.

Political communication to the masses in Jamaica continues to be by word of mouth and other forms of interpersonal behaviour.

From information available to me it appears that little has changed over the last decade and that Jamaican Creole continues to play a very subordinate role in the mass media.

The case history of Tok Pisin illustrates a very different society. The principal initiative for the use of this language in the mass media came from the Catholic mission and the missions continue to dominate the scene. Following the decision to make Pidgin a mission medium and to standardize its orthography and lexicon, the first periodical was published by the Alexishafen mission in 1935, *Frend bilong mi*, a monthly magazine of stories and songs. It continued, except for the war years, until 1952. Also at Alexishafen, the shortlived first cartoon, *Pigtel*, was published in the 1930s. From the Vunapope (near Rabaul) mission came the monthly journal *Katolik: Buk long Tok Pisin*, published in 1940-41. It continued after the war as the *Katolik Nius*.

These early mission publications contained not current news but inspirational and doctrinal discourse. Thus, a large part of the March 1949 edition of *Katolik Nius* is devoted to the discussion of the meaning of Lent rather than current events.

The first government use of mass media was the leaflet campaign by Australian and American armed forces during the Second World War. Shortly after the First World War, the first genuine newspapers appeared. They included *Rabaul News* (1946-59) and the *Lae Garamut* (1947-56). Others were the shorter-lived *Lagasai* (Kavieng, 1947-48), *Buka News* (1948-49), *Madang Matau* (c 1948 and 1952) and *Wewak News* (c 1948). They were all mimeographed weeklies.

Let us do a brief contents analyis of a typical issue, the Saturday 10th September, 1949 edition of the *Lae Garamut*. (Vol. 3, no. 35). Altogether there are six pages. Page 1 is devoted entirely to an article entitled *Stamp bilong putim long letter* reminding the reader that letters must have stamps, page 2 has a half-page news story about the explosion of a petrol tank in Lae. The other half is assorted news from Madang such as school outings, an old woman having been bitten by a snake and the erection of a new school building. *Madang news* continues on page 3, followed by a section called *General news* dealing with the comings and goings of high colonial officials. The last third of the page is devoted to *Police news*, page 4 is *Sports news* dealing with local football matches and page 5 is again Police news, followed by a traditional story from Wewak continued on the last page. Notably absent are world news, advertisements and editorials. The impact of these newspapers was considerable. Writing about the *Rabaul News*, Baker (1953: 196) reports:

> At the beginning of 1950, about 950 copies of the paper were being brought out each Friday night - on a Gestetner. The reading public of these 950 copies was estimated at "at least eighty thousand". An administration officer told me, "I myself have seen natives in outlying districts gathering in the hundreds to hear one man reading from a single copy".

In spite of their success most of these regional newspapers closed down in the mid-50s as a result of the disapproval expressed by the United Nations. The gap was filled by a nation-wide government sponsored free monthly paper *Nius Bilong Yumi* which appeared from 1959 to 1982. Other journals which began to appear around this time were *Wastaua* (1963), a monthly Tok Pisin version of the Jehovah's Witnesses publication *The Watchtower*, and the weekly *United Nations Nius na Nots long Tok Pisin* (1967) put out by the UN Information Centre for Papua-New Guinea, Port Moresby. At the same time, Tok Pisin was used increasingly in hitherto English publications.

The years immediately preceding independence saw a considerable increase in publishing. Most important are the party newspaper *Pangu Pati News*, the bilingual Hiri Motu/Tok Pisin *Poroman* and, above all *Wantok*, first monthly, then published fortnightly, now weekly with a circulation of over 10,000. The day to day problems of editing this newspaper are discussed by Mihalic (1977). Whilst *Wantok* is still very much a Catholic publication, it differs considerably from both earlier church and government publications. Let us briefly list the contents of the edition of 7th January, 1984.

Front page	apology for price increase
	report on rapid rise in the price of betelnuts (equivalent of beer in terms of popularity and social importance)
	half-page cartoon of events affecting Papua New Guinea in 1983
page 2-6	Papua New Guinea News, political and social
page 6-7	summary of events in PNG in 1983
page 8	modern short story, PNG news, ads
page 9-10	advertisements
page 15	wallchart of college of external studies for use in schools
page 11-13	sport
page 14	advertisement for heavy motor vehicles
page 16-17	readers' letters
page 18	advertisement for motor cycles
page 19	survey of world events in 1983
page 20	world news and medical information (VD)
page 21	advertisement for small buses
page 22	illustrated bible and religious news
page 23	traditional story and advertisement
page 24	photographs of world events in December

To turn to other mass media, the first radio broadcasts were made in 1944 from a station set up by the Allies in Port Moresby. Until the end of the war, there were approximately one and a half hours a day of broadcasts for the indigenous people of Papua and New Guinea (Siegel 1985 and n d) Over the years, both the number of stations and the hours broadcast in Tok Pisin increased steadily, particularly after the introduction of short wave services in 1961. Siegel (1981:14-15) reports:

> By 1973 there were stations in 12 districts and approximately 75 000 radio receivers in the country. The daily listening audience was approximately 340 000.

In December 1973, the National Broadcasting Commission (NBC) was established, paving the way for more Papua New Guinean programmers and announcers, and more use of Tok Pisin, especially on the district level. Today, Tok Pisin is heard extensively on 15 of the 19 provincial radio stations. Nine of these broadcast in Tok Pisin almost exclusively. Five use Tok Pisin along with various indigenous languages. One uses it in addition to English and Hiri Motu. Although English remains the main language of the national service, Tok Pisin is used not only in news broadcasts, but also in some interviews and advertisements. It can also be heard in the broadcasts of parliamentary debates and sporting events. Obviously, mass communication does not solve all the problems of a young country such as Papua New

Guinea, but the fact that news about political and social changes has been available to large proportions of the population for many years is certainly one of the reasons for its continued political stability. Other Pidgin- and Creole-speaking countries would be well advised to take a close look at the policies of Papua New Guinea.

Summary and conclusions

The observations made in this chapter about the use of Pidgins and Creoles in literature and for literary purposes are, to a large extent, part of the more general problem of socially subordinate dialects and languages with little or no literary tradition. The development of such varieties into literary languages (in the widest sense) inevitably involves both formal adjustments (such as the standardization of writing and grammar), as well as attitudinal ones; languages which have been held in low esteem over generations are not readily accepted as carriers of information previously reserved for more prestigious varieties.

In the case of Pidgins andCreoles, there are a number of special problems, particularly the fact that they often exist in a diglossic situation with a lexically related superordinate language. Quite frequently, speakers do not even recognize that they are dealing with two separate systems but regard the Pidgin or Creole simply as a corruption of the high variety. Other problems include the relative structural instability of some of these languages, their association with non-egalitarian relationships and their small speech communities.

Much of this chapter has discussed stereotyped views of the structures and use of Pidgins and Creoles and it has been shown that such views persist in perpetuating inefficient patterns of communication, militating against modernization and development of democratic societies and preventing artists from finding an outlet in their own language. Such disadvantages are greatly reduced in countries where literary forms of Pidgins and Creoles are encouraged. My own experience lies in the Pacific region and I may at times have underestimated the literary achievements of other Pidgin- and Creole-speaking areas. This chapter also highlights the necessity for close collaboration between linguists and students of literature. An inter-disciplinary project could provide valuable literary accounts and linguistic analyses of the special pidginizing and creolizing registers in the world's literatures. The greatest need at this point is that of case stories for individual varieties, preferably combining data collection with information about the socio-historical context of their use. Both literary studies and Creolists can only profit from such an approach.

10 Conclusions and outlook

Almost every detail of the formation, nature and function of the marginal languages is a subject of disagreement. Many baseless or outworn ideas are still current about these forms of speech.
(Reinecke 1937:40)

Two key conclusions

The following conclusions are derived from explicit as well as implicit statements made earlier in this volume. First, Pidgins and Creoles, like other human communication systems, are open systems in the technical sense. They are influenced by, and intertwined with, a large number of internal factors; are liable to change and fuzziness; and are generally ill-defined. The general points raised by Hockett (1968:44ff) against Chomsky's views on language seem even more powerful in the context of Pidgin and Creole studies. These languages, more than any others, reflect the human ability for rule-changing creativity.

Second, available models of linguistic and sociolinguistic description are typically designed for closed systems and, as such, are ill-suited to the needs of Pidginists and Creolists. Whereas the need for abstraction and stream-lining in model-making is not denied, it is felt that adequate accounts of these languages call for some radical rethinking. It should be remembered that such models are also needed for other means of human communication, although on a scale of open-endedness Pidgins and Creoles would rank higher than most of these. Particularly problematic aspects of most available models are the traditional dichotomies of competence versus performance, synchronic versus diachronic or grammatical competence versus communicative competence. Whatever their usefulness has been in linguistic model-making, they are of very limited relevance to the study of Pidgins and Creoles, as I have argued in much greater detail in Mühlhäusler (1992b).

Related to the above two points is the observation that the evidence from Pidgins and Creoles appears to favour the dependency hypothesis: that is, the view that some linguistic structures are to be explained by language-external parameters. Pidginists and Creolists should remain at the forefront for those who study the cultural prerequisites to grammatical analysis, and not be seduced by the promises of "scientific linguistics".[1]

Pidgins and Creoles, particularly in their earliest stages, develop in a maximally culture-neutral context and are therefore maximally "natural" communication systems. Their naturalness is related to the fact that, under pressure for communication, the least costly solutions tend to be favoured. After their initial crystallization, Pidgins and Creoles are subject to numerous cultural forces. Thus, the older languages of this group exhibit a mix of cultural and natural grammar similar to that found in other languages.

---

[1] A more detailed discussion of this topic is given by Silverstein (1977) and in the writings of Harris (e.g. 1980).

Because of their greater initial naturalness, Pidgins and Creoles afford highly interesting insights into language universals. Contrary to many claims, language mixing is not an important factor in all areas of grammar and in enduring many developmental stages. Instead, the encounter of languages and communicative patterns that gives rise to Pidgins and Creole tends to result in new systems. To the extent that mixture is involved, it appears to be of the '"chemical compound" rather than "mechanical mixture" type. At present, the analytic apparatus capable of dealing with non-mechanical mixture is lacking.

Next to solutions reflecting the biological and neurological roots of human communication, Pidgins and Creoles also reflect the ability of people to regress to earlier stages of development of communicative behaviour. Such regressive behaviour is particularly strong in initial Pidgin formation.[2] The fact that regression is traditionally seen as deviation (performance or *parole* in linguistics) has prevented its wider discussion.

For most of their history, Pidgins and Creoles have been severely misunderstood by laymen and experts alike. These everyday prejudices have exercised a very considerable influence on linguistic thought and continue to be reflected in some scientific writings.

The study of Pidgins and Creoles has concentrated on relatively few questions. Such questions as were asked reflect its dependence on general linguistics rather than on other disciplines such as anthropology, sociology, literary studies or communication studies. It is hoped that a wider basis can be found for the study of these languages.

The practitioners of the field in most instances have been outsiders. The insider view, which has begun to emerge comparatively recently, may force considerable re-thinking of a number of widely held assumptions.

Finally, contrary to some claims, Pidgin and Creole studies has a large number of potential applications involving, among others, the fields of second language learning, cross-cultural and international communication, understanding of social-control mechanisms, and language planning. The minimal financial investment by governments and universities in Pidgin and Creole research is hardly in tune with the potential benefits – financial and other – one can anticipate. What the study of Pidgins and Creoles can be good for has been discussed by Mühlhäusler (1992a).

Conclusions on a number of other issues were more difficult to arrive at, as certain areas still await the attention of Pidginists and Creolists. It is to these that I now turn.

The metalanguage of Pidgin and Creole linguistics

Throughout this book I have drawn attention to instances where our metalanguage and everyday metaphors suggest problematic interpretations of Pidgins and Creoles. Perhaps the most serious is to regard languages as objects (reifications) rather than processes; this is closely followed by a tendency to locate such objects in a well-defined area of time and space.

The most thorough examination of the metalanguage used in the Pidgin and Creole field is provided by Tabouret-Keller (1980:313-27). She draws

---

2   Some interesting support for this view comes from a study of the interlanguage behaviour of Japanese learners of English (Neustúpny 1983: 29).

attention to the fact that a considerable amount of psychological vocabulary has been carried over into Pidgin and Creole studies, including terms such as need (need for communication), imitation, and identity. Although Pidgin and Creole linguistics owes a great deal to insights from psychology, there is the danger that such terminological innovations "may also smuggle into a discipline notions which, if they are isolated from the epistemological interrogation on which they were based, lack vitality and obstruct discussion" (p 323).

An equally problematic consequence is that questions of language and cognition have been given considerably more attention than the social forces shaping these languages. This is a serious matter in view of their often brief life-span and the drastic changes in social setting brought about by the advent of independence in Pidgin- and Creole-speaking countries.

Next, I would like to mention the metalanguage derived from the conduit metaphor (Harris 1982; Reddy 1979), that is, the view of human communication models as analogues of technological ones such as telegraphy. Such a model is particularly unsuited to the Pidgin situation, where there are notorious discrepancies between the messages sent by the transmitter and those interpreted by the receiver. Moreover, in the critical stages, communication proceeds with no single code and considerable discrepancies between message and signals. The success or non-success of Pidgin communication can hardly be explained in terms of simplistic concepts such as "noise". The prevailing static models of communication have also tended to deflect emphasis from the dynamic and changing character of both Pidgins and Creoles. These languages do not just provide examples of how human beings employ a code to its limits, but, more significantly, of how human beings construct and change codes in order to meet certain communicative requirements. Rule-changing creativity, which was traditionally associated with the marginal or secondary areas of parole and performance, should really be the focus of Pidgin and Creole linguistics.

Martyn-Jones & Romaine have drawn attention to another dangerous metaphor, the container metaphor:

> From the perspective of the history of science, it is perhaps not surprising that the container metaphor should be applied to notions of linguistic competence. Lakoff & Johnson (1980) claim that the container metaphor is a basic one in the human conceptual system, without which we couldn't function or communicate. It has been a dominant mode of conceptualizing human intellectual capacities in other scientific fields. One needs only to think of craniometry as a good example of a literal application of the metaphor, "the mind is a container" (1984:11).

This metaphor has been particularly powerful in the discussion of the educational role of Pidgins and Creoles. Most of those who have argued that knowledge of a Pidgin or a Creole prevents children from acquiring the related lexifier language properly were guided by it.

Finally, and related to the container metaphor, there is the gift metaphor, where the transmission of a European language to non-Europeans is seen as an act of giving a valuable present to a group of 'undeserving' recipients. The gift metaphor is particularly dangerous, since it suggests that the only active and constructive partner is the expatriate, and that the role of the indigenes is one of corruption and debasing.

I have argued for a better understanding of the metalanguage for Pidgin and Creole studies in Mühlhäusler (1995b). Such an understanding will involve the recognition of the metaphorical character of most of our discourse and the deconstruction of the language, professional politics and practices of Pidgin and Creole linguists.

Understanding naturalness

As observed by Reddy (1979:296), "shifts in the notion of what a thing does naturally, that is, if left to its own devices, are the stuff of which scientific revolutions are made". In the history of Pidgin and Creole studies, there have been a number of views about naturalness in these languages, and it would seem worth while to look at these briefly. For a more detailed discussion, see Mühlhäusler (1989a).

Initially, and until relatively recently, the natural state of both Pidgins and Creoles was perceived to be that of grammarless languages. What little grammar some of them had was said to have been borrowed from the lexically related superstratum language. This view, that one was dealing with simplified versions of more sophisticated, usually European models, was largely replaced in the late 1960s and early 1970s by the idea that Pidgins and Creoles represented some universal deep structure, that they shared most (in the case of Pidgins) and all (in the case of Creoles) deep properties of human languages, but lacked certain late transformations. Put differently, they possessed all essential phrase-structure rules but few non-essential transformations. Their grammar was thus optimal rather than deficient or lacking, as in the previous view.

A third view, which is gradually making itself felt, combines the earlier two. In as much as Pidgins and Creoles are used by actual human beings in highly complex communicative situations, rather than by ideal speaker-hearers in a communicative vacuum, they will always fail to be totally natural. Next to the strategy of reverting to one's biological roots when constructing a new first or second language, many other culture-related strategies enter the formation process of actual Pidgins and Creoles, most notably strategies of linguistic regression. It is further felt that the emergence of biologically founded grammar, if such grammar should exist at all, is subject to a triggering of social and socio-psychological factors. Put differently, all languages leak, although some Pidgins and Creoles may leak somewhat less in the early stages of their formation.

This emergent view also acknowledges that no language is a perfect code. Instead, particularly in the case of incipient Pidgins and post-Pidgin and post-Creole continua, a considerable looseness – and even lack – of structuring can be observed. This lack of linguistic grammar is partially compensated by greater appeal to non-verbal channels of communication, although in many instances we can simply observe non-optimal communication, a feature widespread in any language, though perhaps more prominent in second languages such as Pidgins.

From this third viewpoint, the natural function of a Pidgin or Creole is to bring about communication. Such communication can be achieved by both

339

verbal and non-verbal means. In as much as there is a biological/natural basis to these, they will be employed in preference to other solutions wherever there is conflict between communicative strategies. Pidgin and Creole development is thus seen as involving a wider communicative context. Verbal forms of behaviour are at least partially dependent on, and interwoven with, extralinguistic and non-linguistic factors. A social vacuum would lead to no language development, rather than the development of ideal natural Pidgins or Creoles.

In comparing these three solutions, it appears that the former two present self-contained wholes, whereas the latter can only hope to identify some of the pieces that make up our intellectual puzzle. However, as the price for internal consistency is the lack of fit between the model and the real world, the last approach would seem preferable. Although explanations can be given only locally, such explanations at least have the advantage of a reasonable fit with observed reality and/or predictive power in a restricted area. In sum, it is concluded that since Pidgins and Creoles are never left to their own devices in real life, direct access to naturalness is not given. However, the forces shaping these languages appear to be quantitatively less prominent than in the case of many older languages with a long history of human interference.

Non-expatriate Pidgin and Creole studies

Pidgin and Creole linguistics, for better and for worse, has been dominated almost exclusively by Westerners, typically speakers of the lexically related standard languages superordinate to the Pidgins and Creoles. Within this tradition, an impressive body of knowledge has been amassed. It would be foolish to ignore or dismiss the contributions of expatriate experts or suggest that they should abandon their work. However, it could be argued that the view they present is subject to a number of limitations, such as are inherent in any work produced by outside observers.

These include the already mentioned limitations imposed by Western metalinguistic and metacommunicative language. Different systems could provide a new and potentially more profitable frame for looking at Pidgins and Creoles. The change from an entity to a process frame provides an example. Second, the elicitation techniques and field methodology employed by many researchers provide, at best, a partial view of these languages. As has been pointed out in a monograph by Duranti (1981), established elicitation techniques may actually distort linguistic data to the extent that they become useless for genuine insights into natively spoken languages. From this limitation, the often heard desire for better, more "natural" data for Pidgins and Creoles often follows. However, as the data become increasingly informal, the ability of outside observers to make sense of them decreases. I have called this the 'Labovian Paradox': the better your data, the less you can do with them.

The systematic training of linguists from Creole-speaking communities could do a lot to alleviate this situation. The work of a growing number of Caribbean scholars working on their Creoles is a very positive development. Their work shows that it is possible to overcome the expatriate models of their languages.

I have argued elsewhere (Mühlhäusler 1983a) that there are additional problems even for inside observers. They relate to the more general principle that what is developmentally early is least accessible to introspection and most likely to go unobserved by adult members of a linguistic community. In as much as the early developmental stages of Pidgins and Creoles are of particular interest to theorists of these languages, we are faced with a very considerable problem. Disregarding evidence, over- and under-reporting, and misinterpretation thus are also likely to occur with inside investigators. These problems can be diminished by appealing to outsiders and by applying experimental techniques, such as hypnosis.

Linguistic experiments

The development of Pidgins and Creoles takes place within a relatively short timespan. This makes them ideal for testing claims about language development and change. However, as in all social sciences, conditions likely to cast light on the problem investigated do not always present themselves and, in the case of Pidgins and Creoles, the very rate of development tends to lead to a rapid replacement of some highly interesting early developments. Many theoretical questions can only be solved by either patiently waiting until a new case emerges or else by deliberate experimentation.

As regards the first strategy, Pidgins and Creoles continue to emerge and/or get known, such that waiting and careful search frequently pays excellent dividends. This point was made in Wurm (1979), where Papua New Guinea, an area with a very high incidence of linguistic encounters, Pidgins and Creoles, was referred to as a "linguistic laboratory". The 1983 York Conference on Urban Creoles (see *York Papers in Linguistics* 11, 1984) identified the large urban centres of both the First and the Third World as another such laboratory.

Regarding experimentation, the first explicit suggestions for experiments with Pidgins and Creoles are those of Voorhoeve (1961:37-60). Voorhoeve, like the transformationalists that were to follow him, was concerned with the inadequacies of linguistic corpora, particularly in the syntactic area, and thus suggested a number of systematic elicitation techniques to obtain lacking information. Experiments of this type, because they provide a distorted context, though undoubtedly useful, have to be made with great care, and evidence thus gained will need to be checked continually against "naturally" elicited materials. Still, large-scale comparative projects involving Pidgins and Creoles can hardly do without experiments.

The question of how to recover earlier developmental stages has thus far received two answers: one is that by Peet (1979), involving controlled regression under hypnotic conditions. For ethical and practical reasons, one can expect only limited information from this technique.

A much more ambitious project, attempting to recreate the genesis of Pidgins and Creoles whilst cutting down socio-historical variables to a minimum, is that described by Bickerton (1979:17-22). This did not get the approval of funding bodies and hence little more can be said about its potential use.

It would seem to me that experiments attempting to solve global issues will run into financial problems, raise difficult ethical problems and not achieve the aim of controlling the variables involved. Thus it might be more realistic to devise smaller, self-contained local experiments of the type that have been customary in neighbouring sciences such as experimental psychology.

On funding Pidgin and Creole studies

The widespread view that Pidgins and Creoles are marginal languages is reflected in their marginal role when it comes to academic funding. Although it would seem unwise to insist on the establishment of a separate new discipline with separate funding, a case could nevertheless be made for giving more recognition to Pidgin and Creole research within established disciplines such as linguistics (where this has happened to a limited extent), communication studies, anthropology, psychology and language-learning studies. It seems anomalous that a country such as Australia, where a large number of Aborigines speak at least four distinct Pidgins and Creoles, should not have an established academic post devoted to these languages. A similar situation holds in most countries where Pidgins and Creoles are spoken. Such a situation, although entirely explicable, is nevertheless deplorable. Now that Pidgin and Creole studies has attained greater academic respectability, the time may have come for more determined promotion, pointing out potential social and financial as well as academic benefits.

Particular attention should be given to informing the wider public of insights to be gained. There is a continued need for sound popular writings, informed discussion of the prejudices that continue to surround Pidgins and Creoles, and a willingness to enter into public debate. It is only once these languages have come to be seen as assets rather than liabilities by a large audience that there will be a genuine chance for expansion of the field.

The primary benefit of Pidgins lies in the fact that they permit communication between speakers of different languages. In highly multi-lingual areas such as Melanesia or West Africa, effective administration would be impossible without the local Pidgins. Moreover, they increase co-operation and reduce socially damaging misunderstandings between groups. The dramatic downturn in tribal warfare in Papua New Guinea, for instance, is a direct consequence of a common language, as my informants have pointed out to me many times. It should be noted that Pidgins, as second languages, really offer the best of worlds to their users: they can communicate with outsiders, while continuing to express their own identity through their vernacular. Those in the business of developing an international auxiliary language can learn a great deal from study of Pidgins.

The social value of Creoles, in contrast to Pidgins, is that of providing a symbol of group identity for displaced and disrupted people, while at the same time providing a certain protection against further disruptive outside influence. A good example is Northern Australian Kriol, which has grown into a marker of Aboriginal identity, following large-scale upheavals in the traditional patterns of communication in the wake of settler, government and mission activities.

This function of Creoles is often ignored even by their speakers, and to make it explicit could help to reduce the pressure from related standard languages, which is suffered by many Creoles. Recognition of their constructive role in the formation and maintenance of stable societies may well bring social and economic benefits. Instead of labelling them as diseconomies and working towards their eradication, government and education bodies should try to use them for constructive purposes. As long as research on Pidgins and Creoles remains insufficiently funded, these languages will remain under-utilised resources.

Outlook

I hope that I have succeeded in demonstrating that Pidgins and Creoles deserve to be taken seriously not only by linguists and sociolinguists, but also by their speakers and the governments of those countries where they are spoken. Whether or not we can learn and profit from the insights afforded by them is our choice. What I mean is that there have been two trends in dealing with them:

(a) mainstreaming; and

(b) recognizing their otherness.

Mainstreaming has meant, among other things, turning highly variable, transnational communication systems into bounded or regional languages. Thus normalized and made into "modern" languages, Pidgins and Creoles will not look very different from English or French, and will confirm the linguists' Eurocentric views.

Recognizing their otherness has involved abandoning notions of mixed grammar, bounded speech communities, systematicity and so on, and will force the analysts to consider situation and macrocontrast as inalienable parts of analysis.

When I drafted the first edition of this book in 1984, I was only dimly aware of the latter possibility. As I learn more from the study of Pidgins and Creoles, I can sense the very genuine potential offered by these languages to bring about a radical reorientation in our thinking about language.

343

Bibliography

Adam, Lucien 1883 *Les idiomes négro-aryen et maléo-ayren*. Paris: Maisonneuve.

Adamson, Lilian & van Rossem, Cefas 1995 Creole literature. Arends et al. (eds), pp 75-84.

Adler, Max K 1977 *Pidgins, Creoles and lingua francas*. Hamburg: Buske.

Adone, Dany 1994 *The acquisition of Mauritian Creole*. Amsterdam: Benjamins.

Agheyisi, Rebecca 1971 West African Pidgin English: simplification and simplicity. Unpublished PhD thesis, Stanford University.

Agheyisi, Rebecca & Fishman, Joshua A 1973 Language attitude studies. A brief survey of methodological approaches. *Anthropological Linguistics* 12:137-51.

Aitchison, Jean 1981 *Language change: progress or decay*. London: Fontana.

—— 1983 Pidgins, Creoles and Child Language. Ms, London School of Economics.

—— 1995 Chimps, children and creoles: the need for caution. Puppel (ed.), pp 1-17.

Aitken-Cade, S E 1951 *So you want to learn the language: An amusing and instructive Kitchen Kaffir dictionary*. Salisbury: Centafrican Press.

Akers, Glenn 1981 Admissibility conditions on final consonant clusters in the Jamaican continuum. Muysken (ed.), pp 1-25.

Albert, H 1922 *Mittelalterlicher englisch-französischer Jargon*. Halle: Niemeyer.

Alleyne, Mervyn C 1963 Communication and politics in Jamaica. *Caribbean Studies* 3(2):22-61.

—— 1971 Acculturation and the social matrix of creolization. Hymes (ed.), pp 169-86.

—— 1980 Introduction. Theoretical orientations in Creole studies. Valdman & Highfield (eds), pp 1-19.

Allsopp, Richard 1980 How does the creole lexicon expand? Valdman & Highfield (eds), pp 89-108.

—— 1983 Review article: Dictionary of Jamaican English. *English World-Wide* 4:92-96.

Amsler, Jean 1952 Schnuckiputzi, ou la naissance d'un sabir. *Vie et langage* 59:71-76.

[Anderson, Samuel] 1885 *L'Evangil sélon S Matthié (dan langaz créol Maurice)*. London: British and Foreign Bible Society.

—— 1888 *L'Evangil sélon S Marc (...)*. London: British and Foreign Bible Society.

—— 1892 *L'Evangil sélon S Luk (...)*. London: British and Foreign Bible Society.

—— 1896 *L'Evangil sélon S Jan (...)*. London: British and Foreign Bible Society.

—— 1900 *L'Ouvraz Apotr (...)*. London: British and Foreign Bible Society.

Anon. 1859 Canton English. *Household Words* 15:450-52.

Anon. [ca 1830] *Hung maou tung yang fan hwa*. [n p]: [n pblr].

Anon. [ca 1935] *Wörterbuch mit Redewendungen*. Alexishafen.

Anthonisz, R G 1907 *Report on the Dutch records in the Government Archives at Colombo*. Colombo: H C Cottle.

Antonissen, Rob 1980 *Die Afrikaanse letterkunde van aanvang tot hede*. Cape Town: Nasionale Boekhandel.

Appel, René & Muysken, Pieter 1987 *Language contact and bilingualism*. London: Edward Arnold.

Appel, René & Verhoeven, Ludo 1995 Decolonization, language planning and education. Arends et al. (eds), pp 65-74.

Ardener, Edwin W (ed.) 1971 *Social anthropology and language*. London: Tavistock.

Arends, Jacques 1993 Towards a gradualist model of creolization. Byrne, Francis & Holm, John (eds), *Atlantic meets Pacific*, Amsterdam: Benjamins, pp 371-80.

—— (ed.) 1995 *The early stages of creolization*. Amsterdam: Benjamins.

—— [*forthcoming*] The origin of the Portuguese element in the Surinam Creoles. Huber & Parkvall (eds).

Arends, Jacques & Bruyn, Adrienne 1995 Gradualist and developmental hypotheses. Arends, Muysken & Smith (eds), pp 111-20.

Arends, J, Muysken, P & Smith, N (eds) 1995 *Pidgins and Creoles. An introduction*. Amsterdam: Benjamins.

[Atkinson, Hoffman] 1879 *Revised and enlarged edition of exercises in the Yokohama dialect*. Yokohama.

Aub-Buscher, Gertrud 1984 Non-Romance elements in the vocabulary of Trinidad French Creole. Unpublished ms.

Aufinger, Albert 1948-49 Secret languages of the small islands near Madang. *South Pacific*, 3:90-95, 113-20.

Australian Government 1932 *Annual Report to the League of Nations*. Canberra.

Baessler, Arthur 1895 *Südsee-Bilder*. Berlin: Georg Reimer.

Bailey, Beryl L 1966 *Jamaican Creole syntax*. Cambridge: CUP.

Bailey, Charles-James N 1973 *Variation and linguistic theory*. Arlington: Center for Applied Linguistics.

—— 1977 Variation and linguistic analysis. *Papiere zur Linguistik* 12:5-56.

—— 1980 The role of language development in a theory of language. *Papiere zur Linguistik* 22:33-46.

—— 1982 *On the yin and yang nature of language*. Ann Arbor: Karoma.

—— 1996 *Essays on time-based linguistic analysis*. Oxford: Clarendon.

Bailey, Charles-James N & Harris, R (eds) 1985 *Developmental mechanisms of language*. Oxford: Pergamon.

Bailey, Charles-James N & Maroldt, K 1977 The French lineage of English. Meisel (ed.), pp 21-53.

Bailey, Richard W & Gorlach, Manfred 1982 *English as a world language*. Ann Arbor: University of Michigan Press.

Baker, Philip 1982 On the origins of the first Mauritians and of the Creole language of their descendants. Baker & Corne, pp 131-260.

—— 1987 Historical developments in Chinese Pidgin English and the nature of the relationships between the various Pidgin Englishes of the Pacific region. *JPCL* 2:163-207.

—— 1990 Off target? *JPCL* 5:107-20.

—— 1993 Australian influence on Melanesian Pidgin. *Te Reo* 36:3-67.

—— 1995a Motivation in Creole genesis. Baker (ed.), pp 3-15.

—— (ed.) 1995b *From contact to Creole and beyond*. London: University of Westminster Press.

—— 1996a Australian and Melanesian Pidgin English and the *fellows* in between. Baker & Syea (eds), pp 243-58.

—— 1996b Productive *fellow*. Wurm et al. (eds), pp 533-36.

Baker, Philip & Corne, Chris 1982 *Isle de France Creole*. Ann Arbor: Karoma.

Baker, Philip & Mühlhäusler, Peter 1990 From business to Pidgin. *Journal of Asian Pacific Communication* 1:87-115.

Baker, Philip & Syea, Anand (eds) 1996 *Changing meanings, changing functions*. London: University of Westminster Press.

Baker, Sydney 1953 *The Australian language*. Melbourne: Sun Books.

Bakker, Peter & Muysken, Pieter 1995 Mixed languages and language intertwining. Arends et al. (eds), pp 41-52.

Balint, Andras 1969 *English, Pidgin and French dictionary of sports and phrase book.* Rabaul: Trinity Press.

Barrena, Natalio 1957 *Gramática Annobonesa.* Madrid: Consejo Superior de Investigaciones Cientificas, (second edition).

Bateson, Gregory 1944 Pidgin English and cross-cultural communication. *Transactions of the New York Academy of Sciences* 2(6):137-41.

Bauer, Anton 1975 *Der soziolinguistische Status und die Funktionsproblematik von Reduktionssprachen.* Frankfurt: Lang.

Baumann, Adelbert 1916 *Weltdeutsch.* Munich: Huber.

Baxter, Alan N 1985 Kristang (Malacca Creole Portuguese). Unpubl. PhD thesis, Australian National University.

—— 1990 Notes on the Creole Portuguese of Bidan, East Timor. *JPCL* 5:1-38.

Bee, Darlene 1972 Phonological interference between Usarufa and Pidgin English. *Kivung* 5(2):69-95.

Bell, Henry L 1971 Language and the army of Papua New Guinea. *Army Journal* 264:31-42.

Bell, Roger T 1976 *Sociolinguistics.* London: Batsford.

Berry, Jack 1971 Pidgins and Creoles in Africa. *Current Trends in Linguistics* 7:510-36.

Bickerton, Derek 1974 Priorities in Creole studies. DeCamp & Hancock (eds), pp 85-87.

—— 1975a Can English and Pidgin be kept apart? McElhanon (ed.), pp 21-27.

—— 1975b *Dynamics of a Creole system.* London: CUP.

—— 1975c Creolization, linguistic universals, natural semantax and the brain. Paper presented at the International Conference on Pidgins and Creoles, Honolulu.

—— 1976 Pidgin and Creole studies. *Annual Review of Anthropology* 5:169-93.

—— 1977 Some problems of acceptability and grammaticality in Pidgins and Creoles. Greenbaum, S (ed.) *Acceptability in language,* The Hague: Mouton, pp 27-37.

—— 1979 Beginnings. Hill (ed.), pp 1-22.

—— 1980 Decreolization and the creole continuum. Valdman & Highfield (eds.), pp 107-28.

—— 1981 *Roots of language.* Ann Arbor: Karoma.

—— 1984 The language bioprogram hypothesis. *The Behavioral and Brain Sciences* 7:173-88.

—— 1989 The lexical learning hypothesis and the pidgin–creole cycle. Pütz & Dirven (eds), pp 11-31.

Bickerton, Derek & Odo, Carol 1976 Change and variation in Hawaiian English. Final Report on NSF Project No. GS-39748.

Bigsby, Christopher W E (ed.) 1980 *The second Black American renaissance: essays in black literature.* London: Greenwood Press.

Bley, Bernhard 1912 *Praktisches Handbuch zur Erlernung der Nordgazellensprache.* Munster: Westfälische Vereinsdruckerei.

Bloomfield, Leonard 1933 *Language.* New York: Holt, Rinehart & Winston.

Bodemann, Y M & Ostow, R 1975 Lingua Franca und Pseudo-Pidgin in der Bundesrepublik. *Zeitschrift für Literaturwissenschaft und Linguistik* 18:122-46.

Bold, J D 1961 *Fanagalo: phrasebook, grammar and dictionary.* Johannesburg: Keartland.

Bollée, Annegret 1975 Reduplication and iteration in Seychelles Creole. Paper presented at the International Conference on Pidgins and Creoles, Honolulu.

—— 1977a Remarques sur la genèse des parlers créoles de l'Océan Indien. Meisel, (ed.), pp 137-49.

—— 1977b Pidgins und Kreolische Sprachen. *Studium Linguistik* 3:48-76.

—— 1980 Zum Projekt eines Dictionnaire étymologique du créole. Bore et al. (eds), *Romanica Europaea et Americana*. Bonn: Bouvier Verlag, pp 68-76.

Borchardt, Karl 1926 Tok Boi Wörterbuch. Unpublished ms, Manus.

—— 1930 Anleitung zur Erlernung des Tok Boi. Unpublished ms, Manus

Braithwaite, E K 1984 *History of the voice*. London: New Beacon Books.

Brash, Elton 1975 Tok Pisin. *Meanjin Quarterly*, 34:320-27.

Breinburg, Petronella 1984 Linguistic shift – urban Creoles and the black child in European inner city schools. *York Papers in Linguistics* 11:31-38.

Brenninkmeyer, Leo 1924 Einführung ins Pidgin English - Ein Versuch. Unpublished manuscript, Kamacham, Papua New Guinea.

Bright, William (ed.) 1966 *Sociolinguistics. Proceeding of the UCLA Sociolinguistics Conference, 1964.* The Hague: Mouton.

Brinton, Daniel G (ed.) 1883 *The Güegüence; a comedy ballet in the Nahuatl-Spanish dialect of Nicaragua.* Philadelphia: D G Brinton.

Bromilow, William E 1929 *Twenty years among primitive Papuans.* London: Epworth Press.

Bruner, Jerome 1981 The social context of language acquisition. *Language and Communication* 1:155-78.

Buchner, M 1885 Kamerun-Englisch. *Deutsche Kolonialzeitung* 2:676-78.

Bushell, Keith B 1936 *Papuan Epic.* London: Seeley, Service.

Butcher, Benjamin T 1963 *We lived with headhunters.* London: Hodder & Stoughton.

Byrne, Francis 1991 Approaches to "missing" internal (and external) arguments in serial structure: some presumed difficulties. Byrne & Huebner (eds), pp 207-22.

Byrne, Francis & Huebner, Thom (eds) 1991 *Development and structures of Creole languages.* Amsterdam: Benjamins.

Camden, William G 1977 *A descriptive dictionary. Bislama to English.* Vila (Vanuatu): Maropa Bookshop.

—— 1979 Parallels in structure of lexicon and syntax between New Hebrides Bislama and the South Santo language spoken at Tangoa. *Papers in Pidgin and Creole Linguistics* 2:51-118 (Pacific Linguistics A-57).

Cameron, Charlotte 1923 *Two years in the South Seas.* London: Fisher Unwin.

Capell, Arthur 1969 The changing status of Melanesian Pidgin. *Mondo Lingvo-Problemo* 1:102-15.

Carr, Elizabeth B 1972 *Da kine talk.* Honolulu: University Press of Hawaii.

Carrington, Lawrence 1992 Images of Creole space. *JPCL* 7:93-99.

Casely-Hayford, Joseph E 1913 *Ethiopia unbound.* London: C M Phillips.

Cassidy, Frederic G 1966 Multiple etymologies in Jamaican Creole. *American Speech* 41:211-15.

—— 1971 Tracing the pidgin element in Jamaican Creole. Hymes (ed.), pp 202-15.

—— 1975 Interjections in Jamaican Creole. Paper presented at the International Conference on Pidgins and Creoles, Honolulu.

Cérol, Marie-Josée 1991 *Une introduction au créole guadeloupéen.* [n p]: Jasor.

Charpentier, Jean-Michel 1984 Le pidgin bichelamar, avant et après l'indépendance de Vanuatu. *York Papers in Linguistics* 11:51-61

—— 1995 [Ms on the Portuguese Creole of Macau, to appear in *Papia*].

Charpentier, Jean-Michel & Tryon, D T 1982 Functions of Bislama in the New Hebrides and in independent Vanuatu. *English World-Wide* 3:146-60.

Chaudenson, Robert 1974 *Le lexique du parler créole de la Réunion.* Paris: Champion, 2 vols.

—— 1979 *Les créoles français.* Paris: Fernand Nathan.

—— 1992 *Des îles, des hommes, des langues.* Paris: L'Harmattan.

Cheshire, Jenny (ed.) 1991 *English around the world.* Cambridge: CUP.

Chignell, Arthur K 1915 *An outpost in Papua.* London: Smith, Elder & Co.

Chomsky, Noam 1965 *Aspects of the theory of syntax.* Cambridge (Mass.): MIT Press.

—— 1968 *Language and mind.* New York: Harcourt Brace.

Chrestien, François 1822 *Les essais d'un bobre africain.* Port Louis: Deroulède.

Churchill, William 1911 *Beach-la-Mar.* Washington, DC: Carnegie Institution.

Clahsen, Harald 1984 Der Erwerb von Kasusmarkierungen in der deutschen Kindersprache. *Linguistische Berichte* 89:1-31.

Clark, Donald H 1955 Pidgin English: South Pacific polyglot. *Pacific Discovery* 8(5):8-12.

Clark, Ross 1979 In search of Beach-la-Mar. *Te Reo* 22:3-64.

—— 1996 English-Maori contact languages in New Zealand. Wurm et al. (eds), pp175-76.

[Clayton, Jean (ed.)] 1996 *Desert schools.* Canberra: National Language and Literacy Institute.

Clements, J Clancy 1991 The Indo-Portuguese Creoles: languages in transition. *Hispania* 74:637-46.

—— 1992 Foreigner talk and the origins of Pidgin Portuguese. *JPCL* 7:75-92.

Clyne, Michael G 1968 Zum Pidgin-Deutsch der Gastarbeiter. *Zeitschrift für Mundartforschung* 35:130-39.

—— 1975 German and English working pidgins. *Linguistic Communications* 13:1-20.

—— 1977 Bilingualism of the elderly. *Talanya* 4:45-56.

—— 1978 Some remarks on foreigner talk. Proceedings of the German-Scandinavian Symposium on Language Problems of Migrant Workers, Roskilde.

—— 1981 Second-generation foreigner talk in Australia. *International Journal for the Sociology of Language* 28:69-80.

Coates, William A 1969 The German Pidgin-Italian of the 16th-century lanzichenecchi. *Papers from the Fourth Annual Kansas Linguistics Conference,* pp 66-74.

Coelho, F Adolpho 1880-86 Os dialectos romanicos ou neo-latinos na África, Ásia e América. *Boletim da Sociedade de Geographia* 2:129-96, 3:451-78, 6:705-55.

Cole, Desmond T 1953 Fanagalo and the Bantu Languages in South Africa. *African Studies* 12:1-9.

Comrie, Bernard 1981 *Language universals and linguistic typology.* Oxford: Basil Blackwell.

Corder, S P 1976 Language continua and the interlanguage hypothesis. Corder & Roulet (eds), pp 11-17.

Corder, S P & Roulet, E (eds) 1976 *The notions of simplification, interlanguages and pidgins and their relation to second language pedogogy.* Geneva: Droz.

Corne, Chris 1982 A contrastive analysis of Reunion and Isle de France Creole French. Baker & Corne, pp 7-130.

—— 1995 A contact induced and vernacalorized language: how Melanesian is Tayo? Baker (ed.), pp 121-48.

Corne, C, Coleman, D & Curnow, S 1996 Clause reduction in asyndetic coordination in Isle de France Creole: the "serial verbs" problem. Baker & Syea (eds), pp 129-54.

Coulanges, J 1967 L'expressivité en créole. Mémoire de sortie présenté à la Faculté d'Ethnologie de Port-au-Prince, Haïti.

Cozzolino, Mimmo with Blaine, Geoff & Adams, Philip 1980 *Symbols of Australia*. Ringwood: Penguin Australia.

Craig, Dennis R 1980 Communication, Creole, and conceptualization. Valdman & Highfield (eds), pp 245-66.

Crawford, James M (ed.) 1975 *Studies in South-Eastern Indian languages*. Athens, Ga: University of Georgia Press.

—— 1978 *The Mobilian trade language*. Knoxville: University of Tennessee Press.

Crowley, Terry 1990a *Beach-la-Mar to Bislama*. Oxford: OUP.

—— 1990b The position of Melanesian Pidgin in Vanuatu and Papua New Guinea. Verhaar (ed.), pp 1-18.

—— 1993 Père Pionnier and later 19th-century Bislama. *JPCL* 8:207-26.

Crystal, David 1992 *Dictionary of language and languages*. Harmondsworth: Penguin.

Culler, Jonathan 1983 *Barthes*. London: Fontana.

Curtis, S 1977 *Genie: a psycholinguistic study of a modern-day "wild child"*. New York: Academic Press.

Daiber, Albert 1902 *Eine Australien und Südsee fahrt*. Leipzig: Trubner.

Dalphinis, Morgan 1982 Approaches to the study of Creole languages - The case of West African language influences. *Occasional Papers on Caribbean Languages and Dialect* 2:8-14.

DeCamp, David 1967 African day names in Jamaica. *Language* 43:137-49.

—— 1971a Introduction: the study of Pidgin and Creole languages. Hymes (ed.), pp 13-39.

—— 1971b Toward a generative analysis of a post-creole speech continuum. Hymes (ed.), pp 349-70.

—— 1974 Neutralizations, iteratives, and ideophones: the locus of language in Jamaica. DeCamp & Hancock (eds), pp 42-60.

—— 1977 The development of Pidgin and Creole studies. Valdman (ed.), pp 3-20.

DeCamp, David & Hancock, Ian F (eds) 1974 *Pidgins and Creoles*. Washington, DC: Georgetown University Press.

Decker, Thomas 1988 *Juliohs Siza*. Umeå: University of Umeå (Krio Publications Series, vol. 4).

Defoe, Daniel 1719 *Robinson Crusoe*. London: W Taylor.

Dekker, G 1958 *Afrikaanse Literatuur - Geskiedenis*. Cape Town: Nasou.

Dennis, Jamie & Scott, Jeme 1975 Creole formation and reorganization: evidence for diachronic change in synchronic variation. Paper presented at the International Conference on Pidgins and Creoles, Honolulu.

De Rooij, Vincent 1995 Shaba Swahili. Arends et al. (eds), pp 179-90.

Devonish, Hubert 1984 Creole language standardization in Guyana. Race, class and urban/rural factors. *York Papers in Linguistics* 11:63-73.

—— 1986 *Language and liberation: Creole language politics in the Caribbean*, London: Karia Press.

Dillard, Joey L 1972 *Black English*. New York: Random House.

Dixon, Robert M W 1971 A method of semantic description. Steinberg & Jakobovits (eds), pp 436-71.

—— 1980 *The Languages of Australia*. Cambridge: CUP.

D'Offay de Rieux, Danielle 1980 Creole and educational policy in the Seychelles. Valdman & Highfield (eds), pp 267-72.

Dorfmann, Ariel & Mattelart, Armands 1975 *How to read Donald Duck*. New York: International General.

Dogberry (pseud.) 1894 *Humours and oddities of the London Police Courts*. London, Leadenhall.

Domingue, Nicole Z 1977 Middle English: another Creole? *Journal of Creole Studies* 1(1):89-106.

Dressler, Wolfgang 1977a Wortbildung bei Sprachverfall. Brekie, H E & Kastovsky, D (eds), *Perspektiven der Wortbildungsforschung*. Berlin: Bouvier, pp 62-69.

—— (ed.) 1977b Language death issue. *International Journal of the Sociology of Language* 12.

Ducrocq, Louis 1902 L'idiome enfantin d'une race enfantine. *Revue de Lille* 20:439-58.

Duranti, Alessandro 1981 *The Samoan Fono: a sociolinguistic study*. Canberra: Pacific Linguistics (B-80).

Dutton, Thomas E 1970 Informal English in the Torres Straits. Ramson, William S (ed.), *English transported*. Canberra: Australian National University Press, pp 137-60.

—— 1973 *Conversational New Guinea Pidgin*. Canberra: Pacific Linguistics (D-12).

—— 1976 Standardization and modernization of Hiri Motu: issues and problems. *Kivung* 9:99-125.

—— 1978 The "Melanesian problem" and language change and disappearance in South-Eastern Papua New Guinea. Unpublished ms, Australian National University.

—— 1980 *Queensland Canefields English of the late nineteenth century*. Canberra: Pacific Linguistics (D-29).

—— 1982 On the frontiers of contact: non-verbal communication and peaceful European expansion in the South-West Pacific. Unpublished ms, Australian National University.

—— 1983a The origin and spread of Aboriginal Pidgin English in Queensland. *Aboriginal History* 7:90-122.

—— 1983b Birds of a feather: a pair of rare pidgins from the Gulf of Papua. Woolford & Washabaugh (eds), pp 77-105.

—— 1985a *Police Motu: iena sivarai (its story)*. Port Moresby: University of Papua New Guinea Press

—— 1985b Teaching and Tok Pisin. Wurm & Mühlhäusler (eds), pp 535-37.

—— 1987 Successful intercourse was had with the natives. Laycock, Donald C & Winter, W (eds), *A world of language*. Canberra: Pacific Linguistics (C-100), pp 153-71.

Dutton, Thomas E & Mühlhäusler, Peter 1979 Papuan Pidgin English and Hiri Motu. Wurm (ed.), pp 209-23.

—— & —— 1984 Queensland Kanaka English. *English World-Wide* 4:231-63.

Dutton, Thomas E & Thomas, Dick 1985 *A new course in Tok Pisin*. Canberra: Pacific Linguistics (D-67).

Dutton, Thomas E & Voorhoeve, C L 1974 *Beginning Hiri Motu*. Canberra: Pacific Linguistics (D-24).

Eades, Diana 1982 You gotta know how to talk... : information seeking in South-East Queensland Aboriginal Society. *Australian Journal of Linguistics* 2:61-82.

—— 1991 Communicative strategies in Aboriginal English. Romaine (ed.), pp 84-93.

Edmondson, Jerry A 1984 Linguistic naturalness. *The encyclopedic dictionary of psychology.* Oxford: Basil Blackwell.

—— 1985 Biological foundations of language universals. Bailey & Harris (eds), pp 109-30.

Edwards, Jay 1974 African influences on the English of San Andrés Island, Colombia. DeCamp & Hancock (eds), pp 1-26.

Edwards, Viv 1981 Patterns of language use in the Black British community. *English World-Wide* 2:154-64.

Edwards, Viv & Ladd, Paddy 1984 The linguistic status of British Sign Language. *York Papers in Linguistics* 11:75-82.

Eersel, Christian 1971 Prestige in choice of language and linguistic form. Hymes (ed.), pp 317-22.

Egger, Emile 1879 *Observations et réflexions sur la développement de l'intelligence et du langage chez les enfants.* Paris: Picard.

Ehrhart, Sabine 1991 The development of the preverbal markers in St. Louis Creole: the formation of a TMA system? Paper presented at the Sixth International Conference on Austronesian Languages, Honolulu.

—— 1992 The development of the preverbal markers in St. Louis Creole: the formation of a TMA system? *Language Sciences* 14:233-47.

—— 1993 *Le créole français de St-Louis (le tayo) en Nouvelle-Calédonie.* Hamburg: Buske.

Ehrhart-Kneher, Sabine 1996 Palmerston English. Wurm et al. (eds), pp 523-32.

Emonts, Johannes 1922 *Ins Steppen – und Bergland Innerkameruns.* Aachen: Xaveriusverlag.

Encina, Juan del 1520 [See Harvey, L P, Jones, R O & Whinnom, K 1967 Lingua Franca in a villancico by Encina, *Revue de Littérature Comparée* 41:573-79 for what is known of this text.]

Escure, Geneviève 1981 Decreolization in a creole continuum: Belize. Highfield & Valdman (eds), pp 27-39.

Faine, Jules 1939 *Le créole dans l'univers.* Port-au-Prince: Imprimerie de l'Etat.

Farrar, Frederic W 1899 *Language and languages.* London: Longmans, Green.

Feist, Sigmund 1932 The origin of the Germanic languages and the Indo-Europeanizing of North Europe. *Language* 8:245-54.

Féral, Carole de 1980 *Le Pidgin-English camerounais.* Nice: Centre d'Etude des Plurilinguismes.

Ferguson, Charles A 1971 Absence of copula and the notion of simplicity. Hymes (ed.), pp 141-50.

—— 1975 Toward a characterization of English foreigner talk. *Anthropological Linguistics* 17:1-14.

—— 1977 Simplified register, broken language and Gastarbeiterdeutsch. Molony, Zobl & Stolting (eds), pp 25-39.

Ferguson, Charles A & DeBose, C E 1977 Simplified registers, broken language and pidginization. Valdman (ed.) [1977b], pp 99-125.

Ferraz, Luiz 1974 A linguistic appraisal of Angolar. Ferraz, Luiz (ed.) *Memoriam Antonio Jorye Dias,* Lisbon: Instituto de Alta Cultura, pp 177-86.

Figueroa, John J 1971 Creole Studies. Hymes (ed.), pp 503-08.

Fillmore, Charles J 1971 Types of lexical information. Steinberg & Jakobovits (eds), pp 370-92.

Fine, M G, Anderson, C R & Eckles, G 1979 Black English on black situation comedies. *Journal of Communication* 27(3):21-29.

Firth, Stewart G 1973 German recruitment and employment of labourers in the western Pacific before the First World War. D Phil thesis, Oxford University.

Fishman, J A, Ferguson, C A & Das Gupta, J (eds) 1968 *Language problems of developing nations.* New York: John Wiley.

Flanigan, Beverly 1981 American Indian English in history and literacy: the evolution of a pidgin from reality to stereotype. PhD thesis, Indiana University.

Fleischmann, Ulrich 1978 Das Französisch-Kreolische in der Karibik. Habilitations thesis, Free University Berlin.

Foley, William A 1984 Nature vs nurture: the genesis of language. A review article. *Comparative Studies in Society and History* 26:335-44.

Foster, Robert & Mühlhäusler, Peter 1996 *Language and Communication* 16:1-16.

Foster, R, Mühlhäusler, P & Clarke, P *[forthcoming]* Give me back my name: the classification of Aboriginal people in South Australia. [Expected to appear in *Papers in Pidgin and Creole Linguistics* 5, Canberra: Pacific Linguistics.]

Fourcade, Georges 1930 *Z'histoires la case.* Saint-Denis: Drouhet.

Frake, Charles O 1971 Lexical origins and semantic structure in Philippine Creole Spanish. Hymes (ed.), pp 223-42.

Franklin, Karl J 1975 Vernaculars as bridges to cross-cultural understanding. McElhanon (ed.), pp 138-49.

—— 1992 *Traim tasol: vocabulary testing in Tok Pisin.* Canberra: Pacific Linguistics (D-85).

French, A 1953 Pidgin English in New Guinea. *Australian Quarterly* 25(4):57-60.

Freyberg, Paul G 1975 Bai yumi mekim wanem bilong helpim Tok Pisin? McElhanon (ed.), pp 28-35.

Friederici, Georg 1911 Pidgin-Englisch in Deutsch-Neuguinea. *Koloniale Rundschau* 3:92-106.

Gaywood, H C 1951 The use of Pidgin English. *South Pacific* 5:101-03.

Gebhard, Jerry G 1979 Thai adaption of English language features: a study of Thai English. *Papers in Pidgin and Creole linguistics* 2:201-16. (Pacific Linguistics, A-57).

Genthe, Siegfried 1908 *Samoa.* Berlin: Allgemeiner Verein für Deutsche Literatur.

Gilbert, Glenn 1980 *Pidgin and Creole languages: selected essays by Hugo Schuchardt.* London: CUP.

—— 1983 Two early surveys of the world's Pidgins and Creoles: a comparison between Schuchardt and Reinecke. Paper presented at the York Creole Conference.

Giles, Howard 1980 Ethnicity markers in speech. Scherer & Giles (eds), pp 251-90.

Gilman, Charles 1978 A comparison of Jamaican Creole and Cameroonian Pidgin English. *English Studies* 59:57-65.

Givón, Talmy 1979 Prolegomena to any sane creology. Hancock (ed.), pp 3-36.

Gonzales, Ambrose E 1922 *The black border: Gullah stories of the Carolina coast.* Columbia (SC): The State Co.

Goodman, J S 1967 The development of a dialect of English-Japanese Pidgin. *Anthropological Linguistics* 9:43-55.

Goodman, Morris F 1964 *A comparative study of Creole French dialects.* The Hague: Mouton.

—— 1971 The strange case of Mbugu. Hymes (ed.), pp 243-54.

Gordon, J C B 1981 *Verbal deficit.* London: Croon Helm.

Greenberg, Joseph H (ed.) 1963 *Universals of language.* Cambridge (Mass.): MIT Press.

Greenfield, William 1830 *A defence of the Surinam Negro-English version of the New Testament.* London. (Reprinted in *JPCL* 1:255-66, 1986).

Grimshaw, Allen D 1971 Some social forces and some social functions of Pidgin and Creole languages. Hymes (ed.), pp 427-46.

Grimshaw, Beatrice 1912 *Guinea gold.* London: Mills & Boon.

Gumperz, John J 1982 *Discourse strategies.* Cambridge: CUP.

Gumperz, John J & Wilson, R 1971 Convergence and creolization: a case from the Indo-Aryan-Dravidian border. Hymes (ed.), pp 151-68.

Haas, Mary R 1975 What is Mobilian? Crawford (ed.), pp 257-63.

Hagen, Gunther von 1910 *Kurzes Handbuch für Negerenglisch.* Berlin: Dingeldey.

Hale, Horatio 1846 *Ethnography and philosophy.* Philadelphia: C Sherman. (vol. 4 of *United States exploring expeditions. During the years 1838, 1839, 1840, 1841, 1842*).

Hale, Horatio, E 1890 *An international idiom. A manual of the Oregon trade language or 'Chinook Jargon'.* London: Whittaker.

Hall, Edward T 1959 *The silent language.* New York: Doubleday.

Hall, Robert A 1943 *Melanesian Pidgin English: grammar, texts, vocabulary.* Baltimore: Linguistic Society of America.

—— 1944 Chinese Pidgin English: grammar and texts. *Journal of the American Oriental Society* 64:95-113.

—— 1948 The linguistic structure of Taki Taki. *Language* 24:92-116.

—— 1953 *Haitian Creole: grammar, texts, vocabulary.* Philadelphia: American Folklore Society (Memoir 43).

—— 1954a The status of Melanesian Pidgin. *Australian Quarterly* 26(2):85-92.

—— 1954b The provision of literature in Neo-Melanesian. *South Pacific* 7:942-44.

—— 1955a Pidgin English in the British Solomon Islands. *Australian Quarterly* 27(4):68-74.

—— 1955b *Hands off Pidgin English.* Sydney: Pacific Publications.

—— 1956 Innovations in Melanesian Pidgin (Neo-Melanesian). *Oceania* 26:91-109.

—— 1958 Creolized languages and genetic relationships. *Word* 14:367-73.

—— 1959 Stori bilong Teseus na Ariadne. *Scientific American* 200:128-29.

—— 1961 How Pidgin English has evolved. *New Scientist* 9:413-15.

—— 1962 The life cycle of pidgin languages. *Lingua* 11:151-56.

—— 1966 *Pidgin and Creole languages.* Ithaca: Cornell University Press.

—— 1972 Pidgins and Creoles as standard languages. Pride & Holmes (eds), pp 142-54.

—— 1975 *Stormy petrel in linguistics.* Ithaca, NY: Spoken Language Services.

Hall, Robert A, Bateson, G & Whiting, J W 1942 *Melanesian Pidgin English short grammar and vocabulary, (...).* Baltimore: Linguistic Society of America.

Haller, Hermann W 1981 Between standard Italian and Creole. *Word* 32:181-94.

Halliday, Michael A K 1974 *Explorations in the functions of language.* London: Edward Arnold.

—— 1976 Anti-languages. *American Anthropologist*, 78:570-84.

—— 1992 New ways of analysing meaning: the challenge to applied linguistics. Pütz, M (ed.), pp 31-58.

Hancock, Ian F 1969 A provisional comparison of the English-based Atlantic Creoles. *African Language Review* 8:7-72.

—— 1971 A map and list of Pidgin and Creole languages. Hymes (ed.), pp 509-624.

—— 1972 Some Dutch-derived items in Java Creole Portuguese. *Orbis* 12:549-54.

—— 1974 Shelta: a problem of classification. Hancock & DeCamp (eds), pp 130-37.

—— 1975 Lexical expansion within a closed system. Paper presented at the International Conference on Pidgins and Creoles, Honolulu.

—— 1976 Nautical sources of Krio vocabulary. *International Journal of the Sociology of Language* 7:23-36.

—— 1977a Appendix. Repertory of Pidgin and Creole languages. Valdman (ed.), [1977b], pp 362-69.

—— 1977b Recovering Pidgin genesis: approaches and problems. Valdman (ed.) [1977b], pp 277-94.

—— 1979 On the origins of the term pidgin. Hancock (ed.), pp 81-86.

—— (ed.) 1979 *Readings on Creole studies*. Ghent: Story-scientia.

—— 1980 Lexical expansion in Creole languages. Valdman & Highfield (eds), pp 63-88.

—— 1987 A preliminary classification of the Anglophone Atlantic Creoles. Gilbert, Gilbert (ed.) 1987 *Pidgin and Creole languages: essays in memory of John F Reinecke*. Honolulu: University of Hawaii Press, pp 264-334.

Harding, E M 1984 Foreigner talk: a conversational-analysis approach. *York Papers in Linguistics* 11:141-52.

Harris, Joel C 1883 *Nights with Uncle Remus (...)*. Boston: J R Osgood.

Harris, John W 1984 Language contact, pidgins and the emergence of Kriol in the Northern Territory. PhD thesis, University of Queensland.

Harris, Roy 1977 *On the possibility of linguistic change*. Oxford: Clarendon Press.

—— 1980 *The language makers*. London: Duckworth.

—— 1981 *The language myth*. London: Duckworth.

—— 1982 The speech-communication model in 20th century linguistics and its sources. Hattori, Shirô & Kazuko, Inoue, *Proceedings of the XIIIth International Congress of Linguists*. Tokyo: CIPL, pp 864-69.

Haugen, Einar 1966 Schizoglossia and the linguistic norm. Bright, William (ed.) *Sociolinguistics*, The Hague: Mouton, pp 63-73.

Hawkes, Terence 1977 *Structuralism and semiotics*. London: Methuen.

Heine, Bernd 1970 *Status and use of African lingua francas*. Munich: Weltiorum.

—— 1973 *Pidgin-Sprachen im Bantu-Bereich*. Berlin: Reimer.

—— 1975 Some generalizations of African-based Pidgins. Paper presented at the International Conference on Pidgins and Creoles, Honolulu.

Hellinger, Marlis 1972 Aspects of Belizean Creole. *Folia Linguistica* 6:22-39.

—— 1979 Across base language boundaries: the Creole of Belize. Hancock (ed.), pp 315-33.

Helton, E C N 1943 *Booklet on Pidgin English as used in the mandated territory of New Guinea*. Brisbane: W H Adams.

Herman, L & Herman, M S 1943. *Foreign dialects: a manual for actors, directors and writers*. New York: Theatre Arts Books.

Herskovits, Melville J 1941 *the myth of the Negro past*. New York: Harper & Brothers.

Héry, M L 1828 *Esquisses africaines*. Paris: J Rigal.

Hesseling, Dirk C 1905 *Het Negerhollands der Deense Antillen*. Leiden: Sigthoff.

—— 1910 Overblijfsels van de Nederlandse taal op Ceylon. *Tijdschrift voor Nederlandsche Taal-en Letterkunde* 29:303-12.

—— 1979 *On the origin and formation of Creoles: a miscellany of articles*. Ann Arbor: Karoma (translated from Dutch by Markey, T L & Roberge, P T).

Hesse-Wartegg, Ernst von 1898 *Schantung und Deutsch-China*. Leipzig: Weber.

—— 1902 *Samoa, Bismarckarchipel und Neuguinea*. Leipzig: Weber.

Hides, J G 1935 *Through wildest Papua*. London: Blackie & Son.

Highfield, Arnold & Valdman, Albert (eds) 1981 *Historicity and variation in Creole studies*. Ann Arbor: Karoma.

Hill, Kenneth C (ed.) 1979 *The genesis of language*. Ann Arbor: Karoma.

Hinnenkamp, Volker 1982 *Foreigner Talk und Tarzanisch*. Hamburg: H Buske.

—— 1984 Eye-witnessing pidginization? Structural and sociolinguistic aspects of German and Turkish foreigner-talk. *York Papers in Linguistics* 11:153-66.

Hockett, Charles F 1950 Age-grading and linguistic continuity. *Language* 26:449-57.

—— 1958 *A course in modern linguistics*. New York: Macmillan.

—— 1968 *The state of the art*. The Hague: Mouton.

Hoeltker, Georg 1945 *Das Pidgin-Englisch als sprachliches Missionsmittel in Neuguinea*. Neue Zeitschrift für Missionswissenschaft 1:44-63.

Hoenigswald, Henry M 1971 Language history and Creole studies. Hymes (ed.), pp 473-80.

Hollyman, K J 1976 Les pidgins européens de la région calédonienne. *Te Reo* 19:25-65.

Holm, John 1978 The Creole English of Nicaragua's Miskito Coast. PhD thesis, University College London.

—— 1980 African features in white Bahamian English. *English World-Wide* 1:45-66.

—— 1988-89 *Pidgins and Creoles*. Cambridge: CUP, two vols.

Holthouse, H 1969 *Cannibal cargoes*. London & Adelaide: Angus & Robertson.

Hosali, Priya 1983 Syntactic peculiarities of Butler English. Paper presented at the York Creole Conference.

Huber, Magnus & Parkvall, Mikael (eds) [*forthcoming*] *Spreading the word*. London: University of Wstminster Press.

Hudson, Joyce 1984 Kriol or English: an unanswered question in the Kimberleys. Paper presented at the 54th ANZAAS Congress, Canberra.

Huebner, Thomas 1983 *A longitudinal analysis of the acquisition of English*. Ann Arbor: Karoma.

Huet, G 1909 La communauté portugaise de Batavia. *Revista Lusitana* 12:149-70.

Hugill, Stan 1977 *Songs of the sea*. New York: McGraw-Hill.

Hull, Alexander 1968 The origins of New World French phonology. *Word* 24:255-69.

Hull, Brian 1968 The use of Pidgin in the House of Assembly. *Journal of the Papua New Guinea Society*, 2(1):22-25.

Hunter, William C J 1882 *The "fan kwae" at Canton before treaty days 1825-44*. London: Kegan, Paul, Tench.

Huttar, George L 1972 A comparative wordlist for Djuka. Grimes, J E (ed.), *Languages of the Guianas*. Norman: SIL , University of Oklahoma, pp 12-21.

—— 1975 Sources of Creole semantic structures. *Language* 51:684-95.

Hyltenstam, Kenneth & Viberg, Åke (eds) 1993 *Progression and regression in language*. Cambridge: CUP.

Hymes, Dell 1971 Introduction to Section III. Hymes (ed.), pp 65-90.

—— (ed.) 1971 *Pidginization and creolization of languages*. London: CUP.

—— 1980 Commentary. Valdman & Highfield (eds), pp 389-424.

Jablonska, Alina 1969 The Sino-Russian mixed language in Manchuria. *University of Hawaii Working Papers in Linguistics* 3:135-64 (translated by Lyovin, A).

Jackson, Kenneth D 1990 *Sing without shame*. Amsterdam: Benjamins.

Jacobs, Melville 1932 Notes on the structure of Chinook Jargon. *Language* 8:27-50.

Jacomb, Edward 1914 *France and England in the New Hebrides*. Melbourne: George Robertson.

Jacques, Norbert 1922 *Südsee: ein Reisebuch*. München.

Jakobson, Roman 1960 Linguistics and poetics. Sebeok, T A (ed.), *Style in language*. Cambridge, Mass.: MIT Press, pp 350-77.

Janson, Tore 1984 A language of Sophiatown, Alexandra and Soweto. *York Papers in Linguistics* 11:167-80.

Janssen, Arnold P 1932 Die Erziehungsanstalt für halbweisse Kinder. Hueskes, J (ed.), *Pioniere der Südsee*, Hiltrup: Herz Jesu Mission, pp 150-54.

Jennings, William 1995 Saint-Christophe: site of the first French Creole. Baker (ed.), pp 63-80.

Jespersen, Otto 1922 *Language, its nature, development and origin*. London: Allen & Unwin.

—— 1948 *Growth and structure of the English language*. New York: Doubleday Anchor Books & Oxford: Basil Blackwell.

Jiménez, Augusto 1846 *Vocabulario del dialecto Jitano (,,,)*. Seville: Gutierrez de Alba.

Johnson, Mary C 1974 Two morpheme structure rules in an English proto-Creole. DeCamp & Hancock (eds), 118-29.

Johnson, Raymond K 1974 *Language policy in Papua New Guinea*. Port Moresby: Teaching Methods and Materials Centre, Faculty of Education, University of Papua New Guinea (Research Report 28).

Jones, Eldred 1971 Krio, an English-based language of Sierra Leone. Spencer (ed.), pp 66-94.

Jones, Frederick C V 1984 Aspects of the morphology of English-derived words in Sierra Leone Krio. *York Papers in Linguistics* 11:181-90.

Jordaan, K 1974 The origins of Afrikaners and their language 1652-1720: a study in miscegenation and creole. *Race* 15:461-95.

Jourdan, Christine 1983 Mort du "Kanaka Pidgin English" à Mackay (Australie). *Anthropologie et sociétés* 7(3):77-96.

—— 1985 Sapos iumi mitim iumi: urbanization and creolization in the Solomon Islands. PhD thesis, Australian National University.

—— 1991 Pidgins and Creoles: The blurring of categories. *Annual Review of Anthropology* 20:187-209.

Kahn, Morton C 1931 *Djuka. The bush Negroes of Dutch Guyana*. New York: Viking Press.

Kang-Kwong Luke 1984 Language mixing in Hong Kong. *York Papers in Linguistics* 11:191-201.

Kay, Paul & Sankoff, Gillian 1974 A language-universals approach to Pidgins and Creoles. DeCamp & Hancock (eds), pp 61-72.

Keane, E 1951 The contribution of the West Indies to literature. *Bim* 4(14):102-06.

Keesing, Roger [n d] Solomon Pidgin pronouns: predicate markers and the Eastern Oceanic substrate. Ms, Anthropology, RSPacS, Australian National University.

—— 1988 *Melanesian Pidgin and the Oceanic substrate*. Stanford: Stanford University Press.

—— 1990 Solomon Pijin and colonial ideologies. Baldauf, R & Lake, A (eds) *Language planning education in Australasia and the South Pacific*. Clevedon: Multilingual Matters, pp 149-65.

Kihm, Alain 1983 De l'interêt d'étudier les créoles, ou qu'ont-ils d'espécial? *Espace créole* 5:75-100.

—— 1984 Is there anything like decreolization? Some ongoing changes in Bissau Creole. *York Papers in Linguistics* 11:203-14.

—— 1991 Présentation. Kihm, Alain (ed.) *La créolisation: théorie et applications*, pp 5-20 (Recherches linguistiques de Vincennes - 20).

—— 1994 *Kriyol syntax: the Portuguese-based Creole language of Guinea-Bissau.* Amsterdam: Benjamins.

King, Joseph 1909 *W G Lawes of Savage Island and New Guinea.* London: The Religious Tract Society.

Klein, Wolfgang 1986 *Second language acquisition.* Cambridge: CUP.

Kloss, Heinz 1978 *Die Entwicklung neuer germanischer Kultursprachen seit 1800.* Düsselforf: Schwann.

Koch, Harold 1984 Central Australian Aboriginal Pidgin. Paper presented at the 54th ANZAAS Congress, Canberra.

Koefoed, Geert 1975 A note on Pidgins, Creoles and Greenberg's universals. Paper presented at the International Conference on Pidgins and Creoles, Honolulu.

Koll-Stobbe, Amei 1988 [Review of Mühlhäusler (1986)] *Freiburger Universitäts-blätter* 102 (December 1988).

Kotzé, Ernst 1989 How creoloid can you be? Aspects of Malay Afrikaans. Pütz & Dirven (eds), pp 251-64.

Kroon, Willem E 1927 *Dos novela.* Curaçao: Drukkerij van het Vicariaat.

Kulick, Don 1990 *Having a head and showing knowledge: language shift, christianity, and notions of self in a Papua New Guinean village.* Stockholm: Department of Anthropology, University of Stockholm.

Laade, Wolfgang 1968 Tales from the west coast of Papua. *Archiv für Volkerkunde* 22:93-112.

Labov, William 1971 The notion of "system" in creole languages. Hymes (ed.), pp 447-72.

—— 1972 Some principles of linguistic methodology. *Language in Society* 1:97-l20.

—— 1973 *Language in the inner city.* Philadelphia: University of Philadelphia Press.

—— 1980 Is there a Creole speech community. Valdman & Highfield (eds), pp 369-88.

—— 1990 On the adequacy of natural languages. Singler, John V (ed.) *Pidgin and Creole tense-mood-aspect systems.* Amsterdam: Benjamins, pp 1-58.

Ladhams, John [*forthcoming*] The Pernambuco connection? Huber & Parkvall (eds).

Landtman, Gunnar 1917 The folk tales of the Kiwai Papuans. *Acta Societatis Scientianum Fennicæ*, vol. XLVII.

—— 1918 The Pidgin English of British New Guinea. *Neuphilologische Mitteilungen* 19:62-74.

Lass, Roger 1979 *On explaining language change.* Cambridge: CUP.

Lawrence, Peter 1964 *Road belong cargo.* Melbourne: Melbourne University Press.

Laycock, Donald C 1970a *Materials in New Guinea Pidgin.* Canberra: Pacific Linguistics (D-5).

—— 1970b It was a peculiarly great year for Pidgin. *Pacific Islands Monthly* 41:45-48.

—— 1977a Me and you versus the rest: abbreviated pronoun systems in Irianese languages. *Irian* 6(3):33-41.

—— 1977b Creative writing in New Guinea Pidgin. Wurm (ed.) pp 609-38.

—— 1985 The future of Tok Pisin. Wurm & Mühlhäusler (eds), pp 665-68.

—— 1987 [Text of radio talk on languages used in writings about various utopias and dystopias] Kamenka, A (ed.) *Utopias*, Melbourne: OUP, pp 144-78.

—— 1989 The status of Pitcairn-Norfolk. Ammon, Ulrich (ed.), *Status and function of languages and language varieties*, Berlin: De Gruyter, pp 608-29.

Lee, Mary Hope 1979 Ethnographic statement in the Nigerian novel, with special reference to Pidgin. Hancock (ed.), pp 295-302

Lee, Robert A 1981 Making language serve the truth of black experience. [Review of Bigsby (ed.) 1981] *Times Higher Education Supplement,* 31 January 1981.

Leech, G & Svartvik, J 1975 A communicative grammar of English. London: Longman.

Lefebvre, Claire 1986 Relexification in creole genesis revisited: the case of Haitian Creole. Muysken & Smith (eds), pp 279-300.

LeJeune, Jean-Marie Raphael 1886 Practical Chinook vocabulary. Kamloops: St Louis' Mission (mimeo).

Leland, Charles G 1876 *Pidgin-English sing-song.* London: Trübner.

Lenz, Rodolfo 1928 *El Papiamento, la lengua criolla de Curaçao.* Santiago de Chile: Balcells.

Le Page, Robert B 1960 *Jamaican Creole.* London: Macmillan.

——— (ed.) 1961 *Proceedings of the Conference on Creole language studies.* London: Macmillan.

——— 1966 Introduction. Bailey, B L , pp v-vii.

——— 1968 Problems to be faced in the use of English as the medium of education in four West Indian territories. Fishman et al. (eds), pp 431-42.

——— 1973 The concept of competence in a Creole/contact situation. *York Papers in Linguistics* 3:31-50.

——— 1980 Theoretical aspects of sociolinguistic studies in Pidgin and Creole languages. Valdman & Highfield (eds), pp 331-68.

——— 1981 *Caribbean connections in the classroom.* York: M Glasgow Language Trust.

——— 1983a Introduction to the York Creole Conference. Paper presented at the York Creole Conference.

——— 1983b Review of Bickerton: Roots of Language. *Journal of Linguistics* 19:258-65.

——— & Tabouret-Keller, Andrée 1985 *Acts of identity.* Cambridge: CUP.

Liem, Nguyen Dang 1979 Cases and verbs in Pidgin French (Tay Boi) in Vietnam. *Papers in Pidgin and Creole Linguistics* 3:217-46 (Pacific Linguistics A-57).

Lightfoot, D 1979 *Principles of diachronic syntax.* Cambridge: CUP.

Lilke, Eleonore 1972 *Buk bilong kuk.* Bad Liebenzell: Liebenzell Mission.

Lincoln, Peter C 1975 Acknowledging dual-lingualism. *University of Hawaii Working Papers in Linguistics* 7(4):39-45.

Lipski, J 1988 Philippine Creole Spanish: reassessing the Portuguese element. *Zeitschrift für Romanische Philologie* 104:25-45.

London, Jack 1909 Beche de mer English. *Contemporary Review* 96:359-64.

Lounsbury, Floyd D 1968 One hundred years of anthropological linguistics. Brew, John O (ed.), *One hundred years of anthropology.* Cambridge (Mass.): Harvard University Press, pp 153-225.

Lüdi, Georges (ed.) 1994 *Sprachstandardisierung.* Fribourg: Swiss Academy of Humanities and Social Sciences.

Ludwig, Ralph 1989 *Les créoles entre l'oral et l'écrit.* Tübingen: Narr. check title

——— (ed.) 1994 *Ecrire le parole de nuit.* Paris: Gallimara.

Lynch, John (ed.) 1975 *Pidgins and Tok Pisin.* Port Moresby: Department of Language, University of Papua New Guinea, (Occasional Paper no. 1).

——— 1979 Changes in Tok Pisin morphology. Paper presented at the 13th Congress of the Linguistic Society of Papua New Guinea: Port Moresby.

——— 1980 Mixed Languages. Lynch, J (ed.), *Readings in the comparative linguistics of Melanesia.* Port Moresby: University of Papua New Guinea, pp 283-96.

——— 1981 Austronesian "loanwords" (?) in trans-New Guinea phylum vocabulary. Daview, H J et al., *Papers in New Guinea Linguistics* 21:165-80 (Pacific Linguistics A-61).

358

—— 1990 The future of Tok Pisin: social, political and educational dimensions. Verhaar (ed.), pp 389-96.

Lyons, John 1981. *Language and Linguistics*. Cambridge: CUP.

Mabbot, T O (ed.) 1951 *The selected poetry and prose of Edgar Allan Poe*. New York: The Modern Library.

MacKnight, C C 1976 *The voyage to Marege*. Melbourne: Melbourne University Press.

Mafeni, B 1971 Nigerian English. Spencer (ed.), pp 95-112.

Magens, J M 1770 *Grammatica over det Creolske sprog*. Copenhagen: Gerhard Giese Salikath.

Malcolm, Ian 1995 *Language and communication enhancement for two-way learning*. Perth: Edith Cowan University.

Malinowski, Bronislav 1923 The problem of meaning in primitive languages. Ogden, C K & Richards, I A (eds), *The meaning of meaning*, London: Kegan Paul, pp 296-336.

Manessy, Gabriel 1977 Processes of pidginization in African languages. Valdman (ed.) [1977b], pp 129-34.

Manfredi, Victor 1993 Verb focus in the typology of Kwa/Kru and Haitian. Byrne, Francis & Winford, Donald (eds) *Focus and grammatical relations in Creole languages*. Amsterdam: Benjamins, pp 3-51.

[Marbot, François-Achille] 1846 *Les bambous*. Fort-Royal: Ruelle & Arnaud.

Markey, Thomas L   1975 Afrikaans: Creole or non-Creole. Ms, University of Michigan [published in 1982, see below].

—— 1980 Diffusion, fusion and creolization: a field guide to developmental linguistics. Unpublished ms, University of Michigan & Technische Universität Berlin.

—— 1981 Review of Muysken (ed.) 1981. *English World-Wide* 2:269-74.

—— 1982 Afrikaans: Creole or non-Creole. *Zeitschrift für Dialektologie und Linguistik*, 49(2):169-207.

—— 1983 Static vs dynamic in Germanic linguistics. *Monatshefte* 75(2):110-14.

—— 1985 On suppletion. Paper presented at the 7th ISHC Conference, Pavia.

Markey, T, Roberge, P, Muysken, P & Meijer, G (eds) 1979 *On the origin and formation of Creoles: a miscellany of articles by Dirk Christiaan Hesseling*. Ann Arbor: Karoma.

Martyn-Jones, Marilyn & Romaine, Suzanne 1984 Semilingualism: a half-baked theory of communicative competence. Paper presented at the fourth Nordic Symposium on Bilingualism, Uppsala.

May, Karl [1886] 1958 *Der Peitschenmüller*. Bamberg: Karl-May-Verlag.

—— [1879] 1959 *Auf fremden Pfaden*. Bamberg: Karl-May-Verlag [includes *Das Kafferngrab*].

Mayers, W F, Dennys, N B & King, C 1867 *The treaty ports of China and Japan*. London: Trübner and Hong Kong: Shortrede.

Mayerthaler, Willi 1978 Morphologische Natürlichkeit. Habilitations thesis, Technische Universität Berlin.

Mayoux, Jean Jacques 1960 *Melville*. The Hague: Mouton.

McDonald, R (ed.) 1977 Georg Friederici's *Pidgin Englisch in Deutsch-Neuguinea*. Port Moresby: University of Papua New Guinea, Department of Language (Occasional Paper no. 14).

McElhanon, K A (ed.) 1975 *Tok Pisin i go we?* Port Moresby: Linguistic Society of Papua New Guinea (Kivung Special Publication no. 1).

McLaren, Jack 1926 *Songs of a fuzzy-top, being, mainly, the love story of a South Sea Islander, told in his own English*. London: Cecil Palmer.

Mead, Margaret 1931 Talk Boy. *Asia*, 31:141-51, 191.

—— 1956 *New lives for old*. New York: W Morrow.

Meillet, Antoine 1921 *Linguistique historique et linguistique générale*. Paris: Champion.

Meisel, Jurgen M 1975 Ausländerdeutsch und Deutsch ausländischer Arbeiter. Klein, Wolfgang (ed.) Sprache Ausländischer Arbeiter. *Lili* 5(18):9-53.

—— 1976 Linguistic simplification. A study of immigrant workers' speech and foreigner talk. Corder & Roulet (eds), pp 83-113.

—— (ed.) 1977 *Pidgins - Creoles - languages in contact*. Tübingen: Narr.

—— 1983 Transfer as a second-language strategy. *Language and Communication* 3:11-46.

Melville, Herman 1847 *Omoo: a narrative of adventures in the South Seas*. New York: Harper & Brothers.

Mesthrie, Rajend 1989 The origins of Fanagalo. *JPCL* 4:211-40.

Michener, James A 1947 *Tales of the South Pacific*. New York: Macmillan.

Mihalic, Francis 1957 *Grammar and dictionary of Neo-Melanesian*. Westmead (NSW): Mission Press.

—— 1969 Neo-Melanesian - a compromise. Mihalic, Francis (ed.) *The Word in the world 1969*, Epping (NSW): Divine Word Publications.

—— 1971 *The Jacaranda dictionary and grammar of Melanesian Pidgin*. Brisbane: Jacaranda Press.

—— 1977 Interpretation problems from the point of view of a newspaper editor. Wurm (ed.) [1977c], pp 1117-28.

Miller, Mary Rita 1967 Attestations of American Indian Pidgin English in fiction and non-fiction. *American Speech* 42:142-47.

Milroy, Lesley 1980 *Language and social networks*. Oxford: Basil Blackwell.

Mintz, Sidney W 1971 The socio-historical background to pidginization and creolization. Hymes (ed.), pp 481-98.

Moeliono, Anton M 1994 Standardization and modernization in Indonesian language planning. Lüdi (ed.), pp 117-30.

Molière, Jean-Baptiste P de 1671 *Le bourgeois gentilhomme*. Paris: P Le Monnier.

Molony, Carol H 1973 Lexical change in Philippine Creole Spanish. Unpublished ms, Stanford University.

Molony, C, Zobl, H & Stolting, W (eds) 1977 *German in contact with other languages*. Kronberg: Scriptor.

Morris, D, Collett, P, Marsh, P, & O'Shaughnessy, M 1979 *Gestures, their origins and distribution*. London: Book Club Associates.

Morrison, Robert 1807 Unpublished journal, Council for World Mission Archives, School of Oriental and African Studies, University of London.

Morrison, John R 1834 *A Chinese commercial guide*. Canton: Albion Press.

Mosel, Ulrike 1980 *Tolai and Tok Pisin*. Canberra: Pacific Linguistics (B-73).

Mosoro, Michael 1975 Caught in-between. *Papua New Guinea Writing* 19:5-7.

Mufwene, Salikoko S 1986 Les langues créoles peuvent-elles être définies sans allusion à leur histoire? *Etudes créoles* 9:135-50.

—— 1989 Equivocal structures in some Gullah complex sentences. *American Speech* 64:304-26.

—— 1991 Pidgins, Creoles, typology and markedness. Byrne & Huebner (eds), pp 123-43.

—— (ed.) 1993 *Africanisms in Afro-American language varieties.* Athens (GA) & London: University of Georgia Press.

Mülhlhäusler, Peter 1974 *Pidginisation and simplification of language.* Canberra: Pacific Linguistics (B-26).

—— 1977a Bermerkungen zum "Pidgin Deutsch" von Neuguinea. Molony, Zobl & Stölting (eds), pp 58-70.

—— 1977b Creolization of New Guinea Pidgin. Wurm (ed.), pp 567-76.

—— 1978a Papuan Pidgin English rediscovered. Wurm & Carrington (eds), pp 1377-446.

—— 1978b Samoan Plantation Pidgin English and the origin of New Guinea Pidgin. *Papers in Pidgin and Creole Linguistics* 1:67-120 (Pacific Linguistics, A-54).

—— 1978c Synonymy and communication across lectal boundaries in Tok Pisin. *Papers in Pidgin and Creole Linguistics* 2:1-20 (Pacific Linguistics, A-57).

—— 1978d The functional possibilities of lexical bases in New Guinea Pidgin. *Papers in Pidgin and Creole Linguistics* 1:121-74 (Pacific Linguistics, A-54).

—— 1979 *Growth and structure of the lexicon of New Guinea Pidgin.* Canberra: Pacific Linguistics (C-52).

—— 1980a Warum sind Pidginsprachen keine gemischten Sprachen. Ureland, P S (ed.), *Sprachvariation und Sprachwandel.* Tübingen: Niemeyer, pp 139-60.

—— 1980b Phases in the development of Tok Pisin. Hullen, W (ed.), *Understanding bilingualism,* Frankfurt: Lang, pp 119-30.

—— 1980c Structural expansion and the process of creolization. Valdman & Highfield (eds), pp 19-56.

—— 1981a Foreigner talk: Tok Masta in New Guinea. *International Journal of the Sociology of Language* 28:93-113.

—— 1981b Melanesian Pidgin English (Kanaka English) in Australia. *Kabar Seberang* September 1981, pp 93-105.

—— 1982a Kritische Bemerkungen zu Sprachmischungsuniversalien. Ureland, P S (ed.), *Die Leistung der Strataforschung und der Kreolistik.* Tübingen: Niemeyer, pp 407-32.

—— 1982b Language and communication efficiency: the case of Tok Pisin. *Language and Communication* 2:105-22.

—— 1983a Stinkiepoos, cuddles and related matters. *Australian Journal of Linguistics* 3:75-92.

—— 1983b The development of word formation in Tok Pisin. *Folia Linguistica* 17(1-4):463-87.

—— 1984a Discontinuity in the development of Pidgins and Creoles. Enninger, W (ed.), *Studies in language ecology,* Wiesbaden: Steiner, pp 118-34.

—— 1984b Tracing the roots of Pidgin German. *Language and Communication* 4:27-58.

—— 1984c Learning to speak about speaking in a Pidgin language. *Papers in Pidgins and Creole Linguistics* 3:93-103 (Pacific Linguistics A-65).

—— 1984d Review of Baker & Corne 1982. *Kratylos* 29:217-19.

—— 1985a Patterns of contact, mixture, creation and nativization: their contribution to a general theory of language. Bailey & Harris (eds), pp 51-88.

—— 1985 Etymologising and Tok Pisin. Wurm & Mühlhäusler (eds), pp 177-219.

—— 1986 *Pidgin and Creole linguistics.* Oxford: Blackwell.

—— 1989a Nature and nurture in the development of Pidgin and Creole languages. Pütz & Dirven (eds.), 54,

—— 1989b [review of Keesing (1980)] *Studies in Language* 13:459-75.

—— 1990 Towards an implicational analysis of pronouns development. Edmondson, J, Feagin, C & Mühlhäusler, P (eds), *Development and diversity: linguistic varieties across time and space*. Arlington: University of Texas & Summer Institute of Linguistics, pp 351-70.

—— 1991 Queensland Kanaka English. Romaine (ed.), pp 174-79.

—— 1992a What is the use of studying Pidgin and Creole languages? *Language Sciences* 14:309-17.

—— 1992b Redefining creolistics. Wolf, George (ed.) *New departures in linguistics*. New York & London: Garland, pp 193-98.

—— 1992c [Review of Mühlhäusler (1974)] Pütz (ed.), pp 109-18.

—— 1993 The role of Pidgin and Creole languages in language progression and regression. Hyltenstam & Viberg (eds), pp 39-67.

—— 1995a Attitudes to literacy in the pidgins and creoles of the Pacific area. *English World-Wide* 16:251-71.

—— 1995b Pidgins, Creoles, and linguistic ecologies. Baker (ed.), pp 235-50.

—— 1996a *Linguistic ecology: language change and linguistic imperialism in the Pacific region*. London: Routledge.

—— 1996b Linguistic adaptation to changed environmental conditions: some lessons from the past. Fill, Alwin (ed.) *Sprachökologie und Ökolinguistik*. Tübingen: Stauffenburg, pp 105-30.

—— 1996c Pidginization. Goebl, H, Nelde, P, Starý & Wölck, W (eds), *Kontaktlinguistik / Contact linguistics / Linguistique de contact*. Berlin: Walter de Gruyter, pp 643-49.

—— 1996d A *fellow's* adventures in South Australia. Baker & Syea (eds) pp 259-68.

Mühlhäusler, Peter & Harré, Ron 1990 *Pronouns and people*. Oxford: Blackwell.

Murphy, John J 1943 *The book of Pidgin English*. Brisbane: Smith & Patterson.

Murray, J H P 1925 *Papua of today*. London: King & son.

Muysken, Pieter 1975 Pidginization in the Quechua of the lowlands of Eastern Ecuador. Paper presented at the conference on Pidgins and Creoles, Honolulu.

—— (ed.) 1981 *Generative studies on Creole languages*. Dordrecht: Foris.

Muysken, Pieter & Smith, Norval 1986 *Substrata versus universals in creole genesis*. Amsterdam: Benjamins.

Muysken, Pieter & Veenstra, Tonjes 1995 Serial Verbs. Arends, Muysken & Smith (eds.), pp 289-301.

Nagara, Susumu 1972 *Japanese Pidgin English in Hawaii: a bilingual description*. Honolulu: University Press of Hawaii.

Namaliu, Rabbie 1970 The good woman of Konedobu. *Kokave* 1(2):44-53.

Naro, Anthony J 1975 The origin of Pidgin Portuguese. Hawaii Conference, ms.

—— 1978 A study on the origins of pidginization. *Language* 54:314-47.

Neffgen, H 1915 Pidgin-English. *Samoan Times*, 23 January and 27 March, 1915.

Neuhauss, Richard 1911 *Deutsch Neu-Guinea*, vol. 1. Berlin: Reimer.

Neumann, Gunther 1965 Russennorwegisch und Pidginenglisch. *Nachrichten der Giessener Hochschulgesellschaft* 34:219-32.

—— 1966 Zur Chinesisch-Russischen Behelfssprache von Kjachta. *Sprache* 12:237-51.

Neustúpny, Jiri V 1983 Communication with the Japanese. *The Wheel Extended*, 8(1):28-30.

Newton, Henry 1914 *In far New Guinea*. London: Seeley, Service.

Nichols, P 1976 Linguistic change in Gullah. PhD thesis, Stanford University.

Noel, John 1975 Legitimacy of Pidgin in the development of Papua New Guinea toward nationhood. McElhanon (ed.), pp 76-84.

Nolde, Emil 1965 *Welt und Heimat*. Cologne: Du Mont, Schauberg.

Noss, Philip A 1979 Fula: a language of change. Hancock (ed.), pp 175-90.

O'Callaghan, Evelyn 1981 A study of Creole in the West Indian novel. MLitt thesis, University of Oxford.

Ochs, Elinor 1979 Planned and unplanned discourse. Givón, Talmy (ed.), *Syntax and semantics*, vol. 12:51-80. New York: Academic Press.

Ong, Walter 1982 *Orality and literacy*. London: Methuen.

Orwell, George 1949 *Nineteen eighty-four*. New York: Hartcourt Brace Jovanovich.

Ostendorf, Berndt [n d] Literary acculturation in America – what makes ethnic literature ethnic? Ms, Amerika Institut, Ludwig-Maximilians-Universität.

Parépou, Alfred 1885 *Atipa*. Paris: Auguste Ghio.

Paul, Hermann 1970 *Prinzipien der Sprachgeschichte*. Tübingen: Niemeyer.

Pawley, Andrew 1975 *On epenthetic vowels in New Guinea Pidgin*. McElhanon (ed.), pp 215-28.

Peet, William 1979 The nominative shift in Hawaiian Creole pronominalization. *Papers in Pidgin and Creole Linguistics* 2:151-61. (Pacific Linguistics A-57).

Pères Blancs 1885 [Catechism]. Algiers: Missionnaires d'Afrique.

Perez, A Q, Santiago, A O & Liem, N G (eds) 1978 *Papers from the Conference on the standardization of Asian languages*. Canberra: Pacific Linguistics (C-47).

Phillipson, Robert 1992 *Linguistic imperialism*. Oxford: OUP.

Piau, Julie & Holzknecht, Suzanne 1985 Current attitudes to Tok Pisin. Wurm & Mühlhäusler (eds), pp 487-93.

Piniau, S 1975 Tok Pisin – wanpela tok inap karimapim yumi olgeta. McElhanon (ed.), pp 96-101.

Pionnier, Jean-Nestor 1913 Pigeon English ou bichelamar. *Revue de Linguistique et de philologie compareé*, 46:9-17, 184-98.

Platt, John T 1975 The Singapore English speech continuum and its basilect "Singlish" as a "creoloid". *Anthropological Linguistics* 17:363-74.

Poe, Edgar Allan 1897 *The gold bug*. New York: Doubleday & McClure.

Politzer, R L 1949 On the emergence of Romance from Latin. *Word* 5:126-30.

Pollard, Velma 1984 Rastafarian language in St Lucia and Barbados. *York Papers in Linguistics* 11:253-64.

Pos, Hugo 1983 De opkomst van de Surinaamse literatuur 1945 - heden. *Oso* 2:11-18.

Posner, Rebecca 1983 The origins and affinities of French Creoles: new perspectives. *Language and Communication* 3:191-202.

Pradelles de Latour, Marie-Lorraine 1984 Urban Pidgin in Douala. *York Papers in Linguistics* 11:265-70.

Pride, J B & Holmes J (eds) 1972 *Sociolinguistics*. Harmondsworth: Penguin.

Puppel, Stanislaw 1995 *The biology of language*. Amsterdam: Benjamins.

Putman, Jacobus J 1849 Proeve eener Hollandshe spraak-kunst. Ms, Santa Rosa, Curaçao, 48 pp.

Pütz, Martin 1989 British Jamaican English: the impact of ideology. Pütz & Dirven (eds), pp 179-205.

—— (ed.) 1992 *Thirty years of linguistic evolution*. Amsterdam: Benjamins.

Pütz, Martin & Dirven, René (eds) 1989 *Wheels within wheels*. Papers of the Duisberg symposium on Pidgin and Creole languages. Frankfurt: Peter Lang.

Raidt, Edith H 1983 *Einführung in die Geschichte und Struktur des Afrikaans*. Darmstadt: Wissenschaftliche Buchgesellschaft.

Ray, Sidney H 1907 The Jargon English of the Torres Straits. *Reports of the Cambridge Anthropological Expedition to Torres Straits,*, Cambridge: CUP, pp 251-54.

—— 1926 A comparative study of Melanesian island languages. Cambridge: CUP.

Reddy, Michael J 1979 The conduit metaphor - a case of frame conflict in our language about language. Ortony, A (ed.), *Metaphor and thought.* Cambridge: CUP, pp 284-324.

Reed, Stephen W 1943 *The making of modern New Guinea.* Philadelphia: American Philosophical Society (Memoir no. 18).

Reinecke, John E 1937 Marginal languages. Unpublished PhD thesis, Yale University.

—— 1964 Trade jargons and creole dialects as marginal languages. Hymes, D (ed.), *Language in culture and society.* New York: Harper & Row, pp 534-42.

—— 1969 *Language and dialect in Hawaii.* Honolulu: University of Hawaii Press.

—— 1971 Tây Bòi: notes on the Pidgin French spoken in Vietnam. Hymes (ed.), pp 47-56.

—— 1980 William Greenfield, a neglected pioneer Creolist. Paper presented at the Conference of the Society for Caribbean Linguistics, Aruba.

—— 1981 Selective chronology of Creole studies, Special supplementary issue to *The Carrier Pidgin,* vol. 9.

Reinecke, J, DeCamp, D, Hancock, I F, Wood, R E 1975 *A bibliography of Pidgin and Creole languages.* Honolulu: University Press of Hawaii.

Reisman, Karl 1974 Contrapuntal conversations in an Antiguan village. Bauman, R & Sherzer, J (eds), *Explorations in the ethnography of speaking.* Cambridge: CUP, pp 110-24.

Rew, Alan 1974 *Social images and processes in urban New Guinea.* St Paul: West Publishing Co.

Rhydwen, Mari 1993 Writing on the backs of the Blacks. PhD thesis, University of Sydney.

Ribbe, Carl 1903 *Zwei Jahre unter den Kannibalen der Salomon Inseln.* Dresden: Elbgau.

Richardson, I 1961 Some observations on the status of Town Bemba in Northern Rhodesia. *African Language Studies* 2:25-36.

Rickford, John R 1977 The question of prior creolization in Black English. Valdman (ed.) [1977b], pp 190-22I.

—— 1983a What happens in decreolization. Andersen, R W (ed.), *Pidginization and creolization as language acquisition.* Rowley: Newbury House, pp 298-318.

—— 1983b Standard and non-standard language attitudes in a creole continuum. *Society for Caribbean Linguistics Occasional Paper* 16:3-30.

—— 1984 Me Tarzan, you Jane! Cognition and expression in the Creole speaker. Unpublished manuscript, Stanford University.

—— 1987 *Dimensions of a Creole continuum.* Stanford: Stanford University Press.

—— & Closs-Traugott, Elizabeth 1985 Symbol of powerlessness and degeneracy, or symbol of solidarity and truth? Paradoxical attitudes toward Pidgins and Creoles. Greenbaum, S (ed.) *The English language today,* pp 252-61.

Rigsby, Bruce 1984 English Pidgin/Creole varieties on Cape York Peninsula. Paper presented at the 54th ANZAAS Conference, Canberra.

Rigsby, Bruce & Sutton, Peter 1982 Speech communities in Aboriginal Australia. *Anthropological Forum* 5(1):8-23.

Riley, Carroll L 1952 Trade Spanish of the Pinaguero Panare. *Studies in Linguistics* 10:6-11.

Roberge, P T 1990 The ideological profile of Afrikaans historical linguistics. Joseph, J & Taylor, T (eds) *Ideologies of language.* London: Routledge, pp 131-49.

Roberts, Julian 1991 The origins of Pidgin in Hawaii. Paper presented at the 6th International Conference on Austronesian Linguistics, Honolulu.

—— 1995 Pidgin Hawaiian: a sociohistorical study. *JPCL* 10:1-56.

Roberts, Peter A 1977 Duont: a case for spontaneous development. *Journal of Creole Studies* 1:101-08.

Robertson, Frank 1971 Comic opera talk talk; English as she is broken is the New Guinea tongue that strangers love. *Asia Magarine*, 22 August 1971, pp 13-16.

Robinson, W P 1974 *Language and social behaviour.* Harmondsworth: Penguin.

Rogers, Everett M (ed.) 1976 *Communication and development.* London: Sage.

Romaine, Suzanne 1982a What is a speech community? Romaine (ed.) pp 13-24.

—— (ed.) 1982b *Sociolinguistic variation in speech communities.* London: Edward Arnold.

—— 1984 [Review of Muysken (ed.) 1981 *Generative studies on creole languages.*] *Australian Journal of Linguistics* 4:116-22.

—— 1987 *Change and variation in the use of* **bai** *in young children's creolized Tok Pisin in Morobe Province.* Oxford: OUP.

—— 1988 *Pidgin and Creole languages.* London: Longman.

—— (ed.) 1991 *Language in Australia.* Cambridge: CUP.

—— 1992 *Language, education and development.* Oxford: OUP.

Ross, A S C 1964 *The Pitcairnese language.* London: Deutsch.

Rowley, Charles D 1965 *The New Guinea villager.* London: Deutsch.

Royal Commission into Labour 1885 Recruiting labourers in New Guinea and adjacent islands. *Votes and Proceedings of the Legislative Assembly, Brisbane* 2:813-987.

Ruhen, Olaf 1976 Pidgin – the livingest language. *Readers' Digest*, March 1976, pp 43-47.

Rushton, Dorgan 1983 *Brush up your Pidgin.* London: Willow Books, Collins.

Russell, Thomas 1868 *The etymology of Jamaican grammar, by a young gentleman.* Kingston: De Cordova, McDougall.

Ryan, John 1969 *The hot land.* Melbourne: Macmillan.

Sadler, Wesley 1973a *Untangled New Guinea Pidgin.* Madang: Kristen Pres.

—— 1973b *Niugini Pisin: lukim, mekim, tokim.* Madang: Kristen Pres.

Saint-Jacques Fauquenoy, Marguerite 1974 Guyanese: a French Creole. DeCamp & Hancock (eds), pp 27-37.

Saint-Quentin, Alfred de 1872 *Introduction à l'histoire de Cayenne, suivie d'un recueil de contes, fables et chansons en créole (...), par Alfred de St-Quentin. Etude sur le grammaire créole par Auguste de St-Quentin.* Antibes: J Marchand.

Salisbury, R F 1967 Pidgin's respectable past. *New Guinea* 2(2):44-48.

—— 1972 Notes on bilingualism and linguistic change in New Guinea. Pride, J B & Holmes, J (eds), pp 52-64.

Samarin, William J 1953 *Learning Sango. A pedagogical grammar.* Bozoum: Mission Evangelique de l'Oubangui-Chari.

—— 1961 The vocabulary of Sango. *Word* 17:7-22.

—— 1966 Self-annulling prestige factors among speakers of a creole language. Bright (ed.), pp 188-213.

—— 1969 The art of Gbeya insults. *International Journal of African Languages* 35:323-29.

—— 1971 Salient and substantive pidginization. Hymes (ed.), pp 117-40.

—— 1975 Historical, ephemeral and inevitable verbal categories. Paper presented at the International Conference on Pidgins and Creoles, Honolulu.

—— 1980 Standardization and instrumentalization of creole languages. Valdman & Highfield (eds), pp 213-36.

—— 1982 Colonization and pidginization on the Ubangi river. Unpublished manuscript, Toronto.

Sandefur, John R 1981 Kriol – an Aboriginal language. *Hemisphere* 25:252-56.

—— 1982 Kriol in education in 1982. Paper presented at the 7th Annual Congress of Applied Linguistics of Australia, Perth.

—— 1984 A language coming of age: Kriol of North Australia. MA thesis, University of Western Australia.

Sankoff, Gillian 1972 Language use in multilingual societies. Pride & Holmes (eds), pp 33-51.

—— 1975a Wanpela lain manmeri i bin kisim Tok Pisin i kamap olsem tok ples bilong ol. McElhanon (ed.) pp 102-07.

—— 1975b Sampela nupela lo i kamap long Tok Pisin. McElhanon (ed.), pp 235-40.

—— 1976 Political power and linguistic inequality in Papua New Guinea. O'Barr, W M & J F (eds), *Language and politics*. The Hague: Mouton, pp 283-310.

—— 1977 Variability and explanation in language and culture. Saville-Troike (ed.), pp 59-74.

—— 1979 The genesis of a language. Hill (ed.), pp 23-47.

—— 1980 Variation, Pidgins and Creoles. Valdman & Highfield (eds), pp 139-65.

Sankoff, Gillian & Brown, Penelope 1976 On the origins of syntax in discourse: a case study of Tok Pisin relatives. *Language* 52:631-66.

Sankoff, Gillian & Laberge, Suzanne 1973 On the acquisition of native speakers by a language. *Kivung* 6(1):32-47.

Sapinski, Tania *[forthcoming]* Aspects of Aboriginal language use in the Riverlands [provisional title], MA thesis, University of Adelaide.

Sato, Charlene J 1985 Linguistic inequality in Hawaii: the post-Creole dilemma. Wolfson & Manes (eds) *Language of inequality*, Berlin: Mouton de Gruyter, pp 255-72.

—— 1990 *The syntax of conversation in interlanguage development*. Tübingen: Narr.

—— 1991 Sociolinguistic variation and language attitudes in Hawaii. Cheshire (ed.), pp 647-63.

—— 1993 Language change in a creole continuum. Hyltenstam & Viberg (eds), pp 122-40.

Saville-Troike, Muriel (ed.) 1977 *Linguistics and anthropology*. Washington, DC Georgetown University Press.

Sayer, Edgar S 1944 *Pidgin English*. Totonto, mimeo.

Schegloff, E A 1978 On some questions and ambiguities in conversation. Dressler, U (ed.) *Current trends in textlinguistics*. New York & London: Academic Press, pp 81-102.

Schellong, Otto 1934 *Alte Dokumente aus der Südsee*. Konigsberg.

Scherer, Klaus R & Giles, Howard (eds) 1980 *Social markers in speech*. Cambridge: CUP.

Schnee, Heinrich, von 1904 *Bilder aus der Südsee*. Berlin: Reimer.

Schneider, Gilbert D 1974 West African Pidgin English. PhD thesis, Hartford Seminary Foundation.

Schouten, Hendrik 1786 Een huishoudelijk twist. *Letterkundige uitspanningen van het genootschap de Surinaamsche lettervrienden*. Paramaribo, pp 33-37.

Schuchardt, Hugo 1882 Sur le créole de la Réunion. *Romania* 11:589-93.

—— 1889a Beiträge zur Kenntnis des englischen Kreolisch: II. MelanesoEnglisches. *Englische Studien* 13:158-62.

—— 1889b Beiträge zur Kenntnis des Kreolischen Romanisch V. Allgemeines über das Indoportugiesische. *Zeitschrift für Romanische Philologie* 13:476-516.

—— 1891 Beiträge zur Kenntnis des englischen Kreolisch: III. Das Indo-Englische. *Englische Studien* 15:286-305.

—— 1909 Die Lingua Franca. *Zeitschrift für Romanische Philologie* 33:441-61.

—— 1979 *The ethnography of variation. Selected writings on Pidgins and Creoles.* Ann Arbor: Karoma (Translated by Markey, T L).

—— [n d] Kreolische Studien X: Ueber das Negerenglische von Westafrika. Unpublished manuscript, Schuchardt collection, Graz.

Schultze, Ernst 1933 Sklaven und Dienersprachen. *Sociologus* 9:378-418.

Schumann, John H 1978 *The Pidginization process.* Rowley: Newbury House.

Schwartz, Theodore 1957 The Paliau movement in the Admiralty Islands - 1946 to 1954. PhD thesis, University of Pennsylvania.

Schwörer, E 1916 *Kolonial-Deutsch. Vorschläge einer künftligen deutschen Kolonialsprache in systematisch-grammatikalischer Darstellung und Begründung.* Munich: Huber.

Scotton, Carol M 1969 A look at the Swahili of two groups of up-country speakers. *Swahili* 39:101-10.

Sebba, Mark 1981 Derivational regularities in a Creole lexicon: the case of Sranan. *Linguistics* 19:101-17.

—— 1987 *The syntax of serial verbs.* Amsterdam: Benjamins.

Sebba, Mark & Todd, Loreto (eds.) 1984 Papers from the York Creole Conference. *York Papers in Linguistics* 11.

Seiler, Walter 1982 The spread of Malay to Kaiser Wilhelmsland. Carle, R, Heinschke, M, Pink, P W, Rost, C, & Stadtlander, K (eds), *Gava* (Festschrift Kähler), Berlin: Reimer, pp 67-86.

Selinker, Larry 1991 Rediscovering interlanguage. London: Longman.

Shaffer, Douglas 1978 Afrikaans as a case study in vernacular elevation and standardization. *Linguistics* 213:51-74.

Shannon, Claude E & Weaver, Warren 1949 *The mathematical theory of communication.* Philadelphia: W B Saunders.

Sharpe, Margaret 1985 Kriol – an Australian language resource. *Papers in Pidgin and Creole Linguistics* 4:177-94 (Pacific Linguistics, A-72).

Shelton-Smith, W 1929 "Pidgin" English in New Guinea. *Rabaul Times*, 24 May 1929.

Shilling, Alison 1980 Bahamian English - a non-continuum? Day, Richard (ed.) *Issues in English Creoles*, Heidelberg: Groos, pp 133-46.

Shnukal, Anna 1984 Variation in Torres Strait Creole. Paper presented at the 54th ANZAAS Conference, Canberra.

—— 1991 Torres Straits Creole. Romaine (ed.), pp 180-94.

Shnukal, Anna & Marchese, Lynell 1983 Creolization of Nigerian Pidgin English: a progress report. *English World-Wide* 4:17-26.

Shrimpton, Neville 1995 Standardizing the Krio language. Baker (ed.), pp 217-28.

Shuy, Roger W & Fasold, Ralph W (eds) 1973 *Language attitudes: current trends and prospects.* Washington, DC: Georgetown University Press.

Siegel, Jeff 1975 Fiji Hindustani. Unpublished ms, University of Hawaii.

—— 1981 Media Tok Pisin. Paper presented at the Australian Anthropological Society symposium: Language in social and cultural context, Canberra.

—— 1982 Plantation languages in Fiji. Unpublished ms, Australian National University.

—— 1983a Koines and koineization. Unpublished ms, Australian National University.

—— 1983b Plantation Pidgin Fijian. Paper presented at the 15th Pacific Science Congress, Dunedin.

—— 1984 Pidgin English in Fiji. Paper presented at the 54th ANZAAS Congress, Canberra.

—— 1985 Media Tok Pisin. *Papers in Pidgin and Creole Linguistics* 3:81-92. (Pacific Linguistics A-65).

—— 1989 Pidgins and Creoles in education in Australia and the southwest Pacific. Paper presented at the Society for Pidgin and Creole Linguistics meeting, Washington, DC.

—— 1993 Introduction. Controversies in the study of koines and koineization. *International Journal of the Sociology of Language* 99:5-9.

Siegel, Jeff (ed.) 1992 *Pidgins, Creoles and non-standard dialects in education.* Melbourne:Applied Linguistics Association of Australia (Occasional Paper 12).

Silverstein, Michael 1972a Chinook Jargon: language contact and the problem of multi-level generative systems. *Language* 48:378-406, 596-625.

—— 1972b Goodbye Columbus: language and speech community in Indian-European contact situation. Unpublished ms, University of Chicago.

—— 1977 Cultural prerequisites to grammatical analysis. Saville-Troike (ed.), pp 139-52.

—— [n d] Who shall regiment language? Intuition, authority and politics in linguistic communication. Unpublished ms, University of Chicago.

Smart, J R 1990 Pidginization in Gulf Arabic: a first report. *Anthropological Linguistics* 32:83-119.

Smith, Albert 1859 *To China and back.* London: the author.

Smith, Geoffrey P 1969 An educational balance sheet. *New Guinea* 4(2):16-29.

—— 1990 *A crash course in Tok Pisin.* Lae: Papua New Guinea University of Technology.

Smith, Ian R 1984 The development of morphosyntax in Sri Lanka Portuguese. *York Papers in Linguistics* 11:291-302.

Smith, Norval 1977a Vowel epenthesis in the Surinam Creoles. *Amsterdam Creole Studies* 1:1-31.

—— 1977b The development of the liquids in the Surinam Creoles. *Amsterdam Creole Studies* 1:32-54.

—— 1995 An annotated list of Creoles, Pidgins and mixed languages. Arends, Muysken & Smith (eds.), pp 331-374.

Snell, Edward 1988 *The life and adventures of Edward Snell: the illustrated diary of an artist, engineer and adventurer in the Australian colonies 1849-1889.* Edited by T Griffiths. North Ryde (NSW): Angus & Robertson.

Solenberger, Robert R 1962 The social meaning of language choice in the Marianas. *Anthropological Linguistics* 4:59-64.

Southworth, Franklin C 1971 Detecting prior creolization: an analysis of the historical origins of Marathi. Hymes (ed.), pp 255-74.

Speiser, Felix 1913 *Südsee, Urwald, Kannibalen.* Leipzig: Voigtlander.

Spencer, J W (ed.) 1971 *The English language in West Africa.* London: Longman.

Spitzer, Leo 1966 Creole attitudes towards Krio: a historical survey. *Sierra Leone Language Review* 5:39-49.

Sreedhar, M V 1977 Standardization of Naga Pidgin. *Journal of Creole Studies* 1:157-70.

—— 1984 Coining of words in Pidgins/Creoles: a case study of Naga Pidgin. *York Papers in Linguistics* 11:303-10

Stauble, Ann-Marie E 1978 The process of decreolization: a model for second language development. *Language Learning* 28:29-54.

Stefánsson, A 1909 The Eskimo trade jargon of Herschel Island. *American Anthropologist*, 2:217-32.

Steffensen, Margaret S 1977 Double talk: when it means something and when it doesn't. *Chicago Linguistic Soeiety, Papers from the Regional Meetings*, 13:603-11.

—— 1979 Reduplication in Bamyili Creole. *Papers in Pidgin and Creole Linguistics* 2:119-34. (Pacific Linguistics A-57).

Stein, Peter 1989 When Creole speakers write the standard language: an analysis of some of the earliest slave letters from Saint Thomas. Pütz & Dirven (eds), pp 153-78.

—— 1995 Early Creole writing and its effects on the discovery of Creole language structure. Arends (ed.), pp 43-61.

Steinberg, Danny D & Jakobovits, Leon A (eds) 1971 *Semantics: an interdisciplinary reader in philosophy, linguistics and psychology.* Cambridge: CUP.

Stetser, Merle 1976 Forty-five bears: a folk tale throughout the ages. *Working Papers in Linguistics* [University of Hawaii] 8(3):81-125.

Stevenson, Robert Louis 1893 *Island nights' entertainments.* London: Cassell [includes The beach of Falesá].

Stewart, William A 1962 The functional distribution of Creole and French in Haiti. *Georgetown Monograph Series on Languages and Linguistics* 15:149-59.

Stockton, Eric 1971 Poe's use of Negro dialect in *The Gold Bug*. Williamson, J V & Burke, V M (eds), *A various language*. New York: Holt, Rinehart & Winston.

Stowe, Harriet Beecher 1852 *Uncle Tom's Cabin.* London: T Barnard [first published in the USA in 1831].

Stross, Brian 1974 Speaking of speaking: Tenejapa Tzeltal metalinguistics. Bauman & Sherzer (eds), pp 213-39.

Stubbs, Michael 1980 *Language and literacy.* London: Routledge & Kegan Paul.

Sutcliffe, David 1982 *Black British English.* Oxford: Blackwell.

—— 1984 Investigating the language use of a British black community: an initial report. *York Papers in Linguistics* 11:311-22.

Sylvain, Suzanne 1936 Le créole haïtien. Wetteren: Imprimérie de Meester.

Taber, Charles R 1979 French loanwords in Sango: the motivation of lexical borrowing. Hancock (ed.), pp 191-200.

Tabouret-Keller, Andrée 1980 Psychological terms used in Creole Studies. Valdman & Highfield (eds), pp 313-30.

Tabouret-Keller, A, Le Page, R B, Gardner-Chloros, P & Varrot, G (eds) 1997 *Vernacular literacy.* Oxford: OUP.

Tauli, Valter 1968 *Introduction to a theory of language planning.* Uppsala: Almquist & Wiksells.

Tavares, Eugénio 1932 *Mornas: cantigas crioulas.* Lisboa: J Rodrigues.

Taylor, Andrew J 1968 A note on the study of sociolinguistics, with particular reference to Papua New Guinea. *Kivung* 1(1):43-52.

—— 1978 Evidence of a Pidgin Motu in the earliest written Motu materials. Wurm & Carrington (eds), pp 1325-50.

Taylor, Douglas 1963 The origin of West Indian Creole languages: evidence from grammatical categories. *American Anthropologist* 65:800-14.

Taylor, Insup 1976 *Introduction to psycholinguistics.* New York: Holt, Rinehart & Winston.

Taylor, Orlando L 1973 Teachers' attitudes towards black and non-standard English as measured by the language attitude scales. Shuy & Fasold (eds), pp 174-201.

Taylor, Talbot & Mühlhäusler, Peter 1982 [Review of Scherer & Giles (1980)]. *Journal of Literary Semantics* 11(2):125-35.

Temple, Sir William 1690 *An essay upon the ancient and modern learning.* London.

Tetaga, Jeremiah E 1971 Prenasalization as an aspect of New Guinea Tok Pisin. Unpublished ms, Linguistics Institute, University of Michigan.

Thamm, Merna 1970 *Pasim bilong Kristen mama.* Madang: Kristen Pres.

Thomas, John J 1869 *The theory and practice of Creole grammar.* Port-of-Spain: Chronicle Publishing Office.

Thomason, Sarah Grey 1981 Chinook Jargon in areal and historical context. *University of Montana Occasional Papers in Linguistics* 2:295-396.

—— & Kaufman, Terrence 1988 *Language contact, creolization and genetic linguisitcs.* Berkeley: University of California Press.

Thompson, Robert W 1961 A note on some possible affinities between the Creole dialects of the Old World and those of the New. Le Page (ed.), pp 107-13.

—— 1967 On the Portuguese dialect of Hong Kong. *Symposium on historical archaeological and linguistic studies on southern China.* Hong Kong: Hong Kong University Press, pp 238-40.

Thurston, William K 1987 Process of change in the languages of north-western New Britain. Canberra: Pacific Linguistics (B-99).

Tilden, Bryant 1831 Journal of fourth voyage to China (...). Unpublished typescript held at the Australian National University, Canberra.

Todd, Loreto 1974 *Pidgins and Creoles.* London: Routledge & Kegan Paul.

—— 1975 Pidgins and Creoles: the case for the creoloid. Paper presented at the International Conference on Pidgins and Creoles, Honolulu.

—— 1979 Cameroonian: a consideration of "what's in a name?" Hancock (ed.), pp 281-94.

—— 1982 The English language in West Africa. Bailey & Görlach (eds), pp 281-305.

—— 1984 *Modern Englishes.* Oxford: Basil Blackwell.

—— [n d] The CM2 process: a selection of riddles in Cameroon Pidgin English. University of Leeds, ms.

Tololo, A 1975 Opening address. Brammall, J & May, R (eds) *Education in Melanesia,* Canberra: Australian National University, pp 3-12.

Tonkin, Elizabeth 1979 Uses of Pidgin in early literate English of Nigeria. Hancock (ed.), pp 303-08.

Toolan, Michael 1996 *Total speech: an integrational approach to language.* Durham & London: Duke University Press.

Traugott, Elizabeth 1976 Natural semantax: its role in the study of second language acquisition. Corder & Roulet (eds), pp 132-62.

—— 1977 Pidginization, creolization, and language change. Valdman (ed.), pp 70-98.

—— & Romaine, Suzanne 1982 Style in sociohistorical linguistics. Unpublished ms, Universities of Stanford and Birmingham.

Traven, B 1934 *The death ship; the story of an American sailor.* New York: Alfred A Knopf.

Trefossa 1957 *Trotji.* Amsterdam: Noord-Hollandsche Uitgevers Maatschappij.

Trollope, Anthony 1859 *The Bertrams.* Tauchnitz edn., 2 vols.

Troy 1992 The Sydney language notebooks and response to language contact in early colonial NSW. *Australian Journal of Linguistics* 12:145-70.

Trudgill, Peter 1977 Creolization in reverse: reduction and simplification in the Albanian dialects of Greece. *Transactions of the Philological Society*, 1975-77, pp 32-50.

——— 1983 *On dialect*. Oxford: Basil Blackwell.

Tryon, Darrell T, Mühlhäusler, Peter & Baker, Philip 1996 English-derived contact languages in the Pacific in the 19th century (excluding Australia). Wurm et al. (eds), pp 471-96.

Tscharke, E G 1972 *Yumi daunim sik*. Madang: Kristen Pres.

Turner, G W 1966 *The English language in Australia and New Zealand*. London: Longman.

Ullmann, Stephen 1957 *Principles of semantics*. Glasgow: Jackson.

Unesco 1963 *The use of vernacular languages in education*. Paris: Unesco (Monographs on Fundamental Education 8).

Unitas Fratrum 1829 *Da Njoe Testament va wi masra en helpiman Jesus Christus*. London: British and Foreign Bible Society.

Upfield, Arthur 1931 *Wings above the Diamantina*. Sydney: Angus & Robertson.

——— 1963 *Bony and the black virgin*. berkeley: Berkeley Publishing Group.

Ureland, P S 1978 Die Bedeutung des Sprachkontakts in der Entwicklung der Nordseesprachen. Ureland, P S (ed.) *Sprachkontakte im Nordseegebiet*, Tübingen: Niemeyer, pp 82-128.

Urry, James & Walsh, Michael 1981 The lost "Macassarese Language" of Northern Australia. *Aboriginal History* 5(2):91-108.

Valdman, Albert 1968 Language standardization in a diglossic situation: Haiti. Fishman et al., pp 155-89.

——— 1977a Creolization: elaboration in the development of Creole French dialects. Valdman (ed.), pp 155-89.

——— (ed.) 1977b *Pidgin and Creole linguistics*. London & Bloomington: Indiana University Press.

——— 1977c Créolisation sans pidgin: le système des déterminants du nom dans les parlers franco-créoles. Meisel (ed.), pp 105-36.

Valdman, Albert & Highfield, Arnold (eds) 1980 *Theoretical orientations in Creole studies*. London: Academic Press

Valkhoff, Marius F 1966 *Studies in Portuguese and Creole*. Johannesburg: Witwatersrand University Press.

——— 1972 *New light on Afrikaans and Malayo-Portuguese*. Louvain: Peeters.

Van Gulik, Robert 1966 *Murder in Canton*. London: Heinemann.

Van Name, Addison 1869 Contributions to Creole grammar. *Transactions of the American Philological Association* 1:123-67.

Van Rossem, Cefas & van der Voort, Hein 1996 *Die Creol Taal*. Amsterdam: Amsterdam University Press.

Verhaar, John M (ed.) 1990 *Melanesian Pidgin and Tok Pisin*. Amsterdam: Benjamins.

Versteegh, Kees 1984 *Pidginization and creolization: the case of Arabic*. Amsterdam: Benjamins.

Vico, G B 1725 *Principi di una scienza nuova....* Napoli.

Vila, Isidro 1891 *Elementos de la gramática ambú ó de Annobón*. Madrid: A Pérez Dubrull.

Voegelin, Carl & Voegelin, Florence 1964 Languages of the world: Ibero-Caucasian and Pidgin-Creole, fascicle one. *Anthropological Linguistics* 6:1-71.

Volker, Craig Alan 1982 An introduction to Rabaul Creole German (Unserdeutsch). MA thesis, University of Queensland.

Von Weise, Benno 1972 *August von Kotzebue – Schauspiele.* Frankfurt: Athenäum Verlag.

Voorhoeve, Jan 1953 *Voorstudies tot een beschrijving van het Sranan Tongo (Negerengels van Suriname).* Amsterdam: Noord-Hollandsche.

—— 1961 Linguistic experiments in syntactic analysis. Le Page (ed.), pp 37-60.

—— 1962 Creole languages and communication. Committee for Technical Cooperation in Africa *Symposium on multilingualism.* London: CCTA Publishing Bureau, pp 233-42.

—— 1971 Church Creole and pagan cult language. Hymes (ed.), pp 323-26.

—— 1973 Historical and linguistic evidence in favour of the relexification theory in the formation of creoles. *Language in Society* 2:133-45.

—— 1981 Multifunctionality as a derivational problem. Muysken (ed.), pp 25-34.

Voorhoeve, Jan & Kramp, André 1982 Syntactic developments in Sranan. Paper presented at the Fourth Biannual Conference of the Society for Caribbean Linguistics, Paramaribo.

Voorhoeve, Jan & Lichtveld, Ursy M (eds) 1975 *Anthology of Suriname Creole literature.* New Haven & London: Yale University Press.

Wales, Kathleen 1980 Exphora re-examined: the uses of the personal pronoun **we** in present-day English. *UEA Papers in Linguistics* 12:21-44 (University of East Anglia).

Walsh, D S 1984 Is "English-based" an adequately accurate label for Bislama? Paper presented at the 54th ANZAAS Congress, Canberra.

Washabaugh, William 1975 Challenges of Pidgins and Creoles to current linguistic theory: for prepositions to become complementizers. Paper presented at the International Conference on Pidgins and Creoles, Honolulu.

—— 1986 *Five fingers for survival.* Ann Arbor: Karoma.

Washabaugh, William & Greenfield, S M 1983 The development of the Atlantic Creole languages. Woolford & Washabaugh (eds.), pp 106-19.

Weber de Kurlat, Frida 1962 El tipo cómico del negro en el teatro pre-lopesco. *Filología* 8:139-68.

Werkgroep Taal Buitenlandse. Werknemers 1978 *Nederlands tegen Buitenlanders.* Amsterdam: Publications of the Institute for General Linguistics 18.

Whinnom, Keith 1956 *Spanish contact vernaculars in the Philippine islands.* Hong Kong: Hong Kong University Press.

—— 1971 Linguistic hybridization and the "special case" of Pidgins and Creoles. Hymes (ed.), pp 91-115.

Whiteley, Wilfred F 1969 *Swahili: the rise of a national language.* London: Methuen.

Williams, Frederick (ed) 1970 *Language and poverty: perspectives on a theme.* Chicago: Markham Publishing Co.

Williams, S W 1837 Gaoumun fan yu tsa tsze tseuen taou, or A complete collection of the miscellaneous words used in the foreign language of Macao. 2. Hungmaou mae mae tung tung kwei hwa, or those words of the devilish language of the red-bristled people commonly used in buying and selling. *Chinese Repository* 6:276-79.

Winer, Lise & Rimmer, Mary 1994 Language varieties in early Trinidadian novels. *English World-Wide* 15:225-48.

Winford, Donald 1976 Teacher attitudes toward language varieties in a Creole community. *International Journal of the Sociology of Language* 8:45-75.

—— 1991 The Caribbean. Cheshire (ed.), pp 565-84.

Wode, Henning 1977 Development principles in naturalistic L2 acquisition. Drachman, G (ed.) *Akten der 3. Salzburger Jahrstagung für Linguistik*, Salzburg: Neugebauer, pp 207-20.

—— 1986 Die menschliche Spracheerlernfähigkeit als Bioprogramm. Boretzky, N, Enninger, W & Stolz, T (eds), *Akten des 2. Essener Kolloquiums über "Kreolsprachen und Sprachkontakte"*, Bocham: Brockmeyer, pp 285-310.

Wood, Richard E 1969 Linguistic problems in the Netherlands Antilles. *Mondo Lingvo Problemo* 1:77-86.

Wood, William M 1859 *Fankwei; or, the San Jacinto in the seas of India, China and Japan*. New York: Harper & Brothers.

Woolford, Ellen 1979 The developing complementizer system of Tok Pisin. Hill (ed.), pp 108-24.

Woolford, Ellen & Washabaugh, William (eds) 1983 *The social context of creolization*. Ann Arbor: Karoma.

Wullschlägel, H R 1858 *Deutsch-Negerenglisches Wörterbuch*. Löbau: T U Duroldt. (Reprinted in Amsterdam: S. Emmering, 1965).

Wurm, Stephen A 1964 Motu and Police Motu: a study in typological contrasts. *Papers in New Guinea Linguistics* 2:19-41 (Pacific Linguistics A-4).

—— 1969 English, Pidgin and what else? *New Guinea* 4(2):30-42.

—— 1970 *New Guinea Highlands Pidgin: course materials*. Canberra: Pacific Linguistics (D-3).

—— 1971 Pidgins, Creoles and lingue franche. *Current Trends in Linguistics* 8:999-1021.

—— 1975 The question of language standardization and pidgin. McElhanon (ed), pp 108-17.

—— 1977a Pidgins, Creoles, lingue franche and national development. Valdman (ed.), pp 333-57.

—— 1977b The nature of Pidgin. Wurm (ed.) pp 511-30.

—— (ed.) 1977c *Language, culture, society and the modern world*. Canberra: Pacific Linguistics (C-40).

—— (ed.) 1979 *New Guinea and neighboring areas: a sociolinguistic laboratory*. The Hague: Mouton.

—— 1980 Standardization and instrumentalization in Tok Pisin. Valdman & Highfield (eds.), pp 237-45.

—— 1983 Grammatical decay in Papuan languages. Paper presented at the 15th Pacific Science Congress, Dunedin.

—— 1992a Some contact languages and Pidgin and Creole languages in the Siberian region. *Language Sciences* 14:249-86.

—— 1992b Changes of language structure and typology in Pacific languages. Dutton, T E (ed.) *Culture change – language change. Case studies from Melanesia*. Canberra: Pacific Linguistics (C-120), pp 141-52.

—— 1994 Graphization and standardization of languages. Lüdi (ed), pp 255-74.

Wurm, S, Dutton, T, Tryon, D, Voorhoeve, C, Laycock, D & Walsh, M 1981 Pidgin languages and lingue franche in Oceania and Australia. Wurm, Stephen A & Hattori, Shirô *Language atlas of the Pacific area*, text for map 24. Canberra: Australian Academy of the Humanities.

Wurm, Stephen A & Carrington, Lois (eds) 1978 *Second International Conference on Austronesian Linguistics: Proceedings*. Canberra: Pacific Linguistics (C-61).

Wurm, Stephen A & Harris, John B 1963 *Police Motu*. Canberra: Pacific Linguistics (B-1).

Wurm, S A, Laycock, D C & Mühlhäusler, P 1984 Notes on attitudes to pronunciation in the New Guinea area. *International Journal of the Sociology of Language* 50:123-46.

Wurm, Stephen A & Mühlhäusler, Peter 1979 Attitudes towards New Guinea Pidgin and English. Wurm (ed.), pp 243-62.

—— & —— 1983 Registers in New Guinea Pidgin. *International Journal of the Sociology of Language* 35:69-86.

—— & —— (eds) 1985 *Handbook of Tok Pisin.* Canberra: Pacific Linguistics (C-70).

Wurm, S, Mühlhäusler, P & Tryon, Daryl T (eds) 1996 Atlas of languages for intercultural communication in the Pacific, Asia, and the Americas. Berlin: Mouton de Gruyter

Zettersten, A 1969 *The English of Tristan da Cunha.* (Lund Studies in English 37).

Zinkel, Calvin D 1977 Pidgin schools in the New Guinea Highlands. Wurm (ed.), pp 691-701.

Zöller, Hugo 1891 *Deutsch-Neuguinea und meine Ersteigung des Finisterre Gebirges.* Stuttgart, Berlin & Leipzig: Union.

Zyhlarz, Ernst 1932-33 Ursprung und Sprachcharacter des Altägyptischen. *Zeitschrift für Eingeborensprachen* 23:25-45, 81-110, 161-94, 241-54.

Index

Words are listed below in strictly alphabetical order, i.e. spaces, hyphens, apostrophes and diacritics are totally ignored for the purposes of alphabeticization. A reference such as 99n5 means "footnote 5 on page 99". Where a name or topic occurs both in the text on a particular page and also in a footnote on the same page, the index gives only the page number. Titles of publications are in italic typeface.

Also included below are the meanings of a number of abbreviations used in this book.

A

ABC islands -> Aruba, Bonaire, Curaçao
Aboriginal(s) 22, 25, 74, 79, 161n24, 197, 199, 241, 254, 271, 289-90, 307-08, 342
Aboriginal English 290
Aboriginal PE 271, 280, 303n1, 304
academic under-achievement 279-80
Achebe, C 310
acrolect(al) 12, 42, 64, 67, 71, 91, 213, 217, 253, 285
Adam, J 91
Adam, L 25, 114, 344
Adams, P 349
Adamson, L 318, 344
Adler, M 4, 344
Admiralities 10
Adone, D 112n20, 344
Africa(n) 22, 29, 54, 73-74, 83, 90, 100, 102, 105-06, 114, 122, 126, 140, 197-98, 224, 245, 262, 265, 296, 303-04, 306, 309-10, 314, 318, 323
African American English 285, 291
African Pidgins 108, 110, 139-42, 147, 176
African languages 16, 117, 122, 126, 179, 184, 189-90, 310 (see also: Bambara, Banda, Bangwa, Bantu, Bolo, Bulu, Douala, Efik, Ewe, Fulfulde, Gbaya, Gbeya, Hausa, Igbo, Kanuri, Kikongo, Kimbundu, Lingala, Mbondu, Ngbandi, Ngombe, Nyakoma, Sama, Sango, Songo, Swahili, Temne, Twi, Yoruba)
Afrikaans 3, 7, 11, 20, 27, 32, 60, 67, 72, 79-80, 90n46, 96, 154, 161, 198, 247n2, 259-60, 273, 275, 278, 290, 300-01, 314, 323, 331
Afrikaners 262
agentive 216
agglutination of articles in French Creoles 154
Agheyisi, R 5, 38, 234, 244-45, 344
Ainsworth [of Papua] 247
Aitchison, J 8n5, 10, 48, 55n5, 112n21, 133, 199, 211, 231-33, 238, 269, 274, 344
Aitken-Cade, S 26, 297, 344
Akan 173n34
Akers, G 213, 344
Alabama 77
Albanian 269
Albert, H 33, 238n10, 344

Alemannic 174n35
Alexishafen 79, 329, 333
Algiers 295
Ali Island 104. 149
Allen, B 317
Alleyne, M 46, 237, 331-32, 344
Allsopp, R 195, 304, 344
America(n) 68, 75, 79, 114, 131, 135-36, 263-64, 270, 297, 303-04, 306, 311-12, 333
American English 80
American Indian 16, 35, 52, 76-77, 132, 270
American Indian PE 155, 305, 311
American Japanese Military Jargon 131
Amerindian languages 72n29, 117, 206
Amigoe di Curaçao 330
Ammon, U 358
Amsler, J 102, 344
Amsterdam 46, 320
Amsterdam Creole Studies 46
Anansi 318
anaphoric pronouns 151-53
Andersen, R 364
Anderson, C 312, 352
Anderson, S 314, 344
Angami 256-57
Anglophone 30
Anglo-Saxon 7, 27, 33
Angolar 209
Annobón Creole Portuguese (Fa d'Ambu) 28-29, 90
Annobonese -> Annobón Creole Portuguese
Anon. [ca 1830] 295, 344
Anon. [1859] 2, 344
Anon. [ca 1935] 182, 344
Anthonisz, R 273, 344
anthropological linguistics 35-36
Antigua(n) 290
anti-language 67n24
Antillean 292
Antilles 194
Antonissen, R 323, 344
Ao 257
aphasia 61
Appel, R 122, 293, 344
Arab(ic) 2, 74, 103, 117, 216, 306
Ardener, E 40, 344
Arends, J 33, 49, 93, 106-07, 118, 345, 349, 363, 369-70
Argentina 130

argot 3
Aruba 292-93
Asia(n) 68, 75, 103, 129, 272-73
Asterix 308
Atkinson, H 314, 345
Atlantic Creoles 56n6, 95, 256, 303
Atlantic PE 17
Aub-Buscher, G 205, 345
Aufinger, A 184-85, 345
Australia(n) viii, 3, 9, 12, 16, 18, 28, 30, 35,
    45, 57, 68, 73-74, 77, 79, 97, 143, 161n24,
    246-47, 263-64, 275, 277, 282-83, 292,
    296-97, 303, 307-08, 313, 331, 333
Australian Creole English 20, 195, 197, 199,
    254
Australian English 2, 75, 241
Australian PE 14, 16-20, 143, 313n3
Austronesia(n) 116, 238

B

"baby-talk" 37, 39, 93, 96-98, 117
backslang 184-85
backsliding 54n4, 69-70, 166
Baessler, A 4, 345
Bagot Creole 17-18
Bahamas 68
Bahamian English 80, 187
Bahasa Indonesia 57, 80, 87, 198, 259, 300,
    331
Bailey, B 38, 41, 345, 359
Bailey, C-J vi-viii, 7, 8n5, 9, 33, 35-36, 43, 104,
    127, 128n3, 165n25, 214, 228, 236, 238-
    40, 286, 345, 351, 362, 370
Bailey, R 345
Baker, P vii, 1 , 4-5, 15, 17-18, 57, 73, 91, 95,
    114, 143, 154, 192, 204-05, 295-96, 312,
    345, 349, 356, 363, 367, 371
Baker, S 333, 345
Bakker, P 34, 346
Baldauf, R 357
Balint, A 25, 346
Balkans 10
Bambara 205
Bamyili 68
Banda 220
bangwa 184
Bantu 11, 67, 90n46, 139, 142, 145, 154, 209
Bantu Pidgins 145
Barbados 279
Barrena, N 28, 346
basilect(al) 12, 42, 46, 64, 71, 211, 213, 217,
    253, 285
Bateson, G 83, 266, 346, 353
Bauer, A 130, 346
Bauman, R 365, 369
Baumann, A 260, 346
Baxter, A 68, 78, 346
Bazaar Malay 31, 275, 328
Beach-la-Mar 15-17, 24, 88, 94, 96, 133, 137,
    155, 252, 270, 304
Bee, D 140, 265, 346
behaviourism/ist 36-37, 39, 97, 113
Beigu 326
Belfast English 242n12
Belize 276
Belize(an) Creole 8, 72, 241, 276

Bell, H 64
Bell, R 80, 346
Bellow 323
Bemba 30
Bengma 256-57
Benin 105
Berbice Creole Dutch 20
Berlin 274-75
Berry, J 45, 140, 142, 346
BEV -> Black English Vernacular
bible 30, 273, 327-30
Bickerton, D vi, viii, 7, 9-10, 35, 39-41, 43, 45-
    48, 62, 64-65, 73, 86, 91, 93, 109, 111-12,
    117, 119-21, 127, 151, 186-87, 198-200,
    202-03, 212, 214-17, 219, 222, 226, 228-
    30, 233, 235, 287, 341, 346
Bidau 12
Bigsby, C 327n11, 346
bilingual(ism) 3, 9, 59, 64n21, 85, 90n46, 104-
    05, 199, 238, 265-69, 280, 282, 288, 290,
    299-300, 311
bioprogram 7, 10, 39, 45, 78, 86, 91, 93, 198-
    200, 202, 219, 229-31, 234, 240
Birmingham 129
Bislama 9, 17, 19, 20, 25, 29, 87, 146, 154, 163,
    167, 174, 176-78, 215, 254-55, 272, 285,
    328, 331
Bismarck Archipelago 17-18, 275, 281
Bissau Crioulo 78
Black (American) English 32, 54, 68, 189, 237-
    38, 240, 300, 306, 308, 311-12
Black English Vernacular (BEV) 289, 291
Bladon, A viii
Blaine, G 349
Blanche Bay 140
Bley, B 296, 346
Bloomfield, L 4, 37, 88, 97, 177, 346
Boas, F 35
Bodemann, Y 102, 346
Bold, J 297, 346
Boletim de Estudos Crioulos 46
Bollée, A viii, 11, 89, 93, 154, 347
Bolo 205
Bonaire 292
Boni 134, 189, 191
Borchardt, K 178, 296, 347
Boretzky, N 374
borrowing 59, 63, 67, 69, 114, 121, 175-76,
    179, 198, 202, 219-20
Botha, R viii
Bougainville 62, 295
Bounty 91
Braithwaite, E 303, 347
Brammall, J 370
Brash, E 6, 347
Brazil(ian) 20, 22, 72n29, 105n9, 106, 130
Brazilian Portuguese 105n9
Breinburg, P 298-99, 347
Brekie, H 350
Brenninkmeyer, L 116, 172, 347
Breton 20
Brew, J 358
Bright, W 347, 354, 365
Brinton, D 314, 347
Britain 53, 68, 246-47, 298, 308
British 30, 57, 67, 73, 79, 94, 131, 206, 246,
    263, 273, 276-77, 299, 321
British and Foreign Bible Society 27

British Honduras 276
broadcasting 185
Broken (Torres Straits PE) 9, 15, 58n9, 73, 163, 168-70, 174, 178, 209, 254, 326
Bromilow, W 246
Brouwer, L 253
Brown, P 166, 175, 366
Bruma, E 320
Bruner, J 210, 347
Bruyn, A 49, 345
Buang 142, 266
Buchner, M 24, 347
Buin 62
Buka 183
Buka News 333
Bulu 206
Burke, V 369
Bushell, K 309, 347
Bush Negro Language -> Saramaccan
Bush Pidgin 53, 65
Butcher, B 247, 347
Butler English 79
Byrne, F 38, 344, 347, 359, 361
Byzantine 32

C

Cacheu 78
Cahan, A 323
Calcutta 68
calques, calquing 177-80, 197-98
Cambridge 36
Camden, W 29, 177-78, 347
Cameron, C 246, 347
Cameroonian -> Cameroons PE
Cameroon(s) 15, 163, 275, 296, 330
Cameroons PE 15, 34-35, 68, 139, 146, 157, 161, 171, 173, 182-84, 197, 227, 232, 274, 296, 330
Campbell, R 358
Canada 21, 270
Canadian 123
Canberra 263n8
Canton 1-2, 295, 315
Cantonese 5n4, 131
"Cape Dutch" Afrikaans 60, 100
Capell, A 12, 347
Cape Possession 77
Cape Town 273
Cape Verde Creole 106n10, 314
Cape Verde Islands 78, 90, 202
Cape York Creole 19, 241
cargo cults/movements 65-67, 185, 327
Carib 276
Caribbean 28, 46, 56n6, 73, 90, 114, 194, 227, 237, 256, 291-92, 298-99, 303-04, 310, 318, 320, 331-32, 340
Caribbean Creole English 227
Caribbean Creole French 303, 321-23
"Caribbean Negro PE" 16
Carle, R 367
Carr, E 226, 347
Carrier Pidgin 46
Carrington, Lawrence 44, 69, 347
Carrington, Lois 361, 370, 373
Casely-Hayford, E 309, 347
Cassidy, F 208, 237, 331, 347

catastrophic principle 54n3
Catholic 29-30, 68, 273, 296, 320, 333-34
Cattle Station English 14
causatives, causativization 119-20, 169-71
Central African Republic 29, 84
Central America(n) 84, 303
Central Atlantic PE 16
Central Australia 288, 313
Central Australian Aboriginal Creole 199, 218
Cérol, M-J 265, 347
Césaire, A 322
Ceylon -> Sri Lanka
Chabacano 107
Chang 256
change of word class 155-56
Charpentier, J-M 78, 215, 254-55, 347-48
Chaudenson, R 11, 225, 348
Cheshire, J 348, 367
Chignell, A 248, 348
child language 23, 48, 80n39, 111, 133, 146, 231-33
China 74, 104, 312, 315
China Coast PE -> Chinese PE
Chinese 1, 15-16, 52, 94, 118, 129, 134, 136, 224, 252, 271, 277, 295
Chinese PE 1-2, 5, 14-17, 19, 36, 57, 72, 96, 103, 105, 119, 135, 137, 140, 146-47, 149, 151, 180, 224, 242, 295, 304, 308, 312, 315n6,
Chinese Pidgin Arabic 76
Chinese Pidgin English -> Chinese PE
Chinese Pidgin German 20, 103
Chinese Pidgin Russian 78, 137, 155, 262
Chinese-Russian (Trade) Jargon (of Kjachta) -> Chinese Pidgin Russian
Chinook Jargon 29, 52, 72, 78, 132, 137, 139, 145, 152, 159-60, 298, 314
Choctaw 77
Chokri 256-57
Chomsky, N 40, 49, 111, 336, 348
Chrestien, F 314, 348
Christian, Fletcher 91
Chukotka Pidgin Chukchee 20
Churchill, W 16, 24, 26, 88, 94, 137, 348
circumlocution 137
Civilisado, El 330
Clahsen, H 144n13, 348
Clark, D 263, 348
Clark, R vii, 18-19, 34, 91, 135, 149, 270, 348
Clarke, P 25, 352
classification 17-19, 74, 80, 86
Clayton, J 288n8, 289, 348
Clements, J back cover, 78, 102, 348
Closs-Traugott, E (see also: Traugott) 244, 364
Clyne, M viii, 68, 97, 99, 149, 233, 348
Coates, W 73n33, 142n12, 315, 348
Cochin 273
Cocoliche 130-31
code-shifting 265, 285, 310
Coelho, F 31, 108, 118, 348
Cole, D 26, 161, 262, 348
Coleman, D 349
Collet, P 361
Columbia [River] 29
Columbian Creole Spanish -> Palanquero
common-core theories 93, 113-14, 116

comparative linguistics 34
comparative method 223, 225
competence 40-41, 336
complementation / complementizers 172-73, 204
complication 128
compounds 177-78, 181
Comrie, B 39, 348
conduit metaphor 228, 242, 338
Confucius 309
conspiracies 126
container metaphor 338
continuity 44, 225-27
continuum -> post-Creole continuum / post-Pidgin continuum
conventionalization 138
Corder, S 4, 39, 235, 286, 348, 360, 370
Corne, C vii, 15, 38, 60, 79, 113n22, 192, 213, 222n1, 345, 348-49
Coulanges, J 322, 349
County Tyrone Irish English 11
Cozzolino, M 307, 349
Craig, D 280-81, 284, 288, 291, 302, 349
Crawford, J 77, 349, 353
creativity 5, 59n12
Creole (definitions of) 6-11; (etymology of) 6
Creole French -> French-based Creoles
Creole Language Library 47
Creole Portuguese 310
creolization 7-9, 33, 78, 85, 111, 117, 120-21, 167, 186-211
creoloid (semi-Creole) 11-12, 58n8, 60, 96, 278
Crioulo 78, 190
critical threshold 231, 233-34
Croat(s) 289
Crowley, T 20, 25, 29, 163, 349
Crystal, D 4, 349
Culler, J 60n13, 349
CUP = Cambridge University Press
Curaçao 292
Curnow, S 349
Curtis, S 51, 349
Cyprus 3, 56n6

D

Dagua 168, 264
Dahomey 105
Daiber, A 25, 349
Dalphinis, M 126, 264-65, 299, 349
Damão 68
Dani Police talk 20
Danish 28, 273-74, 314
Danish Antilles 12, 273
Darnley island 254, 326
Daru 247
Darwin 18
Das Gupta, J 352
Daview, H 359
day-names 207
Day, R 367
DeBose, C 97, 352
DeCamp, D viii 1, 9, 12, 42, 45, 63n19, 198, 208, 211-13, 219, 228, 241-42, 254, 268-69, 346, 349, 351, 354, 356, 365-66
Decker, T 325, 349

decreolization 64n21, 125, 203, 204n42, 211-15, 217, 221, 239, 269, 274, 287
definitions of 'Pidgin' and/or 'Creole' 1, 3-11
Defoe, D 305-06, 308, 349
De Katolieke Waarschuwer 320
Dekker, G 323, 349
Denmark 68
Dennis, J 5, 349
Dennys, N 2, 360
depidginization 212, 221, 274, 287
derivational morphology 214-16
derivational shallowness 141
De Rooij, V 68, 349
Deshima ii
Deutsche Kolonialzeitung 25
developmental hierarchy 81, 85-86
development of Pidgins and Creoles 51-92, 119, 122, 125, 127-221
Devonish, H 331-32, 349
dialectology 67
diffusion 56, 144, 223
diglossia 64n21, 265-69
Di Lasso, O 315
Dillard, J 300, 306, 311-12, 349
Dirven, R 229, 346, 357, 362, 363, 369
discontinuities 54, 76, 103, 127, 225-27, 234
Dixon, R 146, 157n21, 349
Diu 68
Djuka 34, 189, 191-92, 206-07, 327n10
D'Offay de Rieux, D 280, 292, 350
Dogberry 307, 350
Domingue, N 33, 350
Dominica 321
Dominican 106n10
Dorfmann, A 310, 350
Douala 184, 205
Drachman, G 374
Dravidian 11, 257
Dressler, W 87, 210, 350, 368
drift 10
dual-lingualism 59, 238
Duaun island 326
Du Bois, W 323
Ducrocq, L 30, 350
Duisburg 46
Duke of York Islands 55
Duranti, A 210, 217n47, 340, 350
Dutch 7, 11-12, 20, 28, 32, 60, 80, 97, 106, 125, 210, 254, 272-74, 276-77, 285, 292, 300, 308-10, 314, 320
Dutch Antilles 33, 251
Dutch Creole 273, 276
Dutch East Indies 80
Dutton, T viii, 13-15, 51, 59, 73n30, 77, 105, 127, 130, 136, 150, 162, 164, 169n29, 174, 238, 246n1, 248-49, 257-58, 271, 284, 297, 318, 350, 373

E

Eades, D 28, 290, 350
East Africa(n) 11, 31, 68, 275
Eastern Europe 260
East Sepik 185, 264
East Timor 68, 277
Ebonic 285, 291

Eckles, G 312, 352
Edinburgh Christian Instructor 27
Edmondson, J 61, 210, 351, 361
education, Pidgins and Creoles in 279-302
Edwards, J 206, 351
Edwards, V 48, 298, 351
Eersel, C 215n44, 254, 351
Efik 205
Egger, E 314, 351
Egyptian 11, 306
Ehrhart(-Kneher), S 8, 39, 90n47, 112, 154, 351
Elema(n) 73n30, 77, 136n8, 150, 155
Elema(n) (Hiri) Trade Language 77, 155
Ellison 323
Emonts, J 296, 351
Encina, J 314, 351
England 68
English 1-3, 5-7, 10, 12-14, 22, 25-26, 29, 32, 41, 45, 53, 56-57, 60, 64 -65, 69, 73-75, 82, 84, 91, 94-95, 101, 103-07, 113, 116-17, 124, 126, 129-37, 139, 144, 146-48, 150, 152, 154-56, 161-62, 164, 168, 171, 177-78, 180, 183, 188-89, 191, 199, 202, 212-13, 215-16, 218-19, 224, 227, 229n6, 232, 236, 240, 245-53, 255, 257-58, 262, 265, 267-68, 273-76, 279-85, 288-92, 296-99, 304-06, 308-10, 315-16, 321, 328, 331-34, 343 (see also Australian English)
English (lexicon/based/derived) Creole(s) 10, 34, 90, 114, 189, 194, 210, 269, 298 (see also under names of individual Creoles)
English-Japanese Jargon 131, 136, 159
English World-Wide 47, 288
Enninger, W 362, 374
environmental linguistics 49-50
ergativity 144
Erima 168
Escure, G 38, 351
Eskimo Trade Jargon 3, 129-30
Esperanto 60, 72
Essen 46
Ethiopia 309
Etudes créoles 46
etymology 1-3, 6
Eurocentricity 46, 343
Europe 52, 75, 102, 128, 285, 293
European(s) 41, 56n6, 66, 73-74, 76-78, 101, 105, 117, 135, 161n24, 176, 202, 205-06, 226-27, 237, 245, 248-49, 251-52, 262, 269-70, 274, 276, 296-99, 303-04, 313, 315-17, 324-25
European languages 22, 24-25, 30, 33-34, 70n27, 108, 117, 124-25, 140, 282, 296, 332
Evans, John viii
Ewe 123, 205-06
expanded Pidgin 6, 9, 12, 85, 88, 163-86

F

Fa d'Ambu -> Annobón Creole Portuguese
Faine, J 95, 194, 351
family trees 16-19, 31, 34-35, 114, 223-26
Fanakalo (Fanagalo) 3, 26, 90n46, 139, 141-42, 151, 154-55, 157, 161, 262, 297

Fanon, F 322
Far East 315
Farrar, F 22, 351
Fasold, R 244, 367, 371
Feagin, C 361
Feist 11, 33, 351
Féral, C 173, 227, 351
Ferguson, C 97-99, 101n7, 126, 129, 351
Fernando Póo PE 15, 82, 274
Ferraz, L 209, 351
Figueroa, J 47-49, 351
Fiji 19, 51, 56n6, 73, 75, 136, 271
Fijian 145, 153, 271
Fijian PE 15, 17, 136, 272
Fijian Pidgin Hindi 73, 136
Fill, A 362
Fillmore, C 126, 351
Fine, M 306, 312, 351
Finschhafen-Sattelberg 281
first law of Creole studies vi
first language acquisition 85
First World War 68, 260, 276, 282, 323, 333
Firth, S 294, 352
Fishman, J 244-45, 280, 344, 352, 359, 371
Fitzroy Crossing 68
Flanigan, B 306, 352
Fleischmann, U 27, 256, 303, 321-22, 352
Foetoe-boi 320
Foley, W 202-03, 352
Fon(gbe) 108n15
Forbes, G 264
foreigner talk 56, 64, 93, 96-102, 129, 146n16, 304, 306, 310, 313
Foster, R 25, 303n1, 309, 352
Fourcade, G 205, 352
Frake, O 107, 208, 239, 352
français tiraillou (tirailleur) 79
France 68
Franklin, K 297, 323, 352
French 22, 26-27, 29-30, 33, 46, 59-60, 74, 82, 94-95, 101, 105-06, 123, 125, 135, 140, 142, 154, 175-76, 183, 192, 205, 224, 255, 268-70, 279, 285, 292, 295, 310, 314, 321-22, 331, 343
French(-based) Creoles 11, 34, 90, 95, 114, 123, 154, 192, 194, 204, 269, 321-23, 331
French, A 279, 352
French Guiana 321
French India 90
French West Indies 323
Frend bilong mi 333
Freyberg, P 30n2, 352
Friday (*Robinson Crusoe*) 305, 309
Friederici, G 16, 25, 80, 249, 296, 352
Fuegian(s) 22
Fula -> Fulfulde
Fulfulde (Fula) 176, 216
functionalism/ist 202-03, 210

G

Garden of Eden 317-18
Gardner-Chloros, P 369
Gauteng 297
Gaywood, H 325, 352
Gazelle Peninsula 55
Gazèt sifon blé 46

Gbaya 220
Gbeya 84
Gebhard, J 75, 136, 352
Geelong 307
genesis of Pidgins and Creoles 93-125
genetic relationships 34
Genie 51
Genthe, S 137, 352
German 2, 3n3, 10, 14, 20, 22, 28-29, 52, 56-58, 60, 61n14, 75, 80, 94, 97-102, 104-05, 135-36, 149, 153, 161, 168, 170, 200-02, 227, 232, 250, 260-62, 274-77, 281, 294, 296, 301, 314-17, 323
German Empire 281
Germanic 11, 33, 238, 303, 330
German-Italian 142n12
German New Guinea 9, 12, 19, 30-31, 58, 80, 104, 174, 274-75, 281, 294, 296
German West Africa 174, 276, 317
Germany 49, 75, 135, 274
Ghana 207
Gilbert, G 32, 352, 354
Giles, H 300, 352, 366
Gilman, C 34-35, 352
Givón, T 6, 38, 45, 91, 149, 206, 218, 352, 363
Gloucester, Duke of 264
Goa 68, 78, 272-73
Goebl, H 363
Gold Coast 309
Gonzales, A 314, 352
Goodman, J 53, 75, 131-32, 136-37, 159, 352
Goodman, M 11, 34, 142, 352
Gordon, J 299, 352
Görlach, M back cover, viii, 345, 370
grammaticalization 107, 120, 127, 138, 143-44, 175, 219
graphization 256
Graz 318
Greece 269
Greek 22, 32, 315
Greenbaum, S 346, 365
Greenberg, J 110-12, 352
Greenfield, S 56n6, 353, 372
Greenfield, W 27
Gregesche 315
Grenada 314
Griffiths, T 368
Grimes, J 356
Grimshaw, A 237, 353
Grimshaw, B 26, 353
Groves, W 282-83
Guatemala 276
guest-worker Pidgins 75, 293
Guinea coast 107n12
Guinea-Bissau 65, 190, 225n3
Gulf Arabic Pidgin 75
Gulf of Guinea 28
Gullah 16, 41, 204, 224, 311-12, 314
Gumperz, J 34, 238, 269, 353
Gunther 283, 314
Guyana 20, 40, 64, 253, 276-77, 279, 285, 318, 331
Guyanais 194
Guyanese (Creole) 41, 43, 216-17, 253
Gypsy 314

H

Haas, M 76-77, 353
Hagen, G von 296, 353
Haiti(an) 65, 264, 268, 285, 321-23
Haitian Creole (French) 27, 36, 65, 87, 106n10, 108n15, 123, 125, 154, 194, 204-05, 224, 247n2, 256, 298, 321-22
Hale, H 52, 314, 353
Hall, E 302, 353
Hall, R viii, 4, 16-17, 23, 27-28, 33-34, 36-37, 40, 87, 95, 103, 113, 130, 172, 213-14, 223-25, 256, 269-72, 283, 297, 324-25, 353
Haller, H 7, 353
Halliday, M 67n24, 80-81, 85, 260, 353
Halls Creek 68
Hamitic 11
Hancock, I 1n1, 17-18, 34, 95, 106, 179, 195, 197, 210, 272, 346, 349, 351, 353-54, 356, 358, 362, 365-66, 370
Harding, E 53, 129, 354
Harré, R 60, 62, 110n19, 124, 345, 363
Harris, Joel 314, 354
Harris, John back cover, 37, 159, 161, 277, 297, 354, 373
Harris, R viii, 14, 55, 225, 228, 336n1, 338, 351, 354, 362
Hattori, S 354, 374
Haugen, E 256, 288, 354
Hausa 147
Hawaii(an) 45, 58n9, 73, 202, 226, 291
Hawaiian Creole English 9, 19, 58n9, 65, 71, 119, 127n2, 187, 199, 202, 216, 226, 233, 292, 319
Hawaiian PE 17-18, 20, 62, 109, 119, 130, 190, 199, 226, 233
Hawkes, T 228, 354
Hebrew 1, 22
Heine, B 30, 83n41, 108, 110, 139, 141, 145, 147, 354
Heinschke, M 367
Hellinger, M 200, 276, 354
Helton, E 297, 354
Herman, L 304, 354
Herman, M 304, 354
Herskovits, M 114, 354
Hervé 310
Héry, M 314, 354
Hesseling, D 25, 32, 96, 273, 354
Hesse-Wartegg, E von 25, 104, 354
Hides, J 248, 354
Highfield, A 344, 346, 349-50, 355-56, 358, 362, 365-66, 369, 371, 373
High German 200, 260
Highlands Tok Pisin 172
Hill, K 346, 355, 366
Hindi 60, 136, 257
Hinnekamp, V 75, 97, 101-02, 136, 145, 160, 262, 310, 355
Hiri Motu 15, 30, 31, 57, 68, 73, 79, 105, 143, 145-46, 157-60, 162-63, 167, 169n29, 171, 175, 240, 246, 248-49, 257-58, 265, 267, 283, 286n4, 297, 329, 332, 334
Hiri trade language(s) 130, 136, 242, 262
historical linguistics 34-35, 223-25, 227
historicity 87

Hjelmslev, 149n18, 232
Hockett, C 14n8, 33n3, 92n48, 97, 226, 336, 355
Hoeltker, G 250, 355
Hoenigswald, H 127, 226, 355
Holland 273
Hollyman, K 15, 149, 272, 355
Holm, J viii, 72n29, 117, 187, 206, 276, 344, 355
Holmes, J 353, 363, 365-66
holophrastic talking 128, 132n6
Holthouse, H 51, 355
Holzknecht, S 244, 284, 364
Hong Kong 2, 78, 118, 131, 274
Hosali, P 79, 355
Huber, M 345, 355, 358
Hudson, J 289, 355
Huebner, T 286n7, 347, 355, 361
Hueskes, J 356
Huet, G 272, 355
Hugill, S 315, 355
Hull, A 95, 355
Hull, B 268
Hullen, W 362
Hunter, W 295, 355
Huttar, G 106, 206, 327n10, 355
Hyltenstam, K 355, 363, 366
Hymes, D back cover, viii, 5, 9, 36, 47, 48, 138, 243, 344, 347, 349, 351-54, 355-57, 361, 364, 366, 368, 372
hypercorrection 244
hypno-elicitation 217

I

Iberian 46
Ibo -> Igbo
Icelandic-Breton Pidgin 20
Igbo (Ibo) 126, 205
Ilocano 130
implicational analysis/scales 42-44, 226, 228, 243
impoverishment 4, 128
India(n) 34, 53, 74, 78-79, 256, 262, 269, 271, 274 (see also American Indian)
Indian Ocean 73, 106, 127, 191-92, 303
Indian Ocean Creoles 15, 90, 205, 213, 256
Indian Pidgin Fijian 271
Indo-Aryan 11, 257, 269
Indo-China 270
Indo-European 32, 100
Indonesia(n) 32, 74, 80, 264, 277, 300
Indo-Portuguese 59, 68, 106n10, 118, 303
inflectional morphology 142-44, 166-67, 192, 195, 214-16
innateness 45, 109, 163, 198, 229, 234
innovations 59
Institut d'études créoles 46
interlanguage 4, 75n34, 123, 231, 235, 286-87, 305
International Journal for the Sociology of Language 47
invariant word order 145
Iran 259
Islam(ic) 31, 314, 328
Italian 7, 22, 100, 130-31, 142

Italian-Portuguese contact language of Brazil 130
Italy 315

J

Jabêm 281
Jablonska, A 129, 133, 355
Jackson, K 303, 355
Jacobovits, L 350, 370
Jacobs, M 159, 355
Jacomb, E 137, 355
Jacques, N 316, 355
Jakarta 272
Jakobson, R 81, 243, 356
Jamaica(n) 45, 67, 208, 242, 279, 285, 304, 330-32
Jamaican Creole 3, 12, 24, 34-35, 38, 42, 54, 72, 106n10, 114, 126, 197, 204, 207-08, 210, 213, 239, 253, 298-99, 331-32
Janson, T 67, 356
Janssen, A 58, 356
Japan 270
Japanese 53, 79, 109, 117, 136, 263-64, 282
Japanese PE 52-53, 75, 131, 180, 262, 271
jargon (stage) 6, 9, 52, 56, 128-38, 143, 177
Java 106, 210, 272-73
Javanese Creole Portuguese 210
Jehovah's Witnesses 333
Jennings, W 51, 356
Jerusalem 314
Jespersen, O 4, 224, 240, 356
Jiménez, A 314, 356
Johnson, M 140, 356
Johnson, R 282n1, 356
Jones, E 174, 245, 356
Jones, F 188, 215-16, 356
Jordaan, K 7, 356
Joseph, J 356, 364
Jourdan, C 36, 67, 270-71, 356
Journal of Pidgin and Creole Languages 46
JPCL = *Journal of Pidgin and Creole Languages*

K

Kachari 256
Kahn, M 207, 356
Kaigey, F 326
Kalaw Kawaw Ya 326
Kamerun -> Cameroons
Kanaka(s) 51, 94, 249
Kang-Kwong Luke 131, 356
Kanuri 206
Karipuna 20
Kastovsky, D 350
Katanga 68
Kâte 281
Katolik: Buk long Tok Pisin 333
Katolik Nius 333
Kaufman, T 35, 61, 107, 370
Kave, E 232
Kavieng 333
Kay, P 38, 109, 141, 146, 356
Kaye, A back cover, vii, 356
Kazuko, I 354
Keane, E 303, 356

Keesing, R viii, 29, 36, 114, 123n31, 143, 152n19, 265, 356
Kenya(n) 141, 145, 147, 151
Kenyan Pidgin Swahili -> see Pidgin Swahili
Keram River 193
Kerema 130
Khezha 256-57
Khiamnagan 256
Kiautschou 20, 104, 108, 275
Kihm, A back cover, vii, 78, 190, 211, 222n1, 224n2, 225n3, 241, 356-57
Kikongo 205-06
Kimbundu 209
King, C 2, 360
King, J 246-47, 357
kitchen jargons 79
Kituba 314
Kiwai 247
Kjachta 136-37
Klein, W 48, 357, 361
Kloss, H 303, 321, 330, 357
Koch, H 199, 218, 357
Koefoed, G 111n20, 112, 148, 357
Koenders 321
koiné(s) 3, 11-12, 32, 79
koinéization 12
Kokopo 282
Koll-Stobbe, A back cover, 357
Kolonialdeutsch 61n14, 260-62
Koloniale Rundschau 317
Konyak 256
Korea 270
Korean Bamboo English 75
Koriki 73n30, 77, 136n8, 150
Koriki Hiri Trade Language 77
Kotzé, E 11, 357
Kramp, A 203, 372
Kreolische Bibliothek 47
Krio 12, 34-35, 174, 184, 188, 194-95, 197-98, 215-16, 227, 245-47
Kriol [of Guinea Bissau] 190, 225n3
Kriol [of northern Australia] 3, 9, 12, 18, 41, 45, 59n11, 64n21, 68, 71, 74, 84, 87, 103, 174, 197, 199, 207, 214, 217, 247n2, 254, 285, 288, 325, 327n10, 342
Kriol [of Western Austalia] 289
Kroon, W 314, 357
Kukukuku 248
Kulick, D 83, 357
Kumar, R ii
Kupwar 34, 238
Kwoma 83, 252, 266

L

Laade, W 36, 357
Laberge, S 70, 165-66, 187, 193, 366
Labour trade 51, 129, 271
Labov, W 36, 39, 69-71, 93, 119, 130, 142, 169, 190, 194, 228, 236, 241, 289, 300, 357
Labovian Paradox 340
Labrador Inuit Pidgin French 20
LAD -> language acquisition device
Ladd, P 48, 351
Ladhams, J 33, 106-07, 357
Lae 193, 199, 333

Lae Garamut 333
La Fontaine 314
Lagasai 333
Lake, A 357
Lamassa 249
Landtman, G 36, 357
language acquisition 109n17, 112, 230-33
language acquisition device (LAD) 39
language attitude studies 244-55
Language Awareness 288n8
language death 61, 87, 210, 238, 269-74, 298
language engineering 255-59
Language in Society 47
language planning 228n4, 230, 255-59
language shift 59
Lass, R 226, 357
Latin 22, 28, 52, 229, 285
Lavwa ka bay 46
Law, J 307
Lawrence, P 65n22, 66, 282, 327, 357
Laycock, D viii, 91, 103, 111, 212, 244, 297, 303, 308, 316, 318, 321n9, 325, 350, 357, 373-74
League of Nations 282
Lee, M 310, 357
Lee, R 327n11
Leech, G 124, 358
Lefebvre, C 108n15, 123, 358
Leiden 32
Le jeune, J-M 29, 358
Leland, C 96, 312, 314, 315n6, 358
Lenz, R 108, 358
Le Page, R vii, 8, 40-42, 44-45, 72, 87, 91, 187, 201, 241-42, 276, 279, 287, 298-300, 303, 331, 358, 369-70, 372
lexicalization 128
lexical semantics 205-10
lexicon 2, 5, 91, 135-37, 153-62, 175-82, 198, 202, 205-10, 219-21, 259
lexico-statistics 106
lexifier language 12, 59, 101, 104, 122n30, 124, 154, 162, 197, 199, 202, 217, 249, 251, 311
Liangmei 256
Liberia 76
Lichtveld, U 303, 321, 372
Liem, N 140, 149, 358, 363
life-cycle 87, 235, 269-70
Lightfoot, D 214, 358
Lilke, E 327, 358
Lincoln, P 59n11, 358
Lingala 73
Lingua Franca 2-3, 96, 103, 147, 151, 155, 270, 295, 314
lingua franca/lingue franche 3, 15, 26, 29, 31, 59, 73, 103, 105, 227, 242, 246-48, 260, 262, 266, 271, 274-75, 277, 281-82, 294, 297
Lingua Geral Brasilica 72
Linguistic Society of Papua New Guinea 284
linguistic theory, relevance of Pidgins and Creoles to 222-43
Lipski, J 107, 358
literacy 89
literature in Pidgins and Creoles 303-35
loanwords (see also: borrowing) 176, 178
London 298
London, J 306, 312, 317, 358

Lotha 257
Lounsbury, F 240-41, 358
Loyalty islands 19, 129n4
Lüdi, G 358, 361, 374
Ludwig, R 303, 321, 358
Lumbee Creole English 20
Lutheran 68, 281, 314
Lynch, J 11, 32, 165, 236, 284n2, 358
Lyons, J 47, 359

M

Mabbot, T 306, 359
Macanese 78, 118, 274
Macassar(ese) 277
Macassarese Pidgin 277, 298
Macau 2, 68, 78, 106n10, 118, 272, 274, 295
Mackay 271
MacKnight, C 274, 359
Madang 66, 68, 253, 284, 333
Madang Matau 333
Mafeni, B 9, 16, 160, 164-65, 176n36, 178-79, 359
Magens, J 28, 359
Makzien vo Kristen-soema 320, 330
Malabang 193-96
Malacca 68, 78, 106n10, 274
Malagasy 59
Malakula 29
Malay 2, 20, 74, 80, 94, 198, 272, 276-77
Malay-Portuguese 273
Malcolm, I 285, 359
Malinowski, B 83, 359
Manam 21
Manchuria 129, 134-35
Manes 366
Manessy, G 140, 147, 232, 359
Manfredi, V 222n1, 359
Manus island 176, 185, 193, 196
Mao 256-57
Maori PE 17
Maprik 168
Marathi 11, 117
Marbot, F-A 314, 359
Marchese, L 292, 331, 367
Marianas 275
maritime French 95
markedness 5, 44, 208
Markey, T 3n2, 7, 11, 31-32, 41, 96, 198, 226, 355, 359
Maroldt, K 7, 33, 236, 238-39, 345
maroon(s) 73, 107, 134, 209
Marsh, P 361
Martinican Creole 314, 321-22
Martyn-Jones 58n8, 338, 359
mass media 330-35
Mattelart, A 310, 350
Mauritian Creole 15, 30, 154, 192, 194, 204-05, 314
Mauritius 30, 50, 94, 154, 321
May, K 99, 359
May, R 370
Maya 276
Mayers, W 2, 359
Mayerthaler, W 71, 191, 359
Mayoux, J 305, 359
Mbondu 205

Mbugu 11
McDonald, R 249, 359
McElhanon, K 284, 346, 352, 359, 363-64, 366, 373
McLaren, J 360
Mead, M 84, 249, 252, 294, 360
Mecca 75n33
Mediterranean 103, 270
Meijer, G 360
Meillet, A 33, 224, 360
Meisel, J viii, 56, 75n34, 109, 119, 123, 128, 157n21, 211, 231, 233n8, 234, 236, 293, 345-46, 360, 371
Melanesia(n) 11, 13, 17, 32-34, 47, 51-52, 56n6, 60, 75, 79, 83, 89, 129n4, 133, 148, 156, 163, 166, 185, 224, 237-38, 249, 252, ·263-64, 267, 271, 324, 342
Melanesian languages 16, 33, 123n31, 143, 196, 236
Melanesian PE 15, 16, 18-19, 36, 79, 89, 94, 101, 103, 119, 123n31, 134, 186, 304, 308
Melilla 21
Melville, H 305, 360
mentalism 39, 97
mesolect(al) 12, 42, 211, 213, 217, 253
Mesthrie, R 262, 360
metaphor 183, 223, 228, 270, 338
Michener, J 306, 360
Mickey Mouse 308, 310
Micronesia(n) 17, 19-20, 275
Micronesia PE 17, 19
Middle English 7, 27, 33, 239-40
Mihalic, F 25, 181, 334, 360
military Pidgins 78-79
Miller, M 305, 311, 360
Milne Bay English 20
Milroy, L 89, 242n12, 360
Mintz, S 237, 360
Mioko island 294
Miskito Coast Creole English 117, 206
mission(arie)s 28-31, 45, 50, 58, 61n15, 64-66, 73, 79, 83, 101-02, 105, 136, 200, 249-50, 262, 275, 281, 283, 288, 293, 296, 326, 328, 333, 342
Mississippi 77
Mitchell, R 326
mixed languages 5, 7-8, 27, 31, 224-25
Mobile 77
Mobilian 76-77
Moeliono, A 259, 360
Molière, J-B 314, 360
Molony, C 78, 107, 352, 360
Moluccas 78, 273
Mombasa 68
monogenesis 45
Montreal 123
Moravian 27, 314, 319
Moresche 315
morphology 123, 142, 166-67, 192-98
Morris, D 51, 360
Morrison, J 1, 360
Morrison, R 1, 360
Mosel, U 116-18, 133, 139-40, 177, 179-80, 360
Mosoro, M 310, 360
Motu 30, 56, 68, 77, 101-02, 105, 136, 162, 240, 247-48, 257-58, 268, 286n4
Motuan(s) 73, 77, 101, 136n8, 248

Mufwene, S 33, 40, 44, 222n1, 360-61
Mühlhäusler, P vii, 1-3, 10, 13, 15, 20, 23, 25,
 27, 30, 33n3, 36, 38, 40-41, 47-50, 53, 55,
 57-60, 62, 64n20, 69, 74n31, 76, 79, 83-84,
 89-91, 98, 101, 107n13, 110n19, 114, 122,
 123n31, 124, 128, 137, 141, 143-44, 147,
 149-50, 164, 166, 169-70, 177, 181, 198,
 206, 222, 227, 229, 234-35, 237n9, 244,
 248-49, 259, 267, 271, 281, 291, 295-96,
 303, 309, 312, 328, 336-37, 339, 341, 345,
 350-52, 361-62, 370-71, 374
Mulga Fred 307
multifunctionality 137, 196-97
multilingualism 163
Murphy, J 297, 325, 362
Murray, J 247-48, 362
Murray island 326
Muslim 277
Muysken, P 34, 38, 41, 93, 118, 122, 174, 344-
 45, 358, 360, 362, 369, 372

N

Nagaland 256
Naga Pidgin 87, 145, 177-79, 256-57
Nagara, S 109, 362
Nahuatl-Spanish 314
Namibia 275, 278
Namaliu, R 310, 362
Naro, A 102, 109, 362
Natal 56n6, 262
nativization 8, 37
natural(ness) 5, 8, 23, 44-46, 48-51, 60-63, 71,
 88, 98, 109-12, 114, 122, 128, 141, 208,
 222, 228-29, 239, 287, 339-41
nautical jargon 19, 93-96
Ndjuka 106-07
Neffgen, H 25, 362
negation 146, 217
Negerhollands 12, 28, 32, 60, 65, 273, 313n1,
 314
Negro 23, 25, 306-07
"Negro-Portuguese" 314
Nelde, P 363
neo-grammarian(s) 32
Neo-Melanesian 15-18, 55, 103, 224, 252,
 324-25
Netherlands 49, 75, 276, 292, 298, 314, 321
Netherlands Antilles 210, 285, 292-93, 298,
 314
Neuhauss, R 281, 362
Neumann, G 78, 135-36, 362
Neustúpny, J 53, 244, 337n2, 362
New Britain 24, 34, 176
New Caledonia(n) 9, 19-20, 39, 51, 58n9, 75,
 133, 135, 152, 154, 272
New Caledonian PE 18
New Caledonian Pidgin French 14-15, 82, 149
New Englishes 11
New Guinea(n) 9-10, 12, 17-18, 20, 23, 28, 54
 -55, 57-58, 64, 67, 73-74, 76, 79, 104, 116-
 17, 149, 161, 247-48, 253, 264 -65, 272,
 275-76, 282-83, 294, 307, 309-10, 316,
 324, 334 (see also: German New Guinea,
 Papua New Guinea)
New Guinea Highland(er)s 54, 265
New Guinea PE -> Tok Pisin

New Guinea Pidgin German 14, 56
New Hanover 65
New Hebrides 19, 129n4, 132, 137 (see also
 Vanuatu)
New Hebrides PE 19
New Ireland 176
New South Wales 15, 271
Newspeak 261-62
New Testament 27
Newton, H 30, 246-47, 362
New World 34, 54 , 76, 192, 208
New Zealand 13, 133, 270
New Zealand PE 16
Ngatik Men's Language 18-20
Ngbandi 141
Ngombe 205
Nicaragua 276, 314
Nichols, P 204, 362
Nigeria(n) 15, 54, 64, 178, 292, 309-10
Nigerian PE 9, 14 , 64-65, 146, 164-65,
 176n36, 178-79, 292, 309-10, 330-31
Nius Bilong Yumi 333
Noel, J 265, 267, 326, 362
Nolde, E 294, 362
non-verbal communication 51-53
Norfolk Island 49
Norfolk Island Creole 18-19
Norman 82
North America 33, 36, 298
Northern Australia 79, 103, 277, 280, 285,
 288, 293
Northern Australian Kriol -> Kriol
North Carolina 20
Northern Territory 18, 79, 277
Norway 252
Norwegian 135
Noss, P 176, 362
Nupela Testament 330
nurture 60-63, 228-29
Nyakoma 140

O

O'Barr, J 366
O'Barr, W 366
O'Callaghan, E 310, 363
Oceania 28
Oceanic 36, 116n24, 270
Ochs, E 231, 363
Odo, C 187, 235, 346
Ogden, C 359
Old World 76
Olewale 283
Ong, W 88, 363
oral traditions 315, 318
origins (theories of) 93-125
orthography 331
Ortony, A 364
Orwell, G 224, 261, 364
O'Shaughnessy, M 361
Ostendorf, B 322-23, 364
Ostow, R 102, 346
OSV word order 145-46
OUP = Oxford University Press

P

Pacific viii, 9, 14-16, 18-19, 24, 35, 45, 51, 56n6, 68, 75, 91, 96, 103, 127, 129, 133, 137, 139, 143-44, 146-49, 152, 163, 232, 270-71, 285, 293, 303, 305, 312-13, 315, 327, 331, 335
Pacific Creoles 20, 170, 256
Pacific PE(s) 17, 19, 116n24, 137, 145, 170, 176, 256, 304
Palanquero 20
Palau 275
Paliau 185
Palmerston Island English 20, 90n47
Pangu Pati Nius 334
panlectal grid 43
Papers in Pidgin and Creole Linguistics 46
Papia 46
Papia Kristang 198, 274
Papiamentu 33, 47, 87, 106n10, 107-08, 210, 251, 285, 293, 314, 330
Papua(n) 13, 20, 25, 30, 36, 56n6, 57, 77, 79, 105, 136, 232, 246-49, 257, 265, 297, 334
Papua New Guinea(n) 5, 13, 30, 40-41, 54, 58, 64, 66, 68, 75, 83, 101, 104, 156, 183, 199-200, 219, 238, 249, 251-52, 258-59, 265-68, 277, 283-85, 293, 295, 297-98, 301, 317, 323, 328, 330, 332-35, 341-42
Papuan PE 13-15, 18-19, 26, 29-30, 36, 57, 105, 150, 162, 180, 232, 246-47
Parépou, A 314, 363
Parkvall, M 345, 355, 358
Passi, G 326
patois 3
Patpatar 140
Paul, H 172n33, 364
Pawley, A 165, 364
PE = Pidgin English
Peace Corps 330
Pearson, J 307
Peet, W 216, 341, 363
Pekan Tugu 272
Pele 185
Pennsylvania Dutch 72
Pères Blancs 314, 363
Perez, A 259, 363
performance 336-37
PEs = Pidgin Englishes
Petit-Nègre 144n14, 310
Philippine (Spanish) Creoles 106n10, 107, 239
Philippines / Philippino 78, 107, 130, 208, 237, 273, 285
Phillipson, R 278. 363
philology 31
Phom 256
phonology 134, 138-44, 163, 187-92, 210, 212-16, 232, 312
phonotactics 140-41, 165
Piau, J 244, 284, 363
Pidgin (definitions of) 1, 3-4, 6
Pidgin (etymology of) 1-2
Pidgin Afrikaans 20
Pidgin Bantu 26
Pidgin-Creole life cycle 81
Pidgin English [PE] -> Australian PE, Chinese PE, Melanesian PE, New Guinea PE, Nigerian PE, South Australian PE,

Tasmanian PE, Victoria PE, West African PE)
Pidgin Fijian 73, 82, 145-46, 156, 271, 298
Pidgin French 82, 139, 149, 270 (see also Labrador Inuit Pidgin French, Vietnamese Pidgin French)
Pidgin French 21, 144n14
Pidgin German 68, 79-80, 99-101, 104 -05, 108, 139, 149, 153, 160, 180, 201-02, 260, 262, 272, 310, 312 (see also Chinese Pidgin German)
Pidgin Hausa 147
Pidgin Italian 75n33, 315
pidginization 12, 33, 109, 152
pidginized Afrikaans 79
Pidgin Japanese 314
Pidgin Koriki 20
Pidgin Macassarese 74, 76, 103
Pidgin Malay 277
Pidgin Portuguese 2-3, 68, 76, 78, 102-03, 105-06, 117, 310
Pidgins and Creoles in Education (PACE) 46, 279
Pidgin Sango 142
Pidgin Siassi 76
Pidgin Spanish/English 21
Pidgin Swahili 141, 145, 147, 150
Pidgin Turkish 101
Pidgin Zulu -> Fanakalo
Piñaguero Panare 153
Piniau, S 252, 363
Pink, P 367
Pionnier, J-N 29, 363
Pitcairnese -> Pitcairn Island Creole
Pitcairn Island 49, 90-91
Pitcairn Island Creole 11, 17, 18-19, 90-91, 133, 187-88, 201, 240
plantations 10, 51, 56n6, 58, 64, 72-73, 75n34, 76, 79-80, 82-83, 106, 107n12, 109, 161, 202, 227, 253, 271, 277, 294, 316
Platt, J 11, 363
plural marking 168, 192-93, 204-05, 215
Poe, E 306, 311, 363
Police Motu 37, 73, 79, 105, 162, 246, 248-49, 265
Politzer, R 33, 363
Pollard, V 67, 363
Polynesia(n) 19, 133
Pondicherry 68
Poroman 334
Port Essington 161n24
Port Moresby 68, 101, 105, 247-49, 257, 283, 333-34
Portugal 6
Portuguese 1-2, 5, 10, 28, 32, 68, 72, 74, 78, 102, 105-07, 130, 202, 209, 251, 272-73
Portuguese(-based) Creoles 10, 33, 68, 78, 90, 103, 108, 118, 194, 272-74, 277
Portuguese Guinea 78
Pos, H 310, 318, 321n8, 363
Posner, R 113, 123-24, 363
post-Creole continuum 11-12, 41, 43n7, 44, 211-21, 226, 253, 268, 285, 287, 289
post-generative models 41-45
post-Pidgin continuum 12, 65, 211-21, 287
Pradelles de Latour, M-L 184, 363
pragmatics 143
"pre-Pidgin continuum" 138

prepositions 149, 218-19
Pride, J 353, 363, 365-66
"primitive" languages 22-23
prior creolization 236-41
pronouns 60, 113n23, 124-25, 147-49, 151-53, 168
Protestant 29-30, 319
Proto-Melanesian 17
Proto-Pidgin English 16-17, 35, 95
Providence Island 90, 276
psycholinguistics 9
Puari River 77
Puppel S 344, 363
Puri 22
Putman, J 314, 363
Pütz, M 67, 229, 299, 346, 354, 357, 361, 363, 369

Q

Quechua 60, 173
Queen 264
Queensland 13, 19, 51-52, 56n6, 75, 79, 241, 271-72, 290
Queensland Kanaka English 13-15, 18, 59n11, 271-72, 291

R

Rabaul 24, 68, 253, 294, 316, 330, 333
Rabaul News 185, 333
Rabaul Times 24, 307
Raidt, E 7, 11, 364
Rambutyo 10
Ramson, T 250
Rarotonga(n) 132
Rastafarian 67, 210, 327n11
Ray, S 32-33, 36, 238, 363
received pronunciation (RP) 298-99
reconstruction 127
Reddy, M 228, 242, 338-39, 364
reduplication 56, 117-18, 179-80, 196-97
Reed, S 60, 83, 156, 252, 260, 266, 282, 364
regression 127
Reinecke, J 4, 15-16, 27, 29, 35, 38, 45, 52, 72, 94-95, 118, 137, 142, 162, 180, 248, 251-52, 270, 273, 291, 308, 313-15, 336, 364
Reisman, K 210, 290, 364
relativization 174, 199, 217-18
relexification 15, 34, 56, 74, 93, 96n3, 103-08, 269, 272
repidginization 10, 54
restructuring 127-28
Reunion 59, 321
Reunion Creole 15, 60, 154, 192, 205, 213, 225, 312, 314
Rew, A 265, 364
Rhydwen, M 14, 45, 74, 254, 285, 288, 364
Ribbe, C 129, 364
Richards, I 359
Richardson, I 30, 364
Rickford, J viii, 43, 173n34, 189, 211, 217, 237-38, 240, 244, 253, 326, 364
Rigo 249
Rigsby, B viii, 241, 254, 326, 364
Riley, C 153, 364
Rimmer, M 304, 372

Roberge, P 7, 355, 360, 364
Roberts, J 20, 109, 227, 364-65
Roberts, P 204, 365
Robertson, F 94, 365
Robertson, I 276-77
Robinson, W 80
Robinson Crusoe 308-09
Rogers, E 324, 365
Romaine, S viii, 10, 14, 41, 58, 67, 69, 166, 241, 281, 284, 338, 351, 359, 362, 365, 367, 370
Romance (languages0 47, 144, 238, 240
Roman empire 22
Romance 3, 33
Rome 75n33, 136
Rongmei 256-57
Roper River Creole 19, 254
Ross, A 11, 133, 188, 365
Rossel Island 26
Rost, C 367
Roulet, E 39, 286n6, 348, 361, 370
Rowley, C 277, 365
Royal Commission into Labour 52, 365
RP -> received pronunciation
Ruhen, O 294, 365
rule generalization 5
rule-governedness 227-28
Rushton, D 25, 365
Russell, T 24, 365
Russian 98, 129, 135-36, 155, 252
Russian-Chinese contact language 136
Russonorsk 78, 135, 262
Ryan, J 264, 365

S

Sabir 3, 314
Sadler, W 295, 297, 365
Saibai 326
Saint Croix 28
Saint Helena 49
Saint-Jacques Fauquenoy, M 194, 365
Saint John 28
Saint Kitts Creole 47
Saint Louis (New Caledonia) 58n9
Saint Lucia 321
Saint Lucian Patwa 126
Saint Paul's (Torres Straits) 58n9, 254
Saint-Quentin, A de 314, 365
Saint Thomas 28, 46, 273
Saipan 275
Salisbury, R 54, 89, 365
Sama 205
Samarai [Papua] 30, 247
Samarin, W 4, 29, 37, 69, 84, 96n3, 142, 175, 220, 365-66
Samoa(n) 13, 19, 24, 51, 58, 75, 90n46, 105, 114, 152, 161, 227, 275-76, 294, 306, 316,
Samoan PPE -> Samoan Plantation PE
Samoan Plantation PE 13, 18-20, 25, 58, 68, 90n46, 114, 130, 137, 147-48, 151, 155, 157, 161, 169, 177, 272, 313
Samoan Times 25
Sandalwood English 16, 19
Sandanista 276
Sandefur, J viii, 59n11, 64n21, 68, 71-72, 74, 79, 84, 208, 214, 254, 280, 285, 288, 366

Sango 29, 37, 73, 140, 142, 163, 175-76, 220, 285
Sangtam 256
Sankoff, G viii, 36, 38, 46, 58, 70, 76, 82, 92, 109, 112, 141-42, 146, 152, 165-67, 171, 175, 187, 193, 266, 357, 366
Santiago, A 363
São Tomé 209
Sapinski, T 244, 366
Sapir 10, 35, 121
Saramaccan 34, 73, 96, 106-08, 122, 189, 191, 327n10
Sato, C 125, 244, 286n7, 291-92, 366
Saville-Troike, M 366, 368
Saxon 27
Sayer, E 304, 366
Scandinavia(n) 49, 75, 315
Schegloff, E 146, 366
Schellong, O 94, 366
Scherer, K 352, 366
schizoglossia 288
Schnee, H 140, 296, 366
Schneider, G 227, 366
Schouten, H 320, 366
Schuchardt, H 2, 3n2, 7, 23, 31-33, 35, 48, 78-79, 82, 96, 108, 114, 122, 132-33, 135, 147, 152, 222, 224, 295, 306, 312, 318, 366-67
Schultze, E 36, 72, 367
Schumann, J 286n5, 367
Schwartz, T 185, 367
Schwörer, E 61n14, 260-61, 367
Scott, J 5, 349
Scotton, C 150, 367
sea shanties 315-16
Sebba, M 38, 195, 197, 367
Sebeok, T 356
secondary hybridization 130
second language acquisition / learning / teaching 23-24, 46, 48, 98, 133
Second World War 52, 79, 105, 248, 252, 262, 282, 297, 333
Seiler, W 31, 277, 367
Selinker, L 286n6, 367
Sema 256-57
semantics 122
semi-Creole -> creoloid
semiotics 60n13
Sephardic Jews 251
Sepik 5, 277, 294
Serb(s) 289
serial verb constructions 218
Seychelles 280, 292, 322
Seychellois 87, 154, 197, 292
Shaffer, D 259, 300, 367
Shakespeare, W 310, 325-26
Shannon, C 243, 367
Sharpe, M 289, 367
Shelta 210
Shelton-Smith 25, 64, 367
Sherzer, J 365, 369
Shilling, A 80, 367
Shnukal, A viii, 170n30, 209, 292, 326, 331, 367
Shrimpton, N 245, 325, 367
Shuy, R 244, 367, 371
Siberia(n) 20, 78

Siegel, J viii, 12, 15, 17, 73, 136, 145-46, 153-54, 185, 218, 271, 279, 285, 334, 367-68
Sierra Leone(an) 12, 34, 54, 76, 245-46, 325
sign language 53
SIL = Summer Institute of Linguistics
Silverstein, M 35, 40-41, 76, 80, 137, 160, 235-36, 336n1, 368
simplicity/simplification 4-5, 128, 234-36
Singapore 11, 20
Singapore Bahasa Rojak 20
Singler, J 39, 130n5, 358
Singlish 11
Sinhalese 118
Sino-Russian (jargon/mixed language) of Manchuria 129, 134-35, 137
SLA -> second language acquisition
slavery/slaves 76, 80, 105-06, 107n12, 122, 313n2, 314, 318
Smart, J 75, 368
Smith, A 2, 368
Smith, G 283, 297, 368
Smith, I 167, 273, 368
Smith, N 20, 93, 118, 133-34, 189, 191-92, 345, 358, 363, 368
Smith, P 358
Snell, E 25, 368
social forces 55
social status 260-65
social typology 72-91
Society for Caribbean Linguistics 46, 288
Society for Pidgin and Creole Languages 46
sociolinguist(ic)s 35-36, 88n43, 90, 244-78
Solenberger, R 275, 368
Solomon Island(er)(s) 13, 17, 19, 264, 271, 298, 331
Solomon Islands PE -> Solomons PE
Solomons PE 9, 16-17, 19, 65, 67, 75, 152n19, 163, 167, 174, 176, 262, 265, 271-72, 317, 327n10, 328, 331
Solomons Pijin -> Solomons PE
Songo 205
Sophiatown 67
Sophocles 325
South Africa 7, 11, 20, 79, 90n46, 262, 273, 278
South America(n) 318
South Australia(n) 14, 280, 303n1, 309
South Australian PE 20, 144, 303n1
South-East Asia(n) 79, 131
South East Australian Aboriginal P E 146
Southern Africa 7, 26, 262, 297
South Seas 1, 94, 262, 275, 306
South Seas Jargon 19
South Seas PE 16, 149, 306, 316
South West Africa 275
Southworth, F 11, 237-39, 269, 368
SOV word order 145
Soweto 67
Spain 28, 275-76
Spaniard(s) 276
Spanish 22, 28-29, 78, 82, 117, 130-31, 153, 208, 229, 251, 273-76, 285, 310, 314
Spanish(-based) Creole(s) 33, 107, 208, 273
"speech community" 44, 241-42
Speiser, F 137, 368
Spencer, J 356, 359, 368
Spitzer, L 244-45, 368
Sprachbund 119

Sranan 10, 12, 27, 30n2, 33, 36, 65, 87, 96, 106-07, 112, 125, 133-34, 159n22, 189-91, 195, 197, 203, 215n44, 224, 254, 285, 298, 310, 314, 318-21, 330
Sreedhar, M 87, 145, 177, 179, 257, 368
Sri Lanka (Ceylon) 56n6, 78, 272-74
Sri Lankan Creole Malay 20
Sri Lankan Portuguese Creole 167, 330
stable/stabilization/stabilized Pidgin 6, 9, 12, 54-55, 119-20, 138-63, 177
Stadtlander, K 367
standardization 87, 89, 256, 258-59, 335
Starý 363
Stauble, A-M 286n5, 369
Stefánsson, A 3, 130, 369
Steffensen, M 117, 195, 197, 369
Stein, P 28, 313n2, 369
Steinberg, D 350, 369
Stephen Island 326
stereotypes 56
Stetser, M 319, 369
Stevenson, R 306, 313, 369
Stewart, W 87-88, 268, 300, 369
Stichting voor Culturele Samenwerking 314
Stockton, E 306, 311, 369
Stolting, W 352, 361
Stolz, T 374
story-telling 317-19
Stowe, H 306, 369
Stross, B 84, 369
structural expansion 128
structuralism 33, 36-38
Stubbs, M 256, 369
stylistic flexibility 182-86
stylistic variation 69-72
substrate (substratum) 32, 37, 39, 93, 114-26, 130-32, 134, 139-40, 144, 152n19, 153-55, 160, 169, 172, 173n34, 177-80, 186-90, 192, 195, 197-99, 202, 205-06, 224-25, 227, 233, 236-37, 239, 323
sugar 56n6, 271
Summer Institute of Linguistics 327
superstrate (superstratum) 114, 116, 125, 139, 144, 169, 172, 177, 186, 225, 227, 233
Surinam(ese) 10, 12, 27, 33, 76, 87, 106, 127, 133-34, 189, 191-92, 210, 215n44, 254, 285, 296, 298, 303, 310, 314, 318-21
Sutcliffe, D 269, 298, 369
Sutton, P 241, 364
Svartvik, J 124, 358
SVO word order 145-46
Swadesh, M 107, 162
Swahili 31, 68, 105, 141, 145, 150, 259-60, 275, 300-01, 328, 331
SWAPO 278
Swedish 315
Swiss 36, 315
Sydney 252
Syea, A 345, 363
Sylvain, S 205, 322, 369
syntax 91, 122-23, 134n7, 144-53, 167-75, 198-205, 216-19
systematicity 227-28

T

Taber, C 175-76, 369
Tabouret-Keller, A 8, 44-45, 72, 241, 256, 276, 337, 358, 369
Tagalog 107, 285
Taglish 11
Tahiti(an) 19, 91, 133, 188, 305
Taiap 83
Taki-Taki 16
Tamil 118
Tanganyika 275
Tangoan 177-79
Tanzania 300-01
Tarawai 277
target language 39, 57, 73, 78, 98, 112, 130, 138, 144, 183, 211, 220, 286-87
Tarzanca 20, 102, 262
Tasmanian PE 20
Tauli, V 228, 369
Tavares, E 314, 369
Tay Boi 180, 270
Taylor, A 68, 101, 268, 369
Taylor, D 33, 125, 369
Taylor, I 191, 369
Taylor, O 291, 370
Taylor, T 64n20, 356, 364, 370
Tayo 8-9, 20, 39, 73, 112, 113n22, 154
Tedesche 315
Temne 216
Temple, W 22, 370
tempo 142
tense, modality, aspect (markers) -> TMA
Ternate 78, 273
Ternateño 273
teriary hybridization 138
Tetaga, J 166, 370
TGG -> transformational generative grammar
Thai PE 75, 136
Thamm, M 327, 370
theoretical linguistics 222
Thomas, D 351
Thomas, J 27, 370
Thomason, S 29, 35, 61, 78, 107, 132, 139, 145, 151, 370
Thompson, R 34, 78, 103, 106n10, 179, 197, 370
Thursday Island 254
Thurston, W 34, 370
Tilden, B 1, 370
Timor 78
Tintin 308, 310
TMA 39, 70-71, 106n10, 166n27, 190, 200, 203
Tobago 197
Todd, L 11, 15, 34-35, 53-54, 93, 163, 166n26, 171n31, 182-84, 219, 227, 274, 368, 370
Togo 275
Tok Boi 252
Tok Masta 101, 251-52, 310
Tok Pisin vii, 1-2, 9-10, 13, 15, 17-19, 27-30, 36, 40, 47-48, 53-55, 57-58, 60, 61n14, 64-67, 69-70, 73-74, 79-80, 82-85, 87, 101, 103-04, 113, 115-20, 126, 133-34, 139-42, 146-48, 152, 154-58, 161-85, 190-96, 198-202, 204, 212-20, 227, 232-33, 239, 244, 247, 249-53, 258-59, 265-68, 272, 277,

281-85, 294-97, 303, 310, 316, 318-19, 321n9, 323, 325-28, 332-34
Tok Vaitiman 251
Tolai 2, 69, 113, 115-18, 120, 126, 133, 139-40, 152, 154-55, 168-70, 177-81, 195, 227, 296, 316
Tololo, A 283, 370
tone 140, 192
Tonga 24
Tonkin, E 309-10, 370
Toolan, M 228, 370
Torres Straits (islands) 36, 58n9, 174, 241, 254, 292, 298, 326
Torres Straits Broken -> Broken
Torres Straits PE -> Broken
Town Bemba 30
Trade Spanish of the Piñaguero Panare 153
Tranquebar 68
transformational generative grammar (TGG) 38-42, 44-45, 108-09, 228, 231, 236
transitivity 144, 170
transmission 44, 103, 119
Traugott, E 4, 69, 150, 219, 235, 370
Travaux de recherche sur le créole haïtien 47
Traven, B 308, 370
Trefossa 314, 320, 370
Trepang English 16
Trinidad 197, 279, 291, 304
Trinidadian Creole French 27, 205
Tristan de Cunha English 90-91
Trollope, A 306, 370
Troy, J 20, 371
Trudgill, P viii, 36, 69, 87, 141n11, 269, 371
Tryon, D vii, 20, 69, 74n31, 76, 79, 149, 254-55, 296, 371, 373-74
Tscharke, E 327, 371
Tsotsi Taal 67
Tubuai(an) 91
Tubuseria 268
Turkish 20, 75, 101-02, 136, 145, 262
Turner, G 55, 371
Twain, M 306
Twi 3, 126, 205, 207-08
Tzeltal 84

U

UK 299
Ullmann, S 230, 371
UN -> United Nations
Unesco 4, 371
uniformitarian (principle) 54, 87, 127, 226
Unitas Fratrum 371
United Nations 28, 281, 283, 333
United Nations Nius na Nots long Tok Pisin 333
United States 24, 28, 35, 189
universals 39, 46, 56, 82, 92, 93, 108-13, 119, 120n27, 122, 125-26, 163, 173n34, 177, 191, 200, 215, 225
Unserdeutsch 9, 20, 58, 73, 200-02, 240
Upfield, A 313, 371
Ureland, P 269, 361-62, 371
Urry, J 74n31, 103, 371
USA 7, 274, 299
US Army 264, 271
Usarufa 140, 265

V

Valdman, A 11, 187, 204, 211, 256, 268, 344, 346, 349-50, 352, 354-56, 358-59, 361, 365-66, 369-71, 373
Valkoff, M 6-7, 11, 27, 32, 272-73, 371
Van der Voort, H 28, 274, 371
Van Gulik, R 76n33, 371
Van Name, A 22, 371
Van Rossem, C 28, 274, 318, 371
Vanuatu 9, 29, 75, 83, 154, 178, 254-55, 264, 272, 285, 331
variation 44, 64-65
Varrot, G 369
Veenstra, T 38, 363
Venezuela 276
verb serialization -> serial verb constructions
Verhaar, J 284, 349, 359, 371
Verhoeven, L 293, 344
Versteegh, K 74, 371
Viberg, Å 356, 363, 366
Vico, G 228, 371
Victoria [Australia] 22
Victoria PE 20
Vietnam 270-71
Vietnamese 162, 180, 270
Vietnamese PE 75
Vietnamese Pidgin French 56, 140, 142, 149, 162, 180, 232, 270, 272
Vila, I 28, 371
Vincent, M 144n14
Virgin Islands 60, 65, 273
Virgin Islands Creole Dutch -> Negerhollands
Voegelin, C & F 16, 371
Volapük 60
Volker, C 200, 371
von Hesse-Wartegg -> Hesse-Wartegg, E von
von Wiese, B 98, 372
Voorhoeve, C 169n29, 351, 373
Voorhoeve, J 30n2, 34, 65, 106-07, 159, 195, 197, 203, 296-97, 303, 314, 321, 341, 372
VSO word order 145
Vunapope 200, 282, 330, 333

W

Wales, K 124, 372
Walmajarri 3
Walsh, M 5, 74n31, 103, 371-73
Wanigera 248
Wantok 185, 250-51, 266, 334
Washabaugh, W 49, 56n6, 172, 204, 350, 372-73
Wastaua 333
Weaver, W 243, 367
Weber de Kurlat, F 310, 372
Weltdeutsch 260-62
Werkgroep Taal Buitenlandse 97, 309, 372
West Africa(n) 3, 15-16, 34, 53, 96n3, 105, 117, 126, 163, 187-90, 207-08, 252, 285, 318, 342
West African Creole [English] 35, 189
West African languages -> African languages
West African PE 9, 15-16, 25, 34-35, 82, 119, 163-64, 169, 171, 173-74, 178, 184, 186, 227, 330

West African Pidgin Portuguese 14, 103, 107
Western Australia 285, 289
Western Cape province 60
Western Grazier 307
Western Samoa 15
West Indian(s) 265, 288, 298
West Indian Creole English 67
West Indian Creoles 16, 34, 103, 125-26, 210, 264, 280, 290, 318
West Indies 67, 106, 285
Westminster 46
Westminster Creolistics 47
West Srian 20
Wewak News 333
Whinnom, K 57, 61n16, 78, 88, 101n6, 130-31, 138, 229, 273, 285n3, 372
Whiteley, W 259, 372
Whiting, J 353
WH-questions 151
Whydah 105
Williams, C 295
Williams, F 300, 372
Williams, S 295, 372
Williamson, J 369
Wilson, R 34, 238, 353
Winer, L 304, 372
Winford, D 38, 256, 291, 331-32, 359, 372-73
Winter, W 350
Witwatersrand 297
Wode, H 222, 231, 373
Wolf, G 363
Wolfson 366
Wölck, W 363
Wood, R 251, 292-93, 365, 373
Wood, W 2, 373
Woolford, E 173, 350, 372-73
word formation 177-79, 198
World Englishes 47
Wullschlägel, H 27, 373

Wurm, S vii-viii, 17-19, 20, 37, 60, 69, 74n31, 76, 78-79, 82-84, 115, 143, 149, 159, 163-64, 166, 172, 225, 240, 244, 246, 252, 255-56, 259, 267, 277, 284, 286n4, 297, 319, 341, 348, 350-51, 358, 360-61, 364, 369-70, 371-74
WWI -> First World War

Y

Yabem 266
Yamparico 22
Yangol 319
Yangoru-Dreikikir 185
Yap 275
Yimchunger 257
Yip 193, 319
Yiyili 289
York 46, 67, 298
Yorke Peninsula 25
York Papers in Linguistics 341
Yoruba 123, 126, 205, 216

Z

Zambia(n) 30, 262
Zamboangueño 208
Zemi 256-57
zero derivation 170
Zettersten, A 91, 374
Zimbabwe 262
Zinkel, C 295, 374
Zipf's law 259
Zobl, H 352, 361
Zöller, H 128, 374
Zulu 3, 139, 141, 154, 161, 262
Zuni 117
Zyhlarz, E 11, 374

Lightning Source UK Ltd.
Milton Keynes UK

176094UK00001B/121/P

9 781859 190838